AF668606

Buddhist Critical Spirituality
Prajñā and Śūnyatā

NORTH AMERICAN INSTITUTE OF ZEN
AND BUDDHIST STUDIES
SERIES 4

Buddhist Critical Spirituality

Prajñā and Śūnyatā

SHOHEI ICHIMURA

MOTILAL BANARSIDASS PUBLISHERS
PRIVATE LIMITED • DELHI

First Edition: Delhi, 2001

ISBN: 81-208-1798-2

Also available at:

MOTILAL BANARSIDASS

236, 9th Main III Block, Jayanagar, Bangalore 560 011
41 U.A. Bungalow Road, Jawahar Nagar, Delhi 110 007
8 Mahalaxmi Chamber, Warden Road, Mumbai 400 026
120 Royapettah High Road, Mylapore, Chennai 600 004
Sanas Plaza, 1302 Baji Rao Road, Pune 411 002
8 Camac Street, Kolkata 700 017
Ashok Rajpath, Patna 800 004
Chowk, Varanasi 221 001

Printed in India

BY JAINENDRA PRAKASH JAIN AT SHRI JAINENDRA PRESS,
A-45 NARAINA, PHASE-I, NEW DELHI 110 028
AND PUBLISHED BY NARENDRA PRAKASH JAIN FOR
MOTILAL BANARSIDASS PUBLISHERS PRIVATE LIMITED,
BUNGALOW ROAD, DELHI 110 007

To My Long Suffering Wife
Jeanne Ann Nailling Ichimura

Contents

SECTION TWO

NĀGĀRJUNA AND MĀDHYAMIKA DIALECTIC OF CRITICAL SPIRITUALITY

SECTION THREE

CHINESE BUDDHIST CRITICAL SPIRITUALITY AND ITS CULTURE

BIBLIOGRAPHY AND INDEX

Introduction

The Meaning of Critical Spirituality

This volume is a collection of fifteen essays which were presented by this author each at different occasions during the past decade. While each essay is complete for the meaning of its own title, some of the articles refer to Indian and South Asian Buddhism, and some others to Chinese and East Asian Buddhism. The essays are arranged in four major sections, irrespective of their chronological order, under the over-all title: "Buddhist Critical Spirituality: *Prajñā* and *Śūnyatā*," on the ground that each of them is concerned with the religious nature of Buddhism, its philosophy and history.

In general, the phrase "religious nature" can be termed as "religiosity," thus calling the religious nature of human kind as "human religiosity" or the nature of Buddhism as "Buddhist religiosity." For the title of this book, however, I applied another term "spirituality," which is more prevalent in America as its equivalent, despite the difference of the connotations of these terms. Here, spirituality refers to a capacity and tendency that is innate and unique to all human individuals. It is due to this spirituality or religiosity or religious nature inherent in all humans that an individual is prompted to move to knowledge, faith, meaning, hope, transcendence, connectedness, love and compassion.

Studying the origin and development of the major existing religious traditions of the world, we are compelled to recognize two different types of spirituality. On the one hand, there is the type of spirituality pertinent to theistic or mono-theistic religion. This spirituality prompts individuals to believe in the existence of the transcendent being and the religious redemption in terms of the grace of that being. On the other hand, there is the type of spirituality that prompts individuals to acquire the knowledge that dispenses with the belief of such a being not only with the universe but also with the belief of human individual soul or self. And yet this spirituality finds the way of realizing the state of emancipation from human imperfection and suffering in terms of self-realization. Buddhism belongs to the latter type of spirituality, perhaps, being only a singular example of non-theistic religion.

The adjectival term "critical" has two different meanings in general. One derives from "crisis" which represents a turning point or decisive moment or crucial time of a change or a state of affair. A good example is the name of "critical theology" coined by a group of theologians during the second quarter of the century. Another meaning of "critical" derives from "critic" (or "to criticize") which refers to a reasoned opinion on any subject matter involving a judgment of its value through evaluation or analysis with respect of its merit and demerit. Needless to say, the term here as "critical spirituality" refers to the latter usage, as in the case of a few examples, "critical analysis of linguistic convention," "critical examination of perception," or "critical investigation of philosophical systems," and so forth. What is common in these usages is the fact that the adjectival term implies rational and impartial treatment of a given subject matter.

Speaking broadly, every religion, more or less, has a critical attitude towards life and society and advocates its own belief and thought as well as a set of norms of action as an answer of its spirituality to the critical evaluation of life and society. Accordingly religion in general is strongly assertive of its belief and thought and likely will not allow a critical re-evaluation of its principle and practice within its own community. In this respect, the Buddha's emphasis on the principle of critical thought and attitude is evident in his admonition given to his disciples. He is said to have warned them not to blindly believe in whatever he taught, and he demanded them to critically examine whatever he said by their own thought and practice before accepting it. To those of us who are concerned with the present day world as torn asunder to all factions pulled by different religions and cultures, races and ethnicities, this practical admonition given by Śākyamuni rings loud and clear.

APOLOGETIC REFLECTION ON METHODOLOGY

Śākyamuni's emphasis on his critical spirituality, however, meant to go beyond the practical level of religious belief and spirituality. During the decade of fifty's, T. R. V. Mūrti published a book entitled: *The Central Philosophy of Buddhism* (1955) and created a new sensation among the post-war scholars of Buddhist Studies. In his daring attempt to parallel Mādhyamika philosophy and modern Western philosophy, he followed the way Stcherbatsky briefly attempted in *The Conception of Buddhist Nirvāṇa* (1927), namely, the ultimate goal to which Buddhist critical spirituality leads. Murti elaborated his writing into a full detailed monograph. At the time when the East-West philosophical and cultural interaction just began, his philosophical interpretation was especially welcomed as a viable approach to the new era of Buddhist Studies. Mūrti emphasized that the critical insight of the Buddha and Mādhyamika like Nāgārjuna applied the dialectical method of treatment to metaphysical problems. He contended that this can be elucidated to the Westerner's mind by comparing it with the critical philosophy and dialectical method of Kant, Hegel, and Bradley in the way they applied it to dealing with similar metaphysical problems, say, *a-priori* categories of the mind and the idea of thing-in-itself.

Philosophically, however, the twentieth century began with an anti-metaphysical movement. The so-called analytical philosophy of the early century asserted that the previous metaphysical problems ought to be approached differently through critical examination of language itself. Bertrand Russell and others thought that metaphysical problems arose due to misuse of language, and hence, some of the problems can be dispensed with. Thus, the clarification of linguistic forms and usages by way of logical analysis became the sole subject of investigation of Analytic Philosphy. Previously, "*a-priori* category" and "thing-in-itself" were central subjects to deal with the problem of epistemology. For Kant, for instance, "thing-in-itself" was the ultimate basis of justification for the validity of knowledge with respect to our empirical perceptions and universal forms of the mind in which things appear. Sensation (say color, sound, etc.) gives an individual idea, while mathematical theory gives a necessary and universally valid perception in reference to the actual world. But these two are ultimately detected to be merely different stages of phenomenal appearance, and "thing-in-itself" in the actual world would never become known.

Dissociating themselves from these metaphysical problems, philosophical movements of the new century turned to the problems of logic and language. By the 1930's, around the time when Stcherbatsky's book came out, the original trend of analytical philosophy was divided into the movement of logical positivism in Europe and that of ordinary language philosophy of England, to both of which the subject matter of philosophy was no longer the idea of reality outside language or the form of representation in the mind. The two main streams of philosophers discarded what was previously central to philosophy, i.e., thing-in-itself and a-priori forms of the intellect. As a result, the methodology that Stcherbatsky and Mūrti adopted was to be well stranded despite some enthusiastic follow-ups in the subsequent decade or two. The logical positivists sought an ideal language that could precisely describe a given state of affair in terms of verification, while ordinary language philosophers tried through linguistic analysis to find what state of affair our ordinary language is really deemed to describe. The idea of logical positivism or search for an ideal language waned during the later half of the 20th century, while the so-called philosophy of language has waxed to become the dominant trend through diversification of ordinary language philosophy toward the enquiry of the relation between language and action or between language and mind. There was, thus, a series of developments from the idea of language as descriptive tool to that of language as action or as intent of action, and further to the new trend of the philosophy of mind and that of the referential theory of language.

Reflecting upon the history of Buddhist Studies during the past half a century, I do not find any specific parallel development of its methodology along with the contemporary philosophical trends as briefly mentioned above. Surely during the 50's and early 60's, some scholars, such as, Nakamura, Robinson, and few others, attempted to apply symbolic logic to understand Mādhyamika dialectic and the syllogistic inference of Buddhist and Indian logic. It is my impression that the professional interest of the most of scholars of Buddhist Studies in the West was related to the discipline of Religious Studies. Accordingly they did not find the aforementioned discipline of linguistic philosophy or analytical philosophy to be especially interesting, in part, because their interest was more theological, and in part, because the general public did not sense an aura of spirituality in the result of these philosophical methods. Accordingly, despite the reverberation created by Stcherbatsky and Mūrti, Buddhist Studies has remained in good majority to be concerned with textual critique, history and culture. In theological studies, the methods of doctrinal exegesis and hermeneutic exploration were more favored, but these were not very well familiarized to scholars of Buddhist studies. The reason is that these are oriented toward biblical and theological study and interpretation and do not fit for measuring the trans-linguistic experience of *Samādhi* and *Nirvāṇa*, nor has there been a clear set of criteria to measure the linguistic expression of transcendent insight, such as, *prajñā* and *Śūnyatā*.

As far as my research and writing are concerned, I am obliged to admit that I have been benefitted from learning some of the Western traditional philosophy and contemporary linguistic and analytical methods of philosophy. I have also been benefitted from exploring the philosophical tradition of Sanskrit grammarians and the insight of Medieval Indian linguists. There is an enormous quantity of literary sources in these fields. I have not, however, fully affiliated myself with any one of the philosophical methods of the contemporary West, nor have I been an advocate of any one of the Indian philosophical traditions. Methodologically, therefore, I am obliged to assert that most of my researches and writings as collected in this book were accomplished by *ad-hoc* adoption of some methods and criteria from the aforementioned dual sources, insofar as they fit to dealing with Buddhist thoughts and insights. The Western philosophical trend has been rather too transient throughout the century, while the Indian grammatical and linguistic philosophy is more or less befitting to the Brahmanical and Hindu thoughts. Within a few years, I am planning to publish another volume under the title: *Nāgārjuna's Philosophy of Śūnyatā and Dialectic*, and I am hoping to present a more comprehensive statement on the methodology of a Buddhist Study at that time.

FUTURE PERSPECTIVE OF BUDDHIST STUDIES

Despite the post-war global expansion of Buddhist thought and activity, the scholarship in Buddhist Studies seems to have been still compartmentalized by being limited to their literary sources, linguistic proficiency, and culturally varied backgrounds. For instance, we have four major groups of Buddhist Studies respectively based on the textual sources of Pāli, Sanskrit, Tibetan, and East Asian languages (Chinese, Korean, and Japanese). It is mainly due to the difficult linguistic barriers that an integral study program has not been sufficiently developed in academic institutions. Even today, the centers where a research scholar can pursue an integral approach are indeed limited in number. In major American universities, for instance, Pāli and Sanskrit Studies have been maintained since the pre-war times, and from the 60's, the discipline of Tibetan textual study began to be incorporated for a wider, integral study program. And yet it is far from actuality insofar as the integration of East-Asian Buddhist Study and the hitherto regarded main stream of Buddhist Studies is concerned. Despite the fact that Far Eastern languages and civilization have been well established in major universities since the early 20th century, this is still the actual state of Buddhist Studies today.

My present fifteen articles are all result of cross-cultural studies of Buddhism based on the scriptural sources in Sanskrit and Pāli on the one hand, and the Chinese scriptural sources on the other. Since these articles mainly dealt with earlier Mahāyāna Buddhism, my research has necessarily relied on Sanskrit and Chinese scriptural sources. The Tibetan Tripiṭaka linguistically preserved the original forms of Sanskrit scriptures very well and recorded intra-Buddhist as well as extra-Buddhist polemics of the later half of Mahāyāna Buddhist history in India. On the other hand, the Chinese Tripiṭaka preserved the Sanskrit scriptures of the earlier half of Mahāyāna Buddhist history, especially those which reflect the formative period of Mahāyāna Buddhism. It is my contention that the Sino-Indian cultural interaction through Buddhism is one area that ought to be fully focused in future global Buddhist Studies. Interactions between India and China, two very different cultural and linguistic zones, ought not to be neglected in our integral study approach, because the outcome of such a study on Buddhist spirituality is far more fruitful than a study derived from a singular compartmentalized source of culture and language.

Although Chinese people are currently adopting the Communist ideology to handle their contemporary political and social problems, they are by no means an exception from human religiosity or Buddhist spirituality. I think some of my articles demonstrate how and why the Medieval Chinese could manage to accomplish a lofty heritage of human spirituality in all forms of expression, in thought as well as action for future humanity. Nor should the current Sino-Tibetan conflict interfere with the direction of future Buddhist Studies, because, during the Yüan dynasty and subsequent periods, Tibetan and Chinese Buddhists evidenced superior and creative cooperation in the absence of contemporary ideological constriction and aggression. One of the areas of East Asian Buddhism, to which I wish to have special attention given today, is the doctrinal systematization of Buddhist thought and spirituality, so called *Chiao-p'an* of Medieval China. Since the times of the 5th century onward, the intellectual and spiritual endeavors of Chinese Buddhists organized a variety of philosophical systems on Buddhist doctrines. Each of these systems invariably demonstrates how and why Chinese Buddhist thinkers endeavored to accomplish their own spiritual wayfaring toward the ultimate insight of Middle Way. It is my belief that these specimens or testaments will rekindle the minds of scholars and students toward Buddhist Studies of this new century.

In publishing this book which comprises fifteen articles, I have an earnest wish to communicate to the readers. It is concerned with the question: How could Buddhist scholars respond to the current trend of religious fervor and sentiment globally observed as having been on the rise? During those five centuries of modern times, we have regained the honor and respectability of rational human person from the Medieval theological domination of human affairs. This has been abundantly evidenced not only by the advancement of various sciences, but also by the greatest liberalization of humanity hitherto accomplished in history from the constriction imposed upon rational faculty, natural emotion, and free moral action. Some thinkers began to call our contemporary period as "post-modern era" as early as the 1970's. Crossing the mark of the twenty-first century since then, we hear this term more often and more extensively, but not necessarily with an open-handed salutation. Subversive resurgence of religious fervor seems to have been steadily undermining human rationality, blaming its imperfection and ineffectuality with the conduct of human affairs in communities, societies, or states. Where we most need workings of harmonious principle and rational reconciliation to deal with the global affairs, we seem to have been pulled asunder by religious and cultural factionalism. The lofty ideal figure of human rationality seems to have been seriously hurt along with its honor and respectability. Once again, we are obliged to look into this reactionary trend of religious fervor and sentiment and deal with it for restoring human rationality and magnanimity on the basis of critical spirituality.

Future religion ought to be one which can support and sustain the rational faculty of human nature to its full capacity and honor against odds of threat and fear. I believe that the papers collected here invariably proposing this earnest appeal.

It has been a long journey for my career of study and research that began during 1950's. Throughout this journey, I have been fortunate to be acquainted with innumerable friends of good will and superior guid, to whom I owe much of benefit to advance my wayfaring. Though this is a preliminary step, I would like to include my profound thanks to those friends, many of whom I miss today with reverence. For now, may I thank Mr. R. P. Jain, director of Motilal Banarsidass, for his welcome agreement to publish this volume of my collected papers.

SHOHEI ICHIMURA
AUGUST 31, 2000

SECTION ONE

BUDDHIST CRITICAL SPIRITUALITY IN HISTORY AND CULTURE

ARTICLE ONE

Śākyamuni's Critical Spirituality and India's Crisis[1]

§1. Introduction

From the religious and social point of view, the major problem that contemporary Indians encounter today is twofold: (1) the social and cultural problem of human inequality reinforced by the age-old custom and disposition of the caste system, and (2) the religious and political problem of dissension and hostility between Hindu majority and Muslims, including some of other religious minorities. It is obvious that neither legal codes and administrative regulations can overcome the culture of inequality insofar as Hindu tradition continues to reinforce and sustain caste system, nor can the conflict of inter-religious ethnic confrontation epitomized between India and Pakistan become a source of creative democracy as far as Indian national unity is pressed by Hindu majority rule. There is no other time as today when India needs an intellectual power of critically examining its own culture, society, and religion. On the part of Buddhists, it is the necessary time for them to participate in the affairs of the country as it did in some ancient and medieval times. The purpose of this paper is to differentiate what Buddhist critical spirituality is from Hindu religiosity, and how and why, as the ethical principle, this critical spirituality may contribute to the realization of undistorted equality and creative democracy of a multi-religious society. As a part of this study, the Buddhist principle of ethics is compared with that of the classical philosophy of Stoicism.

§2. Śākyamuni's Renunciation as Historical Breakthrough

According to Oswald Spengler, the historic religions, such as, Buddhism, Christianity, and Islam, were a result of a genuine act

---

[1] Presented at the 2nd International Seminar on Buddhsim at the Bauddha Mahotsava 1999, Banaras Hindu University, Nov. 2-5, under the title: "Critical Spirituality as the Ethical Principle of Theravāda and Mahāyāna Buddhism compared with that of Stoic Philosophical Insight."

of creation preceded by the history of each culture, and hence, the rise of Buddhism was an Indian creation resulted from a grand procession of preceding thought movements embodied in the Ṛg-Veda, Brāhmaṇas, and Upaniṣads. In his interpretation, the rise of Buddhism embodied "India's cultural destiny."[2] In opposition to this "destiny" interpretation, Arnold Toynbee recognized a deliberate configuration of societal problem solution in every epoch-making historical event as a response to the challenge of history. If such response is inadequate, he said, the result is bound to be a failure in the form of some aborted phenomena, or an eventual disintegration of a given culture and its civilization. He was convinced that, just like any other world religion, the beginning of Buddhism was the most remarkable response of the human race towards "a state of society in which the whole of mankind would be able to live together in harmony as members of a single all-inclusive family."[3]

These interpretations obviously represent a macrocosmic and pan-Indian generalization on the origin of Buddhism. I am disappointed, however, with Spengler's idealist interpretation, because his interpretation does not differentiate Buddhism from other manifestations, such as, Hinduism. He regards Buddhism and Hinduism as essentially identical on account of their common culture. I hold that Spengler's view is inadequate to explain the historical meaning of Buddhist spirituality, and that it does not contribute to eradication of a wrong cliché that Buddhism is a part of Hinduism. I am therefore ready to explore Toynbee's empiricist theory of "historical challenge and response." Consider the evidence. Hinduism has all been confined to the subcontinent. Wherever else it was transmitted, it ceased to exist or was switched to Buddhism, for instance, in Burma, Malaya, Indonesia, and Indo-China. Buddhism, on the other hand, wherever it was transmitted, has become a major religion in all parts of the world, not only in Asia but also in Europe and America today. In short, Buddhism embodies its unique spirituality that cannot be identified with that of Hindus.

My preference on the empiricist principle of historical interpretation further has its justification, because the empirical principle is cogent and especially matches the sociologist and anthropologist points of view. It has been nearly a century since modern sociology

---

[2] Oswald Spengler: The Decline of the West, abridged English edition prepared by Arthur Helps, from the translation of Charles Francis Atkins; N.Y.: Alfred A. Knoph, 1962, p. 244.

[3] Arnold Toynbee: A Study of History, abridged one-volume edition by the author and Jane Caplan, Oxford University Press, 1972, p. 44.

began investigating religious phenomena more effectively. Sociology is fundamentally concerned with that part of human phenomena which manifests as social action. Sociologists are interested in the potential force of religion effecting social change. Max Weber, for instance, introduced a concept of "breakthrough" and a theory of religious typology in order to explain ways religion in general contributes to social change.[4] Any historic religion (and in this matter any epoch-making movement) began by way of breaking away from the established normative order under the founder's claim for his moral and spiritual legitimacy. The ways of expressing this legitimacy or the ways religious orientation can exert leverage effecting evolutionary social change constitute variations of religious types.

Weber then outlined four types of solutions or individual paths by cross-tabulating the distinction between asceticism and mysticism and between other-worldliness and inner-worldliness. In this scheme he categorized ancient Buddhism as "other-worldly mysticism." What he meant by this type of religion is that it is an ascetic religion seeking to avoid subjective desires, because these interfere with the pursuit of salvation, and that it also seeks to dissociate one's self totally from the worldly concern.[5] This categorization is satisfactory as far as the direction of religious transcendence is indicated, but I am not satisfied with the withdrawal aspect from the world. The term 'mysticism' does not fit with Buddhism as a whole. If Śākyamuni's action is regarded to have been a total breaking away from secular society as an exemplary mystic, it is wrong and even misleading. In my view, his renunciation and eventual formation of Buddhist Saṅgha must have meant to be the way of his response to the challenge of history imposed upon him. Then, what was the historical challenge he encountered? Before answering this question, I ought to introduce some of the anthropologist point of view on culture and human action.

Anthropology today is a fairly comprehensive field of enquiry, dividing itself into multiple disciplines, such as archeology, linguistics, psychology, physical and cultural anthropology, etc. From the time of Edward Taylor,[6] cultural anthropologists have maintained their

---

[4] Max Weber, The Socioology of Religion (tr. by F. Fischoff), Beacon Press, 1963, p. 51. Esp. see Introduction by T. Parsonns, pp. xlvi-lii.

[5] Weber, ibid., esp. Introduction by T. Parsons, p. lii.

[6] Edward Burnett Taylor (1832-1917) has so often been called the father of this disicpline. Cf. *Image of Man (A history of Anthropological thought)*, by A. de Waal Malefjit, NY: Alfred A. Knopf, 1976, p. 139 ff.

fundamental conviction that culture is the product of social learning rather than biological heredity, and hence it is a complex whole including all socially learned behaviors, such as family, kinship, social organization, agriculture, militarism, law, language, religion, and so forth. This insight, I believe, is parallel with Toynbee's empiricist understanding of history. The problem, however, is that we cannot find an appropriate concrete description of facts in Śākyamuni's biography, except some legendary stories collected in the Jātakas. More precisely speaking, if Śākyamuni's renunciation and formation of the Saṅgha were his response to some historical challenge in terms of concrete crisis and ordeal, it is imperative to determine such a crisis and ordeal as the cause of his breakthrough action .

As Coomaraswamy eloquently said, the time of the Buddha was the final stage when the fusion of the Aryan and indigenous races was nearly complete,[7] and that Śākyamuni's religious movement and the expansive network of his Saṅgha became the road-mark of a new age and paved the way to the harmonization of the two opposing cultures in the Mauryan universal welfare state.[8] All this may be true. Consider, however, how could this kind of pan-Indian generalist's causal abstraction explain the way an individual person ignites a flame of passion to take the course of life like that of Śākyamuni? Some scriptural accounts refer to Prince Siddhārtha's excursion tours and his awareness of human suffering, misery of sickness, despair of death, and so forth. However, could this kind of general human affairs motivate a person to ignite his mind of resolution toward the goal of religious salvation? There seems to be an unbridgeable chasm between the scriptural accounts given in general terms and an actual ordeal experienced by an individual in concrete terms. I am justified, therefore, to look into the more tangible and tragic context of Śākyan society, of which obviously Śākyamuni was a very important member, and see a historical meaning of breakthrough action in his legendary flight from his homeland.

---

[7] Ananda K. Coomaraswamy: *Yakṣa*, Smithsonian Miscellaneous Collections, vol. 80, no. 6, pp. 1-3.

[8] They argue that the Buddha's spiritual path was precisely what the ancient sages had gone through, and that his religion can be interpreted somewhat in similar terms as those of the Upaniṣadic reform of Brahmanism, provided that his higher insight was meant to resolve the antithesis of conservative Brahmanism and nihilistic materialism.

§3. ŚĀKYAN TRAGIC FATE AND ŚĀKYAMUNI'S RENUNCIATION

I think it is still a mystery why traditional and modern scholarship did not attempt a re-evaluation of Śākyamuni's renunciation and his eventual establishment of Buddhist Saṅgha in reference to the tragic ordeal of Śākyan society and the destruction of their state. It is also strange that the ordeals of Śākyan society were preserved only in the form of legendary Jātaka stories, and the meaning of these records were never brought forth for analysis and study as historical facts.[9] In fact, Śākyamuni's biography comprises two contradictory accounts. As is well known, Aśvaghoṣa's *Buddhacaritam* depicts Śākyamuni to have been Prince Siddhārtha of the kingdom of the Śākyas, and all accounts of his youth refer to his monarchical background. On the other hand, Jātaka stories refer to the Śākyan republican polity and its collective decision making as parliamentary, and scholars argued that some of these proceedings were adopted by Buddhist Saṅgha as model of their autonomy.

From all available sources, both Buddhist and Brahmanical, the Śākyan society at the time of Śākyamuni was clearly under the threat of the assimilatory force of Brahmanism, socially, culturally, and politically. In this particular context, there were two major forces that exercised influence resulting in the disappearance of the clan society of the Śākyas: (1) the religious force exerted by the Brāhmaṇa stratum, which sought to build up its influence without regard to their clan membership, and (2) the monarchical force of the Kosala kingdom which was the Śākya's overlord and encouraged disintegration of the clan to develop a uniform bureaucracy. The conflict took place between two corollary agents: (1) Brāhmaṇa assimilatory society consisting of four major caste divisions (Varṇas) and (2) Śākyan tribal society spell bound for its integrity.

The evolution of Śākyan society was relatively independent of that of the Brāhmaṇical society that spread in the subcontinent.[10]

---

[9] Mahānāman's daughter born of a slave woman, became the queen of the Kosala king Prasenajit and bore the prince, who later on destroyed the Śākyan autonomous state. This may have happened while the Buddha was still active. Cf. (Bhaddasālajātaka No. 465, IV, 144-153).

[10] In older scriptures like *Suttanipāta* 991, the Buddha is often called a descendant of the Sun dynasty (ādityabandhu in Sanskrit) in the lineage of Okkāka or Īṣvāku). The House of Ikṣvāku, for instance, appears in the Ṛg Veda X, 60, 4. A detailed history of the Śākyas is given in Buddhaghoṣa's Sumaṅgalavilāsinī (ed. by Rhys Davids and Carpenter, PTS. Pt. I, 258 ff) and *Paramaṭṭha-jotika* (Commentary on *Suttanipāta*) I, 232-6. Also Dīgha Nikāya III, 16. The banished four princes of King Okkāka, third successor of the Ikṣvāku, went away toward the Himālayas taking their five sister

This can be inferred from the fact of the unique social structure of the Śākyas, besides the legendary account of the Śākyan origin. Their society consisted of three strata: (1) landed clansmen in the position of the governing councilors who were engaged in military service for the protection of their farm territory; (2) regular clansmen who were either voluntarily or physically unable to maintain such role and were engaged in cultivation; and (3) household slaves or workers whose status was either due to capture, debt, voluntary self-degradation, or judicial punishment. Importantly, Śākyan society did not comprise either the stratum of Brāhmaṇa or that of Vaiśya or that of Śūdra. In Buddhist literature, social order always begins with Kṣatriya first and then Brāhmaṇa, and so on, whereas in Hindu literature, it always begins with Brāhmaṇa and then Kṣatriya and so on. In short, Śākyan society obviously developed as a separate entity from the evolution of the Brāhmaṇical society.

The Śākyan clansmen maintained a shrine of their own tutelage, Śākyavardhana, "the one who strengthens the Śākyas," and conducted a type of ancestor worship which was inseparably tied to their clan membership. Clan membership was inseparably attached not only (1) to the political right to participate in the republic, but also (2) to the economic privilege based on the patrimonial proprietorship, as well as (3) to the socio-religious status derived from the strict accordance to clan tutelage and ancestor worship.[11] The ultimate basis of clan polity and its legitimate membership was the principle of endogamy (i.e., marriage within kinship or with agnate tribes), with which socio-economic implications had been well institutionalized in their clan society. It follows that the matter of endogamy could become a monumental obstacle against necessary adjustments imposed by history.

The Bhaddasāla Jātaka narrates that the Kosala king Prasenajit (Passenadi in Pāli) requested the Śākyas to send their maiden with proper familial background to become his first queen. In their

---

princesses with them. They founded Kapilavastu on the site occupied by Sage Kapila. These princes married their sisters respectively and made the eldest princess Queen Mother. This peculiar custom was not without parallel, because the Ptolemies are said to have held a similar custom to maintain the purity of the royal blood among them. Cf. Weber, *General Economic History* (Glencoe, Ill.: Free Press, 1950; p. 35). Being informed of his sons' success in their new settlement and maintenance of their race, King Okkāka rejoiced in uttering "Aha smart men (Śakyā)," i.e., "Able men." This term is said to have become the origin of their clan name.

[11] Weber, *General Econoimic History*, p. 47. For similar cases, the Chinese and Roman types of ancestor worship can be cited as to their economic implications.

parliamentary argument the Śākyan clansmen were split into two groups as pro and con and thus unable to reach a decisive conclusion. Accordingly, the Śākyan elder Mahānāman,[12] sought a solution by himself, sending to Kosala his daughter (Bhadasāra by name) born of a slave woman. Besides a series of cover-ups for concealment of the real status of this lady, the Pāli Jātaka explains the Śākyan predicament by referring to a deadly dilemma, namely: If the Śākyas refused, the Kosalas would invade to destroy the Śākyan polity, and if they accepted, their acceptance would necessarily be leading to the eventual disintegration of their clan state.[13] It follows that the only way to cope with the dire situation would be to reform the clan society by amending or adjusting the tribal principle of endogamy. The time of history was such that the Śākya clan society was pressed not only from outside but also from within, to break out from this fateful orientation.

One of the major negative characteristics of Indian civilization was and has been a peculiar passion for regionalism. This is evident not only in the varieties of dialects, subspecies of both Indo-European and Dravidian speech having survived for millennia, but also in a contemporary manifestation of political and social diversities. In this respect, as Coomaraswamy and others suggest, the pre-Buddhist Brahmanism can be regarded as an initial step towards a form of universal society despite its caste structure, and the historical role of the Buddhist movement was to complete the task by eradicating caste mentality. The most negative aspect of Indian civilization, however, was and has been the superstitious belief in magic, especially in the magic of blood in terms of endogamy.[14] Weber keenly diagnosed that this superstitious belief has continually enforced caste mentality. It is evident that the primary force that regulates the members of each caste to comply with his caste norms (*dharma*) is neither individual's rational

---

[12] According to one souçe, Mahānāman is said to have been the son of Dhotodana (3rd brother of Śuddhodana), *Vinaya in Four Divisions* (Ch. 15), in Chinese translation (Taisho. vol. 22, p. 101b), Buddhaghoṣa, however, reported him as the Buddha's paternal uncle. Fleet, *JRAS,* 1906, p. 168.

[13] *Jātaka* IV, 145. See Buddhaghoṣa's account [Fleet, *JARAS*, 1906. [p. 172-173)].

[14] Endogamy, says Weber, has existed only under certain conditions, but by no means always for the tribe as a whole. Rules of endogamy, however, always form the essential basis of a caste. Dietary rules and rules of commensality are always characteristic of the caste but are by no means characteristic of that tribe. . . In contrast to the tribe, a caste is usually related intimately to special ways of earning a living, on the one hand, and to social rank on the other. *Ibid.*, p. 33.

judgement nor ethical virtue. It is fundamentally the superstitious belief in magic. The fact that the Śākyan clansmen were unable to make an appropriate response in reply to Kosala's marital proposition precisely points to this feature. King Prasenajit was befriended with Śākyamuni throughout his life and made invaluable contribution to the initial development of the Buddhist Saṅgha. Thus, it is said in the scripture that Śākyamuni was obliged more than once to the king by explaining his point of view about the lady and his kinsmen's breach of action.

According to Weber, there are three criteria for conducting the analysis of breakhrough in general: (1) Under what cultural definitions of the religious situation the process of change and breakthrough takes place; (2) Through what agency and form of organization the process of change and breakthrough could take place; (3) In what situation would breakthrough be most probable.[15] By combining these criteria with Toynbee's theory of "historical principle of challenge and response," I think it is far more cogent and effectively explains Śākyamuni's breakaway from his Śākyan society as his dissociation from the spell bound mentality of the clansmen and his finding of the way to change it by dealing with the tragic course of Śākyan society. It also explains the nature and function of his organized Saṅgha through which he implemented his solution as the most effective agency to respond to the given historical challenge.

He promoted not only his personal influence upon the contemporaries, like Magadhan king Bimbisāra, Kosala king Prasenajit, the Elders of the Vajjian Republic, and so forth, but also steadily expanded the network of Buddhist Saṅghas across different regions, tribes, and professions by raising status-free professional nucleus (i.e., Bhikkhus and Bhikkhūṇīs) and supporting lay communities. The members of the Buddhist Saṅgha were strictly regulated by the Vinaya code of disciplines to be celibate, dissociated from any profession, subsisting solely on daily alms-begging and accepting whatever alms food from whatever household in due order. These rules were the effective counter-measures to deal with the afore-mentioned magic-ridden mentality and social compartmentalization.[16]

Śākyamuni neither thought that it was possible to reform his

---

[15] *Ibid.*, p. xxx-1.

[16] One of the Caste rules is commensalism which requires that one may sit at the table only with one's caste members, prohibitting otherwise. The status of the cook too was regulated in the matter of food. Transgression requires a set of ritualistic cleansing.

own society while being himself in it, nor could he expect to find ways to rescue it from the on-coming crisis by joining the Brahmanical tradition which was equally irrational, being bound to caste mentality. For him and others, he believed that the status-free (renunciation) position and concomitant religious organization alone could serve as the only possible agency to transform both Śākyan as well as Brāhmaṇical society to be integrated without warfare and bloodshed and guide both of them towards a wider and more universal society. In a way, this goal was achieved two centuries later by the advent of the Mauryan Buddhist state. In this respect, the Pan-Indian generalist views ought to be regarded as valid. But, without knowing the Śākyan context, I believe, Śākyamuni's action of renunciation and formation of the Buddhist Saṅgha cannot be fully understood. Hence, I think that it is necessary to evaluate Śākyamuni's spirituality and philosophical insight in reference to that historical context. Moreover, it is important to critically examine how and why the same successful institution failed to do a similar function when Hindu and Muslim societies squarely confronted toward the end of Medieval India.

§4. Buddhist Saṅgha and Assimilatory Secular Hinduism

Ever since the fall of the Mauryan Buddhist state the exuberant revival of Brahmanism took its course as secular Hinduism and began to restructure and consolidate the society under the four Varṇas with subdivided multiple caste regulations.[17] It was the dark age to the Buddhists, because the early Buddhist Saṅgha was no longer fit to the new situation well. Buddhists launched the Mahāyāna grass-root movement successfully to counter the Hindu Epic movement by compiling a series of Mahāyāna scriptures and developing a set of reformed teaching as "Bodhisattva Way." Nevertheless, since the Buddhist Saṅghas honorably adhered to the same Vinaya code of the Sarvāstivāda orthodoxy, irrespective of different branches as Hīnayāna (orthodox or scholastictic schools) or Mahāyāna,[18] the Buddhist monastic institution did not change its

---

[17] Manu's *Dharmaśāstra*.

[18] Fa-hsien visited India, starting in 400 over the land route and returned in by way of Sinhara, Java, over the ocean route. When he was studying Sanskrit scriptures at the Mahāyāna temple in Pāṭaliputra during the three years from 405, he recorded that there were two Buddhist temples respectively Hīnayāna and Mahāyāna, in Pāṭalilputra, the capital of Magadha, where altogether six or seven hundred practitioners resided,

nature and function; the resident monks and nuns were gradually alienated from the supporting lay communities. One thing is very clear that this monastic life style was to become an irretrievable weakness of the Buddhist Saṅgha in relation to the aggressive social processes of secular Hinduism which steadily eroded Buddhist lay communities.

A little over a decade ago, Lokesh Chandra published a remarkable monograph *The Thousand-Armed Avalokiteśvara*,[19] in which he advocated a theory that the Buddhist hypostasis as Avalokiteśvara was a metamorphosis of the Hindu god Brahmā.[20] He was brilliant in proving that Avalokiteśvara's multifarious manifestation in Indian iconography was due to the potency ascribed to that deity. To substantiate his theory, he borrowed Alicia Matsunaga's thesis on the Buddhist assimilation method. According to Matsunaga, the Buddhist method of assimilation that worked in Japan to absorb native gods and various other rites into Buddhism began in India and had its origin in the framework of that early philosophy.[21] Here, Lokesh Chandra formulated his own, by asserting that Avalokiteśvara's successful assimilation of popular Hindu deities was rather based on Brahmā's potency[22] than on the Buddhist philosophical framework. In fact, his theory has another application to explain how and why abrupt speedy switch occurred from the Buddhist cult to that of the Hindus. He suggested that at some later period, the Hindu deity Śiva was assimilated to Buddhism and gave rise to the name Avalokiteśvara (the lord Avalokita), thereby allowing the emergence of the thousand-armed Bodhisattvas,

---

and that both groups of practitioners were strictly adhering to the Sarvāstivāda Vinaya code. In daily liturgical performance, they differ only in some different *Sūtra* chantings. Cf. The *Biography of Fa-hsien* (or *the Record of his Journey to India*), especialhy, the section of "Magadha."

[19] Delhi: Indira Gandhi National Center for Arts, 1988.

[20] Cf. Lokesh Chandra: *The Thousand-Armed Avalokiteśvara*. Delhi: Indira Gandhi National Center for Arts, 1988. Cf. Chap. 2; esp. p. 20. In reference to the sections of "*mantra, dhāraṇī*, or hymns," in both the *Lotus Sūtra* and the *Pureland Sūtra*, Lokesh Chandra regards Avalokiteṣvara as the "master of logos" (*mantra-dṛaṣṭā*) (in parallel to Brahmā in the Brāhmaṇical system), the Seer (*avaloktṛ*) of Sound (*svara*), who assimilated Hindu deities (lokeśvara) by pronouncement of each sacred hymn (*hṛdaya* or *mantra*) unique to each deity.

[21] Chandra: *op. cit.*, p. 42. Cf. Alicia Matsunaga: *Buddhist Philosophy of Assimilation of the Honji-Suijaku Theory* (*The Historical Development*): Tokyo: Sophia University, C.E. Tuttle, 1969.

[22] See *Ibid*., Chap. 2, esp. p. 20; the Seer (avalokitṛ) of the Sound (svara), who assimilated Hindu deities (Lokeṣvara) by pronouncement of each sacred hymn (*hṛdaya* or *mantra*) unique to each deity.

as well as several other types of images parallel with those of Hindu iconography, namely, the images of thousand eyes, four faces, eleven faces, horse-head, fearless lion head, blue neck, and so on.[23] He informs us that Avalokiteśvara sometimes appears as a Buddha and at other times as Hindu deity Īśvara or Maheśvara (Śīva) without clear reason,[24] and that it was a simple switch on the part of the devotees to change from a Buddhist cultic practice to that of Hindu's.

What I am getting at is that if the Buddhist spirituality engaged in the cult of Avalokiteśvara is not distinguishable from that of Hindu cult, nothing can stop the former to switch its affiliation to the latter, and *vice versa*. By implying that the spiritual basis of the Buddhist cult of Avalokiteśvara is identical with that of Hindu cult on account of Brahmā's potency, Lokesh Chandra seems to suggest that it does not matter whether the cult of Avalokiteśvara is Buddhist or Hindu in the religious culture of India, and that Buddhist spirituality is essentially identical with Hindu's as part of the common culture. What I am trying to prove is that his interpretation is wrong, and that my point of view can be substantiated by referring to the same cult of Avalokiteśvara popularized in China.

When cultural value is transmitted from one place to another or from a prior to a posterior period, unlike scientific technology, it cannot sustain a similar definitive quality due to some degree of increment of vulgarity. This process was inevitable in the history of Indian Buddhism, because Buddhism was perpetually affected by Hinduism ever since the latter's revival from its predecessor 'Brahmanism.' The unique Buddhist spirituality was only articulated within the Buddhist Saṅgha alone as symbolically distinguishing it from other Indian religions, whereas the spirituality of Buddhist lay community was quickly assimilated to secular Hinduism. These two became indistinguishable soon to the eyes of lay communities. A similar development was also visible in the theoretical processes of Buddhist teachings. Indeed, some medieval works of Buddhhist philosophy seem to have been affected by Hindu counterpart.

A couple of decades ago, some Japanese scholars of Buddhist

---

[23] For variations of Avalokiteśvara in India, see Gusto Liebert: *Iconographic Dictionary of the Indian Religions, Hinduism-Buddhism-Jainism*. Asian Arts & Archaeology Series No. 5. Delhi: Indian Books Centre, 1976; pp. 29-30.

[24] Chandra: *ibid*., pp. 15-16; Hsüan-tzang's travel record reveals that he encountered this kind of indiscriminate enshrinement of Kuan-yin in various sites. Cf. *op. cit*., p. 114, Note.

Studies began to critically examine the Buddhist teaching of Karman as to whether or not the accepted Buddhist tradition in Japan contributed more often to the complacency of social injustice, inequality, and discrimination in Japanese society,[25] or whether it really contributed to the critical rectification of these violations. Their research and scrutiny through Buddhist literatures, lectures, and sermons, unfortunately turned out to be the former. The popular notions of Karman and Saṃsāra which prevailed in the Brahmanical and Hindu traditions were conveniently adopted by Buddhist preachers in their sermons in Japan. The research found that the popular notion of Karman was prevalently used to legitimize individual's fortune or fate, health or illness, and so forth in reference to his or her past Karman across past, present and future, exceeding the boundary of ethical rationalization. Thus, their task has been a self-criticism by way of probing scrutiny of non-Buddhist elements and proving their admixture.

In ancient India, human thought gradually precipitated the Upaniṣadic thought of reality as *brahman* or *ātman*. The idea of *ātman* was theorized to be the *a-priori* principle of all humans, and yet despite this insight of universal reality, the four Varṇas were also ascertained to be the *a-priori* statuses of individuals and order of society. These unequal statuses and discriminations were established and sanctioned on the basis of Karman, and so were the magico-ritualistic divisions of caste system. Śākyamuni challenged these irrational concepts by posing the principle of Anātman (Non-self) and introduced the caste-proof Saṅgha as his new religious order. Today, even after caste system is condemned by the contemporary Constitution, the age-old culture lingers, incurring violent conflicts which would likely continue toward eventual eradication. Japanese Buddhists have been now aware how non-Buddhist elements could affect their thought to perpetuate the injustice, inequality, and

---

[25] In 1979, the chief delegate of Japanese Buddhists made an irresponsible statement at the Third World Religious Conference for Peace, asserting that Japanese society had no social problem of injustice like that of inequality or discrimination. This was not true in the light of historical facts, because social segregation of some communities of Japanese as many as rhree million has been continually practiced, and in the matters of profession, marriage, and social association, their individual members have been subjected to unbearable suffering due to unequal treatment and discrimination by prejudice. Since such hidden practices of injustice are clearly against the legality of the Japanese constitution, some Buddhist schools have been compelled to examine their past teachings and practices as to whether their sectarian tenets transgressed the spirit of humanity of the constitution

discrimination in a community of Japanese people.[26]

Besides the doctrine of Karman, the Japanese scholars of "critical Buddhism" have been also engaged in scrutinizing the principle of "Buddha-nature" or "original enlightenment," both of which are of the Mahāyāna Buddhist origin. They boldly denounced that the Japanese uncritical acceptance of these doctrines may have been the primary cause of their failure not to recognize the existence of social injustice as well as that of their inability to face the matter of its proper rectification. They argue that these concepts were likely affected by Hindu conceptions in the course of theorization.[27] They assert that Buddhist spirituality in India eventually succumbed to Hindu influence and developed Buddhist thought in the fashion of 'Dhātu-vāda,' i.e., a doctrine of a singular reality that produces multifarious phenomena as their foundation (*dhātu*), or simply a theory of existential monism or that of fundamental reality.[28] It was this type of the Upaniṣadic doctrine, namely, Brahman or Ātman, that Śākyamuni himself criticized as his main target of repudiation. In fact there is a good deal of similarity between the thought of Tathāgatagarbha and Ātman of Upaniṣadic philosophy. It follows that the theory of Tathāgatagarbha itself ought to be critically examined as to how and why it comprises non-Buddhist thought elements. Since influence and affectation are visible even at theoretical level, how much more affected Buddhist spirituality was at the level of popular practice in late Medieval India. While the Saṅgha as an institution was distinguishable, the Buddhist spirituality was indistinguishable to the eyes of lay practitioners from that of Hindu's. Such was a critical factor of Buddhism's demise in India.

---

[26] The group of people referred to here is believed to be as many as three million Japanese, who have been discriminated for centuries in profession, marriage, association, education, and so on. Although the evolution was nothing to do with Buddhism, the records show that these Japanese were mistreated even in the matter of funerals at Buddhist temples.

[27] Two agendas central to their task of the movement are: (1) critical examination of the doctrine of "original enlightenment" inculcated in the *Mahāyāna-śraddhotpāda-śāstra* (*The Treatise on the Awakening of Faith in Mahāyāna*) and (2) that of the doctrine of "Buddha nature" (*buddha-dhātu*) introduced in the *Śrīmālādevīsiṃhanāda-sūtra* and *Mahāyānaparinirvāṇa-sūtra*, and later on, theorized in the *Mahāyānottaratantra-śāstra*,, *Mahāyāna-sūtrālaṅkāra*, and so forth.

[28] Matsumoto, Shirō: *Engi-to-Kū* (「縁起と空：如来臓批判」 or *Dependent Origination and Śūnyatā: Critical Examination of Tathāgata Garbha*), Tokyo: Daizō Shuppan Ltd., 1989.: p. 13. Matsumoto explains the concept of Dhātuvāda as follows: 「単一な実在である基対 (*dhātu*) が多元的な*dharma* を生ずる」と主張する説。簡単に「発生論的一元論」とか「根源実在論」を指す。」

§5. BUDDHISM'S DISAPPEARANCE UPON HINDU-MUSLIM CONFRONTATION

The initial decline of Buddhism was due to the invasion of the Ephthalite (White Hun) led by Mihilakula (502-545), and the rule lasted half a century. The Mahāyāna Buddhist Saṅgha in Gandhāra region could never recover from the destruction as recorded by Hsüan-tzang, and the Sarvāstivādin Orthodoxy in Kashimīr was totally destroyed. Mihilakula not only treacherously murdered the king who once pardoned his life, and plundered the entire country, but also destroyed the Buddhist establishments which had lasted since Aśoka's time, murdered the Arhat, head of the Saṅgha, and demolished the begging bowl, symbol of the Dharma succession. Ironically, some of the records inform us that this inglorious Ephthalite ruler generously granted lands and temples to the Śaiva school, worshippers of god Śīva. The regions became soon the supporting ground of the Hindu sect of Śaivism. The revival of Buddhism took place now in Eastern India under the patronage of the Guptan rulers. The Nālandā University was built, and the Bodhagayā temple was refurbished. Nevertheless, this revival never meant to be a real grass-root recovery, because, by then, people had mostly been subjected to Hindu social processes and lost their free contact with the Buddhist Saṅgha due to the tightened caste structure.

The second and fatal blow that accentuated the real disappearance of Buddhism was the Muslim military assault that likely occurred around the years from 1199 to 1200. It is difficult to determine in precise terms when and how Buddhism disappeared from the subcontinent. In fact, Buddhism did not totally disappear and continued to survive through the periods of Muslim domination and British colonialism as scattered regional pockets throughout the subcontinent. I am inclined, however, to place the turning point of Buddhism's disappearance at the time of the destruction of Nālandā University and the assault of Bodhagayā Temple by a Muslim expedition led by Muhammad Bakhtyar Khilji.[29] According to the historians, it occurred likely in the fall-winter season of the year

---

[29] Cf. Narendra Krshna Sinha and Anil Chandra Banerjee: *History of India,* Calcutta: A. Mukherjee & Co., 1952 (4th ed); p. 216. This adventurer was a Turk, a troop leader under the Governor of Oudh, and held a fief in the Mirzapur district, U.P. At the time, South Bihar was practically unprotected, because the Pāla dynasty was probably extinct, and the Sena Kingdom lay to the east.

1199-1200.[30]

We have another source of information in the *Biography of Dharmasvāmin* written by a Tibetan scholar monk Chag-lo-tsa-ba Chos-rje-dpal, in which he gives his direct accounts from his witnessing of these terrifying events.[31] The decline of Buddhism was already witnessed several centuries earlier by the renowned Chinese scholar monk Hsüan-tzang who visited India from 629 through 645[32] In order to know about the general situation of Buddhism in the 12th and 13th centuries and the last phase of Buddhist establishments in Southern Magadha, I consider Dharmasvāmin's account[33] as an invaluable source of information.

When Dharmasvāmin arrived at Bodhagaya, the area was totally vacated. Only four Sinhalese monks were remaining to complete their task in tightly closing up the inner and the outer entrance by bricks and plaster, and drawing the image of Maheśvara over the walls, warding off Hindu hooligans from damaging the monument. Dharmasvāmin saw Buddhasena, governor of Bihar, near the Diamond Seat under the Bodhi tree. When a warning reached them regarding the marching Muslim troops, Buddhasena withdrew to some nearby forest to avoid direct encounter, and Dharmasvāmin together with

---

[30] There is some question regarding his dating. Since Dharmaswamin's visit to India is said to have been from 1234 to 1236, there is a difference of thirty and some years between his dating and the historian's reference to Mohammad Bakhtyar Khilji who died in 1206. According to the authors of the above book, the year of 1234 was that King Iltutmish of Delhi (ruled from 1211 through 1236), known as the builder of the Qutb Minar during 1231-32 in honor of a Muslim saint, invaded Malwa and plundered the cities of Bhilsa and Ujjain. This king is said to have acquired the control of Bengal after the death of Nasir-ud-din, governor of Oudh, in 1229. Since these dates are relatively correct, Dharmaswāmin's chronology ought to be further examined.

[31] The date requires a scrutiny but it may have likely been in the year of 1199-1200, because a record is found in Bihar, indicating that in the year of 1202 the Magadhan King Jayasena, son of Buddhasena, contributed a village in honor of thè Diamond Seat for the sake of up-keeping of the Bodhagaya monument, and the excess harvest was designated to be used for that purpose under the control of a Theravādin monk Maṅgalasvāmin, superintendent of the Bodhagaya Temple. Incidentally, he was a Sinhalese Bhikkhu.

[32] Hsüan-tzang took two years to reach India and studied at Nālandā University and traveled various regions as well as Sinhala country during the following thirteen or fourteen years till 645. Cf. *The Ta-t'amg-hsi-yu-chi* (「大唐西域記」 12 fasc.), [Taisho (No. 2067)]. *The Buddhist Records of the Western World during the Great T'ang Dynasty*, translated by Samuel Beal, originally published 1884 London; Two volumes bound in one, Motilal Banarsidass, Delhi: 1981.

[33] Cf. *The Biography of Dharvasvāmin*, English translation by A. Roerich and A.S. Altekar, Patna: 1959.

those monks sheltered themselves in a secluded place for seventeen days till normalcy returned. That year the Tibetan monk took residence at Bodhagaya for the rainy season retreat and witnessed as many as three hundred Sinhalese service men to stay within the temple compound during the night. Since twelve residential buildings near the compound were well preserved, but nearly all empty with only ten to fifteen occupants, he decided that security was the main reason.

When Dharmasvāmin reached Nālandā, it was after the initial assault of the campus by the Muslim troops. They killed several hundred monks and students and burnt down the library and all of its books. He witnessed the scene that many buildings were still smoldering. He met Śrībhadra of ninety years of age, erudite scholar and head of the university, who was remaining in the ruins together with other seventy or so survived faculty members and students. Buddhasena and a wealthy Brahmin family had been looking after them. According to the semi-contemporary Muslim historian, the soldiers and the leader of the expedition did not know what they were assaulting. The following is a record of that Muslim historian quoted in the *History of India* by Sinha and Banerjee[34]:

> The great number of the inhabitants of that place were Brahmans, and the whole of those Brahmans had their heads shaven, and they were all slain. There was a good number of books there, and when all these books came under the observation of the Musalmans, they summoned a number of Hindus, that they might give them information respecting the import of those books; but the whole of the Hindus had been killed. On becoming acquainted (with the contents of those books), it was found that the whole of the fortress and city was a college, and in the Hindi tongue they call a college Bihar.

From the eleventh century onward, the new conflict began between the Hindu and the Muslim societies in the subcontinent. Both Hinduism and Islam are a secular religion in the sense that (1) each has a body of religious scholars respectively as Brāhmins and Ulamās; (2) neither is a celibate priestly office, but each holding a professional livelihood, (3) both are concerned with the matter of secular affairs while actually living within the secular world. The difference between the two was that Hindu society was

[34] *Op. cit.*, p. 216.

compartmentalized with rigid caste rules, whereas Muslim society was rather open with comparatively liberal norms of Koran. With confrontation of the two societies, as Hindu society had no comparable political power or military might, the only way to survive was to tighten the caste structure and prevent the societal disintegration.

In ancient India, it was the contest between the Indo-Arian Kṣatriya's despotic imperialism and the Brāhmaṇa stratum with their legislative superiority by controlling social structure. The *Ambaṭṭha Sutta* suggests such a legislative control of the masses through the use of superstitious magic against the political and military power of the king (Kṣatriya).[35] The problem of Śākyan clansmen, and in this matter, of any of the existing tribal communities, was a squeeze from both sides: one from the Brahman stratum who sought to build up its magico-ritualistic office without regard to clan membership, and another from the imperialist campaign of Kśatriyas who sought to establish its bureaucratic system by edging clan societies towards disintegration.[36] The Śākyas had no chance to survive, so were any of those existing tribal clans. The Buddhist Saṅgha and society actively participated in the social and political policy of the Mauryan Buddhist ruler Aśoka in developing the status-free open society and the paternalistic welfare state by theorizing the ideal of Cakravartin.[37]

The Brāhmaṇa stratum began all out campaign to repudiate this new order by propagating the literature of the four Varṇa codes (*Mānava-dharmaśāstra*), voluminous Epics *Mahābhārata* and *Rāmāyaṇa*, then followed by the compilation of the *Śāstras* and Purāṇas, and so on. The Ephtalite invasion helped Hindus by reducing Buddhist Saṅgha's influence to the lay society, and the Muslim invasion perfected it by appropriating the land estates of Buddhist establishments. By the time of the eleventh century, there was no longer a challenging military might under the social and legislative power of Brāhmaṇa stratum to resist the force of Muslim army. The only way to prevent a total collapse was to tighten the

---

[35] *Ambaṭṭhasutta* (Dīgha Nikāya III, 9607), in which Kanhāyana as the Brāhmaṇa ancestor is depicted as the revolutionary to reşist the despotic power of a legendary Indo-Aryan king Okāka whom Śākyans believed to have been their ancestor.

[36] Cf. Weber, *General Economic History*, The Gree Press, 1950, p. 45. Weber points out that these two major processes are universally observable in other civilizations.

[37] The ancient mythological name of the universal King; Wherever he directs his expedition, the golden wheel with a thousand spokes turns in mid-air to proceed; he is victorious even without a battle.

social structure. Since Buddhist establishment solely depended on such grants, having no grass-root support, when their economic source was once seized, there was no chance for Buddhist Saṅghas to survive along with the Islamic secular religion which allowed no separate priestly status.

§6. CRITICAL SPIRITUALITY AS BASIS OF POPULAR KUAN-YIN[38] CULT IN CHINA

In China, the cult of Kuan-yin Bodhisattva is believed to have begun shortly after Dharmarakṣa's translation of the *Lotus Sūtra* in 286, but most certainly after the more lucid translation of the same text by Kumārajīva in 406 and quickly spread over the divided continent in the north as well as in the south from the fifth century onward.[39] I believe that the dominant cultural force of that early Medieval China was motivated by two major sources of Buddhist spirituality, one being the insight of Prajñāpāramitā and another being Kuan-yin's activist love and compassion. It was the strike of ingenuity that these spiritual phases were symbolically brought into fusion by Kumārajīva's translation of the Hṛdaya Sūtra.[40] Kuan-yin as Avalokiteśvara in India was a male figure and remained to be so throughout the millennia wherever the image was transmitted. In China, however, despite some of the Indian

---

[38] Two different names are ascribed to this Bodhisattva. The earlier name which appears in Kumārajīva's translation is Avalokitasvara (kuan-shih-yin or Kuan-yin), meaning "one who illumines the voice of the world) and the later one which Hsüan-tzang applied in his version is Avalokiteśvara (kuan-tzù-tsai) meaning "one who excels in illumination). In this paper, the former is invariably used to designate the particular Bodhisattva, except when specification is necessary.

[39] The bibliographical records suggest that there were six translations of the same text, but only three translations ascribed to Dharmarakṣa (「正法華経」 translated in A.D. 286), Kumārajīva (「妙法蓮華経」 in 406), and Jñānagupta and Dharmagupta (「添品法蓮華経」 in 601) are extant. Nāgārjuna quotes this Sūtra, more often than any other scriptures, in his commentary *Upadeśaśāstra* (「大智度論」) of the *Mahā(pañcaviṃśati-sāhasrikā)-prajñāpāramitāsūtra* [「大品般若経」(translated also simultaneously by Kumārajīva in 404)].

[40] The actual title of the short text is the Great Wisdom Prayer Sūtra (「大明呪経」). Since it is identical with Hsüan-tzang's translation *Heart Sūtra* (「般若心経」、*Prajñāpāramitā-hṛdaya-sūtra*), the text in question is invariably called "*Heart Sūtra*" in this paper.

forms of Avalokiteśvara were availed to Chinese Buddhist worship,[41] they developed their own image as an effeminated figure during the T'ang dynasty in accordance with their own cultural and aesthetic taste. This feminine image, or sexually neutral figure, precisely ascertains the fact that the spirituality that underlies the Chinese Kuan-yin cult was and has been the insight of Prajñāpāramitā personified as the epithet of activist love and compassion.[42]

Although Lokesh Chandra theorized that the Indian Avalokiteśvara was a metamorphosis of Brahmā, I am obliged to disagree with his view by asserting that the Indian Buddhist cult of Avalokiteśvara and the East Asian cult of Kuan-yin are not monolithic in spirituality. As I understand Chap. 25 of the *Lotus Sūtra*, Avalokiteśvara's sole concern is to rescue all humans who are in all forms of suffering. Avalokiteśvara's virtue of love and compassion is not a self-serving manifestation of some transcendent agent or principle. As a Bodhisattva, his virtue must be balanced with the insight of *Śūnyatā*, without which he loses his status and *raison-détre* as a Buddhist personification of love and compassion. As to Lokesh Chandra's theory that, only by being a metamorphosis of Brahmā, Avalokiteśvara could successfully assimilate Hindu deities, I disagree first with his extension of this interpretation to the East Asian cultural context, and second, I hold that Avalokiteśvara or Kuan-yin Bodhisattva is supposed to embody the insight of the four holy Truths in terms of *Anātman* as well as in terms of *Śūnyatā*, both of which are imbedded in the *Heart Sūtra*. To substantiate my point of view, I shall introduce Edward Conze's remarkable article on the text of *Prajñā-pāramitāhṛdaya-sūtra*.

In his article included in *JRAS* of 1948, he differentiates seven sections in the *Heart Sūtra* and probes their parallels in the *Large Prajñāpāramitā-sūtras* known as the *Ta-p'in-pan-jo-ching* translated

---

[41] The Hindu deity Śiva was assimilated to Buddhism and gave rise to the name Avalokiteśvara (avalokita-īśvara, Lord Avalokita), thereby allowing the emergence of the thousand-armed Bodhisattvas. Lokesh Chandra asserts that "this Avalokiteśvara sometimes appears as a Buddha and at other times as the Hindu deity Īśvara or Maheśvara (Śiva), without clear reason." So came to being several types of Kuan-yin images that were linked to Hindu iconography, like those endowed with one thousand arms, thousand eyes, four faces, eleven faces, a horse-head, a fearless lion head, a blue neck, and so on.

[42] As Kuan-yin moved east, further new variations arose, including the white-robed Kuan-yin, Kuan-yin holding a willow leaf, Kuan-yin with a fishing basket, and the Kuan-yin of easy child-bearing. This last figure, holding a baby in her arm, was sometimes called "Maria Kannon" in Medieval Japan.

from the *Pañcaviṃśatisāhasrikā-prajñāpāramitā-sūtra.*[43] He demonstrates that all the words, phrases, and lines of the short text were extracted from that larger text. Accordingly, this *Heart Sūtra* is meant to be, as Conze says, "a restatement of the four holy Truths for beginners on the method of bearing this teaching in mind as well as on the spiritual advantages of following it."[44] Conze brilliantly dismisses Tantric influence[45] on this text and substantiates his point of view by proving that both terms, '*vidyā*' and '*mantra*' which appear toward the end of the text, were already in use with similar meaning in the early Pāli scripture like the *Niddessa*,[46] in which '*paññā*' or '*prajñā*' is equated with '*mantra*.' Further, he points out that an earlier section of the *Saṃyutta Nikāya* comprises a section called "the first turning of the wheel of the Law" (*Dhamma-cakka-ppavattana-vaggo*), and that here the knowledge of four holy Truths is equated to *vijjā* (*vidyā* or insight or knowledge).[47] In these texts, neither '*mantā*' (*mantra* in Sanskrit) nor '*vijjā*' (*vidyā*) was intended to mean "a secret, mysterious lore of magical potency which can be compressed into a magical formula, a spell." Rather, these two meant respectively "the knowledge of the four holy Truths which is the fundamental insight (*vijjā*) of the Buddha," and parallel to this first turning of the wheel (*dharma-cakra-pravartana-sūtra*), the main subject of which is the *four holy Truths*'[48] the Mahāyāna Buddhists regarded the *Heart Sūtra* as "the second turning of the wheel of the law." This Mahāyāna Buddhist thought

[43] *Ta-p'in-pan-jo-ching* (「大品般若経」、「摩訶般若波羅蜜経」、*Pañca-viṇśati-sāhasrikā-prajñāpāramitā-sūtra*) translated by Kumārajīva, 404. Taishō. 8, (No, 223).

[44] Edward Conze: "Text, Sources, and Bibliography of the *Prajñāpāramitā-hṛdaya*," *Journal of Royal Asiatic Society*. 1948, p. 47.

[45] The closing passage of the *Hṛdayasūtra* comprises a few Tantric terms in stating that "the Prajñāpāramitā is the *mahā-mantro*, the *mahā-vidyā-mantra*." Many argue that these terms indicate some degree of Tantric influence.

[46] Of the two extant commentaries of the *Sutta-Nipāta*, the *Niddesa* is the earlier one, ascribed to Sāriputta, a direct disciple of Śākyamuni, and the *Paramatthajotikā* is the later one ascribed to Buddhaghoṣa of the 5th century. Unlike the latter, the *Nidessa* is confined to some parts of the *Sutta Nipāta*.

[47] *Ibid.*, p. 46. *Dhamma-cakka-ppavattana-vaggo* (*Saṃyutta Nikāya*.: Book XII, Chap. 2: Tathāgatena vutta Nos. 11 and 12): The Initial Turning of the Wheel of Dharma (*Saṃyutta-Nikāya*). The equivalent Chinese translation appears as the *Sūtra of the Initial Preaching of Dharma* (「初転法輪経」) in the *Saṃyukta-Āgama*, No. 15 (「雑阿含経」NO. 15, Sect. 17).

[48] *Ibid.*, p. 48.

enormously appealed to the minds of Chinese and East Asian Buddhists. Since East Asian Buddhists were not affected by Hindu culture and belief, the fundamental insight of Śākyamuni was and has been upheld ever since its authentic transmission despite the different culture and thought of East Asia.

In the history of Buddhist teachings, the negation of reality was accomplished twice, and these two stages can be correlated with the development of the Buddhist virtue of love and compassion. According to the Mahāyāna Buddhist thinker, such as Nāgārjuna,[49] there are three motivational contexts of love and compassion which encompass the entire range of material and spiritual fulfillments of human happiness and well-being. In the twentieth fascicle of the *Ta-chih-tu-lun*, for instance, he summarily gives these three motivational contexts as: (1) the love and compassion that is motivated by the similarity of one's self with other selves, i.e., common humanity (*sattva-ālambana*); (2) the love and compassion that is motivated by the sameness of the psycho-physical elements which form the basis of human existence, i.e., five Skandhas (*dharma-ālambana*); and (3) the love and compassion that is motivated by neither of these two contexts, i.e., independent of motivational context (*anālambana*).[50]

The initial context is based on human rationality, which requires no negation, hence universal to all religions and thoughts. In human science, human love is classified into five distinct categories of separate affectional systems, namely, maternal love, infant-mother love, age-mate or peer love, heterosexual love, and paternal love.[51] Taking these basic bonds of love as a foundation, human interaction evolved to create the bonds of family, neighborhood, community,

---

[49] His active life may be referred to the period of AD 50 through 150, and was the greatest Mahāyāna thinker, the originator of the Mādhyamika school, the author of *Mūlamadhyamakakārikāśāstra* (「中論」) translated by Kumārajīva in 409 and many other texts. His most voluminous commentary *Mahāprajñāpāramitopadeśaśāstra* (「大智度論」) is only avalable in Chinese translated by the same master in 404.

[50] Taishō. 25, p. 209a: 「無尽意菩薩問中説、慈有三種、一者修生縁、二者法縁、三者無縁」 As given in parenthesis, Lamotte correctly gives the respective Sanskrit terms *sattva-ālambana*, *dharma-ālambana*, and *anālambana*. *Ālambana* is an epistemic term to signify cognitive object to be seen, heard, etc. by sense faculties. I introduced the above three criteria by adding the "motivational context" to each of them, because human love and compassion is generally activated in observing, hearing, or knowing some form of imbalance in a given context of some other persons.

[51] *International Encylopedia of Psychiatry*, London: Roughsh Co., 1972. p. 445.

society, and so on, and simultaneously developed ethical principles or normatives of action to regulate human interaction at all levels of human organization. Although neighborly love appears to be largely accepted as a universal phenomenon and thus as a self-evident moral principle, one must still ask: By what justification should such love become a norm in practical ethics? In early Buddhism, the answer was rather simple. The bottom line is that one's self is dearest to every person, and that love of one's self is common to all humans. It follows that since there is nothing more important than one's self, no one would wish to be harmed by another, and neither would anyone wish to harm anyone else on account of that similarity. Accordingly, for early Buddhists, neither a metaphysical principle nor a theological being was necessarily required as a foundation for the principle of neighborly love. The principle simply relied on the fact that one's self and the selves of others are the same, equally giving rise to suffering and rejoicing in their very humanness.

The next higher motivational context is anchored in the insight of *dharma*-theory, requiring the initial negation. The Buddhist insight of Non-self derives from the fact that an individual person is a composite entity comprising multiple phenomenal elements classified into five aggregates (*pañca-skandha*), and that a human person is causally manufactured out of these sensory and mental propensities without any core substance like "self." An individual's self is nothing more than a fictitious designation imposed upon the five aggregates of psycho-physical elements (*rūpa-caitasika-dharmā*).[52] This second motivational context of love and compassion is a step removed from the context of humanity in the common sense world, because an individual person is now viewed in terms of multiple building blocks organized by inner causality. The previously independent human individual is lost here in the wider and more universal landscape of physical, biological, and mental data or elements, becoming an illusory non-existent being. Being thus totally

---

[52] Pañca-skandhas: (1) an aggregate of physical or material facts (*rūpa-skandha*) arising from the contact of six faculties with their objects of seeing, hearing, smelling, tasting, touching, and awareness; (2) an aggregate of facts of sensation (*vedanā-skandha*) arising from subjective impressions of contact as either favorable (kuśala), unfavorable (akuśala), or neutral (avyākṛta) to one's disposition; (3) an aggregate of facts of perception or ideation (saṃjñā-skandha) arising from diverse cognitive assimilation involving naming and differenting; (4) an aggregate of facts of mental activities or forces [usually given in plural (*saṃskāra-skandha*)], crucial to the function of bringing together, formulating or constructing conceptual, linguistic, and volitional responses; (5) an aggregate of facts of awareness, cognition, or consciousness (*vijñāna-skandha*).

freed from the causes of moral and spiritual defilement (*anāsrava*), they see that all humans are merely aggregations of continual flows of sensory and mental elements and ultimately of the empty nature without any substance of identity. This meant that at this stage, the ideal Buddhist human type of the orthodoxy, called 'Arhat,' is one who is totally liberated and independent of all entrapment, social, cultural, and so forth, being exclusively confronted by the bottom line. It was this realization that was the content proclaimed and taught by Śākyamuni at his initial turning of the wheel as the four holy Truths. Why, however, was it necessary to repudiate the reality of *dharmas* for the second time from the point of view of the Mahāyāna thinkers?

§7. *Śūnyatā* as Critical Spirituality: Principle of Communication and Reconciliation

Ancient Greeks thought that the highest good is the human happiness or well being that comes from the fulfillment of all human potential. Aristotle dealt with theoretical and practical virtue as the major subject matter of human ethics. He was convinced with the faculty of reason as the ultimate criterion for theoria as well as for praxis. Reason develops itself partly as rational action and partly as rational thought toward perfection. The Stoic philosophers (nearly all Romans) closely followed the Greeks in harvesting the fruits of enquiry by Socrates, Plato, and Aristotle. They introduced an ideal human type, Stoic sage, who exemplifies theoretical and practical virtue in perfected harmony with nature and reason.

Some great Romans, such as, Marcus Aurelius, Ceneca, Epictetus, and so on, came to experiment the goal of Magnanimity in political action. For them, reason and nature, synonymous in their meaning, embody the ultimate ethical principle. Reason was regarded as "nature" not only of man, but of the universe in general. Nature means "universal Nature, the creative, cosmic power, the world-thought acting according to ends."[53] They were convinced that life according to Nature and according to reason is a duty which the wise man has to fulfil, a law to which he has to subject himself in opposition to his sensuous inclinations. The concept of Natural Law

[53] W. Windelband, *A History of Philosophy* translated into English by James H. Tufts, New York: Macmillan Co., 1956; p. 171. [orignally written in German and publlished by Macmillan, 1893].

we have today to guarantee Human Rights originated in those classical philosophers.

The problem of Stoicism, however, was to show how and why the universe is of such a nature that ethical progress is reasonable. Though they were convinced of harmony with nature or following nature by reason, they could not say what nature is except that it is an abstract system. The Stoic ideal figure was too lofty and strong a character for average people and did not offer a regard for human sympathy and human weakness. When the ideal of magnanimity with political action faltered, the idea of tragedy set in, leading to fear and open the way to a life with faith. In our contemporary world too, I am afraid that the global communities are facing two alternative principles of action in order to survive through global turmoils and conflicts, namely, either to make the principle of faith or the principle of reason as basis of collective action. Religious extremism is on the rise. Would reason hold its primary role? Consider if it would be possible to open dialogue to establish communication between Hindu and Muslim based on their respective religious principles. Human rights based on reason are at bay!

At the time of Marcus Aurelius (160-180), Christians were challenging the Roman religious cult and the Imperial authority, and the philosopher ruler reflected upon his Stoic principle of reason and the Christian principle of faith. His Reflection[54] reminds us that Romans were facing similar alternatives. He says, we Stoics accept death in a disinterested manner, if it is the most reasonable choice. Christians, however, seem to accept death blindly without making their decision on reason, believing that it is the gate-way to heaven, or at least, a release from hell. Stoics think that man is wholly capable of autonomy, but Christians insist upon the fragility and weakness of humans to need some transcendent aid. Stoics allow prayer of thanksgiving but not for intercession, because making the nature conform with human wish is not possible, but Christians allow both prayers. Moreover, Stoics have a sense of tragedy to accept fate, but Christians have neither.

I am, of course, aware that classical rationalism based on objective observation and modern rationalism based on inner awareness are different, and that ancient philosophers were not

---

[54] Marcus Aurelius Antoninus the Stoa mounted the Roman imperial throne. His work is said to be the characteristic monument of this eclectic-religious Stoicism. English translation by G. Long. *The Thoughts of the Emperor*, M. Aurelius Antoninus.

subjected to the problem of language and logic. The matter of communication, however, necessarily becomes an issue when any kind of interaction is undertaken between two humans or groups of humans. Logically, what is essential to valid communication between two interlocutors is that whatever is under discussion must be identical in the minds of speaker and listener. But often times, this simple criterion is hard to come by. Even when the subject matter is expressed by one and the same term, the respective predications create different meanings, resulting in a discrepancy between their references. Here is an example of logical dispute that took place in Medieval India. It is the well known controversy between the Naiyāyika and Mīmāṃsaka, on the subject of Śabda or the "vocal word." The former empiricist school held that "an uttered vocal word is impermanent" because no sooner it comes into being than as a sound made by human enunciation, it perishes. However, the latter transcendentalist school vehemently countered with their assertion that "Śabda is permanent" because it elicits the same meaning in the mind of all listeners in any place at any time. Logically, is it possible to implement communication?

The Buddhist logicians offered the following way to make both parties meet again. They approached the above logical dispute with three cautious considerations which seem to be especially relevant to the context of inter-religious dialogue. (1) They lay emphasis on the respective reasons, namely, "being a product" and "being audible," but not on the syllogism as a whole, because each syllogism is valid in the light of syllogistic rules. (2) They also accepted their simultaneous validity within each system of philosophical presuppositions referring to their underlying thoughts, i.e., "Whatever is a product is impermanent," and "Whatever is audible is permanent." (3) They shifted both the mental process and the logical meaning on to a different plane from that of logical laws, i.e., to the pre-linguistic process of the mind. In other words, the Buddhist logicians intended to resolve the confrontation, not in the logical and linguistic domain, where contradiction holds, but in the subliminal domain prior to the logical and linguistic process. This is one way to create a middle ground where mutual toleration becomes possible.

Buddhists were keenly aware that perceptual and conceptual error or difference is likely to occur in the subliminal plane of consciousness due to a variety of biases. Even a spontaneous perception is an interpretative and unconscious version of what we do after we have perceived. It follows that whatever is asserted by naming is more than likely non-existent, because whatever is designated is a result of defiled mental propensities. This Buddhist approach was important, because the shifting of the problem of contradiction to the subliminal plane provides a logical and psychological middle ground for both parties. This Buddhist approach is dialectical because it involves negation of both assertions on the basis of their mutual contradiction. The Buddhist thinkers thought that reconciliation or communication is only possible at a different level of cognitive process where both assertions ought to be negated, because their claimed reality is equally absent. This is a practical exercise of Buddhist critical spirituality.

The foregoing treatment by Buddhist logicians can be traced to the original Śākyamuni's insight, such that Ignorance (*avidyā*) is the fundamental cause of suffering. Ignorance (lack of wisdom) means uncritical belief in or blind conviction in the existence of one's self and of things that belong to the self (*kāya-dṛṣṭi*). The entire Buddhist system of thought and practice is directed to the matter of how and why we should eradicate this erroneous conviction. Śākyamuni provided the eight-fold holy path,[55] which the orthodoxy expanded into the more elaborate thirty-seven auxiliary practices, required to rid the false conviction in the reality of self[56] The Mahāyāna theorists later introduced the more simplified system of practice as the six norms of perfection (*ṣaḍ-pāramitā*).[57] These six Pāramitās are divided into two groups pertaining to theoretical and practical virtues.[58] Although these two groups of practices ought to be carried out simultaneously, practical virtue was often emphasized as a precondition for the advancement of theoretical virtue. What is

---

[55] 「八聖道」

[56] *Saptatriṃśikabodhipakṣika-dharmā* (三十七菩提分法): An arrangement of the seven sets of practices comprising thirty-seven items. (1) *catvāri smṛtyupasthānāni* (四念住) or four kinds of mindfulness concerned with breathing, posture, etc., (2) *catvāropradhānāni* (四精勤) or four kinds of diligence toward moral perfection, (3) *catvararddhipadaḥ* (四神足) or four kinds of supernormal powers acquired through samādhi), (4) *pañcaśraddhā-indriya* (五根) or five kinds of faculty of enlightenment, (5) *Pañcabala* (五力) or five kinds of superior power to realization of Nirvāṇa, (6) *saptabodhyaṅgāni* (七覚支) or seven disciplines for acquisition of equanimity of the mind toward enlightenment, and (7) *aṣṭaṅgika-ārya-mārga* (八正道) or eight holy paths of the Buddhas.

[57] In his *Ta-chih-tu-lun* (「大智度論」), Nāgārjuna explains that the practices of charity (*dāna*), morality (*śīla*), and patience (*kṣānti*) constitute the norms of practical virtue, whereas diligence (*vīrya*), meditation (*dhyāna*), and insight (*prajñā*) are the norms of theoretical virtue.

[58] *Ta-chih-tu-lun*, *op. cit.*, fasc. 27, p. 262c - p.263a:「初発阿　多羅三藐三菩提意、欲度一切衆生老病死等身心諸苦、作大誓荘厳功徳慧明二事、因縁故所願皆満、是二事有六分修行、名六波羅蜜、布施持戒忍辱是功徳分、精進禅定智慧是慧明.」

unique with Buddhist theoretical virtue is the insight of non-duality or the absence of reality in all things.

A similar problem of communication can occur in the popular cult of Kuan-yin in the mind of devotees. Nāgārjuna notes some sceptical views about the possibility of communication between human prayer wishing salvation and Kuan-yin's transcendent love and compassion. He says: Although the great love and compassion are the foundation of the Buddha-Dharma, some think that these must be of the defiled nature, like lotus flowers, because these are rooted in impure mud. Surely the flowers are pure, but the mud itself cannot be said to be pure. Hence, the Buddha's love and compassion must be of the defiled nature, as far as its origin is concerned.[59] Again, since the Buddha comes into being because of his love and compassion for fellow humans, his love and compassion must be of the defiled nature.[60] The underlying thought of these words is that communication, in general, ought only to be possible between minds which share the same convention.

The dispute between Naiyāyika and Mīmāṃsaka is human communication in horizontal terms, whereas the human prayer toward Kuan-yin Bodhisattva, and in this matter, the Christian prayer to God too, is vertical between human and transcendent. How can we expect that communication goes through from the totally defiled faculty to the undefiled transcendent faculty (of Kuan-yin)? The locus of Kuan-yin's promises is in the human world, but his love and compassion seems to be consistent with the transcendent love and compassion of the Buddhas, for whom the abode is non-duality based on two consecutive negations of this human world and the other world. Returning to the *Hṛdaya Sūtra*, in the first half of the text, it repudiates the reality of the five Skandhas, the twelve chains of causation, and that of the four holy Truths. In this manner the doctrine of the orthodoxy is altogether repudiated. In the latter half of the text, it begins with the merit of the foregoing negation as follows: "On account of this unreality of 'acquisition' and 'non-acquisition,' the Bodhisattva relies on the practice of Prajñāpāramitā introspection, and thereby has his mind liberated from obstacles. Having no obstacle, he has no fear and is free from all up-side-down delusion, and eventually ultimate deliverance from suffering and distress."[61] This is the Buddhist

---

[59] *Ibid*., fasc. 27, p.257b: 「大慈大悲雖是仏法之根本、故是有漏、如水於泥中生蓮華、不得言泥亦応妙、大慈大悲亦如是。」

[60] *Ibid*., fasc. 27, p. 257b: 「仏以慈悲心為衆生故生応是有漏。」

[61] *na jñānaṃ na prāptir nāprāptiḥ tasmāc chāriputra aprāptitvād*

answer, to the question about the notion of tragedy and that of fate. It must be noticed, however, that Buddhist answer is different from that of Christians as to why, despite the fact that both reply "No."

§8. CONCLUSION

My lengthy analysis of the Śākyan tragedy in the early part of this paper is intended to show how and why cultural and ethnic difference could be a monumental cause of human suffering, and it is so tragically similar between twenty-five centuries ago and today as witnessed within the past decade. I have also attempted to show that sociological and cultural analyses can sufficiently prove how and why Śākyamuni's spirituality was motivated to take the course of renunciation as breakthrough action and to organize the Buddhist Saṅgha as his educational institution. Empiricist theory too explains this epoch-making event as an appropriate response to historical challenge. It follows that upon its origination, Buddhist spirituality was necessarily ethical in the sense that it is inseparable from Śākyamuni's action. Why should Buddhist spirituality be regarded as "critical" instead of "positive."?

The *Heart Sūtra* provides the answer. As suggested by Conze, the textual contention was "the second turning of the wheel of Dharma." Initially, Śākyamuni is said to have given his discourse for the first time at the Dear Park (Sarnath). This is the so called "initial turning of the wheel of Dharma" on his central teaching consisting of the four holy Truths. The teaching is directed toward the eradication of false conviction in one's self and about things believed to belong to that self. Now, the above text, which professes "the second turning of the wheel of Dharma," concisely summarized the Mahāyāna reformist point of view of the same four holy Truths in terms of eradication of the false conviction in the reality of elements of the five aggregates. This insight into the voidness of reality (*Śūnyatā*) is deeper, thorough, and universal as critical negation.

Life in general carries varieties of suffering. From the immemorial past, humans have continually sought solutions within the material environment of external nature and within the immaterial inner sphere of human nature. In this human context, Buddhism shares

---

bodhisattvo prajñāpāramitām āśritya viharaty acittāvarvaraṇaḥ, cittāvarṇa-nāstitvād atrasto viparyāsa-atikrānto, niṣṭhā-nirvāṇaḥ//

with the classical philosophers the freedom from sufferings and the fulfillment of happiness on the basis of rational faculty. How, then, should Buddhist critical spirituality go along with the faculty of reason in practical life? The Buddhist critical insight, which attempted twice to eradicate the false conviction in human reality in terms of *anātman* and transcendent reality (five Skandhas) in terms of *śūnyatā*, sees neither reality in "attainment" nor in "non-attainment," because "attainment" conceptually implies duality in itself as "a thing to be attained" and "an agent of attaining," And these correlatives too are seen as unreal in terms of *śūnyatā*. This was the Buddhist way of overcoming the fear of fate and tragedy theorized by ancient Grecian and Roman thinkers.

Buddhist critical insight has a positive aspect as well as sustaining force of the activist life embodied in "Bodhisattva Way." What we learned from the history of Indian Buddhism is that withdrawn into the pacifist monastic life style, Buddhist Saṅgha suffered irretrievable weakness and was unable to re-assert its active engagement in people's life. Secular Hinduism wielded its influence to convert society through Hindu social processes and successfully severed the link between the Saṅgha and lay communities. It was in this context that Mahāyāna movement began under the banner of Bodhisattva Way centered on the moral and spiritual paradigm of Śākyamuni. The life-style of the Bodhisattva embodied the ideology of those reform-oriented activists who opposed the pacifist monastic tradition and spontaneously emphasized the virtue of love and compassion maximally exemplified by Śākyamuni's early career of spiritual pursuit as a Bodhisattva. This movement was, however, bound to be one-half revolution, because the practitioners, even following Mahāyāna Buddhism, remained in monastic institution. I believe, therefore, if Buddhism should revive to its full extent in India, it ought to take the form of a lay Buddhist Saṅgha and an activist moment engaged directly in secular society.

Indian society began with caste norms and social compartmentalization. If history embodies a system of progress toward the ideal of human equality and open society based on human reason, Indian history had a good beginning due to the successful Buddhist movement in ancient India. Soon after that success, however, Indian history seems to have ironically taken the course of counter movement. Of course, there were sufficient causal factors to strengthen this counter movement due to the continual inflow of foreign races and cultures or political and military interventions or colonial domination. Hindus and Muslims lived side by side in the subcontinent till half a century ago, but they formed two independent nations as India and

Pakistan by partition. Now, it is likely the time for India as well as for Pakistan to take its natural course of development to give remedy to the past, especially because the world communities as a whole have been advocating Human Rights today as natural and common to all humans.

Every religious tradition advocates a theme "to return to the original spirituality." The more intensified in disputes and confrontations within or without, the more dogmatic and self-assertive it likely becomes in dealing with the problem of differences. As a result, religious believers likely become hostile and belligerent toward human rationality or secular reasoning. It is unfortunate to see time again how more often human rationality has been muffled, smothered and yielded under the pressure of blind inclination and demand. Critical reasoning is not enough today or at any past period to prevent such courses of development. This is the reason to present the thesis of this paper as the critical spirituality of Buddhism. Reason ought to be the bottom line to deal with human affairs, and human spirituality ought to assist reasoning in thought and action.

ARTICLE TWO

Nāgārjuna's Historicity on the Basis of *Suhṛllekha* and *Ratnāvalī*[1]

§1. Introduction

Despite the paramount importance of Nāgārjuna's contribution to the history of Buddhism, we are painfully aware that no tangible evidence is yet found about his life career in terms of historical fact, nor has any theory been developed to circumscribe his existence from the point of view of human terms. The reason is very clear that whatever knowledge we have today as accumulated in the course of a century from the times of La Vallée-Poussin and Stcherbatsky is all compartmentalized. There has not been a theory that successfully linked the four different phases of Nāgārjuna as the career of a single person, namely: (1) a logician to whom the *Upāyahṛdaya-śāstra* is ascribed, (2) a definitive dialectician who wrote the *Madhyamaka-śāstra*, *Vigrahavyāvartanī*, etc., (3) a learned commentator who compiled the encyclopedic *Prajñāpāramitopadeśa-śāstra* and *Daśabhūmikavibhāṣā-śāstra*, and (4) a political and religious councilor who wrote the *Suhṛllekha* and the *Ratnāvalī* for his patron ruler or respectively for two different recipients. In order to break through the aforementioned problem of compartmentalized fields of knowledge, we need some historical context as a beginning point of decipherment to configurate jig-zag puzzles into a whole and evaluate Nāgārjuna's life career beyond those literary works that have been the only avenues to us in modern enquiry.

The purpose of this paper is to demonstrate an attempt for constructing a single human career as Nāgārjuna's out of multiple elements of knowledge that have been hitherto available to us in terms of compartmentalized bits of a whole. In this task, I am initially obliged to set forth an innovative hypothesis that Nāgārjuna may have had an association with the Śaka Satrap of Ujjayinī besides the Śātavāhana king of Andhra country, and thus, as their

[1] Presented at the International Seminar on Contribution of Andhra Desa to Buddhism under the title: " Nāgārjuna as author of *Suhṛllekha* and *Ratnāvalī* and his Eventual Center of Activity as Southern Kosala," Hyderabad, Dec. 26-28, 1997.

counsellor, he wrote the *Suhṛllekha* and the *Ratnāvalī* respectively for the rival contenders of political and military supremacy over Western India. My effort is directed to analyze what cogent and tangible historical context is available to us in reference to the Śaka-Pahlava period in order to substantiate the above hypothesis.

§2. NĀGĀRJUNA'S DATES REVIEWED FROM LITERARY CONTEXTS

Re-examining the period of Nāgārjuna, I came to see that his life career ought to be placed between the middle of the first and that of the second century (A.D. 50-150), and to this effect, I have already published two papers in proposing this hypothesis.[2] There are three premises for that hypothesis: (1) that Nāgārjuna shared a period of his earlier life with the Kuṣāṇa ruler Kaniṣka and a period of his later life with one or more of the Śātavāhana kings, for whom he is traditionally believed to have written the *Suhṛllekha* (*Friendly Epistle)*; (2) that Nāgārjuna's life should fit this time-span between Kaniṣka's supremacy in power and the political and military rivalry of the *Śātavāhana* kings of the South and the Śaka Satraps of Western India over the coastal regions, both periods nonetheless falling within the range of a possible human life-span, i.e., 70-100 years of age; (3) that if Nāgārjuna happened to be associated with a *Śātavāhana* king, say Gautamīputra Śātakarṇi (who ruled the South between A.D. 106-130) or his successor Vāsiṣṭhīputra Pulumāyi (who ruled between 130-159), he was likely associated with some notable rival Śaka ruler, such as, Rudradāman, great Satrap of Ujjayinī, (who ruled during the period 130-155), and thus wrote for ḥim the *Ratnāvalī* (the *String of Pearls*), an exhortation on Buddhist doctrines and principles of governance.

It is well known that Nāgāruna was author of several important dialectical treatises and was traditionally revered not only as founder of the Madhyamaka school of Buddhism but also as that of Mahāyāna Buddhist tradition. Despite his reputed contribution accomplished by his works in the history of Buddhism, it is hardly known how and why he created or innovated his definitive method of dialectic (*prasaṅga-vākya*). Even though he was an extraordinary

---

[2] Ichimura: "Re-examining the Period of Nāgārjuna: Western India, A.D. 50-150," *Journal of Indian and Buddhist Studies* (*Indo-gaku Bukkyōgaku* ***Kenkyū***), Vol. 40, No. 2, March 1992; "The Period of Nāgārjuna and the ***Fang-pien-hsin-lun*** (「方便心論」) or *Upāyahṛdayaśāstra*,," *loc. cit.*, Vol 43, No. 2, March 1995. [*The journal is abbreviated* henceforth as *JIBS*.]

man of capacity, surely such an important innovation to the polemical method as well as the method of expression for the insight of *Śūnyatā* could not have come suddenly out of nowhere. There must have existed a preceding stage of his career. On the basis of this assumption, I searched for a clue to decipher his dialectic in two directions. One is the problem of logical deadlock which was left unsolved by the editors of the *Kathāvatthu.*[3] Another is the problem of authorship of the logical theory of *Upāyahṛdaya-śāstra* ascribed to Nāgārjuna. The latter text was translated by Kiṅkara and Tan-yao in 473 A.D., seventy years after the translation of Nāgārjuna's major works by Kumārajīva (344-413). In his early career, Nāgārjuna must have been trained in the Ābhidharmika tradition, and if he somehow participated in the fourth Buddhist Council held in Kaśmīra, and, especially, along with Pārśva and Aśvaghoṣa, in the editorial task to compile the *Mahāvibhāṇyāśāstra,* he was surely aware of the doctrinal problem that continued to haunt the Ābhidharmika tradition from the preceding third Buddhist Council. In addition, as it was the post-Epic period, Nāgārjuna was compelled to encounter the intellectual activities of Hindu schools of philosophy and science, which Vidyabhusana characterized in terms of Indian age-old *Ānvīkṣikī* tradition.[4]

The *Upāyahṛdayaśāstra* was definitely a product posterior to the early archaic system of logic included in the *Vimāna* section, the third Book of the *Carakasaṃhitā,*[5] because the logical text in question proposed an innovative system apart from that of Hindu logical development, and it consisted of two primary criteria that became crucial to the later development of Buddhist logic. First, the requirement of "instantiation" (*dṛṣṭānta*), which all Indian schools, Buddhist as well as Hindu, adhered to in terms of corroboration through similar and dissimilar instances (*anvaya* and *vyatireka*), was made the primary principle of the eight categories of its logical theory. In the traditional five-membered syllogism (*pañcāvayavin*)

---

[3] Ichimura: "Ābhidharmika Logical Deadlock in *Kathāvatthu* and Nāgārjuna's Madhyamaka Dialectic," Journal of Indian and Buddhist Studies (*JIBS* in Japan), Vol. 39, No. 2, March 1991. Also see another article: "The Madhyamaka and the Future," *Buddhism into the Year 2000* (*Studies in Buddhology*), Bangkok: Dhammakāya Foundation, 1994, pp. 67-85.

[4] Satis Chandra Vidyabhusana: *A History of Indian Logic,* Motilal Banarsidass reprint, 1971 [Originally published by the University of Calcutta in 1931].

[5] Agniveśa's *Carakasaṃhitā: Text with English Translation and Critical Expression based on Cakrapāṇi Datta's Āyurveda,* Varaṇasi: Chowkhamba Sanskrit Series, 1976, Book 3, Chap. 8, Specific Requirements for Treatment; Esp. passages 27 ff.

of inference, instantiation (*dṛṣṭānta*) constitutes the third statement (*udāharaṇa*) after the position of a thesis (*pratijñā*) and the reason (*hetu*). But the *Upāyahṛdayaśāstra* theorized the primary business of logic as the principle of instantiation in terms of classifying the similar group (*sapakṣa*) and dissimilar group of instances (*vipakṣa*), and thus determining a given subject of inference as a class member of *sapakṣa*, and (2) secondarily positing a reason (*hetu*) that implies its conclusion (*sādhya*) in reference to that substratum. Second, the number of syllogistic statements was reduced down to three by the criterion of "linguistic excellence" (*vākya-praśaṃsā*) together with its contrary "linguistic deficiency" (*vākyadoṣa*). Accordingly, Arnold Kunst asserts that Dignāga's theory of three-membered syllogism was deeply influenced by Nāgārjuna's *Upāyahṛdayśāstra*. The fact that Buddhist logicians revealed an indisputable, common inclination toward the effort of eliminating verbal elements from the syllogistic formula so as to precipitate the purely logical process of the mind was foreshadowed by Nāgārjuna's logical and dialectical insight.[6]

Nāgārjuna's critique against the Naiyāyika system of logic expressed in the *Vigrahavyāvartanī* and *Vaidalyaprakaraṇa* also determines the period of his polemical interaction. Today, the following are generally accepted: (1) Nāgārjuna not only knew the sixteen categories of the Nyāya system, and hence he knew the *Nyāyasūtra*'s Chap. 1, but he also knew Chap. 5, consisting of *Jāti* and *Nigrahasthāna*. (2) The *Nyāyasūtra's* Chaps. 2 through 4, however, may have been written after Nāgārjuna's death. Thus, the *Vigraha-vyāvartanī* 30-51 and the *Nyāyasūtra's* Chap. 2: Sect. 1, Sūtras 8-19, reflect disputes between Nāgārjuna and the Naiyāyikas at much the same stage, but not necessarily one referring to another.[7]

Refuting Vidyabhusana, Prof. H. Ui argued in 1925 that the *Upāyahṛdayaśāstra* was not Nāgārjuna's work in light of his adeptness in the use of logic and knowledge, but it was due to some Ābhidharmika who appeared after the compilation of the *Carakasaṃhitā*.[8] I came to know, however, that Ui failed to see the

---

[6] Arnold Kunst: "The Two Membered Syllogism," *Rocznik Orientalistyczny*, XV (1939-40), p. 76; and also his preface to a Sanskrit edition, *Mélanges Chinois et Bouddhiques* (1948-1951).

[7] Cf. A. Kunst's preface to a Sanskrit edition, *loc. cit.*, and also Yuichi Kajiyama's "Cognition and Logic," *The Collection of Lectures on Buddhism* (『仏教講座』), Vol. 9, 1984

[8] Hakuju Ui: "A Study on the *Hōben-shin-ron* with Annotations" (「方便心論の註釈的研究」); Publilshed as part of his monograph, *Indian*

logical nature of *dṛṣṭānta* as exclusively concerned with linguistic expression or description about similar (*sapakṣa*) and dissimilar (*vipakṣa*) classes of instances, and hence, have agreed with Vidyabhusana and Kunst in that Nāgārjuna was its author. Logical understanding may require some length of time. In his earlier days, Nāgārjuna began to master the science of logic on the basis of the logical system compiled in the *Carakasaṃhitā*. His innovative dialectical method may have been the product of long, arduous search and contemplation.

What I am getting at is that Nāgārjuna's polemical activities with non-Buddhist philosophers, ought to be placed between the time of *Carakasaṃhitā,* contemporaneous to King Kaniṣka, and that of the completion of the pre-classical *Nyāyasūtra* by Akṣapāda around the mid-second century at Prabhāsa in the region of Kāthiawār, West India.[9]

§3. NĀGĀRJUNA'S DATES REVIEWED FROM HISTORICAL CONTEXTS

Nāgārjuna's dates have hitherto been influenced by the dates of Kaniṣka, and according to the current consensus, his active life is placed in the later half of the second century. In refuting this hypothesis, I resorted to Prof. A. Basham's two articles which are the most persuasive,[8] and I have set the time of Kaniṣka's political and military supremacy coinciding with the beginning of the Śaka era (A.D. 78). Basham argued (1) that Kaniṣka and Rudradāman, great Śaka Satrap of Ujjayinī, cannot be considered contemporaneous, because both were characters of such high caliber that peaceful coexistence would have been well nigh impossible, (2) that Rudradāman's Sanskrit panegyric found in Girnar, Kāthiāwār, the locality known to us by Aśoka's inscription, ought to be dated as A.D. 150 in reference to the *Śaka* era 72, and (3) that the only occurrence of the Roman title "Caesar" in India, as adopted by Kaniṣka II in *Śaka* era 41 (i.e., A.D. 119) in Ara inscription, can

---

Philosophical Studies II (「印度哲学研究」), pp. 472-585.

9 Vidyabhusana notes that the abode of Akṣapāda known as Prabhāsa was situated beyond the rock of Girnar in Kathiawar, where we come across all the edicts of Aśoka as well as the Sanskrit inscription of Rudradāman, great Śaka Satrap of Ujjayinī. The date of the latter's panegyric, given as Śaka era 72nd year, corresponds to the year 150 A.D. Thus, the hypothesis of Nāgārjuna's association with Rudradāman as recipient of his *Ratnāvalī* finds a further support from the foregoing cross-philosophical investigation.

only be meaningfully understood in reference to the Romans' victorious conquest over Parthia (including Armenia, Mesopotamia, and Babylonia) under Trajan, because his long expedition and victory took place in the years of A.D. 113 to 117. Hence, Basham concludes that the two other datings, A.D. 128 by S. Konow and A.D. 144 by R. Ghirshman cannot be supported.

The dates of Rudradāman cannot be moved, not only because the *Śātavāhana* king Vāsiṣṭhīputra Pulumāyi (130-159) is recorded in the *Geography of Ptolemy* (VII, 1, 82) as a king Ptolemaius, ruler of the Deccan in the mid-second century, but also because his queen was Rudradāman's daughter.[9] Gautamīputra Śātakarṇi who ruled South India (100-130) prior to Vāsiṣṭhīputra Pulumāyi, is known to have been a great conqueror, of the Brāhmaṇic tradition, asserting the social system of *Varṇas*, conducting the rite of *Aśvameda*, and his early panegyric does not reflect a Buddhist affiliation at all. In the course of military conflict between the Śaka Satraps and this *Śātavāhana* king over the coastal region, Rudradāman of Ujjayinī made peace with him through a matrimonial alliance by sending his daughter to be the queen to his successor Vāsiṣṭhīputra Pulumāyi, whereas the other *Śaka* ruler Nahapāna, of the House of *Kṣaharāta*, in the regions of Mahārāṣtra and Saurāṣtra was destroyed by Gautamīputra Śātakarṇi in A.D. 124. It was only after this time that this king's *Prākrit* inscriptions began to appear in the Buddhist rock-cut temples, recording donations, etc.

If Rudradāman of Ujjayinī, great Śaka Satrap, was indeed the ruler for whom Nāgārjuna wrote the *Ratnāvalī*, then Nāgārjuna's active times may be identified once and for all, in conjunction with the presence of the Śātavāhana kings, to have been in the first half of the second century in the region of Western India. Rudradāman, however, left no words describing himself as a supporter of Buddhism, perhaps due to the fact that the House of Chaṣṭana had been of the Jaina tradition for generations. It is noteworthy, though, that he remained silent about his religious affiliation, including the Jaina. A Sanskrit inscription found in one of the Kāṅheri rock-cut temples [north of Bombay (Lüders, No. 994)], however, implies Rūdradāman's daughter, queen of Vāsiṣṭhīputra Śātakarṇi, to have been a supporter of the Buddhist Saṅgha. Despite the fact that the House of Śātavāhana relied on *Prākrit* for all inscriptions, the queen's record in Sanskrit reflects upon the probable cultural background of Rudradāman's household.

One of the great contributions that Prof. Lamotte made in his well known book, *History of Indian Buddhism,*[10] is his periodization of Śaka-Pahlava Period over the first and second centuries in reference to the Northern and Western India. He especially called attention to the western and coastal regions. Despite the fact that politically, the Kuṣāṇas arrived as latest foreign migrants but established their supremacy obtaining the support of the prior migrants of Scythians (Śaka) and Partians (Pahlava) who actually held real power over regional governance and economic and social function. To characterize in a word, the region of Western India from the mid-first century A.D. through mid-second century, it was an arena of political and military contests between the *Śaka Satraps* of Saurāṣṭra and Ujjayinī of foreign origin on the one hand and the native *Śatavāhana* king of South India on the other, vying for supremacy over the western coastal regions and benefits of maritime trading. Under such a circumstance, historically two processes are inevitable. While political and cultural conflict goes on, there proceeds simultaneous synthesis or assimilation. Lamotte's detailed descriptions of various Hīnayāna Saṅghas on the basis of the variety of inscriptions recorded on the sites of rock-cut temples and the panegyrics of the Śātavāhanas, Buddhist communities were thriving supported by varieties of racial backgrounds, such as, Indians, Greeks, Partians, Sythians, and so forth. Buddhism seems to have uniquely provided a catalytic principle for political mediation and cultural synthesis, while Buddhist communities provided a buffer zone to prevent outright conflicts between the adversaries.

If the life of Nāgārjuna is placed within the time range from the mid-first century A.D. up to the mid-second century, especially in conjunction with Western India, one ought to see (1) evidence of a society as diverse and as attuned as that for which Nāgārjuna wrote his major treatises, i.e., the *Madhyamakakārikā, Vigraha-vyāvartanī* as well as the encyclopedic *Prajñāpāramitopadeśaśāstra* and *Daśabhūmikavibhāṣā-śāstra,* and also (2) see the presence of two rival political and military leaders who created a historically unique environment in Western India, during which time Nāgārjuna was compelled to write his exhortations on religion, ethics and principles of governance for two different patron rulers.

After a few centuries of the Epic period, much of which is still closed to modern historical investigation due to scantiness of

---

[10] *Histoire du Buouddhisme Indien, des Origines á l'ére Śaka,* originally published in 1958 as part of publication of the Oriental Institute of Louvain. An English translation by Sara Webb-Boin came out in 1988 as 36th volume of the institute.

chronologically reliable records, the Śaka-Pahlava era witnessed hordes of tangible historical records. We have series of epigraphies that began to evidence from around that period about the Buddhist institutions, communities and activities, along with political and military records at several localities concentrated in the western coastal regions. This new trend was facilitated by or coincided with, the new Buddhist architecture, such as rock-cut cave temples (*caityagṛha* or *cetiyaghara*) and monasteries (*vihāra*), which provided an excellent medium for carving inscriptions.

To provide only a glimpse of the panoramic phenomena, I shall limit myself to sketching the Buddhist communities of Western India during this Śaka-Pāhlava period:

(1) The Nāsik cave complex consists of 33 caves belonging to Hīnayāna schools [i.e. Pravrajitabhikṣu of the Caturdiśa-saṅgha (the community of monks of the four quarters)]: those belonging to the schools of the Bhadrāyaṇīyas and Caitikas], and included epigraphic records belonging to the Śātavāhana kings [i.e. Kṛṣṇa (37-27 B.C.), Gautamīputra Śātakarṇi (106-130 A.D.), Vāsiṣṭhīputra Pulumāyi (130-159), Yajñaśrī (A.D. 165-194) and also those belonging to the Kṣaharāta Satraps, Nahapāna (119-124 A.D.) and Uṣavadāta.[11]

(2) The Junnar cave complex, located in the 25 miles east of Bombay, consists of some structures that belonged to the Saṅghas of the Dharmottarīyas, Caitikas, Apajītas or Aparājita Schools. The records of donors included the names of Greeks, Śakas, and Pahlavas besides indigenous Indian names, e.g., a *Śaka* named "Ayama" who was Nahapāna's minister; the complex also included some inscriptions of the Satrap Nahapāna (ca A.D. 124).[12]

(3) The Kārli cave complex, called "Valūraka Leṇa Caves," near *Malavli* Station in linking Bombay and Poona, consists of structures that belonged to the Mahāsaṅghika school supported by the people of Dhānyakaṭaka (the region down stream of the Kṛṣṇā River in the Southeast). It also includes structures which belonged to the Dharmottarīyas and Sauvarṣakas Schools, and inscriptions belonging to Nahapāna Satrap and Śātavāhana kings, such as Gautamīputra Śātakarṇi and Vāsiṣṭhīputra Pulumāyi.[13]

---

[11] Heinrich Lüders: *List of Brahmī Inscriptions from the Earliest Times about A.D. 400 with the Exception of Those of Aśoka*, Indological Book House, Varanasi, 1973; pp. 122- 130; No. 1122 - No. 1149. Lamotte: op. cit., pp.509-512

[12] Lüders: *Ibid.*, pp. 130-136, Nos. 1150 - 1183; Lamotte: *Ibid.*, pp. 507-509

[13] Lüders: *Ibid.*, pp. 115-120, Nos. 1086 - 1108; Lamotte: *Ibid.*, pp. 512-514

(4) The Kānheri cave complex, located on the *Salsette* Island 16 miles north of Bombay and 6.25 miles northwest of Thānā ("kānheri" derived from the Sanskrit name Kṛṣṇa-śaila or Kanhasala), consists of structures which belonged to the local Saṅgha and the universal *Saṅgha* of the four quarters (*caturdiśasaṅgha*). There also are structures belonging to the Schools of Bhadrāyanīyas and Aparaśailas and supported by the local people of Nāsika, Kalyāṇa, and the people of Kārṇata and Dhānyakaṭaka of South-eastern India, and included epigraphic records of Vāsiṣṭhīputra Pulumāyi, and Yājñaśrī (165-194), which constitute a veritable merit book (*puṇyapustaka*) specifying donations and individual donors by name.[14]

In addition to these, there are the Bhājā cave complex in the Western Ghāṭs between Bombay and Poona; the *Bedā* complex near the *Bhājā*; the Kondāne cave complex 10 miles northwest of Kārli; the Pitakhorā cave complex which included inscriptions of various families from the region of Pratiṣṭhāna (present day Paithan), and the Ajantā cave No. 1 at the center of the complex for various Hīnayāna schools.[15]

From the inscribed names, it is difficult to determine the racial background of each donor, except those ruling families, such as Nahapāna and Uṣavadāta of the Kṣaharāta as well as Rudradāman, Jayadāman, Rudrasena of the Chaṣṭana, or the ministers and officials with specified titles and familial backgrounds. Nevertheless, western India during the initial two centuries was in the veritable Śaka-Pahlava period in the sense that the descendants of these races dominated the economic and political dimensions of society and actively participated in supporting the Buddhist Saṅghas by providing them with housing, a supply of funds for maintenance and repair, as well as daily needs of the monks.

More importantly, the agents of these recorded deeds of religious piety represent not only the Śaka-Pahlava populace but indeed also many individuals, merchants and craftsmen, men of all walks of life from South India, referring to the reigns of Śātavāhana kings in their records. In short, each and every record informs us of the ongoing phenomenal co-enterprise devoted to the support of Buddhist Saṅghas, transcending racial, political, cultural, and social differences. This was an impressive development out of the religious, cultural and social conflict that preceded it in the earlier period.

---

[14] Lüders: *Ibid.*, pp. 101-109, Nos. 984 - 1034, Lamotte: *Ibid.*, pp. 514-515

[15] Lamotte: *Ibid.*, 504-507

§4. ŚĀTAVĀHANA KINGS VERSUS ŚAKA SATRAPS:: POLITICAL AND CULTURAL CONFLICT

Although the Śakas entered into the subcontinent after the Pahhlavas, the two races did not distinguish their cultural bearings but equally adopted the Indo-Helenic civilization and the Persian system of administration, and thus ruled over the conquered land by dividing it into a number of provinces by governorship (Satrap), and rapidly assimilated themselves with Indian civilization. In the year of 58 B.C., a native ruler called Vikramāditya briefly succeeded in having the *Śakas* withdraw from the regions of Saurāṣṭra and Mālwā and made the beginning of the native calendar called Vikrama era.[16] But one hundred thirty-five years later, a Śaka king reconquered the same regions and placed his capital in Ujjayinī. This victory is said to have occurred in 78 A.D., but there is an ambiguity about whether this new Śaka era was made to commemorate the point of departure of the Śaka victory, or to commemorate the beginning of Kaniṣka's Kuṣāṇa suzerainty.[17] In any case, the Śakas produced two Satraps: (1) the House of Kṣaharāta which ruled over the regions of Saurāṣṭra and as far as Sindhu, and (2) the House of Chaṣṭana which established its rule in Mālwā by making its capital at Ujjayinī.

Of the two political and military forces of the Śaka Satraps in Western India, Nahapāna and his son-in-law Uṣabhadāta of the House of Kṣaharāta actively affiliated themselves with Buddhism and generously supported Buddhist Saṅghas with gifts of caves,

---

[16] The aforementioned Jaina text *Kālakācāryakathānaka* also refers to the conflict between the Śakas and a native king of Mālwā Vikramāditya and to the latter's victory, over the invading Śakas by the year 58 B.C. This event is believed to have marked the inauguration of a new, so-called, Vikrama era. A. L. Basham, however, discredits this native era, because, he asserts, it was not known till the fourth century A.D. and only after its adoption by local clans, such as Mālwā, in that century and onward. Hence, there is no evidence of whether and when the Vikrama era really began. Basham: "A New Study of Śaka-Kuṣāṇa Period," *loc. cit.*, pp. 7-8; also see É. Lamotte's translated excerpt from the *Kālakācāryakathānaka* in his *History of Indian Buddhism*, pp. 454-455.

[17] Lamotte takes information that the native Vikrama era was passed over to the Śaka era after 135 years, from The Periplus of the Erythraean Sea §41 (Cf. Lamotte, *op. cit.*, p. 455). If the Śaka era marks the beginning of the Śaka victory over the native ruler in Mālwā, the number of 135 years of Vikrama era from its beginning 58 B.C. and the beginning of Śaka era (A.D. 78) do not match. Some ambiguity lingers. Cf. the preceding note.

and so forth. They assumed the rank and title of Kṣatriyas,[18] whereas the members of the House of Chaṣṭana seem to have generally remained affiliated with Jaina religion for generations. The conflict between the Śaka Satraps and the Śātavāhana kings apparently took a collision course when the *Kuṣāṇa* political and military supremacy began to diminish. When the second Kuṣāṇa ruler Vāsiṣka was still in full power with the imperial title (*mahārāja rājādhirāja devaputra ṣāhi*) as evidenced in an inscription of Sāñcī by the 28th year of Śaka Era (A.D. 105), Rudradāman, Satrap of Ujjayinī, the House of Chaṣṭana, was still a vassal under the Kuṣāṇa overlord. Around this time, the name of Gautmīputra Śātakarṇi, who reigned in 106-130, began to appear in inscriptions with his title as "king of kings, lord of the Vindhya range, lord of the south (Dakṣiṇāpathapati)."

The House of Śātavāhana which belonged to the Andhra tribe descended from the Brahmin family, originally the Andhrans inhabited the region of Vindhya and the neighboring Deccan territories. After Pushamitra of the Śuṅga usurped the Mauryan throne (187-185 B.C.), the period entered the age of rival chieftains between Śātavāhana and Kaliṅga, and within a century, the founder of the former dynasty, known as Sīmuka (60-37 B.C.), put an end to the insignificant Śuṅgas and the derivative Kaṇvas in the region of Vidarbha. It was, however, the third ruler Śātakarṇi (27-17 B.C.) who raised its power and prestige by staving off the assault of meteorite Khāravela of Kaliṅga (ca. mid-first century B.C.), and then launched his extensive conquests from Eastern Mālwā to the present Hyderābad in the south, passing through the Maratha country, performing the rite of Aśvamedha.[19] The Śātavāhana, however, experienced temporary

---

[18] The Buddhist Saṅgha inherited theoretical and practical goals and tasks from its founder. The Śākyan clan, from which Śākyamuni came, had a republican form of society consisting of Kṣatriya clansmen. There was neither the class of Brāhmaṇas (highest in Brahmanical ideolgoy) nor that of Śūdras (lowest in the same). In Buddhist texts, the social order always begins with the Kṣatriya first, then Brāhmaṇa, Vaiśya, and Śūdra, in opposition to the Brahmanical order which enumerates Brāhmaṇa first, then Kṣatriya and so forth. Thus, it was easier and more convenient for those alien conquerers to assume the Kṣatriya title, which was most respected in Buddhist communities. Moroever, Buddhist communities in general minimized the Brahmanical status of Śūdras, accepting alien migrants more or less on equal terms.

[19] Some historians doubt if the Śātavāhanas were an Andhra stock, and think that they were probably of the Brāhmaṇa with a little admixture of Nāga blood, because "Andhra" is absent in all of their epigraphic records which are uniformly recognized as Śātavāhana.[N. K. Sinha, and A. Ch. Banerjee: *History of India*, Calcutta: A.R. Mukherjee, 1952; p. 93]. Lamotte

eclipse between 17 B.C. through 106 A.D. till the accession of Gautamīputra Śātakarṇi (106-130). Affiliated with the Brahmanical culture, this king's personality can be glimpsed from his panegyric that goes as follows:

> He crushed down the pride and conceit of the Kṣatriyas, furthered the interests of the twice-born [Brāhmaṇas] as well as the lowest orders, and stopped the contamination of the four castes.[20]

This panegyric seems to have commemorated his victory over the Satrap Nahapāna of the House of Kṣaharāta in A.D. 124. By implication, this single panegyric seems to have epitomized the existing cultural and religious conflict that had lasted up to that time for a few centuries between alien Śaka-Pahlavas and native Indians.

His similar panegyrics appeared nearly a decade later in two Nāsik inscriptions (Lüders: Nos. 1125 and 1126), informing us that after overthrowing the Satrap Nahapāna, he granted a certain field confiscated from that ruler to a Buddhist Saṅgha of the Bhadrāyanīya Sect. Gautamīputra Śātakarṇi's name then appeared more frequently in various localities, perhaps, initially buying the hearts of Buddhist communities over the influence of the destroyed Kṣaharāta rulers. But later on there is evidence of a more genuine generosity toward Buddhist Saṅghas on behalf of his queen mother, etc. This turning point coincided with his acceptance of peace with Rudradāman (A.D. 130-155) of the House of Chaṣṭana, ruler of Ujjayinī, on the basis of a matrimornial alliance by receiving the latter's daughter as wife of his successor, Vāsiṣṭhīputra Pulumāyi.

Whereas Gautamīputra Śātakarṇi was a valiant conqueror with native sensitivity, Rudradāman was a learned governor (Satrap) who combined his administrative skill with military valor. He left by far the most unique panegyric by the 72nd year of Śaka era (A.D. 150) on the rock of Junāgaḍh in Girnār, famous as the site of the inscription of Aśoka's edict. In alliance with Gautamīputra

---

thinks that Sātakarṇi's capital was at Pratiṣṭhāna (present-day Paithan or Baithan) upstream of the Godawarī, 100 miles east of Bombay. This might have been the case at the time of Vāsiṣṭhīputra Pulmāyi, but at the time of his predecessor, Gautamīputra Śātakarṇi, their capital was at a different locality, called Southern Kosala, according to Hsüan-tzang's travelogue. In fact, the later generations of the Śātavāhana gradually moved their capital further south-east-ward in the regions of Nāgārjunikoṇḍa along the Kṛṣṇā River.

[20] Sinha and Banerjee: *Ibid.*, p. 94. Also see Lüders: *op. cit.*, p. 94 (No. 1125); and L.M. Joshi: "Life and Times of the Madhyamaka Philosopher Nāgārjuna," *Maha Bodhi,* 73, 2(1966), 42-49; esp. p. 45.

Śātakarṇi of the South, he subsequently consolidated his dominion at Ujjayinī and extended it to the regions of Kāthiawār, Sindhu, Eastern and Western Mālwā, and even Rājasthan to the north. He twice rebuffed the challenge of Vāsiṣṭhīputra Pulumāyi (his son-in-law, A.D. 130-159) but, in principle, sustained a peaceful balance with the southern power, leaving to it the administrative prerogative of maritime trading and commerce in the coastal regions of the Indian Ocean.

Rudradāman's inscription, written in *Brāhmī* script, was the earliest record ever written in perfect Sanskrit as a literary composition of a learned nature and became the model for the Guptan rulers who followed it a few centuries later. This inscription conveys, among other things, two important messages to our study. It recorded that the Satrap had his minister restore the lake Sudarśana located near Girinagara by defraying the cost from the Satrap's own treasury,[21] and that he twice defeated Śātakarṇi, the lord of the South (Dakṣiṇāpatha-pati), but on account of the nearness of their relation, he did not destroy him; and that he himself acquired the title of *Mahākṣatrapa*. The Śātavāhana king referred to here was obviously his son-in-law Vāsiṣṭhīputra Pulumāyi, whom the *Geography of Ptolemy* recorded as an excellent administrator in promoting maritime trade in Western India and the coastal regions.

As mentioned before, Rudradāman did not mention his religious affiliation with the Buddhist Saṅgha, perhaps because the House of Chaṣṭana had been affiliated with Jaina religion for generations. But, in the matter of religion, neither did he mention his affliation with Jaina at all. On the other hand, his daughter's name appears, with the title as the queen of Vāsiṣṭhīputra Pulumāyī, in the inscriptions in Sanskrit at the Kanheri cave temple, with an apposition as "daughter of the *Mahākṣatrapa* Rudradāman" (Lüders, No. 994). It is an interesting but enigmatic inscription. Despite the fact that the Śātavāhanas used Prākrit exclusively as their official language for public statements, and despite the presence of several Prākrit inscriptions recording the construction of the cave temple, and referring to the reign of Gautamīputra Śātakarṇi (Lüders, No.

---

[21] The lake originally constructed by the Vaiśya Puṣyagupta, the provincial governor (rāṣṭriya) of the Maurya king Candragupta, and subsequently adorned with conduits by the Yavana (Greek) king Tuṣāspha for Aśoka the Maurya, had been destroyed during a storm at the date given above by the waters of the Suvarṇasikatā, Palāśinī and other streams of Mount Ērjayat. The work was executed by the minister (amātya) Huviśakha, the son of Kulaipa, a Pahlava, who had been appointed by the king to rule the whole of Ānartta and Surāṣṭra.

987), the Sanskrit language was used for inscribing the name of Rudradāman's daughter, as "Queen (*devī*) of [*Vā*]*sishṭhīputra Srī-Sāta*[*karṇi*], descended from the race of the Kāraddamaka kings (*rājan*), daughter of the Mahākshatrapa Ru . . ."

With the foregoing brief sketch of the rock-cut temples in association with epigraphic records, it becomes possible to assert that the Buddhist communities of professional Bhikṣu Saṅgha and supporting lay population, not only flourished despite the ongoing conflicts between the Satraps of the West and the Śātavāhana kings of the South, but also gradually transformed the political and cultural conflicts in the direction of accommodation and reconciliation. While the aforementioned epigraphic records of the period reflect the interaction of two political and military contenders, if Nāgārjuna happened to be associated with a Śātavāhana king, Gautamīputra Śātakarṇi (ca. A.D. 106-130) or his successor Vāsiṣṭhīputra Pulumāyi,[22] writing the *Suhṛllekha* for either one, it is indeed possible to hypothesize that he may also have had some association with the great Satrap of Ujjayinī, Rudradāman (A.D. 130-155), writing for him the *Ratnāvalī,* an exhortation on Buddhism and state governance. In short, there was a cogent political, social, and cultural reason to hypothesize that these two writings respectively and gradually acculturated the two different camps of political and military leaders toward peaceful co-existence and prosperity.

§5. *SUHṚLLEKHA* AND *RATNĀVALĪ* RESPECTIVELY WRITTEN FOR HĪNAYĀNA AND MAHĀYĀNA ORIENTATIONS

Three different translations of the *Suhṛllekha* are included in the Chinese *Tripiṭaka*, comprising more or less identical contents, but the names of the king to whom each text refers are all different.[23] On the other hand, the *Ratnāvalī* has but a single

[22] According to Bu-ston (A.D. 1329-1384), Nāgārjuna was forced by a young prince Śaktimān, son of King Antivāhana or Udayanabhadra, to commit suicide. Joshi: *Ibid.* Hsüan-tzang also recorded a similar narrative that a young prince, tired of waiting for his accession to the throne, obtained from his mother the secret of his father's longevity which had been helped by Nāgārjuna's magical knowledge of medicine. Thus, he met the master and urged him to die, so that his father king also die. Nāgārjuna is said to have cut his head off using a dry reed leaf! S. Beal: *op. cit.*, vol 2, p. 214.

[23] They are respectively translated (1) by Guṇavarman (367-431), A.D. 431, under the title *Bodhisattva Nāgārjuna's Essential Teaching in Verse for King Ch'an-t'o-chia-wang* (「龍樹菩薩為禅陀迦王説法要偈」 1 fasc.), Taisho. 32,

version translated by Paramārtha in 558-569, entitled *An Exhortation for King Pao-hsing* or *Ratnāvalī* [*Rāja-parikathā-ratnāvalī* (the *Necklace of Jewels, the Religious Counsel for the King*) as Sanskritized from Tibetan translation].[24] There was an interval of a hundred and twenty-seven years between the initial translation of the *Suhṛllekha* in A.D. 431 by Guṇavarman from Kashmir, and the translation of the *Ratnāvalī* in 558 by Paramārtha, a native of Ujjayinī. When Guṇavarman left Kaśmir for China, it was the reign of Candragupta II (A.D. 380-413) in the subcontinent, the third ruler of the Guptan dynasty. While keeping Pāṭaliputra as his capital, Candragupta II conducted his rule from Ujjayinī by subsuming the Śaka rulers of the Chaṣṭana and Western India and thus extended his power over the coastal regions as well as the south as far as Hyderabad. When Paramārtha left Ujjayinī, it was just after the devastating Hun invasion had been barely contained by Skandagupta (435-467) of the Guptan dynasty, and the historians say that the Guptan state and society were rapidly declining. Wherever Paramārtha obtained the original text of the *Ratnāvalī*, there was an ample period of time through the reigns of Śaka and Guptan rulers during which the contents of the text could be modified, if so indeed.

(No. 1672), pp. 745b-748a; [*Aryanāgārjuna-bodhisattva-suhṛllekha*] ; (2) by Saṅghavarman, (A.D. 434), under the title *The Essential Teaching in Verse Recommended to all Kings* (「勧発諸王要偈」*Lung-shu-p'u-sa-h'üan-fa-chu-wang-yao-chieh* (1 fasc.), Taisho. 32, (No. 1673), pp. 748a-751a, in which the name "Ming-sheng" (明勝、Udayana?) appears in the first verse; and (3) by I-ching (635-713), A.D. 637, under the title *Bodhisattva Nāgārjuna's Exhortation in Verse for the King*,(「龍樹菩薩勧誡王頌」*Lung-shu-p'u-sa-ch'üan-chieh-wang-sung*, 1 fasc.), Taisho 32, (No. 1673), pp.751a-754b. Although no name is given in this version, I-ching specified in his note that the person to whom the epistle is addressed is "Royal Friend of Ch'êng-t'u Country of South India" (寄与南印度親友乗土国王) and further in his *Nan-hai-chi-kuei-nei-fa-ch'uan* (「南海寄帰内法伝」4th fasc.) he gives it as "King Shih-yen-tê-chia of the house of Sha-to-p'o-han-na" (Śātavāhana).

[24]In Tibetan version, the Sanskrit title is *Rājaparikathā-ratnamālā*, while Chinese title was given as *Pao-hsing-wang-chêng-lun* (「宝行王正論」1 fasc.); author's name missing, translated during 558-569 by Paramārtha (A.D. 499-569); Taisho 32, No. 1656. Some Sanskrit fragments of the *Ratnāvalī* have been discovered by G. Tucci, and he subsequently published its edited text and English translation in *Journal of Royal Asiatic Society* 1934, pp. 307-325; 1936, pp.237-252, also 423-435. There are some missing portions in this manuscript, hence it is not a complete text. Since the *Suhṛllekha* versions all agree in regard to its authorship by Nāgārjuna, there seems to be little doubt about the textual authenticity, whereas it is necessary to examine the contents of the *Ratnāvalī* in order to ascertain its authorship as Nāgārjuna. This can be accomplished in reference to the definitively dialectical portion of the text.

In examining and comparing both texts, one can easily notice differences in the teaching, audience, and method. The *Ratnāvalī* is a well organized treatise comprising the advanced Mahāyāna doctrine of *Śūnyatā* and Bodhisattva practice through the Ten Stages (*daśa-bhūmis*) as well as advanced Buddhology. On the other hand, the *Suhṛllekha* presents the Śrāvakayāna doctrine for the laity written almost like a catechism in a simple itemization of points of the teaching. I judge Guṇavarman's translation to be best in terms of the clarity of the meaning of each passage and the identifiability of the Chinese terms and phrases with those of Buddhist usage in Sanskrit. The text consists of versified lines throughout, each comprising seven characters. It is a small text, filling less than three pages in the Taishō Daizōkyō edition. The *Ratnāvalī* translated by Paramārtha, on the other hand, is a longer text of thirteen pages, divided into five chapters.[25] It consists of versified lines, each of which cosisted of five characters. These texts can hardly be called identical in contents even after discounting the probable portions of modification. If these two texts are to be attributed to Nāgārjuna, I cannot help thinking that they were written by the same author but respectively for two separate recipients with different types of personalities.

In order to distinguish the *Suhṛllekha* as a text addressed to a person of a Hīnyāna orientation and the *Ratnāvalī* as another text addressed to a person of a Mahāyāna orientation, we shall keep two criteria in mind: (1) whether the goal of religion is given in terms of Śrāvakayāna anticipating the Arhat's path, or Mahāyāna anticipating Bodhisattva's path; (2) whether the governing principles and practical policies inculcated in each text can be linked to Śrāvakayāna or Bodhisattva-yāna respectively.

First, although the *Suhṛllekha* refers to the six norms of practice

---

[25] Here, Paramārtha's Chinese translation is exclusively used as source of the *Ratnāvalī* passages. Cf. G. Tucci's edition of the Sanskrit frgments and English translation ["The Ratnāvalī of Nāgārjuna: Part I," *Journal of the Royal Asiatic Society*, 1934, 307-325; "Part II," ibid., 1936, 239-252]; Michael Hahn's new edition of Nāgārjuna's Ratnāvalī, [Vol 1, The Basic Texts (Sanskriṭ, Tibetan, Chinese); Bonn: 1982, which also contains the text of the canonical Tibetan version and a photocopy of the Chinese translation by Paramārtha] The five chapters are entitled as follows: (1) An-le-chieh-t'o P'in (Chap. Well-being and Ultimate Release) [Taisho 32, p. 493b], (2) Tsa P'in (Chap. Miscellanea) [Ibid. p. 495b], (3) P'u-t'i-tzú-liang P'in (Chap. Pre-requisites of Enlightenment) [Ibid. p.497c], (4) Chêng-chiao-wang P'in (Chap. Straightforward Teaching to the King) [Ibid. p.500a], and (5) Ch'u-chia-chêng-hsing P'in (Chap. Renouncing Familial Life and Straightforward Practice) [Ibid. p. 502c]

(*ṣaḍ-pāramitā*) in the beginning part of the text,[26] these are neither specified as belonging to the Mahāyāna teaching nor as the norms to be practiced by the Mahāyāna Bodhisattva. They are given in conjunction with other sets of norms, e.g., six kinds of mindfulness,[27] ten good norms of conduct,[28] and eight observance-day rules for laity.[29] The author then states that if one believes in the efficacy of these norms of conduct as taught by the Śākyan sage (i.e., the Buddha) and practice them diligently, one will be born in heaven and eventually reach Nirvāṇa.

The *Ratnāvalī* is definitely a Mahāyāna text. While the *Suhṛllekha* does not use the term "Mahāyāna" in any of its passages, the *Ratnāvalī* clearly expresses the author's intent by using the term "Mahāyāna" at the beginning of the third chapter ("Prerequisites for Enlightenment") and thereafter. In parallel with the *Suhṛllekha*, the text initially gives the goal of religion in the first chapter: "Well-being and Ultimate Release," in reference to (1) ten good and bad kinds of conduct and purification of three *Karmas*, i.e. thought, speech, and action,[30] to accomplish preliminary realization of human well-being (*an-le*).[31] Having set forth this preparatory method toward the goal, the text begins to expound the method for realizing the final goal of religion, entitled as "the ultimate insight for deliverance, extremely subtle and most difficult to see," and introduces the Mahāyāna philosophical insight in detail in the first and well into the second chapter.

Starting with the basic Buddhist insight, i.e., absence of reality of one's self (*ātma*) and of anything that belongs to that self (*ātmīyam*),[32] the *Ratnāvalī* expounds the unreal nature of all psycho-

---

[26] *Suhṛllekha:* Taisho 32, p.745b (24-28); charity (*dāna*), morality (*śīla*), perseverance (*kṣānti*), endeavor (*vīrya*), concentration, (*dhyāna / samādhi*) and insight (*prajñā*).

[27] *Suhṛllekha:* Taisho 32,. p. 745b (21). Six kinds of mindfulness (*liu-nien / ṣaṭ-smṛti*): Three Treasures (*tri-ratna*: Buddha, Dharma, and Saṅgha), Charity (*dāna*), Morality (*śīla*), and Birth-in-Heaven (*devajanman*).

[28] *Daśa-kuśala-karma-pathāḥ:* (1) *prāṇātipātāt prativirataḥ*, (2) *adatta-ādānāt*, (3) *kāma-mithyā-cārāt*, (4) *anṛta-vacanāt*, (5) *sambhinna-pralāpāt*, (6) *paruṣa-vacanāt*, (7) *piśuna-vacanāt*, (8) *abhidhyātaḥp*., (9) *vyāpādāt*, and (10) *mithyā-darśanāt*, p. 745b (22)

[29] *Suḥrllekh*a: Taisho 32, p.745c (2-3).

[30] *Ratnāvalī*: Taisho 32, p. 493b-c (up to 21).

[31] (i) Freedom from the four lower cycles of life, like hellish life, etc., (ii) receipt of heavenly and human rulership endowed with wealth and happiness, (iii) realization of Brahmaloka (an ecstatic psychic state) based on the practice of concentration (*samādhi*). *Ratnāvalī:* Taisho 32, c (22-26).

[32] *Ibid.*, p. 494a (1).

physical elements (*sarva-dharma-śūnyatā*).[33] The remaining philosophical exposition covers the subject of causality,[34] the passage of three time moments (past, present, future) and the conventionally indeterminate questions of existence and non-existence (*avyākṛta-vastūni*),[35] the relation between the self and the *Skandhas*, between phenomena and four gross elements (*mahābhūta*), as well as between the forms (*rūpa*), corresponding sense faculties (*āyatana*), and resulting cognitions (*vijñāna*),[36] [by entering into the second chapter "Miscellanea" (雜品)], the non-substantiality of all psycho-physical elements (*sarvadharma-nairātmya*), the dualization in varieties of conceptual formulation, the magical configuration of the world whose appearance and disappearance are cognized but without their realities, the meaning of the Buddha's fourfold method of logical analysis (*catuṣkoṭi*) and the ultimate truth that transcends conventional determination. In short, all the foregoing constitute the contents of ultimate insight.[37] These subjects are all equally treated in the *Madhyamakakārikā-śāstra* wtihout exception.

As to its philosophical doctrine, the *Suhṛllekha* can hardly be said to emcompass the Mahāyāna philosophy, nor even the Ābhidharmika philosophy. The text, however, presents a series of realistic descriptions on the temporary and impermanent nature (*anityatā*) of life referring to the human body, and of material possessions in reference to the problems induced by them, and of the precarious kingly status, in reference to the endless life cycles (*saṃsāra*). Not even heavenly being can escape from the fate of falling into the states of animals, hungry ghosts, or sufferers of the Avīci hell.[38] Doctrinal exhortation in the *Suhṛllekha* is hardly

---

[33] *Ibid.*, p. 494a (2) - b (1). By seeing the unreality of the Skandhas, an end can be brought to the wrong view of self's existence; as long as one is attached to the reality of the Skandhas, there is no end of such wrong view, and the same is true with the view of reality of action (karman) and existence (bhāva); the cycle of Saṃsāra, life and death, continues like a ring of whirling torch, but there is neither its beginning, nor middle, nor end, nor is there in reality any of its past, present or future moment in the phenomenon of that fiery ring; the ring of fire appears, as it were, only through mutual interdependence of those points of reference. When one's insight truly penetrates into this matter, the wrong view of self's existence is bound to cease; when the ideas of reality of "self"and "Skandhas" are brought to an end through this insight, there arises the state of total freedom from attachment, which the Buddha taught as "Nirvāṇa."

[34] *Ibid.*, p. 494b (2) - c (8).

[35] *Ibid.*, pp. 494c (9) - 495a (14).

[36] *Ibid.*, p. 495a (15) - b (28).

[37] *Ibid.*, pp. 495b (29) - 496a (5).

[38] *Suhṛllekha*: Taisho 32, pp. 746c (28) -747b (27).

anything abstract and intellectual, but is very concrete and realistic in depicting the process of the deteriorating human body to explain the temporality of life, or briefly enumerating the doctrine of the Skandhas and absence of individual self, the twelve chains of causation (*dvādaśāṅga-nidāna*), the four noble truths (*catvāri āryasatyāni*), and the eight noble paths (*āryāṣṭāṅga-mārga*).[39]

The textual contents of the *Suhṛllekha* can be regarded as rather introductory, intended for lay beginners with a Śrāvakayāna orientation. This is shown by the elaborate description given of the fateful *Saṃsāric* cycles of life from the glorious heavenly beings down to the detailed features of sufferings in the animal, ghostly, and hellish worlds in ever realistic representations.[40] The author seems to dramatize the effect of Karmic retribution, such that no one, even the king, could escape from such a fate *vis-à-vis* this transient world of existence, from the fate of causal effectuation brought about by one's conduct. Thus, he is able to urge the audience to seek the goal of Nirvāṇa through moral fortitude, the practice of concentration, and cultivation of wisdom.

In the *Suhṛllekha*, "Nirvāṇa" is defined as the state where all human suffering, e.g., life, oldage, death, and suffering and lamentation, is absent (transcended), nor is there in that state anything like hills, rivers, sun and moon, altogether.[41] Significantly, the author states after this definition: "If one wishes to realize the insight to approach that goal, and yet has no due teacher, he ought to make available to himself any of the 'seven auxiliary sets of practice for enlightenment,' (*sapta-bodhy-aṅgāni, satta-bojjhaṅgā*) and concentrate on practicing it, because it is much easier for him to cross the ocean of life and death as soon as one acquires any of these vessels."[42] The foregoing briefing is sufficient to point out that

---

[39] Respectively: *Suhṛllekha*: Taisho 32, pp. 746b(29)-c(9); Taisho 32, p.746b (11-16); ibid. p. 747c (8-11)

[40] *Ibid.*, pp.746c (28-29) -747b (1-27).

[41] *Ibid.*, p 746c (2-3).

[42] *Ibid.*, p. 746c (4-5). *Saptabodhyaṅgāni* (*satta-bojjhaṅgā*): (1) *smṛty-sambodhy-aṅga* (abiding in the mindfulness of discerning insight (*prajñā*) and retaining previous experiences in good memory; (2) *dharma-viniścaya-sambodhy-aṅga* (differentiating through the insight those experiences of psycho-physical elements retained in memory as to their being true or false); (3) *vīrya-sambodhy-aṅga* (exerting one's effort in pursuit of the practice of critically discerning right dharmas from false ones); (4) *prīti-sambodhy-aṅga* (abiding in the delight born of practising the preceding ones); (5) *praśrabdha-sambodhy-aṅga* (becoming free from bodily and mental disturbance while accompanying the preceding moment of delight); (6) *samādhi-sambodhy-aṅga* (deepening mental concentration through calming the physical and mental state); (7) *upekṣā-sambodhy-aṅga* (maintaining

the contents of the *Suhṛllekha* is befitted to laity and Śrāvakayāna orientation.

In striking contrast, the description of Saṃsāric cycle of lives, such as animals, ghosts, and hellish sufferers, is significantly absent in the *Ratnāvalī*. This significant absence of Saṃsāric description isconsistent with the grand synthesis of an ideal path-finder Bodhisattva, the religious figure of Mahāyāna Buddhism, with the secular ideal of universal monarch, the myth of Cakravartin.[43] The *Ratnāvalī* does not dramatize the Saṃsāric cycle of life to make it the crucial moment of religious conversion on the part of audience, but expounds the doctrine of universal emptiness of psycho-physical elements (*sarva-dharma-śūnyatā)*, the insight that underlies the whole being of a Bodhisattva, as the crucial moment of his conversion. Simultaneously it introduces an ideal ruler actively engaged in the task of state-governance in whom a linkage is accomplished between the profound Mahāyāna insight and the magnanimous secular ideal of Cakravartin. This is the hallmark of the exposition given in the *Ratnāvalī*.

Now, the king is advised to engage himself in the practice of "four kinds of immeasurable thought or contemplation" (*catuvāri apramāṇāni*),[44] to involve himself in religious tasks, such as, enshrining the image of the Buddha, building the sacred sanctuary (*caityagṛha*), and monastic residence (*vihāra*) with best endowments, and so

---

mental equanimity and equilibrium).

[43] Mahāpuruṣa Cakravartin, "the superman turning the wheel," goes back to the pre-Vedic, pre-Āryan traditions of India being reflected in various Buddhist and Jaina writings as well as in Hindu Purāṇas. In the Buddhist conception, this universal monarch is secular counterpart of the Buddha who is said to have "set in motion the wheel of the sacred doctrine." Cf. Dīgha Nikāya No. 17: Mahā-sudassana-sutta ("The great Sun" = Sudassana = Cakravartin), and No. 26: Cakkavatti-sīhanāda-sutta ("The Lion's Roar of the Universal Ruler"); [Dialogues of the Buddha II, III tr. by T. W. S. and C. A. F. Rhys Davids; The Sacred Books of the Buddhists III, IV), London 1910 & 1921]. See also Heinrich Zimmer, Philosophies of India, edited by Joseph Campbell, New York: Meridian Books, 1957, pp. 127-139

[44] *Catvāri Apramāṇāni* (*cattasso apamaññā*), [*maitrī, karuṇā, muditā,* and *upekṣā*]: four kinds of immeasurable or infinite mind or thought: (1) *maitrī* or *maitrā* (*mettā*): love or benevolence; the desire of bringing (to one's fellow-men) that which is for their welfare and good (*hita-sukhōpanaya-kāmatā*); (2) *karuṇā*: an exalted state of compassion for all beings, all that is encompassed in the sphere of one's good influence or the desire to remove bane and sorrow (from one's fellow-men): *ahita-duḥkha-apanaya-kāmatā*; (3) *muditā* (originally *mṛdu-tā* – delicate, tender, gentle): sympathy in joy, happiness, complacency; and (4) *upekṣā* (*upekkhā*): equanimity, free of love and hate or joy and sorrow.

forth.[45] Such practices are archaeologically attested to in the rock-cut temple architecture that, as mentioned before, began to evolve in Western India during the Śaka-Pahlava period.

Subsequently in the second chapter, the *Ratnāvalī* provides an elaborate system of Mahāyāna Buddhology consisting of thirty-two superior marks as well as eighty additional marks, the image of Buddhahood, the ultimate goal attainable by the merit of the Mahāyāna path. At the beginning of the third chapter: "Prerequisites for Enlightenment" (「菩提資糧品」), the text advises the king to accept the Mahāyāna path on account of its meritorious qualities, which are then far richer than and superior to, those of Śrāvakas and Pratyekabuddhas.[46] In this connection, toward the end of the third chapter, it exhorts the importance of raising the thought of enlightenment (*bodhicittotpāda,* 「菩提発心」) and being steadfast with it.[47]

Throughout the fourth chapter: "Right Teaching for the King" (「正教王品」), the courteous exhortation repeats how the king ought to nurture and cultivate himself morally and spiritually in dealing with his own salvation as well as that of the mundane world. Toward the end of the chapter, it introduces a detailed account of the six *Pāramitā,* norms of *bodhisattva* practice, fitting the foregoing context and the integration of Hīnayāna tradition within that of Mahāyāna.[48] Entering into the last chapter: "Renouncing Familial Life and Right Practice" (「出家正行品」), the *Ratnāvalī* extols in detail the training of the monk who renounced familial life and his pursuit of the religious goal as a Mahāyāna bodhisattva.[49] Toward the end, it finally introduces the Ten Stages (*daśabhūmi*) of the Bodhisattva, the stratified stages of spiritual attainment, paralleling the ten *Pāramitās.*[50]

---

[45] *Ratnāvalī*: Taisho 32, p.498b (25-29) - c(1-5).

[46] *Ibid.*, p. 497c (25-29)

[47] *Ibid.*, p. 499c (22-23).

[48] *Ibid.*, p. 502a (15) - c (2).

[49] The fifth chapter begins with the enumeration of fifty-seven minor faults which a bodhisattva ought to overcome. Cf. An English translation by Michael Hahn from Sanskrit fragments corroborated by the Tibetan version, verses 1 through 34: "A Numerical Problem in Nāgārjuna's Ratnāvalī," Indological and Buddhist Studies (Volume in Honour of Professor J. W. de Jong on his Sixtieth Birthday), Delhi-India: Sri Satguru Publications, 1982, pp. 161-185.

[50] *Ibid.*, pp. 503c (6-29) - 504b (1); Daśa-bhūmi-s: *pramuditā-bhūmi* (Joyful), *vimalā-* (Pure or immaculate), *prabhākarī-* (Light-giving or Luminous), *arciṣmatī-* (Radiant or Effulgent), *sudurjayā-* (Very-difficult-

The ten stages inculcated in the *Ratnāvalī* are identical with those advanced forms of ten stages propounded in the *Daśabhūmika* chapter of the *Buddhāvataṃsaka-sūtra* (*Hua-yen-ching*,「華厳経」), and also with those which are found in the large *Prajñāpāramitā-sūtra*[51] (*Pan-jo-ching*,「般若経」) as well as in the *Upadeśaśāstra* (*Ta-chih-tu-lun*「大智度論」). The Mahāyāna Bodhisattva career and its path are thus brought into a single text as the underlying integral thought of the author. These items of exhortation are totally absent in the *Suhṛllekha*.

§6. GOVERNING PRINCIPLES INCULCATED IN *SUHṚLLEKHA* AND *RATNĀVALĪ*

As to the practical matter of governing the state, the *Suhṛllekha* gives a few basic principles or policies which the king ought to adopt. It does not provide any criterion for the ideal of a welfare state, but places its emphasis exclusively on king's moral and religious conduct. The king is advised to practise speech that reflects good intentions and truthfulness, but not one devoid of truth or reality. He is advised to apply his thought to judge situations as well as people in terms of the logical method of four-fold alternative analysis (*catuṣkoṭi*).[52] He is also advised to practise contemplation on offensive objects, i.e., the impurity of human physical features (*aśubhabhāvanā*) in women, to regard them as his sister or mother, and overcome his passion just as he overcomes his enemy on the battlefield.[53] He is also advised not to indulge in the habits of gambling, drinking, etc., which distract him from attention to his religious salvation and moral practice.[54] The

---

feat-of-overcoming), *abhimukhī-* (Face-to-face or turning toward); *dūraṅgamā* (Far-going or far reaching), *acalā-* (Immovable or steadfast), *sādhumatī-* (Good being or good thoughts), and *dharmameghā-* (Cloud of the doctrine or cloud of virtue). Cf. Har Dayal: *The Bodhisattva Doctrine in Buddhist Sanskrit Literature* (originally published in 1932 by Routledge & Kegan Paul, London), Reprint by Delhi: Motilal Banarsidass, 1970; pp.283-291.

[51] The "large *Prajñāpāramitā*" text (Ta-p'in-pan-jo, (「大品般若経」) means the *Pañcaviṃśati-sāhasrikā-prajñāpāramitā-sūtra* consisting of 25,000 verses. This is so-called in distinction from the small Prajñāpāramitā text (「小品般若経」) consisting of 8,000 verses (i.e., *Aṣṭasāhasrikā-prajñāpāramitāsūtra*).

[52] *Suhṛllekha*: Taisho 32, p. 745c (12-18).

[53] *Ibid.*, p.745c (19-26).

[54] *Ibid.*, p. 746a (16-17). Gambling parties featuring the game of "*akṣa*," i.e., throwing dice (originally throwing hard nuts), played a significant

Ratnāvalī also makes a brief recommendation against indulgence in alcohol and playing dice, but provides a far more detailed account of women, cautioning the king not to be swayed by passion due to their physical attraction. This is done by enumerating offensive objects associated with women similar to those of contemplation on impurity (*aśubhabhāvanā*).[55] It is apparent that this detailed presentation is an expansion of a few corresponding passages in the *Suhṛllekha*.[56]

The *Ratnāvalī*'s exhortation on practical tasks and policies prescribed for an ideal monarch has no parallel in the *Suhṛllekha*. The *Ratnāvalī* includes religious as well as secular tasks such as carving images of the Buddha and Bodhisattvas, building sanctuaries (*caitya-gṛha*) and monasteries (*vihāra*), decorating these structures with flowers and paintings, illuminating them with lights,[57] disseminating the practice of copying and chanting the scriptures by making gifts of papers and pencils, building schools, and hiring teachers.[58] As to social and welfare policies, it mentions promoting medicinal and medical science, knowledge of the calendar and arithmetic so as to measure the field of cultivation, rescue young and old from illness, building roads and highways, public rest houses, groves and ponds and providing means of livelihood, room and board, etc. in accordance with the size of each province; benefitting the populace by supplying water for distant regions through digging wells, attending the sick, relieving the fear of starvation, and so forth through stocking up medicines of all kind, staple foods, vegetables, fuel in properly conditioned storages, and so forth.[59] It is apparent that these agencies and facilities embody

---

part in the ritual of the royal consecration ceremony, to the extent that the gambling hall is attached to the king's palace in the later Vedic period. The Mahābhārata provides evidence that many kings indulged in the habit of playing dice. Cf. A.L. Basham, *The Wonder that was India (A survey of the culture of the Indian sub-continent before the coming of the Muslims)*, London: Sidgwick and Jackson, 1954, pp. 207-208.

[55] *Ratnāvalī*: Taisho 32, pp.496c (6-29) - 497a (1-24).

[56] *Suhṛllekha*: *ibid*. pp. 745c (27-29) - 746a(1-4). Aśubha-bhāvanā or saññā is one of the five necessary practices prescribed as a beginning part of the Śrāvakayāna path; contemplation of offensive things, specially of human corpses in various states of disintegration; there are nine (in some text, ten) such monkish disciplines, elsewhere called simply *nava saṃjñāḥ*; the nine concepts of offensive things; *vinīlaka-, vipūyaka-, vipaḍumaka-, vyādhmātaka-, vilohitaka-, vikhāditaka,-, vipṣiptaka-, vidagdhaka-, asthi-saṃjñā-bhāvanā*.

[57] *Ratnāvalī*: Taisho 32, p.498b (26-29) - 498cc (1-4).

[58] *Ibid*., p. 498c (11-14).

[59] *Ibid*., pp. 498c (15-29) -499a(1-4).

the heart of the state's welfare policy, because these were deemed to be managed by trustworthy directors and dispensed by them at times of natural disaster, famine, flood, epidemic as well as man-made disasters, such as robbery.[60]

The enumeration encompasses also economic and distribution policies, such as, providing farmers with tools of cultivation in cases of disasters, reducing of levies and taxes by adjusting their burdens according to each situation, improving distribution systems and transportation, various methods of price stabilization, and so forth.[61] Moreover, in the 4th chapter, on treating criminals, the king is repeatedly advised to apply compassion in sentencing and punishing an individual as to whether he be chained, whipped, beaten with a stick, etc., no matter how atrocious and dangerous a criminal might be.[62] Furthermore, in case of detention, if a detainee is poor, he must be released within five days, and even when such a criminal is chained in prison, he must be provided with sanitary condition, food and drink, medicine and a fan for relieving the heat, and so on.[63] In short, despite its relatively short exhortation, the *Ratnāvalī* includes many of the basic principles and policies regarded as adequate for the enlightened ruler from the Buddhist point of view and necessarily to be kept in mind and practiced as the standard conduct of the Bodhisattva ruler.

§7. POINTS OF HISTORICAL REFERENCE FOR NĀGĀRJUNA'S DATES IN *SUHṚLLEKHA* AND *RATNĀVALĪ*

Having surveyed the contents of the two texts attributed to Nāgārjuna, I am ready to lay down a set of evaluations conducive to approximation of the times and contexts of his writings. First, since neither text includes the Vijñānavāda doctrine, it may safely be determined that they were both written in the period prior to the appearance of the Vijñānavāda system of Buddhist philosophy. The fact that the *Ratnāvalī* refers to the schools of Sāṃkhya, Vaiśeṣka and Jaina of the pre-Classical period[64] is historically relevant in parallel with Aśvaghoṣa's reference to the Sāṃkhya

---

[60] *Ibid.*, p. 499a(5-9).
[61] *Ibid.*, p. 499a (10-19).
[62] *Ibid.*, p. 501a (3-8).
[63] *Ibid.*, p. 501a (9-14).
[64] *Ibid.*, pp. 494c (9-12).

system of Arāḍa in his *Buddhacarita*[65] and also his or Kumāralāta's reference to the Sāṃkhya, Vaiśeṣika, and Naiyāyika schools in the second topic of the *Sūtrālaṅkāra-śāstra* (or *Kalpanā-maṇḍitikā* enlarged by Kumāralāta?).[66] The fact that the *Ratnāvalī* criticizes the Jaina system of philosophy along with the foregoing two schools is not a difficult problem if the text itself was addressed to some Śaka ruler of western India during the Śaka-Pahlava period, because the early Śaka rulers of Western India were closely related to the Jaina teachers from the first century B.C. onward, as recorded in the Jaina text *Kālakācāryakathānaka*.

Rudradāman's silence in his epigraphic records about his attitude toward Buddhist communities may have meant that he might have been a Jaina follower, because a second Junāgaḍh Sanskrit inscription seems to link some descendants of the House of Chaṣṭana with the Jaina teachers.[67] Although Buddhism seems to have held sway in Western India from the second century onward through the Gupta period, there continued to be a strong Jaina affiliation in the Śaka-Pahlava population of those regions.

The *Ratnāvalī* refers to the Vaiyākaraṇa system (the science of grammar) in the fourth chapter. It simply draws a parallel case in reasoning that the Mahāyāna teaching is superior to the Hīnayāna, on the ground that it includes the Hīnayāna teaching within itself, whereas the latter does not include the former. The science of grammar compiled by Pāṇini in the 4th century B.C. consisted of two main bodies of works: (1) the list of words (*pada-mātṛka*), such as verbal roots (*dhātupāṭha*) and nominal bases (*gaṇapāṭha*), and (2) the grammatical rules (*pratyāhāra-sūtras*).[68] The former ought

---

65 Cf. *Buddhacarita*: VII: "Visit to Arāḍa" in E. H. Johnston's The Buddhacarita or Acts of the Buddha, Pt I (Sanskrit edition) and II (English translation): Canto i to xiv translated from original Sanskrit supplemented by the Tibetan Version; published by the Univ. of Punjab, Lahore: Calcutta: Baptist Mission Press 1936.

66 *Ta-chuang-yen-ching-lun* (「大荘厳経論」)translated by Kumārajīva, A.D. 381-401; Taisho 257, No. 201, (15 fasc.) p. 258c ff.

67 Cf. Lüders: No. 966; A Junāgaḍh Jain(?) inscription in Sanskrit at Girnār: The fragment "mentions some Mahākṣatrapa, the grandson of Kshatrapa Svāmi Jayadāman, the great grandson of . . ., Svāmi-Caṣṭana, moreover Girinagara, and those who have obtained the knowledge of the Kevalins.

68 *Ratnāvalī*: Taisho 32, p. 502b (16-19). Pāṇini's system of grammar consists of the lists of verbal roots (*dhātupāṭha*) and nominal bases (*gaṇapāṭha*) and the rules of grammar (*pratyāhāra-sūtras*). Logically, the study of the former is preliminary to that of the latter. In Buddhist textual tradition, there developed two concepts of classification, i.e., the class of "*neya-artha*" and that of "*nīta-artha*," respectively "textual meaning having

to be studied first, and only then can the rules of grammar be studied. The Satrap of Ujjayinī Rudradāman had his panegyric carved in standard Sanskrit and recorded, among other things, that he mastered the science of grammar. This fact somehow matches the *Ratnāvalī*'s use of an analogy by referring to the Vaiyākaraṇa discipline. Thus, irrespective of whoever the ruler was, for whom Nāgārjuna wrote the exhortation, he knew his patron monarch was well-acquainted with the discipline of Sanskrit grammar and its curriculum.

Excluding two Sanskrit records in Girnār, Rudradāman's (No. 965) and a stone inscription (No. 966: Jaina's record?), there are only five Sanskrit inscriptions throughout Lüders' collection of *Brāhmī* records in Western India. One of those five (Lüders: No. 994) implies that, as referred to before, Rudradāman's daughter, queen of the Śātavāhana king Pulumāyi, was a supporter of a Buddhist Saṅgha, while three other inscriptions refer to two Śākyan (not Śaka) monks, recording their donation of a Buddha-statue (Lüders: Nos. 989, 990). The remaining two records are respectively an inscription of a universal prayer (Lüders: 992) and some Buddhist creed, though not clearly legible (Lüders: No. 991). The Sanskrit inscription that mentioned Rudradāman's daughter as affiliated with a Buddhist Saṅgha seems to imply that this great Satrap was an anonymous Buddhist or held an anonymous affiliation with Buddhist doctrines.

The *Ratnāvalī*'s principles of a welfare state and its policies seem to be concretely demonstrated in the restoration work of the Sudarśana lake by Rudradāman as part of irrigation system. The inscription is found as parallel to that of the Mauryan inscriptions

---

not yet (clearly) established or fulfilled (by inference or the like)" and "textual meaning having been well established or fulfilled." In Mahāyāna tradition, the Hīnayāna texts are included in the class of "*neyārtha*" that ought to be fulfilled in Mahāyāna texts that are "*nītārtha.*" Preceding the passage in question, the *Ratnāvalī* refers to the four bases of reliance for the path of the Bodhisattva. [Taisho 32, p. 502b (12)]. This means that the Mahāyāna Bodhisattva relies on the set of four bases (*catvāri pratisaraṇāni*), namely, (1) on meaning rather than on word (*arthapratisaraṇena bhavitavyaṃ na vyañjana-pratisaraṇena*), (2) on knowledge rather than on consciousness (*jñānapratisaraṇena bhavitavyaṃ na vijñānapratisaraṇena*), (3) on those texts whose meaning is well established rather than those whose meaning is not fully established (*nītārthasūtra-pratisaraṇena bhavitavyaṃ na anītārthasūtra-pratisaraṇena*), and (4) on the nature of dharmas rather than on the individual person (*dharma-pratisaraṇena bhavitavyaṃ na pudgala-pratisaraṇena*). The analogy which the author draws by referring to the Vaiyākaraṇa system of grammar is that the Mahāyāna teaching includes the Hīnayāna texts as its preliminary subject of study, but the latter does not include the former.

by Aśoka, referring to the public work of the Vaiśya Puṣyagupta, the provincial governor of the Maurya king Candragupta, subsequently adorned with conduits by the Greek king Tushāspha for Aśoka the Maurya. Considering the fact (1) that Candragupta Maurya was a Jaina follower and himself joined the Jaina Saṅgha after abdicating his throne, (2) that the name of the lake "Sudarśana" is another name of the sun or Cakravartin, and (3) that Rudradāman had his panegyric inscribed in Sanskrit along with the Aśokan edict at the site, we cannot help hypothesizing some degree of linkage between the idea of Cakravartin inculcated in the Ratnāvalī and the Satrap's unique personality and deed as governor (Satrap) or ruler (Mahārāja) of that region during the Śaka-Pahlava period.[69]

The *Suhṛllekha* does not mention the appearance of rock-cut temples at all, nor does it refer to images of the Buddha, whereas the *Ratnāvalī* openly promotes the building of such structures as meritorious deeds on the part of donors, thus supporting the archaeological evidence of those cave temples initiated during the Śaka-Pahlava period. Though we have no direct record of Rudradāman's relation to Buddhist Saṅghas, we have ample evidence for the fact that a good portion of the Śaka-Pahlava population of Western India affiliated themselves with the Buddhist faith. We notice that not only Rudradāman's daughter (Lüders: No.994) but also the Satrap of the House of Kṣaharāta, Nahapāna, his daughter and son-in-law Uṣabhadāta, supported Buddhist Saṅghas. The latter was especially generous in donating the caves and sanctuaries, villages and various endowments to the Buddhist Saṅghas.[70] The Śātavāhana kings also supported the Buddhist Saṅgha by donating caves, sanctuaries, as well as various endowments, which are verified in Buddhist cave inscriptions widely scattered throughout Western India. These Buddhist cave inscriptions, with the sole exception of five which were carved in Sanskrit, were all equally carved in the medium of mixed dialect or *Prākrit*, of which the latter constitutes the majority.

The Śātavāhana kings exclusively relied on *Prākrit* to record their panegyrics and continued to patronize this language throughout

---

[69] According to historians, the regional council did not agree with the reconstruction of the lake, but Rudradāman instructed his official, his appointed local governor Suviśākha, the son of a Pahlava, to carry out the task anyway, bearing the entire expense from his own royal treasury. He is said to have been an accomplished scholar, renowned for his knowledge of Sanskrit grammar, and he did not kill men except in battle. [N. K. Sinha and A.C. Banerjee: op. cit., p.101]

[70] Cf. Lüders: op. cit. See Nos. 1099, 1131, and 1133.

their dynastic history. If there was any ruler who could be the recipient of the *Ratnāvalī* during the Śaka-Pahlava period, it is apparent that he cannot be identified with the same Śātavāhana king for whom the *Suhṛllekha* is supposed to have been written. This hypothesis, I believe, can easily be proven by the general cultural background of the Śātavāhana kings as distinguished from the Satraps of Western India.

§8. NĀGĀRJUNA'S BIOGRAPHY AND SOUTHERN KOSALA

One of the best research articles on Nāgārjuna's biography in the post-war era was written by Professor L. M. Joshi and was published as part of *Mahā Bodhi* in 1965 [Vol. 73, Nos. 1 (pp. 13-20, and No. 2 (pp. 42-49)]. As historian, he traced the layers of Nāgārjuna's biographical references chronologically through Tibetan sources by demonstrating how the medieval Tibetan writers errored in juxtaposing more than two Nāgārjunas as a single person. The pre-war scholarship of G. Tucci, Max Walleser, Winternitz, and so forth, already suggested that there could have been four different Nāgārjunas: the Buddhist philosopher, the *Tantric* master, the medieval erotic writer and the alchemist, and that they were uncritically juxtaposed one after another just because of the identity of their names.[71] In this respect, Joshi's research did not produce anything new but confirmed the point that the Mādhyamika forefather, author of the dialectical treatises at the time of early Mahāyāna teaching ought to be distinguished from the Tāntrika master, Bhadanta Nāgārjunapāda, who was the author of the Vajrayāna system of Buddhist teaching. The problem is that this Tāntrika master was, at least, five centuries posterior to the former.

Another acceptable research article on Nāgārjuna's life career was due to Prof. D. Ruegg and was published as part of *Indological and Buddhist Studies in honor of Prof. de Yong's 60th Birthday* in 1982.[72] Ruegg takes up Lamotte's hypothesis that there could have been two Nāgārjunas, one being the author of the dialectical treatises distinguished as Nāgārjuna I, and another, being a Sarvāstivādin Ābhidharmika and author of the *Prajñāpāramitopadeśaśāstra* which is extant only in Kumārajīva's Chinese translation *'Ta-chih-tu-lun'*

---

[71] *A History of Indian Literature*, v. II, Calcutta , 1933, pp. 343-344

[72] "Towards a Chronology of the Madhyamaka School," ibid., pp. 505-530; Delhi: Sri Satguru Publications, Indological & Oriental Publishers, 1982

(「大智度論」). Lamotte's hypothesis derived from the fact that this voluminous text cites some passages from the works of Āryadeva and Rāhulabhadra known as Nāgārjuna I's disciples and junior to him. Ruegg, however, dismissed Lamotte's theory, because, as far as these two kinds of authorship are concerned, the single person theory simplifies the historical context, and I agree with him that it is certainly more economical than postulating two Nāgārjunas within so close a vicinity in time.

Joshi and Ruegg differ in their conclusions regarding the times of Nāgārjuna. Although Lamotte did not place much historical value to the Chinese biographical texts on Nāgārjunà, Aśvaghoṣa, or Āryadeva,[73] he had a great confidence in the encyclopedic *Prajñāpāramitopadeśa-śāstra* (*Ta-chih-tu-lun* 「大智度論」) only extant in Kumārajīva's translation, and the *Mahāvibhāṣā-śāstra* (*T'a-p'i-po-sha-lun* 「大毘婆沙論」) or the *Great Commentary on Abhidharma*)[74] again only extant in Hsüan-tzang's translation. In the epilogue of his translation, Hsüan-tzang notes that the great assembly of the Elders took place in Kaśmīra four hundred years after the Parinirvāṇa under the auspice of King Kaniṣka of the Kuṣāṇas.[75] Lamotte correctly determined Nāgārjuna to be contemporaneous with Aśvaghoṣa, Āryadeva and the *Mahāvibhāṣāśātra* on the basis of common usage of Sanskrit as means of doctrinal propagation, but he wrongly placed the reign of Kaniṣka in the year of 128-151 A.D. on the basis of S. Konow's pre-war theory on that date. Ruegg seems to have the same choice for approximating Nāgārjuna's time in the later half of that century. On the other hand, Joshi held that Kaniṣka's reign began by the Śaka era, equivalent to A.D. 78, and relying on the textual tradition of *Laṅkāvatāra-sūtra*, and so forth,[76] concluded that Nāgārjuna appeared

---

[73] *History of Indian Buddhism from the Origins to the Śaka Era*, translated into English by Sara Webb-boin, Universitér Catholique de Louvain, Institut Orientaliste, Louvain-La-Neuve, 1988, p. 593

[74] *Abhidharma-mahāvibhāṣā-śāstra* or a detailed commentary on the *Abhidharma-jñānaprasthāna-śāstra* that belonged to the Sarvāstivāda school.

[75] The date of *Mahāvibhāṣā-śāstra* noted by Hsüan-tzang and that of Nāgārjuna given in the *Laṅkāvatāra-sūtra*, etc., both of which refer to a period of four hundred years from Parinurvāṇa, must have come from the common Buddhist tradition at that time. Unlike modern scholarship, the tradition set only a century between Asśoka's reign and the Buddha's Parinirvāṇa, instead of two as known to us today. Hence, "three hundred years between Ashoka and Kaniṣka" or "five hundred years with an additional century after Parinirvāṇa" was a quite accurate tradition, except the omission of the second Buddhist Council held in Vaiśālī.

[76] Joshi: *loc. cit.*, pp. 40-41

four hundred years after the Buddha's Parinirvāṇa. Accordingly, he postulated a life span of 200 years to his existence from the middle of the first century B.C. to the middle of the second century A.D., somehow inclining toward the legendary longevity attributed to Nāgārjuna.

With Chinese tradition, the main source on the life and times of Nāgārjuna is the *Biographical Record of Bodhisattva Nāgārjuna* (*Lung-shu-p'u-sa-chuang,*「龍樹菩薩伝」) translated into Chinese by Kumārajīva in 405 A.D. along with two other biographies on Aśvaghoṣa and Āryadeva.[77] By discounting legendary elements, there is general agreement with as well as specific difference from, Tibetan tradition:

(1) According to the biography, Nāgārjuna was born in a Brāhmaṇa family in South India, endowed with extraordinary capacity as being able to understand the meaning of the four Vedas still in childhood while in chanting.

(2) After narrowly escaping from a severe punishment due to his adolescent act of mischief at the king's palace, he joined Buddhist monk-hood upon ordination and studied all of the Tripiṭaka scriptures within ninety days. Unsatisfied, however, he travelled to the Himālayan region where he was introduced to Mahāyāṇa texts by an old monk of a Stūpa shrine.

(3) Unable to understand the doctrine fully, he further ventured to visit the Nāga king's palace in the bottom of ocean and studied the innumerable Mahāyāna texts at his library in search of the profound insight for ninety days.[78] Thus, he reached satisfactory understanding and realized the two-fold transcendent insight that *dharmas* neither arise nor perish, neither non-arising nor non-perishing (*anutpattika-dharma-dvaya-kṣānti* 「無生二忍具足」).[79]

---

[77] *The Lung-shu-p'u-sa-chuang* (1 fasc.), Taisho 50 (No. 2047), p. 184a-185b; a second version, one fasc/ also translated by Kumārajīva, *ibid.* pp.185b-i86c.; *The Ma-ming-p'u-sa-ch'uan (The Biography of Aśvaghoṣa)* (1 fasc.), Ibid. (No. 2046), pp183; *Ti-p'o-p'u-sa-chuan (The biography of Deva Bodhisattva Āryadeva)* (1 fasc.), *Ibid*. (No.2048), pp. 186f.

[78] The number of seven used in describing the number of book storages and that of beautiful book chest (「開七宝蔵、発七宝華函」) reminds us a similar usage in the *Eight Thousand Verses Prajñāpāramitā Text* (「八千頌般若経」). The passage here goes: "Opening the seven library storages and taking out seven beautifully decorated chests of texts, the Nāga king handed to Nāgārjuna those many sacred scriptures that comprise comprehensive and profound expositions on immeasurable subtle truths."

[79] Realization of the twofold insight of *Śūnyatā*; *anutpattika-dharma-*

(4) Upon returning to South India escorted by the Nāga king, he actively propagated the Mahāyāna doctrine in the southern regions through repudiating heretic doctrines and composing the *Upadeśaśāstra*, *Madhyamakaśāstra*, and so forth.[80]

(5) Then, he converted the king of South India and was successfully engaged on innumerable occasions in defeating heretics. Approaching his death and facing a Hīnayāna monk's hatred in rivalry, he passed away in a solitary room unattended.[81]

(6) A single sub-note, though unknown by whom and when, is attached at the end of this biography, stating: "According to the *Historical Record of Patriarchal Successions* [*pu-fa-ts'ang-ch'uan*], he is the thirteenth patriarch and enjoyed longevity due to his dietary and medicinal knowledge, still living today by two hundred years of age (現住長寿二百歲)."[82]

According to the biography, Nāgārjuna acquired some knowledge of magical chemistry and medicine at his youth, but this is not linked to his legendary longevity. It is apparent, however, that the Chinese biography does not comprise any of the career of a Tāntrika master that predominates in Tibetan sources.

The same biographical narrative in Chinese version that Nāgārjuna had an opportunity to visit the Nāga's world and procured some

---

insight of non-arising of psycho-physical elements. This insight, however, is dual: (1) the insight that repudiates both arising non-perishing regarding all phenomenal elements (破生滅) and simultaneously (2) that further liberates the logico-linguistic process holding on the thoughts of "non-arising" and "non-perishing" (言語道断). It is the insight of *Śūnyatā* through which one sees all phenomenal elements not only as "neither arising nor perishing" but also "neither non-arising nor non-perishing" and thus understands them ultimately as pure and immaculate like Nirvāṇa (一切法如涅槃). This insight of *Śūnyatā* represents the entering into the initial stage of Bodhisattva (菩薩初位) chracterized as non-falling back (不退転位).

[80] "In order to expound the Mahāyāna doctrine, he composed *Upadeśa-śāstra* (「大智度論」) consisted of 10,000 verses, and also *Chuang-yen-fo-tao-lun* (「荘厳仏道論」五千偈),, *Ta-tzú-fang-pien-lun* (「大慈方便論」五千偈」), and *Madhyamaka-śāstra* (「中論」),, each consisting of 5000 verses, whereby he let the teaching spread in Southern India, and again composed the *Akutobhayā* (Self-commentary on *Madhyamakaśāstra* (「無畏論」) consisting of 10,000 verses, but the *Madhyamakaśāstra* excels most among all of his works." The list of Nāgārjuna's works are not limited to the above. *Chuang-yen-fo-tao-lun* and *Ta-tzú-fang-pien-lun* are not extant or unidentifiable with any of other works.

[81] Nāgārjuna asked the Hīnayāna monk, saying: "Do you wish me to live on further for a long time to come?" His reply was: "Candidly replying, I do not wish so."

[82] *Ibid.*, p. 185b (6-7).

profound texts from the Nāga bodhisattva king,[83] finds its parallel expression in the *Harṣacarita* (*The Life of King Harṣa*) written by Bāṇa Bhaṭṭa probably in the late 7th century A.D., in which the narrative was linked with Nāgārjuna's offering of a pearl necklace (*ekāvalī*) to the king of South India. The eighth book (*Ucchvāsa* or "Exhilaration") of this drama-poetry comprises an allegorical story alluding to the legendary association of Nāgārjuna with the king of the House of Śātavāhana. The chapter depicts a scene in which, in the course of dialogue, King Harṣa was given a pearl necklace, an antidote of all sufferings for all beings (*sarvasattva-saṅtāpahāriṇī*), from the Buddhist saint Divākaramitra, who was once a Vāsuki-nāga, the serpent king of the under-world. Parallel seems to hold with the legendary narrative that Bhikṣu Nāgārjuna was taken to the realm of the serpent king (Nāgarāja), that he was given that pearl-necklace (*ekāvalī*), and that, upon returning to the human world, he offered it to the king of śātavāhana who was "the lord of three oceans."[84] The problem is that in all the legends of Nāgārjuna, the name of Rudradāman never occurred, and that both the *Suhṛllekha* and the *Ratnāvalī* have been assumed to be written for and given to, a single Śātavāhana king. Lamotte only speaks of the *Suhṛllekha* and does not mention the *Ratnāvalī* in connection with the Śātavāhana king, perhaps becasue he was aware of the different contents of these texts.

As another element of the biography that Nāgārjuna sojourned in the Himālaya region may be paralleled with a legend recorded in the *Rājataraṅgiṇī* (*The Records of Kaśimīra Kings*) completed by Kalhaṇa, Kaśmiri historian, in 1150. According to his writing, after one hundred fifty years from Śākyasiṃha's *Nirvāṇa*, Nāgārjuna resided at Ṣaḍarhadvana (the Six-Arhats forest) and engaged in propagation of Buddhism and defeated all non-Buddhist opponents in public debate, and that he protected the Buddhists in the Kaśmīra country under the mandate of Kuṣāṇa rulers and was praised by the people as the lord of the earth.[85] Although Kalhaṇa

---

[83] *Ibid.*, p. 184c (7-15).

[84] *Harṣacarita*, (Chaukhamba ed., Varanasi, 1958), Ucchvāsa (8th bk.), pp.439-440: /*kiyaty api kāle kadācin māmaikāvalīṃtasmān nāgarājān nāgārjuno nāma nāgair evānītaḥ pātālatalaṃ bhikṣur abhidāta lebhe ca/ nirgatya ca rasātalāt trisamudrādhipataye śātavāhana nāma narendrāya suhṛde sa dadau tām,*/ See also V.S. Agarwala, *Harṣacarita Eka Sāṃskṛitika Adhyayana*, Patna, 1953, pp.197-198. The passage is quoted from Joshi: *loc. cit.*, p. 46.

[85] Joshi, *loc. cit.*, II, p. 46. His note gives the Sanskrit passage from *Rājataraṅginī*, book I, verses 168-173 and 177-178, verses 172-173 and 177. /*tadā bhagavataḥ śākyasiṃhasya parinirvṛte, asmin mahīlokhyatau*

wrongly put the time as 150 years after the Buddha's Parinirvāṇa perhaps due to the remoteness of the time, his specification of the Kuṣāṇa period was correct. This legend surely can facilitate some basis to support how and why Nāgārjuna had a good knowledge, as revealed in the *Ratnāvalī*, about actual workings of governing principles and policies for the life of people.

In Indian historical scenes, we know through the biography of a 13th century Tibetan monk pilgrim, Dharmasvāmin or Chag-lo-tsa-ba Chos-rje-dpal, that a Nāgārjuna referred to in his book was associated with the Vajrayāna system of the Guhyasamāja and likely identified with the Tāntrika Siddha and author of such Vajrayāna texts.[86] Since Dharmasvāmin's life preceded all of those Tibetan historians, the confusion of two Nāgārjunas in their tradition may have had its origin in the accounts of his diary. This remarkable Tibetan monk is said to have witnessed the last phase of Indian Buddhism in the heart of its birthplace in Magadha. When he arrived at Nālandā in 1234 just after the initial raid of this great university by the Moslem expedition led by Muhammad Bakhtyar Khilji,[87] he witnessed the devastating sight where smokes were still rising from the burning library. During repeated raids by the Moslem army, he singlehandedly helped the aged monk scholar Śrībhadra,[88] head of the university, to escape the slaughtering ground by carrying him on his back and subsequently received personal instruction from this profound scholar monk for two years before returning to his land. In other words, during the thirteenth century, the information which Dharmasvāmin collected on Nāgārjuna as included in his biography may have already been a well established tradition in the Nālandā circle of the medieval Buddhist world.

As it was, in the Tibetan tradition, the figure of Nāgārjuna is hopelessly entangled with legends and histories through coalescence of more than two different personalities across their different time periods and doctrinal adherences. For instance, confused details of the life and times of a Nāgārjuna are recorded in the *History of*

---

sārdha varṣaśataṃ hayagāt /

[86] *The Biography of Dharmasvāmin* (Chag-lo-tsa-ba Chos-rje-dpal) English translation. by George Roerich, Patna, 1959, p. 107 and p. 110. Cf. L.M. Joshi: *loc. cit*, p. 15.

[87] Historians (Cf. Sinha and Banerjee [*op. cit.*, p. 216] found a contemporary Moslem historian's note that refers to the library of Nālandā University which was destroyed by the expedition led by Muhammad Bakhtyar Khilji who held a fief somewhere in south Bihar.

[88] Cf. Sri Chaturbhuj: "The last Abbot of Nalanda," *Maha Bodhi*, 82, 6(1964), 241-242.

Buddhism (*Chos-ḥbyun*, or literally *Record of the Doctrine*) by Bu-ston (AD 1290-1384), in the *Blue Annals* by Gos-lo-tsa-ba gZon-nu-dpal (AD 1392-1481), in the *Mystic Tales* by Tāranātha (circa. AD 1574), in the *History of Buddhism in India* by Sumpā-mKham-po (AD 17th or 18th century), and so forth.[89] It is apparent that these sources mixed up the Mādhyamika dialectician who composed the *Madhyamaka*śāstra with another Nāgārjuna, a Tāntrika master, who was connected with composition of some number of Tantric texts, and whose existence is attested by an epigraphical inscription in Amarāvatī Cave addressing to him as "*Bhadanta Nāgārjunācārya.*"[90] The Tibetan tradition as a whole accepted a Nāgārjuna to whom some of the Mahāyāna treatises, such as *Madhyamaka* texts, those of *Vajrayāna Tantras* as well as secular treatises of medicine and alchemy are equally attributed.

As to Nāgārjuna's biography,[91] the Tibetan tradition held the following points in general: (1) that Nāgārjuna appeared four hundred years after the Buddha's Parinirvāṇa in a Brāhmaṇa family by caste, to the south of Vidarbha, lived mostly on the mount Śrīparvata or that of the neighboring mountain Śrī Dhānyakaṭaka [all in vicinity of Amarāvatī by the bank of the Kṛṣṇā River in the south-east although he travelled widely, (2) that he was instrumental in propagation of the Mahāyāna Buddhist doctrine through advocating the *Prajñāpāramitā* scriptures, composing various *Mādhyamika*

[89] Cf. Joshi presents in his article a detailed study on Tibetan tradition in reference to the sources written by these Tibetan historians, "Life and Times of the Madhyamaka Philosopher Nāgārjuna," *Maha Bodhi* 73, 1(1965), 15-16.

[90] Cf. Ruegg, D. Seyfort gives a concise evaluation on the dating of the inscription in his article: "Towards a Chronology of the Madhyamaka School," *Indological and Buddhist Studies* (*Volume in Honor of Professor J.W. de Jong on his Sixtieth Birthday*), Bibliotheca Indo-Buddhica No.27, Delhi: Indian Books Centre, 1982, esp. pp. 505-509; notes 9 and 10, where he gives sources for dating the inscription as 600 A.D.: by Burgess: Notes on the Amarāvatī Stūpa (Madras 1882), p. 57; and The Buddhist Stūpas of Amaravati and Jaggayyapeta (Archaeological Survey of Southern India, London 1887), pp. 111-112. or 450-500 A.D. suggested by Tucci: Minor Buddhist Texts, II (Rome 1958), p. 284.

[91] Cf. Joshi's survey covers the following: Bu-ston: *History of Buddhism*, Eng. trans. by E. Obermiller, Heidelberg, 1932, Pt II, pp.120-130; Go-lo-tsa-ba gZon-nu-dpal: *The Blue Annals*, Eng. trans. by G. N. Roerich, 2 parts, Calcutta, 1949, 1953; Tāranātha: *Mystic Tales*, Engl. trans. by B. N. Dutt, Calcutta 1944, pp. 8-11; *Geschichte des Buddhismus in Indien*, German transl. by Von A. Schiefner, St Petersbury, 1869; Engl. Trans. by N. Dutta and U. N. Ghoshal in *IHQ* of the relevant portion in *Indian Historical Quarterly* XXVIII, 1952 p.41 ff; Sumpā-mKhan-po: dPg-bSam-ïJon-bZan, ed. by S. C. Das, Calcutta, 1908; S. K. Pathaka, "Life of Nagarjuna" from Pag Sam Jon Zang, *IHQ* XXX, p. 93f.

treatises as well as Tāntrika texts; (3) that he was in possession of some supernormal psychic powers and knowledge of chemical or medicinal sciences, and enjoyed a very long life, and (4) that he held close association with and influence on the king of South India but died under somewhat unusual circumstance in which the king's prince was directly involved.

It was the Tibetan sources that referred Nāgarjuna's birthplace to the "region south of Vidarbha," but Tāranātha gave another version about his birthplace as well as his career. Nāgārjuna is said to have been born in a Brāhmaṇa family from Kahora, part of Kāñcī, in the south of Vaidarbha, entered the Nālandā when he was seven years old to receive instruction from Rāhula on the Tāntrika scripture, *Aparimitāyur-dhāraṇī*. After many years of literary as well as evangelical activities, he spent the last part of his life in the monastery built on the *Śrīparvata* by the bank of the Kṛṣṇā River near Dhānyakaṭaka in Āndhradeśa. It was at this multi-chambered rock-cut monastery at Mt. Śrīparvata, a mountain of Nāgārjunikoṇḍa, when Nāgārjuna allowed himself to have his head cut off by Prince Suśakti or Śaktimān, son of Antivāhana or Udayanabhadra.[92] It is most likely that this Nāgārjuna, whose name was recorded as *"Bhadanta Nāgārjunācarya"* in the Jaggayyapeta Stūpa near Amarāvatī was not a *Mādhyamika* dialectician but a Tāntrika Siddha, to whom authorship is ascribed for a number of Tāntrika treatises as well as medical and metallic science.

Lamotte, however, correctly noted that the topographical description of the Tibetan sources is different from Hsüan-tzang's record which depicts far more complicated scenes. Traveling from Tāmralipti (south of present-day Calcutta), Hsüan-tzang arrived at Southern Kosala[93] by passing through Uḍra (Orrisa), Kōnyōdha, and Kaliṅga

---

[92] Tāranātha wrote that Nāgārjuna lived his last 200 years at Śrīparvata practising Tantras with Yoginīs till he was beheaded by prince Suśakti, the grandson of king Udayana. Cf. Tāranātha: *History of Buddhism*, chap. xv, *IHQ*. xxviii, 1952, transl. by N. Dutt and U. N. Ghoshal, pp. 41-50 [Joshi, *ibid*., p.17]; Bu-ston wrote that Nāgārjuna was murdered by prince Śaktimān, a son of King Antivāhana or Udayanabhadra. Cf. *History of Buddhism* (tr. Obermiller), II, pp. 120-130. [Joshi, *op. cit*., p. 16.]; Lamotte: Webb-boin's English translation: *op. cit*., pp. 345-346.

[93] Hsüan-tzang's itinerary which began from Tāmralipti (south of todays' Calcutta) goes as follows [Here, Chinese 5 lis constitutes a mile: *op. cit*., II, p. 209, Note 70.]:

Traveling to the northwest for 140 miles (700 lis) to reach Karṇasuvarṇa, traveling toward the southwest for 140 miles (700 lis) to reach Uḍra (Orrisa);

Traveling toward the southwest for 240 miles (1200 lis) to reach-

and wrote that the capital of Kosala was about 40 Li (8 miles) around, and that the population of Bhikṣus was 10,000 residing in one hundred Saṅghārāmas. He visited an old Saṅghārāma not far to the south from the city, where Nāgārjuna stayed, and a Stūpa that was built by Aśoka standing by its side. He witnessed the place where he received Āryadeva who came up from further south and became his successor of Dharma-lineage.

Immediately after this, however, Hsüan-tzang narrated a legend as to how Nāgārjuna ended his life. The story dramatically differed from that of Kumārajīva's translation. Nāgārjuna is said to have been well practiced in the art of medicines. On the basis of his secret medicinal compound, he nourished himself for many hundreds of years, and so did the Śātavāhana king who was his patron and recipient of the mysterious medicine. Now the king's young son, impatient of his time of accession to the throne, was told by his mother queen that his father king would live as long as Nāgājuna would. Since all this was the result of the master's religious power, the day the master dies, the king would also succumb to death. Nagārjuna is said to have accepted the prince's request to forsake his life, and he cut his head off by means of a dry plant leaf.[94] This incredible legend continued to survive in I-ching's travelogue written a century later and in the aforementioned Tibetan sources as well.

By far more important is the description about the monastery that the Śātavāhana king is said to have constructed for Nāgārjuna. This was located about 300 Li (60 miles) to the southwest. The monastery was built within the solid rocky mountain, called Bhramaragiri ("dark-peaked hill"), that stood out as a solitary peak with mighty precipice. He described the Saṅghārāma as consisting of five-layered structure, each storey as tunnelled into a massive rock, equipped with four halls where a golden Buddha statue was set respectablely, and connected through corridors. From the high peak of the hill, streamlets flowed down like small cascades, through the different storeys, winding round the side galleries, and then discharging themselves out. Because of scattered light-holes,

---

Kōnyōdha, traveling toward the southwest for 280 miles (1400 lis) to reach Kaliṅga, traveling toward the northwest for 180 miles (900 lis) to reach Southern Kosala.
From here, Hsüan-tsan further traveled toward the south for 380 miles (1900 lis) to reach Āndhra, traveling toward the south for 200 miles (1000 lis) to reach Dhanyakataka by the Kṛṣṇā river.

[94] *Ibid..*, II, pp.212-214

the rooms are well illumined."[95] It is for this engineering feat of construction that Nāgārjuna was said to have transformed ordinary rocks into gold so as to ease the king's financial drain.[96] We have a couple of other records which seem to have referred to this same monastic establishment. Fa-hsien, who traveled to India (399-413) two centuries before Hsüan-tzang, recorded about the monastery of the southern country in his diary. Though he did not actually visit there because of some difficult conditions imposed on travellers, such as, dangerous roads, custom payments, requirement of escort service, etc.,[97] he included in the diary what he was informed about the monastic structure from someone from that country:

Arriving at Kauśāmbi, Fa-hsien said: By the distance of two hundred *Yojana* (about 1,000 miles), one reaches the country of the south (*dakṣiṇa*). The monastery was built into a massive rock hill called "dark peak hill" as a five-storey structure. These storeys comprise 500 rooms on the first floor, then 400, 300, 200, and then 100 rooms on the top floor. There is a fountainhead on the very top, from which a cascade of water flows down in front of each rock-cut room and into the gutters of each compartment, and then from the corner of each storey down to the lower storey, and so forth. Each room and floor corridor has windows cut through the rock wall, and it is brightly lit everywhere by day light.[98]

Hye-ch'o (Hui-ch'ao), a Korean pilgrim native of Shin-la of the eighth century, also left a comment in reference to this monastery.[99] He left South China in 724 for India by Southern Sea like I-ching did before (629-645) and returned through Central Asia to An-hsi in Chinese territory in December 727. From Central India, he walked for more than three months to arrive at the kingdom of the south whose territory extended to the southern, the eastern, and

95 *Ibid.*, p. 215.

96 Samuel Beal: *op. cit.*, pp.214-217

97 The last known Śātavāhana was Yājñaśrṭ Śātakarṇi who ruled 165-194 [Sinha and Bernagee, *op. cit.*, p. 94, whereas Lamotte gives it 174-203. *op. cit.*, p. 509]. From the mid-third century, the Śātavāhana was replaced by the house of Vākāṭakas of the Central India. Rudrasena II made a marital alliance with Candra Gupta II (380-413). It was during this period that Fa-hsien visited India and stayed for three years in the monastery in Pāṭaliputra to learn Sanskrit and copy the Vinayas.

98 Kazutoshi Nagasawa: *The biography of Fa-hsien and Travelogue of Sung-yun* (「法顕伝、宋雲行紀」), Tokyo: Heibonsha1971, p.126.

99 *The Hye Ch'o Diary: Memoir of the Pilgrimage to the Five Regions of India*, translated text and editing by Yang, Han-sung, Jan, Yün-hua and Iida, Shotaro and Laurence W. Preston. Seoul, Korea: Asian Huamanities Press, Po Chin Chai Ltd., ?

the western sea, and to the northern borders of central, western and eastern India. The following is his description in brief: "In the mountains there is a large monastery which was constructed by Yakṣas under order from the Bodhisattva Nāgārjuna and not built by human beings. Moreover, the pillars were cut from [rocks of the] mountain and built in three storeys. The monastery is over three hundred paces in circumference. . . But, at present the monastery is ruined and there are no monks. Seven hundred years after Nāgārjuna this place began to decay."[100]

General Cuningham attempted to identify Southern Kosala with the modern province of Berar or Gondwana, place it at Chāndā, a walled town 290 miles to the northwest of Rājamahendri, capital of Kaliṅga, with Nāgpur, Amarāvatī, or Ilichpur as alternatives.[101] Despite other theories postulated by others posterior to Cuningham, Southern Kosala has not yet been identified for certainty even today. Another important locality which lies contiguous to this region of Southern Kosala was Vidarbha, an indicator that refers to Nāgārjuna's birthplace. Hsüan-tzang, however, did not mention anything about the region of Vidarbha, the name of which did not appear in Chinese sources as a whole. It was the Tibetan source that informed the birthplace of Nāgārjuna as "south of Vidarbha." From the historical point of view, Vidarbha was an important locality, because it was not only the center of Hindu culture during the post-Epic and Classical period, but also the center of the sub-continent between north and south as well as between east and west. There has been discrepancies as to where precisely this historically familiar region is today. Lamotte refers it to the Wardhan region south-west of Nagpur. The author of Monier Williams Sanskrit Dictionary refers it to the region south of the Vind*ya* mountain range known as the homeland of the Nala-Damayantī story. Historians, such as N. K. Sinha and A. Ch. Banerjee, think that it was the eastern Madhyapradesh. The last two seem to agree regarding the general area that has been irrigated by the two rivers Narmadā and Tāpti.

Geographically, Simuka, founder of the house of Śātavāhana,

---

[100] *Ibid.*, p. 43. According to the notes 54 and 56 (p. 64), the locallity likely was in the eastern Chalukyas if it refers to the Bhramarā hill「跋邏末羅」which means "black bees"). The following additional information is given: "The cave temple actually exists today in the mountain of Undavilli near Bẹzwada. As noted by Sadakata, the hill is still called 'black hill' (Telegu "Malla-Malai") by the locals.

[101] *Ibid.*, pp.209, Note 70.

extended its expedition to that region to destroy the Kaṇvas that ruled there nearly half a century. According to the panegyric of Gautamīputra Śātakarṇi, the Śātavāhana ruled over a vast territory as far as the Vindhya in the north and as far as the three coastal regions in the south. Pratiṣṭhāna (present Paithan), Vāsiṣṭhīputra Pulumayi's seat of administration, was an important junction on the north-to-south highway (Dakṣiṇāpatha) and also sufficiently closer to the western coastal regions to regulate the maritime trading. During the time of his predecessor Gautamīputra Śātakarṇi, however, the Śātavāhana's capital city was much more in the hinterland as attested by Hsüan-tzamg's calcuation of distances and recording of directions of his journey from Tāmralipti. When the king's expedition reached the Vindya mountain as claimed in his panegyric, the distance to Ujjayinī, capital of *Satrap* Rudradāman, was only forty or fifty miles northward. Ujjayinī was the place of the Mauryan viceroy a few centuries before their times, and before his accession to the Mauryan throne, Aśoka stationed there as governor overseeing the western coastal regions and southern India. Buddhist communities evolved in Vidiśā and Ujjayinī since ancient times, because these cities were on the highway between Kauśāṃbī (Alahabad) and Pratiṣṭhāna and further to the south beyond.[102] Elder *Bhikṣu* Mahinda, Aśoka's son, had an enduring connection to the Ujjayinī Saṅgha before taking up his mission to the island country Siṃhala. Despite all these contextual relations, we have still no tangible evidence to substantiate the linkage of Rudradāman to the Buddhist community, nor to Nāgārjuna. I believe, however, that it would be the first step to determine the archeological site of Southern Kosala and the monastic site that the Śātavāhana king built for Nāgārjuna sixty miles to the south-west of that city.

§9. CONCLUSION

After more than one half of a century during the post-war research accomplishment, it has no longer been the problem of four different Nāgārjunas with which we should be concerned today.[103]

---

[102] *Ibid.*, pp. 210-211.

[103] É. Lamotte suggested in the preface to his French translation of the *Ta-chih-tu-lun*, Vol. III, that two Nāgārjunas can be hypothesized. G. Tucci further suggested the existence of three Nāgārjunas, a Mahāyāna philosopher, a Vajrayāna Siddha, and an alchemist. Still further M. Winternitz says: "Most likely the Buddhist philosopher, the Tantric writer, the medieval

What we are facing today is the problem of compartmentalized jig-zag puzzles of knowledge, fragmented elements of Nāgārjuna, without a configurated personality as human. Accordingly, a bloodless pale image of a mythical figure appears here and there without coherent and consistent linkage in human terms.

According to the Chinese textual catalogue, we recognize four types of texts ascribed to Nāgārjuna: (1) the type of logical treatise, such as *Upāyahṛdayaśāstra*, (2) the type of dialectical treatises with focus on the *Madhyamaka* doctrine, (3) the type of minor didactic and expository texts, under which the *Suhṛllekha* and the *Ratnāvalī* can also be classified along with a number of other works, (4) the type of grand commentary, expository treatises, such as, the *Mahāprajñāpāramitopadeśa-śāstra* and *Daśabhūmikavibhāṣā-śāstra* (both extant only in Chinese), which elucidate the Mahāyāna teachings and the practice of Bodhisattva. As said before, the fifth type of Tantric works ascribed to Nāgārjuna ought to be excluded.

The subject of Nāgārjuna and *Madhyamaka* was once the heart of Buddhist Studies in the post-war era, but the force of interest and enthusiasm for it seems to have waned, precisely because of aforementioned compartmentalization of past researches. In order to reverse this trend, I believe, it is absolutely necessary to reconcile those bits of knowledge accumulated in the past into the career of a single person as Nāgārjuna. In this regard, the *Ratnāvalī* provides an excellent specimen in which the four strands (i.e., logician, dialectician, learned commentator, and political and religious counsellor) are brought together in a single miniature form. From my analysis of the contents of both the *Suhṛllekha* and the *Ratnāvalī*, I have shown why we cannot simply assume or claim that Nāgārjuna wrote both the texts. It is even worse to assume that both texts were written for one and the same recipient. Given the stature of Nāgājuna as great master, I believe that it may not be inappropriate to assume his authorship for both texts, one for Hīnayāna orientation and another for Mahāyāna orientation. Logically, therefore, I have proposed the hypothesis of two different recipients and demonstrated how useful these two texts can be for conducting research into the historical panorama of the Śaka-Pahlave period. They serve as dual beacons in looking for the two different personalities of the recipients of the respective texts and also allows us to reflectively determine the dates of their authors. When all other approaches are exhausted,

---

writer and the alchemist were four different men, who were confused owing to the identity of names." History of Indian Literature II, Univ. of Calcutta Press, 1933, pp. 343-344).

I believe that the method I have proposed is a new approach worthy of testing, even though it may have to wait for the discovery of some tangible evidence to be vindicated.

The birth place of Nāgārjuna is relatively unimportant in comparison to Southern Kosala or the monastic establishment where he eventually made his center of activity. For, it may allow us to review the entire political and geographical contexts that encompass Western and Southern India during the Śaka-Pahlava period. Though it is legendary, I believe that there is some clue in his venture to visit the *Nāga*'s territory for deepen his understanding of Mahāyāna Buddhism. Who could mediate Nāgārjuna and Rudradāman? What was Nāgārjuna as human, who wrote and acted in human terms?

ARTICLE THREE

Buddha's Love and Human Love with Focus on Kuan-yin Bodhisattva[1]

§1. Introduction

Kuan-yin Bodhisattva is one of the most enduring members of the Buddhist Pantheon. Across boundaries of land and ocean, he has continued to be the focus of cultic devotion among Buddhists for two millennia, and is perhaps second only to Śākyamuni Buddha in popularity. Ever since the invocation in ancient India of his name, Avalokitasvara in Sanskrit in the Samanta-mukha Section of the *Lotsu Sūtra*,[2] he has been known in the Mahāyāna branch of Buddhism as the embodiment of the supreme virtue of love and compassion. Traces of belief in and worship of this Bodhisattva are found in all regions where Mahāyāna Buddhism once spread,[3] and are a living practice in East Asian countries today, despite contemporary political, social and economic changes.[4] Kumārajīva

---

[1] Presented at International conference of philosophy and psychotherapy held at Nan-hua college, Taiwan, October 16 through 17. The theme of the Conference: was "Life, Love, and Death," October 16, 1998. The article is included in *Chung-Hwa Buddhist Journal*, No. 13, pp. 195-254; Taipei: The Chung-Hwa Institute of Buddhist Studies, March, 2000

[2] Fa-hua-ching（「法華経」shortened from「妙法蓮華経」); the Sanskrit text: *Saddharmapuṇḍarīka-sūtra* in Sanskrit: edited by Kern and Nanjō, 1912, Bibliotheca Buddhica 10. Three Chinese versions: (1) *Chêng-fa-hua-ching* (「正法華経」in 10 fascs.), Taishō. 9 (No. 263), translated by Dharmarakṣa in AD 286; (2) *Miao-fa-lien-hua-ching* (「妙法蓮華経」in 7 or 8 fascs.), Taishō. 9 (No. 262), translated by Kumārajīva in 406; (3) *T'ien-p'in-miao-fa-lien-hua-ching* (「添品妙法蓮華経」in 7 or 8 fascs.), Taishō. 9 (No. 264), by Jñānagupta and Dharmagupta in 601. In this paper, Kumārajīva's textual translation is the main source of reference. The chapter 'Sammanta-muckha' is the 25th in Kumārajīva's text, and it is translated as "All gates through which the Bodhisattva contemplates the voices of the world" (「観世音菩薩普門品」); in Dharmarakṣa's text, it is the 23rd chapter, and the title is given "All gates through which the Bodhisattva illumines the voices of the world" (「光世音普門」), and in the last translation of 601, it is the 24th chapter with the same title as that of Kumārajīva.

[3] Cf. Tay, C.N. "Kuan-yin: the cult of half asia," *History of Religions*, No. 162 (now 1976) 147-177

[4] Blofelt, John: *Compassion Yoga; the mystical cult of Kuan Yin*. London

(CE 406) and Hsüan-tzang (between 645-664) respectively rendered the Sanskrit Avalokitasvara or Avalokiteśvara in Chinese as kuan-shih-yin (or in shortened form as kuan-yin) and Kuan-tzŭ-ts'ai. While the virtue of love and compassion continued to be praised, hypostatized and depicted in human form for countless ages, the iconographic image of this Bodhisattva rapidly multiplied into varied forms in India through assimilation of Hindu deities. In China, during the latter half of the first millenium, his standard image radically changed from that of an austere male figure to that of an effeminate figure with a maiden-like smile and refined celestial womanhood. Regarding their initial encounter with Kuan-yin, some writers in the West wrote of being "profoundly affected" by the artistic representation of the figure and its enchanting spell.[5]

The popularity of the cult of Kuan-yin Bodhisattva is due primarily to the dual virtues that Mahāyāna Buddhism ascribed to the ideal of this Bodhisattva. Love and compassion constituted his practical virtue, while the insight of *Śūnyatā* was his theoretical virtue. The ideal of Kuan-yin Bodhisattva fared well among Mahāyāna Buddhist followers by attracting their belief and devotion, whether in high or low culture and South or East Asia. The said two virtues, interdependent like the two wheels of a cart, represent the two expedient means or criteria (*upāya-kauśalya*) essential to any Bodhisattva's career. What makes the Bodhisattva's dual virtues unique among all human systems of thought is the very insight of *Śūnyatā* (emptiness), the principle that whatever is is devoid of its own nature (*niḥsvabhāva*).

In this paper, I am concerned with the subject of Kuan-yin Bodhisattva's virtue as invariably expressed in "the vow of self-abnegation for love and compassion toward all sentient beings, especially those in suffering and distress." Because of his vow not to cross to Nirvāṇa, despite his full capacity to do so, Kuan-yin is said to hold mid-stream until all other beings have been successfully rescued and have crossed to the yonder shore. I think that Kuan-yin's virtue as the embodiment of Buddhist love and compassion is the bridge that links human virtue to that of the enlightened and perfected (Buddhas, Tathāgatas). This paper has three main points: (1) distinguishing love and compassion of Buddhas from that of humans in terms of non-duality between the agent of love and the recipient; (2) analyzing this principle in reference to the three

(1977) Alternative title, *Bodhisattva of compassion; the mystical tradition of Kan Yin.* Boulder, Colo (1978) 158 p; Esp. p. 19.

[5] *Ibid*, p, 14.

recipient; (2) analyzing this principle in reference to the three motivational contexts of love and compassion; and (3) evaluating Buddhist love and compassion in terms of perfect communication based on the insight of *Śūnyatā*.

§2. LOVE AND COMPASSION THROUGH FOUR CONTEMPLATIVE DISCIPLINES[6]

In Chinese Buddhist literature, the Buddhist virtue of love and compassion is generally expressed by a compound of '*tz'ŭ*' and '*pei*'[7] (compassion and commiseration) rather than the singular term '*ai*'[8] (love). The reason for this is that the term '*ai*' was used to represent one of the twelve members of Buddhist causality, i.e., dependent origination (*pratītyasamutpāda*).[9] The term *tṛṣṇā* in Sanskrit or *taṇhā* in Pāli, which refers to this eighth term within the series of twelve, was translated as '*ai*' or '*k'o-ai*'[10]. The term denoted an innermost blind force of "craving", like thirst, which triggers "attachment" (*upadāna*) first to "existence" (*bhava*), then to the mass of sufferings represented collectively by "birth and death" (*jarā-maraṇa*), namely, grief, lamentation, misery, detachment and despair (*śoka-parideva-duḥkha-daurmanasya-upāyāsa*). The force of "craving" is said to arise from the "feeling" (*vedanā*) of external contact (*sparśa*) through the six-fold sensory and mental faculties (*ṣaḍāyatana*) in the context where "name and form" (*nāma-rūpa*) are dualized within "consciousness" (*vijñāna*). This conscious moment is said to arise from a configuration of multifarious inner workings of Karmic (essentially mental) propensities (*saṃskāras*) within the subconscious domain, triggered by ignorance (*avidyā*) about the foregoing process. Thus, Buddhist writers refrained from using the term '*ai*' to express the sublime virtue of love, but instead resorted to either a compound of *tz'ŭ* and *pei*, or another compound consisting of '*tz'ŭ*' and '*ai*.'[11] I am inclined to think that "love" is an effective word for the purpose of communication, because it has been commonly used by other religious traditions among English speaking peoples.

---

[6] Four immeasurable thoughts or contemplations (*catvāri apramāṇāni*, 四無量心): Maitrī, Karuṇā, Muditā, and Upekṣā.

[7] 「慈悲」

[8] 「愛」

[9] 「十二縁起」

[10] 「渴愛」

[11] 「慈愛」

In this paper, therefore, whenever I use the phrase "Buddhist virtue of love and compassion," I refer to either a compound of '*tz'ŭ-pei*' or 'tz'ŭ-*ai*.'

'*Tz'ŭ*' stands for '*maitrī*' in Sanskrit (*metta* in Pāli) and means an active wishing for the welfare and happiness of others (*hita-sukha-upanaya-kāmatā*), whereas '*pei*' stands for '*karuṇā*' (same in Pāli) and means a passive wishing for the absence of illfare and unhappiness in others (*ahita-dukkha-apanaya-kāmatā*). These slightly different connotations are also found in Mahāyāna usage. For instance, in the 20th fascicle of the *T'a-chih-tu-lun*, Nāgārjuna explains '*maitrī*' and '*karuṇā*' as part of the four disciplines of "boundless contemplation" or "immeasurable mind" (*catvāri apramāṇāni*). '*Tz'ŭ*' means "boundless contemplation of love or good will toward all beings," a constant seeking for security and benefit that contributes to their well-being. '*Pei*' means "a boundless thought of compassion or commiseration toward all beings"[12] who are subjected to physical and mental sufferings in all walks of life (literally, the five cycles of life).[13] In Chinese translations, *tz'ŭ* and *pei* are almost always compounded in the translation of *maitrī* or *karuṇā* or both taken together, because, as pointed out by H. Nakamura, conceptually the two meanings are equally anchored in a common motivational sentiment.[14]

In early Buddhism, the practice of *maitrī* and *karuṇā* were prescribed for lay Buddhists as well as professional monks as basic norms of human ethics. However, two other disciplines of sympathetic joy (*muditā*) and equanimity (*upekṣā*) were added gradually to these norms to form a set of four standard practices for monks under the rubric of "four immeasurable thoughts or contemplations" (*catuvāri apramāṇāni*). Thus defined as part of the four disciplines and prescribed for those who were engaged in the path of scholastic

---

[12] Etienne Lamotte's French translation: of the *T'ā-chih-tu-lun* (the 20th fascicle), Taishō. 25, (No. 1509p. 208c]: *Le Traité de la Grande Vertu de Sagesse de Nāgārjuna* Tome III, Institut Orentaliste, Louvain, 1970, p. 1242. La *maitrī*, c'est penser avec amour aux êtres et toujours rechercher la sécurité (*yogakṣema*) et des choses heureuses (*sukhavastu*) pour leurx faire due bien; La *karuṇā*, c'est penser avec pitié aux êtres qui subissent dans les cing destinées (*gati*) toutes sortes de doullelurs corporelles (*kāyikaduḥkha*) et due douleurs mentales (*caitasikaduḥkha*).

[13] '五道.' Five realms of existence or life styles or courses of life cycle through which all sentient beings were classified in ancient India. Usually six realms as for gods (deva), human (*jana*), animal (*tiryak*), hungry ghost (*preta*), perpetual fighter (*asura*), and hell-gound (*naraka*). Here the asura is included in hell (*naraka*).

[14] Nakamura, Hajime: Jihi (「慈悲」、Buddhist Love and Compassion). Kyoto: Heirakuji Shoten (11th ed), 1994. pp. 22-23.

orthodoxy (Hīnayāna), the disciplines of *maitrī* and *karuṇā* were practiced within the pacifist framework of the Buddhist monastery[15] to guide and regulate the minds of practitioners toward sublime spirituality. In the course of history, Mahāyāna movements began around the first century B.C. and compiled their respective scriptures in various parts of India almost simultaneously, the earliest of these scriptures being the *Prajñāpāramitā-sūtra* (henceforth *Wisdom Sūtra*), *Saddharmpuṇḍarīka-sūtra* (*Lotus Sūtra*), *Buddhāvataṃsaka-sūtra* (*Hua-yen Sūtra*), and *Amitāyus-sukhāvatī-vyūha (Pureland Sūtra)*.[16] By the time of Nāgārjuna (ca. CE 50-150), the greatest Mahāyāna thinker, these textual sources became the scriptures held in common by those Mahāyāna activists who challenged the scholastic pacifist tradition of the orthodoxy.

These Mahāyāna movements advocated a new career of spirituality, called the Bodhisattva Way (*P'u-sa-tao*),[17] centered on the moral and spiritual paradigm of Śākyamuni (the Sage of the Śākyas), historical founder of Buddhism. In short, the lifestyle of the Bodhisattva embodied the ideology of those reform-oriented activists opposed to the pacifist monastic tradition. It was natural then for the virtue of love and compassion to be maximally emphasized in the context of Śākyamuni's early career of spiritual pursuit as a bodhisattva. Thus, the activist virtue began to be differentiated from the pacifist vehicles of Śrāvaka and Pratyekabuddha on the basis of the Mahāyāna insight of *Śūnyatā*.

In the 27th chapter of the *Ta-chih-tu-lun*, Nāgārjuna sets forth thirty-three question-and-answers and differentiates the perfected virtue of love and compassion ascribed to the enlightened and perfected (Buddha and Tathāgata) on the one hand, and the imperfect human virtue of love and compassion and the imperfect virtue of the Śrāvaka and Pratyekabuddha vehicles on the other.[18] He provides detailed arguments by defining the Buddha's perfected virtue in terms of*Ta-tz'ŭ* (*mahā-maitrī*) and *Ta-pei* (*mahā-karuṇā*) [*ta,* meaning

---

[15] The tradition, to which the monastic system refers here, is the Sarvāstivāda which spearheaded the Buddhist orthodoxy from the second century BC to the third century AD in northern India.

[16] *Prajñāpāramitā-sūtra*, (*The Perfection of Prajñā Insight*, 「般若経典」), *Saddharmpuṇḍarīka-sūtra* (*The Lotus Flower of the Wondrous Dharma*, 「妙法蓮華経」), *Buddāvataṃsaka-sūtra* (*The Buddh's Flower Garland* 「華厳経」), and *Amitāyus-sukhāvatī-vyūha* (*The Manifestation of Pureland* 「(「浄土経」).

[17] 「菩薩道」 Bodhisattvayāna, Boddhisattva Way or Bodhisattva Path or Bodhisattva Vehicle..

[18] Śrāvaka-yāna and Pratyekabuddha-yāna which constitute two vehicles.

"great" or "superior"] and the imperfect human virtue as *shao-tz'u* and *shao-pei* [*shao,* meaning small or inferior]. In his French translation of the *Ta-chih-tu-lun*, Etienne Lamotte renders these terms respectively as *"grande bienveillance"* and *"grande compassion,"* and *"petite bienveillance"* and *"petite compassion."*[19]

As to the distinction of these two virtues, superior and inferior, Nāgārjuna asserts that *Ta-tz'ŭ* and *Ta-pei* belong to Buddhas and Bodhisattvas, whereas *shao-tz'ŭ* and *shao-pei* belong to ordinary humans as well as to those who advocate the Śrāvaka and Pratyekabuddha vehicles.[20] The lesser virtue of love and compassion is a part of the four disciplines of "immeasurable thoughts," whereas the superior virtue is a part of the eighteen epithets of Buddhahood shared by no one else (*aṣṭādaśa āveṇikā buddha-dharmāḥ*).[21] Nāgārjuna, however, specifies the difference between the virtue of the Buddha and that of Bodhisattva by saying that "it is an expedient definition to call Bodhisattva's virtue superior (*ta-tz'ŭ* and *ta-pei*), because, though it is lesser than that of the Buddha, by comparison to that of the two vehicles, it is (much) greater."[22] In short, he elucidates the fundamental difference between the two as follows:

> The great virtue of love and compassion ascribed to the enlightened is alone true and greatest. Again, the lesser virtue of love (*shao-tz'ŭ*) means a mere wishing in thought to make people happier, without the actual ability to do so. The lesser virtue of compassion (*shao-pei*) means to empathize with the various physical and mental sufferings which people undergo and feel sympathy for them, without the actual ability to help the people be rid of these. In the case of the superior virtue of love, the Buddha wishes people to be awarded with security and happiness and, in actuality, helps them realize these. Likewise, with the great virtue of compassion, the Buddha empathizes with people's misfortune and, in actuality, assists them to be rid of their suffering.[23]

---

[19] *"la Grande Bienveillance* and *la Grande Compassion,"* *op. cit.*, p. 1705.

[20] 「凡夫二乗」

[21] *Aṣṭādaśa āveṇikā buddha-dharmāḥ* (十八不共法): *daśa-balāni* (十力), *catvāri vaiśāradyāni* (四無畏), *trīṇi smṛty-upasthānāni* (三念住), and mahākaruṇā (大悲).

[22] Taishō. 25, fasc. 27, p. 256 b: 「菩薩大悲者於仏為小、於二乗為大。此是仮名為大」

[23] *Ibid.*, p. 256b-c: 「仏大慈大悲真実最大、復次小慈但心念与衆生楽実無事楽、

Here, one of Nāgārjuṇa's criteria to differentiate Buddha's love and compassion from human love and compassion is clearly expressed in terms of ultimate effectuation. This distinction between the two qualitatively different virtues of love and compassion can further be observed in the three motivational contexts of love and compassion.

§3. THREE MOTIVATIONAL CONTEXTS OF BUDDHIST LOVE AND COMPASSION[24]

Mahāyāna thinkers differentiated three motivational contexts of love and compassion by emcompassing the entire range of material and spiritual fulfilments of human happiness and well-being. In the twentieth fascicle of the *Ta-chih-tu-lun*, Nāgārjuna summarily gives three criteria for the Buddhist virtue of love and compassion in terms of its motivational contexts: (1) the love and compassion that is motivated by the similarity of one's self with other selves, i.e., common humanity (*sattva-ālambana*); (2) the love and compassion that is motivated by the sameness of the psycho-physical elements which form the basis of human existence, i.e., five Skandhas (*dharma-ālambana*); and (3) the love and compassion that is motivated by neither of these two contexts, i.e., independent of motivational context (*anālambana*).[25]

First, in human science, human love is classified into five distinct cateogries of separate affectional systems, namely, maternal love, infant-mother love, age-mate or peer love, heterosexual love, and paternal love.[26] Taking these basic bonds of love as a foundation, human interaction evolved to create the bonds of family, neighborhood, community, society, and so on, and simultaneously developed ethical principles or normatives of action to regulate human interaction at all levels of human organization. Although neighborly love appears

---

小慈名観衆生種々身苦心苦、憐愍而已不能令脱。大慈者念令衆生得楽亦与楽事。大悲憐愍衆生苦亦能令脱苦。」

24 「三種之慈悲」

25 Taishō. 25, p. 209a: 「無尽意菩薩問中説、慈有三種、一者修生縁、二者法縁、三者無縁」 As given in parenthesis, Lamotte correctly gives the respective Sanskrit terms *sattva-ālambana*, *dharma-ālambana*, and *anālambana*. *Ālambana* is an epistemic term to signify cognitive object to be seen, heard, etc. by sense faculties. I introduced the above three criteria by adding the "motivational context" to each of them, because human love and compassion is generally activated in observing, hearing, or knowing some form of imbalance in a given context of some other person.

26 *International Encylopedia of Psychiatry*, London: Roughsh Co. , 1972. p. 445.

to be largely accepted as a universal phenomenon and thus as a self-evident moral principle, one must still ask: By what justification should such love become a norm in practical ethics?

In early Buddhism, the answer was rather simple. The bottom line is that one's self is dearest to every person, and that love of one's self is common to all humans. It follows that since there is nothing more important than one's self, no one would wish to be harmed by another, and neither would anyone wish to harm anyone else on account of that similarity. Accordingly, for early Buddhists, neither a metaphysical principle nor a theological being was necessary as a foundation for the principle of neighborly love. The principle simply relied on the fact that one's self and the selves of others are the same, equally giving rise to suffering and rejoicing in their very humanness. Nāgārjuna explains the virtue of love and compassion in this initial motivational context as follows:

> In reference to people of all regions and all walks of life (lit., the five cyclical courses of life),[27] one ought to regard them as if they were one's father and mother, brothers and sisters, nephews and nieces, and friends. One ought always to wish that they find happiness in whatever they desire and obtain benefit and security, in this manner extending one's mind as widely as possible over the vast numbers of peoples in all regions. This kind of thought of love and compassion ought to be based on the likeness of all people. It is in this motivational context that not only ordinary people in action but also professional monks who have not reached the state of sainthood (Arhat) are said to activate their love and compassion toward other peoples.[28]

What holds here is the age-old principle of ethics, such that "one ought not to do unto others what one does not wish others to do unto one's self" and that "one ought to do what is good for others in the same way one wishes others to do for one's self." This is the first motivational context in terms of human similarity.

Second, the next higher motivational context is anchored in the insight of *dharma*-theory. The Buddhist insight of Non-self derives

---

[27] Wu-tao (五道) : from bottom:, the life of hell, hungry ghost, animal, human, and heavenly being. These states of existence may be conceived as different life styles or states of life resulting from varieties of causes and conditions in the human world.

[28] *Ta-chih-tu-lun* (20th fasc.), Taishō. 25, p. 209b. 「十方五道衆生中、以一慈心視之、如父如母如兄弟姉妹子姪知識、常求好事、欲令得利益安隱。如是心遍滿十方衆生中、如是慈心名衆生縁。多在凡夫人行処有学人未漏尽者」

from the fact that an individual person is a composite entity comprising multiple phenomenal elements classified into five aggregates (*pañca-skandha*), and that a human person is causally made out of these sensory and mental propensities without any core substance like "self." An individual's self is nothing more than a fictitious designation imposed upon the five aggregates of psycho-physical elements (*rūpa-caitasika-dharmā*), namely: (1) an aggregate of physical or material facts (*rūpa-skandha*) arising from the contact of six faculties with their objects of seeing, hearing, smelling, tasting, touching, and awareness; (2) an aggregate of facts of sensation (*vedanā-skandha*) arising from subjective impressions of contact as either favorable (*kuśala*), unfavorable (*akuśala*), or neutral (*avyākṛta*) to one's disposition; (3) an aggregate of facts of perception or ideation (*saṃjñā-dharma*) arising from diverse cognitive assimilation involving naming and differenting; (4) an aggregate of facts of mental activities or forces [usually given in plural (*saṃskāra-skandha*)], crucial to the function of bringing together, formulating or constructing conceptual, linguistic, and volitional responses; (5) an aggregate of facts of awareness, cognition, or consciousness (*vijñāna-skandha*). This second motivational context of love and compassion is a step removed from the context of humanity in the commonsense world, because an individual person is now viewed in terms of multiple building blocks organized by inner causality. The previously independent human individual is lost here in the wider and more universal landscape of physical, biological, and mental data or elements, becoming an illusory non-existent being.

Again, I quote a passage of Nāgārjuna from the same text to explain this second motivational context:

> Acting in this motivational context of *dharma*-theory, those saints, like Arhats, Pratyeka-buddhas, and Buddhas, have eradicated all impure, defiled propencities (*āsrava*), annihilated the notion of self or I-ness, liberated from thoughts of identity and difference [regarding things experienced],[29] and understood

[29] In the earlier part of the 20th fascicle, [*ibid.*, *Ta-chih-tu-lun, Ibid.*, p. 206b], Nāgārjuna explains the practice of transcending the dual features of identity and difference as to any phenomenon [*Animita-samādhi* (無相三昧)] as follows: "The practitioner ought to contemplate like this: 'Since every *dharma* arises by depending on causes and conditions, it cannot be really an existent; but it is merely an unreal aspect [without its substance]. Moreover, grasping this aspect alone as real, people insist on their view that one's self and things belonging to it really exist. Now I ought to investigate whether or not I can really take hold of this particular aspect as belonging to a real substance.' No matter however in detail one

> that human desires arise depending upon continual momentary causes and conditions. In reference to this causal structure of a human person, the enlightened Buddhas are aware that people are merely continual flows of factual elements and, hence, of the empty nature without substance of self-identity. Despite the truth that the five aggregates make up a human being, ordinary people neither see this empty nature of the human individual, nor accept the insight that an individual is a mere configuration of momentary flows of causes and conditions. Accordingly, they frantically look for happiness, each to his own fulfilment of desires at all times. Moved by a sense of pity for this state of affairs, those who are wise activate their love and compassion for people and help them realize whatever happiness they wish to realize [within the world in which they live]. This is the second motivational context of love and compassion based on the bottom line of human existence (*dharma-ālambana*).[30]

Third, the highest motivational context is paradoxically the absence of motivational context. In activating the virtue of love and compassion toward people, the enlightened and perfected neither relies on the nature of common humanity, nor on the insight of *dharma*-theory, precisely because he holds the insight of *śūnyatā*. Nāgārjuna explains this, in relation to the preceding two motivational contexts, as follows:

> There are three kinds of love and compassion, the first which depends on the similarity of fellow humans (*sattva-ālambana*), the second which depends on the universal basis of sensory and

---

investigates into it, one realizes that nothing can be grasped as a real thing. Nor is it possible to really prove whether there is a substance for the aspect of maleness or that of femaleness, that of identity or that of difference, etc. The reason is that all those [sensory and mental] dharmas (facts) are without a substance or without anything belonging to it, hence the said aspects are unreal and non-existent. Because of their nature of emptiness, there is neither a man nor a woman. Identity or difference is only a name referring to non-existent substance, and hence, [it does not matter whether] it is asserted as identical or different. Because of this, it is not possible to grasp a substance called as "man" or "woman," "identical" or "different." 「行者思惟作是念、諸法従因縁生無有実法、但有相、而諸衆生取是相著我我所。我今当観是相有実可得不。審諦観之都不可得。若男相女相一異相等、是相実皆不可得。何以故、諸法無我我所故空。空故無男無女、一異等法我我所中名字。是一是異、以故男女一異法実不可得。」

[30] *Ibid.*, fasc. 20; p. 209b-c: 「行法縁者、諸漏尽阿羅漢辟支仏諸仏、是諸聖人破吾我相、滅一異相故、但観従因縁相続生諸欲。以慈念衆生時、従和合因縁相続生但空。五衆即是衆生、念是五衆以慈念。衆生不知是法空而常一心欲得楽、聖人之令随意得楽。為世俗法故、名為法縁。」

mental elements (*dharma-ālambana*), and the third which relies on neither. Ordinary humans rely on the aspect of human features. The Śrāvaka and Pratyekabuddha as well as Bodhisattva initially rely on the first motivational context but, later on, rely on the second motivatonal context, namely, the bottom line of factual psycho-physical elements. In the case of Buddhas, being thoroughly immersed in the contemplation of the insight of ultimate emptiness, they are said to depend on no motivational context.[31]

Here I am obliged to examine why the Buddhist virtue of love and compassion was initially differentiated between the first and second motivational contexts. Nāgārjuna asserts that the human virtue of love and compassion must depend on the criterion that all humans are similar, but establishes a second stage for the vehicles of Śrāvaka, Pratyeka as well as Bodhisattva, noting that they initially rely on the first criterion and then move to the second criterion later. Those who have not yet become Arhat, and hence, have not accomplished total emancipation, are still bound and entrapped by the influence of morally and spiritually defiled propensities (*āsrava*).[32] In activating their love and compassion, these practitioners cannot do away with the first motivational context because they are concerned with some particular humans, and must naturally be influenced by the ideas of the particular humans with whom they are concerned. This means that these practitioners may not transcend the various influencing factors derived from the social and cultural contexts in which the lives of those persons with whom they are concerned are intertwined.

In the second motivational context, there are those practitioners who have realized the state of Arhat, eradicated the idea of self or I-ness, and hence transcended the aspects of identity or difference in the things they experience. Being thus totally freed from the

---

31「慈悲心有三種、衆生縁法縁無縁、凡夫人衆生縁、声聞辟支仏及菩薩初衆生縁後法縁。諸仏善修行畢竟空故、名為無縁。」

32 *Yu-lou* (「有漏」) *Sāsrava* in Sanskrit, āsava in Pāli, means the state of being affected or influenced by passion, defilements, in which the process of life is in full swing; verbal and mental defilement which cause obstruction to enlightenment. Here it is given as "morally and spiritually defiled propensities." 漏尽 (*lou-chin*) or 無漏 (*wu-lou*), opposite of yu-lou., the state of being unaffected or uninfluenced by passion, defilement, in total transcendence from the process of life. *Āsrava* means 'flowing,' 'running,' 'discharge' and is applied in analogy to the discharge or outflow of passions and their faith, impure flux from sense faculties and the mind. It is synonymous with *kleśa* or defilement. *Āsrava* denotes the state of *Sāsrava*.

causes of moral and spiritual defilement (*anāsrava*), they see that all humans are merely aggregations of continual flows of sensory and mental elements and ultimately of the empty nature without any substance of identity. Here, Nāgārjuna obviously meant that at this stage, those saints who are totally liberated become independent of entrapment, social, cultural, and so forth, because they are confronted exclusively by the bottom line, i.e., the five aggregates of sensory and mental operations, neither defiled nor undefiled. One might say that this is the ultimate principle of universality common to all humans, beyond all differences of religion, culture, society, and so forth. This retrospective insight is the second motivational context, within which practitioners are supposed to reassess the world and meet fellow humans with love and compassion.

For Buddhist thinkers, however, this was not enough. Thus came the third non-motivational context only attributable to Buddha's love and compassion. Nāgārjuna continues:

> The virtue of love and compassion that is activated without any motivational context [unlike the former two], belongs only to the Buddha. The reason is that the mind of Buddha ought not to abide either within the domain of or dinary consciousness (*saṃskṛta*)[33] or within the domain of the transcendent (*asaṃskṛta*). His mind relies not on the past, present or future world, because he knows that motivational contexts [of the human world] are unreal, up-side-down, and illusory. Hence, the mind of Buddha does not depend upon any of these unreal motivational contexts. Since ordinary people do not know how transcendentally real these sensory and mental elements are, they stray into all walks of life (literally, the five cyclical courses of life), attach themselves to sensory and mental elements, discriminating one from another for selection, [thus unable to see *things as they really are* (*yathābhūtam*)].[34] Hence, it is the Buddha's virtue of love and compassion to help humans acquire the same insight, [concerning the reality of elements totally freed from

[33] *Saṃskṛta* (有為): phenomenal, affected, composite existence is an interplay of multiple subtle, ultimate, not further analysable, elements of *nāma-rūpa* (mind and matter) and forces derived from the given causal concatenation of multiple elements. Whatever is phenomenal is therefore subject to the causality of dependent origination.*Asaṃskṛta* (無為): Unaffected, non-composite, absolute, unconditioned, and unlimited, and hence transcendent. Only three *dharmas* were accepted by the Abhidharmists, such as Sarvāstivāda

[34] 「諸法実相.」

defilement]. This is called the independence from motivational context."[35]

In the history of Buddhist doctrines, the negation of reality has been done twice. In the first case, as negation of the reality of empirical self on the basis of multiplicity of sensory and mental elements. Here, the pscyho-physical elements are regarded as real (*dharma-svabhāva*), but a human person is considered unreal (*anātman*). A human is as unreal as a cart which, when broken down into its component parts (wheels, axle, frame, etc.), is after all only a name. This was the position of the orthodox insight of *dharma-svabhāva*.[36] The aforementioned second motivational context represents this first negation. In the second case, the Mahāyāna insight of *Śūnyatā* repudiated the reality of these psycho-physical elements or *dharmas* (*dharma-niḥsvabhāva*).[37] Then, the non-motivational context of the Buddha's virtue of love and compassion may be inferred as derived from the second negation, i.e., unreality of psycho-physical elements (*dharma-śūnyatā*).

§4. BUDDHA AND BODHISATTVA DIFFERENTIATED AS TO THEIR LOVE AND COMPASSION

In scholastic Buddhism (Hīnayāna), Bodhisattvas were stereotyped together with Śrāvakas and Pratyekabuddhas as "three vehicle followers" (*tri-yāna* or *yāna-traya*). It was in Mahāyāna Buddhism that the Bodhisattva ideal was reconceptualized as a threshold Buddha, one who is on the verge of Buddhahood, and was thereby clearly differentiated from the orthodox ideal of discipleship (Śrāvaka) or of the solitary practitioner (Pratyekabuddha).[38] In this respect,

---

35 *Ibid.*, fasc. 20. p. 209c.「無縁者、是慈但諸仏有。何以故、諸仏心不住有為無為性中。不依止過去世未来現在世、知諸縁不実顛倒虚誑故、心無所縁。仏以衆生不知是諸法実相。往来五道、心著諸法分別取捨、以是諸法実相智恵。令衆生得之。是名無縁」

36「人空法有」

37「法空」

38 Śrāvaka (Sāvaka iṇ Pāli, 声聞), originally both lay and monk who listened to Śākyamini's teaching and instructions. The goal was to realize the ideal of Saint as Arhat through rigorous regulation of one's moral and spiritual life toward the insight of Fourfold holy Truths. The type of practice and style of life centered to the self-improvement and advancement, and this was criticzed by the Mahāyāna followers as self-centered. Pratyekabuddha (Pacceka-buddha in Pāli, 辟支仏、独覚、縁覚) one enlightened by himself through the insight of "Dependent Origination," but dies without proclaiming the truth to the world. This reclusive nature was criticized by Mahāyāna followers.

Nāgārjuna was an uncompromising Mahāyāna advocate; he grouped Buddhas and Bodhisattvas together over and against the group of Śrāvakas and Pratyekabuddhas. In early Buddhism, as noted before, the principles of *maitrī* and *karuṇā* were taught as the basic norms of human ethics, but were soon combined with sympathetic joy (*muditā*) and equanimity (*upekṣā*) as part of four disciplines by the orthodoxy.[39] These four disciplines then became prescribed practice for professional monks cultivating mental and spiritual aptitude for religious salvation. Nāgārjuna informs us in detail about how these disciplines were put into practice.[40]

When a practitioner (1) conducts contemplation of *maitrī* or loving friendliness, he wishes happiness for others beginning with his close relations and then expanding his wishing outward, eventually to encompass all humans. When he (2) conducts contemplation of *karuṇā* or compassion, he empathizes with the suffering of some particular individuals and then expands his empathy outward to eventually encompass all humans. When he (3) conducts contemplation of *muditā* or sympathetic joy, he holds joy for some particular person and for his successful deliverance from suffering, then expands this outward to eventually encompass all humans. Finally, when he (4) conducts contemplation of *upekṣā* or equanimity, he transcends or dissociates himself from the foregoing states of mental involvement, modeling his practice after that of some person who has managed to transcend both suffering and rejoicing.

The last of these four practices was clearly established to help maintain a lifestyle of mental balance and spiritual enhancement. It was with respect to these essentially passive disciplines that I earlier characterized the monastic lifestyle of the Śrāvakas and the solitary withdrawal from life of Pratyekabuddhas as the pacifist approach to spiritual advancement.

Now, I am obliged to briefly introduce another objective Nāgārjuna has in mind. He points out that these four disciplines are constructive for the inner growth and cultivation of human spirituality, but that they are too contemplative in nature because they do not actually

---

[39] Four immeasurable contemplation (四無量心): p.758 fasc. 20. '喜' embodies the third discipline and '捨' the fourth discipline.

[40] In the Ta-chih-tu-lun, fasc. 20, Nāgārjuna as commentator deals with the threefold Samādhi (三三昧), four-fold Dhyāna (四禅), four-fold Aatvāri apramāṇāni (四無量心), and four higher Ārūptya-Samādhi (四無色定). The disciplines of Four Immeasurables is found in Fasc. 20 (Chap. 33), Ibid., pp. 208c through 211c

effect or bring about anything in practical terms.[41] If one really wishes happiness for others, whether a person, family or community, and wants to do something practical about this, perhaps by helping others overcome preexistent problems and suffering, Nāgārjuna enthusiastically endorses direct involvement in the activist lifestyle of a Bodhisattva. He inculcates the activist virtue of Bodhisattva in the 27th fascicle of the *Ta-chih-tu-lun*, where, if we keep the paradigm of Śākyamuni in mind, the underlying intent of his message is loud and clear:

> Love and compassion are the foundation of the Buddha's Way. The reason is that the Bodhisattva (e.g., Śākyamuni as a young man) initially observes varieties of human suffering, like old age, sickness, and death, physical and psychological [problems], the present life and the life beyond, and whatever distress accompanies these sufferings. He then activates his "great love and compassion" (*ta-tz'ŭ* and *ta-pei*) for fellow humans and vows to rescue them from these sufferings. In order to actualize his vow, he resolves to seek the way of emancipation and eventually realizes the supreme enlightenment. Because of this activist great love and compassion, the indomitable mind of the Bodhisattva is never defeated throughout the duration of incalculably many cycles of life-circumstances (*asaṃkhyā-lokā*). Because of his love and compassion, he also makes a vow not to enter Parinirvāṇa [until the rest of human kind have accomplished it before him].[42]

The above passage reveals the linkage between the activist Bodhisattvas and the enlightened Buddhas. Previously, the Buddha's virtue of love and compassion was called "*mahā-maitrī*" and "*mahā-karuṇā*," differentiating it thus from the lesser virtue of common humans as well as from that of the Śrāvaka and Pratyekabuddha. But it is not quite clear how and why the Buddha's virtue of love and compassion is distinct from that of the Bodhisattva. In Mahāyāna scriptures, we often encounter those celestial Bodhisattvas like Samantabhadra (Pu-chien or Pien-chi), Manjuśrī (Man-shih-li) or Mañjughoṣa, and Avalokiteśvara (Kuan-yin),[43] and those Bodhisattvas

---

[41] *Ibid.*, p. 210b. 「此但憶想未有実事。」

[42] *Ibid.*, p. 256c: 「慈悲是仏道之根本。所以者何。菩薩見衆生老病死苦、身苦、心苦、今世後世苦等 諸苦所悩。生大慈悲救如是苦。然後発心求阿　多羅三藐三菩提。亦以大慈悲力故。於無量阿僧祇世生 死中心不圧没以大慈 悲力故。久応得涅 槃而不取証。以之故。一切諸仏法中慈悲為大。若無大慈大悲、弁早入涅槃。」

[43] Samantabhadra (Pu-chien, 普賢 or Pien-chi, 遍吉), Manjuśrī or

who have reached the final ten sublime stages (*daśabhūmis*).[44] They are endowed with the merits of the ten special faculties of the Buddhas.[45] Nonetheless, Nāgārjuna categorically asserts in the fortieth fascicle of the text that the Buddha is not challengeable, saying:

> Although these Bodhisattvas are greater than the other Bodhisattvas, when they are compared with the Buddha, their faculties are still far short of the Buddha's. It is like the moon which, though great, is no match before the sun, disappearing in the sun's light.[46]

The Bodhisattvas' virtue of love and compassion is obviously distinguished by their vow of self-abnegation with respect to the final Enlightenment and Nirvāṇa. But what is the merit of this vow of self-abnegation? What is the merit of the Buddha's virtue of love and compassion? After all, though once a Bodhisattva, he has now obviously gone beyond his vow and has accomplished Buddhahood.

In the forty-fourth fascicle of the *Ta-chih-tu-lun*, Nāgārjuna addresses the subject of Bodhisattva and replies to the question: What does the word *bodhisattva* mean?

> According to Indian grammar, a number of words are compounded to make up a phrase. '*Bo*' is a letter, '*dhi*' is another letter. Only when these two are compounded does the word '*bodhi*' come to be. In China,[47] this is equivalent to the meaning of "ultimate insight." '*Sattva*' means either a "sentient being"[48] or

---

Mañjughoṣa (Man-shih-li, 文殊師利), and Avalokiteśvara (Kuan-yin, 観音).

[44] Daśabhūmis (十地): Ten stages or grounds of Bodhisattva career, each of which embodies his realilzation of the respective practice or virtue assigned to it. Historically the idea of ten stations evolved gradually from the initial appearance in the *Mahāvastu* (「大事」 ca. 150 B.C.). The final forms of the ten Bhūmis were completed in the *Buddhāvataṃsaka-sūtra*. In the Ta-chih-tu-lun, Nāgārjuna often times refers to the third ground of Non-Sliding-Back (avaivartya-bhūmi) which was the older form.

[45] Ten faculties or *daśa-balas*: (十力の功徳) (1) *sthāna-asthāna-jñāna-bala,* (2) *karma-vipāka-jñāna-bala,* (3) *dhyānavimokṣasamādhi-samāpatti-jñāna-bala,* (4) *indriya-parāpara-jñāna-bala,* (5) *nānādhimukti-jñāna-bala,* (6) *nānādhātu-jñāna-bala,* (7) *sarvatra-gāmini-pratipaj-jñāna-bala,* (8) *pūrva-nivāsa-anusmṛti-jñāna-bala,* (9) *cyuty-upapatti-jñāna-bala* and (10) *āśraya-kṣaya-jñāna-bala.*

[46] *Ibid.*, 「是諸菩薩於余菩薩為大。比於仏不能遍知、如月光明雖於日則不現。」

[47] It is obvious that the translator Kumārajīva's commenting is implicated here.

[48] 「衆生」

a "great mind."[49] For the sake of the ultimate insight, whoever resolves to seek the ultimate enlightenment is called *bodhisattva*. He who wishes to help fellow humans and for that purpose joins the practice of the highest way, this is called Bodhisattva.[50]

In the fortieth fascicle, Nāgārjuna gives the following summary as to how a Bodhisattva's career advances through a series of ever higher insights:

> Observing with his human eyes how those who are near him undergo varieties of suffering in this world, he is motivated with love and compassion for them. The great Bodhisattva being initially resolves to pursue the path of enlightenment and undertakes the practice of meditation and concentration to acquire the supernormal eye (*divya-cakṣu*).[51] Thus, surveying widely how all other humans undergo varieties of physical and mental suffering by straying into the six spheres of life cycles, the Bodhisattva is all the more motivated with love and compassion for their suffering, and further pursues the way to acquire the wisdom eye so that he may rescue those sufferers. Having acquired the wisdom eye (*prajñā-cakṣu*),[52] the Bodhisattva realizes how varied and diverse the characteristics of human minds are, and thus further pursues the way to acquire the transcendent eye (*dharma-cakṣu*)[53] so that he may help sufferers realize deliverance by acquiring the same insight of their own.[54]

The transcendent eye means the insight of *Śūnyatā* by which the Bodhisattva enters into the first stage of the final ten sublime states of the Bodhisattva career. Here he is expected to be able to see the characteristic of ultimate reality (*tattva-lakṣaṇam*) as it really is (*yathābhūtam*)[55] through this insight. At this initial stage,

---

49 「大心」

50 Taishō. 25, p. 380b-c: 「天竺語法衆字和合成語、衆語和合成句。如菩為一字、提為一字。是二不合則無語。若和合名為菩提。秦言無上知恵。薩た或名衆生、或是大心。為無上知恵故出大心名為菩提薩　。願欲令衆生行無上道。是名菩提薩　。」

51 *divya-cakṣu* (天眼) consisted of five kinds of supernormal power.

52 *prajñā-cakṣu* (慧眼

53 *dharma-cakṣu* (法眼)

54 *Ibid.*, fasc. 40, p. 349a-b: 「菩薩初発心時、以肉眼見世界衆生受諸苦患、心慈愍、学諸禅定、修得五通、以天眼遍見六道中衆生、受種々身心苦、益加憐愍故、求慧眼以救済之。得是慧眼已、見衆生心相種々不同、云何令衆生得是実法。故求法眼引導衆生令入法界中、故名法眼。」

55 *chu-fa-shih-hsiang* (「諸法実相」): Both compounds *tattva-lakṣaṇam* and *yathābhūtam* are often come up with verbal terms to see, view,

the Bodhisattva should be endowed with the two-fold expedient means (*upāyakauśalya*).[56] From the very beginning of his career, he is prescribed to practice the six normative practices of perfection (*ṣaṭ-pāramitā*), namely, charity (*dāna-pāramitā*), morality (*śīla-p.*), patience (*kṣānti-p.*), diligence (*vīrya-p.*), meditation (*samādhi-p.*), and insight (*prajñā-p.*).[57] While engaging himself in these practices, he acquires the capacity to know the characteristics of all things as they really are and this new capacity activates the mind of great compassion (*mahā-karuṇā*)[58] for all people. Unless one knows the ultimate nature of things as they really are, one is mired in attachment to the false appearances of the ordinary world and, as a result, must undergo varieties of physical and mental suffering.

Now, the two-fold expediency of the Bodhisattva means (1) the transcendent knowledge or *prajñā* insight into the *Śūnyatā* of all *things (dharma-cakṣu, fa-yen)*, the culmination of the foregoing practice of the six Pāramitās, and (2) the great compassion (*mahā-karuṇā, ta-pei*), the very source of the Bodhisattva's original resolution. On account of this two-fold expediency, the Bodhisattva shall not fall into attachment to things of a temporary nature, and neither shall he abandon people as a result of that capacity. While not abandoning his compassionate concern for people, he is, however, fully aware of the unreal nature of all things and of the nature of emptiness (*śūnyatā*). The Bodhisattva maintains these expedient means in proper balance in order to enter into the initial stage of Bodhisattvahood.[59]

The foregoing features of the activist career of the Bodhisattva ought to have two balanced competences. To repeat, the Bodhisattva sees emptiness in all things he experiences, and hence he is free from attachment; however, he is still said to retain his interest in and compassion for the happiness and well-being of fellow humans.

Previously, it was noted that the Buddha's virtue of love and compassion is motivated neither by common humanity nor by the

---

understand, etc. meaning: to intuit the characteristic of ultimate reality as it really is without superimposing one's prejudice or preconception, etc. which necessarily distorts truth to create error.

[56] *Upāyakauśalya* (方便): skill-in-means, appropriate and excellent expediency, based on the true insight and leading to the goal of religious truth; expedient method to help fellow beings toward the goal of enlightenment.

[57] *Ṣaṭ-pāramitā* (六度), namely, *charity* (*dāna*, 布施) morality (*śīla*,持戒), perseverance (kṣānti, 忍辱), endeavor (vīrya, 精進), mediation (samādhi, 禅定), and insight (prajñā, 智慧).

[58] *Mahāmaitri* (大悲心)

[59] *Ibid.*, fasc. 27. Cf. p. 246: 「具足般若波羅蜜多故、知諸法空。大悲心故憐愍

ultimate factual basis of human existence. How then can the Buddha's virtue of love and compassion be distinguished from that of the Bodhisattva, whose basic qualification has been explained above as balancing two expediencies? Again, previously, it was noted that the Buddha mind is not confined to ordinary consciousness (*saṃskṛta*), because whatever arises in the human world based on morally and spiritually defiled propensities is unreal, up-side-down, and illusory (the first negation), but also is not confined to the transcendent (*asaṃskṛta*), because the psycho-physical elements, though transcendent of empirical perception and conception, are ultimately non-substantial and empty (the second negation). As we have seen above, the Bodhisattva's two-fold expedient means has both of these dimensions as well. What then is the difference? Nāgārjuna finally specifies that the difference between Buddha mind and Bodhisattva mind lies in the fact that the Bodhisattva, by his own choice, does not assume enlightenment, and hence does not use the Buddha eye:

> By acquiring supernormal powers, the Bodhisattva is supposed to know various expedient ways in which to assist fellow humans. But he has not realized Buddhahood, and hence does not have the Buddha eye. He views the world and people with the wisdom eye and the transcendent eye, but is unable to use the Buddha eye. He has reached the ultimate insight that nothing arises or perishes (*anutpattika-dharma-kṣānti*)[60] and thereby clearly sees the causal context in which people [each respectively] realize the utlimate enlightenment. Thus he applies this knowledge to rescue them in various ways, but by not realizing Buddhahood, does not use the Buddha eye.[61]

§5. BUDDHIST CULT OF KUAN-YIN BODHISATTVA AND HUMAN CULTURES

Setting aside theoretical inquiry for the moment, I am obliged to investigate some historical and cultural aspects of the Buddhist cult that centered upon Kuan-yin Bodhisattva and continued for two millennia in the Asiatic continent. In the fortieth fascicle of his

---

衆生。於是二法以方便力不生染著。雖知諸法空、方便力故亦不捨衆生。雖不捨衆生亦知諸法実空。若於是二事等即得入菩薩位。」

[60] *Anutpattika-dharma-kṣānti* (無生法忍)

[61] *Ibid.*, fasc. 40. p. 351a: 「得菩薩神通知種々度衆生道。未得成仏故無仏眼慧

commentary, Nāgārjuna refers twice to the name of Kuan-shih-yin along with Samantabhadra[62] and Mañjuśrī[63] while discussing the Buddha's sublime virtue of love and compassion. Kuan-shih-yin or "one who envisions the voices of the world" (abbreviated as 'Kuan-yin' in Chinese, or 'Kannon' in Japanese), is a celestial Bodhisattva endowed not only with the ten special faculties ascribed only to the Buddhas, but also with the sublime stature and superior physical marks characteristic of the Buddhas.[64] Moreover, by his own resolution to neither assume the supreme enlightenment nor enter the goal of Nirvāṇa till all others accomplish it, he is supposed to remain forever active in the human world.[65] The Bodhisattva inherited the activist role, in a manner of speaking, to exercise his two-fold expediency for the sake of Buddhist salvation in lieu of Śākyamuni who had passed on to Parinirvāṇa. It was in the *Lotus Sūtra* that the activist role of the Kuan-yin Bodhisattva was established for the first time as an important part of the scriptural scenario. His name also appears in the *Pureland Sūtras*[66] in which his relationship to Amitābha Buddha (A-mi-t'o-fo) is depicted like that of Maitreya

---

[62] Samantabhadra (普賢菩薩): this Bodhisattva seems to have held no histroical bearing, but was regarded a figure of personification of his epithet as commanding all vows and his omnipresence as guadian wherever Buddhist Vihāras were located.

[63] Mañjuśrī (Wên-chu-shih-li, 文殊師利 or Mañjughoṣa, 妙音): This bodhisattva seems to have been an actual person who advocated the Mahāyāna teaching. In ancient Mahāyāna scriptures, he invariably appears as the head monk of all assemblies, and seems to be especially linked with the Prajñāpāramitā scriptures. After 450 years from the time of Śākyamuni's Parinirvāṇa, this Bodhisattva appeared in the Himalaya region and taught the twelve classes of Buddhist scriptures (十二分教) to the five hundred sages. Then he returned to Kausala, his birth place, and entered Parinirvāṇaā. The *Lotus Sūtra* (Fasc. 4), the *Flower Garland śūtra* (Fasc. 45), as well as the *8000 śloka Prajñāpāramitā Sūtras* or *Tao-hsing-pan-jo-ching* (「道行般若経」 Fasc. 4) tell that the Bodhisattva assembled the scripture in Southern India.

[64] For instance, the mark of a wheel consisting of a thousand spokes like the vehicle of legendary Cakravartin (千輻輪相) is generally drawn under the foot on the pedestal.

[65] Taishō., p. 350a:「如遍吉菩薩観世音菩薩文殊師利菩薩等、見是菩薩如諸仏相、知当成仏。*Ibid.*, 350b: 十住菩薩与仏、無有差別。如遍吉文殊師利観世音等、具足十力功徳等、而不作仏為広度衆生故。」

[66] Amitābha Buddha (阿弥陀仏): According to Staël-Hostein's argument, the earliest occurrence of Chinese name kuan-shih-yin (観世音) is equivalent to 'avalokita-īśvara' in the larger *Sukhāvatī-vyūha-sūtra*. Cf. "Avalokita and Apalokita," Harvard Journal of Asiatic Studies, vol 1 (1936), 350-362..] Cf. p. 351

(the future Buddha)[67] to Śākyamuni. Being the guide and savior of all, the Bodhisattva seems to have been fashioned after Amitābha who was once the Bodhisattva Dharmākara[68] in another legendary context aeons ago. In the *Flower Garland Sūtra* too, Kuan-yin's name appears as one of the fifty-five teachers to whom the youthful saint Sudhana-śreṣṭhi-dāraka[69] paid his pilgrimage in Southern India to seek enlightenment. It was, however, the *Lotus Sūtra* that made Kuan-yin by far the champion guardian and Buddhist savior of all human beings.

In Chinese, the name of this Bodhisattva was rendered as (1) Kuang-shih-yin[70]: "one who illumines the voices of the world" by Dharmarakṣa (ca. 288), (2) Kuan-shih-yin[71]: "one who surveys (envisions) the voices of the world" by Kumārajīva (406), and (3) Kuan-tzŭ-tsai[72]: "one who excells in [*prajñā*] illumination"[73] by Hsüan-tzang (between 645-664). In the *Lotus Sūtra* as well as the *Ta-chih-tu-lun*, Kumārajīva applied *'kuan-shih-yin'* equally to Avalokitasvara, and Nāgārjuna refers to this Bodhisattva as the major dispenser of the Buddha's love and compassion in the human world. The original Sanskrit name is still a problem, because two terms of reference appear in the extant Sanskrit texts as Avalokitasvara and Avalokiteśvara.[74]

---

[67] Maitreya (Mi-lê, 弥勒): According to the *Hsien-yu-ching* [「賢愚経」13 fascs, Taishlō. 4, (No. 202)] or Avadāna Collection called *Damamūka-nidāna-sūtra*, No. 57, Fasc. Po-p'o-li-p'in (「波婆離品」) comprises a story of Maitreya who was a disciple of Śākyamuni. Born as a son of a minister of the king of Vārāṇasī and became a student of a Brāhmaṇa scholar, but one day attended Śākyamuni's lecture at the Gṛdhrakūṭa in Rājagṛha, he became a disciple. Cf. *Ta-chi-tu-lun* (the 29th fasc.).

[68] Fa-ts'ang P'u-sa (法蔵菩薩).

[69] Shan-ts'ai-t'ung-tzù (善財童子)

[70] Kuang-shih-yin (光世音菩薩)

[71] Kuan-shih-yin (観世音菩薩)

[72] Kuan-tzŭ-tsai (観自在菩薩)

[73] Hsüan-tzang explains his translation of Kuan-tzù-tsai for Avalokiteśvara as correct, saying: "Avalokiteśvara is called in T'ang language as 'Kuan-tzù-tsai. Avalokita is kuan (観), īśvara is tzù-tsai (自在). In the olden translation, it was Kuang--shih-yin (光世音) or Kuan-shi-yin (観世音) or Kuan-shih-tzù-tsai (観世自在) are wrong.." In his commentary on the *Mahāprajñāpāramitā-hṛdaya-sūtra* by his disciple K'uei-chi (窺基、632-682). [「般若心経幽賛巻上」Taishō. 33 (No. 1710)], 'kuan' means illumining (照), namely, an insight that clarifies non-existence and existence (了空有) and 'tzù-tsai' means the proficiency of doing things at one's will (従任).

[74] The *Lotus Sūtra* has the former name in the Nepalese manuscript, while the latter name appears in the manuscript of the *Pureland Sūtra*. Despite the fact that both scriptures were most likely compiled during the first century B.C., since it is difficult to determine exactly to what period

According to Lokesh Chandra, Avalokitasvara may have been the original or an early name, whereas Avalokiteśvara was a later name influenced by the Hindu deity Śiva, the lord of the world (*lokeśvara*). Use of Avalokiteśvara was already prevalent at the time of Hsüan-tzang when he visited India in the second quarter of the seventh century (between 629-643).[75] Some scholars attempted to trace the etymological origin of *avalokita* to shed some light on the problem. Har Dayal argued in his book *Bodhisattva Doctrine* that the name '*avalokitasvara*' ought to bear a religious meaning like savior or salvation. Yet, he concluded with some scepticism that, "The compound of '*avalokita*,' which means "to see," and '*svara*' meaning "sound" is a queer sort which would convey no clear meaning to an Indian."[76] Following Dayal's lead, Staël-Holstein also pursued the religious connotations of '*avalokitasvara*' in an article exploring the Pāli verbal roots *apalok* and *olok* (*avalok* in Sanskrit)[77] and the causative form *avalokayati*, which apparently occurs twice in *Divyāvadāna*."[78] In my opinion, however, these terms do not convey any specific religious connotation intended to galvanize a successful cult movement of a major magnitude.[79]

From the Buddhist spiritual point of view, it is advisable for research purposes to approach the Buddhist cult of Kuan-yin Bodhisattva by differentiating its Indian and Chinese developments, because the respective cultural orientations of the cult in India and in China seem to have been quite different. This difference was unmistakably manifested in the iconographic history. During the

---

each of the manuscripts belonged, we cannot decide which term was original.

[75] Lokesh Chandra: Cf. Chap. 2 in the *Thousand Armed Avalokiteśvara*. Delhi: Indira Gandhi National Center for Arts, 1988. Esp. p. 20. According to this author, when these two names were being used in confusion, 'Avalokita' alone began to be used in later medieval India like the case of the Bodhicaryāvatāra by Śāntideva (c. 650-750).

[76] *Bodhisattva Doctrine in Buddhist Sanskrit Literature*, originally published by Routledge & Kegan Paul Ltd., London 1932. pp. 47-48.

[77] Staël-Holstein, A. von. "The etymological origin to two Pāli verbal roots apalok and olok," *Harvad Journal of Asiatic Studies* 1(1936) 350-362. Esp. p. 357. [Henceforward as *HJAS*]

[78] Staël-Holstein: *loc. cit,* pp. 360-361; apalok or olok means "to grant freedom, take leave of or get leave to go," and the causative form avalokayati means "asking somebody for permission or freedom to do something" in the textual context.

[79] The Sanskrit manuscript of the *Prajñāpāramitāhṛdaya-sūtra* comprises a similar verb like vyavalokayati which is practically identical in meaning as avalokayati, namely, to look upon or look at, view, behold, notice, observe. Cf. Eddward Conze: "Text, Sources, and Bibliography of the *Prajñāpāramitā-hṛdaya*," *JRAS*, April 1948; p. 34.

period of the Mauryan Buddhist rulers (B.C. 273-183), the Buddhist world was perpetuated through the professional monks' Saṅgha and the cult of Stūpa worship by the Buddhist laity. But after the rise of Hindu political power, and during the following dark age, the Buddhist world was gradually undermined by Hindu mythological and cultic movements for religious revitalization. The time of the Buddhist compilation of Mahāyāna scriptures and promotion of anthropomorphic Buddhist cults coincided with the rising tide of Hindu religious influence in society. According to Lokesh Chandra, Avalokitasvara Bodhisattva was a metamorphosis of Brahmā, Lord of the Earth, who was known also as the Hindu deity Lokeśvara or Lokanātha (the lord or savior of the world). The Hindu deity Śakra or Indra was the incarnation of stamina (*sthāman*) and represented the will-to-power and the central active figure of the ethereal world. From Buddhist legend as well as iconographic representation, we know that Śākyamuni was flanked by Indra and Brahmā before he decided to proclaim his Dharma to the world. Thus, asserts Lokesh Chandra, "with the transcendence of Śākyamuni to Amitābha, Indra and Brahmā were transformed into Mahāsthāmaprāpta and Avalokitasvara."[80]

At some later period, the Hindu deity Śiva was assimilated into Buddhism and gave rise to the name Avalokiteśvara (*avalokita-īśvara*, the lord Avalokita), thereby allowing the emergence of the thousand-armed Bodhisattvas. This Avalokiteśvara sometimes appears as a Buddha and at other times as the Hindu deity Īśvara or Maheśvara (Śīva), without clear reason.[81] So came to being several types of Kuan-yin images that were linked to Hindu iconography. Avalokiteśvara, however, also appeared as an acolyte for Śākyamuni, of course. According to Hsüan-tzang's travel record, when he visited the site of the Bodhi tree and Mahābodhi temple at Buddhagaya, he witnessed on the eastern side of the tower both the statue of Avalokiteśvara and that of Maitreya (the future Buddha). Both were made of white silver and were ten feet high, placed respectively in the right and left niches outside the gate of the upper chamber

---

[80] Chandra, *op. cit.*, p. 11. In the Pureland iconography, Avalokitasvara (觀世音) and Mahāsthāmaprāpta (勢至) are the members of the triad as Amitābha's acolytes. The two figures are depicted as sublime as Amitābha and are in possession of a similar set of superior marks only ascribed to the Buddhas. Avalokiteśvara is always on the right of Amitābha while Mahāsthāmaprāpta, a little smaller figure, on Amitābha's left side.

[81] Chandra. *ibid.*, pp. 15-16; Hsüan-tzang's travel record reveals that he encountered this kind of indiscriminate enshrinement of Kuan-yin in various sites. Cf. *op. cit.*, p. 114, Note.

where Śākyamuni was enshrined.[82] This was the standard Buddhistic image of Avalokiteśvara shown always with a lotus stalk in the left hand and the right hand held up over the chest.[83] By the mid-seventh century when Hsüan-tzang was traveling in India, the images of Avalokiteśvara had already multiplied into many forms, including those endowed with one thousand arms, a thousand eyes, four faces, eleven faces, a horsehead, a fearless lion head, a blue neck, and so on.[84] One might say that on the Indian scene, at this time, the Buddhist cult of Avalokitasvara was already irretrievably entangled with cults of various Hindu deities. As John Blofeld asserts, the transference of these Indian variations to the Chinese and East Asian cultural environments definitely ran into limitations.[85]

In China, the cultic worship of Kuan-yin Bodhisattva is believed to have begun shortly after Dharmarakṣa's translation of the *Lotus Sūtra* in 286, but most certainly after the more lucid translation of the same text by Kumārajīva in 406, quickly spreading during the fifth century.[86] From the time this *Sūtra* became the doctrinal basis for the T'ien-t'ai School of Buddhism, and after Chih-i wrote his powerful exposition on the *Lotus Sūtra* and the vows of Kuan-yin near the end of the sixth century, the cult of Kuan-yin became a

---

[82] Hsi-yu-chi (「西遊記」), Buddhist Records of the Western World. trans. by Samuel Beal, originally published 1884 London; Two volumes bound in one, Motilal Banarssidass, Delhi: 1981. Vol 2, p. 119. The monumental tower of Śākyamuni's enlightenment was originally a Sasanian architectural structure of Persia (ca. 2nd to 4th cent.) but at the time of its modern restoration, it was changed to the present structure as we have today. Unlike the square entrance of the building in Indian architectural form, the upper layer entrance was in the dome shape like Iranian mosques we observe today, and Śākyamuni's statue was enshrined in that inner compartment. Hsüan-tzang then observed the two statues outside niches set on both sides of the entrance. See Ichimura: Buddhagaya Temple in Indian Buddhism (1-10), *World Buddhism* (Sri Lanka) XVIV, 4-12, 1975 and XXV, 1 (1976).

[83] 「正観音」or「聖観音」

[84] For variations of Avalokiteśvara in India, see Gōosta Liebert: Iconographic Dictionary of the Indian Religions, Hinduism-Buddhism-Jainism. Asian Arts & Archaeology Series No. 5. Delhi: Indian Books Centre, 1976; pp. 29-30.

[85] John Blofeld: op. cit., p. 41

[86] The bibliographical records suggest that there were six translations of the same text, but only three translations ascribed to Dharmarakṣa (「正法華経」286), Kumārajīva (「妙法蓮華経」406), and Jñānagputa and Dharmagupta (「添品法蓮華経」601) remain as extant. Nāgārjuna quotes this Sūtra, more often than any other scriptures, in his commentary *Upadeśaśāstra* (「大智度論」) of *Mahāprajñāpāramitāsūtra* [「大品般若経」(translated by Kumārajīva, A.D. 402-412)].

major source of Buddhist spirituality in Medieval China.[87] By the seventh century, I believe, Chinese Buddhist thought had already set in motion the subsequent development of the East Asian Kuan-yin cult in terms of the "Bodhisattva ideal." The reason is that, except for some of the Indian forms of Avalokiteśvara to which they duly paid respect, Chinese Buddhists developed their own images according to their own cultural and aesthetic taste; the best known example of Chinese aesthetic influence being the female Kuan-yin. Though often called a "goddess of mercy," this feminine form has remained the dominant image of Kuan-yin in China and, from the ninth century onwards, spread to the entire continent as well as eastward to Korea and Japan. As Kuan-yin moved east, further new variations arose, including the white-robed Kuan-yin, Kuan-yin holding a willow leaf, Kuan-yin with a fishing basket, and the Kuan-yin of easy child-bearing. This last figure, holding a baby in her arm, was sometimes called "Maria Kannon" in Medieval Japan.

It is somewhat ironic, I think, that the Buddhist cult of Avalokiteśvara which originated in India eventually lost its Buddhist spirit under Hindu cultural influence and was quickly reclaimed as a Hindu deity by their cults. In contrast, despite the radical change in its iconographic representation and its increasingly diverse cultural environment, the cult of Kuan-yin Bodhisattva has survived well in East Asia retaining its Buddhist spiritual essence. There are a few interpretations of how and why the transformation from the male to the female Kuan-yin occurred in China. According to Palmer and Ramsay, it was a result of the cultural melting pot in northwest China during the centuries of the T'ang dynasty (618-907), where a host of different religions rubbed shoulders. The landscape included Buddhism and Taoism, alongside Shammanism and Bon, the indigenous religion of Tibet, and Christianity and Manichaeism, alongside Islam and Zoroastrianism.[88] This hypothesis is generally

[87] Chih-i (538-597) systematized the T'ien-t'ai Classification of Buddhist Dcotrines known as "Fivefold Periods and Eight Teachings" (「天台五時八教教判」) on the basis of the *Lotus Sūtra* and *Nirvāṇa Sūtra* (*Ni-p'an-ching*, 「涅槃経」). His authorship covers many writings, but the Profound Meaning of *Lotsu Sūtra* (*Miao-fa-lien-hua-ching-hsüan-i* 「妙法蓮華経玄義」) in 593 [Taishō. 33 (No. 1716)] and *The Profound Meaning of Kuan-yin* [*Kuan-shih-yin-hsüan-i* 「観音玄義」), its commentary (*Kuan-yin-i--shu*, 「観音義疏」), and the *Short Commentary on the Chap. of Samanta-mukha* (*P'u-mên-p'in-su*, 「普門品疏」 Taishō. 34, No. 1728) are regarded to have contributed to the Kuan-yin cult movement.

[88] Martin Palmer and Jay Ramsay with Man-ho Kwok: Kuan Yin: Myths of the Chinese Goddess of Compassion. London: Thorsons, an

accepted. John Blofeld also thinks that the transformation must have occurred in China from around the eighth century through the late eleventh century, since the male form of Avalokiteśvara spread independently to Tibet and Mongolia and later to Champa and Cambodia during the ninth and tenth centuries, and has remained male to this day.[89]

Palmer and Ramsay call particular attention to the figure of Madonna, the one who holds a child in her arm. They think that this representation was itself originally taken from Egyptian statues of the goddess Isis and her divine child Horus. They argue that it is possible to interpret the transformation of Kuan-yin from male to female in a manner consistent with the way in which Virgin Mary became the focus of cultic worship in Christianity. Since Taoist concepts of female deities existed in China before the time of Kuan-yin, the case in question may show that the divine and feminine, once established in a culture, necessarily re-emerge and take on new forms in response to elements of cultural suppression.[90] Blofeld, however, seems to disagree by asserting that the main source of influence came from the female Bodhisattva Tālā of Tibet. Blofeld may have considered the religious and cultural affinity too remote in the hypothesis of an Isis-to-Madonna-to-female-Kuan-yin evolution.[91] There is yet a third view on this matter, as proposed by Elena Schmidt in her article on the Art of Asia, that the main source of influence may have been the combined forms of the Iranian water goddess Anahita and the Greek fertility goddess Artemis.[92] However the course of evolution, the sudden appearance of a female Kuan-yin during the T'ang dynasty in China poses as much difficulty as the initial appearance of Avalokitasvara within the ancient Indian Buddhist domain as a personification of Buddhist love and compassion.

Palmer and Ramsay enthusiastically invite more studies on this neglected subject noting that study of the feminine Kuan-yin in Chinese religion will open not only an exploration of other feminine divinity within China but also an exploration of aspects of feminine

---

Imprint of Harper-Collins Publishers, 1995; p. 19.

89 John Blofeld: *op cit.*, p. 49.

90 Palmer and Ramsay: *op cit.*, p. 21. The authors suggest that among other reasons, popular Buddhism needed a female image to compete with the Taoists and their successful goddesses, such as the Queen Mother of the West.

91 *Ibid.*, p. 40.

92 Elena Schmidt: "The Little Known Binglingsi, Buddhist Caves," *The Art of Asia*, Vol 27, No. 4, July-August 1997; pp. 132-137.

divinity which transend diverse religions and cultures.[93] The longing for a female deity is strong within most cultures as evidenced by goddess Isis of Egypt, the cult of Virgin Mary in Christianity, that of Sophia Wisdom in the Judaism of the Diaspora, that of the various Tārās in Tibetan Buddhism, and the role of the goddesses in Hinduism.[94] In the age of feminist movements today, the subject may very well become a new trend in religious studies for the coming new century.

Having thus surveyed the Kuan-yin cults of the first millennium, what I intend to demonstrate is that the Indian and Chinese Buddhist cults were culturally and spirtually different. Lokesh Chandra provides a very persuasive analysis of the origin of the cult of Avalokiteśvara and its iconographic history. But he seems to have missed the fact that the Indian Buddhist cult of Avalokiteśvara and the East Asian cult of Kuan-yin are not monolithic in spirituality. He is brilliant in proving Avalokitasvara as a metamorphosis of Brahmā, and in setting forth that the phenomenon of his multifarious manifestation in Indian iconography is due to the process of assimilation and interiorization by the potency of Brahmā. In this connection, Lokesh Chandra quotes Alicia Matsunaga's thesis that the Buddhist assimilation that worked in Japan to absorb native gods and various other rites into Buddhism began in India, and that the Buddhist theory of assimilation had its origin in the framework of that early philosophy.[95]

Lokesh Chandra invoked in part the potency pertaining to the substratum of the metamorphosis, namely, Brahmā, and in part the philosophy of assimilation such that the transcendent noumenon descends into the temporary domain as phenomenal manifestation.[96] Here, I must pose the following question: Is Brahmā's potency, which was the essential core of Avalokiteśvara, identical in spiritual basis to that which Buddhist thinkers ascribed to Kuan-yin in China? In reference to the sections of *mantra*, *dhāraṇī*, or hymns, in both the *Lotus Sūtra* and the *Pureland Sūtra*, Lokesh Chandra regards Avalokitasvara as the "master of logos" (*mantra-draṣṭā*) (in parallel to Brahmā in the Brahmanical system), the Seer (*avalokitṛ*)

---

93 Palmer and Ramsay: *op. cit.*; Cf. the introductory statement.

94 *Ibid.*, p. 17.

95 Chandra: *op. cit.*, p. 42. Cf. Alicia Matsunaga: *Buddhist Philosophy of Assimilation of the Honji-Suijaku Theory (The Historical Development)*: Tokyo: Sophia University, C.E. Tuttle, 1969.

96 *Honji-suijaku* (本地垂跡): The transcendent noumenon descends nanifesting itself in the phenomenal domain.

of the Sound (*svara*), who assimilated Hindu deities (*lokeśvara*) by pronouncement of each sacred hymn (*hṛdaya* or *mantra*) unique to each deity.

As I understand Chap. 25 of the *Lotus Sūtra*, Avalokitasvara's sole concern is that he is determined to rescue all humans who are in trouble and suffering. Avalokitasvara's virtue of love and compassion is not a self-serving manifestation or self-serving emanation of some transcendent agent or principle. As a Bodhisattva, his virtue must be balanced with the insight of *Śūnyatā*, without which he loses his status and *raison-d'étre* as a Buddhist personification of love and compassion. The Kuan-yin cult in China was rooted in the insight of *Śūnyatā* and the belief in the original enlightenment proclaimed in the *Lotus Sūtra*, the dual source of the vow of the Bodhisattva career.

§6. KUAN-YIN BODHISATTVA DEPICTED IN THE *LOTUS SŪTRA*

In the history of Mahāyāna Buddhism, no other scripture has ever been so studied as the *Lotus Sūtra*. The popularity of the text lay in its twofold theoretical framework. First, it illuminated the appointed time at which the original and timeless Dharma revealed by ancient Buddha in the immemorial past would converge with the historical or contemporary Dharma currently realized by Śākyamuni through his enlightenment[97] (Chap. 11: "Beholding the Jewel-inlaid Stūpa"). This moment was symbolized by the dramatic event in which the two Buddhas, trans-historical and historical, would be seated together within the gigantic jewel-inlaid Stūpa that would spring forth from the earth to fill the sky. Second, the *Lotus Sūtra* foretold that at that moment, the immeasurable numbers of Bodhisattvas who had never before been seen would suddenly arise everywhere through the cracked earth from below, to middle of the sky, surounding the Stūpa (Chap. 15: "Bodhisattvas from Under-ground"). The scenario points (1) to the beginning of change from the cult of relic worship toward the cult of the anthropomorphic image, (2) to the beginning of revelation of the trans-historical Dharma of original enlightenment by way of the currently revealed Dharma of the enlightened Śākyamuni, and finally (3) to the beginning of the active propagation of the Dharma of the new age by the host of Bodhisattvas charged with the vow of activism for

---

[97] The transcendent domain (本門) and the phenomenal domain (跡門).

love and compassion. It would be in this dramatic and imaginary arena that Śākyamuni would introduce Kuan-yin Bodhisattva before the multitude of participants (Chap. 25: "Avalokitasvara Bodhisattva").

The 25th Chap. of the *Lotus Sūtra* begins with the Buddha's reply to Akṣayamati Bodhisattva regarding the meaning of the name Avalokitasvara. The reply points primarily to love and compassion as Kuan-yin's epithet, since he is ever alert to the imploring of all sufferers and, should they wholeheartedly chant his name, beseeching him for deliverance, he will come to help them be free from their suffering. He is endowed with the transcendent faculty to immediately perceive all voices and, in no time, come to the rescue of all callers. I shall herewith simplify and enumerate all circumstances of suffering noted in the Sūtra.

First, the Bodhisattva can and will render assistance to anyone who suffers in the circumstances of human jeopardy as follows:

> (1) When one is surrounded by a great fire, (2) when one is swept away by flood waters, (3) when one's ship has been blown away by a cyclone and stranded on the island of the Rākṣasa (cannibals), (4) when one faces assault by a robber bearing a sword or other weapon, (5) when one is disturbed by ill-minded Yakṣas (demi-gods of some power) and demons like the Rākṣasa, (6) when one is bound by fetters and chains, or (7) when one's caravan is about to be assaulted by highway-men.

Further, the verse section introduces additional circumstances as shown in the subnote,[98] but in all cases, it is utmost emphasized that one should cry out for help in genuine faith to the Bodhisattva's love and compassion, so that one will be rid of the foregoing

[98] Continued from the above: (8) When one is thrown into a fiery pit, (9) when one floats on the waves by a shipwreck, (10) when one is pushed over a precipice, (11) when one is chased and falling from a hilltop, (12) when one is surrounded by the swords of enemies, (13) when one is about to be executed due to a king's ill will, (14) when one is imprisoned with fetters and chains, (15) when one is poisoned or cursed unto injury or death, (16) when one encounters evil Rākṣasas, poisonous Nāgas, ghostly demons, etc., (17) when one is attacked by a horde of wild animals, (18) when one has stepped into a pile of venomous insects, snakes, or scorpions, (19) when one encounters a fearful storm with thunder, lightening, hail and rain, (20) when one is totally exhausted by pain and fatigue, (21) when one is suffering the evil cycles of life, such as hell, ghost, and animal, undergoing birth, old age, sickness, and death, (22) when one faces legal suit at the government office and is threatened by the military court, and (23) when one meets all kinds of suffering and dangers with threat of death.

circumstances of human jeopardy.[99]

Second, the Bodhisattva's transcendent power will assist anyone in dealing with the three fundamental forces of human predicament (*kleśa*):

> (1) When one is afflicted by ineradicable sensual desire, (2) when one falls into a fit of outrage, or (3) when one is entrapped in serious delusion. If one chants or recollects the name of the Bodhisattva and reminds oneself always of his power of love and compassion, one will be liberated from the predicament of these passions.

Third, the Bodhisattva's transcendent power of love and compassion will grant whatever one sincerely wishes for one's self, as for instance:

> (1) When a woman wishes to bear a boy or (2) when she wishes to bear a girl.

Brofeld informs us that the practice of this type of Kuan-yin cult is still found in some regions in contemporary China.[100]

Fourth, the Bodhisattva's transcendent power of love and compassion guarantees that:

> (1) One who venerates him and retains his name in one's mind shall be rewarded with merit as great as that which another person creates by venerating myriads of myriads of Buddhas with alms-offerings, and (2) the merit that one creates by

---

[99] Takakusu gives some of the iconographic records of the Kuan-yin cult derived from the Samantamukha chapter of the Lotus Sūtra. "In the so-called Buddhist litany represented in some sculptured reliefs of Ajanta (no. 4), Ellora (No. 3): Dangers from an elephant, a lion, an enemy with a sword, and a young man against a woman, on one row, and those from a fire, a snake, a flood, and a female against a male, while a standing figure of Kuan-yin is represented at the center. Aurangābād (No. 7): the eight scenes are specified by a fire, a sword, a thief, and a shipwreck on the right, and a lion, a snake, an elephant, and a man with a woman on the left, Kuan-yin is flying towards the center to their rescue. Kānheri (No. 4), one of the 108: the scenes are ten instead of eight, a girl with a man; a man in a striking attitude before a snake-king; a man brandishing a sword against a female with a child, a man with a stick before another who is prostrating himself, an elephant, a lion, a serpent, a man visible, probably drowned; a man with his hands raised probably in a pushing attitude." ["Kuan-yin," Encyclopedia of Religion and Ethics, p. 764]. Although Takakusu estimated the time of these records to have been in the 7th or 8th centuries. I think that some of them go back much earlier periods, possibly into the third century, so-called Śaka-Palhava Era created by the new arrivals of Scythians and Parthians in western India and coastal regions.

[100] Blofeld: op. cit., p. 19

> venerating him and being mindful of him shall be as inexhaustible as that which another person has accumulated by venerating myriads of myriads of Buddhas with all alms-offerings and being mindful of them.

Fifth, perhaps the most important aspect of this chapter is the ways of manifestation in which Kuan-yin Bodhisattva is said to fulfil his virtue of love and compassion. Altogether, thirty-three forms of manifestation or appearance are mentioned in Kumārajīva's text, through which he is said to teach the Buddha-Dharma to all sentient beings:

> (1) The appearance of a Buddha for those who are familiar with the Buddhas, (2) likewise the appearance of a Pratyekabuddha for those who are familiar with the Pratyekabuddhas, (3) the appearance of a Śrāvaka for those who are familiar with the Śrāvakas, (4) the appearance of Brahmā for his believers, (5) the appearance of Śakra (Indra) for his believers, (6) the appearance of Īśvara for his believers, (7) the appearance of Maheśvara (Śiva) for his believers, (8) the appearance of a commander-in-chief (*cakravartin* or *senāpati*) for his subordinates, (9) the appearance of Vaiśravaṇa (Kubera) for his followers, (10) the appearance of a Brāhmaṇa for his coalleagues and associates, and (11) the appearance of a Vajrapāṇi for his associates.

These eleven forms of manifestation are equally found in the Sanskrit text discovered in Nepal[101] as well as in Kumārajīva's translation, but the latter comprises further additional forms, making up altogether thirty-three.[102]

---

[101] The Nepalese Sanskrit text generally agrees with the prose section, but additionally comprises a verse section; however, neither the translation by Dharmarakṣa (CE 286) nor that by Kumārajīva (406) included the section. The verse section was later added according to the third translation ascribed to Jñānagupta and Dharmagupta and accomplished in 601.

[102] Here, No. 17 and No. 33 are included in the above enumeration, but in order to show the order given in the Chinese text, these are repeated as part of additional series: (10) the appearance of a ruler for his associates or governors (rājā), (11) the appearance of a merchant or (12) a female merchant for his or her colleagues and associates, (13) the appearance of a retired man or (14) a retired woman for his or her friends, (15) the appearance of a minister or (16) a minister's wife for his or her government officials and colleagues, (17) the appearance of a Brāhmaṇa or (18) a Brāhmaṇa's wife for his or her colleagues, (19) the appearance of a mendicant or (20) a female mendicant for his or her associates, (21) the appearance of an Upāsaka (a layman) or (22) an Upāsikā (a laywoman) for his or her associates, (23) the appearance of a boy, (24) the appearance of a girl, (25) the appearance of a Deva (god) for his associates, (26) the

The popularity of Kuan-yin cult can be inferred from a record by Guṇabhadra of the 5th century, who was engaged in the work of translation during the years of 367-431. He crossed Southern Ocean by boarding a ship from Sinahala and arrived in Kuan-chou by 435. During the voyage, he is said to have chanted the name of Kuan-yin Bodhisattva.[103] The popularity of the cult goes further back to the 4th century, or even the 3rd century in India, because Kānheri and Aurangābād cave temples began as early as the second century Śaka-Pahlava period in western regions and bear various bas-reliefs describing the scenes of the Kuan-yin chapter of the *Lotus Sūtra*.[104]

Among those other sources, like the *Pureland Sūtras,*[105]etc., in which Kuan-yin Bodhisattva's virtue of love and compassion is described, I consider the *Lotus of Mercy (Karuṇāpuṇḍarīka-sūtra)*[106]

---

appearance of a Nāga (tribe) for his associates, (27) the appearance of a Yakṣa (demon), (28) the appearance of a Gandharva (heavenly musician), (29) the appearance of an Asura, (30) the appearance of a Garuḍa, (31) the appearance of a Kinnara, (32) the appearance of a Mahoraga (great serpent), (33) the appearance of a Vajrapāṇi for his associates. The thirty-three forms of Kuan-yin were created and often represented in art. In Japan there are thirty-three sacred places of pilgrimage where various images of Kuan-non (観音) are enshrined and worshipped.

[103] Cf. a brief biography attached to the Kuo-ch'ü-hsieny-tsai-yin-kuo-ching (「過去現在因果経」), Taishō. (「大正新修大蔵経」) Vol. 3, (No. 189), p. 620. Kuan-yin Bodhisattva is called the grantor of fearlessness and safety (abhayaṃdada) to any and all sentient beings.

[104] Cf. Note 98. During the Śaka-Palhava period, ca. from the 2nd CE through 3rd, the bearers of history were those new immigrated peoples of Scythians (Śaka) and Parthians (Palhava) who were engaged in sea-faring and caravan land traders in Indian Oceans. The Kānheri complex, located on the Salsette Island 16 miles north of Bombay and 6.25 miles northwest of Thānā consists of structures which belonged to the local Saṅgha and the universal Saṅgha of the four quarters (caturdiśasaṅgha), belonging to the Orthodox schools, supported by the local people of Nāsika, Kalyāṇa, and the people of Kārṇāṭa and Dhānyakaṭaka of South-eastern India, and included a good number of epigraphic records of that period (165-194). The cult of Avalokitasvara in the religion seems to have been supported mainly by sea-faring communities.

[105] Practice of Contemplation on the Buddha of Immeasurable Longevity (*Amitāyurbuddhadhīna-dūtra*) After the teaching how to envision the Buddha of immeasurable longevity, Śākyamuni begins to teach on the characteristic of Kuan-shih-yin Bodhisattva in the latter chapter. The description of this Bodhisattva is no different from any of the sublime Buddhas, and then Śākyamuni goes on to Mahāsthāpanaprāpta, whose feature is also no different from the sublime Buddhas. These two together with Amitābha are called the Pureland Triad Buddhas (浄土三尊). 「観無量寿仏経」 Taishō.12 (365).

[106] Pei-hua-ching (「悲華経」 or 「大乗悲分陀利経」 or 「悲蓮華経」) 10 fasc., translated by Dharmarakṣa 414-426. Taishō. 3, (No. 157), Section 3: the

as a unique scripture, because it comprises the quintessential formula of his vow. The scripture inculcates that in his former life, Kuan-yin who was an eldest son and heir prince of a certain universal ruler Cakravartin who became Amitābha Buddha subsequently, resolved his mind to take up a Bodhisattva career. The vow laid down by Kuan-yin upon his initial moment of resolution is as follows:

> May I resolve my vow for the Bodhisattva career. Should anyone be subjected to suffering, fear and so forth, thereby being forced to abandon the right Dharma, thus to fall into darkness and lose all reliance and protection, yet should he uphold my name in his mind and chant my name, and then shall it be heard by my transcendent faculty of audition and vision, and should he yet remain unliberated from suffering, fear and so forth, shall I not take the supreme enlightenment unto myself.[107]

There seems to be an insurmountable chasm in communication between human wishes and Kuan-yin Bodhisattva as the dispenser of love and compassion. For, whereas the former is totally adrift amidst the five cycles of life, the latter seems to be free of these cycles? Irrespective of whether people's desire is spiritual or secular, their calling for help may likely be under the influence of their defiled mental propensities (*kleśas*) anchored in the three forces of craving, anger and delusion. Would Kuan-yin Bodhisattva allow himself to step down to the level of humans since the latter cannot reach his level? If his virtue of love and compassion could actively respond to the needs of people despite their minds being under the influence of moral and spiritual defilement, should not his virtue and motivation be activated in a state of mind similar to that of his recipient human beings? Insofar as communication is required, would his actions not have taken place under the influence of defilement? As a matter of fact, Nāgārjuna poses a similar question for the sake of his readers: "Though I do not intend to be disrespectful to the Buddha, since he was motivated by love and compassion for his fellow humans and realized enlightenment to discover the way to overcome their suffering, his love and compassion must be in full communication with their minds which are under

---

Records of the Original Certification of Bodhisattvas for Buddhahood.

[107] *Ibid*. (fasc. 3): Taishō. 3, p. 185c: 「願我行菩薩道時、若有衆生受諸苦悩恐怖等事。退失正法堕大暗処、憂愁孤窮無有救護無依無舎、若其為我天耳所聞天眼所見、是衆生等若不得免斯苦悩者、我不成阿　多羅三藐三菩提。」

the influence of defilement."[108]

§7. KUAN-YIN BODHISATTVA AND THE *PRAJÑĀ HEART SŪTRA*

Although the *Heart Sūtra* is the shortest scripture on the doctrine of *Śūnyatā*, it is the only Sūtra in which Kuan-yin Bodhisattva actively participates as the chief exponent of the insight of *Śūnyatā*. According to the Taishō Tripiṭaka, the *Heart Sūtra* was translated eight times during a period of four and a half centuries ending in 861, beginning with Kumārajīva's version and including Hsüan-tzang's version in 649.[109] On average, two new versions of the *Heart Sūtra* became available to the public every one hundred years, each with some incremental improvements. Because of its brevity and preciseness, the text was popular and most widely circulated in China. However, the state of affairs in China was quite different from the situation Buddhism was facing in India during the same period.

When Hsüan-tzang traveled to India, esoteric Buddhism was at its zenith, but signs of the impending decline of Buddhism were already quite visible. During the few centuries before and after Hsüan-tzang's visit, Hindu iconography and cult movements gradually reclaimed their deities and institutions. In China, on the other hand, esoteric Buddhism was just being introduced during the seventh century. Its influence was constrained in part by the exoteric Buddhism that had preceded it and established the powerful traditions of the T'ien-t'ai, Hua-yen, San-lun, and Wei-shih (*vijñāna-mātra*) systems of thought. Esoteric Buddhism was further constrained by the Chinese cultural environment which was radically different and alien from that of India.

The *Heart Sūtra* was the pan-sectarian text accepted by all Buddhist schools in China as the essential core doctrine of Mahāyāna Buddhism, not only by the above scholastic traditions but also by the practical traditions of Ch'an and Pureland. As it is concise and short, the text was fit for memorization and chanting by an individual or community of people. Lay people as well as priests and nuns frequently combined chanting of the *Heart Sūtra* with

---

108 *Ibid*., p. 257, Fasc. 27, 「我不敢不敬。仏以慈悲心為衆生故生、応有漏」

109 Cf. *Bukkyō Kaisetsu Daijiten* (*Dictionary of Buddhist Books with Expositions*) vol. 9, Tokyo: Daito Shuppan, p. 82 and vol. 10, p. 274.

chanting of the *Kuan-yin Sūtra,*[110] a section of the *Lotus Sūtra* extracted and used as an independent text. The widespread use of these Sūtras was one of the distinctive features of Chinese Buddhist culture in the later half of the first millennium.

In his article of 1948, Edward Conze differentiates seven sections in the *Heart Sūtra* and proves their parallels in the *Large Prajñāpāramitā-sūtras.*[111] He demonstrates that all the words, phrases, and lines of the short text were extracted from the larger text. Accordingly, this *Heart Sūtra* is meant to be, as Conze says, "a restatement of the four holy Truths for beginners on the method of bearing this teaching in mind as well as on the spiritual advantages of following it."[112] Conze brilliantly dismisses Tantric influence on this text, despite the fact that the closing section comprises a few Tantric terms, as for instance in the following sentence: "The *Prajñāpāramitā* is the *mahā-mantra*, the *mahā-vidyā-mantra.*"[113] In support of his view, Conze refers to a similar usage in the *Niddessa*[114] and Pāli commentaries, wherein *paññā* (*prajñā* or 'insight' in Sanskrit) is called *mantra*. Further, he points to one of the earliest Saṃyutta Nikāya texts in Pāli, "The First Turning of the Wheel of the Law" (*Dhamma-cakka-ppavattana-vaggo*), in which the knowledge of four holy Truths is equated to *vijjā* (*vidyā* or knowledge in Sanskrit).[115] In both of these texts, the term *mantā* (*mantra* in Sanskrit) or *vijjā* (*vidyā* in Sanskrit) is not intended to mean, "a secret, mysterious lore of magical potency which can be compressed into a magical formula, a spell." Rather, the term is intended to mean, "the knowledge of the four holy Truths which is the fundamental insight (*vijjā*) of the Buddha." In parallel to this first turning of the wheel

---

110 「妙法蓮華経観音普門品」、「観音経」

111 *Ta-p'in-pan-jo-ching* (「大品般若経」or「摩訶般若波羅蜜経」), *Pañca-viṃśati-sāhasrikā-prajñāpāramitā-sūtra* (「二万五千頌般若」) translated by Kumārajīva, 402-412. Taishō. 8, (No, 223).

112 Edward Conze: "Text, Sources, and Bibliography of the Prajñā-pāramitā-hṛdaya," *JRAS,* 1948, p. 47.

113 *Ibid.*, p. 37: *mahā-mantro mahāvidyā-mantro anuttara-mantro samasama-mantraḥ sarva-duḥkha-;raśamanaḥ satyam amithyātvāt prajñāpāramitāyām ukto mantraḥ. tadyathā oṃ gate gate pāraget pārasaṃgate bodhi svāhā.*

114 Of the two extant commentaries of the *Sutta-Nipāta*, the Niddesa is the earlier one, ascribed to Sāriputta, a direct disciple of śākyamuni, and the *Paramatthajotikā* is the later one ascribed to Buddhaghoṣa of the 5th century. Unlike the latter, the *Nidessa* is confined to some parts of the *Sutta Nipāta.*

115 *Ibid.*, p. 46. *Dhamma-cakka-ppavattana-vaggo*: The Initial Turning of the Wheel of Dharma (「初転法輪経」).

(*dharma-cakra-pravartana-sūtra*), the main subject of which is the four holy Truths,[116] the Mahāyāna theorists regarded the *Heart Sūtra* as "the second turning of the wheel of the law." This Mahāyāna Buddhist thought enormously appealed to the minds of Chinese and East Asian Buddhists.

The *Heart Sūtra*'s scenario holds that at one of the Dharma sessions held on Vulture Peak in Rājagṛha, Śākyamuni suggested that Śāriputra, who held the first seat, request Kuan-yin Bodhisattva to give a lecture on the insight of *Śūnyatā*. In reply to Śāriputra, the Bodhisattva, who was engaged in deep contemplation surveying the distress calls of sentient beings, expounded the meaning of the four holy Truths from the point of view of *Śūnyatā*, the second negation of reality according to Mahāyāna insight.

My purpose in discussing the *Heart Sūtra* here is two-fold. First, I hold that the Kuan-yin Bodhisattva who became the center of the cult in China was not a metamorphosis of Brahmanical magical potency. While Lokesh Chandra argued that only Avalokiteśvara as a metamorphosis of Brahmā could have enabled successful assimilation of Hindu deities, I disagree with his extension of this metamorphosis to the East Asian cultural context. Second, from the foregoing analysis of the *Heart Sūtra*, I hold that Avalokiteśvara or Kuan-yin Bodhisattva was meant to embody the insight or knowledge of the four holy Truths in terms of No-self as *Vidyā*, and the second insight or knowledge of the four holy Truths in terms of *Śūnyatā* as *Mantra*. Because of different historical and social conditions, the Kuan-yin Bodhisattva in China and East Asia should be understood in terms of the dual (not double) negations and not in terms of the Brahmanical or Hindu esoteric assertion or potency.

How then should we view the two faces of Kuan-yin Bodhisattva, one as dispenser of love and compassion, as depicted in the 25th Chap. of the *Lotus Sūtra*, and the other as expounder upon the insight of *Śūnyatā,* as depicted in the *Heart Sūtra*? I think that the *Heart Sūtra* provides a point of reconciliation, a balance that is extensively attested to in Nāgārjuna's *Ta-chi-tu-lun*. The point of differentiation that requires some reconciliation lies in two human requirements. *First*: Life in general carries varieties of suffering, for which humans have continually sought solutions within the material environment of external nature and within the immaterial inner sphere of human nature. In this human context, Kuan-yin Bodhisattva's vow and skill-in-means is directed toward the fulfilment

[116] *Ibid.*, p. 48.

of the mundane needs of individuals and human-kind in the eradication of suffering and the ensurement of their well-being. *Second*: Kuan-yin Bodhisattva's insight of the four holy Truths is two-fold: (1) the eradication of false conviction in one's self and about things believed to belong to that self (*first negation*), and (2) the eradication of false conviction about the reality of elements of the five aggregates (*second negation*).

In his article on the *Heart Sūtra*, Conze calls attention to the section which immediately follows the four holy Truths, and he traces in. the *larger Prajñā Sūtra*, among others, two important points of discussion on the Bodhisattva insight of *Śūnyatā*: First, (1) that there is "no attainment" in actual fact, because "attainment" conceptually implies duality in itself, like the duality between "things to be attained" and "an agent of attaining"; and second, (2) that there is "no desire for any attainment" on the part of the Bodhisattva, because of his insight of non-duality and hence non-attainment.[117] Here, I must call attention to the fact that a dual negation of "neither nor" underlies the above two points; that is, the use of "neither attainment" and "nor desire of attainment" in the repudiation of both the subjective sphere and the objective sphere. This dual negation is extended to encompass loving and loved, knowing and known, acting and acted upon, and so on. I understand from extensive comments made by Nāgārjuna in his *Ta-chih-tu-lun* that it is on these grounds that we speak of the Bodhisattva's abnegation of his own enlightenment and Nirvāṇa for the sake of others.

The Chinese Mahāyāna Buddhists composed the four-fold Bodhisattva vow in verse which has been adopted without exception by all schools in East Asia. The early original form of the four-fold vow can be traced back to the *Eight Thousand Verse Wisdom Sūtra* (Fasc. 8),[118] *Lotus Sūtra* (Chap. 3), and so on, but it is clearer still in the *Bodhisattva Ornament Sūtra* (vol. 1 of two vols.).[119] In this

---

[117] *Ibid*., p. 45.「無智亦無得、以無所得故」in Hsüan-tsang's translation.

[118] *Aṣṭasāhasrikā-prajñāpāramitā-sūtra* (*Tao-hsing-pan-jo-ching*,「道行般若経」10 fasc.) or *Eight Thousand Verse Prajñāpāramitā-sūtra* (「八千頌般若経」), translated by Chih-lou-chia-ch'en in A.D. 179, [Taishō. 8, (No. 224)]. Cf. Fasc 8.

[119] *P'u-sa-ying-lo-pên-yeh-ching* (「菩薩瓔珞本業経」or *the Sūtra on the Original Action of the Garland of the Bodhisattva* (2 fasc.) translated by Chu-fo-nien (Buddhasmṛti) in 376-378. Taishō. 24 (No. 1485),1010 ff. ['Garland' (mālā) mentioned in the title is the jewel-ornament consisting of crown, necklet, and bracelets of the Boddhisattvas This Sūtra was composed to manifest the Original Action (Pên-yeh) of the Bodhisattvas.

Sūtra, the Bodhisattva's vow is formulated with reference to the goals of the four holy Truths as follows:[120]

> May I help all those who have not overcome suffering overcome it;
> May I help all those who have not understood causal aggregation understand it;
> MayI help all those who have not settled firmly in the path settle upon it;
> May I help all those who have not realized Nirvāṇa realize it.

This original form was eventually refined into the presently practiced formula of the four-fold vow in verse as follows:[121]

> However innumerable the sentient beings might be, I vow to rescue them from suffering;
> However inexhaustible the inner defilements might be, I vow to terminate them;
> However unlimited the subjects of practice might be, I vow to master them;
> However infinite the height of the Buddha way might be, I vow to realize it.

In the T'ien-t'ai tradition, Chih-i has an excellent elucidation of this vow.[122] In the Ch'an tradition, the sixth patriarch's *Platform Sūtra*[123] comprises it, and the Esoteric tradition has extended it to

---

[120] Cf. *The Mochizuki Bukkyō Daijiten*, vol. 2, p. 1755b. "*Ssŭ-hung-shih-yüan*" or "*Shigu-seigan*" (四弘誓願).

[121] 「衆生無辺誓願度、煩悩無尽請願断、法門無量請願学、仏道無上請願成」 This is in Ch'an tradition.

[122] "The five Skandhas, from which a nihilistic view arises, is the suffering (*duḥkha*), the ten kinds of defiled propensities (*anuśaya*) operate in the causal aggregation (*samudaya*), the quiet contemplation of mindfulness (*smṛty-upasthāna*) belongs to the path (*mārga*), and the anihilation of four upside-down views (*catur-viparyāsa*) leads to the cessation (*nirodha*). The vow ought to be raised in regard to these four. For instance, first, a nihilistic view ought to be repudiated at each and every moment when the five-defiled-skandha continues to be configurated for hundred thousand of myriad times within a day and night. Each skandha configuration is a single moment of an individual person. So should there be incalculable numbers of persons occurring and perishing during a day and night. How much more should there be such occurrences if it is for an entire life time, and how much more so if it is for the incalculable cycles of life!" Cf. Chih-i: *Mo-ho-chih-kuan* (「摩訶止観」), Fasc. 10, No. 2 of two vols: [Cited from the *Mochizuki Bukkyō Daijiten*, vol. 2, p. 1755c].

[123] 「六祖法宝檀経」

five lines with a few minor differences in phrasing. The Pureland has it verbatim, but with two lines appended to fit their tradition.

Despite the common use of the Bodhisattva vow, I have long wondered whether it should be regarded as a vow to be taken by a single individual, or rather as a vow to be taken collectively by all mankind. It would seem that the weight and scope outlined in the verse is beyond the scope of an individual. In our human world, generations of humans are expected to come into this life and leave, with ever greater numbers of humans to come tomorrow, next year, and so on, *ad infinitum*. It is therefore more closely within the bounds of comprehension if we consider Kuan-yin Bodhisattva's vow not to attain Nirvāṇa himself but to continue his task for the sake of others within the collective human context.

§8. KUAN-YIN'S LOVE AND COMPASSION BASED ON THE TRANSCENDENT INSIGHT OF *ŚŪNYATĀ*

There is remarkable similarity among human thought systems with respect to the relationship beween thought and action. Every system teaches theoretical virtues through which humans are expected to identify appropriate goals consistent with the highest good, and practical virtues with which humans may select the best action required to meet individual goal. Ancient Greeks thought that the highest good is the human happiness or well-being that comes from the fulfilment of all human potential. In the *Nichomachean Ethics*, Aristotle dealt with two major subjects, namely, theoretical and practical virtue as the subject matter of human ethics. His system of thought is characterized by a boundless confidence in the faculty of reason as the ultimate criterion for theoria as well as for praxis. Reason develops itself partly as rational action and partly as rational thought toward perfection. Further, correct determination of the will for action must come from rational insight rather than the desire arising from erroneous knowledge. Thus, in Aristotle's view, erroneous knowledge leads to failure to achieve human potential and thus necessarily to a failure to achieve happiness.

In a similar fashion, Buddhists consider ignorance (*avidyā*) the fundamental cause of suffering. Ignorance (*avidyā*) means the uncritical belief in or blind conviction in the existence of one's self and of things that belong to the self (*kāya-dṛṣṭi*). The entire Buddhist system of thought and practice is directed to the matter of how and why we should eradicate this erroneous conviction.

Śākyamuni provided the eight-fold holy path,[124] which the orthodoxy expanded into the more elaborate thirty-seven auxiliary practices, required to rid one of the false conviction in self.[125] The Mahāyāna theorists later introduced the more simplified system of the six norms of perfection (*ṣaṭ-pāramitā*).

These six Pāramitās are divided into two groups pertaining to theoretical and practical virtues. In his *Ta-chih-tu-lun*, Nāgārjuna explains that the practices of charity (*dāna*), morality (*śīla*), and patience (*kṣānti*) constitute the norms of practical virtue, whereas diligence (*vīrya*), meditation (*dhyāna*), and insight (*prajñā*) are the norms of theoretical virtue.[126] Although these two groups of practices ought to be carried out simultaneously, practical virtue was often emphasized as a precondition for the advancement of theoretical virtue. What is unique with Buddhist theoretical virtue is the insight of non-duality or the absence of reality in all things.

As the *Prajñā Heart Sūtra* says, acquiring the insight of the four holy Truths, one comes to know that there is no object to be obtained, nor is there any agent who obtains it. In the ordinary human world, with the idea of obtainment, an agent acts upon a certain object that can be obtained. Within this fundamental context, all moral and ethical theories are developed. Again, based on Nāgārjuna's statement in the same commentary, I shall paraphrase the inner thoughts of a Bodhisattva:

> Having gone through the six norms of practice, I see the true aspect of things as they really are[127] and must remind myself of the original vow I took when I resolved to seek the way of Enlightenment for the purpose of rescuing others from their

---

124 「八聖道」

125 *Saptatriṃṣikabodhipakṣika-dharmā*「三十七菩提分法」: An arrangement of the seven sets of practices comparising thirty-seven items. (1) *catvāri smṛtyupasthānāni* (四念住) or four kinds of mindfulness concerned with breathing, posture, etc., (2) *catvāropradhānāni* (四精勤) or four kinds of diligence toward moral perfection, (3) *catvārarddhipadaḥ* (四神足) or four kinds of supernormal powers acquired through samādhi), (3) *pañcaśraddhā-indriya* (五根) or five kinds of faculty of enlightenment, (5) *Pañcabala* (五力) or five kinds of superior power to realization of Nirvāṇa, (6) *saptabodhyaṅgśni* (七覚支) or seven disciplines for acquisition of equanimity of the mind toward enlightenment, and (7) *aṣṭaṅgika-ārya-mārga* (八正道) or eight holy paths of the Buddhas.

126 *Ta-chih-tu-lun*, Taishō. 25, fasc. 27, p. 262c - p.263a: 「初発阿　多羅三藐三菩提意、欲度一切衆生老病死等身心諸苦、作大誓荘厳功徳慧明二事、因縁故所願皆満、是二事有六分修行、名六波羅蜜、布施持戒忍辱是功徳分、精進禅定智慧是慧明.」

127 「諸法実相」

> suffering. Having arrived at the height of insight, I do not see anyone as really existent and wonder, thus, what I should do about the people for whom I originally vowed to render help. From the true aspect of things as they really are, those whom I originally thought were suffering are not. But, since they do not know the true aspect of things as they are, I must help them see and understand this. Then, they should be able to rescue themselves with their own insight.[128]

In medieval India, a violent philosophical controversy occurred between the two Hindu schools of Naiyāyika and Mīmāṃsaka on the subject of *Śabda* or the "vocal word." The former empiricist school held that "an uttered vocal word is impermanent" because no sooner it comes into being, as a sound made by human enunciation, than it perishes. However, the latter transcendentalist school vehemently countered with the assertion that "Śabda is permanent" because it elicits the same meaning in the mind of any listener in any place at any time. In convention, the above two assertions are contradictory and cannot be reconciled, especially because both parties have legitimate grounds for the assertion of their views. From the logical point of view, what is essential to valid communication between two interlocutors is the condition that whatever is under discussion must be identical in the minds of speaker and listener. But often, this simple criterion is hard to meet. As is evident in the above controversy, even when the subject matter is expressed with one and the same term, respective predications create different meanings, resulting in a discrepancy between their references. It is obvious that there is no reference that may simultaneously satisfy the assertions that "x is impermanent" and "x is permanent."

Here, Buddhist logicians offered a unique approach to deal with the problem. They attempted to resolve the sectarian logical deadlock first by admitting that both assertions were true in their respective contexts, but not within one and the same context; second, they shifted the controversy to the subliminal plane of consciousness where perceptual and conceptual error or difference is likely to occur due to a variety of biases. For, even a spontaneous perception is an interpretative and unconscious version of what we do after we have perceived. It follows that whatever is asserted by naming is more than likely non-existent, because whatever is designated is of

---

[128] *Ibid.*, fasc. 27, p.263a: 「菩薩以般若波羅蜜、知諸法相念其本願、欲度衆セイ作是思惟諸法実相中衆生不可得当云何度。亦作此念諸法実相中衆生不可得当云何度、復作此念、諸法実相中衆生雖不家得、而衆生不知是諸法相故、欲令知是実相。」

defiled mental propensities.

This Buddhist approach was important, because the shifting of the problem of contradiction to the subliminal plane provided a logical and psychological middle ground for both parties. This Buddhist approach is dialectical because it involves negation of both assertions on the basis of their mutual contradiction. The Buddhist thinkers thought that reconciliation or communication is only possible at a different level of reality where both assertions are negated in regard to their claimed reality. The virtue of love and compassion ought to be considered in a similar manner, because the Buddhist ultimate love and compassion is based on the principle of non-duality between the loving and the loved.

It is in a similar context, I presume, that Nāgārjuna notes some sceptical views. Although the great love and compassion are the foundation of the Buddha-Dharma, some think that these must be of the defiled nature, like a blooming lotus flower rooted in impure mud. Surely the flower is pure, but the mud itself cannot be said to be pure. Hence, the Buddha's love and compassion, as far as its origin is concerned, must be of the defiled nature.[129] Again, since the Buddha comes to being because of his love and compassion for fellow humans, his love and compassion must be of the defiled nature.[130] The underlying thought here is that communication, in general, ought only to be possible between minds which share the same convention. Hindu philosophical controversy of medieval India demonstrates well how and why convention implies contradiction in itself, and shows how the ultimate reconciliation or communication may have to be made through the negation of the reality of the two adversarial assertions. The sublime virtue of love and compassion ascribed to Kuan-yin Bodhisattva may have to be evaluated in similar terms.

Kuan-yin's virtue of love and compassion as described in the *Lotus Sūtra* is sublime in light of his transcendent power to survey the world and detect cries of distress. I have long wondered about his vow and its parallel with that of Amitābha, who was once Dharmākara Bodhisattva. According to the *Pureland Sūtras*, Avalokiteśvara is a deputy dispenser of love and compassion in lieu of Amitābha Buddha, and bears a miniature image of Amitābha in his crown. In the Pureland tradition, Amitābha is singularly concerned

---

[129] *Ibid.*, fasc. 27, p.257b: 「大慈大悲雖是仏法之根本、故是有漏、如水於泥中生蓮華、不得言泥亦応妙、大慈大悲亦如是。」

[130] *Ibid.*, fasc. 27, p. 257b: 「仏以慈悲心為衆生故生応是有漏。」

with and absolutely promises ultimate salvation to all sentient beings to be received in his transcendent domain. Although the locus of Kuan-yin's promise is in the human world, his love and compassion seems to be consistent with the transcendent love and compassion expressed by Amitābha Buddha.

In *Nichomachean Ethics*, Aristotle speaks of the outcome of the perfection of the two virtues. By perfecting practical virtue, we humans are capable of enjoying ideal friendly association with other humans, while by perfecting theoretical virtue, we attain an ideal contemplative life immersed in matters of heavenly and natural law. Representing the Buddhist point of view, Nāgārjuna says that the Buddha revealed three levels of human happiness and well-being, namely, (1) happiness of a human level, (2) happiness of a heavenly level, and (3) happiness of an emancipated level.[131] The Bodhisattva should be able to help other humans in their conversion to humanly and heavenly attainment as well as to emancipation. Nāgārjuna then sums up the general difference between the Buddha and the Bodhisattva in relation to common humans, with the following words:

> The Bodhisattva has not attained the state of Buddhahood, nor has he attained the Buddha eye. Hence, he is himself afforded three kinds of happiness and well-being, wherefrom he shall help other humans in their conversion, whereas the Buddha helps all humans attain the same conversion while remaining in the state of emancipation.[132]

We understand that a Bodhisattva comes into being when he has been awakened to the fact of human suffering in life and death, and motivates himself to feel love and compassion toward all living beings. Upon learning the Buddha's insight, he acquires equivalent insight of sameness (*sama-citta*) toward sentient beings in terms of Non-Self, understanding that every individual self is merely a designation with no everlasting reality. In understanding the dependently arising elements of the five aggregates, he further acquires the insight of *Śūnyatā*, that all elements of the Skandhas have no reality of their own (*niḥsvabhāva* or *śūnyatā*). Thus, his insight into all things comprises awareness of the sameness of all

---

[131] *Ibid.*, fasc. 40, p. 355b-c; 「人楽、天楽、涅槃楽」

[132] *Ibid.*, fasc. 40. p. 355c: 「是菩薩未成就仏道、未得仏眼故、以三種楽故。教化可度衆生諸仏但以解脱楽教化衆生。」

humans and the sameness of all elements.[133] Now, he approaches the state of non-duality by transcending the duality of the ordinary world and human convention. By transcending various discriminations like long and short, white and black, male and female, and so on, he thus envisions the non-dual aspect or rather no-aspect (*wu-hsiang*) of all things; in this non-dual context, reconciliation or communication is perfected. Ultimately, this insight is what he wishes all fellow humans to attain.[134] Nāgārjuna explains this dialectical process by referring to the relationship between this world and the other world:

> What is the way to transcend this world (or convention)? Knowing what this world really is is the way to transcend it. For, the wise know that even if they seek to grasp this world and the other world, they cannot obtain either one. Since the two worlds cannot be obtained, the said two worlds ought to be known for the sake of practicality as this world or as the other world. It is simply for the sake of repudiating this world that the other world is refered to. The aspect of this world is in itself the other world, and there is no place other than this world. The reason is that the aspect of this world cannot be obtained, nor can the aspect of this world and the other world be obtained. Because both are always empty, no fixed aspect of this world of things is obtainable. Thus, the practitioners who practice with this insight do not obtain this world, nor do they attach themselves to the other world.[135]
>
> This world is called the five aggregates. Even if all the Buddhas of ten regions look for this aspect of the five aggregates, they cannot grasp where it comes from, where it stays, and where it goes away. When one does not see the aspects of where it originates, where it stays, and where it goes away, this is the other world. [At that moment,] when a practitioner contemplates

---

[133] Cf. *Ibid.*, fasc. 40, p. 393a: 「所謂大慈悲故、初発度一切衆生心故。学諸仏等心観衆生故、一切法自性空故、如是等因縁故、於一切衆生中生等心、得是等心巳、得一切衆諸法等。一切諸法者、如先説衆生等法等義。」

[134] Cf. Ibid., fasc.40, p. 393b: 復次、「衆生中行忍辱慈悲等福功徳無量、功徳無量故心柔軟、心柔軟故疾得禅定、修禅定故心如意調柔、心如意調柔故、破世間長短男女白黒等。入一相法所謂無相、得是法等巳、令一切衆生得是法等。」

[135] *Ibid.*, fasc. 27, p 258c 「何等是出世間道、如実知世間、即是出世間道、所以者何、智者求世間出世間、二事不可得、若不可特、当知仮名為世間出世間、但為破世間故、説出世間、世間相即是出世間、更無所復有。所以者何。世間相不可得。是出世間、是世間相常当空。世間法定相不可得故、如是行者不得世間、亦不著出世間。若不特世間、亦不著出世間」

> this world and the other world, he does not see either world, nor does he see this world converging with the other world, nor does he see the other world converging with this world, nor does he see the other world as other than this world, nor does he see this world as other than the other world. In this manner, he has no cognition either of this or of that as "This is this world," and "that is the other world." If one forsakes this world and yet does not take the other world, this is called the other world.[136]

This is how Nāgārjuna explained the Buddhist goal of the middle.

§9. CONCLUSION

Despite the age of industrialization and instant communication tools, we seem to have developed the problem of human alienation by eroding the fabrics of bonds in all spheres of human life and activity. Besides the problem of domestic affairs, we have also been experiencing a period of the fragmentation of international community due to different religions and cultures, races and nationalities. In no other time than today in history, do we need some means of effective antidote to deal with these problems and establish human unity. In this respect, it is a worthy cause to re-investigate the Buddhist virtue of love and compassion.

Every individual builds his own history and culture from cradle to death through a series of unique experiences not shared by any other person. Hence, human love is always based on partial communication due to each individual's Karmic propensities. Because of such a partial communication between loving and loved, Buddhist thinkers theorized the Buddha's love in terms of ultimate effectuation over and against human love. What makes communication imperfect in one case and makes it perfect in another case? I have pursued the point of difference in the two-fold expediency of the Bodhisattva: (1) the great compassion (*mahā-karuṇā, ta-pei*), the very source of the Bodhisattva's original resolution; and (2) the transcendent

---

136 *Ibid.*, fasc. 27「世間名五衆、五衆相仮令十方諸仏求之、亦不可得。無来処無住処、亦無去処。若不得五衆来住去相。即是出世間。行者爾時観是世間出世間、実不可見、不見世間与出世間合。離世間亦不見出世間、離出世間亦不見世間、如是則不生二識所謂世間出世間、若捨世間不受出世間、是名出世間、[若菩薩能如是知、則能為衆生分別世間出世間道、有漏無漏一切諸道亦如是人一相是名道種慧」

knowledge or *prajñā* insight into the *Śūnyatā* of all *things*. The representative Mahāyāna thinker like Nāgārjuna conceived these features as respective foundations of Buddhist practical and theoretical virtues to be perfected by the practice of the six-fold *Prajñāpāramitā* norms. What is trustworthy with the Bodhisattva ideal is first that his entire concern is concrete and factual, as anyone's or like ours, regarding human suffering, like old age, sickness, and death, and so on; and second, that his insight of *Śūnyatā* is another factor for the trustworthiness of the ideal, because it is based upon non-duality of all things.

I have probed the insight of *Śūnyatā* as the theoretical basis of Buddhist love and compassion by contrasting the Kuan-yin cult in China whose quintessence is the insight of *Śūnyatā* over and against Lokesh Chandra's theory that Hindu Brahmā's potency was the essential core of Avalokiteśvara. In this connection, I have a hunch that the feminine form of Kuan-yin likely evolved along with the notion that the *Prajñāpāramitā* scripture was respected and worshipped in ancient India and later in Tibet as mother of the insight and of the enlightened one.

Although the locus of Kuan-yin's promises is in the human world, his love and compassion seems to be consistent with the transcendent love and compassion of the Buddhas, for whom the abode is non-duality based on the dual negation of this world and the other world. The ultimate purpose of Buddhist love and compassion is to help others to reach an understanding of the four holy Truths in terms of Non-self and *Śūnyatā*, so that each individual helps one's self rid of ignorance and realize emancipation.

The matter of communication necessarily becomes an issue when any kind of interaction is undertaken between two humans or groups of humans. Capable of moving between the three motivational contexts of love and compassion, the Kuan-yin Bodhisattva attends anyone's mental action without either discrepancy or discordance but with perfect communication in terms of non-duality. What is essential to the Buddhist love and compassion is the balanced activism imbued with the insight of *Śūnyatā*.

Section Two

NĀGĀRJUNA AND MĀDHYAMIKA DIALECTIC OF CRITICAL SPIRITUALITY

ARTICLE FOUR

NĀGĀRJUNA'S DIALECTIC ANALYZED IN TERMS OF *ANVAYA-VYATIREKA*[1]

§1. INTRODUCTION

Although the metaphor of light and darkness has been extensively used in religious and philosophical literature throughout the world, it seems to have contributed more dramatizing the dichotomous view of the world than reducing tension or resolving such antitheses. It was Nāgārjuna, the forefather of Mādhyamika tradition, who philosophically brought attention to this metaphor and demonstrated how and why the dichotomy of good *versus* evil, knowledge versus ignorance, can be resolved on the basis of critical examination rather than one-sided belief and conviction. The metaphor in question with which this article is concerned appears in part in the Madhyamaka treatises attributed to Nāgārjuna and in part in the *Nyāyasūtra* and its commentary *Nyāyabhāṣya* by Vātsyāyana. The heart of the problem is the nature of cognition that arises from the faculty (*pramāṇa*) acting upon its object (*prameya*). The metaphor of the light of a candle's flame refers to the faculty of cognition and the darkness refers to object of cognition. The question is concerned with the fact of cognition or knowledge in which it is taken for granted that both the faculty and objects are somehow brought to a contact. The Naiyāyika logicians upheld that an individual cognizes an object by means of cognitive faculty, and that a cognition of an object is acquired by the *pramāṇa*, means of cognition, as an instrument, and Nāgārjuna repudiates this Naiyāyika theory of *pramāṇa*.

There is good reason to believe that Nāgārjuna favored this metaphor for his dialectical treatment, because it appears not only in his *Vigrahavyāvartanī* and *Vaidalyaprakaraṇa* in which the Naiyāyika notion of *pramāṇas* is directly criticized, but also in his definitive work *Mūlamadhyamaka-kārikā-śāstra*.[2] The way in which

---

[1] *Amalā Prajñā Aspect of Biddhist Studies* (Professor P. V. Bapat Felicitation Volume; Bibliotheca Indo-Buddhica No. 63), Edited by N. H. Samtani and H.S. Prasad, Delhi Indian Book Center, 1989; pp. 325-341.

[2] *Vigraha*. kārikās 36-39: *Vaidalya-sūtras* 6-10, esp., comment.; and *MK* VII, 8-12.

Nāgārjuna applied his dialectic to this metaphor, I believe, represents one of his model formulas of dialectic applied to religious and philosophical arguments, and that by logically analyzing it, it is possible to determine what is operationally and theoretically crucial to his dialectical method. Although it appears to be paradoxical, I contend that the *logical criteria of anvaya and vyatireka* (positive and contrapositive exemplifications or verifications) constitute the crucial principles of his dialectical method of refutation. In this sense, I believe his method of refutation had an intrinsic relationship with the convention of Indian syllogistic formula of inference and demonstration and necessarily influenced the theory of ontology and epistemology attributed to Buddhist logicians.

By "dialectic" I am referring to the Nāgārjunian method of *reductio-ad-absurdum* argument (*prasaṅga-vākya*). The purpose of this paper is primarily to demonstrate how and why his dialectic is based on the logical criteria of *anvaya* and *vyatireka* in reference to the aforementioned metaphor, and also thereby how the Mādhyamika dialectic influenced the system of Buddhist logic.

§2. BUDDHIST CONCEPT OF *ŚŪNYATĀ* AND ITS INFLUENCE UPON BUDDHIST LOGIC

One of the major difficulties that modern scholarship has encountered in Mādhyamika Studies has been the seeming violation of logical laws committed by the Mādhyamika dialecticians. The laws of logic, such as, contradiction,[3] identity and excluded middle have been carefully guarded in the West as the supreme criteria for ensuring the basis of reality for thought processes. If one cannot maintain these laws in his thinking and speech, whatever he thinks or says will be regarded as having no validity. When A's existence and A's non-existence are asserted at once as true, this implies that affirmation and negation correspond to nothing outside of the mind, since there is neither agreement nor disagreement between one's thought and its object. It may be condemned as

[3] The laws of identity and excluded middle are equally reducible to that of contradiction. Here I am referring to the following two Aristotelian expressions of the principle of contradiction: (1) The same attribute cannot simultaneously belong and not belong to the same subject and in the same respect. (2) It is impossible to affirm and deny the same predicates at the same time of the same thing. Cf. I. M. Bochenski, *A History of Formal Logic*, tr. and ed. by T. Thomas (New York: 1956), p. 612.

referring to nothing but an illusion. It was precisely toward such a conclusion that Nāgārjuna tried to show us about cognition by way of treating the metaphor of the flame of a lamp whose light is believed to illumine objects by breaking darkness.

Although convention *a-priori* accepts that light and darkness should encounter to explain the fact of illumination, Nāgārjuna examined this conception as to whether these two really have a point of their contact, only to conclude that insofar as light and darkness possess their respective beings or self-identity (*svabhāva*), they could never meet. The only way to reverse this absurdity is to repudiate this self-identity principle (*svabhāva*) respectively ascribed to these opposite entities and instead to accept their functional interdependence (*parasparāpekṣatā*), because these two contrary entities are simultaneously identical and different, namely, *niḥsvabhāva* (i.e., without *svabhāva*) *and śūnyatā* (i.e., emptiness or voidness).[4] Then, the concept of *śūnyatā* appears to be implying an obvious transgression of those logical laws. The question is: Whether or not the concept of *śūnyatā* really violates those laws of thought and subverts the reality of thought and annihilates constructive thinking itself. Nāgārjuan did not think so, declaring rather that the truth of *śūnyatā* is the basis of our conceptual world as well as that of external phenomena.[5]

Profs A. Kunst and H. Nakamura are among the fewer numbers of scholars who made important progress for understanding this Nāgārjunian claim. They clarified some of the influences which the

---

[4] S. Schayer gives his symbolic notation to this dialectical relationship as (x,Y). xRy. ....–(xy̌). –(x=y) in reference to MK 14: 5b. The verse 5 of the Chap. 14 reads in its entirety as follows:

anyad anyat pratītya anyan na anyad anyaṛte 'nyat́aḥ/ 5a
yat pratītya ca yat tasmāt tad anyan nopapadyate// 5b
'x' is different from 'y' by depending on 'y'; 'x' is not different from 'y' without 'y,' (5a) When 'x' depends on 'y,' it is not possible that 'y' is different from 'x.' (5b) In short, when 'x' is depending on 'y,' 'x' is neither 'y,' nor '–y.'

The symbolic notation means this under-dotted conclusion.
"Über die Methode der Nyāya-Forschung," *Zeitschrift Winternitz*, (Leipzig: 1932), p. 250. Nakamura also seems to have agreed with Schayer's interpretation. Cf. "The Influence of the Concept of Śūnyatā on Buddhist Logic," *Bukkyo no Kompon Shinri* (*The Fundamental Truth of Buddhism*), Tokyo: 1956, p. 32, and also *Indian Buddhism: A Survey with Bibliographical Notes*, (Osaka: 1980), p. 249.

[5] MK IV, 9 and XXIV, 14:
vyākhyāne ya upālambhaṃ kṛte śūnyatayā vadet/
sarvaṃ tasyānupalabdhaṃ samaṃ sādhyena jñāyate// MK 4: 9ab
sarvaṃ ca yujyate tasya śūnyatā yasya yujyete/
sarvaṃ na yujyate tasya śūnyaṃ yasya na yujyate// MK 24:14ab

concept of *śūnyatā* and the dialectical exposition exercised upon the way Buddhist logicians dealt with the logical principle of contradiction, excluded middle or identity. Both agreed that these logical laws are heterogeneous to the philosophical domain to which the concept of *śūnyatā* is supposed to have been applied. Kunst openly cast a doubt to the dogmatic application of logical laws to the analysis of Buddhist doctrine, because Buddhist thoughts and theories are based on a different kind of logic, so-called *catuṣkoṭi*, logic of four-fold truth-value, which admits four standard classifications: "Something is A, -A, both A and -A, and neither A nor -A,"[6]

In demonstrating his point of view, Kunst appealed to the way Buddhist logicians dealt with two contradictory assertions respectively attributed to the Naiyāyika and Mīmāṃsaka schoolmen on the definition of *Śabda* in syllogistic formulations.[7].

Naiyāyika definition: *Śabdo 'nitya kṛtakatvāt*:
An utterance is impermanent,
because it is a product,
like a pot is.
Mīmāṃsaka definition: *Śābdo nityaḥ śravaṇatvāt śabdatvavat*:
An utterance is permanent,
because it is audible
like anything that is audible.

For the empiricist Ṇaiyāyika, an utterance (a vocal word) is a temporary modification (*guṇa*) produced upon a permanent substance (*dravya*), such as ether (*ākāśa*), like a pot is a product out of a material substance of clay. The transcendentalist Mīmāṃsaka, on the other hand, maintained that any audible, that is, communicable, sound carries its transcendental ideation as its essence, which, for them, was permanent.

From the traditional logical point of view, these two assertions (i.e., *śabdo 'nityaḥ* and *śabdo nityaḥ*) are contradictory as regards to their common substratum. Hence, it would be natural and logical to

---

[6] Cf. Kunst: "The Concept of the Principle of Excluded Middle in Buddhism," *Rocznik Orientalistycny* XXI, (1957), p. 141.

[7] *Ibid.*, p. 146. These examples are given in the *Nyāyapraveśakasūtra*: Gaekwad Oriental Series, 38 (1930), pp. 3-4. Although, strictly speaking, *śābdo anityaḥ kṛtakatvāt ghaṭavat*, is a Vaiśeṣika siddhānta, since the Naiyāyika accepted the metaphysical system in *toto*, I present it as the Naiyāyika view of language, especially, in correlation with Nāgārjuna's refutation of *śabda* in the *Vigrahavyāvartanī* as discussed in the later part of this paper.

decide either one of them to be false. Kunst, however, pointed out that Buddhist logicians took a more cautious approach in taking three considerations:[8] (1) Buddhist logicians lay emphasis on the respective predications, such as "being a product" and "being audible," and not on the syllogisms as a whole, because each syllogism is valid in the light of inferential criteria (which I shall discuss later); (2) They also accepted their simultaneous validity within each system of philosophical presuppositions (*siddhānta*), i.e., respectively: "Whatever is a product is impermanent" and "Whatever is audible is permanent"; (3) They, however, shifted both the mental process and the logical significance on to a different plane from that of those logical laws, namely, to the so-called pre-linguistic process of the mind.

These steps which Kunst brilliantly recognized reflect an authentic Buddhist articulation regarding (1) the philosophical meaning and the structural feature of Indian syllogism, (2) the problem of antithesis inherent in syllogistic formulation and (3) the way Buddhist tried to resolve such antithesis for the goal of freeing human consciousness. I am obliged to point out, however, that these Buddhist considerations were gradually advanced historically from the pre-Classical Abhidharmist through Mahāyāna theorists search of break-through over the barrier of convention and transcendence in human consciousness. As I pointed out elsewhere,[9] in the pre-Classical times, it was the norm for doctrinal disputes among Buddhists to formulate their assertion and refutation according to the rules of *anvaya* and *vyatireka*. In the *Kathāvatthu*, for instance, I recognize that the logical principle of *anvaya* and *vyatireka*, crucial to valid inference, were already put in practice as the basic rule of logically valid thesis, and that the logical and linguistic convention was strictly operated with the categories of assertions and assertion-variables.

The logical problem of which the orthodox Theravādin and the heterodox Pudgalavādin experienced an insurmountable antithesis over the subjects of *dharma* and *pudgala*, was, in fact, identical with the problem of the aforementioned Naiyāyika and Mīmāṃsaka controversy, namely, discrepancy of the respective variables despite the identical subject term. In case of such referential discrepancy, ensued polemics could lead nowhere for determining which assertion

---

[8] *Ibid.*

[9] Ichimura: "A Study of the Mādhyamika Method of Refutation, Especially of its Affinity to that of Kathāvatthu," *Journal of International Association of Buddhist Studies* III, 9(1980), 7-15.

is valid or invalid. I believe it was one of Nāgārjuna's objectives to resolve such a deadlock among the Abhidharmists. Kunst seems to have recognized this Nāgārjunian endeavor reflected in Buddhist logician's approach as he cited a link in Nāgārjuna's aximomatic statement as follows:

> In teaching the doctrine (*dharma*), the Enlightened Ones rely on the two truths, empirical and transcendent. Those who do not differentiate these two truths do not understand the profound reality (*tattva*) in the doctrine of the Buddha. Without relying on the empirical truth, the transcendental truth cannot be shown; without relying on the transcendental truth, the *Nirvāṇa* cannot be realized.[10]

Kunst's interpretation that Buddhist logicians attempted to treat the problem of contradiction in the transcendental direction was attested by Nakamura somewhat in a complementary manner. In his study on "The Influence of the Concept of *Śūnyatā* on Buddhist Logic,"[11] Nakamura mainly examined Dignāga's system of logic with focus on some of the points of which Hindu philosophers made special issues, because such points of controversy could be selected as the likely areas the concept of *śūnyatā* influenced. Kunst and Nakamura agreed that Buddhist logicians allowed contradiction in the domain of ultimate facts, because it is purely philosophical matter how to interpret namings of facts since factual existence precedes inferential process in which naming occurs. As far as the logical domain is concerned, however, Nakamura emphasized that it is universal to any system of philosophy, whether Hindu or Buddhist, as it is governed by the laws of logic.[12] According to Kunst, it was permissible for Buddhist logicians not only to juxtapose against reality two different arguments (*hetu*), which are mutually contradictory, to prove one thesis (*sādhya*), but also to pose one argument to prove two theses which appear even mutually exclusive,[13] although this would not be permissible within a system

---

[10] MK 24: 8,9,10; and *Vigraha*. 28 (=MK 24: 10):
dve satye samupāśritya buddhānāṃ dharmadeśanā /
lokasaṃvṛti-satyaṃ ca satyaṃ ca paramārthataḥ //8
ye 'nayor na vijānanti vibhāgaṃ satyayor dvayoḥ/
te tattvaṃ na vijānanti gambhīraṃ buddhaśāsane //9
vyavahāram anāśritya paramārtho na deśyate /
paramārtham anāgamya nirvāṇaṃ nādhigamyate //10

[11] Nakamura: *op. cit*., p.329.

[12] *Ibid.*

[13] Kunst: *loc. cit.*, p. 142.

simultaneously.

In any case, what Kunst contended was that in order to determine validity or invalidity for two seemingly contradictory assertions, Buddhist logicians did not apply the so called objective criterion independent of human mind, but sought it in the mind making reality only partly a function of extraneous phenomenon. It is obvious that this approach of the Buddhist logicians required a new insight and new theories of ontology and of language. Nakamura determined that this underlying insight was the concept of *śūnyatā* which resulted in Dignāga's theorization of *pratyakṣa* and *apoha*.[14]

There are two fundamental reasons as to why these theories embody the insight of *śūmyatā*: (1) that ultimate facts of experience (*pratyakṣa*) transcend epistemic and mental process, and (2) that the use of logico-linguistic expression has no objective reference except its negated contraptions (*apoha*). Dignāga defined *pratyakṣa* as "free from conceptual bifurcation" (*kalpanāpoḍha*) to which Dharmakīrti added his own as "non-contradicted" by the underlying essence of reality (*abhrānta*).[15] It is such an ultimate fact of experience in which alone absolute particular (*paramārthasat*) or thing-in-itself (*svalakṣaṇa*) is pertained as an instantaneous (*kṣaṇika*) efficient moment (*arthakriyākārin*), and hence, through which alone man comes into touch with such transcendental reality. Insofar as the given moment is real, having its efficiency, *pratyakṣa* is immediately followed by an epistemic dichotomy into the object (*prameya*) and the subject (*pramāṇa*) as a characteristic of cognitive process. This mental process is synthetic in that it links an immediate sensation (*nirvikalpaka-jñāna*) with subsequent mental construction (*savikalpaka-jñāna*) or an act of referring an image or universal (*sāmānya*) to that sensation.[16] Linguistically it is the judgmental process (*niścaya*) which links the subject of proposition with its predication as universal.

Dignāga determined this epistemic and linguistic process as an inference being solely mental, having no corresponding referential entity.[17] For, this linguistic process (*nāmakalpanā*) depends upon

---

[14] Nakamura: *op. cit.*, p. 329.

[15] *Pramāṇasamuccaya* 13; Cf M. Hattori, *Dignāga, On Perception*, Harvard Oriental Series 47 (1968), p. 25, esp. Note 1, 25 in p. 82f; Nyāyabindu 14. Cf. Th. Stcherbatsky: *Buddhist Logic* II, esp. Note , p. 19.

[16] *Pramāṇa-s.*: 1. 3: *nāmajātyādiyojanā / kalpanā* is nothing but the process of associating with an object linguistic symbols of five categories: *nāma, jāti, guṇa, kriyā,* and *dravya*, which Dignāga is said to have adopted from the Vaiyākaraṇas. Cf. Hattori: *op. cit.*, p.82.

[17] *Pramāṇa-s.*: V. 1 (cited in *Tattvasaṅgraha-pañjikā* (GOS, 30-1,

exclusion of its contraposition. For instance, a predication "p" in an assertion is supposed to have arisen through negation of its contraposition "–p." This constitutes the theory of *Apoha*. Although it appears to be paradoxical to say that an ultimate fact which transcends mental process is also immanent in this process by way of negation, this is what Buddhist logicians in effect proposed in their ontology and logic, and I believe, this is what Nāgārjuna intended to demonstrate through his dialectic.

§3. BUDDHIST REDUCTION OF THE FIVE-MEMBERED SYLLOGISM TO TWO-MEMBERED FORMULA

The foregoing interpretations attributed to Kunst and Nakamura are complementary in equally focusing on the crucial domain, of which the concept of *śūnyatā* is believed to have influenced on theorization in the system of Buddhist logic. Kunst suggested that it was this domain where ultimate solution may be transcendentally at hand for the problem of contradiction created at the level of propositional assertions. Nakamura determined that this was the same domain where an instantaneous ultimate moment is immediately translated into propositional assertions though by way of negation. I consider that it is the domain where *anvaya* and *vyatireka* operations take their spontaneous course either for logical construction or dialectical repudiation.

My primary task is therefore to clarify as to why, despite their being logical processes, they can be the structural basis of Nāgārjuna's dialectical method. In view of the influences which the concept of *śūnyatā* exercised upon logical theories, I think the concept itself is essentially of a logical nature. Suggesting a similar insight, Kunst pointed out that Buddhist logicians consistently simplified the members of syllogistic inference in the course of theoretical refinement. Reduction was accomplished from the traditional five-membered syllogism (*pañcāvayava*) eventually down to the singular one consisting only of *hetu* statement. He was convinced that it was Nāgārjuna who initially noticed the redundancy of verbal elements in syllogistic demonstration and gave a stimulus to its thorough revision.[18] Kunst, however, did not fully clarify the philosophical implication of this

---

1926)], p. 441, 6-7.

na pramāṇāntarair śabdam anumānāt tathāhi tat /
kṛtakatvādivat svārtham anyāpohena bhāṣate /

[18] Kunst: "The Two-Membered Syllogism," *RO*, XV, (1939-40), p. 76.

unmistakable tendency, which I shall examine as to its relation to the Nāgārjunian method of dialectic.

If we can differentiate our thought category into five levels of reality, namely, (1) linguistic symbols, (2) subjective mental entity, (3) objective meanings, (4) phenomenal realities, and (5) transcendental entities, we can reduce, on the one hand, the initial three levels to a single category that consists of symbols or concepts, and, on the other hand, the remaining two to another category that consists of ontological fact. Then, it is possible to treat our world of experience in terms of interaction between these two dimensions. It was Stanislow Schayer who initially noted that ancient and Medieval Indian logicians generally treated their subject upon the two categories of assertive sentences and their variables.[19] Since I hold that the Mādhyamika dialectic shares the core structure of Indian syllogistic inference, I am prepared to apply symbolic notation to my analysis as far as it is helpful in terms of propositional logic with restricted variables.[20]

Indian syllogistic inference as distinguished from the Western type is based on the relation of concomitance (*vyāpti*) between Reason (*hetu*) and Conclusion (*sādhya*) and not that of entailment or implication derived from tautology. It is rather pragmatic because its validity depends on whether a given argument (*hetu*) and conclusion (*sādhya*) are supported by the evidence of every day occurrences or commonly experienced facts of life. In this paper, I shall consistently express this *concomitance* in terms of conjunction: "p and q" or its contraposition "–q and –p," instead of conditional implication, such as "if p then q" [i.e., 'p ⊃ q'] or "if –q then –p" [i.e., '–q ⊃ –p'] respectively. While the general relation "p•q" guides an inferential process from "p" to "q," what underlies this process is the *anvaya* and *vyatireka* operations, whose importance as the core operation of inference was ever more clearly made visible in the course of reduction applied to the members of syllogism.

The early Nyāya logicians theorized an inferential process as consisting of the five-membered statements (*pañcāvayavas*).[21]

1. *pratijñā*: The hill's having fire. "q(a)," ['a' = a hill; q = "having fire"]
2. *hetu*: The hill's having smoke. "p(a)," ['p' = "having smoke"]
3. *udāharaṇa* (*dṛṣṭānta's* dual application):

[19] Cf. Schayer: "Über die Method der Nyāya-Forshung," op. cit., pp. 247-257.

[20] Cf. Bochenski, op. cit., p. 323.

[21] Cf. Schayer's notation, op. cit., p. 254.

Wherever smoke there is fire: (x){p(x)•q(x)} [*vyāpti* = "p • q"]
Anvaya: like in a kitchen: (α){p(α)•q(α)] [α = a kitchen]
Vyatireka: unlike on a lake: (β)[–q(β)•–p(β)] [β = a lake]

4. *upanaya*: So, the hill is having smoke: (α)p
5. *nigamana*: Therefore, the hill is having fire: (α)q

The essential operation of syllogistic inference as a means of demonstration is found in *udāharaṇa* and *upanaya* of the Naiyāyika's or in the *dṛṣṭānta* and *hetu* of the Buddhist formulation. Dignāga theorized the basic rules of valid inference as *trairūpa*, of which Śaṅkarasvāmin concisely laid down as (1) *pakṣadharmatva*, (2) *sapakṣe sattvaṃ*, and (3) *vipakṣe asattvaṃ*.[22]

As a method of demonstration, the Rule 2, which is *anvaya*, determines in a *dṛṣṭānta* (a kitchen) the class of *sapakṣa*, of every member of which the two concomitant propositions: "'x' possessing smoke" and "'x' possessing fire," are jointly true, i.e., (x){p(x)•q(x)} exemplified by p(α)•q(α).

The Rule 3, which is *vyatireka*, on the other hand, determines in a contrapositive *dṛṣṭānta* (e.g., a lake) the class of *vipakṣa*, of every member of which those two propositions are equally false, i.e., (y){–q(y)•–p(y)} exemplified by (β)[–q(β)•–p(β)}. The dual exemplifications *ipso facto* determines the given *pakṣa* or substratum (a hill or the value of 'x') within the class of *sapakṣa* (similar) but not of *vipakṣa* (dissimilar).

The Rule 1, lastly, prescribes that the assertion "p" (*hetu*, reason), whose relationship with "q" (*sādhya*, conclusion) has been simultaneously validated through *anvaya* and *vyatireka* and is to be applied to the particular *pakṣa* in question as "p(a)."

In theorizing these rules Dignāga already eliminated three members

---

[22] Pramāṇa-s: III: quoted in *Nyāyabinduṭīkā* on I, i,. 35:
sapakṣe san nāsan dvedhā pakṣadharmaḥ punas tridhā /
pratyekam asapakṣe ca sadasad dvidhātvataḥ //
Quoted in Vidyabhusana: *A History of Indian Logic*, (Calcutta, 1921), p. 283]. Nyāyapraveśā, op. cit., p. 1.
(1) *Pakṣa-dharma-tva* means the positing of a *hetu* or Reason, an assertion specifying the object to be inferred qualified by a predication; e.g., an assertion of a hill having a "smoke" implying a fire; ....(a)p [... (a)q].
(2) *Sapakṣesattva* means that the substratum in question must be found among the similar class members, like kitchen, etc...........(a, b, c, etc.){p•q}.
(3) *Vipakṣe asattva* means that the substratum is never found among the dissimilar class members, like lake, water tank, etc........(r, s, t, etc.){–q•–p}.

from the Naiyāyika syllogistic formula. *Nigamana* and *Upanaya* were immediately eliminated on the ground that the former was a mere repetition of *pratijñā* (subject to be proved) and the latter only a pedagogical indication of the qualifier of the valid *hetu*. Next, *pratijñā* was to be forsaken because it was non-essential to demonstration. The reason is that in telling others that there is a fire on the hill, one depends on the general relation of smoke and fire already known to one's audience through common experience, and hence, the *pratijñā* whose role is to tell the subject matter is redundant.[23] The whole process of inference was thus brought down to two members, *hetu* and *udāharaṇa* of the Naiyāyika's five-membered formula. The following is the two-membered syllogism of the post-Dignāgan Buddhist logic:

1. *Vyāpti*: Wherever there is smoke, there is fire: (x){p(x)•q(x)}
   Anvaya: Like in the kitchen where both likely are: p(α)•q(α)
   Vyatireka: unlike in a lake where neither is: –q(β)•–p(β)
2. *Hetu* (implying *sādhya*): There is smoke that implies fire. p(a)•q(a)

The Naiyāyikas vehemently objected to Dignāga's new formula by insisting that *pratijñā* is necessary to indicate *sādhya* as well as to determine the validity of *hetu*. Dignāga assigned class determination to the *anvaya-vyatireka* statement, whereas the Naiyāyika assigned *concomitance* verification to it. As to the second statement, Dignāga assigned laying down *hetu* which implies *sādhya* with reference to its *pakṣa*, whereas the Naiyāyika assigned *hetu* verification by the *sādhya* determined by the preceding *anvaya-vyatireka* procedure. From these differences it is easy to see why Dignāga defined the *prameya* (object of inferential knowledge) as a *pakṣa* marked by *hetu* which implies *sādhya:* "(a)p" {–>(a)q}. Dignāga gave three reasons: (1) when the concomitance of "p" and "q" is known universally, the "q" should be implied in the statement of "p(a) (*hetu*); (2) when "q" is known universally to be found in a *dṛṣṭānta*, the *pakṣa* in question [= 'a' or a hill] should be the object to be cognized; and (3) if the object of an inference is the relationship between hill and fire in "q(a)," there is no element here capable of making an inference possible, nor is there anything to be inferred. It follows that the connection between the *dharmin* 'a' and the *dharma* "q" need not be expressed, nor should it be accompanied by *hetu*.[24]

---

[23] Cf. Kunst: *loc. cit.*, pp. 79-80.

[24] *Pramāṇa-s*: II, 8-11: (quoted in Vidyabhusana: op. cit., pp. 281-282; Cf. H. Kitagawa: *A Study of Indian Classical Logic* – Dignāga's System, (Tokyo: 1965), pp. 103-4, esp. , Note 95.

The foregoing Dignāgan conception further allowed his successors, such as Dharmakīrti and Ratnākara, to consider that both *pakṣavacana* (verbal statement of substratum) and *dṛṣṭānta* (examples) would be non-essential to the validity of demonstration and, hence, could be forsaken. Dharmakīrti is said to have thought that inductive knowledge which determines universal relations is good for an inference for oneself (*svārthānumāna*) but in instructing others (*parārthānumāna*), any deductive universal propositions, i.e., (x){p(x) • q(x)}, and *hetu*-laying, p(a), are sufficient for its singular conclusion q(a).[25] A few centuries later, Ratnākara advocated a similar idea that in *dṛṣṭānta* one grasps the elements of *vyāpti, i.e.,* "p" and "q," but in the *pakṣa* one grasps concomitance indicated by *hetu.*[26] Then it is mere matter of choice what one substitutes for (x){p(x)•q(x)}, namely, whether to use a *dṛṣṭānta* 'α' (= kitchen) or a *pakṣa* 'a' (= hill). Thus, the member of a syllogism which was not questioned throughout was the *hetu* alone.

§4. LOGICAL LIMIT AND DIALECTICAL METHOD UPON *ANVAYA* AND *VYATIREKA*

Although the foregoing is a sketchy presentation, I believe it is sufficient to show some causal relationship between the gradual reduction of the members of syllogism consistently observed and some philosophical motive which may have guided such direction. Kunst attributed to Buddhist logicians two apparent motives as to why they eschew psychological elements from symbolic formulation and avoid repetitions (*punarvacana*) of items that another member of syllogism may express or implicitly contain.[27] He, however, only alluded to a possibility of some metaphysical or ontological reason. The use of linguistic symbols is in part referential and in part tendentious (purposive). When a *hetu* is given, I am certain that for

---

kecit dharmāntara meya liṅgāvyabhicārataḥ /
sambandhaṃ kecid icchanti sidhatvād dharmadharmiṇoḥ //
liṅgaṃ dharme prasiddhaṃ cet kim anyat tena mīyate /
atha dharmiṇi tasyaiva kim arthaṃ nānumeyatā //
sambandhe 'pi dvayaṃ nāsti ṣaṣṭhī śruyeta tadvati /
avācyo 'nugṛhītatvān na cāsau liṅgasaṃgataḥ //
liṅgasyāvyabhicāras tu dharmeṇānyatra dṛśyate /
tatra prasiddhaṃ tad yuktaṃ dharmiṇaṃ gamayiṣyati //

25 Kunst: "The Two Membered . . ." *loc. cit.*, p. 82.

26 *Ibid.*

27 *Ibid.*, p. 75

Buddhist logicians it means that there is already something factual in the ultimate sense, instantaneous and efficient, which calls for its being, and that this *hetu* assertion in turn has implied in itself its concomitant assertion revealing the tendentious frame of human mentality. This is consonant with the way Dharmakīrti attributed an ultimate efficiency to the instantaneous moments as singularly capable of creating purposive mental processes.

Toward the end of the theoretical refinement of Buddhist logic, Ratnākara considered that the inner concomitance (*antarvyāpti*) can dispense with *dṛṣṭānta* for those entities of which momentariness (*kṣaṇikatva*) can be predicated.[28] Thus, it seems that Buddhist logicians were thinking of inferential process as wide as can include spontaneous thought movements. It is our common experience that a rapid flow of linguistic symbols in speech or audition is regulated for their orderly appearance in our consciousness along with grammatico-linguistic rules and categories. Irrespective of whether a thought movement from one moment in which smoke is perceived to another moment in which an outbreak of fire is inferred happens to be spontaneous or deliberate, there should be underlying a certain process which binds thought movements or regulates their proper linkages within the stream of consciousness (*skandhasantāna*) as basic to any higher complex relations and linkages. This reasoning allows me to assert that it is the *anvaya* and *vyreka* operations, which underlie a given linkage in reference to dynamic instantaneous moments of consciousness.

In the light of this interpretation, we may have the deductive or logical process in the following form:

1. $p(a)$ .... *pakṣadharmatva*
2. $(x)\{p(x) \cdot q(x)\}$ and $p(\alpha) \cdot q(\alpha)$........................ *sapakṣe sattvaṃ*
3. $(y)\{-q(y) \cdot -p(y)$ and $-q(\beta) \cdot -p(\beta)$........................*vipakṣe asattvaṃ*
4. $q(a)$..*sādhya*

Here, however, by making the value of 'x' as well as 'y' each an instantaneous moment, both affirmative and negative *dṛṣṭāntas* [i.e., "$p(\alpha) \cdot q(\alpha)$" and "$-q(\beta) \cdot -p(\beta)$"] can be dispensed with. What underlies the mental process to regulate tendentious imputation as "$p \cdot q$" [as "$p \supset q$" or "$p \rightarrow q$"] is the dual processes of *anvaya* and *vyatireka* simultaneously juxtaposed on the linkage between "p" and "q." Thus, the above formula can be further simplified for the inner concomitance to the following formula:

---

[28] *Ibid.*, p. 83. Ratnākara: *Antarvyāptisamarthana*, edited by Haraprasad, Bibliotheca Indica new series, No. 1226; (Calcutta: 1910), p. 103 (15-16).

$(x)\{p(x)\bullet q(x)\} \bullet (y)\{-q(y)\bullet -p(y)\}$.

As to the question of why the above operation is crucial, I have found an answer in the pre-Classical Abhidharmist logico-philosophical problem as recorded in the *Kathāvatthu.* The crux of the Abhidharmist problem was that the Theravādin who stood for the orthodoxy of *anātman* and the Pudgalavādin who advocated the semi-transcendent agent of *pudgala,* were logically deadlocked on the subject of *pudgala.* By postulating a semi-metaphysical agent as '*pudgala,*' the latter intended to explain the causal continuity of instantaneous *Skandha* configurations of human consciousness. Thus, the theory of *pudgala* was blamed to be a heresy against the Buddhist orthodoxy of *anātman.*

The logical indeterminacy between the orthodox Theravādin, to whom *dharmas* are alone real, and the heterodox Pudgalavādin, to whom *pudgalas* are also real, was therefore not only a logical problem but also a serious doctrinal problem, because the very fact that *dharmas* are indistinguishable from empirical entities such as *pudgalas* could undermine the transcendent status of *dharmas* and the authority of the religion itself. The ambivalent nature of *pudgala,* however, is that its unreality is known only through the transcendental insight in which the *dharmas* are known to be ultimately real. The cause of the indeterminacy between the status of *dharmas* and that of pudgala was derived from the fact that the argument could not make a clear-cut distinction or difference between the classes of *dharmas* and *pudgalas*.

In order to make a brief but intelligible account of the Abhidharmist logical problem, I shall rely on similar notation as before. Let a transcendent and an empirical entity respectively be a member of the class of *sapakṣa* and that of *vipakṣa,* and let two concomitant assertions "p" and "q," respectively as (1) that 'x' "is known in the sense of a genuinely real thing (i.e., a class memer of *dharmas*)," and (2) that 'x' "is known in the same way as a genuinely real thing is known."[29] The Theravādin set forth these concomitant propositions, because if 'x' is a transcendent *dharma*, both propositions are true (i.e., "p•q"), whereas if 'x' is an empirical *pudgala,* they expected that both propositions ought to be negated as "–q•–p."

The Pudgalavādin asserted the first proposition as "p" on *pudgala*,

---

[29] *Kathāvatthu* I,1:
puggalo upalabhati saccikaṭṭhaparamaṭṭhenāti /
yo saccikaṭṭtho tato sopuggaalo upalabhati saccikaṭṭhaparamaṭṭhenāti //
The English translation of the two propositions is taken directly from Rhys Davids's translation: The Points of Controversy or Subjects of Discourses. PTS, 1915]:

but negated the second as "–q," because, although they postulated a *pudgala* as real, but this was "not a result acquired through the same way as a transcendent *dharma* is known." Now, to the Pudgalavādin's rejoinder, the Theravādin negated the first proposition as "–p" on *pudgala*, but was compelled to assert the second as "q," because an empirical *pudgala* is known as unreal "through the same way as a transcendent *dharma* is known as real." Thus, the resulted concomitant formulas, i.e., Theravādin's "–p•q" and Pudgalavādin's "p•–q" are mutually invalid from the point of view of *anvaya-vyatireka* requirement: i.e., "if a *pudgala* is known as real, it ought to be known in the same way a *dharma* is known as real," and "if 'x' is not real, it ought not to be known as a *dharma* is known as real."

In view of an efficient method of refutation, the Theravādin's matching up the Pudgalavādin's thesis "p" with a concomitant proposition "q"[30] can be interpreted as a subtle trick to let his adversary lay down the class boundary of *pudgala* in admixture with that of *dharma*. The Theravādin expected that even if their adversary affirmed "p," they were obliged to negate the second proposition as "–q," and hoped to claim that the Theravādin won a victory upon the logically invalid concomitance of the Pudgalavādin's assertion, i.e., "p•–q." This invalid concomitance means that the substratum in question (i.e., *pudgala*) was classified in part as a member of *sapakṣa* (i.e., *dharmas*) by affirming the first proposition, but in part a member of *vipakṣa* by negating the second proposition (i.e., *pudgala*). On the part of the Theravādin too, in part, classifying *pudgalas* in the class of empirical ("–p"), they were compelled in part to classify them to share the same predication as that of *dharmas* ("q"). I believe that this was the main reason that Nāgārjuna did not allow the qualification of partial identity between two related entities which are brought into the sphere of logical operation. It would have been due to the same reason that Buddhist logicians guarded the dual rules of exemplification as the supreme criteria for the logicality of inference or demonstration.

It was, however, an ingenious counter-argument on the part of the Pudgalavādin, when they questioned the Theravādin regarding the second proposition first: "In your thought, should a *pudgala* be known as unreal in the same way a *dharma* is known as real," i.e., "q,' which the Theravādin could not negate, and yet ought to negate

---

30 "a *pudgala* "is known in the sense of a genuinely real thing" and "a *pudgala* "is known in the same way as a genuinely real thing is known""

the first proposition: "*pudgala* is known as real" as "–p." Thus, their mutual invalidation was complete between the Theravādin's propositions as "(*pudgala*){–q•p}" and the Pudgalavādin's counter argument as "(*pudgala*) {p•–q}." Their refutations were completely balanced on a par. The Theravādin blamed the Pudgalavādin, saying that their assertion was wrong, because "if p, then q," but their conclusion is "p and –q." The Pudgalavādin too countered the Theravādin, saying that their assertion was wrong, because if "–p, then –q," but their conclusion is "–p and q.' Since "p•q" and "–q•–p" are mutually contraposition endowed with identical truth value, the Abhidharmist method of argument was very much standard based on syllogistic formula of demonstration.

I contend, therefore, that Nāgarjuna's method of dialectic had its theoretical as well as practical purpose in part to deal with the foregoing logical problem of mutual invalidation. I have shown that the problem of logical indeterminacy or mutual invalidation boils down to the level of referential variables. There is a clear parallel between the Abhidharmist problem on *pudgala* and that of the Naiyāyika *versus* Mīmāṃsaka on *śabda*. In both cases, despite the common subject term, the two involved parties brought in different classes of variables in asserting their respective concomitance. What is required at this juncture would be to eliminate the existing difference in the referential level. My hypothesis is that the way to resolve the doctrinal antithesis at the propositional level and to strike down the discrepancy at the referential level would be the principle of complete identification of the different variables.

§5. NĀGĀRJUNA'S REFUTATION OF NAIYĀYIKA LOGIC: DIALECTICAL CONTEXT *VERSUS* LOGICAL CONTEXT

Nāgārjuna's critique of the Naiyāyika concept of *pramāṇa* generally represents the Buddhist critical attitude toward the grammtico-linguistic convention upon which the system of *pramāṇa* was founded. This is inferable from the fact that Vātsyāyana tried to defend the validity of *pramāṇa* ultimately in reference to the grammtico-linguistic principle, namely, syntactical categories (*kāraka*) and the significative power (*samākhyānimitta*) of linguistic symbols. In the *Nyāyasūtra* II, 1, 8-11, some of Nāgārjuna's passages that appeared in the *Vigrahvyāvartanī* are concisely rephrased as follows:

> Perception cannot be established in past and future, because it arises only from the contact of sense-faculty and its object, which

is confined to the present moment. But if perception and its object are simultaneous since there is a fixation between cognition and its object, there is no successive occurrence of cognition.[31]

To this Mādhyamika critique, Vātsyāyana argued that the role of *pramāṇa* need not be fixed to the present moment as long as it is fixed to the syntactical category, such as, the instrumental case.[32] A musical instrument, for instance, can be *pramāṇa* for producing the sound of a tune, but the sound itself can be *pramāṇa* for identifying the instrument which is being played.[33] It is up to the speaker's intention that one thing can become a *pramāṇa* at one time and a *prameya* at another time respectively in different contexts.[34] In support of this defense, Vātsyāyana further argued that *pramāṇa* and *prameya* are equally instrumental to realization of action (*kiryāsādhana*), and yet the former has a distinction (*kiryāviśeṣa*) as a means of cognition (*upalabdhisādhana*), whereas the latter, its object (*upalabdhiviśeśa*). Thus, the point of confrontation between the Naiyāyika and Nāgārjuna was whether *pramāṇa* and *prameya* are fixed within a given syntactical context, and whether they reciprocate their functional identities within one and the same context. There is an obvious categorial difference between the two propositions. I shall briefly make this point clearer.

In the *Vigrahavyāvartanī*, Nāgārjuna applies two types of dialectic

---

[31]*Nyāyasūtram* II. i. 8-11; Kashi Sanskrit Series Vol. 43 (1942), II. 52. 3:
pratyakṣādīnām aprāmāṇyam traikālyāsiddheḥ /8
pūrvaṃ hi pramāṇasiddhau nendriyārthasannikarṣāt pratyakṣotpattiḥ /9
paścātsiddhau na pramāṇebhyaḥ prameyasiddhiḥ //10
yugapatsiddhau pratyarthaniyatatvāt kramvṛttitvābhāvo buddhīnām /11

[32] *Nyāyabhāṣya* II. i. 8-11 (*Ibid.*, pp. 53-4):
samākhyāhetos traikālyayogāt tathābhūtā samākhyā / .... *pramito 'nenārthaḥ pramīyate pramāsyata iti pramāṇam* /
pramītaṃ pramīyate pramāsyata iti ca prameyam/
traikālyānabhyanujñāne ca vyavahārānupapattiḥ/
Nyāyabhāṣyam II. i. 16 (*Ibid.*, p. 57): *tathā ca kārakaśabdā nimittavaśāt samāveśena vartanta iti*/ . . *kārakaśabdaś caivaṃ pramāṇaṃ prameyam iti*/ *sa ca kārakadharmaṃ na hātum arhati*/ *NBh* II. i. 19 (*Ibid.*, pp. 58-60).

[33] *NBh* II. i. 15 (*Ibid.*, pp. 56):
śabdād ātodyasiddhitvāt iti/ *yathā paścāt siddhena śabdena pūrvasiddham ātodyam anumīyate*/ *sādhyaṃ ca ātodyam, sādhanaṃ ca śabdaḥ* . . . /

[34]*Nbh*. II. i. 15 (*Ibid.*):
pramāṇaṃ prameyam iti ca samākhyā samāveśena varttate samākhyānimittavaśāt/ *samākhyānimittaṃ tūpalabdhisādhanaṃ pramāṇam upalabdhaviṣayaś ca prameyam iti*/ *yadā ca upalabdhiviṣayaḥ kvacid upalabdhisādhanaṃ bhavati tadā pramāṇaṃ prameyam iti caiko 'rtho 'bhidhīyate*/

arguments, one of which may be called the analytic method since it is based on the Abhidharmist causal concept of *hetupratyayatā*.[35] This method has one single purpose, namely, to reduce every entity to its constituent elements and thereby to make known the nominalistic nature of every object and universal. It is intended to repudiate the Naiyāyika notion of *śabda* postulated as possessing its self-identifying principle (*svabhāva*) and linguistic efficiency. Nāgārjuna argues that there is no essential being in a linguistic utterance (*śabda*) because it arises out of multiple material factors (*mahābhūta*) and human anatomical efforts.[36] The genesis of vocal symbols as thus analyzed could dismiss an uncritical belief in the existence of a core substance (*svahbāva*) but may not be able to do so with linguistic efficiency evidenced in communication.

Nāgārjuna, however, switches here to the second type, *reductio-ad-absurdum* argument, pointing to a categorially different dimension with which the Buddhist in general was concerned. When we question whether something really is or is not, we generally resort to the criterion of its cognizability, namely, whether it can be perceived or not. This initial type of demonstration can be accomplished by such an empirical criterion, but not the case of linguistic efficiency, because it involves cognitive processes in which a speaker arouses a similar reaction in the listener's mind as that which is aroused by an actual sequence of words itself. Communication is nothing but a parallel occurrence of similar cognitive processes in the minds of the two people. Nāgārjuna must have considered the case of linguistic efficiency in above terms.

Thus, the difference between the two schoolmen was whether linguistic efficiency derives from the grammtico-linguistic rules and postulates with which the Naiyāyika aligned the nature and function

---

[35] As shown in Note 37 here, Nāgārjuna analyzes a composite into its constiuents, i.e., direct (*hetu*) and indirect (*pratyaya*) causes, and consisThe Vigrahavyvartanī of Naāgārjuna with the author's commentary, Edited by E.H. Johnston and Arno,d Cunst; tently refers to the absence of an entity in each of them or both or outside them. *Vigraha*. 1 [Cf. Nāgārjuna's autocommentary, an edition by Johnston and Kunst, *Mélanges Chinois et Buddhiques* IX, 1951, pp. 99-152, especially, p. 10]:

na hi bīje hetubhūte 'kuro 'sti, na pṛthivyaptejovāyoādīnām ekaikasmin pratyayasaṃjñite, na pratyayaeṣu samagreṣu, na ca hetupratyaya-sāmagryām, na hetupratyaya-vinirmuktaḥ na pṛtageva ca /

[36] *Ibid.*,

tad api hetau nāsti mahābhūteṣu samprayukeṣu viprayukteṣu vā, pratyayeṣu nāsty uraḥkaṇṭhauṣṭhājihvādantamūlatālunanāsikāmūrdha-prabhṛtiṣu yatneṣu, ubhayasāmagryāṃ nāssti, hetupratyayavinirmuktaṃ pṛthag eva ca nāsti /

of *pramāṇas*, or whether it derives from the more fundamental epistemic dimension in which sense faculties and incoming external stimuli are supposed to interact to create subsequent logico-linguistic mental processes. Such ultimate factual dimension cannot be gauged by an empirical cognition. From this point of view, Nāgārjuna's method of dialectic, especially in the sense of *reductio-ad-absurdum* argument, can be justifiably accepted in view of creating self-contradiction in the level of propositional assertions.

Although Nāgārjuna gives no clear hint about the formula of *anvaya* and *vyatireka* in his dialectic, it is possible to detect them from the way he manipulates propositions for inducing the dialectical context. By dialectical context, I mean a necessary condition in which both referential variables of *sapakṣa* and *vipakṣa* ought to be simultaneously present in one and the same spatio-temporal sphere, thus necessarily creating total contradiction. In the *Vigraha-vyāavartanī* (*kārikās* 31-324), Nāgārjuna initially brings up a dilemmatic question as to whether a *pramāṇa,* say a perception, is self-understood. If not, there should be a need of another set of *pramāṇas* to understand the initial set of cognitions, and so on *ad infinitum.*[37] In responding to this charge, the Naiyāyika introduced the metaphor of a candle's flame that can illumine an object as well as itself in order to support their point of view that a *pramāṇa* is self-understood. The light of a candle has a self-reflexive apprehension (*svasaṃveda*), because the light illumines itself as well as others.[38] In this context, it is possible to formulate two concomitant propositions: (1) "p" = 'light' "illumines itself" and (2) "q" = 'it' "illumines others."

Now, Nāgārjuna matches up the metaphor of 'light', which constitutes an entity 'x' of the class of *sapakṣa*, with another metaphorical entity 'dark' as an entity 'y' of the class of *vipakṣa.* 'Dark' is supposed to function in obstructing the light's illumination against others as well as itself, thus formulating the contrapositive concomitance as "–q•–p." This means that, as an opposite entity of light, 'dark' obstructs illumination against others as well as itself. It is a stroke of ingenuity with Nāgārjuna that he creates a

---

[37] *Vigraha.* kārikās 31-32:
yadi ca pramāṇatas te teṣāṃ teṣāṃ prasiddhir arthānām/
*teṣāṃ punaḥ prasiddhiṃ būhi kathaṃ te pramāṇaānām//*31
anyair yadi pramāṇaiḥ pramāṇasiddhir bhavet tad anvasthā/
*nādehḥ siddhis tatrāsti naiva madhyasya nāntasya//*32

[38] *Vigraha.* kārikās 35:
yadi ca svātmānam ayaṃ tvad vaacanena prakāśayaty agniḥ/
*param iva nanv ātmānaṃ paridhakṣyaty api hutāśaḥ//*35

dialectical context by juxtaposing 'light' and 'dark' in reference to one and the same spatio-temporal sphere, because, in convention, 'light' and 'dark' are taken for granted to encounter at some point, establishing a contact. The following is a simplified translation of *kārikās* 36 through 39 accompanied by my two supplementary arguments on the left side column and their symbolic notation on the right side column.[39]

kārikā 37. *Anvaya* and *Vyatireka* Co-present:

Where Total contradiction resulting:..(x){p(x)•q(x)}.• (y){–q(y)•–p(y)}
Lght 'x' illumines itself and others: ....(x) {p (x)•q(x)}
Dark 'y' also obstructs both from illumination:...(y){–q(y)•–p(y)}

k. 37. *Anvaya* Only (*Vyatireka* negated):

Wherever light 'x' illumines itself and others.........(x){ p(x)•q(x) }
No dark is supposed to remain in operation....–[(y) { (–q(y)•–p(y) }]
How can light illumine anything?....................(xy) {p (xy)•q (xy)}.

Supplement: *Vyatireka* Only (*Anvaya* negated):

Wherever dark 'y' obstructs lights from both..........(y){(–q(y)•–p(y)}
No light is supposed to be capable of illumining..........–[(x){p(x)•q(x)}]
How can light illumine anything?.....................(yx){–q(yx)•–p(yx)}

K. 38. *Anvaya* and *Vyatireka* Co-present:

Does llight illumine dark at its moment of arising?.........(x){p(x)•q(x)}
No, light does not reach it from the beginning..........(y){–q(y)•–p(y)}
Total contradiction resulted:............(x){p(x)•q(x)}.• (y){–q(y)•–p(y)}

k. 39. *Anvaya* Only (*Vyatireka* negated)

If light illuimines dark without reaching it.................(x){p(x)•q(x)}
No dark is supposed to remain in operation.......–[(y){–q(y)•–p(y)}]
This light is supposed to illumine all the world......(xy){p(xy)•q(xy)}

Supplement. *Vyatireka* Only (*Anvaya* negated)

---

[39] *Vigraha*. kārikās 37-39:
yadi ca svaparātmānau tvad vacanena prakāśyayaty agniḥ/
pracchādayiṣyati tamaḥ svaparātmānau hutāśa iva // 36
nāsti tamaś ca jvalane yatra ca tiṣṭhati parātmani jvalanaḥ/
kurute kathaṃ prakāśaṃ sa hi prakāśo 'ndhakāravadhaḥ// 37
utpadyamāna eva prkāśayati agnir ity asadvādaḥ/
utpadyamāna eva prāpnoti tamo na hi hutāśaḥ// 38
aprāpto 'pi jvalano yadi vā punar andhakāram upahanyāt/
sarveṣu lokadhātuṣu tamo 'y.am iha saṃsthito hanyāt// 39

If dark here destroys light without reaching it............(y) {(–q(y)•–p(y)}
No light is supposed to be capable of illumining.......–[(x){p(x)•q(x)}]
This dark is supposed to obstruct light in all the world....(x){–q(yx)•–p(yx)}

The formula expressed in *kārikās* 36 and 38 equally read as: Wherever light 'x' illumines itself and others (which means "p•q"), darkness 'y' also obstructs illumination from both (which means "–q•–p"). It is obvious that this predicament is created by an unexpected contradiction implied in our logical and linguistic convention, and that this is suddenly disclosed in the dialectical context when two mutually opposite entities, i.e., light and dark are juxtaposed over the same sphere and moment of illumination. Since an interaction of *pramāṇa* and *prameya* is an *a-priori* condition for any form of cognition, there is no sophistry in this dialectical context, which, however, efficiently demonstrates the fact that our linguistic expression, such as "light illumines darkness," has no independent referential object, except the two entities totally identified. This peculiar absence of a referential object is further demonstrated in the subsequent *Kārikās*. Of the *Kārikās* 37 and 39 as well as my two supplements, it is logically correct to think that, being mutually exclusive, light and darkness cannot be found at the same space and time, and yet leads to an absurdity that the phenomenon of illumination is unaccounted.

Although it is not detectable in linguistic expression, the symbolic notation for these *kārikās* reveals two significant insights behind their apparent absurdity: (1) that the affirmative formula: (xy){p(xy)•q(xy)}, and the negative one (yx){–q(yx)•–p(yx)}, are equally derived through negation of their respective contraposition; and (2) that despite the fact that the variable 'x' and 'y' are mutually exclusive (*sapakṣa* and *vipakṣa*), they are co-present in both phenomena, exchanging their natures and functions to make their illumination or its obstruction asserted. It follows that there is only one condition for the fact of illumination, such that 'x' and 'y' are identical while at the same time different. This amounts to saying that they could reciprocally assume each other's nature! In support of my foregoing demonstration I shall quote a passage from *Vaidalyaprakaraṇa*, especially, Nāgārjuna's auto-commentary on the Sūtra 2:[40]

---

[40] Cf. S. Yamaguchi: "Nāgārjuan's Śāstra on the Nyāya School *Vaidalyaprakaraṇa*, (Shōrigakuha ni taisuru Ryūju no Ronshō I)." *Buddhist Studies* (*Bukkyō Kenkyū*), IV, 2(1927), 243. Also, Y. Kajiyama (ed): "The Vaidalyaprakaraṇa of Nāgārjuna," "Tibetan passage in the appendix; *Miscellanea Indologica Kiotiensia*, Nos. 6-7 (1965), 134 (16-22).

> *Pramāṇa* and *prameya* cannot exist by themselves since they interact. (*sūtra* 2) When there is a *prameya*, a *pramāṇa* becomes a (real) *pramāṇa*, or when there is a *pramāṇa*, a *prameya* becomes a (real) *prameya*. (Thus) the *pramāṇa* is established by (the function of) *premeya*, and the *prameya* by (the function of) *pramāṇa*. Thus, by being mutually dependent, each one obtains its own existence as *prameya* or *pramāṇa*. Therefore (one and the same) *pramāṇa* becomes both and so does *prameya*. Thus, *pramāṇa* and prameya are established upon reciprocal dependence (*apekṣāsiddhi*) and are brought into existence through mutual dependence (*anyonyotpādaka*). Therefore, *pramāṇa* cannot be established independently.

§6 CONCLUSION

It is our common experience that in order to have successful communication between two people, proposing an identical statement is not sufficient because it cannot ascertain whether they equally had the same referential object in mind. Indian logicians in ancient and classical periods considered that at least two statements were necessary for making this examination possible. Here, however, Hindu and Buddhist logicians disputed as to the logical operation of *anvaya* and *vyatireka* which underlie the respective concomitant statements as well as the object of inferential reasoning and demonstration. Hindu logicians maintained that the business of logic is to deal with abstract entities and relations which they regarded as real on the basis of grammtico-linguistic rules and postulates. Buddhist logicians, on the other hand, regarded undifferentiable dynamic moments alone as real and the business of logic as determining the way in which they would be translated into our static construction of the world. Buddhist logicians did not recognize *śabda* as an independent *pramāṇa* and included it in inference (*anumāna*). This theoretical development was initiated in the Nāgārjunian critique of logico-linguistic convention. If the real is momentary and is bound to disappear upon its very appearance, the very coming into being is contradictory to its simultaneous going to non-being. Nāgārjuna's dialectical treatment of the metaphor of illumination seems to have contributed to the clarification of this essential self-contradiction, of which I consider that the following three points are of primary importance:

1. That any given moment of consciousness is ultimately dualistic

comprising both *anvaya* and *vyatireka* processes with reference to their respective variables;

2. That these variables, respectively representing the classes of *sapakṣa* and *vipakṣa*, are invariably co-present in consciousness exchanging their functions reciprocally;

3. That every concomitant assertion "p•q" or negation"–q•–p" is accompanied by the exclusion of its contraposition.

I believe that these points are self-explanatory in ascertaining the influence which the Nāgārjunian method of refutation exercised upon the theoretical development of Buddhist logicians.

The Mādhyamika method of refutation as expressed above is neither nihilistic nor hostile to our convention but reveals how the deductive force of the mind is generated through the *anvaya* and *vyatireka* operations to sharpen philosophical and logical antithesis at the referential level. At the same time, however, they seem also to show us some significant way in which we may accomplish our freedom of consciousness over any doctrinal and ideological antithesis. Consider the fact that both *anavya* and *vyatireka* operations sharpen philosophical and logical antithesis at the referential level. At the same time, however, they seem also to show us some significant way in which we may accomplish our freedom of consciousness over any doctrinal and ideological antithesis. Considering the fact that both *anavya* and *vyatireka* were originally derived from the grammarians' technical term usage, I think it is of a great interest to see why Buddhist masters, such as Nāgārjuna, regarded the type of critical examination of human convention as an essential path to their goal of religious emancipation. In this paper, I have covered some of the points once again which were already treated in my preceding articles published elsewhere, hoping that this would more systematically clarify the theoretical basis which justifies my thesis that the logical principle of *anvaya* and *vyatireka* is crucial to the nature and function of Mādhyamika dialectic, and also that the Mādhyamika treatment of human convention in turn contributed to the Buddhist refinement of logical thoughts and systems.

ARTICLE FIVE

Ābhidharmika Logical Crisis and Mādhyamika Dialectical Solution[1]

§1 Introduction

The term *'madhyamaka'* generally indicates whatever is centered between two opposing extremes, i.e., the medial; but within Buddhist usage, it denotes the insight and practice of the Middle Way (*madhyamā-pratipad*). In the developmental history of Buddhist Doctrine, this fundamental concept evolved through two major stages, passing from the Ābhidharmika to the Mādhyamika[2] school. The *Kathāvatthu* preserved in Theravādin Abhidharma literature clearly demonstrates a crisis within early Buddhist Doctrine, a 'logical deadlock' resulting from failure to establish a clear distinction between trans-empirical *dharmas* (psycho-physical elements) and the empirical *pudgala* (*person*) in Theravādin-*versus*-Pudgalavādin dispute. The purpose of this paper is primarily to elucidate the nature of this logical deadlock and present the Madhyamaka solution, an innovative dialectic introduced by Nāgārjuna (ca. second century Western Era).[3]

---

[1] The original paper was given under the title "The Mādhyamika and The Future" at the International Buddhist Conference sponsored by Dhammakāya Foundation, Bangkok, Thailand, Febrauary 1990. It was published as part of the Conference Proceedings, *Buddhism Into The Year 2000,* Dhammakāya Foundation, 1994.

[2] In this paper both *'madhyamaka'* and *'mādhyamika'* are used with some different meanings. 'madhyamaka' signifies 'the middle way' with a connotation of Buddhist doctrine, whereas *'mādhyamika'* refers to a group of Buddhists who advocated the doctrine of the middle and especially those who resorted to the critical method of dialectic.

[3] At least, four or five different groups of texts, belonging to different periods, were ascribed to the name of Nāgārjunas: (1) the author of the definitive dialectical texts, *Mūla-madhyamaka-kārikā-śāstra*, *Vigraha-vyāvartanī,* and a number of dialectical treatises, as well as the author of the *Suhṛllekha* (the *Friendly Epistles*) addressed to a monarch and traditionally identified as belonging to the house of Śātavāhana, and the *Ratnāvalī (the String of Pearls)* addressed to another ruler of the mid 2nd century, who might have been Rudradāman, Śaka Satrap of Ujjayinī; (2) the scholar trained in the Sarvāstivādin Ābhidharmika tradition who then turned to Mahāyāna and wrote the encyclopaedic *Mahāprajñāpāramito-padeśaśāstra*, as well as the commentary on t he *Daśabhūmika-vibhāṣā-sāstra*;

This paper, however, has a secondary prospect, because the way ancient Buddhist thinkers resolved the said crisis was not an isolated event of the past but has its direct implication with our contemporary Buddhist endeavor in the effort of preserving not only Buddhist tradition but also all human cultures as a whole. In general, every religious tradition has been concerned with the linkage between the spiritual and secular domain in their own terms. Today, however, each religion is not only facing all other faiths and varied ways of life different from its own, but also altogether facing an inescapable trend of secularization, the process that has been resulted from rapid industrialization and social modernization working hand-in-hand to transform traditional society and culture. The teaching and practice of religion can no longer elude the challenge posed by these powerful forces of social and cultural change.

In the Buddhist world, the Theravādin and Mahāyāna traditions hitherto have continued to uphold somewhat different ways to link the spiritual and secular domain, but with a growing awareness of the forces of change, leaders in both traditions, whether professional monks or lay devotees, have found it necessary to review old forms of expression and seek new approaches so as to accommodate on-going change with a new set of appropriate meanings and directives. It is my contention that while learning the problem ancient Buddhists faced and the way they resolved it, we are able to renew a long overdue critical examination of the existing forms of linkage between the spiritual and the secular, whereby to advance a step toward the reform that is necessary to the future growth of Buddhism and a step toward the unification of the two traditions through the creation of a viable avenue of communication and mutual cooperation.

Moreover, the task has grown today because of the physical presence of the Buddhist tradition expanding globally, moving beyond

---

(3) the author of some Tantric texts, who was known as a Tantric siddha, and called Bhadanta Nāgārjunācārya in a 7th century inscription discovered a century ago in South India. (4) In addition to these figures, there is another Nāgārjuna whom Kalhaṇa (ca. 12th century), author of the *Dynastic History of Kāśmīra Kings Rājataraṅgṇī*, recorded as a confidant of the Kuṣāṇa ruler Kaniṣka of the first century, together with the famous Buddhist poet Aśvaghoṣa, and was active in the propagation of Buddhism in Kāśmīra region. [Cf. L. M. Joshi, "Life and Times of the Madhyamaka Philosopher Nāgārjuna," *Maha Bodhi* 73, 1(1965), 15-16; Ruegg, D. Seyfort: "Towards a Chronology of the Madhyamaka School," *Indological and Buddhist Studies*, Bibliotheca Indo-Buddhica No.27, Delhi: Indian Books Centre, 1982, esp. pp. 505-509.]

the geographical confines of the past, and reaching to all parts of the world. In the recent decades, Buddhist tradition has acquired increasing respect as an equal among the other religious traditions of the West. If the Buddhist tradition as a whole, Theravādin and Mahāyāna, can hope to offer a service to humanity on global terms, it will do so through examination and assessment of this issue of the linkage between spiritual transcendence and secular engagement by introducing new directions and new forms of expression for the period to come.

§2 COMMUNICATION-BREAKDOWN AS EXPRESSED IN THE *KATHĀVATTHU*[4]

It is generally believed that during the history of Buddhism in India there was no direct contact between the Theravādin tradition dominant in Southeast Asia, and the Mahāyāna tradition transmitted and preserved in East Asia. I am obliged, however, to point out that a thread of continuity in doctrinal development existed, spanning the crisis in Theravādin orthodoxy, recorded in the *Kathāvatthu*, and the successful solution of the problem through the Madhyamaka dialectic (ca. A.D. 2nd century). I believe it is ever more relevant today to address this dialectical method as a first step in establishing communication between the Theravādin and Mahāyāna traditions.

The compilation of the *Kathāvatthu*, attributed to Moggaliputta-tissa,[5] who chaired the third Buddhist Council (ca. mid-third century

---

[4] Edited by A. C. Taylor for PTS, 1894-97; reprint by Routledge & Kegan Paul, 1979. According to Mrs. Rhys-Davids, the text was compiled when the contents of, at least, parts of the *Dhammasaṅgaṇi* (first book), *Vibhaṅga* (second one) and *Paṭṭhāna* (seventh one) of the Abhidhamma Piṭaka were already established as orthodox Buddhist doctrine. [Cf. Prefatory Note, *Points of Controversy or Subjects of Discourse*, being a Translation of the *Kathāvatthu*, London: PTS, Luzac & Co., 1960.] In his commentary *Kathāvatthu-ppakaraṇa-aṭṭhakathā*, however, Buddhaghoṣa conveys the tradition, stating that the *Kathāvatthu* was compiled as a pre-emptive measure of refuting heresies (*āyatilakkhaṇa*), this having been after the compilation of the *Puggala-Paññatti* in succession to the *Dhammasaṅgani*, *Vibhaṅga*, and *Dhātukathā*. [Cf. *Kathāvatthuppakaraṅa-Aṭṭhakathā* included in *Pañcappakaraṅa-aṭṭhakathā* named *Paramaṭṭhadīpanī* and critically edited by N. A. Jayawickrama (Text Series No. 169); London: PTS, Routledge & Kegan Paul, 1979, p. xv.]

[5] According to the *Dīpavaṃsa* (The Chronicle of Ceylon), Moggaliputta-tissa, a councilor to King Aśoka, ordained the king's son, prince Mahinda, in Aśoka's sixth regnal year (262 B.C.E.). After retirement, upon the king's request, Moggaliputta-tissa attempted to reform the Saṅgha which had been unable to conduct the *Uposatha* meeting for seven years due to

B.C.), was, perhaps, the boldest and most courageous task ever undertaken by the editorial authors of the Pāli Abhidhamma Piṭaka. This text was translated into English as *The Points of Controversy* by Mrs. Rhys-Davids[6] and is known as the record of extensive doctrinal disputes exchanged among various Buddhist schools on standard logical proceedings. I say that this undertaking was the "boldest and most courageous task," precisely because those points of controversy, left unresolved as they were, could have undermined the religious authority of the orthodoxy and the position of the editors themselves by allowing leeway for the espousal of heretic views. In this connection, I am obliged to emphasize again the significance and relevance of the dialectical method in establishing communication between Theravādin and Mahāyāna traditions, now more than ever before.

We all know that Buddhist doctrine fundamentally consists of the insights of the Four Holy Truths (*catur-ārya-satya*), Dependent Origination (*pratītyasamutpāda*), Five Aggregates (*pañca-skandha*), Twelve Bases of Cognition (*dvādaśa-āyatana*) and Eighteen Categories of Reality (*dvādaśa-dhātu*). The very reason that the metaphysical principle of 'self' (*atta* or *ātma*) was rejected in Buddhism in terms of *anattā* was due to the insight that an individual person (*puggala* or *pudgala*) is an organized aggregation of the five Skandhas (*upādāya-skandha-s*). Hence, the psycho-physical elements of the five Skandhas (i.e., those categories of *rūpa*, *vedanā*, *saṃjñā*, *saṃskārā* and *vijñāna*) were regarded more real than an individual person [*puggala*], because the latter is nothing but a product of multiple psycho-physical elements organized through their direct and indirect causal networks (*hetu-pratyaya-tā*) and hence, merely a pseudo-entity which has been given a linguistic name. Viewing every object of experience as arising from the causality of dependent origination (*pratītyasamutpāda*) was the essence of the doctrine of right view (*samyag-dṛṣṭi*), and training oneself to see things as they really are (*yathābhūtaṃ*) was the essence of the practice of the middle way (*madhyamā-pratipad*).

---

obstruction by evil-minded monks; he did this by organizing and chairing a council consisting of a thousand qualified elders. The council was completed over a nine month period during Aśoka's seventeenth regnal year (251 B.C.E.); Moggaliputta-tissa was then at 72 years of age. He is also known to have compiled the *Kathāvatthu*, promoted the establishment of the Kāśmīra-based Saṅgha, and to have become the first patriarch of the Dharmaguptaka school.

6 See Note 1 above; PTS Text Series V, jointly translated by Shwe Zan Aung and Caroline Augusta Foley Rhys-Davids, originally published 1915.

Thesis: 'Vocal word' [śabda] is permanent..................*śabdo nityaḥ*
Reason: because it is audible (or communicable)[10]........*śravaṇatvāt*
Example: just as vocal word is (that is audible)........*śabdatvavat*

This is an excellent example of communication-breakdown between two different cultures or systems of thought. One schoolman presupposes that from the empiricist point of view, "whatever is produced is impermanent." Since a vocal word (a set of sounds forming a symbol) is a product of human effort, it is therefore impermanent; just as a pot which is once shaped eventually breaks down, a word disappears no sooner than it is uttered. The other schoolman, however, presupposes from the transcendentalist point of view that a word-symbol transmits a command to another person, eliciting its meaning, i.e., the essential ideation which the word-symbol is supposed to elicit. For him, therefore, a vocal word ought to be transcendent of space and time, and hence, permanent. Despite one and the same subject term '*śabda*,' the two different presuppositions lead the two schoolmen to the drawing of mutually contradictory predications: "is impermanent" and "is permanent."

In Indian logical terminology, the logical linkage between reason and thesis, (namely, "whatever is a product is impermanent" and "whatever is audible is permanent,") is called 'pervasion' or 'concomitance between two terms' (*vyāpti*). The very contradiction manifested in the two theses, which are induced from the two different logical relations (*vyāpti*), despite the same subject term, obviously caused communication-breakdown. Thus, when two people respectively hold different presuppositions or logical linkages due to their respective cultural upbringings, this difference is likely to lead to a breakdown in communication between the two. Take the case

---

[10] The Mīmāṃsā schoolmen, along with the Vaiyākaraṇas (Grammarians), postulated the transcendental existence of ideas and concepts in a similar manner to Plato's postulate of the world of eternal ideas. The schoolmen favored a *vox archetypa* rather than the *vox ectypa* which the Naiyāyika favored. Bhartṛhari, a grammarian of the 6th century, theorized three stages of verbal sound [*trayī vāc*], through which the archetypical essence of a word, initially abiding as supreme consciousness [*śabdabrahman*] (.i.e., the stage of *paśyantī*), subsequently becomes an awakening consciousness accompanied by a subtle movement (i.e., that of *madhyamā*, where the eternal word [sphoṭa] appears), and finally, manifests itself as an audible verbal sound by taking its phenomenal expression (i.e., that of *vaikharī*). Any audible sound-word is therefore regarded as carrying its paradigmatic meaning by virtue of its communicability to everyone at any time within a linguistic community. Cf. *Vākya-padīya:* Kārikā 143 (Kāṇḍa 1): *paśyantī, madhyamā,* and *vaikharī*. K. Kunjuni Raja parallels these stages respectively with sphoṭa, prākṛta-dhvani, and vaikṛta-dhvani. [K.K. Raja: Indian Theories of Meaning, Adyar Library and Research Center, 1963.]

of Moslem-Hindu communal violence in India, that of Moslem-Jewish violence in Lebanon, or that of ethnic and religious confrontation in Northern Ireland, as well as in Balkan regions; the root cause of human tragedy and disaster can, indeed, be identified as the manifestation of communication-breakdown resulting from different cultural and religious presuppositions. In this context, I am convinced that the task of establishing communication between Buddhist and non-Buddhist cultures and religions can be carried out in a manner similar to that in which the said logical dispute was resolved.

Returning to the logical problem of *Kathāvatthu*, it is apparent in the previous example that, in order to accomplish communication between two people, one party's logical linkage from reason to conclusion ought to be a universal kind that can also apply to the other party. When one lets a group of people to know an outbreak of fire over a distant hill, one ought to show the presence of a smoke over that hill. If the causal linkage of smoke and fire is common knowledge to the people, they will immediately grasp the conclusion of an outbreak of fire on that hill. This would mean that they are able to judge whether or not the referred linkage of smoke and fire is possible in the area in question. I can now sum up the basic rules of logic which make communication between two people possible:[11]

1. The logical or causal linkage of two terms (e.g., smoke to fire) must be commonly known to both parties with reference to a class of objects, like a kitchen, where both smoke and fire are always observed to occur together.

2. The contrary negative linkage, "When there is no fire, there is no smoke," must be equally known to the same people with reference to another class of objects, like a lake, where neither fire nor smoke is possible at any time.

If these dual conditions, which can safeguard our thinking process from falling into error, are not met, communication-breakdown again ensues. When a public argument takes place between two parties, the thesis of whichever party that fails to comply with the

[11] These examples are given in the *Nyāyapraveśakasūtram*: Gaekwad Oriental Series, 38 (1930), pp.3-4. Although strictly speaking, 'śabdo anityaḥ kṛtakatvāt ghaṭavat,' is a Vaiśeṣika presupposition [*siddhānta*], since the Naiyāyika accepted the metaphysical system in toto, it is presented as the Naiyāyika view of language. Cf. A. Kunst: "The Concept of the Principle of Excluded Middle in Buddhism," Rocznik Orientalistyczny XXI, (1957), p. 146.

foregoing dual rules is invalid and hence failed in defeat. The logical deadlock recorded in the *Kathāvatthu* was due to failure of both parties with respect to the said logical rules, thus mutually invalidating their intended theses. The initial dispute quoted in the *Kathāvatthu* was the Theravādin's refutation of the Pudgalavādin's heresy that the '*puggala*' (an individual person) is a semi-trans-empirical entity.

The *Kathāvatthu* logical argument is so repetitive and intricate as a proceeding, any one would easily be lost amidst unfamiliar method and expression. However, I found its proceeding as consistent and meaningful with respect to its singular objective, namely, the linkage between the trans-empirical psycho-physical elements (*dharmas*) and the empirical person (*pudgala*). The linkage of spirituality and convention was thus epitomized by the said problem of linkage between *dharmas* and *pudgala*. In order to refute the Pudgalavādin, the Theravādin orthodoxy initially prepared two-fold concomitance for their own propositions in complying with the logical rules.

1. 'x' (a subject term) is known as a genuinely real thing;[12]
2. 'x' is known in the same way as a genuinely real thing is known.[13]

These two statements can be respectively given notation as "p(x)" and 'q(x)." Here, the Theravādin was referring as the value of 'x' to a trans-empirical *dharma* (such as, *rūpa*, *vedanā*, etc.) in the Skandha categories, believing that these two qualifying propositions could distinguish clearly any entity which belongs to the trans-empirical domain from any entity which belongs to the empirical, such as a *puggala*. The Theravādin wanted to use this concomitance as their criterion to test the thesis of the Puggalaādin's contension on pudgala in notation as a variable 'y' here.

The Theravādin questioned the Puggalavādin, asking: "Is '*puggala*' known as a genuinely real thing?" The Puggalavādin replied

---

[12] These two rules are a paraphrasing of the valid syllogistic principles of '*anvaya* and *vyatireka*,' or 'similar and dissimilar instantiation' or 'method of agreement and that of difference.' Cf. Th. Stcherbatsky, Buddhist Logic, Vol I, pp. 283-287. [Śaṅkarasvāmin [probably Dignāga's disciple] defined these two rules in his concise *Nyāyapraveśaka-sūtram* as /*sapakśe sattva*/ *vipakṣe 'sattvam*/ "two concomitant propositions ought to be jointly verified by the class of similar instances" and "the same propositions equally falsified by the class of dissimilar instances." [Gaekwad Oriental Series vol. 33, 1930, p.1]

[13] '*saccikaṭṭho paramaṭṭho tato so (dhammam) upalabbhati saccikaṭṭhaparamaṭṭhena*'

affirmatively, "Yes, it is so known" [notation as 'p(y),' 'puggala' being a value of 'y']. The Theravādin again questioned the Puggalavādin, asking: "Is '*puggala*' known in the same way as a genuinely real thing (i.e., a *dhamma*) is known?" The Puggalavādin cannot give a similar affirmative reply, hence, "No, not so" [notation as '–q(y)']. With this expected negative answer, the Theravādin declares that the Puggalavādin has suffered defeat by failure to comply with the two logical rules, quoting:

> You, Puggalavādin, are wrong, because if you affirm the first proposition as "p(y)," you ought to also affirm the second one as "q(y)," but you instead affirmed the former while negating the latter, i.e., "p(y) • –q(y)." If you are to negate the latter, you ought also to negate the former, i.e., "–q(y) • –p(y),' but you instead affirmed the former and negated the latter as "p(y) • –q(y)."[14]

Ingeniously, however, in the second round (i.e., the Pudgalavādin's rejoinder the Puggalavādin rebutted the Theravādin through similar tactics, asking: "Is '*puggala*' not known as a genuinely real thing?" The Theravādin replied, "No, it is not so known," [–p(y)]. The former again questioned the latter, asking: "Is '*puggala*' not known in the same way as a real thing is known?" Here the Theravādin could not give a similar confident reply, because the unreality of "empirical self" is known through the same trans-empirical insight in which *rūpa-dharma*, etc. are known as genuinely real thing. Hence the Theravādin was forced to reply affirmatively as: "Yes, it is not not so known in the same way" through double negation. Thus, the Puggalavādin successfully induced a defeat upon the Theravādin on the same grounds, i.e., the Theravādin's failure to complying with the logical rules in their reply as "–p(y)•q(y)." The Puggalavādin censured the Theravādin, saying:

> If you, Theravādin, negate the first proposition [that is our thesis], you ought also to negate the second one as "–p(y) • –q(y),"

---

[14] In Indian logic, logical relation was not conceived in terms of comprehension of the minor term or proposition by the major, but in terms of concomitance, concurrence, or accompaniment of two terms or propositions, although the latter relation can be translated into the former—comprehension of a minor universal by a larger one. Hence, a conditional statement: "if 'p,' then 'q'", was not conceived in terms of comprehension expressible by the 'containment of' symbol '⊃,' but, strictly speaking, in terms of conjunction expressible by the conjunctive symbol of ' • .' Here, the containment symbol is used with an intention to express the conditional force of the logical rule, and the argument in question ought to be understood as: "'p• –q' is false, because 'p • q.'"

but you instead, while negating the first, affirmed the second as "–p(y) • q(y)." If, on the other hand, you wish to affirm the second proposition, you ought also to affirm the first one as well, as "q(y) • p(y)," but you instead, while negating the first, affirmed the second as "–p(y) • q(y)." Since you affirmed the second while negating the first, you failed to accomplish your thesis.

The Puggalavādin further proceeded to press the Theravādin in the third round (*niggaha*: refutation), the fourth round (*upanaya*: application of the Theravādin's reasoning to their own case), and then the fifth round, the conclusion (*niggamana*).[15]

Since the beginning of this century, Buddhist scholars have long been puzzled over the nature and origin of the logical method which the pre-Classical Ābhidharmikas applied to the proceeding of their public debate. Relying on her Burmese co-translator's analysis, Mrs. Rhys-Davids briefly discussed the nature of this logical method in her prefatory note to *The Points of Controversy*.[16] The analysis failed, however, to grasp the underlying logical rules of *anvaya* and *vyatireka*, thus blurring somewhat the doctrinal issue concerning the inseparable tie of the transcendent and empirical domain to the limit and the range of logical reasoning. In order to clarify the way mutual invalidation took place, I reproduce here a chart which I included in one of my articles published elsewhere.[17] Since the only variable used in the logical arguments here is the single entity '*puggala*' symbolized by 'y', it is dropped from successive notations to simplify the logical processes of the arguments.

Table of Mutual Invalidation

Theravādin *versus* Pudgalavādin
"Whether *Puggala* is Empirical or Transcendent"

---

[15] For the foregoing initial session [*Paṭhamo Niggaho*], see the *Kathāvatthu* in Pāli, *op. cit.*, pp. 2-4, where there follow the subsequent sessions, including the second refutation [No. 6 through No. 10 (*ibid.*, pp. 4-7)] and the short refutations which constitute the third, fourth, and so forth, up to eighth (*ibid.*, pp. 7-11), before proceeding to the subject of identity or difference between *puggala* and *dhammas* (*ibid.*, No. 17 onward, pp. 11f). The method in which the initial topic *puggala* is discussed in detail according to the full process of logical analysis, each discussion of a subsequent topic thereafter being progressively condensed with the understanding that the framework follows the analysis of *Puggalakathā*, and is called *peyyālamukha* or 'successive discourse.' Jayawickrama, *op. cit*, p. xviii.

[16] *Op.cit.*, pp. xlvii-li.

[17] Cf. Ichimura: "A Study of the Mādhyamika Method of Refutation, Especially of its Affinity to that of *Kathāvatthu*," *Journal of International Association of Buddhist Studies*, III, 2(1980), 10-15, esp. pp.10-11.

1. Theravādin Refutation

Puggalavādin thesis 'p•–q'
is false, because 'p ⊃ q';
'p•–q' is false, because '–q ⊃–p';
Hence, the thesis 'p•–q' is false.

2. Puggalavādin Rejoinder

Theravādin refutation '–p•q'
is false, because '–p ⊃–q';
'–p • q' is false, because 'q ⊃ p,'
Hence, the refutation '–p•q' is false.

3. Puggalavādin Refutation

Theravādin's refutation '–p•q'
can be refuted, because '–p ⊃ –q.'
Theravādin's refutation '–p•q'
is false, because 'q ⊃p.'
Hence, '–p•q' can be refuted.

4. Puggalavādin Application

Our thesis 'p•–q' is not falsified;
Your refutation '–(p•–q)' is
not acceptable, because 'p⊃q'
and also because '–q ⊃ –p';
Hence, '–(p•–q)' is not acceptable.

5. Puggalavādin's Conclusion

Our thesis 'p • –q' is not refuted,
because 'p• q' is not compelled;
Your refutation –(p• –q) is not convincing,
because '–p• –q' is not compelled;
Hence 'p•q' and '–q• –p' are not convincing

The subject of dispute then moves on to the five Khandhas (*Skandha*: *rūpa*, *vedanā*, *sañjñā*, *saṃskāra*, and *vijñāna*), Twelve *Āyatanas*, Eighteen *Dhātus*, and then to the physical body (*kāya*), examining the issue of whether *puggala* is known differently or identically with respect to each set of *dhammas* in these categories.[18] Next, the subject of dispute moves to the matter of transmigration:

puggalo sandhāvati asmālokā paraṃ lokaṃ
parasmā lokā imaṃ lokan ti?
Āmantā; So puggalo pe? Na h'evaṃ vattabbe.[19]

And further to the subject of favorable (*kusala* or *kuśala*), unfavorable (*akuśala*), and indeterminate (*avyākata* or *avyākṛta*) *dhammas*, and so forth, continuing with good conduct (*kalyāṇa-kamma*) and bad conduct (*pāpaka-kamma*), supernormal powers (*ṣaḍabhiññā* or *abhijñānuyoga*), and all stages of saintly attainments, and so forth. The way in which these disputes were carried on was precisely identical, and thus, every dispute ended in logical deadlock through the same kind of mutual invalidation as encountered

[18] *Kathāvatthu* up to No.157,. p.28.
[19] *Ibid.*, up to No.169, p.34.

above, each party failing to comply with the two logical rules.

§4. SOLUTION BY THE MĀDHYAMIKA DIALECTICAL METHOD

In order to explain the nature of the Abhidharmist logical deadlock, I shall resort to the well known stock example of smoke-fire relation as briefly applied before. According to some Buddhist logicians like Śaṅkarasvāmin, the business of syllogistic inference is defined primarily as "determining the class of things in which both smoke and fire can occur, like a kitchen, a hill, a house, etc. and simultaneously the class of things in which neither fire nor smoke can ever occur, like a lake, water tank, desert, etc. These two opposite groups of things are called respectively "similar class" and dissimilar classes" (*sapakṣa* and *vipakṣa*). Observing a billow of smoke over a yonder hill and wishing to let others know that the hill is on fire, what one ought to do is to let them see the smoke and the hill, that is all needed. Thus, for valid logical inference as well as demonstration, it is indispensable to have a group of examples which corroborate the smoke-fire relationship.

Let the class of affirmative examples, say, a kitchen, etc. be a variable 'x' and that of contraposition like a lake, etc. be an opposite variable 'y.' Assuming that the linkage between smoke and fire is a well-established universal, we express this linkage by means of two concomitant propositions: "wherever a smoke is," and "there a fire is," and respectively give them a notation as "p" and "q." When these concomitant propositions "p" and "q" are applied to any one of the similar class members, say, a value of 'x' as 'kitchen (α), 'both "p' and "q' are verified as true, i.e., $(\alpha)\{p(\alpha)\bullet q(\alpha)\}$. This constitutes an affirmative corroboration, and called '*anvaya*,' meaning connection, linkage, sequence. Next, a similar operation ought to be applied to corroborate the same concomitant propositions to be tested by a variable of the dissimilar class members, say, a value of 'y' as a lake (β). This ought to result in the negation of both propositions as not true, i.e., $(\beta)\{-q(\beta)\bullet -p(\beta)\}$, which means: "neither a smoke nor a fire is to be found in the locus of a lake, and so forth. This is a contrary or negative corroboration, called '*vyatireka*,' meaning disconnection, absence of linkage or sequence.

To answer how and why these two, affirmative and negative, corroborations are necessary, it is sufficient to point out that when one wants to know whatever object through valid inference, one ought to be sure that the object in question is a member of the similar class and not a member of the dissimilar class. Otherwise, even when one observes a smoke, one may not find fire, and *vice versa*. Therefore, besides the two opposite classes of things, 'x' and 'y', the Buddhist thinkers also kept in mind that there are always two other classes of referential variables, which, however, do not serve as valid inferential condition. Let me lay down the four different classes of variables with respect to the logical universal between smoke and fire: (1) those which can be predicated as having both smoke and fire, like a kitchen, etc.[20]; (2) those which can never be predicated as having either one, separately or jointly, like a lake, a water tank, etc. As said before, these two classes of things correspond to the dual rules of valid inference as *anvaya* and *vyatireka*[21]; (3) those which can be predicated as having smoke but no fire, which can be transcribed as "p(χ) • –q(χ)"; and (4) those which can be predicated as not having smoke but having fire, which is transcribed as "q(δ)• –p(δ)."

In the light of these four classes of variables, the cause of mutual invalidation between the Theravādin and Pudgalavādin can be explained by the last two classes of variables and the two sets of concomitant propositions. It was in this way that the subject term *puggala* was thrust into the arena of public debate as an ambiguous and very upsetting topic. The Puggalavādin asserted in part that '*puggala*' is a trans-empirical entity like a *rūpa-dhamma*, while in part accepting its denial through inability to assert the

---

20 Buddhist logicians called this positive class of referential entities the class of 'similar instances' [*sapakṣa*] (which are symbolized as 'x'), and defined its function as verifying the two logically related propositions 'p • q' as true; i.e., "x has smoke" and "x has fire" are equally true [(x)p • (x)q], if 'x' is a member of the 'similar class,' such as, a kitchen, a hill, etc. This constitutes the logical criterion of *anvaya* or 'affirmative instantiation.'

21 In addition to the principle of anvaya, logically valid inference requires the principle of vyatireka or 'negative instantiation,' calling for the presence of the class of negative instances [*vipakṣe*] (which are symbolized as 'y'). Buddhist logicians defined the function of contrapositive instances as verifying the absence of concurrence of fire and smoke in any member of that class, hence simultaneously falsifying the two logically related propositions, stating that "'y' has no fire" nor does "'y' have any smoke" ['(y) –q • (y) –p']. Here 'y' is a member of the 'dissimilar class.' The presence of the contrapositive class is very important for valid logical inference as part of inductive reasoning in distinguishing the logical boundary between a group of similar entities and that of dissimilar ones. Take a hill for example.. The hill may be observed on some occasions as having smoke but no fire, and *vice versa* on some other occasions. Despite this kind of irregularity, we cannot preclude on this basis the possibility of the concurrence of smoke and fire. Thus, when we see a billow of smoke rising on the hill, it is probably correct to infer an outbreak of fire there. This probability can be asserted only when negative instances, such as, a water tank, are known as having neither fire nor smoke jointly or separately.

second proposition, i.e., 'p•–q'! Moreover, the Theravādin failed to prove that a *rūpa-dhamma* alone is real and trans-empirical, because the unreality of empirical entities can also be accomplished in a similar way. Although the Theravādin could repudiate a *puggala* as not a trans-empirical entity, the very fact that he could not repudiate the second related proposition did not clearly separate the logical boundary between *dharma* and *puggala*. In short, the Theravādin failed to clearly distinguish the status of trans-empirical *dhamma* and the status of empirical *puggala* in logical terms.

Now, I must point out that the heart of controversy between the two Hindu schools and the controversy within the Ābhidharmika schools are identical in essence. This means that although the two Hindu schoolmen began to debate on the same subject term, say, '*śabda*,' what the Nyāya logicians referred to as 'impermanent śabda is different from what the Mīmāṃsā linguists referred to as 'permanent *śabda*.' The referential discrepancy between the Theravādin and Puggalavādin is far more complicated than the logical deadlock of the Nyāya *versus* Mīmāṃsā, because the syllogistic arguments presented by the Nyāya and Mīmāṃsā schoolmen are both correct in terms of logical rules, and also because their concomitances are totally different and unrelated, (1) whatever is a product is impermanent, and (2) whatever is audible is permanent. The following chart reveals the point of discrepancy more clearly:

Naiyāyika	Mīmāṃsaka
'a' = Naiyāyika's *śabda*	'b' = Mīmāṃsaka's *śabda*
p = "whatever is a product"	π = "whatever is audible"
$-\theta$ = "is impermanent."	θ = "is permanent."

The problem arises from the fact that both parties are convinced that they are talking about one and the same subject term '*śabda*,' *although actually not*. If, however, it is assumed that both are talking about one and the same subject term, contradiction is inevitable as impermanent *versus* permanent. But since their respective statements of reason are totally unrelated, there is no way to determine their respective theses either as valid or invalid in logical terms. Buddhist logicians in general voiced that in debate, the reason statement ought to be at least agreed upon between two contesting parties. In any case, the fundamental cause of their discrepancy is cultural, the choice of a concomitance for the best of their respective interests.

Applying a similar analysis and symbolism, we have obtained the Theravādin argument referring to a *puggala* as negating the first proposition but affirming the second, i.e., "(y){ –p(y) •q(y)}," and the Pudgalavādin's argument as "(y){p(y)•–q(y)}." In order to determine the fundamental cause of their discrepancy, I shall go back to the very ambiguious statement which the Pudgalavādin quoted as the Buddha's word. The Pudgalavādin questioned the Theravādin, saying: Isn't a *pudgala* known as a genuinely real thing? and after the Theravādin replied "No," the Pudgalavādin pressed the Theravādin by saying the following:

> Was it said by the World-honored One that there is the person (*puggala*) that goes along (with an aggregation of Five *Khandhas*) for the sake of an individual's self (*atthi puggalo attahitāya paṭipanno*), and the *rūpa dhamma* (and so forth) are known in the sense of a genuinely real thing?

The Theravādin was compelled to answer affirmatively "Yes." Then the Pudgalavādin further pressed the opponent, questioning:

> "Is the *rūpa-dhamma* one thing? Is the *puggala* another?"[22]

It is clear that the ultimate cause of the discrepancy was how each of them responded to this question. In short, the discrepancy derived from their different choice out of two alternative interpretations. The Theravādin regarded *dhamma* and *puggala* as different on the ground that one is trans-empirical and another is empirical, whereas the Pudgalavādin interpreted them as identical on the ground that a *puggalo* goes along with *dhamma*, etc. It is profoundly interesting and intriguing that no official reconciliation or determination was offered within the orthodoxy despite the fact that the problem continued to haunt the tradition.

Now let us hear how and why Nāgārjuna provided the Mādhyamika solution to the mutual invalidation by way of his dialectical method. The following passages are quoted from his definitive work *Madhyamaka-kārikā-śāstra,* Chap. 10: (Examination of Fire and Fuel" (*Agnīndhana-parīkṣānāma*), which dealt with the relationship between *pudgala* and *Skandhas* (i.e., *rūpa-dharmas*, etc.). He uses the metaphor of fire and fuel, respectively exemplifying a *pudgala* and a group of Skandḥas, both of which are supposed to be simultaneously on-going affairs. The multiple psycho-physical elements of the Skandhas are meant to be fuel, while an empirical self or *pudgala* is fire. The phenomenon of combustion somehow occurs

---

[22] *Puggalo n'upalabbhati saccikaṭṭhaparamaṭṭhenāti? Vuttaṃ Bhagavatā*: *Atthi puggalo attahitāya paṭipanno, rūpañ ca upalabbhati saccikaṭṭhaparamaṭṭhenāti? Aññaṃ rūpam añño puggalo ti?*

through the contact of fuel and fire, just as the activity of a '*pudgala*' occurs along with the group of 'Skandhas.' In the said chapter, Nāgārjuna argues as follows:[23]

> If fuel is identical with fire, the fire, agent of burning, and the fuel, object being burned, would become identical. [For,] if fire is different from fuel, there should be fire without fuel. (Verse 1)
>
> [If this were so,] fire would continue to burn forever, burning without any fuel or without the meaning (necessity) of burning fuel again, and it would thus become one which has no function of burning. (V. 2)
>
> Here, if that fuel which is being burned is identical with this fire, when that fuel is being burned alone, by what agent of burning could it be burned further? (V. 3)
>
> [If fuel is different,] fire does not reach it; the unreached cannot be burned. Moreover, whatever abides unburned cannot be extinguished; being inextinguishable, it must remain, indeed, like one that has its own mark (i.e., self-existent; *svaliṅgavān*; i.e., *svabhāvatas*). (V. 5)

In this way, Nāgārjuna gradually induces a realization of the 'interdependence' of two related things in the reader's mind, but again repudiates this conception as well, quoting:[24]

> If fire depends on fuel, and fuel on fire, which one of these two [fire or fuel] should come into existence first; depending on which does fire burn fuel? (V. 8)
>
> Fire does not arise by depending on fuel, nor does fire arise without depending on fuel, nor is fuel burned depending on fire,

---

[23] *yad indhanaṃ sa ced agnir ekatvaṃ kartṛ karmaṇoḥ /*
anyaś ced indhanād agnir indhanād apy ṛte bhavet // 1
nityapradīpta eva syād apradīpanahetukaḥ /
punar ārambhavaiyarthyam evaṃ cākarmakaḥ sati // 2
tatraitasmād idhyamānam indhanaṃ bhavatīti cet /
kenedhyatām indhanaṃ tat tāvan mātram idaṃ yadā // 4
anyo na prāpsyate 'prāpto na dhakṣyaty adahan punaḥ /
na nirvāsyaty anirvāṇaḥ sthāsyate vā svaliṅgavān // 5

[24] *yadīndhanam apekṣyāgnir apekṣyāgniṃ yad indhanam /*
katarat pūrvaniḥpannaṃ yad apekṣyāgnir indhanam // 8
apekṣye 'ndhanam agnir na nānapekṣyāgnir indhanam /
apekṣyendhanam agniṃ na nānapekṣyāgnim indhaṇam // 12
āgacchaty anyato nāgnir indhane 'gnir na vidyate /
atrendhane śe am uktam gamyamānagatāgataiḥ/ 13
indhanaṃ punar agnir na nāgnir anyatra cendhanāt /
nāgnir indhanavān nāgnav indhaṇāni na teṣu saḥ // 14

> nor does it burn without depending on fire. (V. 12)
>
> Fire does not arise from anything other than itself, nor is fire found anywhere in the fuel. Of this fuel, every alternative feature has already been said just as it was examined in the passage of present, past, and future of motion.[25]
>
> Again, fuel is not fire, nor is fire found elsewhere other than fuel. Fire does not possess fuel, nor is fuel found in fire, nor is fire found in fuel. (V. 14)

Originally the concept of *pudgala* was introduced to explain the continuity of an empirical person along with the group of psycho-physical elements (*rūpa-dharmas*, etc.) which were defined as momentary (*anitya*), arising and perishing in time. The pertinent question is now: "By repudiating any linkage whatsoever between the two, what does Nāgārjuna intend to accomplish?"

Another example is to be quoted here from the *Vigrahavyāvartanī*. In this text, Nāgārjuna refutes convention in which illumination is thought as arising out of a contact of light and darkness. By applying his dialectic to this metaphorical relation, he argues in Verses 36 through 39 as follows:[26]

> If, as you say, fire illumines both other things and itself, then darkness will cover both other things and itself. (V. 36)
>
> There is no darkness in light nor in something else in which light abides. How [then] can it illumine? For, illumination is destruction of darkness. (V. 37)
>
> It is wrong to say that light illumines in the very process of its origination. For, in the very process of its origination, light does not come into contact with darkness. (V. 38)
>
> Even if light destroys darkness without coming into contact

---

[25] Referring to Chap. II, "Examination of past and future motions" (*Gatāgata-parīkanāma*)]. (V. 13) in the *Madhyamakakārikā-śāstra*.

[26] The verses in English are quoted from K. Bhattacharya's work of translation: *The Dialectical Method of Nāgārjuna*: *Vigrahavyāvartanī* (2nd edition.), Delhi: Motilal Banarsidass, 1978, pp. 117-119.
yadi ca svaparātmānau tvadvacanena prakāśayaty agniḥ /
pracchādayiṣati tamaḥ svaparātmānau hutāśa iva // 36
nāsti tamaśca jvalane yatra ca tiṣṭhati parātmani jvalanaḥ /
kurute kathaṃ prakāśaṃ sa hi prakāśo 'ndhakāravadhaḥ // 37
utpadyamāna eva prakāśayaty agnir ity asadvādaḥ /
utpadyamāna eva prāpnoti tamo na hi hutāśaḥ // 38
aprāpto 'pi jvalano yadi vā punar andhakāram upahanyāt /
sarveṣu lokadhātuṣu tamo 'yam iha saṃsthito hānyāt // 39

with it, this light, abiding here would destroy darkness in all the worlds. (V. 39)

Here, in the *Vigrahavyāvartanī*, Nāgārjuna refutes the Naiyāyika system of logic by dialectically treating *pramāṇa* (means of cognition) and *premeya* (object of cognition). In so doing, he uses the metaphor of candle light and that of nightly darkness in parallel with frequent literary expression, such as, "Wisdom destroys darkness of ignorance," and so forth. Since it is taken for granted in convention that an illumination occurs upon the contact of light and its object of illumination, he exhaustively repudiates the relationship between the two. In our convention, we explain the fact of illumination by referring to the point of contact of light and darkness at some spatio-temporal sphere. We conceive of the fact of perception with reference to the spatio-temporal sphere wherein the visual faculty and its object somehow find contact. So once again, Nāgārjuna leads his argument toward the same goal, namely, that irrespective of whether light and darkness are different or identical, the very condition of illumination which requires the assumption of a contact between the two cannot be accomplished insofar as they are believed to be in possession of their own being or exclusive nature. Thus, the question is raised once again: "By repudiating any relational circumstance between light and darkness, what does Nāgārjuna hope to accomplish?"

5. THE COMMON STRUCTURAL FOUNDATION OF LOGIC AND DIALECTIC

In Medieval India, Mādhyamika dialectical method was called '*prasaṅga-vākya*' ("*reductio-ad-absurdum* argument" being the closest rendering). However, I have been calling it as 'dialectical method' for the following reason. As has been demonstrated elsewhere,[27] there is a common structural foundation for inferential logic and dialectic. The logical structure consists of two conditions as explained above: Firstly, it consists of the dual rules of valid inference; namely, (1) affirmative linkage of two terms, e.g., "if smoke, then fire," and (2) negative linkage of two terms, e.g., "if no fire, then no

[27] Cf. Ichimura: "An Analysis of Mādhyamika Dialectic in terms of the Logical Principle of Anvaya and Vyatireka," *Amalā Prajñā Aspects of Buddhist Studies* (*Professor P.V. Bapat Felicitation Volume*) edited by N. H. Samtani and H. S. Prasad [Bibliotheca Indo-Buddhica No. 63; Delhi: Indian Book Centre, 1989, pp. 325-341], esp. 336-337.

smoke." Secondly, it consists of two clearly distinguished classes of referential variables for the respective linkages: (1) those which, like a kitchen, are capable of having both smoke and fire; and (2) those which, like a pond, are incapable of having both fire and smoke. Indeed, Nāgārjuna's dialectic is anchored in this logical structure. The difference between logic and dialectic arises in respective logical and dialectical contexts.

In the logical context, the two sets of referential variables are strictly separated through positive and negative concomitant linkages. No cross-logical boundary is permitted, because a cross-logical boundary brings about a context similar to that of the Theravādin *versus* Puggalavādin dispute, resulting in logical fallacy or, at best, logical indeterminacy. In the dialectical context, however, both positive and negative sets of referential variables are totally identified through juxtaposition of both positive and negative propositional linkages with reference to the sphere wherein the two sets of variables are conventionally presupposed to have a contact. Nāgārjuna, however, allows no conceivable linkage between light and darkness or between fire and fuel. When he posits a concomitance in which light is said to illumine others and itself, he places, without fail, an opposite concomitance in which darkness obstructs others and itself from illumination. In so doing, he creates a thought in the mind of the audience, that there must be a meeting point in space and time where light and darkness come together, because, if it were not so, our convention fails to explain the fact of illumination. In like manner, the audience is caught in a thorough repudiation of the linkage between fire and fuel [i.e., between *pudgala* and *skandha*], to be forced into a thought that there must be some point in space and time where an empirical person and the on-going totality of psycho-physical elements (*skandhas*) are conjoined, because, otherwise, it would be impossible to explain the existence of an individual person consisting of multiple facts of thought and perception.

I must call attention to this point of contact in space and time as conceived by us in our convention. It is here in the referential domain of nature where the mind of the audience is pressed by the dialectic to expect the point of contact through juxtaposition of the two opposing sets of propositional linkages. The result is that the audience is compelled to acknowledge a dual-natured variable, like fire, being simultaneously identical with and different from, fuel, or *vice versa*. The discrepancy between two opposite variables can thereby be totally eliminated in theoretical terms.

The Buddhist logicians of Medieval India approached the problem with three cautious considerations which seem to have approximated the Mādhyamika approach and especially relevant to inter-cultural or inter-religious dialogue today: [28]

1. They placed emphasis on the respective reasons, namely, "śabda is a product," and "śabda is audible," but not on the syllogism as a whole, because each syllogism is valid within its own system of inferential rules.

2. They simultaneously accepted the validity of the two theses, "śabda is impermanent" and "śabda is permanent," within their respective systems of philosophical presupposition, expressed in the concomitant linkages "Whatever is a product is impermanent" and "Whatever is audible is permanent."

3. They shifted both the mental process and the logical meaning to a different plane, separate from that of logical laws, because referential force of logic sharpens the sense of difference. This means that Buddhist logicians intended to resolve the confrontation of the two Hindu adversaries within the trans-empirical plane of their minds.

Thus, it is apparent that Buddhist logicians found it permissible to juxtapose against reality two different arguments which are mutually contradictory. Both Buddhist logicians and Mādhyamika dialecticians seem to have agreed in their ways of resolving antithesis by identifying the referential variables (say, fire and fuel) by juxtaposing the opposite theses (i.e., fire and fuel are totally different) on to the point of contact in referential domain. As mentioned before, this Buddhist logicians' treatment of the problem of communication-breakdown is not essentially different from the Mādhyamika dialectic, because inducing a contradiction in the logico-linguistic sphere of the mind to bring about total identification within the referential sphere of the mind, is effectively the same thing as shifting the matter toward the trans-empirical sphere.

It is clear that the Mādhyamaka dialectic does not repudiate the empirical world, and that what it repudiates or treats is the underlying mental force of linguistic behavior and culture formation, namely, the referential force of the mind toward its objective referent and the tendentious or purposive force of the mind which links one symbol with another. The Ābhidharmika disputes on their different theses which invariably originated due to these two forces of the mind, the circumstance of which the Madhyamaka dialectic

---

[28] Cf. A. Kunst: "The Concept of the Principle of Excluded Middle in Buddhism," *Rocznik Orientalistyczny* XXI, (1957), 146.

is designed to dissolve by bringing about a more conciliatory state of the mind. By disclosing the hidden contradiction in each symbol-usage, the dialectic intends to annihilate each sharpened discrepancy between two different assertions.

It should be additionally noted that Nāgārjuna's solution is not to abandon the orthodox insight of *Skandhas* (*khanda-s*), *Āyatanas*, and so forth. As a Mādhyamika, Nāgārjuna demonstrated the empirical status of these *dharmas* discussed along with *pudgalas* as essentially limited to the empirical and linguistic domain, and thus he attempted to restore the status of real *dharmas* to the trans-empirical and non-linguistic domain as a matter of the transcendental insight of Ābhidharmika elders.

Although we have no tangible evidence of history regarding the precise date of this innovator of the dialectic, called Nāgārjuna, his philosophical and religious personality, and his logical thinking are felt vivid and unique even within a few authenticated texts as quoted here. To understand his doctrine of *śūnyatā* and his method of dialectic, it is sufficient to take up the *Treatise on the Fundamental Middle Through Versified Composition* (*Mūla-madhyamaka-kārikā-śāstra*), and the *Treatise on Turning Around (Doctrinal) Disputes* (*Vigrahavyāvartanī*).[29] These two works, identical in method and style as well as in versified composition, suggest that Nāgārjuna was trained within the Ābhidharmika tradition during his early career but subsequently to be drawn toward the Mahāyāna.

Nāgārjuna may have been a contemporary of the generation of Aśvaghoṣa, renowned Buddhist poet, and the Kuṣāṇa ruler Kaniṣka. The Chinese text *Fu-fa-ts'ang-yin-yüan-chuan* (*Record of the Histories of Dharma-Transmission* translated into Chinese in A.D. 472)[30]

---

[29] Respectively, the former being contained in Candrakīrti's *Prasannapadā* which was edited by Louis de La Vallée Poussin [Bibliotheca Buddhica, IV, St-Pétersbourg, 1903-1913], the latter being edited by E. H. Johnston and A. Kunst, a Romanized Sanskrit text, *Mélanges Chinois et Bouddhiques*, Vol. IX (1951), Appendix [also, see K. Bhattacharya's edition and translation: *The Dialectical Method of Nāgārjuna: Vigrahavyāvartanī* (2nd edition.), Delhi: Motilal Banarsidass, 1978, and Chr. Lintner's edition accompanied by the Tibetan version, *Nagarjuniana, Studies in the Writings and Philosophy of Nāgārjuna.* (Buddhist Traditions Vol. II), Motilal Banarsidass, 1982, pp. 76-86].

[30] The text in question [Taishō. 50; p. 297 ff (No.2058)] is recorded as having been jointly translated by Chi-ch'ieh-yeh and T'an-yao during the period of Northern Wei. In 1911, however, H. Maspero challenged the authenticity of this text as a work of translation, concluding that it was a composition and compilation in China. Be that as it may, there is no doubt that the text contains some degree of historical information. [Cf. Maspero: "Sur la date et l'authenticité du *Fou-fa-tsung-yin-yüan-chuan*," *Mélanges*

listed Nāgārjuna as fourteenth and Aśvaghoṣa as twelfth in the patriarchal genealogy of *Dharma* transmission. Aśvaghoṣa is known to have been one of the favored confidants of the Kuṣāṇa ruler, along with Vasumitra, Sarvāstivādin head-monk, who presided over the Fourth Buddhist Council in Kāśmīra, and chief editor of the *Mahāvibhāṣāśāstra* according to Paramārtha. The *Rājataraṃgiṇī* (*The Dynastic History of the Kāśmīra Kings*) which was written by Kalhaṇa in the twelfth century, implies that Nāgārjuna was one of the inner circle of Kaniṣka's advisers and actively engaged in the propagation of *Dharma* in Kāśmīra. In one of the passages in his *Hsi-yu-chi*, Hsüan-tzang recorded that Nāgārjuna was the renowned Buddhist master in Western India. This particular passage challenges the hitherto commonly held tradition that his major activity took place in Southern India.

In chronologically placing Nāgārjuna, I am inclined to think that he lived from the middle of the first century to that of the second and was associated with the Śātavāhana kings (either Gotamīputra Śātakarṇi or Vāśiṣṭhīputra Pulumāyī) and the Śaka Satrap Rudradāman of Ujjayinī, for whom he left each respectively as their religious counselor a discourse entitled as the *Suhṛllekha* and *Ratnāvalī*. Some decades ago, A. Basham reconfirmed that the era of Kaniṣka began during the later half of the first century, i.e., A.D. 78, instead of 144, and the period of the above two groups of rulers cannot be moved from the mid-second century because of the record of the *Ptolemy's Geography*.. The period from the first and second century was regarded the Śaka-Phalhava Era during which the foreign races, Parthians and Scythians, together with Kuṣāṇas, actively participated in Indian civilization under the guidance of Buddhist spirituality. It was also during the period when the *Nyāyasūtra*, a Hindu logical text, in which Nāgārjuna's critique is cited more than once, was in the process of formation in the region of Western India. It was the likely era during which the intellectual and evangelical activities of Nāgārjuna can best be placed

6. CONCLUSION

The root cause of the *Kathāvatthu* 'logical deadlock' was the different presuppositions on the status of *dhammas* and that of *pudgala,* both of which were crucial to the Buddhist spirituality and the goal of religious emancipation. The doctrinal crisis was not

---

d'Indianisme, Paris.]

of the nature of an isolated past event, but of a contemporary nature evidenced in the communication-breakdown among intra-Buddhist sectarian branches as well as inter-religious and cultural problems of confrontation. Antithesis is easily sharpened and magnified through the logical and linguistic behavior of the human mind. To deal with this kind of problems, historically the Buddhist tried to uphold the practice of examination of the problems at the trans-empirical level, allowing two contesting forces to be successfully reconciled.

The ancient tradition of the Theravādin Abhidharmists left the *Kathāvatthu* types of doctrinal disputes unresolved and without a form of systematic reconciliation. It has been handed to each of the later generations to resolve the problems by themselves, just as it was done by Nāgārjuna with his dialectical method. Considering today's trends of secularization and social change, I believe that communication between the Theravādin and Mahāyāna traditions ought to be the foremost important step for establishing linkage between the spiritual and secular consciousness, and that the Mādhyamika method of dialectic may serve with a viable catalytic function to bringing about communication between the two traditions. It is hoped that the Mādhyamika dialectical method can simultaneously provide a similar catalytic effect in communication between Buddhist and non-Buddhist religions and cultures.

Finally, I am obliged for two reasons to pay tribute to those elders who were engaged in assembling the *Kathāvatthu* disputes: Firstly, they provided a very open display of the doctrinal crisis, through which they intentionally demonstrated the fundamental problem inherent in the linkage between the world of Buddhist transcendence and the world of convention. They deliberately prepared an arena in which future generations would grapple with the problem and seek its solution. Secondly, while our intra-Buddhist task is to review the relation between the transcendent value (*paramārtha-satya*) and that of convention (*laukikasāṃvṛti-satya*), our task ought to involve communication with non-Buddhist religions and cultures as well. It should be remembered that the Saṅgha which the elder Mogaliputta-tissa led was located in Mathura, later to be the summer capital of the Kuṣāṇa rulers. It was in this progressive circle of the Buddhist world in ancient India that the Graeco-Indian text, the *Milinda-pañha*, was created. In this connection, I am indeed convinced that the role of the Mādhyamika dialectic holds new meaning for our time and for the future.

ARTICLE SIX

NĀGĀRJUNA AND *UPĀYAHṚDAYAŚĀSTRA*[1] (*FANG-PIEN-HSIN-LUN*「方便心論」[2])

§1. INTRODUCTION

As an earliest study on the *Upāyahṛdayaśāstra*, in his renowned book, *History of Indian Logic* published in 1921, Prof. Vidyābhūṣaṇa briefly referred to its authorship on the basis of the textual contents.[3] Four years later then, Prof. H. Ui published in 1925 a research article on the same text under the title: "An Annotated Study on the *Hōben-shin-ron*."[4] The opinions of these two scholars regarding the authorship of the text were widely different. On the one hand, Vidyābhūṣaṇa inclined to believe that the author was Nāgājuna,[5] while, on the other hand, Prof. Ui categorically denied it and asserted instead that the original text should be ascribed to some Hīnayāna Ābhidharmist who had appeared prior to Nāgārjuna.[6] Secondly, Vidyābhūṣaṇa was conviced that this logical text ascribed to Nāgāarjuna advocated the three-membered formula of syllogistic inference,[7] whereas Ui atated that it was based on the traditional five-membered syllogism similar to that of the *Carakasaṃhitā* as

---

[1] Presented at the Annual Convention of Indogaku-Bukkyōgaku Gakkai (Japanese Association for Indian and Buddhist Studies), Musashino Women's College, Tokyo 1994 ; The orignal paper was entitled "The Period of Nāgārjuna and the Fang-pien-hsin-lun (「方便心論」 or *Upāyahṛdayaśāstra*)," and appeared as a shortened form in *Japanese Journal of Indian and Buddhist Studies,* Vol. 43, No. 2, 1995, pp. 2033-2028.

[2] Translated (1 fasc.) by Kiṅkara (Chi-chia-yeh) (吉迦夜), A.D. 472; ***Taishō***.32, No. 1632, pp. 23b-28c.

[3] Satis Candra Vidyabhūṣaṇa: *A History of India Logic*, Calcutta University Press, 1921; pp. 118-120 and 259-261. (Reprint from Motilal Banarsidass, 1971)

[4] 「方便心論の註釈的研究」 or A Study on *Hōbenshinron* by Ui, Hakuju,included in his monograph, *Indian Philsoophical Studies* II (「印度哲学研究」), pp. 472-585.

[5] Vidyabhūṣaṇa, *op, cit.*, p. 259; He comments in Note 1: "Some suspect that the work was not composed by Nāgārjuna whose name, though mentioned by some Chinese editors, does not appear in the Chinese version. In the absence of any introduction to the Chinese version we cnnot deny altogether the authoriship of Nāgārjuna. . ."

[6] Ui: *op. cit.*, p. 493.

[7] Vidyābhūṣaṇa, *op, cit.*, p. 119.

well as that of *Nyāyasūtra.*[8] In 1930, Tuci published his Sanskritization of the *Fang-pien-hsin-lun* along with other texts, but regarding the question of its authorship, he just simply followed Ui's opinion as he said so in his introduction.[9] Then, after more than half a century, Y. Kajiyama brought forth a new study in 1984 and challenged the hitherto uncontested Ui's opinion in terms of three points: (1) that it is possible to regard Nāgārjuna as the textual author, (2) that the text advocates the three-membered syllogism rather than the five-membered one, and (3) that it constitutes an anti-logical text (反論理学書) in that it was written not for recording the theories on the logical methods of debate prevailing in the author's peirod but for the sake of critically examining such theories from the Buddhist point of view.[10]

In my study on the text, I have independently arrived at a similar conclusion as far as the initial two points are concerned, because, though regrettable, I was unaware of the existence of Kajiyama's article.[11] My conclusion is, however, more categorical, (1) drawn from examining the author's theory of instantiation (*dṛṣṭānta*, 喩), of which Kajiyama did not outright refute Ui's misinterpretation, (2) from clarifying the meaning of "linguistic excellence" (*vākyapraśaṃsā*, 語善)[12] and its implication in reference to the Buddhist logic of the later periods, and (3) from tracing identical phrases and itemization of Buddhist system (*siddhānta*) in Nāgārjuna's *Suhṛllekha.*

My investigation is concerned with the initial four of the eight

---

[8] Ui: *op. cit.*, p. 511.

[9] Tucci, G.: *Pre-Diṅnāga Buddhist Texts on Logic from Chinese Sources, Translated with an Introduction, Notes and Indices*; Baroda: Gaekwad Oriental Institute, 1929; pp. xi-xii.

[10] Yuichi Kajiyama: "Epistemology and Logic" included in *the Lectures on Mahāyāna Buddhism* IX (「講座大乗仏教」第九巻), Tokyo: Shunjūsha, 1984; pp. 12, 15, and 17-18.

[11] I am obliged to mention that Profs. E. Katsura and A. Saito kindly informed me of Prof. Kajiyama's article after my presentation of the paper during the conference.

[12] The translator of the *Carakasaṃhitā* renders "syntactical excellence" as *vākyapraśaṃsā* [*Carakasaṃhitā*, Vimāna Section, Text with English Translation and Critical Exposition based on Cakrapāṇi Datta's *Āyurveda*; Varanasi: Chowkhamba Sanskrit Series, 1976; p. 232. It is obvious as asserted by Prof. Ui that the textual author may have taken this particular term from the *Carakasaṃhitā*. However, I render it as "linguistic excellence" instead of "syntactical excellence," precisely because the word order is concerned from the logicl point of view rather than from the grammatical point of view.

criteria the author presented as essential to his logical method of argument, in part because my thesis can be ascertained on the result therefrom and, in part, because the remaining subjects were already dealt convincingly by Kajiyama.

§2. SIMILAR (*SAPAKṢA*, 同喩) AND DISSIMILAR INSTANCE (*VIPAKṢA*, 異喩)

The dual instantiation (*anvaya* and *vyatireka*, i.e., corroboration through similar and dissimilar instances) was regarded by all schools, Hindu as well as Buddhist, to be one of the essential members of the syllogistic inference in ancient India. In the traditional five-membered formula (*pañcāvayavin*, 五支作法), it is the third statement (*udāharaṇa*) immediately following the statement of the *Hetu* (reason).[13] The reason for which Ui denied the author of the *Fang-pien-hsin-lun* to be Nāgārjuna and asserted that it would have been some Hīnayāna scholar, was that, among others, the theory of *dṛṣṭānta* is set forth as the primary of the "eight logical criteria for logical argument" (八種論法), is defective, thus lacking the adeptness of Nāgārjuna, greatest Mahāyāna dialectician.

Unlike the other logical texts, like the *Carakasaṃhitā*[14] and *Nyāyasūtra*, the present text only enumerates the *dṛṣṭānta*, omitting the remaining four members of syllogism.[15] Because of this, Ui was

---

[13] The five-membered syllogism consisted of the following: 1. *Pratijñā* (Thesis): "Fire on the hill"; 2. *Hetu* (Reason): "Because smoke on the hill"; (3) *Dṛṣṭānta* or *Udāharaṇa* (Corroborative Instance or Dual Instantiation): "Wherever there is smoke there is fire, just as in a kitchen"; "Wherever there is no fire, there is no smoke, just as in a water tank"; (4) *Upanaya* (Application): "So, smoke on the hill"; (5) *Nigamana* (Conclusion): "Therefore, fire on the hill."

[14] The *Carakasaṃhitā* or *Compendium of Medical Science* which was redacted from Ātreya's *Ayurveda* by Caraka, renowned authority of the science, identified as one of Kaniṣka's Court Councilors along with Aśvaghoṣa, etc. The text is divided into eight parts, of which the method of debates is included in Part III, Chap. 8: Vimāna Sthāna (Science of Right Measures), under the Procedure of Debate (*sabhāśāvidhimata* Nos. 15-67). *Op. cit.*, pp. 225-249

[15] The *Carakasaṃhita*, Vimāna Sthāna Nos. 27 and 31, provides forty-four logical terms, among which the five members of syllogism (*avayava*) are enumerated as follows: *Pratijñā* (proposition), *Sthāpānā* (justification) which is consisted of four, *Hetu* (statement of probans), *Dṛṣṭānta* (corroborative instance), *Upanaya* (subsumptive correlation), and *Nigamana* (final conclusion). *Ibid.*, pp. 232 and 234. The *Nyāyasūtra* provides sixteen categories of logical system, among which example (*dṛṣṭānta*), tenet (*siddhānta*) and the five members of a syllogism (*avayava*) are enumerated respectively in this order.

suspicious of the authenticity of this logical theory. Kajiyama, however, interpretes it as an intentional omission, chacracterizing the text to be "anti-logical" rather than "logical." In any case, the author theorizes this initial criterion (*dṛṣṭānta*) to be of two kinds (喻有二種): (1) a kind that is accepted by all (具足喻), and (2) a kind that is accepted by some (小分喻). The theory inculcates these two as well as the similar (*sapakṣa*, 同品) and dissimilar classes (*vipakṣa*, 異品) of instances approximately as follows[16]:

> A *dṛṣṭānta* must be understood by ordinary men as well as holy men [of superior insight], so that [the subject of inference] can subsequently be explained.[17] For instance, a *dṛṣṭānta* statement: "the ordinary mind starts and issues like a whirl-wind," is admissible to every one, because [even] ordinary men all know how such a wind moves. Thus, [through such an instance] every one decisively understands how frivolous and restless the ordinary mind is. Unless every one knows what such a whirl-wind is like, the instance does not serve [the purpose of demonstration] as an [appropriate] similar instance. [for explaining what the ordinary mind is like].[18]

As quoted before, an instance, such as "whirl wind," [which ordinary as well as men of spiritual insight equally understand,] constitutes a similar instance, whereas an instance, Nirvāṇa, which only the holy men understand, and which the ordinary men do not, is called a dissimilar instance.[19]

In commenting on these definitions, Ui made a serious misinterpretation, quoting: The pair of "similar and dissimilar instances" (同異喻) and the pair of "those which are accepted by all (具足) and those which are accepted by some" (小分喻) are entirely different in conception. The latter [distinction] should rather be based on the "total and partial identity" between that which is compared (所喻) and that with which it is compared (喻), whereas the former is based on the "identity and difference between the two."[20]

Although Kajiyama does not offer any new insight on this matter, he points out that the *Fang-pien-hsin-lun*, *Carakasaṃhitā*,

---

[16] *Taishō*. 32, p. 23c, lines 6-7.

[17] 「凡聖同解、然後可説」

[18] 「如言是心動発猶迅風、一切凡夫知風動故、便得決了心為軽躁、 若不知不得為喻」Cf。*Ibid*., lines 18-21.

[19] 「如前風喻名之為同、聖得涅槃而凡不得、是名為異」Cf. *Ibid*., lines 24-25.

[20] Ui: *op. cit*., p. 485.

Vaidalya-sūtra, and *Nyāyasūtra*, all agree on the definition of *dṛṣṭānta*, i.e., "that which the ordinary as well as the wise commonly know," and that it is only the *Fang-pien-hsin-lun* which alone advocates the above two kinds of *dṛṣṭānta*, i.e., "one accepted by all and another accepted by some."[21] Moreover, by referring to Nāgārjuna's argument in the *Vaidalyasūtra*, he points out that the master seems to have held the above definition in mind when he repudiates the cases of *dṛṣṭānta* not only in total identity (*sūtra* 26), total difference (*sūtra* 27 and 29), but also in partial difference (*sūtra* 28).[22]

§3. LOGICALITY OF *DṚṢṬĀNTA*: A *SAPAKṢA* ACCEPTED BY ALL (具足) BUT A *VIPAKṢA* BY A FEW (小分)

From the logical point of view, inferential instantiation is not concerned with the similarity of physical forms between the two that are compared, but exclusively with the similarity of linguistic expressions or descriptions regarding respective referential substrata. For instance, when Nāgārjuna refutes the Naiyāyika notion of *pramāṇa* in the *Vigrahavyāvartanī*, he takes up the relationship between "light" (an agent of illumining) and "dark" (an object illumined) to instantiate the relationship between visual faculty (*pramāṇa*) and its object (*prameya*) and demonstrate that the relationship cannot be established either on their identity or difference. His dialectic points to the nature of linguistic convention which invariably and *a-priori* presumes their contact for the phonomenon of cognition or that of illumination in parallel with an expression: "Wisdom dispels ignorance," and so forth.

Take another stock example based on similarity. When one

---

[21] Kajiyama: *op. cit.*, p. 20. he gives his source in reference to the *Vaidalyaprakaraṇa* (27, 29), where it is said: neither the total identity nor partial identity of resembrance makes an instantiation possible.

[22] If that which is compared and that with which it is compared are [totally] identical, [the purpose of] instantiation cannot be achieved because fire cannot instantiate another fire (*sūtra* 26). Nor even if they are totally different, just as water cannot instantiate fire (*sūtra* 27). Nor, even if partially identical, just as between a mountain and a bundle of hairs which are partially identical in terms of existence, singularity, or physical configuration (*sūtra* 28). Cf. S. Yamaguchi: "Nāgārjuna's Treatise Challenging the Naiyāyika School - on the *Vaidalyasūtra* (*Shōrigakuha-ni-taisuru-Ryūju-no Ronsho - Vaidalya ni-tsuit*) *Shūkyō Kenkyū* (*Journal of Religious Studies*) 4, No. 1 (Tokyo: 1927), 80-100, and No. 2 (1927), 87-110; esp. pp. 99-100; Y. Kajiyama's Tibetan edition: The *Vaidalyaprakaraṇa* of Nāgārjuna, *Indogaku-Shiron-shū* (*Miscellanea Indologica Kiotiensia*, Nos. 6-7 (Kyoto, 1965), 129-155

perceives a rising smoke on a distant hill, one reasons that there should be an outbreak of fire there and tries to convey this information to one's audience by citing kitchen as a similar instance. Although the hill and the kitchen have no common physical or conceptual form of identity, they can be classified into the same group of similar instances (*sapakṣa*) by virtue of potentially having a causal concomitance in common as expressed in language: "A hill having smoke likely is on fire," "a kitchen having smok likely has fire in the hearth," and so forth. It is the same with a dissimilar example, such as, a water tank, a desert field, and so forth, where, everyone knows, neither fire nor smoke is possible at all times. The water tank and the desert field have no common physical or conceptual form of identity, they can be classified into the same group of dissimilar (or counter) instances by virtue of having a causal concomitance in common as expressed in language: "a water tank can not be a locus of fire, hence, not a locus of smoke," "a desert field is not a locus of fire, hence, not a locus of smoke," and so forth.

Ui made a serious error in the logical nature of instantiation, especially on dissimilar examples (異喩). He explains his point of view, saying: It is not only wrong to theorize simmilar class (同品喩) and dissimilar class of instances (異品喩) respectively in terms of "accepted by all" (具足) and "accepted by some" (小分), but also actual things do not allow us to classify a whirl-wind and Nirvāṇa respectively as simmilar and dissimilar instances.[23] He reasons first that the whirl-wind and the mind must be regarded only as partially identical and never be regarded totally identical; secondly, that the example of Nirvāṇa contradicts the definition of *dṛṣṭānta* in general, i.e., "to be understood by both ordinary as well as holy men" (凡聖同解). Nirvāṇa ought to be taken for its immovable and eternal quality as contrary to the ever changing and transient nature of the mind. Hence, it is wrong to theorize similar and dissimilar classes of examples in terms of "accepted by all" and "accepted by some."[24]

Kajiyama, as mentioned before, partially rectifies Ui's overstatement by confirming that Nāgārjuna consistently held, in his other treatises, the two kinds of instances in terms of "accepted by all" and "accepted by some" in the same way as those which are defined in the *Fang-pien-hsin-lun*. Kajiyama, however, does not

---

[23] Ui: *op. lcit.*, .p. 485.

[24] *Ibid.*

mention as to why the textual author's definition of dissimilar instance is admissible, i.e., Nirvāṇa can be a dissimilar instance in contradistinction to a similar instance, such as, whirl-wind.

Here, three points must be taken for consideration. First, the textual author's theory of logic is concerned and deals with those established sectarian systems of teachings (*siddhāntas*, 所執 or 定說). Each school upholds its own system of thought and teaching, and such core belief and teaching cannot be accepted by any other school which upholds a different system of belief and teaching. Second, from ancient times in India, every philosophical and religious school compiled its own sacred literature (*āgama*) and made it a valid source of knowledge (聖教量). Each school thus could rely on such source of knowledge as a valid ground for public debates, despite the fact that one source of knowledge is incompatible with another and mutually inadmissible. Third, even within one and the same religio-philosophical tradition, variation is innevitable as regards to its followers. Some gifted persons understand its truth, experiencing transcendent insight, whereas some others don't. The textual author obviously anticipated these conditions.

Let us see whether Nirvāṇa, which common men cannot fathom, can be applied as a dissimilar instance in contrast to a similar instnce "whirl-wind." Validity of an instance indeed depends on what aspect of an object of inference is compared with. Though the text does not specify what is instantiated by a dissimilar instance Nirvāṇa, it is logically apparent that the mind of quietude and stillness in concentration (寂定心) is the object of instantiation in contra-distinction to the ordinary mind that incesantly moves and changes like an whirl-wind, which men of ordinary mind can understand. Though the state of Nirvāṇa is beyond their understanding, they may accept this counter instance to demonstrate the mind of stillness in concentration, insofar as men of extraordinary insight accept it as valid counter instantiation.

In order to substantiate the foregoing contrast, I am obliged to make a reference to a verse in Nāgarjuna's *Suhṛllekha*, where the master instructs his patron king as follows[25]:

---

[25] There are three Chinese texts presumably translated from the similar Sanskrit original: (1) by Guṇavarman (求那跋摩、367-431), A.D. 431, under the title *Bodhisattva Nāgārjuna's Essential Teaching in Verse for King (Lung-chu-p'u-sa-wei-ch'an-t'o-chia-wang-shou-fa-yao-chieh* (1 fasc.); Taisho. 32, No. 1672.] ; (b) by Saṅghavarman (僧伽跋摩), A.D. 434, under the title *The Essential Teaching in Verse Recommended to all Kings* (*Lung-shu-p'u-sa-h'üan-fa-chu-wang-yao-chieh* (1 fasc.); Taisho. 32, No. 1673, and

> Concentrate [your] mind diligently in the practice of *Śīla*, *Dhyāna-samādhi,* and *Prajñā*. With the mind of quietude and stillness in concentration, [you] ought to seek the path of Nirvāṇa.[26]

There is no illogicality on the part of textual author in citing the dual *dṛṣṭānta* as whirl-wind and Nirāṇa respectively for instantiating the ordinary mind of frivorous change and the mind of concentration that abides still.

In contemporary life circumstances too, we frequently meet such occasions, in which people accept a dissimilar instance even if it is beyond their understanding, insofar as it is accepted by the wise and the professional endowed with special training and insight. For instance, a kitchen as a similar instance can be accepted by all, wise and fool, for instantiation of the smoke-fire concomitance. So too is acceptable to both a dissimilar example, such as, a water tank, where neither fire nor smoke is possible. Suppose, a scientist astronomer cites here Mars' atmosphere as a dissimilar example to demonstrate the same contraposition ("Wherever there is no fire there is no smoke either") on the basis that Mars has no air of oxigen. Ordinary citizens may accept such a counter instantiation as valid in good faith on the basis of his authority as a scientist.

In short, the textual author correctly advocates that in logical debate between two different systems of thought or belief, the similar instance ought to be accepted by all, wise and fool, for its effectiveness, but a dissimilar instance, insofar as it is acceptable to men of superior insight, serves the purpose of demonstration as counter instantiation.

§4. LINGUISTIC EXCELLENCE (*VĀKYAPRAŚAṂSĀ*) AND THREE-MEMBERED SYLLOGISM

The developmental history of Buddhist logic reveals a unique trend of thought in reducing the number of inferential statements involved in a syllogism. In introducing the formula of three-membered syllogism, Buddhist logicians, such as, Dignāga, initially dismissed the fourth and fifth statements, i.e., application (*upanaya*) and

---

(3) I-ching (義浄、635-713), A.D. 637, under the title *Bodhisattva Nāgārjuna's Exhortation for the King in Verse* (*Lung-shu-p'u-sa-ch'üan-chieh-wang-sung* (1 fasc.); Taisho 32, No. 1673.

[26] Saṅghavarman's translation「勧発諸王要偈」1 fasc.,Taishō. 32, No. 1673, p. 750 c, lines 4-6.「専心勤修習戒品禅定慧、寂静調不動当求涅槃道」

conclusion (*nigamana*) out of the traditional five member statements. However, he even considered that the thesis statement (*pratijñā*) is linguistically superfluous.[27] The only items which escaped from the critical dismissal of superfluous statements as linguistically indispensable were the reason statement (*hetu*) and the corraborative statement of dual instantiation (*anvaya* and *vyatireka*). It was the *Fang-pien-hsin-lun* which enunciated the principle of such reduction for the first time, because the reduction of linguistic excess is quite in accordance with the principle of "linguistic excellence" (*praśaṃsā*).

In his article, "The Two-Membered Syllogism,"[28] Arnold Kunst points out that Dignāga's theory of three-membered syllogism was deeply influenced by the *Fang-pien-hsin-lun* as well as Maitreya's theory of three-membered syllogism inculcated in the *Yogācārabhūmi-śāstra* in Chinese translation (「瑜伽師地論」). He says:

> The decision to purge the verbal instruction of all redundant elements led to the exclusion from a syllogism of all those members the functions of which were superseded by the function of another member. Thus *nigamana* went, which (according to some) was a mere repectition of *pratijñā*, and thus *upanaya* went, which was only a pedagogical indication of the qualities of the correct *hetu*. It was apparently Nāgārjuna who first noticed the redundance of these members, and gave a stimulus to a thorough revison of the verbal instruction.

Dṛṣṭānta is regarded in Buddhist logic to be specially important in syllogistic inference because, different from Hindu logicians' view, they considered the main business of inference:

(1) to determine a given subject of inference by means of its similar (*sapakṣa*) and dissimilar instances (*vipakṣa*) and

(2) to posit a reason (*hetu*) that implies its conclusion (*sādhya*).[29]

---

[27] Dignāga's refutation against the Naiyāyika insistence on the ncessity of Pratijñā is quoted by Vācaspati Miśra in his *Nyāyavārtikatātparyaṭīkā*. Cf. Vidyābhūṣaṇa, *op. cit.*, pp. 281-282.

[28] *Rocznik Orientalistyczny* XV (1939-1940), 72-83; esp. p. 76.

[29] In opposition to this Buddhist logicians' view in assigning class determination of a given substratum to the *Anvaya* and *Vyatireka* procedures as the primary task of inference, the Hindu logicians assigned to them the verification of the universal relation (*Vyāpti*) between smoke and fire. Moreover, in opposition to Buddhist logician's view in regarding the laying down of a Reason as the main body of an inference, Hindu logicians interpreted it as verification of a given reason by means of the conclusion. Dignāga refuted this Hindu logicians' view, stating: The object of inferential

To repeat, in case of an inference for others (*parārthānumāna*), these two statements are of real necessity, i.e., to corraborate a general rule through dual instantiation and to apply a reason to an individual substratum. But, in case of an inference for one's self (*svārthānumāna*), the reason statement can even be omitted, precisely because the dual instantiation *ipso facto* posits the *hetu* in the process of class determination of a given subject (a hill). Thus, repetition is avoided in one's silent thought movement.

Kajiyama characterizes the *Fang-pien-hsin-lun* as an enigmatic text, because the logical theory in it does not enumerate any syllogistic members other than the *dṛṣṭānta*. He reasons that the author must have a different purpose in mind, namely, a critique of the existing methods of debate; hence it is an anti-logical text. The author of the *Fang-pien-hsin-lun*, however, lays down his justification at the beginning of the text as "preventing heterodoxies and seductive rhetorics" and "spreading and defending Buddhist orthodoxy."[30] Moreover, before commenting on the eight principles, he states as follows:

> I shall briefly explain the eight subtle principles of this treatise for the sake of "exposing the various systems of thought and belief" and "for the sake of terminating conceptual obsession."[31]

I can agree with Kajiyama's above labeling of the text as far as the author's justification is identical with Nāgārjuna's goal of dialectical treatises. Yet, I consider that the textual goal is further set forth to be a Buddhist logical method, in part, for the sake of cross-sectarian debates and, in part, for the sake of an innovation preliminary to the method of dialectic. For, in the second criterion, the author introduces ten religio-philosophhical systems of teaching and belief (*siddhānta*) including the Buddhist's own as the subject matters of his method of debate. Moreover, in the third and fourth, he prescribes two sets of three criteria to explain the principle of linguistic excellence (*vākyapraśāṃsā*)[32] and a set of three criteria to

---

reasoning is neither the properties of a given substratum between "smoke-fire" and a hill, but the substratum itself characterized by the conclusion. Cf. Vidyābhūṣaṇa, *op. cit.*, pp. 281-82. Dignāga's refutation is quoted by Vācaspati Miśra in his *Nyāyavārtikatātparyaṭikā*.

30 「防邪智巧弁、欲令正法流布於世,、欲護正法」

31 The Chinese text quoted in Ui's text, *op. cit.*, p. 478 and his Japanese rendering, *ibid.*, p. 479. 「八種甚妙論法我当略説、為開諸論門、為断戯論故」

32 *Taisho*. *op. cit.*, p. 23, lines 9-10. "Linguistic excellence means that

explain the principle of linguistic deficiency (*vākyadoṣa*, 言失).[33]

Linguistic Excellence means (1) Freedom from "three aspects of defficiency" (減有三種相), (a) defficient reasoning (*hetu-nyūna*, 因減), (b) defficient instantiation (*dṛṣṭānta-nyūna*, 喩減), and (c) defficient linguistic expression (*vākya-nyūna*, 言減); (2) Freedom from "three aspects of superfluous excess" (增有三種相), (a) superluous reasoning (*hetu-adhika*, 因增) (b) superfluous instantiation (*dṛṣṭānta-adhika*, 喩增), and (c) superfluous linguistic expression (*vākya-adhika*, 言增).

Linguistic Defectiveness means (a) repetitive statement (*punar-ukta,* 重言), (b) meaningless statement (anartha-ukta, 無義), and (c) incoherent statement (*apārthaka*, 欠義).

Taking all of these criteria into account, it is plain to any one that the principle of linguistic excellence means to prescribe reason, instance, as well as wording (linguistic expression), to be neither more nor less, but most precise and appropriate to a given subject of inference. It is also apparent that these criteria are primarily concerned with two members of syllogism, *hetu* and *dṛṣṭānta*, for which linguistic expression is prescribed to be precise, no more no less. As Kunst states, these criteria are identifiable as the motivating force of Buddhist theoreticians in Classical and Medieval India.

§5 CONSIDERATION OF NĀGĀRJUNA'S EXCHANGE OF ARGUMENTS WITH THE NAIYĀYIKAS

The very hypothesis that the real author of the *Upāyahṛdayaśātra* (*Fang-pien-hsin-lun*) was the same Nāgārjuna who also wrote among others the *Madhyamaka treatises*, *Suhṛllekha* and *Ratnāvalī* need be ascertained historically to be compatible with the dates of the textual origin within the century from A. D. 50 through 150 by way of cross-philosophical investigation of Buddhist and Hindu logical texts. As Ui asserts, the composition of the text is posterior to the *Carakasaṃhitā*,34 but prior to the *Nyāyasūtra.* The latter text,

---

the words (precisely) follow an (intended) meaning" (語善者謂語順於義). As specified in Note above, the word order is concerned with logic rather than grammar.

[33] *Taisho*. *Ibid*., line 11. "Linguistic defficiency is defined as any statement that contradicts logicality" (言失者謂乖於理).

[34] *Op. cit*., p. 484. Prof. Ui questions the meaning of 「然後可説」 but suggests to interpret it in the way the *Carakasaṃhitā* meant. "Description

however, has been studied by many scholars since the initial quarter of this century to reveal its complex nature and composite structure, with the result of widely varied dates of its origin.

Vidyābhūṣaṇa, for instance, determines the dates of the *Nyāyasūtra* in the mid-second century A.D., redacted by Akṣapāda35 from the *Ānvīkṣikī* tradition that goes back to the aphorims of Medhātithi Gautama. The primary reason that Vidyābhūṣaṇa determines the origin of the *Nyāyasūtra* in the mid-second century A.D. and attributes it to Akṣapāda, is that the designated period was also the times when the Hindu literature of the *Purāṇas* and the *Śāstras* were compiled by the assemblies of Brāhmaṇa scholars in the region of Vidarbha.36 Vidyabhuṣaṇa persuasively proposes this hypothesis by referring to four historical conditions: (1) that the mid-second century was the period of cultural and intellectual revival of Brāhmaṇas in Western India and the border region known as Vidarbha (Berar) to Southern India, (2) that this revival movement was directly motivated under the influence of the Fourth Buddhist Council which was held in Jālandhara in Kāśmīra half a century before under the auspices of the Kuṣāṇa ruler, Kaniṣka; (3) that the Brāhmaṇa sages met together in groups under the leadership of Jātūkarṇya Vyāsa, whose name prevailed in the region of Vidarbha as having compiled the *Purāṇas* and other *Śāstras*; and (4) that while Medhatithi Gautama was a native of Mithilā, Northeastern India in the sixth century B.C., Akṣapāda, a different indivdual, flourished at Prabhāsa in the region of Kāthiawār,[37] Western India

---

of universal truths comprehensible to the wise and ignorant alike is known as *dṛṣṭānta* or example; it illustrates the object." (*dṛṣṭānto nāma sa yatra mūrḍhaviduṣāṃ buddhisāmyaṃ, tenaiva yad varṇyam varṇayati*); *Carakasaṃhitā op. cit.*, 235.

[35] *Ibid.*, p. 50.

[36] Vidarbha is the region located on the border line (*dakṣiṇapatha*) between Middle India and South India. In Buddhist tradition in Tibet, Vidarbha was regarded to be Nāgārjuna's native region.

[37] *Ibid.*, p. 49. Vidyābhūṣaṇā notes that "Prabhāsa was situated beyond the rock of Girnar in Kathiawar, where we come across all the edicts of Aśoka as well as an inscription of Rudradāman which, supposed to be the first inscription in Sanskrit about 150 A.D., mentions Candra Gupta [the first Mauryan monarch] and Aśoka by names. . ." Cf. *Archaeological Survey of Western India*, Vol., II, p. 128. Vidyābhūṣaṇa also alludes that the region was a center for philosophical enquiry by referring to the *Bhāgavata Purāṇa*'s narrative about the discipline of logic, namely: Dattāteya, who was junior to Kapila (a Sāṃkhya sage), taught to Alarka the discipline of Ānvīkṣikī (here, a philosophical disquisition on soul, *ātmavidyā*). The sage is said to have resided on the Girnar hills in Kathiawar, and a temple associated with his name is said to be still existing there. *Ibid.*, p.10-11.

during the second century A.D.

It is problematic, however, that Vidyābhūsana estimates the dates of Nāgārjuna a whole century posterior to the *Nyāyasūtra* as about A.D. 250-320[38] .He knows not only that Ui places the date of the *Nyāyasūtra* after Nāgārjuna whom he approximated as about A.D. 113-213 on computing dates given by Kumārajīva, but before Vasubandhu.[39] But he also knows that Herman Jacobi places the *Nyāyasūtra* between 200 A.D. and 450 A.D. on the ground that the *Nyāyasūtra* refutes the *Śūnyavāda*, hence posterior to Nāgārjuna.[40] Despite the studies accomplished by these scholars, Vidyabhuṣaṇa upholds his view that it was Akṣapāda's system which Nāgārjuna criticised as regards to the Naiyāyika notion of *Pramāṇa*, and hence that Nāgārjuna was posterior to Akṣapāda.

In defending his point of view, Vidyābhūṣaṇa introduces an interpolation theory to explain why the *Nyāyasūtra*, Chap. II, Sect. i, comprises the *Sūtras* 8-11 which reiterate Nāgārjuna's critique in the *Vigrahavyāvartanī* as well as the *Sūtras* 12-19 which defend the Naiyāyika point of view.[41] He argues that though it was Akṣapāda's theory which Nāgārjuna criticized, the said portion of the *Nyāyasūtra* may have been interpolated into the chapter (*Adhyāya*) when Vātsyāyana was writing his commentary around A.D. 400, so that he could refute the Buddhist critique in defense of his tradition.[42]

The cross-philosophical investigation into the times of Nāgārjuna and the dates of the *Nyāyasūtra* was followed by the works of Theodor Stcherbatsky,[43] and H. N. Randle,[44] and sustained a ferver

---

[38] *Ibid.*, p. 51 and also pp. 251-252.

[39] Cf. *Ibid.*, p. 50, note 2. Ui: *Vaiśeṣika Philosophy according to the Daśapadārthaśāstra.* Royal Asiatic Society, London, 1918, p. 43; Cf. also H. N. Randle: *Indian Logic in the Early Schools*, (originally pub. from Oxford Univ. Press, 1930). New Delhi: Oriental books Reprint, 1976, p.15.

[40] Vidyābhūṣaṇa: *Ibid*. p. 50, note 2. Cf. also H. Jacobi: "On the Dates of the Philosophical Sūtras," *Journal of the American Oriental Society*, 31, (1911), pp. 2-3.

[41] The *Nyāyasūtras* II, i, 8-11 are supposed to have reiterated Nāgārjuna's critique expressed in the *Vigrahavyāvartanī*, Especially verses 12-19 and 36-39.

[42] Vātsyāyana was well prepared in his *Nyāyabhāṣya,* on Sūtra 19, which asserts the proper Naiyāyika theory of Pramāṇa, and exhibits his *tous de force* in the effort of refuting the Buddhist critique.

[43] *Buddhist Logic* (I and II), originally published by the Academy of Sciences of the USSR, Leningrad as Bibliotheca Buddhica XXVI (Pts I and II) and by Constable and Company ltd. in England, 1930, and its reprint by Dover Publications, Inc., 1962.

[44] *Indian Logic in the Early Schools: A Study of the Nyāyadarśana in its Relation to the Early Logic of Other Schools*, originally published by Oxford

throughout the pre-world war period. After three decades in the post-war era, Buddhist scholars of the fifty's were better equipped in reading into the polemical interactions between the Naiyāyika and the Mādhyamika. The question whether the *Nyāyasūtra* II, i. 8-19 of that composite work was in existence when Nāgārjuna wrote the *Vigrahavyāvartanī* was already dealt by S. Yamaguchi in his note,[45] by Tucci on pp. 34 ff of the notes on his translation,[46] and by Rāhula Sāṅkṛtyāyana in his introduction.[47]

Whatever has been academically accoomplished since then with the matter in question is best expressed by Arnold Kunst in his introduction to the Sanskrit edition of the *Vigrahavyāvartanī* co-authored by N. H. Johnston in 1952:[48]

> All that can safely be said is that the two works reflect the dispute between the two schools at much the same stage, but not necessarily with reference by one to the other. But one point is certain and that is that Nāgārjuna took some of the Naiyāyika arguments from a different work of that school. For he quotes a verse from it just before kārikā 34[49] and the Naiyāyikas evidently admitted the validity of his criticisms, since the views put forward in that verse are mentioned by Vātsyāyana only to be rejected as incorrect[50] and are stated by Vācasptati Miśra, Tātparyaṭīkā on II, i, 19, to have been held by an *ācāryadeśiya* [a pseudo-Naiyāyika teacher].[51] It appears

Univ. Press in 1930, and by Oriental Books Reprint Corporation in 1976.

[45] *Vigrahavyāvartanī*, French translation of the Tibetan translation, by Susumu Yamaguchi, *Journal Asiatqiue*, 215, p. 1-86. Also, "Shōrigakuha ni taisuru Ryūju no Ronsho: Vaidalia," Pts 1 and 2, (Nāgārjuna's Treatise against the Naiyāyika School), *Shūkyō Kenkyū*, IV, 2 & 3 (1927), resp. pp. 240-260 and pp.407-430.

[46] *Vigrahavyāvartanī*, Tibetan translation in G. Tucci, *Pre-Dinnāga Buddhist Texts on Logic from Chinese Sources*, Gaekwad's Oriental Series, 49. Baroḍa: Oriental Institute, 1929.

[47] *Vigrahavyāvartanī*, Sanskrit text, ed. Rāhula Sāṅkṛtyāyana, *Journal of Bihar and Orissa Research Society,* XXIV, No 3(19**). Appendix, Introd. pp. i-x; Text: pp. 1-31.

[48] E.H. Johnston and Arnold Kunst (eds): The *Vigrahavyāvartanī* of Nāgārjuna with the author's Commentary, [*Mélanges Chinois et Buouddhiques*, 1951, (Appendix, pp. 99-152)]. Esp. Kunst's introduction to the edition, *Ibid.*, p. viii.

[49] *Vigrahavyāvartanī*, verse 33:
teṣām atha pramāṇair vinā prasiddhir vihīyate vādaḥ/
viaṣamikatvaṃ tasmin viśeṣahetuś ca vaktavyaḥ// 33

[50] *Nyāyabhāṣya* II, i, 19

[51] Vācaspati Miśra: *Tātparyaṭīkā* II, i, 19.

therefore that the verse in question is quoted from some treatise by this discredited teacher, whose name we are never likely to learn. [The bracketing is this writer's.]

§6. FURTHER CONSIDERATION OF NĀGĀRJUNA'S EXCHANGE OF ARGUMENT WITH THE NAIYĀYIKAS

There is another portion in the *Nyāyasūtra,* namely, V, 1. 9-17, which Nāgārjuna is supposed to have known when he wrote the *Vigrahavyāvartanī* (esp. *kārikās* 34-39) and *Vaidalyaprakaraṇa* (*sūtras* 6-10). The heart of critique is concerned with whether a means of cognition (*pratyakṣa,* etc.) is self-evident (*svataḥpramāṇya*) or requires a secondary source for its ascertainment. The *Nyāyasūtra* passages in Chap. V assert that the *pramāṇa* is self-evident, requiring no second *pramāṇa* like a candle flame which illumines both itself and others. Nāgārjuna refutes not only this self-evidence of cognition but also its contrariety, i.e., requiring another (*parataḥpramāṇa*). In other word, he knew the portion of *Nyāyasūtra* 5. The aforementioned *Nyāyasūtra* 2 then rebutted Nāgārjuna by means of a candle flame which illumines others but is also perceived by human faculty, ultimately then on the basis of convention, such as, the Kāraka system.[52]

In his article of 1985, Kajiyama summarily dealt with the *Nyāyasūtra* V, 1. 9-17, calling attention to the fact that Nāgārjuna definitely knew this portion and possibly the most of Chap. 5 together with Chap. I, but that Nāgārjuna did not know Chap. II when he wrote the aforementioned dialectical texts. Thus, Kajiyama concludes that the first and fifth chapters of the *Nyāyasūtra* were already in existence in its basic form prior or contemporaneous to Nāgārjuna, whereas the second through fourth chapters were compiled after Nāgārjuna's death.53 In any case, it is clear that the foregoing state of affairs presents no serious obstacle, however, but offers a more cogent reason for me to uphold the proposed hypothesis that Nāgārjuna's literary activity, not only the composition of our concerned text *Upāyahṛdayaśāstra* but also the other dialectical treatises, can be approximated as likely contemporaneous with the earlier formative period of the *Nyāyasūtra* during the mid-second century A.D.

---

[52] Vātsyāyana defends the theory of *parataḥprāmāṇya* in *Nyāyabhāṣya* II, i. 16-19 by introducing the Kāraka system at length while commenting sūtra 16.

[53] *Op. cit.*, pp. 48-49.

The two initial centuries of the Western era constitute the crucial period for the developmental history of Indian philosophy as well as logical enquiry, because initially the *Carakasaṃhitā* and then the *Nyāyasūtra* contributed to the refinement of the Naiyāyika system of logic, so that a couple of centuries later Vātsyāyana could improve the theory further to become the Classical system of Nyāya logic. I think that it is more cogent to link Nāgārjuna's existence and active composition of his works with such a period of intellectual turmoil and search of theoretical perfection.

Finally, I am concerned with the representative Buddhist system of teachings (*siddhānta*, 定說) enumerated in the second of the eight criteria for the method of debate (八種論法) along with nine other sectarian systems of his times. The author ennumerates Buddhist system as four holy truths (四諦), twelve causes and conditions (十二因緣), thirty-seven auxiliary methods of enlightenment (*bodhipakṣikas*, 三十七菩提分法), and four sacred spiritual states of realilzation (四聖果). Ui regarded these items to be the basis of the author's being a Hīnayāna follower, while Kajiyama rather accepts them as authentic representation of the Buddha's teaching.[54]

On this subject matter, I am obliged to make an additional comment on the basis of the *Suhṛllekha* attributed to Nāgārjuna. In my previous paper that appeared in this journal, I proposed a theory that the *Suhṛllekha* and *Ratnāvalī* are written by Nāgāejuna for the sake of two contemporary rulers, hypothetically presented as a Śātavāhana king of the south, e.g., Gotamīputra Śātakarṇi, and a Śaka Satrap of Western India, i.e., Rudradāman, endowed with their unique personalities respectively suited to Hīnayāna and Mahāyāna orientation. What the *Suhṛllekha* mainly inculcates is the early orthodoxy upheld through the Ābhidharmika period, precisely because Nāgārjuna refers toward the end of the epistle to all of the aforementioned teachings. Nāgārjuna counsels the king by saying that "Nirvāṇa' is the state where all human suffering, e.g., life, old-age, death, and suffering and lamentation, is absent (transcended), nor is there in that state anything like hills, rivers, sun and moon,

---

54 *Op. cit.*, pp. I do not understand why it is wrong for Nāgārjuna to ennumerate these as genuinely Buddha's teachings (正義). Irrespective of whether Mahāyāna or Hīnayāna, there is no mistake in regarding these to be the Buddha's real teachings (正義). The *biography of Nāgārjuna* by Kumārajīva records that he is said to have studied Hīnayāna Sūtras and Śāstras before he became a Mahāyāna follower. This is also apparent in his various writings. Throughout the passages of this text, I do not find anything wrong for Nāgārjuna to write this text.

altogether." Accordingly, it is evident that Ui cannot hold his point of argument.

§7. CONCLUSION

The cross-philosophical enquiry on the interaction between Nāgārjuna and the Naiyāyikas reveals the probability that Nāgārjuna's logical and dialectical treatises fit best between the time of the *Carakasaṃhitā* and that of *Nyāyasūtra*. Vidyabhūṣaṇa notes that the abode of Akṣapāda known as Prabhāsa was situated beyond the rock of Girnar in Kathiawar, where we come across all the edicts of Aśoka as well as the Sanskrit inscription of Rudradāman, great Śaka Satrap of Ujjayinī. The date of the latter's panegyric, given as Śaka Era 72nd year, corresponds to the year 150 A.D. Thus, the hypothesis of Nāgārjuna's association with Rudradāman through his *Ratnāvalī* in the regions of Western India finds a further support from the foregoing cross-philosophical investigation.

The textual author of the *Upāyahṛdayaśāstra* justifies his treatise on the method of debate by setting his purposes as (1) preventing heretics and seductive rhetorics, (2) discriminating good and bad and neutral, (3) exposing the methods of other systems and terminating conceptual obsession, and (4) ultimately enabling the right *Dharma* to prevail in the world [*Taishō*. 32., p. 23, lines 15 ff]. I can agree with Kajiyama's descriptive term "anti-logical" insofar as Nāgārjuna theorized his method of debate for the purpose of combating misleading heretical teachings and their conceptual obsession. However, I disagree with his perspective in that I view the *Upāyahṛdaya-śāstra* to essentially be intended as a logical text to prescribe the ground rules for Buddhist debators in contest with Hindu adversaries. More importantly, I see that the *Upāyahṛdayaśāstra* was the ground work for Nāgārjuna to later on develop his method of dialectic in which he maximized the use of *dṛṣṭānta*.

ARTICLE SEVEN

STRUCTURAL LINKAGE BETWEEN NĀGĀRJUNA'S DIALECTIC AND LOGIC[1]

§1. TWO KINDS OF LOGICAL IMPASSE AND NĀGĀRJUNA'S DIALECTIC

In my last article that appeared in this journal [*JIBS*., 43., 2. (March 1995), 20-25], I tentatively suggested that the *Upāyahṛdaya-śāstra* (「方便心論」) was Nāgārjuna's ground work for his later innovation of a dialectic and that the logical principle of instantiation (*dṛṣṭānta*, 喻法) was maximized in his method. It is the purpose of this paper to substantiate these hypotheses by proving how and why his dialectic in part resolved the intra-Buddhist logical impasse recorded in the *Kathāvatthu* (「論事」) and in part also resolved the extra-Buddhist logical impasse like encountered by the author of that text. In short, as its author, Nāgājuna was compelled to innovate his dialectic to deal with the problem of these logical impasses.

As evidenced in the *Kathāvatthu* long before the times of Nāgārjuna, and before the early Nyāya logical system theorized in the *Carakasaṃhitā*, the principle of dual instantiation (*i.e., anvaya,* 同喻法; *vyatireka,* 異喻法) was the essential part of Indian logic. This principle can be analyzed into two mental processes: *Tendentious* and *Referential*. Take for example the Vaiśeṣika school's argument regarding "vocal word" (*śabda*): "Śabda is impermanent, because it is a product, just as a pot (anything that is molded) is" (*śabdo 'nitya kṛtakatvāt ghaṭavat*). Focusing on *Śabda*, this realist Hindu school distinguishes similar and dissimilar classes of variables by positively linking two propositions (*anvaya*): "if anything is a product of human effort" (*p*), then "that is impermanent (*q*)," like a pot, etc, and simultaneously by linking two contrapositive propositions (*vyatireka*): "if anything is not impermanent (–*q*)," then, "that is a non-product (–*p*)," like a god, etc. *Anvaya* verifies two assertions to

[1] This is a composite article of three minor papers included in the *Journal of Indian and Buddhist Studies* with the following titles: "On the Relationship between Nāgārjuna's Dialectic and Buddhist Logic (1)," Vol.45, No. 2, 1997, pp. 1029-1025; "Nāgārjuna's Dialectic and Indian Logic (2)" Vol. 46, No. 2, 1998, pp. 1024-1020; "Nāgārjuna's Dialectic and Buddhist Logic (3)," Vol. 47, No. 2, 1999, pp. 1021-1016.

be logically concomitant in reference to the members of the similar class of instantiation (*sapakṣa*), whereas *Vyatireka* also verifies two contrapositive assertions to be logically concomitant in reference to the members of the dissimilar class of instantiation (*vipakṣa*). In this logical context, the dual symbolic process of the mind is in part referential towards the respective classes of variables, and in part tendentious or purposive in linking the two respective propositions.

Historically, the logical impasse was created in two different ways. First, in challenge to the above Vaiśeṣika thesis, for instance, the Mīmāṃsaka transcendentalist argued on the same subject as follows: "*Śabda* is permanent, because it is audible (i.e., communicable to any one at any time), just as any vocal word (that is audible) is" (*śabdo nityaḥ śravaṇatvāt śabdatvavat*). The two schools therefore ended up with mutually contradictory definitions. The question is: "Are these schools really arguing about one and the same thing?" My answer is "No," because, even though the subject term bears the same name, what they really meant was in actuality two different things as is evident in their respective predications, i.e., "impermanent" and "permanent." This truth may not be generally known to the engaging contestants. Moreover, since the syllogistic formulas presented by both parties are error-free, it is not possible to resolve their contradictory definitions in terms of logic as to which is true or false. This impasse was caused by the difference of their presuppositions, expressed in different logical concomitances (*vyāpti*), i.e., "Whatever is a product is impermanent" (Vaiśeṣika) and "Whatever is audible is permanent" (Mīmāṃsaka). It was this type of logical impasse which the author of the *Upāyahṛdayaśāstra* likely encountered.

In my article, I suggested that the author's theory of logic was concerned with addressing to established sectarian doctrines (*siddhānta*, 定說) and with propagating right views against heretical views through public debate, and that the author theorized the class of similar instances to be a kind that is acceptable by all (凡聖同解) but the class of dissimilar instances to be a kind acceptable to a few (聖得凡不得). By implication, "acceptable by all" may be extended to prescribe that similar instance ought to be acceptable to all sectarian advocates. For instance, exemplifying an ordinary mind by a whirl-wind is acceptable equally to the wise as well as to the fool or to a Buddhist and to a non-Buddhist as true. The problem is the kind of dissimilar instances, because the author of *Upāyahṛdayaśāstra* theorized that it is permissible to apply a sectarian principle or presupposition as a dissimilar instance, insofar as it is admissible to the few wise. For instance, to the mind of Buddhist believers, the example of "*Nirvāṇa*" is acceptable, because it exemplifies the stillness of the mind in concentration (定心), as a means of contrast to the description of the ordinary mind as frivolous (散心) like a whirl-wind. In short, ultimately Buddhist sectarian principles cannot apply as a dissimilar instance in extra-Buddhist logical disputes and *vice versa*.

The second type of logical impasse can be created when it is concerned with the linkage between the trans-empirical (*paramārtha*) and empirical consciousness (*saṃvṛti*). The best example is an impasse created by mutual invalidation between the Theravādin and Pudgalavādin on the subject of *pudgala* (empirical self). Although I once treated this subject in "Ābhidharmika Logical Deadlock in *Kathāvatthu* and Nāgārjuna's Madhyamaka Dialectic,"[2] I shall recapitulate the essential points of their logical impasse. The initial dispute recorded in the *Kathāvatthu* was the Theravādin refutation against the Pudgalavādin heresy that the '*pudgala*' is a semi-trans-empirical agent. For the Theravādin orthodoxy, those trans-empirical *dharmas* of the Five Skandhas (*rupa*, *vedanā*, etc.), are alone real while an individual self, consisting of these psycho-physical elements, is merely an unreal phenomenon designated by name. The Theravādin was compelled to defeat the Pudgalavādin heretical view.

The Theravādin strategy was to adopt two concomitant propositions which jointly reveal the transcendent nature of *dharmas*: (1) if anything is known in the sense of a genuinely real thing (*upalabbhati-saccikaṭṭha-paramaṭṭhena*, "*p*"), then (2) it ought to be known in the same way as a genuinely real thing is known (*saccikaṭṭho paramaṭṭho-tato-so-upalabbhati-saccikaṭṭhaparamaṭṭhgena*, "*q*"). They expected that if a given variable is a *dharma*, the two propositions must be equally affirmed as "*p•q*," whereas if it is an empirical *pudgala*, both the propositions must be negated as "–q•–p." The Pudgalavādin asserts "*p*" as to the nature of *pudgala*, but he is obliged to negate the second as "–q," because, as Buddhist, he cannot assert that a *dharma* and a *pudgala* are identical. Thus, the Theravādin strategy induces an illogical concomitance as "p•–q" in the Pudgalavādin, hoping the latter to concede their defeat. In the second round, however, the Pudgalavādin rebutted the Theravādin by similar tactics, questioning: "Is a *pudgala* not known in the sense of a genuinely real thing?" The Theravādin denies it as "*–p*," but ought to affirm the second question: "Is a *pudgala* not known

[2] *Ibid.*, 39, 2 (March 1991), 20-24.

in the same way as a genuinely real thing is known?" as "q," because a *pudgala* is known as unreal only in the same way as *dharmas* are known as real.

This mutual invalidation seriously undermined the orthodoxy upheld by the Theravādin, because it blurred the distinction between the nature of transcendent *dharmas* and that of empirical self (*pudgala*). It is my contention that when contradiction or mutual invalidation ensues in the logical context and cannot be resolved in logical terms, it becomes the dialectical context. Here, the dialectic is necessarily and justifiably called for. In the simplest terms, the dialectic offers either to totally identify the dual referential variables or to juxtapose the dual propositional linkages. Although it is beyond the scope of this paper to fully explain Nāgārjuna's dialectical forms, I am obliged to point out what his dialectic can accomplish with regard to the logical impasse created by the foregoing two cases.

The reason that I call Nāgārjuna's method a "dialectic" is that it is anchored in the logical structure. In the use of language, the symbolic process of the mind necessarily operates in the logical context as consisting of the dual corroborations separated by similar and dissimilar referential variables. But when an impasse arises and cannot be resolved by logic, which I call "dialectical context," the dialectic is called for. As an explanation, I call attention to the way Buddhist logicians of Medieval India tried to resolve the Vaiśeṣika and Mīmāṃsaka confrontation: (1) Buddhist logicians placed emphasis on their respective reasons: "'*śabda*' is a product," and "'*śabda*' is audible," but not on the syllogism as a whole, because each syllogism is valid in the light of logical rules; (2) they accepted simultaneous validity for the contradictory theses but within each system of philosophical presuppositions, i.e., "Whatever is a product is impermanent" (Vaiśeṣika) and "Whatever is audible is permanent" (Mīmāṃsaka); (3) through identifying the two variables as real, they tried to shift both the mental process (corroborations) and the logical meaning (variables) on to a different domain transcending that of logical laws. In short, it was intended to shift the mind from the logical context in which the sense of difference is sharpened towards the trans-empirical domain. The dialectic performs the same function.

The dialectical method as well as the Buddhist logicians' approach was intended to bring forth a more reconcilable state of the mind. This, however, cannot be achieved while referential and tendentious forces of the mind are in full operation. The primary task that the dialectic is supposed to accomplish is to induce total contradiction in the logical and linguistic sphere of the mind. For instance, following a linguistic convention to explain a phenomenon of illumination by a contact of 'light' and 'dark,' the dialectic leads to the total incompatibility of the two, yet secondarily implies that they ought to be identified for the sake of convention. This actually does the same thing, shifting the matter of contradiction towards the trans-empirical sphere. In fact, the theoretical basis of the logicians was originally developed from the dialectical method. When an object of reference is perceived as having an independent nature (*svabhāva*) through a symbolic system, we call it empirically existent. When it is intuited as having merely dependent nature (*pratītyasamutpāda*) because of causes and conditions (*hetupratyayatā*), we call it transcendentally non-existent (*śūnyatā*) by discounting the reality of the symbolic system. What Nāgārjuna's dialectic repudiates is the two symbolic forces of mental behavior and culture formation, namely, the referential and tendentious forces of the mind.

The Mahāyāna Buddhist insight is generally distinguished from the Ābhidharmika's in terms of the unreality of both *dharmas* and *pudgala* (人法二無我). When we see how and why the Nāgārjunian dialectic can resolve the *Kathāvatthu*'s logical impasse, it becomes clear to us that the solution is not to abandon the orthodox insight of *dharmas*. On the contrary, it was intended to restore their status to the trans-empirical and non-linguistic domain as the sole concern of saintly insight, by totally distinguishing true *dharmas* from the empirical and linguistic domain where their status is subjected to controversy through admixture with *pudgalas* whose status is essentially limited to the empirical and linguistic domain.

§2. LOGICAL DISPUTE CITED AS TOPIC 2 IN THE *KALPANĀMAṆḌITIKĀ* (*TA-CHUAṆG-YEN-LUN-CHING*, 「大荘厳論経」)

The second topic of the *Ta-chuang-yen-lun-ching* translated by Kumārajīva or known as *Kalpanāmaṇḍitikā* in Sanskrit ascribed to Kumāralāta[3] by H. Lüder, consisted of a doctrinal dispute on causality between a new Buddhist convert, Kauśika by name, and his old Brahmanical colleagues. According to the story, Kauśika

[3] *Kalpanāmaṇḍitikā (Ta-chuang-yen-lun-ching*, 「大荘厳論経」) Taishō: Vol. 4 (No. 201) p. 258c - 261a.

happened to read the *Sūtra of the Twelve-Membered Causality*[4] and drawn to the practice of concentration. Going through the twelve causal linkages (*aṅga*) serially by way of phenomenalization (*anuloma*) as well as by way of dephenomenalization (*pratiloma*), he acquired an insight into the causality of dependent origination (*Pratītyasamutpāda*). Thus, he became a Buddhist upon his own conversion but was inevitably faced with a challenge from his former colleagues. He was obliged to respond to their challenges raised from the point of view of the Vaiśeṣika pluralist theory of causality and that of the Sāṃkhya monist theory of causality.

What is unique about the polemic cited in this story is that the method of argument undertaken against the Vaiśeṣika and Sāṃkhya theories of causality represents a miniature form of the Nāgārjunaian treatise. In addition, the argument reveals the relationship between Indian logic and Buddhist dialectic more clearly, because of its brevity and conciseness. The purpose of this paper is to lay out some important points of identity between the method of argument applied in this polemic and Nāgārjuna's dialectic and clarify the relationship between Buddhist dialectic and Indian logic.

In the classification of the philosophical schools in Classical India, the Vaiśeṣika was linked with the Naiyāiyika school of logic, because the former provided the metaphysical basis while the latter the logical superstructure. Kauśika declares to his Brahmanical colleagues that the Buddha's teaching of "twelve-membered Causality" is alone the true insight of causality, and that the rest of all other theories are false. The essential points of Kauśika's argument against the Vaiśeṣika goes briefly as follows:

> The Vaiśeṣikas are confused about cause and effect, because they do not understand the Buddhist *dharma* theory [i.e., *Skandhas, Āyatanas,* and *Dhātus*]. They brag about their inductive method [i.e., rendered by Kumārajīva as 'method of approximation' on a jar (瓶因果浅近之法)],[5] but it can only deal with the causality of things and not with that of human senses and intellect

---

[4] 「十二因縁経」 or 「貝多樹下思惟十二因縁経」 1 fasc., Taishō. 16 (No. 213) translated by chih-tien of Wu (呉支謙)

[5] From the logical point of view, the law referred to by Kumārajīva and translated by him as 「瓶因果浅近之法」 must be that of inductive logic, which is crucial to scientific knowledge. A causal law in science requires repeated experiment and approximation as to a given hypothesis. For instance, knowledge of the causal relationship between a jar and broken pieces of clay depends on repetition and approximation.

inherent in human body.[6] The material cause of a jar may be known by observing its prior presence and its break-down into pieces of clay later, just as this cloth here is made of those threads, vertical and horizontal, inter-woven line after line. If, however, a jar is here alone [without broken pieces], how can you determine its material cause as pieces of clay? Again, since broken pieces of clay do not function as a jar, by merely observing their presence from the point of view of a jar's function, how can you decide if these pieces might be the material cause of a jar?[7]

Indian logic is known to be double-featured, inductive as well as deductive. In order to demonstrate a causal relation between a rising smoke over the yonder hill and an outbreak of fire there, it is required to give an example from the similar class of things (*sapakṣa*), say, a kitchen, where both smoke and fire are generally co-present, and also an opposite example from the dissimilar class of things (*vipakṣa*), like a water tank, where neither fire nor smoke is observed. Induction demands validation of a given thesis in reference to *Sapakṣa* and *Vipakṣa* according to the rules of *Anvaya* and *Vyatireka* respectively, while deduction is simply an application of a given universal to a given object of inference. In short, the efficacy of a logical demonstration depends on how effectively a given example convinces the listeners regarding the certainty of co-presence of cause and effect in a given object in question.

Unlike the case of smoke and fire, however, a jar and its broken pieces of clay cannot be co-present despite their causal relationship. If an unbroken jar is present, there can't be pieces of clay, and if it is broken into pieces of clay, there can no longer be a jar. This inherent incompatibility is precisely identical with that incompatibility between *light* and *dark* which Nāgārjuna applied in his *Vigrahavyāvartanī* in order to refute the Naiyāyika and demonstrated the absurdity of their causal contact (*Kārikās* 37-39).

The similarity of argument here with that of Nāgārjuna becomes more convincing when we read the fifteenth verse of the tenth

---

[6] *Ibid.*, p. 259b: 26-29:「彼毘世師論極有過患。云何乃用比仏語。如毘世師論不知法相錯乱因果。於瓶因果浅近之法。尚無慧解分別能知。況解人身身根覚慧因果之義　」

[7] *Ibid.*, p. 259c: 1-9:「憍尸迦言。汝毘世師論実有是語。然無道理。汝今且観如因於縷以為経緯然後有畳。瓶瓦亦爾。先有瓶故然後有瓦、若先無瓶云何有瓦。復次破無用瓶瓦無用瓶瓦有用。是以破瓦不得為因。現見陶師取泥成瓶不用破瓦。又見瓶壊後有破瓦。瓶若未壊云何有破。」

chapter of his *Madhyamaka-śāstra*: "By means of an example of fire and fuel, all possible relationship between self and five Skandhas have been repudiated without a remainder, including causal examples of a jar and a cloth." In the chapter in question, neither a jar nor a cloth is actually treated, but both are especially taken up in Kauśika's polemic, the similarity of dialectic is beyond mere coincidence.

The Sāṃkhya philosophy, as linked with the Yoga school of practice in Classical India, theorized human cognition and consciousness in terms of spontaneous transformation of the single universal medium (*pradhāna*) triggered by its linkage with an individual spirit (*puruṣa*). The medium automatically changes itself into the subjective and the objective worlds of human experience. Sensation created by a sense faculty in correspondence to its object is to be unified by the ego principle (*ahaṅkāra*) and relayed to the faculty of intellect (*buddhi*) for cognition. Kauśika refutes this Sāṃkhya theory of causality and their logic of deduction approximately as follows:

> The Sāṃkhyas claim that the five-membered syllogism [i.e., proposition, reason, exemplification, application, and conclusion] explains everything. But they cannot provide an adequate example for validating their theory like "dewlap" which can determine the class of all cattle at once, because their metaphysical theory is logically self-contradictory. They postulated the primary principle (*pradhāna*) as unborn like a permanent principle, and as omnipresent everywhere, and yet, they say, it transcends every phenomenon simultaneously. Since "omnipresent" and "not omnipresent" are two contradictory features, the theory becomes meaningless by itself. If there is anything like that at all, it must be nothing but impermanent as an instantaneous thing.[8]

Though the absence of a logical example appears to be a minor offence, it is the major logical deficiency in Indian logic, because it not only disqualifies the logicality of a given thesis but also its syllogistic demonstration. From Kauśika's point of view, logic is supposed to deal with the world of empirical facts (三界 or 五趣).

---

[8] *Iibid*., p. 259c: 22-29 -260a: 1-7:「憍尸迦言、如僧佉経説有五分論義得尽。第一言誓。第二因。第三喩。第四等同。第五決定。汝僧佉経中無有譬喩可得明了如牛髯。況辨法相而能明了。何以故。汝僧佉経中、説鉢羅陀那不生如常遍一切処。亦処処去。如僧佉経中説鉢羅陀那不従他生而体是常。能生一切遍一切処去至処処。説如是事多有僭過。何以故。於三有中無有一法但能生物不従他生。是故有過。復次遍一切処能至処処。此亦有過。何以故。若先遍者去何所至。若去至者遍則不遍。二璃相違其義自破。若如是者則無常。」

According to the Sāṃkhya, however, the primary principle (*pradhāna* or *prakṛti*), by definition, transcends all phenomena as *noumenon* and yet simultaneously resides as immanent in all spheres of human experience. Thus, their causal theory of identity between cause and effect (*satkārya-vāda*) faces serious problem, precisely because there is no adequate example to exemplify transcendent *noumenon* in the original state (*pradhāna*) and multifarious variation of its evolved state in phenomena in terms of co-presence. It was Nāgārjuna's primary method to explore whatever self-contradictory concept is inherent in a given subject of examination and thereby demonstrate why it becomes impossible from the empirical point of view.

Although Kauśika's logical refutation ends after the foregoing two, his subsequent polemic reveals further points of similarity with Nāgārjuna's method. It was customary throughout ancient and medieval India that Brahmanical tradition invariably criticized Buddhism on account of the two basic doctrines, (1) that there is neither beginning nor ending with the succession of life and death (生死無有本際) and (2) that there is no self-identifying essence in a person as well as in all things (又復説一切法中悉無有我). In explaining these two, Kauśika applies the metaphor of "seed and sprout,"[9] which Nāgārjuna also used in his *Vigrahavyāvartanī*.[10]

Perhaps, the most significant similarity between Kauśika's polemic and the dialectic of Nāgārjuna ought to be sought in the way the latter placed the 26th and 27th chapters as conclusion of his *Madhyamakaśāstra*. In the 26th chapter, he does not apply his dialectic to any of the serial linkages of the twelve members of Dependent Origination, but simply presents them in due sequence for both phenomenalization (*anuloma*) and dephenomenalization (*pratiloma*). Kauśika too concludes his polemic by simply reciting the twelve members in both ways.[11]

Finally, after reciting the twelve links in the causation, Kauśika invokes a warning precisely like Nāgārjuna did in the 27th chapter, shunning the wrong view that the body really exists as belonging

---

[9] *Ibid*., p. 260b: 1-5: 「我於今者。楽説譬喩以明斯義。譬如穀子衆縁和合得生芽。然此種子実不生芽。種子滅故芽便増長。子滅故不常。芽生故不断。仏説受身亦復如是。雖復無我業報不失。」

[10] Cf. Nāgārjuna's auto-cmmentary on *Kārikā* 1, *Vigrahavyāvartanī*.

[11] *Ibid*., p. 260b: 19-25: 「時憍尸迦即為十二縁経而言。無明縁行。行縁識。乃至老生縁老死憂悲苦悩滅。無明滅則行滅。乃至老死滅故憂苦悩滅。以従衆縁無有宰主。弁於其中解悟無我。非経文中但説無我。復次以有身故則便有心。以有身心諸根有用識解分別。我悟斯事便解無我。」

to one's self (*sat-kāya-dṛṣṭi,* 有身見). Insofar as one is attached to the existence of self, one is under the spell of primordial desire and is totally involved in the process of life and death. It is therefore primary for the path of emancipation to eradicate the notion of "real existence of self."[12]

From the foregoing points of identity between Kauśika's method of argument and that of Nāgārjuna, the following points may be concluded: (1) the author of the *Kalpanāmaṇḍitikā* may have been nearly contemporaneous to Nāgārjuna, well acquainted with the latter's writings and understood the essentials of the doctrinal implication. (2) Just as the core process of Indian logic is the principle of *dṛṣṭānta*, the Nāgārjunian dialectic also structurally has the same principle in its core. In the logical context, cause and effect ought to be co-present in the class of *sapakṣa*, whereas in the dialectical context, cause and effect are forced to mutually contradict and exclude each other from their co-presence, on account of which a given causal relation is repudiated. The dialectical negation of a given relationship suggests an important rule that the necessary change from the logical to the dialectical context seems to take place when a given example is viewed in reference to its instantaneous space and time. (3) Since logic deals with the world of common sense phenomena, Buddhist dialectic must be deemed to deal with the world of instantaneous succession of the five Skandhas. Nāgārjuna's dialectic has all its goal as the method of entering the world of five Skandhas and has its justification within its instantaneous succession.

§3. THE MEANING OF METAPHORICAL EXAMPLES IN NĀGĀRJUNA'S DIALECTIC

Metaphorical examples that Nāgārjuna uses in his dialectical treatises seem to bear a similar function as that of logical examples (*dṛṣṭāna*). In his voluminous commentary *Mahāprajñāpāramitotpāda-śāstra,* especially in the 6th fascicle, he enumerates as many as ten metaphorical examples as adequate comparisons for corroborating the insight of *śūnyatā or niḥsvabhāva.*[13] What is common in the use

---

[12] *Ibid.*, p. 260b: 27-29 - c: 1-4: 「又問。若如汝言生死受身相続不断。設有身見有何過咎。答曰以身見故造作諸業。於五趣中受善悪身形。得悪形時受諸苦悩。若断身見不起諸業。不起諸業故則不受身。不受身故衆患永息。則得涅槃。」

[13] *Ta-chih-tu-lun* (「大智度論」): Taoshō 25 (No. 1509), 101c - 105c: *māyā*

of these metaphorical examples is to disclose the *dual natured reference*, such that whatever is experienced bears formal appearance, and yet it is simultaneously devoid of substantial existence, i.e., apparent existence and real non-existence. In this paper it is intended to clarify the theoretical basis of Nāgārjuna's metaphorical examples, such as, *māyā*, applied in his dialectical treatises. Whether did Nāgārjuna think of a theoretical basis for his use of metaphorical example as parallel with that of logical demonstration (*dṛṣṭānta*)? This question, I think, is relevant, because, being an adept logician and dialectician, he must have examined the efficacy and the validity of metaphorical examples applied in his treatises in parallel with those of logical examples. As an indirect piece of evidence for asserting that *māyā* example is based on a similar theoretical basis as that of logical demonstration, I call attention to Bhāvaviveka's syllogistic formula of demonstration in which the use of metaphorical examples occurs. The purpose of this paper is to prove the meaning of Nāgārjuna's *māyā* metaphor in parallel with the principle of logical example.

In general, the propositional symbol (sentence) is conceived as embodying the relationship of subject and predicate terms. The subject term refers to non-linguistic items such as things or facts, whereas the predicate term relates general conceptions to it. Grammatically, the former is introduced by nouns or substantivals through nominalization, while the latter, by verbs or verb-like, adjectival, participial, etc. Based on these two criteria, i.e., categorial and grammatical, J. F. Staal tried to establish in 1960[14] that in Sanskrit, like other Indo-European languages, nominalized elements appear as the subject, and only elements which are not nominalized as the predicate. In this connection, he determined also that the function of a Sanskrit sentence is predicative and that its negation is the negation of its predicate and not of its subject. Thus, the view of Schayer (1932) and Kunst (1959) that Indian logic operates as a rule with propositional assertions and their variables, has been attested in a wider context. It was due to the same theoretical basis that I transcribed into symbolic notation the initial round of arguments between the Theravādin and Pudgalavādin schools as

---

(如幻), *marīci* (如焔 or 蜃気楼), *dakacandrā* (如水中月), *ākāśa* (虚空), *pratiśruthā* (如響), *gandharvanagara* (如乾闥婆城), *suvapnachāyā* (如夢影), *pratibimba-nirmāṇa* (如鏡中像), and *upamadharma-adhimukutir* (如化).

[14] "The Construction of Formal Definitions," *Transactions of Philological Society*, p. 91.

recorded in the *Kathāvatthu*.[15]

In 1997, I presented another paper on a Buddhist critique against the Vaiśeṣika and Sāṃkhya systems of philosophy as recorded in the *Kalpanāmaṇḍitikā*.[16] The refutation is unique in the sense that the causal theories of both the schools were repudiated on the ground that both systems lacked an adequate example. Logical exemplification *(dṛṣṭānta)* means (1) corroboration of the linkage of two propositions as "p ⊃ q" (if smoke, then fire) in reference to a given class of variables 'x' (*sapakṣa*: a kitchen, etc.) and likewise (2) contrapositive corroboration of the linkage of two negated propositions as "–q ⊃ –p" (if no fire, then no smoke) in reference to the opposite class of variables 'y' (*vipakṣa*: a water tank, etc.). For repudiating the Sāṃkhya causality, the Buddhist critique points out that there is no example to corroborate the two contradictory propositions referring to the Sāṃkhya monistic principle, namely: "*Pradhāna* (*noumenon*) is permanent and immanent in all phenomena," and "is simultaneously transcendent from all of them." These contradictory propositions preclude the possibility of an empirical example for corroborating the Sāṃkhya primary principle. As to the Vaiśeṣika causality, the Buddhist critique questions about the validity of inductive method which the school-men prided as capable of discovering all things, causalities, relations, and so forth. Taking up the causal relation between a jar and broken pieces of clay as an example, the critique questions: How could a proposition that refers to the presence of an unbroken jar be linked with another proposition that refers to broken pieces of clay? When an unbroken jar is present, there should be no broken piece of clay, and *vice versa*. In this context, no linkage is ascertained between two propositions as true, irrespective of whether the linkage means identity or causality. This mutual exclusion of the two referential variables has its well known parallel in Nāgārjuna's use of a metaphor of light and dark. In his *Vigrahavyāvartanī*, Nāgārjuna dialectically repudiates a possibility of co-presence of light and dark on the basis that their natures mutually exclude each other, although convention takes their contact for granted to explain a fact of illumination. If light and dark are respectively symbolized as variables 'x' and 'y,' I contend that an assumption of their co-presence creates the dialectical context, in which 'x' and 'y' are not separated but coalesced in the

---

[15] Cf. "Ābhidharmika Logical Deadlock in Kathāvatthu and Nāgārjuna's Madhyamaka Dialectic," *JIBS*, 39 (No. 2), 1991; pp. 20-24.

[16] Cf. Note 3 above.

mind, as dual natured reference 'xy.'

Among the Mādhyamika school-men, Bhāvaviveka, who initiated the Svātantrika tradition, advocated the syllogistic formula of demonstration for the insight of *śūnyatā* in contrast to the Prāsaṃgikas who exclusively advocated the *prasaṃga* method (i.e., *reductio-ad-absurdum argument*). Bhāvaviveka is known to have upheld that in public debate, the Mādhyamikas may have to debate with other philosophical schools through a syllogistic formula equipped with thesis, reason, and example. In his *Karaṭala-ratna,*[17] Bhāvaviveka presented two model arguments to demonstrate the insight of *śūnyatā*. In one, the subject term is a variable of empirical things, and in another, it is a variable of trans-empirical *dharmas*, but both the predicates are identical in terms of *śūnyatā* (devoid of existence or reality). This negation is characterized by a conditional adverbial term as '*paramārthatas*' or '*tattvatas*' (from the point of view of ultimate truth) and exemplified by metaphorical examples.[18]

In my article of 1991, I proved that Nāgārjuna's dialectic was in part intended to resolve the logical deadlock of the Abhidharmist controversy between the Theravādin orthodoxy and Pudgalavādin heterodoxy. The Theravādins upheld that *dharmas* alone are real. The school-men were compelled to defeat the Pudgalavādin's heresy that *pudgalas* too are somehow real and transcendent. In that same article, I introduced a view that Nāgārjuna's method of dialectic contributed to the solution of the *Kathāvatthu* logical deadlock. I believe that the syllogistic formulas of the Svātantrika not only support my point of view but also explain the meaning of the metaphorical examples.

Briefly explaining the origin of the logical deadlock, first, the Theravādin prepared two propositions in order to defeat the

---

[17] Cf. N. Aiyaswami Sastr: *Karatalaratna of Bhavya*, Visva-Bharati Annals II (1949), i-xvi, 1-124; The text of Sanskritizatiion from the Chinese Tripiṭaka *Ta-ch'êng-changchen-lun* (「大乘掌珍論」) *or The Mahāyāna Treasure within the Hand,* Taishō. 30 (No. 1578), 268 ff.

[18] (1) *tattvataḥ saṃskṛtā śūnyā māyāvat pratyayodbhavāt/* (真性有為空、如幻縁生故)

Thesis: In ultimate truth, whatever is empirical is devoid of its existence,

Reason: Because its origination depends upon causes and conditions,

Example: Like a magical apparition (that is devoid of real existence).

(2) *asaṃskṛtās tv asvahbhūtāḥ khapuṣpavat//* (無為無有実、不起似空華)

Thesis: [In ultimate truth,] whatever is transcendent has no existential reality,

Reason: Because it is devoid of [empirical] origination.

Example: Like sky-flowers [that is devoid of existential reality].

Pudgalavādin:[19]

(1) *upalabbhati-saccikaṭṭhaparamaṭṭhena-ti* (Whatever is known in the sense of a genuinely real thing);

(2) *saccikaṭṭho paramaṭṭho tato so upalabbhati saccikaṭṭha-paramaṭṭhena-ti* (Whatever is known in the same way as a genuinely real thing is known).

Transcribing the referential entity '*dharmas*' as the members of a variable 'x' and the two related propositions respectively as "p" and "q," I can simplify the linkage of the two propositions as "(x)p• (x)q." This means that the two propositions can be linked as true when the reference is transcendent *dharmas* 'x'. On the other hand, when the variable 'y,' such as empirical *pudgalas*, is applied to the same two propositions, the Theravādin hoped to see the result as "(y)–q• (y)–p." This means that the class of *pudgalas* 'y' is clearly determined as empirical, and the Pudgalavādin's claim that *pudgalas* are also real and transcendent is falsified. But the Pudgalavāsdin's arguments in rejoinder ingeniously leads to an unexpected mutual invalidation and logical deadlock. The following chart is a reproduction of one that has already been cited in the article 5 before. Since the variable *pudgala* 'y' is all common in all arguments, it is dropped from the formula of symbolic notation.

Mutual Invalidation in Chart

1. Theravādin Refutation

Puggalavādin thesis 'p•–q'
is false, because 'p ⊃ q';
'p•–q' is false, because '–q ⊃–p';
Hence, the thesis 'p•–q' is false.

2. Puggalavādin Rejoinder

Theravādin refutation '–p•q'
is false, because '–p ⊃–q';
'–p • q' is false, because 'q ⊃ p';
Hence, the refutation '–p•q' is false.

3. Puggalavādin Refutation

Theravādin's refutation '–p•q'
can be refuted, because '–p ⊃ –q.'
Theravādin's refutation '–p•q'
is false, because 'q ⊃p.'
Hence, '–p•q' can be refuted.

4. Puggalavādin Application

Our thesis 'p•–q' is not falsified;
Your refutation '–(p•–q)' is
not acceptable, because 'p⊃q'
and also because '–q ⊃ –p';
Hence, '–(p•–q)' is not acceptable.

5. Puggalavādin's Conclusion

---

[19] [Cf. Rhys Davids's translation: *The Points of Controversy or Subjects of Discourses.* PTS, 1915].

Our thesis 'p • –q' is not refuted,
because 'p• q' is not compelled;
Your refutation –(p• –q) is not convincing,
because '–p• –q' is not compelled;
Hence 'p•q' and '–q• –p' are not convincing

As evident in this chart, the logical principle of dual corroborations (*anvaya-vyatireka*) was already strictly adhered to by Buddhist debaters at the time of *Kathāvatthu*. If the dual corroborations result in the form of "(x){p• q}" and "(y){–q•–p}," the demonstration is valid, i.e., because *dharmas* and *pudgalas* are clearly differentiated. If, on the other hand, the corroborations result in either "(y){p• –q}" or "(y){q• –p}," the demonstration is invalid, because the given variable 'y' is cross-boundary, i.e., partially identified with 'x.' Thus, the Pudgalavādin insisted that although their thesis is cross-boundary as "(y){p•–q}," insofar as the Theravādin's thesis on *pudgala* remains also to be cross-boundary as "(y){–p• q}," they did not feel compelled to acknowledge defeat. Thus, it became the major Abhidharmist task how to deal with this problem of cross-boundary, mutual invalidation on the nature of *pudgalas*. It was necessary either to clearly separate the class of *dharmas* 'x' and that of *pudgalas* 'y' respectively into the transcendent and empirical domain. Or, since this separation is not possible as long as it is dealt by logical convention as evident in the above chart, it was inevitable to bring the status of *dharmas* down toward the empirical domain through total identification but *upon one single condition, such that both variables are devoid of reality*. This was what Nāgārjuna accomplished through the dialectic of *śūnyatā*.

Bhāvaviveka's two model arguments concisely express the same.

(1) *tattvataḥ saṃskṛtā śūnyā, māyāvat pratyayodbhavāt/*
An empirical object (有為) is ultimately (真性) devoid of existence (空);
Because its origination depends on causes and conditions (縁生故);
Like a magical apparition (如幻) [that is devoid of real existenc];

(2) *asaṃskṛtās tv asvahbhūtāḥ khapuṣpavat//*
A transcendent entity has no existential reality (無為無有実);
Because it is devoid of [empirical] origination (不起故).
Like sky-flower (似空華) [that is devoid of existential reality].

The given examples are respectively "magical apparition" (*māyāvat*) and "sky-flower" (*kha-puṣupavat*), which are included in Nāgārjuna's list of metaphorical examples. Thus, Bhāvaviveka's two syllogistic demonstrations incorporated metaphorical examples in parallel with the regular logical demonstration.

Three points are in order: First, in the *Kathāvatthu*, the Theravādin regarded *dharmas* 'x' and *pudgalas* 'y' as the variables of position and contraposition respectively, but as evident in the Svātantrika formula, the Mādhyamika retained the classes of variables 'x' and 'y' as distinct in the subject term and yet totally identified these in the predicate in terms of *śūnyatā*. The use of metaphorical examples, such as *māyā*, is obviously meant to corroborate the insight of *śūnyatā*. Second, in the Mādhyamika demonstration, each distinct variable in the subject term is justified to lose distinction by the universal predication of *śūnyatā* with adverbial terms like '*tattvatas*' and '*paramārthatas*.' This modificational term is identical with the *Kathāvatthu*'s usage of '*saccikaṭṭhaparamaṭṭhena*' and obviously implies a contextual change from the empirical to the transcendent and from the logical to the dialectical context. Third, this adverbial term "from the point of view of ultimate truth" also is designed to imply a unique sentential construction, such that while the subject refers to empirical objects, the predicate is oriented toward the trans-empirical. Although this sentential construction was one of the major targets of the Prāsaṃgika criticism, it may have some significant meaning in the way of dealing with the logico-linguistic propensity of human mind. While *śūntyatā* is obviously different from ordinary negation, what is essential to the linkage of moments, spaces, cognitions, and sentences ought to be the *dual natured reference* as "simultaneously existent and non-existent," or "identical and different." It must be an intermediary object of reference brought forth by the dialectical context and exemplified by a magical apparition.

Section Three

CHINESE BUDDHIST CRITICAL SPIRITUALITY AND ITS CULTURE

ARTICLE EIGHT

The Significance of Chinese Buddhist Philosophy for the Contemporary World[1]

§1. Introduction

In the early 1960's when I was engaged in doctoral thesis research, I came to know a work of Prof. Hu Shih (胡適), eminent historian and philosopher, on the subject of ancient Chinese logic.[2] For the first time, I became aware that the Mohist school of logic, founded by Mo-tzŭ,[3] a contemporary of Confucius (K'ung-tzŭ),[4] prospered in ancient China for a few centuries prior to the Ch'in dynasty (255-209 B.C.) and that of Han.[5] While perusing the text, I was struck by the fact that the ancient China already developed a logical system comparable to that of ancient India as well as ancient Greece, and that the Chinese actively applied the logical method not only to advance scientific knowledge but also to resolve social and political problems.

In the same work, Hu Shih pointed out that from the logical point of view, the Confucian and Mohist, though rival, nevertheless complemented each other by their respective contributions to the development of logical thought. Where Confucian thinkers set forth the principle of "names" and "predicables," the Mohist thinkers discovered the principle of "subject term." Thus, despite their adversarial positions, their theories precisely contributed to the advancement of Chinese logical thought in terms of the logical structure of propositions.

Although Buddhism appeared in China several centuries after these pre-Han philosophical schools, its philosophical insights further

---

[1] Presented at the 8th International Conference for Chinese Philosophy, Beijing University, Aug. 9-13, 1993; published as part of *Journal of Chinese Philosophy*, under the title Contemporary Significance of Chinese Buddhist Philosophy, 24 (1997) 75-106.

[2] Hu-shih (胡適): *The Development of the Logical Method in Ancient China*, Shang-hai: The Oriental Book Co., 1928.

[3] 墨子(ca. 480-390 B.C.), native of Lü (魯).

[4] 孔子(ca 551-479 B.C.), posthumous name: 至聖文宣王, native of Lü.

[5] The former Han held its sovereignty from 206 B.C. to A.D. 23; the latter Han from A.D. 25 to 220.

contributed to the Chinese logical and linguistic understanding. It is important for students of Chinese philosophy to focus more attention on the Buddhist philosophical insights in Medieval China in the area of pre-linguistic and pre-logical phases[6] which underlie the ordinary mental, logical and linguistic functions as a way to evaluate the moral and religious thoughts of the Chinese.

The purpose of this paper is threefold: (1) to examine briefly the Confucian and Mohist thoughts on logic and language; (2) to present the Classical Chinese Buddhist thought on logic and language as an important complement to ancient Chinese logical thoughts, and (3) to evaluate the contemporary relevance and significance of Chinese Buddhist thought and insight.

§2.. CONFUCIAN AND MOHIST THOUGHT ON MORAL AND CULTURAL PROBLEMS

As is known among historians, during the period of the sixth century B.C., the central power of the Chou dynasty (周) was steadily declining and the feudal state was rapidly disintegrating. The Chou aristocracy and culture, the revival of which Confucius dreamed, were no longer cohesive. There developed the multi-independent states each equipped with a bureaucratic system and each fought against every one else throughout the period of social and political uphearvals. This chaotic state of affairs eventually ended in the rise of Ch'in, a centralized and bureaucratic empire just preceding the great Han Dynasty (漢). Facing the ills of the times, Confucius and Mo-tzŭ were equally engaged in the task of restoring the order of society and reforming its system by advocating two widely different philosophical and practical orientations.

Confucius (ca. 450 B.C.), a teacher of young nobles in the state of Lu (魯), devoted his life to defining and refining the values embodied in the proprieties and culture of the Chou aristocracy. Behind these norms of conduct and culture, he perceived an ideal "true gentleman" (Chün-tzŭ, 君子) guided by such inherent principles as benevolence, etc. ("Love others" and "Do not do to others what you would not wish them to do to you.") and reasoned that the ills

[6] As to the meaning of "pre-linguistic phases," see Ichimura: "*Śūnyatā* and Paradigm-Shift: Dialogue between Buddhism and Science" included in *Śramaṇa Vidyā Studies in Buddhism, Prof. Jagannath Upadhyaya Commemoration Volume I*, Sarnath, Varanasi, India: Central Institute of Higher Tibetan Studies, 1987, pp. 81-100.

of the society derived from the prevailing negligence on the part of the aristocratic members of society, the failure to adhere to the norms of proprieties and maintain cultural forms of harmony such as music (*le*, 楽). Thus, his major effort was directed toward the restoration of the codes of honor (positive rules of propriety) to be practiced by the true "gentlemen." Confucius was convinced that as the ruling class of landed gentlemen mutually support each other through normative proprieties, the masses would spontaneously follow the rules of law.

Chou society was divided into the classes of landed aristocrats and the masses. The members of aristocracy regulated their own conduct based on a body of positive rules of propriety, i.e., a "code of honor" (*li*, 禮), while the masses were imposed legal codes which provided for the "five kinds of penalties with their 'three thousand' classified degrees." Under this dual system of morality, along with the division of the society into "superior men" and "little men," the former was governed by a code of honor alone whereas the latter or the masses by the fear of punishment. If the people are governed by laws and their conduct regulated by punishment, Confucius reasoned that the idea of "government by law" will become highly undesirable because to him it seemed evident that the masses would try to evade the penalties without the sense of shame. In any case, he did not think of the law as an effective instrument. Thus, he concluded that the best way to lead the masses was by virtue and the rules of propriety, enabling them to feel shame and thus try to be good.[7]

Standing on the other side of the aisle, Mo-tzŭ and his followers neither shared the culture of Chou as understood by the Confucians nor desired to complicate their lives with elaborate etiquette, such as the duty to mourn one's father for three years. Their guiding principle was always practical utility combined with pragmatic criterion, such that the meaning of every institution lay in what was good for itself, and the meaning of every conception or belief or policy lay in what kind of conduct or character it was fitted to produce. Mo-tzŭ said: "Any principle which can elevate conduct should be perpetuated. That which cannot elevate conduct should not be perpetuated. To perpetuate anything that cannot elevate conduct is nothing but waste of speech."[8] The Mohists felt a deep objection not only to the class division of the aristocratic members and the masses, but also to the aristocratic moral code because it

---

[7] Cf. Hu Shih: *Ibid.*, p. 47.

[8] *Ibid.*, p. 65.

was divisive, requiring the gentleman to put his duties to his family and his lord before the interests of anyone else. Accordingly, each family as well as each state was obliged to prefer itself over others and to be drawn into conflict with others, a conflict in which, it was the common people who always suffered.

In contrast to the Confucian principle of gradation of love, decreasing with the remoteness of relationship, the Mohists introduced the idea of universal concern or love, loving others just as one's self. "Chien-ai" (兼愛) means "to love others just as one's self," having as much regard for others, say, father, elder brother, lord, vassar, and so forth, as for one's self, having as much regard for other families as for one's own, and so on.[9] The term signifies a principle that applies to all, thus it is translatable as "universal love." But it was also on this same principle of "universal concern" that aggression (*kung,* 攻), namely, one state attacking another state simply in order to benefit at its expense, was condemned by the Mohists as a crime no different from the private robberies and murders committed and punishable by the state. Although Mo-tzŭ and his followers were not people with warm sympathies towards everyone, their personal affection was disciplined by a stern sense of justice and equality. In theory, they did not tolerate the idea of a state or government which did not benefit all but a limited class of citizens.

The Mohists believed that a government originated from the need to unify the "different moralities" (*i-i,* 異義) of individuals competing in the primitive war of all against all, and that its function is to "unify and assimilate morality throughout the empire" (*i-t'ung-hsia-chih-i*).[10] He treated anarchy as a conflict not of interests but of "moralities," by which he meant not moral codes but the conflicting family or state loyalties within the traditional love which the Confucians advocated.[11]

§3. CONFUCIAN AND MOHIST CONTRIBUTION TO LOGIC AND LANGUAGE

Philosophically, both Confucius and Mo-tzŭ contributed to the logical and linguistic reflection. Confucius sought to "rectify the

---

[9] Cf. A.C. Graham: *The Later Mohist Logic and Science*; Hong-kong: Chinese University Press, 1978; p. 12.

[10] 一同天下之義、Cf. *ibid.*, p. 13.

[11] *Ibid.*, p. 8.

names" as the task which he considered so necessary in order to realize moral and political reform. Thus, as Hu Shih puts it, "Confucius sought to make the language as exact means and an integral part of the logical philosophy."[12] He used the written words and judgments (i.e., propositions) so judiciously and so juridically to imply moral judgment, to approve and condemn as the laws of a State ought to approve and condemn.[13] The events in the *Chun-Chiu* (「春秋」) are not merely recorded with linguistic exactitude, but also at the same time with ethical judgments. The judgments are implied in the wording itself. He registered his disapproval and condemnation of wars carried on by one state against another as "invasions and aggressions." Only those wars led by princes who had received at least nominal sanction from the Emperor were recorded as "punitive expedition." In short, the *Chun-Chiu* is said to have been intended by Confucius to embody his doctrine of "rectifying names and judgments" and "to reform a corrupt age and restore it to rightness." The underlying methods are (1) to apply exact use of language, (2) to give implicit ethical judgments, and (3) to lay out ideal relationship.

As evident, Confucius' motive was an intellectual reorganization of society by means of "names" and "judgment," which he truly believed to be the key to the solution, namely, "to reform a corrupt age and restore it to rightness." He and his followers attempted to discover through the study of names what things ought to be and sought after in order to reform the social and political order of the day. They furnished the society with an elaborate and rigid system of ideal relationship (*li*, 理).[14] These two tasks were carried out by the Confucian scholars in the following centuries in terms of (1) teaching the judicious use of the written word as exemplified in the *Chun-Chiu*, and (2) editing and codifying elaborate customs, moral precepts, rituals, ceremonies, etc. into a system of propriety (*li*, 禮). Their motto was: "Set up what is righteous, and consider not its beneficial results."[15]

Mo-tzŭ was quite dissatisfied with this Confucian method and approach. He instead sought for a criterion by which the truth and falsity as well as the right and wrong of beliefs, theories, institutions,

---

[12] Hu Shih: *op. cit.*, p. 50 .

[13] *Ibid.*, pp. 48-49.

[14] *Ibid.*, p. 67. Aslo see Herbert Fingarette: *Confucius – the Secular as Sacred*, Harper Torchbook, 1972, esp., the concept of Li[fb] in Confucius' thought.

[15] Hu Shih: *op. cit.*, p. 64.

and policies could be *tested* either to be so or not to be so. Accordingly, Mo-tzŭ's motto, as quoted before, was: "Any principle which can elevate conduct should be perpetuated. That which cannot elevate conduct should not be perpetuated. To perpetuate anything that cannot elevate conduct is nothing but waste of speech." Unlike the Confucians, they always considered the pragmatic principle and kept their eyes on the end results or beneficial results which might come by choosing the proper course of action. Thus, the practical consequence was the sole criterion of value and worth of principles and institutions. Consequently, Mo-tzŭ and his followers were always aware of the importance of the motives of action as "foreseen ends which call for the endeavor." This was Mo-tzŭ's distinct contribution to the philosophical insight of moral action beyond that of Confucius.

From the logical point of view, the Confucian contribution was the discovery of the significance of "names" or "predicables" which become the indices to classify things and actions. But the Confucians failed to see that the predicables detached from their practical bearing upon the "predicated" are empty and meaningless. It was left to Mo-tsŭ and his followers to introduce the term "subject" or the "predicated" (*shih*, 実) into their logic. Quoting from Hu Shih's translation, Mo-tzŭ defined the subject term and the predicate term, respectively, as "that by which something is said (about something) is the predicate (name); that about which something is said, is the subject or the predicated (real)."[16] For students of philosophy, it is evident that the Confucian attempt of discovering the original meaning of a word is a futile task. Even if it is found, the original meaning can have very little more than mere etymological interest. If we abandon the strictly etymological approach, we are compelled to resort to arbitrary meanings by attributing them to conceptual references as ideals.

According to Hu Shih, therefore, Mo-tzŭ's contribution was to check this irresponsible one-sided emphasis of the empty predicables by discovering "subject term" to which names or predicates are to be predicated. A predicate must be taken with reference to the predicated, and a judgment must be taken with reference to its practical consequences. Knowledge ought to consist not in learning predicables and universals, but in the ability to use these things in real life, namely, "to elevate conduct." A man is said to "know" things "not because of his ability to name them, but because of his

---

[16] *Ibid.*, p. 67.

ability to choose them."[17]

The ancient Confucians will say to those who powerlessly stand by watching moral chaos, violent bloodshed, and meaningless destruction, to educate yourselves to the meanings of human rights, freedom, justice and ultimately, to understand the underlying universal law, through the study of these conceptual names and predicates, and thereby seek to reform the global social and political order with an elaborate and rigid system of ideal relationship confronting multi-racial, multi-cultural, multi-religious or multi-national encounters. The Mohists, however, would further say: This is not enough. You ought to be able to distinguish the right from the wrong by enquiring into the causes of a good government as well as a bad government. By examining the relations between names (predicables) and substances (subjects), one ought to be able to determine the good and the evil in reference to actual agents, things or events and deal with difficult and doubtful situations.[18]

But how can we do these things? The Mohists then provided us with their theory of logical method, through which we may be able to discover ways to deal with these multiple tasks. Mo-tzŭ developed a system of logic, the only logic developed in the history of Chinese thought. Rephrasing Hu Shih's translation of the crispy textual statement, I put the Mohist definition of inferential logic as follows:

> The reasoner ought to note and observe the happenings (literally becoming so) of all things, seek the order or relation between the various judgments, define the subject with the predicate to express his meaning in a proposition by giving the reason [i.e., by the statement to begin with 'because' (*ku*, 故)] in a premise, and support the reason-conclusion relation *by selecting instances on the principles of agreement* (*t'ung*, 同) *and difference* (*i*, 異) [The *italic* is this writer's.].[19]

This constitutes the essential element of Mohist logic. The surprise

---

[17] *Ibid.*, p. 93.

[18] *Ibid*, and also Graham, *op. cit.*, p. 40. Graham especially calls attention to the Mohist introduction of the 'tz'ŭ' (辞) or "speech, sentence or proposition" for the first time distinguished from the name. He states: The distinction, grammatically less marked in Chinese than in Indo-European languages, seems to have attracted attention only after it was noticed that "knowing is different from having a pictorial idea," and with this discovery, "the Mohist's attention shifts to the similarities and differences, not between objects or names, but between the propositions by which we describe.

[19] Hu Shih: *ibid*, p. 93; Also Cf. Graham's above note and its follow-up, *ibid.*, p. 40.

is that this Mohist method of inference is indeed comparable to the Buddhist method of inference (*anumāna*) developed in India.

§4. COMPARISON BETWEEN CHINESE AND INDIAN LOGIC

The Indian logic of inference in general was theorized on the dual principles of *anvaya* and *vyatireka*. The terms, '*anvaya*' and '*vyatireka*,' originally belonged to the vocabulary of the science of grammar in ancient India and signify respectively "connection" and "separation."[20] As philosophical reflection developed, these terms were used by Buddhist as well as Hindu logicians to mean the dual procedures of similar and dissimilar instantiations for logically valid reasoning. As referred to before, these two operations correspond exactly to the Mohist principles of agreement (*t'ung*) and difference (*i*)[v]. As will be made clear below, irrespective of Indian or Chinese language, these operations are fundamental to the mental process of classifying referential objects by means of naming and hence indispensable to the practical use of language (*vyavahāra*).

In the Indian logical context, the positive and negative instantiations represent not only inductive but deductive reasoning as well. For instance, in an inference to reason from rising smoke perceived over the slope of a distant hill, one may infer an outbreak of fire there. First, the reasoner seeks to determine whether it is valid to assert the two related predications (i.e., "something has smoke" (Reason) and "something has fire" (Conclusion) in reference to an object of reference (a distant hill). So one tests this causal concomitance of "smoke-and-fire" (i.e., "Wherever there is smoke, there is fire") by referring it to similar instances, such as, a kitchen where the two always concur. In addition, one is also obliged to test the contraposition: "If no fire, then no smoke" by referring it to dissimilar instances, such as a water tank, where the two concomitants never occur separately or jointly. Having done so, only then, in reference to a given subject term (i.e., here 'a hill'), the reasoner can safely assert the reason (*hetu*): "Because of a rising smoke over the hill-side," and the conclusion (*sādhya*): "an outbreak of fire on that hill." In Indian syllogism, this combined procedure of inductive and deductive reasoning, i.e., citing similar and dissimilar examples, was required at all times.

---

[20] Cf. G. Cardona: "Anvaya and Vyatireka in Indian Grammar," *The Adyar Library Bulletin*, 31-32, 1967-68, 313-352.

The Mohist principles of agreement and difference likewise constitute an inductive reasoning. As a minor difference from Indian logic, however, the Mohists did not include the dual instantiations in the syllogistic formula, theorizing instead a valid inference to be based on a Hsiao[w],[21] i.e., an inductively well proven causal or logical relation based on the method of agreement and difference. In this respect, Indian and Chinese forms of syllogistic inference are fundamentally the same, reflecting the universal nature of logic and language.[22] With this understanding, the meaning of the Mohist's criticism against the Confucian doctrine of names can be more clearly grasped by consulting with a Hindu-Buddhist dispute that occurred in Medieval India. There is an instructive parallel between the difference of Mohist and Confucian logical thought on the one hand and that of Buddhist and Hindu logical thought on the other.

One of the heated disputes between Buddhist and Hindu logicians in Medieval India was focused on the question: Whether the Buddhist three-membered syllogism innovated from the traditional Indian five-membered logic is valid. The traditional Indian syllogism consisted of five statements:

(1) Thesis (*pratijñā*): "Fire on the hill,"
(2) Reason (*hetu*): "Smoke on the hill,"
(3) Examples (*udāharaṇa*): "Wherever there is smoke, there is fire, like in a kitchen," and "Wherever there is no fire, there is no smoke, like near a water tank.
(4) Application (*upanaya*): "There is smoke on the hill,"
(5) Conclusion (*nigamana*): "Therefore, there is fire on the hill."[23]

Critically examining this formula, the Buddhist logician, Dignāga (ca. 5th century), introduced a three-membered formula as follows:

(1) Examples: similar instantiation (*anvaya*) and dissimilar instantiation (*vyatireka*),
(2) Reason which implies its Conclusion as applicable to a substratum,

---

[21] Cf. Hu Shih: *op. cit.*, p. 99; also Graham: *op cit.*, pp. 470-473.

[22] Cf. S. Ichimura: "On the Paradoxical Method of the Chinese Mādhyamikas: Sêng-chao and the Chao-lun Treatise," *Journal of Chinese Philosophy* 19 (1992) 51-71.

[23] Of these five-membered statements, Dignāga eliminated initially the *Nigamana* (conclusion) and *Upanaya* (application of concomitance or *vyāpti*) on the grounds that the former is a mere repetition of the *Pratijñā* (thesis) and that the latter is only a pedagogical indication of the qualilties of the valid *Hetu*.

(3) Conclusion.

The dispute in question arose between Hindu logicians who upheld that what is to be proven (thesis) must be initially proposed and the Buddhist logicians who countered that it is not necessary. The reason that this difference became a heated dispute is that it was correlative to another difference concerning the object of inferential knowledge.

In reply to Hindu logicians' criticism, Dignāga and Buddhist logicians in subsequent periods defended their theory by stating that real and necessary members of a syllogism or inference, are only of two types, namely, (1) the general rule expressed in the statement of similar and dissimilar instances (*dṛṣṭānta*) and (2) its application to an individual substratum by stating a reason (*hetu*). When a universal relation of smoke and fire is known to a community of people, in order to let them know a conclusion that "a distant hill is on fire," it suffices to inform them that "a distant hill has a billow of smoke (*hetu*)." For, in this very reason (*hetu*), its conclusion (*sādhya*) that "the hill is on fire" is already implied.[24]

In opposition to this Buddhist logicians' view in assigning class determination of a given substratum to the *anvaya* and *vyatireka* procedures as the primary task of inference, the Hindu logicians (Naiyāyika) assigned to them the verification of the universal relation (*vyāpti*) between smoke and fire. Further, in opposition to Buddhist logicians' view in regards to the laying down of a Reason (*hetu*: "a hill having a smoke") as the main body of an inference, Hindu logicians interpreted it as verification of a given Reason (smoke on a hill) by means of its Conclusion (*sādhya*: fire on a hill) determined by the previous (*anvaya-vyatireka*) procedure. Dignāga refuted this Hindu logicians' view by stating: The object of inferential reasoning is neither the properties of a given *substratum* (e.g., "smoke-then-fire" of a hill) nor the connection (*sambandha*) between the "smoke-fire" relation and a 'hill,' but the substratum itself characterized by the conclusion (*sādhya*: "a hill having fire").

The reason is threefold: (1) When the concomitance of smoke and fire is known universally, the conclusion should be implied in the statement of a reason, i.e., "(a)P then (a)Q"; (2) When "Q" is known universally to be found in a similar instance, say, a kitchen as "(b)Q" [where 'b' is a kitchen], the substratum 'a,' which is one of

---

[24] Dignāga's refutation of Hindu Nyāya logic on this matter is quoted by Vācaspati Miśra in his *Nyāyavārttikatātparyaṭīkā*., p. 169 (24) - p.180 (10). Cf. Vidyabhusana, *History of Indian Logic*, pp. 281-82..

the similar class members as 'b' is, should be the object to be cognized by inference; and (3) If the object of an inference is the hill-fire relation, there is no element capable of making an inference possible, nor is there anything to be inferred. It follows that the connection need not be expressed as Thesis (*pratijñā*), nor should it be accompanied by Reason (*hetu*).[25]

The point intended here is that for Medieval Indian Buddhist logicians, it is not the purpose of an inference to know a given universal relation (If smoke, then fire) as valid, because such a universal ought to be already known by a community of people through induction. Hence, it is the purpose of inference to let them know whether a given substratum, say, a yonder hill, is a member of the similar class of things like a kitchen and not a member of the dissimilar class like a water tank. Hence, the main element of an inference is the laying down of a Reason on the basis of the class determination of a given substratum, and not the verification of the Reason (*hetu*) in relation to Conclusion (*sādhya*) as held by Hindu logicians. This difference exactly parallels the difference found between the Confucian and Mohist views of logic.

Recapitulating the foregoing points, the Confucians discovered the significance of "names" or "predicables" or "universals" which are the indices to classify things and actions. But they failed to see why cultural and ethical universals, which guide human conduct, become empty and meaningless statements when detached from their practical context of an agent or substratum. The Mohists criticism precisely pointed to this by introducing the idea of subject term as object of an inferential knowledge and defining the logic of inference as follows: It is the task of inference to express one's meaning in a proposition by giving the reason in a premise [i.e. by the statement to begin with 'because,' i.e., "*ku* . ."], and support the reason-conclusion relation *by selecting instances on the principles of agreement* (*t'ung*) *and difference* (*i*)[y]."[26] Here too, the essential business of the Mo-tzŭ's theory of inference is twofold: (1) class-determination of a given subject term and (2) laying down of an inferential reason. It follows that the Mohist criticism was justified against the Confucian theory of the primacy of naming or universal relation, precisely because a name or a relation without its *substratum* has no reality nor efficacy.

---

[25] *Ibid.*

[26] The italics are this writer's.

§5. CHINESE BUDDHIST CONTRIBUTIONS TO LOGIC AND LINGUISTIC

The religion of the Buddha was officially recorded to have been introduced to China in AD. 156 in the reign of Han emperor Ming (*Ming-ti*, 明帝). Yet, it would take a few centuries for Chinese Buddhism to acquire its generic feature. During the period of two centuries, from the end of the 4th to the 6th, the period of so-called "Six Dynasties," also known as the period of "Divided China of North and South," multifarious forms of Buddhism, Hīnayāna as well as Mahāyāna, along with their scriptures and cultures, were introduced piecemeal to the divided regions of North and South with no clear reference to scriptural origin, developmental history and sectarian affiliation. Thus, it became the major task of scholar monks and intellectual Buddhists to sort out the translated texts into textual groups and to correlate them into a certain order for the developmental history of the scriptures relative to the teachings purported in them. The more comprehensive the system was, the more superior and satisfactory it was for Buddhist scholars to classify the doctrinal teachings and practices in the attempt to fathom the religion and culture of Buddhism.

By the time of the mid-sixth century, two clear features characteristic of Chinese Buddhism emerged out of this situation. The first was the so called '*Chiao-pan*' or in full '*Chiao-hsiang-pan-shih*, 教相判釈), namely, systematic and critical classification of Buddhist doctrines. The second was the primacy of Mahāyāna Buddhism over Hīnayāna, although, in practice, the latter tradition was also given due importance. From the doctrinal point of view, Chinese Buddhists adopted Mahāyāna Buddhism as superior to that of Hīnayāna for two basic reasons: (1) the Mahāyāna insight of *dharma-śūnyatā* (*k'ung-hsing*, 空性) is superior to the Hīnayāna insight of *dharma-svabhāva* (*yu-tzŭu-hsing,* 有自性) and (2) the Bodhisattva-yāna path of practice (*p'u-sa-ch'êng*, 菩薩乗) is superior to the Śrāvaka-yāna path of practice (*sheng-mên-ch'eêg*, 声門乗) .

The term *śūnyatā*, compounded of *śūnya* (empty, void, hollow) and an abstract suffix *tā* (equivalent to *ness*), was almost invariably translated into Chinese as *kung-hsing* (emptiness, voidness, or vacuity). The concept of this term was essentially both logical and dialectical. The difficulty to understand this concept is due to its transcendental meaning (*paramārtha*) in relation to the logico-linguistic meaning (*vyavahāra*), especially because the etymological tracing of its meaning [i.e. *śūnya* meaning "vacuous or hollow within a shape of things"] provides no theoretical or practical addition to one's understanding of the concept.

The normative set of practices of Bodhisattva-yāna [(vehicle, *ch'êng*, 乘); (*mārga*, *hsing*, 道); (*caryā, hsing*, 行), consisted of six standard forms committed by "One who seeks to realize ultimate insight" (*bodhi-sattva*, *p'u-sa*). The six forms of practice (*ṣaṭ-pāramitās*: *liu-t'u* (六度) or *liu-po-lo-mi* (六波羅蜜) which represent the broadest categories of virtues enumerated in the *Prajñāpāramitā-sūtras* and other Mahāyāna scriptures are charity (*dāna*, *pu-shih*, 布施) morality (*śīla*, *ch'ih-chieh*), perseverance (*kṣānti*, *jen*, 忍), endeavor (*vīrya*, *ching-ching*, 精進), meditation (*dhyāna-samādhi*, *ch'an-t'ing*, 禅定), and wisdom (*prajñā*, *chih-hui*, 智慧), to which four more were added later on resulting in the Ten Pāramitās (*shih-po-lo-mi,* 十波羅蜜): expediency (*upāya*, *fang-pien*, 方便), vow (*praṇidhāna, yüan*, 願), might (*bala*, *li,* 力), and insight (*jñāna*, *chih*, 智). The body of normative practices, however, prescribes no set of detailed specifics of human conduct or moral action. Whatever specific action a Bodhisattva takes to apply within a given situation is left to his insight of *śūnyatā*. The special faculty to be acquired through this insight is defined as "skilfulness in expedient means," or "skilfulness in the choice and adoption of the means or expedients for converting others or helping them" (*upāya-kauśalya*, *shan-ch'iao-fang-pien*、善行方便).[27] The concept of "expedient means" does not simply mean ordinary conduct based on reason and rational calculation. But because it is anchored in the insight of śūnyatā, the "skilfulness in means" is a special faculty imbued with the nature of transcendence. Moreover, this faculty is also pragmatic, because whatever specific action it is to take, is adopted by a Bodhisattva as best fit to a given situation as well as to a specific foreseen goal. The concept is thus dual-natured, empirical and trans-empirical.

In the history of Chinese Buddhism, two stages are recognized for full comprehension of the Mahāyāna insight of *śūnyatā*. First, toward the end of the fourth century, Kumārajīva (鳩摩羅什), foremost exponent and translator of the Mādhyamika treatises, arrived in Western China and completed the translation of the dialectical treatises in A.D. 409, while raising a group of excellent scholar monks under his guidance. Among these disciples, Sêng Chao (僧肇、383-413), whom the teacher praised as foremost in the understanding

[27] Cf. Har Dayal: *The Bodhisattva Doctrine in Buddhist Sanskrit Literature*, orginally published in London, 1932; Motilal Banarsidass, 1970. p.248 ff.

of the doctrine, left a treatise called *Chao-lun* (「肇論」) on the Mādhyamika philosophy of *śūnyatā*.28 In this text, he innovated a unique method of paradoxical argument, which I believe has the best fit with respect to the linguistic system of Chinese for the demonstration of the dialectical meaning of *śūnyatā*.

Toward the end of the sixth century, then Chih-i (智 、531-597), the third patriarch of the T'ien-t'ai school(天台宗) and a contemporary of the San-lun (三論宗) master Chi-tsang (吉蔵、549-623), wrote a series of texts on the T'ien-t'ai doctrines, establishing an elaborate system of teachings endowed with the classification of "five periods and eight teachings" (*wu-shih-pa-chiao*, 五時八教). The system classifies the five periods of doctrinal development, the four methodical teachings of religious practice (*hua-i-ss„-chiao,* 化儀四教), and the four doctrinal teachings of religious conversion (*hua-fa-ss„-chiao,* 化法四教). Philosophically, the T'ien-t'ai system is understood to be a type of Buddhist phenomenology, such that a moment of thought or human consciousness was analyzed into three thousand phenomenal dimensions (*I-nien-san-ch'ien*, 一念三千), and that all these multiple phenomena are theorized to interact in perfect permeation (*Yüan-jung-san-ti*, 円融三諦), embodying the threefold truth of "dependent origination" (*pratītyasamutpāda, yüan-ch'i*、縁起), namely, the three aspects of "emptiness" (*śūnyatā* or *k'ung,* 空), "linguistic practicality" (*prajñapti, chia*, 仮), and "middle path" (*madhyamā-pratipad, chung-tao*, 中道). Chih-i adopted these definitions of "dependent origination" (*pratītya-samutpāda, yüan-ch'i*) from Nāgārjuna's *Chung-lun* (「中論」), Chap. 24, Verse 18.[29]

Although the insights of *śūnyatā* (*k'ung*), *prajñapti* (*chia*), and *madhyamā* (*chung,* 中), were taken from Nāgārjuna's *Chung-lun*,

---

[28] *The Chao-lun* or *The Treatise of Sêng-Chao* consists of four short essays and two epistles written on Buddhist doctrines, regarded as the earliest extant Chinese Mādhyamika text composed by the native Chinese mind. 1 fasc., Taishō Daizōkyō 45, (No. 1858), p. 150 ff. See Ichimura, *op. cit.*

[29] Verse 18, Ch. 24 reads as follows:
yaḥ pratītyasamutpādaḥ śūnyatāṃ tāṃ pracakṣmahe//
sā prajñāptir upādāya pratipat saiva madhyamā//
"That which has arisen through dependent origination, we call Emptiness; it is a linguistic convention based on [causal] configuration; it is indeed the middle path."

Cf. Alternative translations, such as, by K. Inada in his *Nāgārjuna: A Translation of His Mūlamādhyamikakārikā* [Tokyo: Hokuseido Press, 1970], or by J. Takakusu in *The Essentials of Buddhist Philosophy*, University of Hawaii Press, 1947, p. 129.

the system of *'I-nien-san-ch'ien* and *'Yüan-jung-san-ti'* ought to be regarded a genuinely original Chinese theory, just as the Hua-yen ten-fold theory of dependent origination (*shih-hsüan-yüan-ch'i*, 十玄縁起) with regards to both the transcendent (*hsing,* 性 or *li*, 理) and the phenomenal (hsiang, 相) or *shih,* 実). During the same century as that of Chih-i, the Hua-yen system was in the process of establishment by Tu-shun (杜順、557-640). It was then further developed by Chih-yen (智厳、602-668) and completed by Fa-tsang (法蔵、643-712) in the middle of the T'ang dynasty. The system consisted of the classification into five teachings and ten schools (*wu-chia-shih-tsung*, 五教十宗). Though it was not as broad as that of T'ien-t'ai, philosophically, it concentrated on the profound analysis of the perfect interdependence of *dharmas* (*dharma-dhātu-pratītya-sam-utpāda*, *fa-chieh-yüan-ch'i*,). Where the T'ien-t'ai system constitutes a grand combination of philosophical and religious elements, it represents a pioneering analysis of the causality of "dependent origination." I believe it is a uniquely Chinese formulation, just as that of T'ien-t'ai. In this paper, however, I shall confine myself to the question: How and why Sêng-chao's method of dialectic and Chih-i's understanding of *śūnyatā* contribute towards the contem-porary world?

§6. LOGICAL AND DIALECTICAL STRUCTURES

The Nāgārjunian method of dialectic shares the same structural foundation as that of logic and language. At the time of Nāgārjuna, Indian logic (Nyāya) nearly reached its full maturation equipped with a unique theory of syllogistic inference. It was unique in comparison with the Aristotelian syllogism, but, as some contemporary logicians hold,[30] Indian logic of inference was essentially not different from that of the Chinese logic developed by Mo-tzŭ, precisely because of two identical procedures of their inference. First, both were theorized to bear the dual principles of similar and dissimilar instantiations (*anvaya* and *vyatireka*) in Indian logic or the dual methods of agreement (*t'ung*) and difference (*i*) in Chinese logic as essential criteria of valid reasoning. Second, both understood the function of inference to cognize a given substratum or a subject term by determining its class as being in parallel with similar examples that belong to the same class in terms of a Reason-to-

[30] Cf. Janusz Chmielewski: "Notes on Early Chinese Logic: I-IV," *Rocznik Orientalistyczny*, especially, No. III [*ibid.* 27, 1(1963)].

Conclusion relation. The only minor difference between the two is that the Indian syllogisim requires similar as well as dissimilar examples at all times for deduction, whereas the Mohist formula calls for an established model form (*hsiao*, 效) for valid deduction, with which a given reason ought to be in agreement.

'*Hsiao*' means "to imitate," "to be similar to," "to be efficacious," "to yield the expected result," or "to verify." Hu Shih translated this important Neo-Mohist logical term as "deduction" or "deductive reasoning," i.e., "an inference to be deduced from a *hsiao* or a mold." He translated the passage of the definition of *Hsiao* (found in the Book 37) as follows:[31]

> The *Hsiao* or reasoning from a mold consists of setting up the form (*fa*, 法). That which is modeled after is that which is to be set up as the form. When the cause or reasón conforms (*t'ung*、同) to the *Hsiao* or Mold, it is right [i.e., the method of agreement]. When it does not conform (*i*, 異) to the *Hsiao*, it is false [the method of difference].

Although the Mohist deductive reasoning requires no dual instantiation, since the reasoner ought to parallel a given object of deduction with a model form (*hsiao*), it is evident that the model form to which the reasoner refers for his inference must be one that has already been well established in convention through the method of induction, i.e., on the basis of the methods of agreement and difference.

The fact that the dual principles of similarity and dissimilarity or that of agreement and difference are commonly found in Indian and Chinese logic suggests that the inferential process of the mind is universal despite the difference of cultural and linguistic forms, and that they are essential to the symbolic process of the mind. For instance, in order for a child to be able to call an animal a cow, he or she must know the convention according to which a certain group of animals with a set of similar properties, like a dewlap, is called a "cow." The process that underlies the child's mind ought to be the process of affirming similar objects and denying dissimilar

---

[31] Hu Shih: *op. cit.*, p. 96. Graham, translating *Hsiao*[fd] as "exemplifying," quotes the Mohist definition of Hsiao from its text along with his translation in his work, *op. ci.*, p. 470[fe] and gives his translation as follows: 'Some' is not all ['stone' when broken up]. The loan-named ['Ch'in horse'] is not now so. An example ['pillar'] is a standard for being deemed such-and-scuh ['wood']; the thing exemplified is the standard by which the example is deemed such-and-such. Therefore if something coincides with an example, it is this thing, and if it does not it is not; this is "exemplifying." (p.471)

objects, such as, horses, etc., and while doing so, he classifies "cows" in contrast to what he has denied. Thus, it is clear that the logical context, in which a child correctly calls an object a "cow," is based on (1) the dual rules of similar (*anvaya*) and dissimilar instantiations (*vyatireka*) or agreement (*t'ung*) and difference (*i*), and on (2) the clear distinction of the class boundary between the two contrary groups of things (e.g., a "cow" and a "horse or non-cow" in the case of naming; and "a kitchen having smoke and fire" and "a water tank neither having fire nor smoke" in the case of inference). This is what I call the *logical context* of syllogistic inference.

Hu Shih pointed out that the Confucian contribution to logic was the discovery of "name" or "predicables" (*ming*, 名) while the Mohist contribution to logic was the discovery of "subject" or "predicated" (*shih*, 実). As briefly mentioned before, Mo-tzŭ defined the subject term and the predicate term respectively as "that by which something is said (about something) is the predicate (name, *ming*)"; "that about which something is said," is the subject or the predicated (fact or substance, *shih*)." When two universals are linked in proper sequence in reference to this subject term, there arises a meaningful statement or proposition. The process, which links these two parts of a sentence, is structurally the logical context in which the two processes are clearly separated.

Language is a system of symbols, semantically agreed for their denotation and for their syntactical stringing into a sentence, and stands in the middle between the spheres of nature and mind. From the immemorial past, the human race has evolved the use of language as the primary tool to depict the world of experiences in abstraction by symbols and to communicate them with fellow humans. Thus, irrespective of whether it is Japanese, Chinese, Indian, or English, every word of language, every common name, expresses the recognition of a class. In fact, the process of classifying things and that of linking words, phrases, or sentences in the use of language is so common that it is performed in most cases unconsciously and spontaneously. Then, what is the role of Buddhist dialectic? How is it related to this structural foundation of logic?

Analyzing Nāgājuna's dialectical treatises over and over again, I am increasingly convinced that one primary principle that underlies all of his *reductio ad absurdum* arguments (*prasaṅga-vākya*) is the *dialectical context* in which the dual instantiations (*anvaya* and *vyatireka*) are simultaneously applied to one and the same spatio-temporal sphere in reference, where two contrary classes of entities are forced to coalesce. The following is the gist of his argument that appears in the *Vigrahavyāvartanī* (*kārikā* 36-39):[32]

> Since an illumining light (a candle light) and dark night are two opposite agents, wherever there is light, there cannot be dark, and *vice versa*. It follows that although conventional knowledge leads us to believe that these two may have contact somewhere, there is no possibility at all for such a contact.

The argument conveys to the reader two things: (1) It is impossible for two different things to be a referent at one and the same place and time; likewise for two contrary or contradictory concepts to be applied to one and the same referent. This is correct from the point of view of the logical context. (2) Despite this convention, Nāgārjuna reminds the reader of the fact that convention itself violates this rule, so that the process of naming (i.e., denoting an object by name) as well as the process of syntactical linkage of a subject with its predicate is found to be ultimately based on the dialectical context.

His dialectical argument gradually compels the reader to become aware that our convention: "light illumines dark," "wisdom dispels ignorance," and so forth, though apparently meaningful, is based on the juxtaposition of two conceptually contrary or exclusive statements, namely, "light illumines dark," and "dark obstructs illumination." This means that convention is invariably anchored in the dialectical context where similar and dissimilar instantiations (*anvaya* and *vyatireka*) are simultaneously referred to one and the same spatio-temporal sphere. Here, two logically distinct classes of entities are no longer held separate in thought but coalesced into one, though empirically impossible and logically meaningless. As a result, there comes into being a dual natured referent, e.g., something that is both 'simultaneously existent and non-existent.'

In other words, the dialectical procedure compels us to realize that every symbolic usage (i.e., naming an entity or classifying a similar instance) is concurred with its contrary (i.e., naming an opposite or classifying a dissimilar instance) in itself. It is for this reason that in order to explain the insight of *śūnyatā*, Nāgārjuna and Mahāyāna Buddhists in general used a class of metaphors that exemplify dual-natured entities in terms of magic, sky-flower, dream, and so forth.

Just suppose that we are listening to an on-going speech, in

---

[32] Cf. Ichimura: *loc. cit.*, p. 57.

which phonemes, words, and sentences are incessantly coming and going. Catching a series of rapid sounds, our mind instantaneously configurates them into a word, a series of words into a sentence, and a series of sentences into a unified meaning. It is within this dynamic flow of speech or thought also that we cannot deny the on-going dual operations of positive and negative instantiations at every moment of consciousness, which vigorous logical reflection alone can abstract *a-posteriori*. Now we can define the dialectical context in terms of two conditions. The conditions are (1) that the dual operations of *anvaya* and *vyatireka* are intuited to be present at every moment of consciousness in terms of linguistic symbols; this is called the juxtaposition of the contraries; and (2) that these two operations in turn refer the two contrary meanings to a given moment of spatio-temporal sphere, forcing the respective referents to coalesce; this is called the dual- natured referent. Thus, a stream of consciousness, a series of moments linked one to another, is understood to be accomplished within the dialectical context.

§7. SÊNG-CHAO'S PARADOXICAL ARGUMENT AND T'IEN-T'AI'S PHILOSOPHY OF ŚŪNYATĀ

Although the Mohist school abruptly disappeared from history after the Ch'in dynasty which was followed by the period of Han, evidence supports the view that the Mohist text circulated in the Neo-Taoist movement during the third and fourth century.[33] Accordingly, some of the Taoist scholars may have been acquainted with the Mohist logical theory. In my article that appeared in this journal,[34] I treated the Madhyamaka treatise by Sêng-Chao (384-413), a Taoist before being converted to Buddhism, and demonstrated his paradoxical method of dialectic that could have been aided by his knowledge of the Mohist logical treatise. First, his method of dialectic is not the form of *reductio ad absurdum* argument on which Indian masters mainly relied, but almost entirely a paradoxical form of argument. Second, he employed the most important technical term of the Mohist, i.e., "*Hsiao*," in the treatise, *Chao-lun*. Though his use occurred only once toward the end of the last article "Nirvāṇa is No-naming" (*Nieh-p'an-wu-ming-lun*, 「涅槃無名論」),[35]

[33] Cf. A.C. Graham: *op. cit.*, p. 66.

[34] *Journal of Chinese Philosophy*, 19 (1992) 51-71.

[35] Although *Nieh-p'an-wu-ming-lun* was translated in that article as

there is good reason to believe, from the view point of the textual context, that his usage of the term seems to exhibit his knowledge of the Mohist method of deduction.

I quote a few of my arguments that appeared in the aforementioned article here in order to render clear the above two points analyzed in this paper. From childhood, we learn the use of language through listening to others, observing their behaviors, and testing out the efficacy of its usage by ourselves, and along with these experiences, we acquire a mind ingrained with conviction that things exist in the way in which language depicts. Sêng-chao's paradoxical method of argument deals with such fixation of our mind by forcing the reader to the maze of paradoxes one after another. Yet, he does not fail to conclude each argument without showing that the dual members of each paradox invariably refer to one and the same reference:

> If we want to express the real (*chên*, 真), we go against convention (*su*, 俗). If we follow convention, we fail to express the real . . . When people say that things are abiding (*chu*, 住), I say that they are 'gone' (*ch'ü*, 去). When they say that things are "gone," I say that they are "abiding." Although "gone" and "abiding" are different in expression, what they mean points to a single reference.

The fact that Sêng-Chao was clearly aware of the dialectical context can perhaps be best demonstrated by referring to the following passages that appear in his essay, "Whatever is Unreal is Emptiness" (*pu-chên-k'ung-lun*, 「不真空論」),in the concluding portion of the essay.

> The expression "existent" (*yu*, 有) refers only to a metaphorical existent (*chia-yu*, 仮有), for it distinguishes "not-nothing" (*fei-wu*, 非無). By the expression "nothing" (*wu*, 無), we distinguish "not-existent" (*fei-yu*, 非有). Though the referential fact is one, the expressions are two.

> We want to say that *dharmas* exist, but their existence is not real production (*fei-chên-sheng*, 非真生). We want to say that *dharmas* do not exist, but phenomenal forms (*shih-hsiang*, 事象) are already configurated. Phenomenal forms cannot be said as "identical with nothing" (*pu-chi-wu*, 不即無), but we only say

title should be translated as "Treatise that *Nirvāṇa* is No-naming" in accordance with the foregoing analysis.

that anything unreal (*fei-chên*, 非真) is not a real existent (*fei-shih-yu*, 非実有). It follows that the meaning of "emptiness of whatever is unreal" is thus revealed.

Accordingly, the large *Prajñāpāramitā-sūtra* (*ta-p'in-pan-jo*, 「大品般若経」) says: *Dharmas* are called metaphorically as "unreal" (*chia-ho-pu-chên*, 仮号不真) just as a magically created man is. For, we cannot say that there is no magically created man, but only that such is not a real man (*fei-chên-jên*, 非真人).

The Buddhist insight of *śūnyatā* does not offer any political statement either to the school of Confucian traditionalism or to Mohist utilitarian pragmatism. Nor does it provide additional definition or form to the Mohist logic or logic in general. The insight of *śūnyatā*, however, proposes to critically examine the use of symbols, the logical and linguistic process of the mind, as is exemplified in Sêng-Chao's treatise.

A century and a half after Sêng-Chao, there arose a number of Chinese Buddhist schools on both sides of the political division of North and South, among which the T'ien-t'ai school was foremost. As briefly mentioned before, Chih-i constructed his system of thought ultimately on the three Nāgārjunian concepts of *śūnyatā*, *prajñapti*, and *madhyamā* (*san-kuan*, 三観). Of the four successive levels of Buddhist doctrines (*hua-fa-ssŭu-chiao*, 化法四教) which he classified in his system, Chih-i placed the threefold Nāgārjunian insight into the highest and perfect teaching (*yüan-chiao*, 円教).[36] According to the T'ien-t'ai master the perfect teaching is explained as follows:[37]

---

[36] (1) *Tsang-chiao* or the practical teaching concerned with the three realms of existence, comprising the teaching of the *Sūtra-piṭaka*, all doctrines of Hīnayāna schools; (2) *T'ung-chiao* or the theoretical teaching concerned with the three realms of existence, comprising the teachings common to the three Vehiclas and the basic Mahāyāna teaching; (3) *Pieh-chiao* or the practical teaching concerned with that which is beyond the three realms of existence comprising purely Mahāyāna teachings specially opened to Bodhisattvas as to the doctrine of *śūnyatā* and middle path; (4) *Yüan-chiao* or the theoretical teaching concerned with that which is beyond the three realms of existence, comprising the Middle path as noumenon, perfectly harmonious, theoretically and practically.

[37] Cf. Bruno Petzold: *The Clasification of Buddhism, Bukkyō Kyōhan, comprising The Classwification of Buddhist Doctrines in India, China, and Japan;* Vol. I, Pt. 4: Tendai Doctrine, Ch. 12, §3, 4 [Edited by S. Ichimura, (Wiesbaden, Germany: Otto Harrassowoitz, 1995)] and J. Takakusu: *op. cit.*, pp. 133-34. Takakusu translates perfect permeation[fo] as "one-in-all all-in-one" (i.e., one element contains all elements). Chih-i: *Ssŭ-chiao-i* (「四教義」) in12 fasc. [Taisho 46 (No. 1929), esp. pp. 760-769].

The term '*yüan-chiao*' is identical with '*yüan-miao*, 円妙' (perfect wondrous), '*yüan-man*, 円満' (perfect, fulfilled teaching), '*yüan-chi*, 円極' (perfect and complete), '*yüan-tun*, 円頓' (perfect, abrupt teaching), and is considered as the highest theory in Mahāyāna Buddhism which exhaustively teaches the true form of the Dharma-world (*dharmadhātu*) and leaves nothing hidden or untaught.

Yüan-chiao explains all phenomena with the truth of '*pu-tan-chung*, 不単中' or "Not mere middle," which means (1) *Chi-k'ung* (即空) or "direct identity with Emptiness," (2) *Chi-chia* (即仮) "direct identity with linguistic convention" (*prajñapti*), and (3) *Chi-chung*(即中) or "direct identity with Middle Path" (*madhyamā*).

This means that every and all phenomena are initially identified directly with Dependent Origination (*yüan-ch'i*); secondly, they are directly identified with Emptiness (*chi-k'ung*); third, they are directly identified with linguistic convention (*chi-chia*); fourth, they are directly identified with Middle or the transcendent (*chi-chung*). Thus, the four categories of theoretical teachings (*hua-fa-ssŭ-chiao*, 化法四教) represent a system of gradual perfection of the causal insight of dependent origination (*yüan-ch'i*, *pratītyasamutpāda*) and are designed to enable practitioners to eventually attain the middle domain where phenomenal occurrence is viewed with an entirely different significance relative to the initial meaning. In this regard, the philosophical culmination in turn becomes religious salvation.

In the initial stage of teaching, innumerable phenomena are viewed through the insight of dependent origination as arising and perishing due to the state of human defilement and delusion. In the last, perfected stage of teaching, however, imbued with the insight of *śūnyatā*, myriads of phenomena or human differentiations are identified with the ultimate true state of things as they are [*chên-jo-shih-hsiang* (真如実相), *tattvasya lakṣaṇam*), perfectly free, unobstructed, and harmonious]. This is the ultimate realization of Middle Path in the system of Mahāyāna Buddhism as intuited and constructed by the great T'ien-t'ai master Chih-i.

§8. CONCLUSION: CHINESE BUDDHISM AND ITS CONTRIBUTION

Śākyamuni Buddha did not express his religious doctrine in terms of *śūnyatā*, but rather by (1) dependent origination (*pratītyasamutpāda* or *Yüan-ch'i* or *Yin-yüan-shêng-ch'i*, 因縁生起) and (2) middle path (*madhya-mārga*, *madhyamā-pratipad* or *Chung-tao*). Several centuries later, a group of Mahāyāna texts, such as, the *Prajnñāpāramitāsūtras* (*Pan-jo-ching*, 「般若経」) and *Buddhāvataṃsaka-sūtras* (*Hua-yen-ching*, 「華厳経」) introduced the doctrine of *śūnyatā*. By the midle of the second century A.D., this was further consolidated by Nāgārjuna, foremost Mahāyāna philosopher, through his dialectical treatises, such as, the definitive *Mūlamadhyamaka-kārikā* (the *Middle Treatise*, *Chung-lun*, or 「中論」).

As referred to before, Nāgārjuna defined the original insight of dependent origination in the *Middle Treatise*, the 18th verse of Chap. 24, by equating it with *śūnyatā* (*k'ung-hsin*), *prajñapti* (*chia-she*, 仮設), and *madhyamā* (*chung-tao*), thus accomplishing the linkage of dependent origination (*yüan-ch'i*) and *madhyamā* (*chung-tao*). Very early on, these four concepts became the primary objects of enquiry for Chinese Buddhists from the times of Sêng-Chao to that of Chih-i of the T'ien-t'ai school, Chi-tsang of the San-lun school, and so forth. According to Sêng-chao and Chih-i, through the insights of *śūnyatā* and *prajñapti*, every phenomenon (*vyavahāra*) in the world of convention can eventually be affirmed to pertain to the nature of transcendence (*paramārtha*, *Chên-ti* or *sheng-i-ti*, 勝義諦) in the middle (*chung*). This middle domain, one might say, is like a locus, without space or time, where the empirical (*laukika-vyavahāra-satya*, *su-ti*, 俗諦) and the transcendent (*paramārtha-satya*, *chên-ti*, 真諦) are said to interact as identical (*t'ung*, 同), while at the same time being different (*i*, 異). The question now is: What does this religious commentary mean from the logical and linguistic point of view?

Nāgārjuna as well as Sêng-Chao invariably introduced the concepts of "secular" (*su*) and "true" (chên) respectively referring to the conventional nature (*vyavahārasatya*) and the transcendent (*paramārthasatya*). They invariably juxtapose two contrary statements in the dialectical context, resulting in a referent in the dual natures, i.e., "something is existent while non-existent," "something is gone (*ch'ü*, 去) while being present (*chu*, 住)," "light (*ming*, 明) is identified with dark (*an*, 暗) while being different from it," and so on.

Language is the medium par excellence for the formation of culture because it depicts, prescribes, and sustains all forms of behavioral patterns that make up and involve all subjective and objective social institutions. Simultaneously, cultural forms reinforce the ways language is used. Though symbols may serve to liberate the human mind for universal communication, more often than not they create bondage and prejudice, interfering with proper communication and mutual understanding. In this sense, even rational and logical thinking often reflects a particular form of culture and convention. An ideology is defined as a systematic body of concepts about human life and culture or systematically integrated assertions, theories, and aims that constitute a socio-political program. As experienced by all of us, the twentieth century has manifested by a variety of ideologies. Today, no sooner had the era of ideological confrontation been over, than has begun the era of uncertainty accompanied by amorphous, even sanguine, confrontations among different ethnic societies and cultures, including different religious beliefs. These conflicts are creating far more formidable human problems than imaginable precisely because of their irrational nature.

The crucial point is how one should deal with the force of a mind tied down to a particular form of ideology, culture, religion, ethnicity or race. How could that mind, compartmentalized within one form or another, be opened to what lies beyond its own culture? Although Buddhist dialectic or the insight of *śūnyatā* shares the same foundation as that of logic and language, it indeed appears to demolish the very foundation of logic and language by juxtaposing contrary predications and thereby inducing a dual natured referent. As evident in the T'ien-t'ai philosophy, however, the Buddhist insight does not repudiate the empirical world (*shih-hsiang*, 事象) where the symbolic system operates but simultaneously accepts the workings of symbols as they are (*chia-she*, 仮設) from the transcendental point of view (i.e., based on *śūnyatā*). Yet it repudiates the underlying mental force that engenders linguistic behavior and culture formation, again in terms of *śūnyatā*. The insight of *śūnyatā* counters the referential force of the mind directed toward its object of reference by its ultimately dual nature, and thus counters the tendentious or purposive force of the mind that links one symbol to another in terms of its ultimate self-contradiction.

What is the characteristic of Chinese Buddhism that is uniquely distinguishable from the Indian counterpart? There should be no difference basically between Indian and Chinese Buddhism insofar as it is concerned with those fundamental insights of dependent origination (*pratītyasamutpāda*), emptiness (*śūnyatā*), linguistic practicality (*prajñapti*), and middle path (*madhyamā*) are concerned. Nevertheless, there is a degree of difference between the practical forms of method resorted to, respectively, and the theoretical contents of ultimate realization.

First, the reason that Sêng-chao resorted to his own paradoxical method of argument rather than the *reducto ad absurdum* argument of Indian masters can be traced in part to the non-inflectional mono-syllabic language and the use of ideographic characters of Chinese language and in part to the influence of the Mohist system of logic, especially the application of *Hsiao* and giving importance to subject terms.

Second, the T'ien-t'ai philosophical system accomplished a total bridging between the phenomenal (*shih*, 事) and transcendent (*li*, 理) in the very practical daily life in terms of the Nāgārjunian threefold truth (i.e., *k'ung-chia-chung*, 空仮中), whereas in Indian Buddhist systems, the state of phenomenal, mundane existence, was not totally identified, except in theory, with ultimate transcendence in the way Chinese Buddhists accomplished.

The practical mentality anchored in factuality (*shih*, 事) is an important asset of Chinese Buddhist spirituality and so is the harmonious orientation exhibited in theorization of facts (*li*, 理), both of which are evidenced in the T'ien-t'ai theory of "harmonious permeation of all phenomena in terms of the threefold transcendent truth" (*yüan-jung-san-ti*, 縁融三諦). The Chinese Buddhist contribution to Chinese philosophy is that while accepting the Confucian and Mohist logical thought, they demonstrated why the ultimate foundation of these two theories ought to be perceived from the standpoint of the Buddhist insight of Dependent Origination and to review their respective theories from the transcendental view of Middle Path, namely, in terms of *śūnyatā* and *prajñapti*. As this twofold Buddhist insight contributed to the history of Chinese philosophy, I believe it can also contribute to the understanding and amelioration of contemporary world problems. The process is painfully slow but it is time for contemporary thinkers to begin to examine insights and events that have moved and molded a culture to supreme heights – in this case, Chinese Buddhism which peaked during the T'ang Dynasty.

ARTICLE NINE

The Chinese Mādhyamika Sêng-chao's Paradoxical Method of Argument[1]

§1 Introduction

Opinions vary among scholars as to the questions: whether Chinese Buddhists correctly understood the Indian Mādhyamika's religio-philosophical system, or whether the Chinese understanding of Buddhist spirituality as a whole was and has been authentic. This question, whether or not the Buddhist religio-philosophical system, comprising the conceptions of dharma, śūnyatā, prajñā, nirvāṇa, and so forth, was communicated across barriers of cultural differences between peoples as divergent as the Chinese and Indian, can be answered in a variety of ways. I hold that the Mahāyāna Buddhist insight of śūnyatā (i.e., emptiness or voidness), with which the Mādhyamika method of dialectic was exclusively concerned, is trans-cultural. By the time of the fifth century, the Chinese Buddhists had come to understand it in such precise terms that it became the religio-philosophical foundation for their own subsequent development. And this achievement was prompted by their intellectual or religio-philosophical concern over the nature of logic and language. The Chao-lun (「肇論」), which is ascribed· to Sêng-chao (僧肇、374-414), is the best evidence to substantiate these points of view.

The *Chao-lun* or *The Treatise of Sêng-chao*, which consisted of four short essays and two epistles written on Buddhist doctrines, is thought by modern scholarship to be the earliest extant Chinese Madhyamaka[2] text composed by the native Chinese mind and an important landmark in the early stages of Chinese Buddhist thought

[1] Originally entitled as "On the Paradoxical Method of the Chinese Mādhyamika: Sêng-chao and the Chao-Lun Treatise" and included in *Journal of Chinese Philosophy* 19 (1992) 51-71.

[2] Two terms '*madhyamaka*' and '*mādhyamika*' are used in this paper with different meanings: '*Madhyamaka*' signifies "middle" or anything that is median, referring to the Middle Way of the Buddhist. Nāgārjuna expressed it as '*madhyamāpratipad*' in the *treatise on the Verses of the middle* (*Madhyamaka-kārikā-śāstra*), whereas '*mādhyamika*', an adjectival derivative, refers to the school that advocated this doctrine and its dialectical method.

formation. Once a Taoist student, Sêng-chao had turned to Buddhism and was trained under Kumārajīva, the greatest textual translator of all times. By assisting his master in the task of translation and attending his teacher's lectures, Sêng-chao became well versed in the Madhyamaka treatises and developed a deep doctrinal understanding. The main body of the *Chao-lun* essays consisted of a series of paradoxical arguments, and this method parallels that of *reductio-ad-absurdum* arguments (*prasaṅga-vākya*) comprised in the Madhyamaka treatises composed by Nāgārjuna (ca. 50-150 A.D.) and his followers in India.

The primary purpose of this paper is to demonstrate how and why Sêng-chao's paradoxical method may have had a direct bearing on Chinese logical and linguistic thinking; and secondarily to clarify both why the Mādhaymika or Buddhist insight of *Śūnyatā* is trans-cultural, and why Chinese logico-linguistic concerns could have helped Sêng-chao understand the insight of *Śūnyatā*.

§2. STRUCTURAL IDENTITY OF INFERENTIAL LOGIC BETWEEN INDIAN AND CHINESE SYSTEMS

In spite of a persistent scholarly interest in Indian Mādhyamika Studies in the West, there has not been a comparable interest in Chinese Mādhyamika Studies. By "Chinese Mādhyamika Studies," I mean the philosophical and doctrinal investigation into the expository works written by Chinese Buddhist thinkers, among whom Sêng-chao is to be included together with other disciples of Kumārajīva as well as the founder of the San-lun school (三論宗), Chi-ts'ang (吉藏), and his followers. I believe the major reason for this retarded interest in Chinese Mādhyamika Studies can be attributed to the misconception that cultural dissemination follows a general rule, such that Buddhist spirituality ought to be most authentic in the Indian Buddhist cultural environment in which it was born, and that the degree of authenticity will probably diminish whenever it is transmitted to an alien or different cultural environment. Since China and India are historically regarded as independent cultural zones, the aforementioned misconception seems to have affected every interpretation on the subject of Sino-Indian Buddhist transmission.

The study of the *Chao-lun* seems to have been similarly affected, because we have only three major post-war works so far available to us: W. Liebenthal published his *Chao-lun*: *The Treatise of Sêng-chao*, comprising a full textual translation in English, from Peking in 1948 (a revised edition published by the Hong Kong University Press in 1968); a group of Japanese scholars led by Z. Tsukamoto published the *Jōron no Kenkyū* (*The Study of Chao-lun*), a full textual translation in Japanese, from Kyoto in 1955; and R. H. Robinson included his study on the *Chao-lun* and its partial translation in English in his *Early Mādhyamika in India and China* from the University of Wisconsin Press in 1967. I am, however, somehow dissatisfied with the way each author has approached the subject matter, especially, on Sêng-chao's paradoxical method of argument. For instance, despite his deep study on Sêng-chao's text and thought, Liebenthal remarks his evaluation in the following word: "A wall of misunderstanding separated the Chinese understanding of Buddhism from that of Indians."[3] Robinson, however, dissented from Liebenthal's conclusion and asserted that Sêng-chao's understanding of the Madhyamaka doctrine and its method is fairly accurate, and yet, he too fell short of a fuller evaluation and failed to see the implication of Sêng-chao's paradoxical method by saying that "his argument is imitative and hence lesser in degree than Indian masters."[4] I believe these scholars may have believed that, as a general rule, cultural dissemination is inevitably affected by a degree of degeneration from the original form and quality. The detailed textual and linguistic research of the Japanese scholars is impressive, but their translation seems to be overshadowed by Taoistic thought and jargon. I fear that this hinders the reader from reaching a proper evaluation of Sêng-chao's treatise.

Having made these critical comments, I must say that I have tried in several papers to develop a more satisfactory approach to Sêng-chao's religio-philosophical insight of *śūnyatā* as well as his dialectical method of paradoxical argument. Along with the underlying three premises which have already been given in my initial introduction, I intend here (1) to demonstrate why the paradoxical method of argument Sêng-chao applied in his exposition of the insight of *śūnyatā* can be theoretically ascertained as an authentic Mādhyamika method of dialectic fit for the Chinese mind and audience; (2) to show why this paradoxical method can be more clearly analyzed in reference to the Chinese language and the Mohist logic of ancient China. I hold an hypothesis that Sêng-chao knew the Neo-Mohist system of logic, and that this knowledge

---

[3] Liebenthal, *op. cit.*, pp. 22.

[4] Robinson, *op. cit.*, pp. 154-55.

helped him formulate his own dialectical method in terms of paradoxical argument.

In a series of research papers written in the early 80's, I explored Chinese Mādhyamika thought in parallel with that of its Indian counterpart. In 1983, I read a paper entitled "Is Sêng-chao's method of demonstration an authentic Mādhyamika?"[5] at the 194th annual meeting of the American Oriental Society, and believe that I proved how and why Sêng-chao's paradoxical method is an authentic Mādhyamika dialectic. My thesis was that the *reductio-ad-absurdum* method of argument which Nāgārjuna initially introduced as the definitive method of Mādhyamika dialectic in India, shares one and the same structural basis as that of the inferential logic, and that 'dialectical thinking' and 'logical thinking' derive from their respective modifications of that common structural basis. Moreover, the structural basis of inferential logic formulated in ancient India is essentially identical with that of the Mohist logic formulated in ancient China. It follows that the working of the human mind in terms of inferential logic is beyond culturally different forms, and that Sêng-chao's paradoxical method of argument can be placed in parallel with the *reductio-ad-absurdum* method of Indian Mādhyamikas, such as, Nāgārjuna.

In India, the core operations of inferential reasoning are seen as the dual principles of *anvaya* (i.e., collaboration by affirmative examples) and *vyatireka* (i.e., collaboration by negative examples). For instance, upon seeing a billow of smoke over a hill, one infers the probable outbreak of a fire on that hill. By minimizing the extra-logical linguistic elements of syllogistic inference, Buddhist logicians in India analyzed this inferential process and reduced the essential mental operations down to two steps as sufficient for valid inference.[6] Let us first analyze the inferential process of the mind in terms of four sequence:

(1) positing a minor term or reason: "the hill has smoke, (a)P; Here, 'a' is a locus or substratum. e.g., the yonder hill, and "having smoke" is its predication. Thus (a)P means to assert that "the yonder hill is having smoke."

---

[5] The article included in T*he Professor L. M. Joshi Memoarial Volume*, Central Institute of Higher Tibetan Studies, Sarnath, Varanasi, India, 1987.

[6] Śaṅkarasvāmin simplified the inferential rules in his *Nyāyapraveśaka-sūtram, Gaekaward Oriental Series*, 33 (1930), p. 1: *pakṣadharmatvaṃ sapakṣe sattvaṃ vipakṣe cāsattvam iti*/

(2) determining if a causal link "if smoke then fire" is applicable to the substratum in question. Here it is to determine whether a substratum or the hill is a similar class member (*sapakṣa:* the variable 'x') like a kitchen (α), etc. where smoke and fire are observed to be likely concomitant. Thus, a universal causal link "(x)P then (x)Q" can be verified by a similar example like 'kitchen' as "(α)P• (α)Q." This affirmative collaboration is called *'anvaya'* or the principle of exemplifying an inferential linkage between "having smoke" (P) and "having fire" (Q) by means of a similar example. This can be formulated in symbolic notation as: (x){(x)P• (x)Q} and (α)PQ;

(3) determining if the substratum in question is not a dissimilar class member (*vipakṣa*: variable 'y') like a water tank, etc., where neither fire nor smoke is ever observed together or separately. This can be put in notation as "–(y)Q•–(y)P" which ought to be verified by a dissimilar example alone like a water tank (β). This negative collaboration is called *vyatireka* or the principle of exemplifying the contra-position, distinguishing the logical boundary between the dissimilar and similar classes. This can be put in notation as: (y) {–(y)Q•– (y)P} and –{(β)QP}.

(4) Finally, drawing a *Conclusion* in terms of the major term (a)Q, to assert that "the hill is on fire."

In our inferential process or demonstration, the initial positing of "having smoke" as Reason (*hetu*) referring to a yonder hill itself is generally known in public to imply its conclusion (*sādhya*) as "having fire." Then, a catechistic statement of the conclusion is superfluous. Moreover, since the hill or a locus to which Reason is initially posited ought to be a member of the similar class (*sapakṣa*). Hence, the initial position of Reason can be substituted by the second step of affirmative collaboration (*anvaya*).

Thus, Buddhist logicians of ancient India theorized that the inferential process can ultimately be reduced to the two steps of *anvaya* and *vyatireka* operations. In an inference, these two operations ought to be clearly separated in reference to their respective variables, i.e., similar and dissimilar loci (*sapakṣa* and *vipakṣa*), here exemplified by a kitchen and a water tank. This is what I call "logical context."

This logical context means clear referential demarcation between the class of things that can be predicated as "having smoke" as well as "having fire" and the opposite class of things that can never be predicated as "having fire" or "having smoke." This context is accomplished by the principle of *anvaya* and *vyatireka*, i.e., application of a logical concomitance "P*Q" and its contra-position "–Q• –P" respectively to the similar and dissimilar classes of referents (*sapakṣa* and *vipakṣa*). This is the characteristic of Indian Buddhist inferential logic.

Coming to the Mohist system of logic, I emphatically point out that the inferential logic of ancient China is essentially identical with respect to the crucial dual operations, and that it is sufficient to refer to a few expositions to substantiate my point of view: *The Development of the Logical Method in ancient China* by Hu Shih (Shang-hai: 1928), *The later Mohist Logic and Science* by A. C. Graham (Hong-kong: 1978), and in addition, Janusz Chmielewski's series of articles: "Notes on Early Chinese Logic (I-VI),"7 *Rocznik Orientalistyczny,* especially, No. III (*Ibidem* 27, 1(1963) 103-121).

Hu Shih translated the dual operations as the *'t'ung'* (同), "method of agreement" and *'i'* (異), "method of difference" and explained that the two methods combined can establish valid inference which the Neo-Mohists regarded as the true method of induction[8]

Graham's understanding of these two methods does not fundamentally differ from Hu Shih's. It was Chmielewski who compared Neo-Mohist logic with its Indian counterpart and demonstrated the important terminological correspondences between Indian and Mohist inferential structure.[9] Their difference is that the principle of exemplification of Indian syllogistic inference is absent from the Mohist system; the Mohists instead apply the principle of *hsiao* (效)[10] a kind of universal statement well established by induction. The normative valid basis of inference, however, does not affect the logic of inferential process and is a correlative factor within the differences between Sanskrit and classical Chinese. It follows that this normative valid basis can serve as a common ground to analyze the *reductio-ad-abusrudum* method and paradoxical

---

[7] *Roznik Orientarist,* Vol. 26, I (1962) 7-22; Vol. 26, 2(1963) 91--105; Vol. 27 1(1963 103-121; Vol. 28, 2(1965) 87-111; Vol. 29, 2(1965) 117-138; Vol. 30, 1(1966) 31-52.

[8] Hu Shih, *op. cit.*, pp. 103-105; Grahm: *op. cit.*,p. 102 and p. 130. Here the principle of agreement and that of difference are translated as "Having respects in which they are the same, i.e., being of the same kind. Not having respects in which they are the same, i.e., not being of a kind," namely,: "having some thing by means of which they are (judged to be) the same," and "having something by means of which they are judged not to be the same."

[9] Chmielewski, *loc. cit.*, "Notes on . . III," p. 109.

[10] *Ibid.*, "Notes on . . III; " the entirety of the article is devoted to the subject of *hsiao*.

method respectively adopted by the Indian and Chinese Mādhyamikas.

§3. LOGICAL CONTEXT AND DIALECTICAL CONTEXT AND RESPECTIVE DUAL CRITERIA

That the Buddhist insight of *śūnyatā* is trans-cultural can be defended by the very fact that the inferential logic of the mind transcends cultural differences, and also that the dialectical method, which is definitive of that insight, derives from the same structural basis as that of logical thinking. This, however, does not mean that the dialectical method can arise directly from the structural basis of the inferential logic. As has been explained before, the inferential process requires two conditions: (1) the clear demarcation of the two sets of loci; and (2) the separate application of *anvaya* and *vyatireka* operations in reference to each respective *locus*. This two-fold condition I called "Logical Context." Then what is the Dialectical Context, in which the dialectical method has its justification? It is radically different from the logical context in two ways.

At the 31st Orientalist conference held in Tokyo in the summer of 1983, I presented my paper entitled: "Buddhist dialectical methods and their structural identity,"[11] in which the dialectical context is theorized in terms of two criteria, namely: (1) that the dialectical context is necessarily created in every logical and linguistic process of the mind as "simultaneous application of *anvaya* and *vyatireka*,' and (2) that these operations in turn create a dual-natured reference" in terms of "simultaneous identity and difference." I contend that it was this characteristic dual-natured reference that was metaphorically exemplified as magical apparition, sky flower, and so forth. Suppose we are listening to on-going speech in which phonemes, words, and sentences are incessantly coming and going. Catching a series of rapid sounds, our mind spontaneously configurates them into a word, a series of words into a sentence, and a series of sentences into a unified understanding. It is within this dynamic flow of speech or thoughts that we have a glimpse of the spontaneous juxtaposition of *anvaya* and *vyatireka*, irrespective of whether or

---

[11] Shohei Ichimura: the résumé of the article included in Proceedings of the 31st International Congress of Human Science in Asia and North Africa (Tokyo: The Toho Gakkai) 1984, pp.149-150; the full text included in *Dr. S. V., Sohoni Felicitation Volume*, Journal of Bihar Research Society, 1987.

not it is actually experienced, at every linkage point of consecutive moments of words or thoughts.

This juxtaposition of two assertions or thoughts is the first criterion of the dialectical context, and is clearly recognized in Nāgārjuna's favored *reductio-ad-absurdum* argument (*prasaṅga-vākya*). Perhaps, the best example of his argument is found in his *Vigrahavyāvartanī* in which he critically repudiates the Naiyāyika theory of *pramāṇa* by demolishing the epistemic relationship between sense faculty (*pramāṇa*) and incoming *stimuli (prameya)*. His *Middle Treatise, and* each of its all chapters, can invariably be analyzed in terms of this criterion as critically examining the Abhidharmist theory of causality of psycho-physical elements (*dharmas*) and the relationship between the Skandhas of these things and an individual self (*pudgala*).[12]

In the *Vigrahavyāvartanī*, Nāgārjuna resorts to the metaphor of light and dark respectively paralleled to the Naiyāyika theory of pramāṇa (means of cognition) and prameya (objects of cognition). Human perception derives from the contact of sense faculty and its object just as a candle's light illumines objects of nightly darkness. Since every religious literature commonly comprises a similar metaphor, like "Wisdom breaks the darkness of human ignorance to shine forth the ultimate spiritual truth," it was admissible for Nāgārjuna to use the metaphor to exemplify *pramāṇa* and *prameya*, perceptual faculty and its object, respectively as light and dark.

The pattern of his argument is precisely identical and consistent. Conceptually, light and dark are incompatible by definition, and yet in convention, the contact of these entities is taken for granted to explain the fact of illumination, just as it is taken for granted between visual faculty and its object. In like manner, Nāgarjuna exemplifies the relationship between human individual (*pudgala)* and underlying psycho-physical elements (*rūpa* and *caitāsika dharmas* of the Skandha) in terms of fire-fuel relationship. In convention, the contact of fire and fuel, which are two different things, is taken for granted to explain combustion. It is the purpose of Nāgārjuna's *reductio-ad-absurdum* method to demonstrate how and why this human convention does not stand dialectical scrutiny. The following

[12] For the dialectical treatment on the relationship between *pramāṇa* and *prameya*, see the *Vigrahvyāvartanī*, partially treated in this article in the following.. For the dialectical treatment of the relation beetween *pudgala* and *dharmas*, see the *Mūlamādhyamikakāerikā* X: *Agnīndhanaparīkṣā*, where Nāgārjuna uses the metaphor of fire and fuel respectively for *pudgala* and *dharmas*.

is a simplified translation for the Kārikās 36 through 39 comprised in the *Vigrahavyāvartanī*, the heart of his critique on the relationship between *pramāṇa* and *prameya:*[13]

36. In reference to the point of contact in space and time, wherever light illumines dark, dark also obstructs its illumination.

The mutually opposite entities 'light' and 'dark' cannot be identified conceptually, and yet convention holds that the two ought to be met to explain the phenomenon of illumination. If each one has its own reality (*svabhāva*) as indicated by each name, they cannot accomplish a contact, mutually repudiating each other in terms of contradiction.

37. Wherever there is light, there should be no dark (because they are mutually exclusive). How could light illumine anything?

38. Does light illumine dark at the moment of its arising? No, it has no contact with dark from the very beginning.

39. If light here illumines dark without a contact with it, this light here could illumine all the world.

It is apparent that the key operation of Nāgārjuna's method of *reductio-ad-absurdum* argument is to have two contrary or contradictory assertions focus on a singular point of reference. Here the metaphor of "a contact between light and dark" is used to exemplify the point of contact between visual faculty and its stimuli as the necessary causal factor of perception. It is apparent that this point of factual contact clearly transcends linguistic convention, because it is conventionally impossible to have these two different things, light and dark, together at one and the same place and time. Thus, Nāgārjuna points out two things:[14] (1) the spatio-temporal

---

[13]*Vigraha*. Kārikās 37-39:
yadi ca svaparātmānau tvad vacanena prakāśyayaty agniḥ/
pracchādayiṣyati tamaḥ svaparātmānau hutāśa iva // 36
nāsti tamaś ca jvalane yatra ca tiṣṭhati parātmani jvalanaḥ/
kurute katham prakāśaṃ sa hi prakāśo 'ndhakāravadhaḥ// 37
utpadyamāna eva prkāśayati agnir ity asadvādaḥ/
utpadyamāna eva prāpnoti tamo na hi hutāśaḥ// 38
aprāpto 'pi jvalano yadi vā punar andhakāram upahanyāt/
sarveṣu lokadhātuṣu tamo 'y.am iha saṃsthito hanyāt// 39

[14] Cf. Ichimura: "An analysis of Mādhyamika dialectic in terms of the logical principle of *anvaya-vyatireka*," in *Studies in Buddhoslogy: Professor P.V. Bapat Felicitation Volume*, ed. N. H. Santani (Delhi: Motilal Banarsidass, 1988), esp. Sect. IV. Also "An Approach to Dōgen's dialectical thinking and method of instantiation (a comparative study of *Shōbō Genzō*)," *JIABS*, IX, 2(1986) 79-80, in which the verses are put into symbolic notation.

sphere to which such a contact is referred is not possible within the logical context, where, because of the *anvaya-vyatireka* principle, the two opposite classes (light and dark) are not permitted to cross the boundary, either light becoming dark, or *vice versa.*, (2) the referential sphere at which light and dark no longer hold respective self-identity which becomes the dialectical context, at which light identifies itself with dark, and *vice versa*, across the logical boundary. Thus, mutual accommodation seems to be possible only within the dialectical context where light and dark are simultaneously identical and different. I think that this ultimate factual reference ought to be regarded as "dual-natured" which transcends logical and linguistic convention. From the Mādhyamika point of view, every perceptual faculty and every object of perception are two different things within the logical context, and yet this logical convention ultimately breaks down, so to speak, to become the dialectical context. In this dialectical context, independent self-identity (*svabhāva*) is no longer held, but reciprocity or mutual accommodation or loss of self-identity (*niḥsvabhāva* = *śūnyatā*) between the two as dual-natured referent. In short, the dialectical context consists of two criteria: (1) juxtaposition of opposite assertions and (2) dual-natured reference.

§4. SÊNG-CHAO'S PARADOXICAL ARGUMENT BASED ON TWO CRITERIA OF THE DIALECTICAL CONTEXT

The *Chao-lun* is regarded as a difficult text not only because of its dialectical content, which it shares in common with the Mādhyamika treatises, but also because Sêng-chao's dialectical method is not the so-called *reductio-ad-absurdum* argument of the Indian masters. He instead relied on the uniquely paradoxical method of argument of his own. And it can be proven to be an authentic Mādhyamika dialectic in terms of the two criteria mentioned above: the juxtaposition of two opposite assertions and the dual-natured reference. Without these criteria, we are unable to properly evaluate the formidable paradoxical argument of Sêng-chao unprecedented in Indian Mādhyamika treatises. Only after a careful analysis of the said dual criteria do we notice a set of the basic patterns as compliant with the same criteria detected in the Indian Mādhyamika method.

In the first essay collected in the *Chao-lun*: "The theory that things (i.e., *dharmas*) do not change,"[15] Sêng-chao deals with the

---

15 「物不遷論」

causality of *dharmas* regarding the phenomenon of "motion" (動) or "change" (遷), the same subject which Nāgārjuna dealt with in the second chapter of his *Middle Treatise*. In this essay, Sêng-chao sets forth a series of paradoxical arguments in terms of very tangible and concrete phenomena. As with Nāgārjuna, Sêng-chao's usual procedure is to match up a contrary or contradictory conception or phenomenon with one that is to be considered. Unlike Nāgārjuna, however, he bypasses the procedure of analysis and repudiation of the syntactical categories (*kāraka-śabda*), but immediately matches the word-meaning of "motion" (動) with its contrary state "stillness" (静). He further introduces a number of similar contraries, like "going" (去) and "abiding" (住); "going" (去) and "coming" (来); "passing" (往) and "staying" (留); "abiding" (住) and "changing" (遷). Sêng-chao presents convention as "things pass away" (物流動), while matching it up with his contrary assertion as "things do not pass away" (物不遷). This essay provides an excellent example of "matching up contraries":

> By motion, people mean that things are in motion and not at rest, because (they think) that past things do not reach the present. For the same reason, however, I claim that it is stillness, meaning that they are at rest and not in motion. (People think that) because things are in motion and not at rest, they do not come (to the present). I think, (however, that) because things are at rest and not in motion, they do not pass away (from the present). (People think that) things do not stay still and hence change, because past things do not come to the present, whereas (I think that) things are still and do not change, because past things did not go away anywhere. It follows that whatever is asserted ("neither reaching to the present nor passing away from the present') is not a different experience but different ways of viewing.[16]

Sêng-chao then argue through his typical form of paradoxical method:

> Things are said to be permanent (常) and yet not abiding (不住); they are said to be passing (去) and yet not changing (遷). Because not changing (不遷), things are passing (去) and yet

---

[16] Taishō., 45 (No. 1858); p. 151a (22-24). 「夫人之所謂動者。以昔物不至今。故曰動而非静。我之所謂静者。亦以昔物不至今。故曰静而非動。動而非静。以其不来。静而非動。以其不去。然則所造未嘗異。所見未嘗同。」

> always at rest (常静). Because not abiding (不住), they are at rest (静) and yet always passing (常往). Because things are at rest (常静) and yet always passing (常往), they are passing and yet not changing (弗遷). Because they are passing (往) and yet always at rest (常静), they are at rest (静) and yet not staying (弗留).[17]

As evident, every formula contained in the series constitutes contradiction, hence logically meaningless. Sêng-chao's method does not mean a logical anarchism, however. In parallel to Nāgārjuna's, his method can be shown as designed to communicate the insight of *śūnyatā* as to the nature of linguistic convention. For, in the essay, more than once, he lets his audience come to term with the fact that the two paradoxical statements, which though referring to two distinct classes of variables (respectively "things in motion" and "things in stillness), accomplish their juxtaposition over the singular spatio-temporal sphere of reference:

> When people say that things are abiding, I say that they are gone. When they say that things are gone, I say that they are abiding. Although 'gone' and 'abiding' are different in expression, what both mean is one reference.[18]

Following Nāgārjuna, however, Sêng-chao also leaves his exposition a little short of explicitly stating such *dialectical context*, except for the fact that the past and the present cannot be reconciled by means of convention, just as 'light' and 'dark' cannot.

> People seek the past in the present and say that it does not abide (不住). I seek the present in the past and know that it is not gone (不去). If the present reached the past, there should be the present in the past. If the past reached the present, there should be the past in the present. Since there is no past in the present, I know that it does not come (不来). Since there is no present in the past, I know it did not pass (不去). If the past does not reach the present, the present also does not reach the past. Each even by nature abides in one time (住於一世). What kind of things could go and come?[19]

---

[17] *Op cit.*, p. 151b (18-21). 「是以言常而不住、称去而不遷、不遷。故雖往而常静。不住。故雖静而常往、雖静而常往。故往而不遷、雖往而常静。故静而弗留牟。」

[18] *Op. cit.*, p. 151c (10-12). 「人之所謂住。我則言其去。人之所謂去。我則言其住。然則去住雖殊其致一也。」

[19] Taishō., p. 151c (12-17). 「人則求古於今。謂其不住。吾則求今於古。知其不

Given the foregoing type of argument, one anticipates a spontaneous objection or skepticism from the conventional point of view. In fact, Sêng-chao addresses to such an objection in the third essay: "*Prajñā* is Not-Knowing."[20] Especially, in the second question-answer session. The question which Sêng-chao raises from the commonsense point of view reflects, I assume, his own intellectual, logico-linguistic concern as it is said:

> Things cannot be used for communication, and hence they are given names. By way of names, people speak of things as referents and communicate with others about them. Although things are not names, they become the objects to be denoted by names (in terms of correspondence). Hence, by a name, if we seek anything, we can obtain something that corresponds to the name.[21]
>
> Now, however, you theorize that the transcendent insight (聖心) is 'not-knowing,' and yet you also said that there is nothing that it does not know. If the *Prajñā* is 'not-knowing,' it must mean not to have ever known anything, and if it is 'knowing,' it must mean to have always been knowing. This is what the Doctrine of Names promulgates, and it is the basic (logical) principle of assertion[22]
>
> Contrary to this common sense, you are saying that 'knowing' and 'not-knowing' are assumed to be identical as one in the *Prajñā* insight. Yet your statement refers to two different meanings. Examining what is said and looking for its reference, I have not found anything that can substantiate what you have so asserted. If knowing should mean to distinguish the nature of the *Prajñā* insight, then 'not-knowing' would not fit to distinguish it, and *vice versa*. If neither does not fit to do so, there is no sense in further discussion.[23]

Sêng-chao replies to this criticism through his paradoxical method of argument, and in doing so, he again applies the dialectical

---

去。今若至古。古応有今。古若至今。今応有古。今而無古。以知不来。古而無今。以知不去。若古不至今。今亦不至古。事各性住於一世。有何物而可去来。」

[20] 「般若無知論第三」Taishō., pp.152a-154c.

[21] *Ibid*, p. 153c (15-17)
「難曰。夫物無以自通。故立名以通物。物雖非名。果有可名之物当於此名牟。是以即名求物。物不能隠。」

[22] *Ibid*., (17-19). 「而論云聖心無知。又云無所不知。意謂無知未嘗知。知未嘗無知。斯即名教之所通。立言之本意也。」

[23] *Ibid*., (19-22). 「然論者欲一於聖心。異於文旨。尋之求実。未見其当。若知得於聖心。無知無所弁。若無知得於聖心。知方無所弁。若二都無得。無所復論哉。」

criterion of juxtaposition. Initially he quotes some textual passage as defining '*prajñā*' in paradoxical terms as "neither nameable nor expressible in language," "neither existent nor non-existent," or "neither real nor unreal."[24] Then, after an apologetic statement, Sêng-chao continues, saying: "Though words cannot explain what the *Prajñā* is, since there is no other way of communication, I am obliged to explain it to you,"[25] quoting:

> The *Prajñā* is subtle and formless and cannot be said as existent. Yet, because it is functionally limitless, it cannot be said non-existent. Because the *Prajñā* cannot be said non-existent, it may have to be said that it is (transcendentally) existent. Because the *Prajñā* cannot be said as existent, the theory of names or language cannot designate it by name. Hence it follows that the *Prajñā* cannot be (an empirical) knowing. If the comprehensive awareness of the *Prajñā* is wished to be expressed, it must be said 'not-knowing' and yet not 'not-knowing.' With respect to its distinguishing of the aspect (of things), it cannot be said as nothing. Because of its comprehensive awareness, it cannot be said as existent. Because it is non-existent, the *Prajñā* is 'knowing' and yet 'without knowing.' Because it is not nothing, the *Prajñā* is 'without knowing' and yet 'knowing. It follows that 'knowing' is identical with 'not-knowing.' Although 'knowing' and 'not-knowing' are different in expression, they are not different in terms of the *Prajñā* insight[26]

§5. THE DIALECTICAL MEANING OF *REDUCTIO-AD-ABSURDUM* AND PARADOXICAL METHOD OF ARGUMENT

Admitting that Sêng-chao's paradoxical method conforms the dialectical criteria of 'juxtaposition' and 'dual nature of reference,' we are confronted with a question as to why Sêng-chao relied exclusively on his distinctive paradoxical form of argument instead of the *reductio-ad-absurdum* form which Indian Mādhyamikas favored. In dealing with this curious difference, I presented another paper at the 33rd annual conference of the Japanese Association for

---

[24] *Ibid.*, p. 153 (23). 「経云。般若義者。無名無説。非有非無。非実非虚。」

[25] *Ibid.*, p. 153 (26-7). 「今試為子狂言弁之。」

[26] *Ibid.*, p. 153 (27-29) to p. 154 (1-4). 「夫聖心者。微妙無相不可為有。用之弥勤。不可為無。不可為無。故聖智存焉。不可為有。故名教絶焉。是以言知不為知。欲以通鑒。不知非不知。欲以弁其相。弁相不為無。通鑒不為有。非有。故知而無知。非無。故無知而知。是以知即無知。無知即知。無以言異。而於聖心也。」

Indian and Buddhist Studies held in Tokyo, 1984.[27] I identified two possible approaches to the problem in question, namely, (1) by exploring formal differences of Sanskrit and classical Chinese, or (2) by exploring cultural differences of the two peoples. On that occasion, I adopted the first approach.

My reason for adopting this approach was that, despite formal differences between classical Chinese and Sanskrit, the human capacity for language and symbol usage is generally accepted to be universal, and the logical laws underlying it are everywhere the same. In case of the difference of cultural forms, on the contrary, it is far more difficult. For instance, the conceptual network of Taoist and that of Indian Buddhist thought cannot be immediately compared due to the lack of any clear criterion shared by the two systems. What regulates cultural differences is far more complicated than logical rules which underlie all forms of language. For instance, the surface structure of syntactical relations may be quite different from one language to another; some languages have an intricate case system, whereas some others a much simpler one. Yet, the deep structure that underlies different languages seems to be universal and common as is confirmed by the fact of translatability from one language to any other language. In any case, my findings are as follows.

Sanskrit is equipped with an intricate system of syntactical categories, i.e., *kāraka-śabda*, accompanied with case inflections, grammatical word classes, and so forth, whereas classical Chinese is mono-syllabic, lacking inflection and grammatical word classes, and so forth. In addition, Chinese ideographical symbols contrast sharply with the phonetic symbols of Sanskrit. The formal aspects of Chinese, however, are not necessarily a disadvantage, because recent studies indicate that certain characteristics of Chinese in question facilitate logical thinking, because they bring classical Chinese closer to the symbolic language of modern logic than any tongue of the Indo-European type. The action-centered sentiential structure of Sanskrit itself was restructured by Buddhist logicians to attain the logically calculational subject-predicate form. On the other hand, the sentential formula of Chinese (esp. classical one) is the logically fit *topic-comment* structure and with no grammatical constriction, such as, copula, inflection, parts of speech, etc., which

---

[27] Ichimura: "A determining factor that differentiated Indian and Chineese Mādhyiamika methods of dialectic as *reductio-ad-absurdum* and paradoxical argument respectively," *Journal of Indian and Buddhist Studies*, 33, 2(1985), 834-84.

are often logically ambiguous or misleading. My tentative conclusion is that the *reductio-ad-absurdum* method is more suitable *vis-à-vis* Sanskrit, whereas the paradoxical method is more fit vis-à-vis classical Chinese.

To say that in Sanskrit, a sentence is action-oriented, means that the syntactical categories (*kāraka-śabda*) were analyzed to be a set of case relations. Thus, a simple statement "He goes" (*gacchati*) is believed in convention to acquire its symbolic power from the *Kāraka* framework, of which *kartṛ* (agent, e.g. "goer" or *gantṛ*), *karman* (recipient of action, e.g., "referential passage" or *gamyamāna*), and *karaṇa* (instrument, "act of going" or *gamana*) and so froth are theoretically abstracted as assisting significative efficiencies. The key operation of Nāgārjuna's dialectic is to repudiate each of the Kāraka categories believed to possess its specific signification in terms of *svabhāva* ("self-identifying efficiency"). Thus, given a single term '*gamyamāna*' (passive reflexive progressive form of √*gam*, to go), not only '*gamana*' (transitive or active progressive form) as well as *gantṛ* (nominative form as agent) are *ipso facto* present as members of the action context, but also determine its action verb as '*gacchati*,' and so forth, according to the rules of proper inflection for person, number, tense, voice and mood.

Nāgārjuna maximizes this linguistic convention in reference to the factual world where the symbolic system of language has its ultimate concern. In the second chapter of his *Middle Treatise*, for instance, he applies a series of *reductio-ad-absurdum* arguments with focus on the *kāraka-śabda*s of a verb √to go. He begins with the action context in which an act of going or a movement (*gamana* or *gati* synonymously given) is concomitant with bodily motion (*ceṣṭā*) and that it is inherent in an on-going referential passage of movement (*gamyamāna*).

> VERSE 2: An act of going (*gati* or *gamana*) is concomitant with bodily motion (*ceṣṭā*), which is inherent in a (referential trace of) on-going movement (*gamyamāne*); such a motion is neither in a past movement (*gate*) nor in any future movement that does not yet come (*agate*). Hence, it ought to be where the on-going movement (*gati*) takes place.[28]

---

[28] *Kārikā* 2 in the chapter entitled as "the examination of gone and yet to come" (
gatāgata-parīkṣa-nāma dvitīyaṃ prakaraṇam):
ceṣṭā yatra gatis tatra gamyamāne ca sā yataḥ/
na gate nāgate ceṣṭā gamyamāne gatis tataḥ// 2

Now, based on this premise, Nāgārjuna induces absurdity by maximizing the significative power of *kārakas*, quoting:

> VERSE 4: Whoever presumes that an act of going (*gamana*) belongs to an on-going trace of movement (*gamyamāna*), he is subjected to an error of admitting that without a motion (*ṛte gates*), there is an on-going trace of movement (*gamyamānam*), because the referential trace is being traversed (without an act of going).
>
> VERSE 5: If the *gamana* is to be found in the *gamyamāna*, this assertion *ipso facto* commits itself to another assertion, that there are two *gamanas*; one *gamana* by which the *gamyamāna* is produced, and another *gamana* which is inherent in the *gamyamāna*.
>
> VERSE 6: When two *gamanas* are assumed, there should follow two goers (agents of action), because no motion is possible without its agent, and *vice versa*.[29]
>
> VERSE 11: [In like manner] if again it is asserted that the goer goes (*gantā gacchati*), it results in a similar predicament such that two acts of going (*gamanas)* are implied, namely, one *gamana* which indicates its agent and another *gamana* which the agent produces.[30]

It is obvious that Nāgārjuna's foregoing *reductio-ad-absurdum* arguments are intended to examine the causal change of things, e.g., psycho-physical elements (*dharmas)* of the Skandha, of human individual, in terms of motion or time passage. He focuses on the *dialectical context* in which motion or an on-going movement (*gamana*) is concomitant with its referential passage of motion (*gamyamāna*) as well as with its agent of going (*gantṛ)*. This contextual fixation which is clearly crucial to Nāgārjuna's method is justified in reference to the factual world, because it is this sole region where alone visual faculty (*pramāṇa*) and its incoming stimuli (*prameya*) establish a contact for the fact of epistemic experience or cognition. It follows

---

[29] *Kārikās* 4, 5, and 6:
gamyamānasya gamanaṃ yasya tasya prasajyate/
ṛte gater gamyamānaṃ gamyamānaṃ hi gamyate// 4
gamyamānasya gamane prasaktaṃ gamanadvayṃ/
yena tadgamyamānaṃ ca yaccātra gamanaṃ punaḥ// 5
dvau gantārau prasajyete prasakte gamanadvaye/
gantāraṃ hi tiraskṛtya gamanaṃ nopapadyate// 6

[30] *Ibid., kārikās* 11.
gamane dve prasajyete gantā yad uta gaccati/
ganteti cocyate yena gantā san yacca gacchati// 11

that the only way to resolve the foregoing absurdity is to recognize the principle of simultaneous identity and difference of referential entities. In other words, when light and dark are posed irreconcilably as contradictors, neither the phenomenon of illumination nor that of dark can be explained. Nor is an antithesis of existent and non-existent meaningful. It would be the same with the antithesis of motion and stillness, and so forth. On the other hand, should the fact of illumination be perceived, it would have involved negation of dark, and *vice versa*. It is precisely what Sêng-chao's paradoxical argument achieves as evident in his paradoxical arguments.

In parallel with Nāgārjuna's argument, it is clear now why Sêng-chao's dialectical method did not resort to the *reductio-ad-absurdum* argument to deal with the conception of motion and stillness, and so forth, precisely because the Chinese language does not depend on the action-centered grammatical system. Despite the universal deep structure of human language, the difference between Sanskrit and Chinese is a serious barrier from the point of view of translation. Even the greatest translator such as Kumārajīva, despite his profound insight and knowledge of both languages, just could not render an exact equivalent of '*gamyamāna*' in strictly grammatical terms, i.e., a reflexive or passive progressive form of √*gam*,[31] but translated it simply as "passing moment" (去時) or "present passing" (現去), precisely because there is no equivalent grammatico-linguistic system, such as that of Sanskrit, in the Chinese language. I am therefore inclined to think that for the same reason the characteristic of the language itself precluded a similar necessity of the Nāgārjunian *reductio-ad-absurdum* method from the mind of the native Chinese Buddhist thinkers.

§6. SÊNG-CHAO'S PARADOXICAL ARGUMENT AND MOHIST LOGICAL PRINCIPLE OF *HSIAO*

It is intriguing whether a special relationship exists between a language and a system of logic developed within that linguistic environment, especially in case of the Mohist system of logic (墨子之論理) in ancient China. Indian logic, as indicated by the terms of *anvaya* and *vyatireka*, evolved initially within the grammarians' discipline to search and organize the rules and principles of Sanskrit

[31] The meaning of gamyamāna is corollary to that of '*gamyate*' (passive reflexive of the verb 'to go'), e.g., *gamyamānam gamyate*, MK II, k. 4.

grammar. If Sêng-chao's paradoxical method is more attuned to Chinese language, it may very well be questioned whether his method was at all based upon the Mohist system of logic, as the Nāgārjunian dialectical method was based upon Indian logic. Charles Graham informs us that the Neo-Mohist text was circulated during the third century.[32] Sêng-chao, who lived in the fourth century and was trained in the Taoist classics might have been exposed to the Mohist logical thought. In a paper I presented at the 36th annual meeting of the Japanese Association of Indian and Buddhist Studies in summer, 1987, entitled "On the dialectical meaning of instantiation in terms of *māyā-dṛṣṭānta* in the Indian and Chinese Mādhyamikas,"[33]

I gave evidence for the fact that Sêng-chao may have known the Mohist system of logic.\Unlike Indian syllogistic inference, the Mohist system did not advocate the principle of instantiation, but provided the principle of *hsiao* (效) as essential to valid inference, which Hu Shih interpreted to mean "model thought" or "standard mode of thought," and Chmielewski interpreted it to mean any universal statement of causality well established by induction.[34] In short, *hsiao* was conceived by the Mohist as true, and hence regarded as a legitimate general premise for deriving any particular statement as valid. According to Sanskrit inferential rules (*anvaya-vyatireka*), each inference must include an affirmative as well as a negative instance, thus combining inductive procedure with deduction. The Mohist system theorized the dual rules as the method of sameness and that of difference, in parallel with Sanskrit counterparts, i.e., affirmative and negative collaborations, but without the principle of instantiation. This may be why Sêng-chao does not appeal to instantiation, except to quote the Sūtra when necessary. For instance, in his second essay: "The theory that whatever is unreal is voidness,"[35] he applies a *māyā* metaphor quite adequately, quoting:

We want to say that *dharmas* exist, but their existence is not a

---

[32] Charles A. Graham: *Later Mohist Logic, Ethics and Science*, The Chinese University Press, 1979, pp.64-66; the Neo-Mohist canon seems to have been circulated at the turn of the 4th cnetury among the Neo-Taoist circles. The San-lun master Chi-ts'ang comments on the Mohist logic in his major work: *The Profound Meaning of Three (Mādhyamika) Treatises* (「三論玄義」), Taishō. 45, No. 1852, p. 6c line 29 - p. 7a line 3: 「難曰く。是有是無名為両是。非有非無名為両非。既墮是非。還同儒墨。答本非二是故有雙非二是既亡。雙非亦息。故知非是亦復非非。」

[33] *JIBS*. 36, (1988), 9-15.

[34] Hu Shih, *op. cit.*, p. 95f; Chmielewski: *loc. cit.*, pp. 106-109.

[35] 「不真空論」第二 : pp.152a-153a.

> real production. We want to say that *dharmas* do not exist, but phenomenal forms are already configured. Phenomenal forms cannot be said as identical with nothing, but we only say that anything unreal is not a real existent. It follows that the meaning of "*Śūnyatā* of Whatever is Unreal" is thus revealed. Accordingly, the *Pañcaviṃśati-sāhasrikā-prajñāpāramitāsūtra* says: "*Dharmas* are called metaphorically as "unreal" just as a magically created man is. For we cannot say that there is no magically created man, but that such is not a real man.[36]

I am convinced that Sêng-chao was acquainted with Mohist logic because of the special context in which he uses the term *hsiao*. Although he does not use *hsiao* to designate an inferential universal or a norm for valid inference, he uses it to designate the dialectical context that validates all dialectical statements. In his last easy, "the theory that Nirvāṇa is name-less,"[37] he considers the relationship between psycho-physical elements (*dharmas*) and an individual self (*pudgala*), while trying to demonstrate the truth of non-duality, by demonstrating that there is no difference between the *pudgala* and the *dharms* from the point of view of the *Prajñā* insight. Sêng-chao initially describes what the perfect man is:

> The perfect man is all void without any form whatsoever, and yet there is none in myriads of things that is not created by his self. Whoever should cause myriads of things to be met with himself and thus realize his own being, would it be such perfected man alone? If a man is not with the true nature of things, he should not be a perfected man. Without a perfected man, there should arise no true nature of things. Whenever there is the true nature of things, there should arise a perfected man; accordingly the perfected man is not different from the true nature of things.[38]

Sêng-chao then quotes a doctrinal query and reply between Indra and Subhūti:

> Then, the lord of gods questioned: "In what reference should I seek the *Prajñā* insight?" Subhūti replied: "You should not seek it in reference to a *rūpa*, nor should you seek it in reference to

---

[36] Taishō., 45, p. 152b (16-20). 「何則欲言其有。有非真生。欲言其無。事象既形。事象形不即無。非真非実有。然則不真空義。顕於茲牟。故放光云。諸法仮号不真。譬如幻化人。非化人非真人也。」

[37] 「涅槃無名論」: Taishō., *op. cit.*, p157a-161b.

[38] *Ibid.*, p. 161a (7-9).

> anything separate from a *rūpa*." Subhūti again said: "Seeing the causality of "Dependent Origination" means seeing the Dharma; seeing the Dharma means seeing the Buddha."[39]

Then, referring to the above triad (i.e., seeing *pratiītyasamutpāda*, seeing *dharmas*, and seeing *buddha*), Sêng-chao designates it in terms of *hsiao*, and says:

> This is the *ultimate spiritual context* (*hsiao*)[40] in which one realizes the insight of non-difference between things (psycho-physical elements (dhamras) and an individual self (pudgala). Therefore, the perfected man puts away[41] subtle primeval forces prior to their signs of phenomenalization and stores them up within the undifferentiated awareness of referential manifestation.[42]

Although no direct hint is found in the passage, I think that Sêng-chao seems to have deliberately used the Mohist logical term *hsiao* to denote the trans-logical, dialectical context as foundation of his paradoxical argument, and that this is in precise parallel with the logical context, of which the Mohist theorized the criterion of *hsiao* for every valid inferential statement. I believe that this hunch is supported by the immediately following statements of Sêng-chao:

Thus, it is said in the Sūtra (?): One realizes Nirvāṇa without separating himself from *dharmas* and also it is said: "Because there is no limit with the (number of) *dharmas*, there is neither a limit with Enlightenment," Thus the path of Nirvāṇa is known as having no limit." .Hence, it follows that things (*dharmas*) are neither different from an individual self (*pudgala*), nor is the self different from

---

[39] *Ibid.*, (10-12). 「故天帝曰般若当於求何。善吉曰。般若不可於色中求。又見縁起為見法。見法為見仏。斯即物我不異之效也。」

[40] According to the Mathew's Chinese English Dictionary, '*hsiao*' (效) means to imitate, to follow an example, and hence used as compounds to mean efficacy (效力), potentiality (效能), fulfilment or verification (效験) or to put forth effort (效労), to devote one's energy or to devote oneself to (效義). Here it is rendered as "ultimate experiential context" either in the sense of "ultimate spirituality" or dialectical context," in which alone the *Prajñā* insight is at hand. The group of Japanese scholars translated this particular passage: "This is, indeed, the evidence of non-difference between *things* and self in the perfected man." Obviously they did not take account of the Mohist meaning of the logical concept of *Hsiao*.

[41] '*chi*' ( ) means to put away weapons (for peace), to cease hostilities, to fold up, to collect onself, to gather elements or people in.

[42] *Ibid.*, (12-16). 「見縁起為見法。見法為見仏。斯則物我不異之也。所以至人玄機於未兆。蔵冥運於即化。」

things, and that things and the self inexpressively meet together[43]

§7 Conclusion

I have refrained to quote Sêng-chao's expository statements which contain Taoist jargon and thereby to keep myself away from an interpretative commitment to his cultural form. I have tried as far as I can to confine my investigation to the forms and functions of his paradoxical method and thereby analyze how successfully he created the dialectical context and revealed the *Prajñā* insight of *śūnyatā* through his own method. Whether his paradoxical method derived from his familiarity with the Mohist inferential logic, or whether it derived from the general cultural form of Chinese people, is still a question. Some contemporary scholars assert that "it is the wisdom of Chinese Philosophy to emphasize the importance of body, and that Chinese thought in general bears a down-to-earth characteristic. On the other hand, some contemporary scholars also assert that there is no special way of expressing counter-factuals in the Chinese language. They argue whether the language has not offered its native speakers incentive for thinking about the world in terms of counter-factuality, and whether this characteristic negatively affected Chinese people to become behind in the development of modern science[44]

I cannot subscribe myself to this point of view, because I know that the Mohist school developed not only an independent logical system, but also a remarkable degree of contribution to human science and mathematics in ancient China. Nevertheless, comparing Nāgārjuna's *reductio-ad-absurdum* method on the *Kāraka-śabdas* and Sêng-chao's paradoxical method on his concerned referential dimension, I am aware of some important difference between the two peoples with respect to Buddhist spirituality. I think that Sêng-chao's use of *hsiao*, the crucial terminology of the Mohist system of logic, fits quite well with the particular passage quoted above, namely: "This is the *ultimate spiritual context* (*hsiao*) in reference to which one realizes the insight of non-difference between

---

[43] *Ibid.*, (16-20).
「経曰、不離諸法而涅槃。又曰諸法無辺故。菩提無辺。以知涅槃之道。。。然則物不異我。我不異物。物我玄会。」

[44] Cf. A. H. Bloom: The Linguistic Shaping of Thought. New Jersey: Lawrence Erlbasum Associates, 1981.

things (psycho-physical elements or *dhamras*) and an individual self (*pudgala*)." The fact that Sêng-chao deliberately applied the Mohist term *hsiao* to designate the dialectical context can be further confirmed by the immediately following dialectical statement:

> "Things (*dharmas*) are neither different from an individual self (*pudgala*), nor is the self different from things, and that things and the self inexpressively meet together.

My research on the relationship between Sêng-chao's paradoxical method and Mohist logic is still incomplete. The origin and role of '*hsiao*' as the valid inferential criterion is still a mystery to me. However, I am certain that it is possible to apply the criterion of structural identity of Indian logic and Indian Buddhist dialectic to that relationship between Sêng-chao's paradoxical method and the Mohist inferential logic.

The ultimate question to those of us who are seriously engaged in the study of religion is the nature of religious truth. It is generally believed that unlike a scientific truth, religious truth cannot be subjected to experimental and logical criteria for its validity. And yet, it is neither acceptable to our intelligence that religious truth is totally outside the faculty of reason, nor that it is totally within it as human experience, whatever this term might mean. Should a given historical religion be autheticated or verified of its possession of a universal nature in terms of human spirituality, this universal nature ought to be established irrespective of different historical and cultural contexts in which it takes its manifestation, insofar as it is spoken and written in logical and linguistic convention.

Between Indian Buddhism that arose in ancient India and developed within that cultural context and that Buddhism which was transmitted to China and developed in that cultural context, there should be some difference. If Buddhism's spirituality is trans-cultural and hence identical between the two, and if the respective forms are culturally bound, the difference between the two ought to be mutually complementary. In view of these points of consideration, the early Chinese Madhyamakika Sêng-chao and his work *Chao-lun* provide further opportunity of research enquiry on Buddhist spirituality with respect of its extra-trans-culturality and intra-trans-culturality.

ARTICLE TEN

Heart Sūtra translated by Hsüan-tzang and Kumārajīva and Its Cultural Impact[1]

§1. Introduction

The last Sanskrit text that Hsüan-tzang completed for his task of translation at Yu-hua-kung (玉華宮) is known to have been the largest, monumental *Mahāprajñāpāramitā-sūtra* of six hundred fascicles.[2] This single scripture comprises the three other scriptures of the same Prajñāpāramitā group, comprising respectively one hundred thousand, twenty-five thousand, and eight thousant verses. Accordingly, this textual translation was Hsüan-tźang's ultimate goal, for which he is said to have originally decided to visit India. He was the best authority in the philosophical aspect as well as the linguistic aspect of the Prajñāpāramitā literature. The focus of my interest in this paper is the *Hṛdaya Sūtra* or so-called *Heart Sūtra,* of which once Edward Conze ascertained that all of its passages are identifiable in *toto* with the contents of another Prajñā scripture, namely, one that consists of twenty-five thousand verses, so called *Larger Wisdom Text* translated by Kumārajīva.[3]

Since the two versions respectively ascribed to Hsüan-tzang and Kumārajīva are so close in terms, phrases, and expressions, I have found that it is futile to seek differences in terms of textual critiques, and hence, directed my enquiry toward the cultural impact which the same text created respectively at the time of Kumārajīva and Hsüan-tzang. From the cultural point of view, the

---

[1] Presented at the 2nd International Academic Conference on Hsüan-tzang Study under the title: "Hsüan-tzang's *Prajñā-hṛdaya-sūtra* compared with That of Kumārajīva from the Point of Vew of Chinese Buddhist Culture," Tong-chuan, Shaanxi Provice, China; March 22 through 25, 1999. It is included in the published proceeding entitled: 「玄奘研究第二届銅川玄奘国際学術研討会文集」、黄心川主編 [陝西師范大学出版社、1999; pp. 331-355].

[2] 「大般若経」 or *Ta-pan-jo-ching*, 「大般若波羅蜜多経」 or *Ta-pan-jo-po-lo-mi-to-ching,* 600 fascicles) Taishō. 5-6-7, No. 220.

[3] The *Pañca-viṃśatisāhasrikā-prajñāpāramitā-sūtra or the larger Prajñā Sūtra (Ta-pin-pan-jo-ching,* 「大品般若経」) *that consists of 25,000 Verses (ślokas).* Conze's analysis appeared in *Journal of Royal Asiatic society*, 1948, pp. 33-51.

Heart Sūtra comprises an important innovation in that the main expositor of the Prajñāpāramitā spirituality was made Kuan-shih-yin Bodhisattva (観世音菩薩) instead of the Buddha. After Hsüan-tzang popularized the *Heart Sūtra*, this Mahāyāna personification of love and compassion became the center of the cultic movement which eventually made its way to all regions of East Asia, becoming a pan-cultural force. What is significant is the fact that the spirit of the *Heart Sūtra* has remained an inseparable element of this cultural force.

In pursuit of the textual meaning of the *Heart Sūtra*, I intend to clarify how and why the meaning of *Śūnyatā* survived without being criticized as nihilism in China, unlike in India where it was unjustly so criticized by the Hindu partisans. I am also concerned with the cultural force of the Kuan-yin, which has survived through countless ages, for finding how and why it could contribute to the solution of the present day problem of prejudice and misconception as continual sources of human suffering.

§2. THE *PRAJÑĀ-HṚDAYA-SŪTRA* WITHIN THE ENTIRE *PRAJÑĀPĀRAMITĀ* LITERATURE

The *Prajñā Heart Sūtra*[4] translated by Hsüan-tzang in the year 649 is perhaps the shortest scripture of all Buddhist texts as it consisted of only 262 characters. Since *Hsüan-tzang* did not incorporate it in his super-voluminous, all inclusive *Great Prajñāpāramitā Sūtra* of 600 fascicles, he must have regarded it as an independent text.[5]

---

[4] *Pan-jo-hsin-chimg* (「般若波羅蜜多心経」), Taishō. 8, No. 251.

[5] The Taishō New Tripiṭaka edition has only two entries for Hsüan-tzang's translation of the Prajñāpāramitā Sūtra. The three volumes (No. 5 through 7) comprise (1) the *Ta-pan-jo-po-lo-mi-to-ching* [「大般若波羅蜜多経」600 fasc. (No. 221-244)], and (2) the shortest *Mo-ho-pan-jo-po-lo-mi-to-hsin-ching* [「摩訶般若波羅蜜多心経」1 fasc. (No. 252) included in the 8th volume along with other Prajñāpāramitā scriptures. Hsüan-tzang systematically collected all sixteen lecture sessions supposed to be held at four different localities (四処十六会). Thus, came to be the stupendous all-inclusive texual edition, which comprised the following three:

(1) the *Śatasāhasrikā-prajñāpāramitā-sūtra* (the *100,000 Śloka Prajñāpāramitā-sūtra* 「十万頌般若」) which corresponds to the initial and primary lecture session and to the initial 400 fascicles of the largest translation;

(2) The *Pañcaviṃśati-sāhasrikā-prajñāpāramitā-sūtra* (the *25,000 Śloka Prajñāpāramitā-sūtra* 「二万五千頌般若」) which corresponds to the 2nd and 3rd lecture sessions (第二、三会) and to the 78 and 59 fascicles of the text

There are eight extant versions of the *Prajñā Heart Sūtra* which are comprised in the 8th volume of the Taishō Tripiṭaka New Edition,[6] and if some non-extant texts[7] are added, the number of its versions is said to go up to as many as thirteen or fourteen,[8] reflecting the enormous popularity of this *short sūtra* in Chinese Buddhist culture.

The oldest extant translation of the text is ascribed to Kumārajīva (AD 344-413) with its title as *Mahāprajñāpāramitā Wisdom Prayer Sūtra.*[9] is known to have represented the anterior olden translations

---

respectively distinguished as the Ta-pin-pan-jo group (「大品般若類」), and

(3) The *Aṣṭāsāhasrikā-prajñāpāramitā-sūtra*. (the *8000 Śloka Prajñāpāramitā-sūtra*「八千頌般若」) which is equivalent to the 4th and 5th lecture sessions (第四、五会), and corresponds to the 18 and 10 fascicles of the Hsiao-pin-pan-jo group (小品般若類).

These fascocles of the text altogether constitute a 94 % of the 600 fascicles and nearly comprehend the whole Prajñā lecture sessions which are consistent among themselves. The Taishō edition vol. 8, which corresponds only to one fourth of the entire Prajñā Sūtra Section, comprises the Ta-pin-pan-jo group (大品般若) and Hsiao-pin-pan-jo group (小品般若) translated by different translators, such as, Kumārajīva (鳩摩羅什) of Yao-ch'in (姚秦) as foremost, Chih-ch'ien (支謙) of Wu (呉), Chih-lou-chia-ch'en (支婁迦讖) of the Late Han, Dharmarakṣa (竺法護) and Wu-la-ch'a (無羅叉) of the Western Chin (西晋) as well as those texts which were regarded as independent outside the aforementioned sixteen lecture sessions. The *Hṛdaya Sūtra* was obviously treated as an independent scripture. How and why Hsüan-tzamg regarded it as an independent text is a matter of dispute.

6 「大正新修大蔵経」

7 For instance, the non-extant texts are *Mahāprajñāpāramitā Prayer Sūtra* (「摩訶般若波羅蜜呪経」) ascribed to Chih-ch'ien (支謙、AD 222-284), a lay in the Prajñā Section, of Wu (呉), regarded by some to have been a version of the *Hṛdaya Sūtra*; *Pan-jo-po-lo-mi-t'o-ching* (「般若波羅蜜多那経」) ascribed to Bodhiruci (菩提流支、572-772); *Moho-panjo--sui-hsin-ching* (「摩訶般若随心経」) ascribed to Śikṣānanda (実叉難陀、652-710), *Fo-shuo-pan-jo-po-lo-mi-t'o-ching* (「仏説般若波羅蜜多心経」) ascribed to I-ching (義浄、624-703) which has been regarded a false ascription because of its total identity with Hsüan-tzang's version, except for a few non-essential additions.

8 Watanabe, Shōgo: An introduction to the theory on the formation of the *Prajñā-hṛdaya-sūtra* (「般若心経成立論序説」), Buddhist Studies (「仏教学」 No. 31, July 1991), p. 42. Also Cf. Kajiwa, Kōun: *A Study on the Formation of Mahāyāna Buddhism* (「大乗仏教の成立史的研究」、Tokyō, Sankibō, 1981), p. 171; Fukui, Fumiyoshi: (「般若心経の歴史的研究」、Tokyō: Shunjūsha, 1987), p. 191.

9 *Mo-ho-pan-jo-po-lo-mi-ta-ming-chou-ching* (「磨訶般若波羅蜜大明呪経」1 fasc., Taishō 8 (No. 250), whose Sanskrit equivalent has been identified as *Mahāprajñāpāramitā-mahā-vidyā-mantra-sūtra*. I rendered the title literally

(旧訳), whereas Hsüan-tzaing ushered the era of the posterior new translations (新訳).[10] After Hsüan-tzang's most popular *Heart Sūtra*, the Taishō Tripiṭaka enumerates six other, similar but little enlarged, versions, on average two new texts every century up to the last translation by Dhānapāla (施護) around 981, each offering some incremental improvements.[11] Mysteriously, however, during the two centuries between Kumārajīva and Hsüan-tzang, no other translation of this *Sūtra* was recorded. Nor was Kumārajīva's translation (「大明呪経」) recorded under his name in the major catalogue of the six dynasties, such as, the *Collection of the Tripiṭaka Textual Records* (i.e.,「出三蔵記集」) compiled by Sêng-yu (僧祐、420-589).[12]Nor Hsüan-tzang himself seems to have known the existence of such a prior translation. The introductory statement attached to the Chinese transliteration of the *Sanskrit Hṛdaya Sūtra,* which Hsüan-tzang is said to have produced his version, informs that the *Sūtra* was

---

in parallel with the compound terms; 'ta' as "great"; 'ming' as "wisdom," "knowledge," "illimuniation," etc.; 'chou' as "a prayer," "a sacred formula" or "mystical verse," or "a magical formula," "incanttion," "charm," "spell," etc.

[10] More precisely analyzing the history of Chinese translations, There were five different periods: (1) ancient translations (古訳、AD 178-375), assembled in Tao-an's catalogue, (2) earlier olden translation (旧訳前期、376-501), marked by Kumārajīca and recorded in Sêng-yu's catalogue, (3) later olden translations (旧訳後期、502-617), recorded in the Catalogue of Various Scriptures (「衆経目録」) sponsored by dynastic edicts; (4) earlier new translations, (新訳前期、618-959), the period being initiated by Hsüan-ts'ang and (5) later new translations (新訳後期, 960-1906). Cf. Ono, Genmyō: "History of transmission and translation of Buddhist Sūtras, *Bussho Kaisetsu Daijiten* (「仏書解説大辞典」), Additional Vol., pp. 7-8.

[11] (1) 「普遍智蔵般若波羅蜜多心経」re-translation by Fa-yueh (法月), T'ang dynasty [Taishō 8, (No. 252)], (2)「般若波羅蜜多心経」 by Prajñā (般若) and Li-yen in 790 [*Ibid*., (No. 253)], (3)「梵本般若波羅蜜多心経」by Prajñācakra (智慧輪) in 861 [*Ibid*., (No. 254], (4)「般若波羅蜜多心経」by Dharmasiddhi ? (Fa-chêng, 法成) in 855 [*Ibid*., (No. 255)], (5)「梵本般若多心経者」by Amoghavajra (不空金剛) in 771-775 [*Ibid*., (No. 256)], and (6) 「仏説聖仏母小字本般若多心経」 by Dhānapāla (施護) in 980-? of Sung dynasty [*Ibid*., (No. 257)] and「仏説帝釈般若波羅蜜多心経」[*Ibid*., (No. 249)].

[12] 「出三蔵記集」(15 fasc.), *Ch'u-san-ts'ang-chi-chi* [Taishō 55, (No. 2145)] which integrated into itself an anterior .catalogue: *the Catalogue of the Various Scriptures through General Survey*「綜理衆経目録」compiled by Tao-an (道安、314-385) on those Buddhist texts brought to China as well as translations, covering the period from the late Han dynasty down to the Eastern Chin (東晋、317-419). The edition *Ch'u-san-ts'ang-chi-chi* (「出三蔵記集」) was compiled during 510-518 by Sêng-yu (僧祐、445-518) of Liang.

orally given to Hsüan-tzang by an ailing monk whom he happened to meet on the way to India.[13] Some contemporary Japanese scholars hypothesized that the *Sūtra* referred to in that introduction was Kumārajīva's translation,[14] but some others are sceptical about it, thinking that it may have been a Sanskrit text or even simply a fragment consisting of its last *Mantra* formula.[15]

That the *Great Wisdom Prayer Sūtra* (「大明呪経」) was Kumārajīva's translation cannot be refuted because of the *verbatim* identity between this version of the *Heart Sūtra* and a portion of the second chapter of the *Larger Prajñāpāramitā Sūtra* of his translation, known as *Ta-p'in-pan-jo-ching* or the *25,000 śloka Prajñāpāramitā-sūtra* in Sanskrit. What is significant with Hsüan-tzang's *Heart Sūtra* is the fact that his translation and Kumārajīva's

---

[13] This *Hṛdaya Sūtra* in Sanskrit transliterated by Amoghavajra (不空), entitled 「唐梵翻対字音般若波羅蜜多心経」 [Taishō 8, (No. 256) discovered from the Tung-huang excavation, S 700)] is said to have been the text which Hsüan-tzang translated (梵本般若多心経者、大唐三蔵之所訳也). The introduction to this text begins, saying: "When the Tripiṭaka master stayed overnight at the Kung-hui-ssù in the province of I (益州) on the way to India, he happened to meet an ailing monk who tried to stop his journey by explaining how and why it was extremely difficult and dangerous to go through the regions. The monk then said: "I have 'the essential truth of spirituality of the Buddhas of three periods' (三世諸仏心要法門). If you upholds this, you should be able to survive your journey for going and returning." Thus, the master received it orally from that monk. In the next morning, he was already gone. In the Nālandā University, when the master was engaged in the act of circumambulating the Sūtra Hall as morning service, suddenly he saw the same monk, who then congratulated him for his successful journey and, upon letting him know that he was the Kuan-yin Bodhisattva, he disappeared into the early morning air (我是観音菩薩言訖冲空). Taishō *op. cit.*, p.851b.

[14] Kajio, Kōun: 「大乗仏教の成立史的研究」山喜房, 1981, p. 171; and Fukui, Bunyū: 「般若心経の歴史的研究」春秋社, 1987, p. 191ff, theorized that Hsüan-ts'ang obtained Kumārajīva's translation from a monk. Challenging this point of view, ShogoWatanabe points out that this may not be the case by referring to the process of gradual alteration of the story regarding the textual sourc of Hsüan-ts'ang's translation in the *Catalogue of Buddhist Scriptures Newly Determined in the Era of Chen-hüan* (「貞元新定釈経目録」, ca. the 9th century). Watanabe: 「般若心経成立序説－「摩訶般若波羅蜜大明呪経」と「大品般若経」との関係を中心として」 [*Journal of Buddhist Studies* (「仏教学」 No. 31, pp. 41-86) especially p. 80, subnote 1. According to Watanabe, the catalogue in question mentions that the *Hṛdaya Sūtra* that Hsüan-ts'ang received from a saintly monk during his journey to India was the text which Kumārajīva translated as the *Great Prajñā Wisdom Sūtra* (「大明呪経」).]

[15] Watanabe: *op. cit.*, p. 8

are not only very close in their use of terms and expressions, but also precisely identical in their meaning as "quintessential of the *Prajñāpāramitā* insight." Trained in Sanskrit and Buddhist Studies in India and experienced in the task of many translations, Hsüan-tzang had no reason to adopt Kumārajīva's use of words and expressions for his version. It is extremely interesting and enticing, therefore, to know how and why similar usage of words and expressions should take place in their respective versions of the *Heart Sūtra*, despite their different centuries, their different cultural orientations, and their different Sanskrit originals.

§3. THE LINKAGE OF THE *PRAJÑĀ HṚDAYA SŪTRA* AND KUAN-YIN BODHISATTVA

Whether it was the same Sanskrit original or two different manuscripts of it, upon which the two masters respectively relied for translation, is a matter of dispute, because copied manuscripts often reveal scribal error, addition, or omission as elements of unavoidable occurrence. In general, it is extremely difficult to determine which one of the two is more original and authentic than the other, unless the place and time are specified for each manuscript's origination. There is, however, a decisive piece of evidence for the fact that Kumārajīva and Hsüan-tzang relied on different Sanskrit manuscripts. In Kumārajīva's translation, the chief expositor of the *Heart Sūtra* is given as 'Kuan-shih-yin' (観世音) [or Kuan-yin (観音) in short], whereas in Hsüan-tzang's translation, it is given as 'Kuan-tzŭ-tsai' (観自在). 'Kuan-shih-yin' and Kuan-tzŭ-tsai' derived from different Sanskrit compounds, are respectively '*avalokita-svara*' and '*avalokiteśvara*' [i.e., *avalolita-īśvara*].

Around A.D. 288, Dharmarakṣa rendered in his translation of the *Lotus Sūtra* (「正法華経」) Kuang-shih-yin (光世音) as translation of *avalokitasvara*, meaning "one who illumines the voices of the world." The use of '光' (*kuang*) essentially connotes an identical meaning as that of Kumārajīva's use of '観' (*kuan*), namely, "spiritual illumination or introspection" '照' (*chao*). Thus, Kumārajīva too rendered 'Kuan-shih-yin Pu-sa' (観世音菩薩) into the Bodhisattva '*avalokitasvara,*' meaning "the Bodhisattva who surveys the [suffering] voices of the world." Kumārajīva applies this same rendering not only in his translation of the *Lotus Sūtra* (「妙法蓮華経」 or *Saddharmapuṇḍariīka-sūtra*), especially, the 25th Chapter "Kuan-shih-yin's Multifarious Manifestation" (「観世音

普門品」) in 406, but also in his voluminous translation of Nāgārjuna's *Grand Treatise on the Prajñā Wisdom and Means of Deliverance* (「大智度論」 or *Mahāprajñā-pāramitôpadeśa-śāstra*) during 402 through 405. It was Hsüan-tzang who made a new rendering in 649 as Kuan-tzŭ-tsai," meaning "the Bodhisattva who excels in [*prajñā*] illumination,"[16] and after his translation, the subsequent translators, such as Fa-yueh, 法月), Prajñā (智恵) and Li-yen (利言), Prajñācakra (智慧輪), Dharmasiddhi (法成), Amoghavajra (不空), Dānapāla (施護), all followed his rendering as 'Kuan-tzŭ-tsai Pu-sa,' except for Prajñācakra who compounded the two alternatives together as 'Kuan-shih-yin-tzŭ-tsai Pu-s.'

There has been a good number of studies as to which of the two Sanskrit terms, *avalokitasvara* or *avalokiteśvara*, was the true original designation of the Bodhisattva that embodies the Buddhist ideal of love and compassion. What has so far been accomplished in search of its answer is the theory that '*avalokitasvara*' (観世音 or 観音 in short) was an older usage, while '*avalokiteśvara*' (観自在) was a posterior one.[17] According to Lokesh Chandra, an Indian scholar who is known to be expert on the iconography of Kuan-yin, the term '*avalokitasvara*' may have been the original or an earlier name, whereas '*avalokiteśvara*' was a later name adopted under the circumstance of increasing Hindu cultic influence of deity Śīva as lord of the world (*lokeśvara*).

It is known from Hsüan-tzang's travel record[18] that the use of

---

[16] Hsüan-tzang asserts his translation of Kuan-tzŭ-tsai for Avalokiteśvara by saying: "Avalokiteśvara ought to be called in T'ang language as 'Kuan-tzŭ-tsai. Avalokita is kuan (観), īśvara is tzŭ-tsai (自在). His disciple (窺基、632-682). defended his master's rendering in his commentary on the *Mahāprajñāpāramitā-hṛdaya-sūtra* [「般若心経幽賛」巻上、Taishō. 33 (No. 1710)]: In the olden translation, it was Kuang--shih-yin (光世音) or Kuan-shih-yin (観世音) or Kuan-shih-tzŭ-tsai (観世自在), which are all wrong. 'Kuan' means illumining (照), namely, an insight that clarifies non-existence and existence (了空有) and 'tzŭ-tsai' means the proficiency of doing things at one's will (従任)."

[17] The *Lotus Sūtra* has the former name in the Nepalese manuscript, while the latter name appears in the manuscript of the *Pureland Sūtra*. Despite the fact that both scriptures were most likely composed during the first century B.C., since it is difficult to determine exactly to what period each of the manuscripts belonged, we cannot decide which of the two names was original from the extant Sanskrit manuscripts.

[18] Cf. *Ta-t'amg-hsi-yu-chi* (「大唐西域記」 12 fasc.), [Taisho (No. 2067)]. *The Buddhist Records of the Western World during the Great T'ang- Dynasty.* trans. by Samuel Beal, originally published 1884 London; Two volumes bound in one, Motilal Banarssidass, Delhi: 1981.

Avalokiteśvara was already prevalent in India in the second quarter of the seventh century (between 629-643).[19] In fact, when these two names were being used in confusion, 'Avalokita' alone began to be used in later medieval India as has been evidenced in the *Bodhicaryāvatāra* by Śāntideva (c. 650-750). It follows that Kumārajīva and Hsüan-tzang were in two different eras when Avalokitasvara and Avalokiteśvara respectively referred to one and the same personification of Buddhist love and compassion.

Accepting the history of the partial change from Avalokitasvara to Avalokiteśvara, we ought to notice that the *Prajñā Hṛdaya Sūtra* made the most significant moment for the history of Buddhist culture in China, because the *Sūtra* depicts the Bodhisattva Kuan-shih-yin or Kuan-tzù-tsai to be the chief exponent of the Prajñā doctrine. In all the texts of *Prajñāpāramitā* literature, there is none other than this single text in which Kuan-shih-yin appears to be the chief expositor of the doctrine. And this same Bodhisattva is depicted in the *Lotus Śūtra*'s 25th Chapter "Kuan-shih-yin's Multifarious Manifestation" (「觀音普門品」) as champion guardian and Buddhist savior.[20] He has inherited the so-called activist role to exercise his two-fold expediency, *Prajñā* (wisdom) and *Karuṇā* (compassion), to help humans escape from sufferings and endeavor his supernormal power for the sake of their salvation in lieu of Śākyamuni after his *Parinirvāṇa*. In the *Prajñā Heart Sūtra*, this activist role of Kuan-yin Bodhisattva was re-cast, for the first time, as an important part of the scriptural scenario of the *Prajñā* doctrine to become the chief exponent of the transcendent insight of *Śūnyatā* as well as the practice of this introspection.

His name also appears in the *Pureland Sūtras*[21] in which his

---

[19] Lokesh Chandra: Cf. Chap. 2 in *the Thousand Armed Avalokiteśvara*. Delhi: Indira Gandhi National Center for Arts, 1988, esp. p. 20. According to this author, when these two names were being used in confusion, 'Avalokita' alone began to be used in later medieval India like the case of the *Bodhicaryāvatāra* by Śāntideva (c. 650-750).

[20] The 25th Chap. of the *Lotus Sūtra* begins with the Buddha's reply to Akṣayamati Bodhisattva regarding the meaning of the name Avalokitasvara. The reply points primarily to love and compassion as Kuan-yin's epithet, since he is ever alert to the imploring of all sufferers and, should they wholeheartedly chant his name, beseeching him for deliverance, he will come to help them be free from their suffering. He is endowed with the transcendent faculty to immediately perceive all voices and, in no time, come to the rescue of all callers. I shall herewith simplify and enumerate all circumstances of suffering noted in the Sūtra.

[21] Amitābha Buddha. or 阿弥陀: According to Staël-Hostein's argument, the earliest occurrence of Chinese name *kuan-shih-yin* (觀世音) is equivalent to *'avalokita-īśvara'* in the larger *Sukhāvatī-vyūha-sūtra*. Cf. "Avalokita and

relationship to Amitābha Buddha (*a-mi-t'o-fo*) is depicted like that of Maitreya (the future Buddha)[22] to Śākyamuni. In the *Flower Garland Sūtra* too, Kuan-yin's name appears as one of the fifty-five teachers to whom the youthful saint Sudhana-śreṣṭhi-dāraka[23] paid his pilgrimage in Southern India to seek enlightenment. But it was the striking ingenuity on the part of the anonymous author of the *Hṛdaya Sūtra* that the great creative force of culture in East Asia was successfully released out of the linkage of the activist role of love and compassion and the transcendent insight of *prajñāpāramitā* introspection. It is almost beyond belief how and why this linkage of transcendent insight and activist compassion has not hitherto been the subject matter of enquiry as culminating Buddhist spirituality. I hold that the meaning of the Heart Sūtra ought to be re-evaluated from the point of view of this linkage of dual sources of Bodhisattva career.

§4. HSÜAN-TZANG'S AND KUMĀRAJĪVA'S *HEART SŪTRA* PARALLELED

The structure of the *Prajñā Heart Sūtra* has been well studied. It has a longer version consisting of twenty-five *Ślokas* as well as a shorter version consisting of fourteen *Ślokas*. There are two different ways of looking at the *Heart Sūtra*, but as my primary focus of interest, I advocate a remarkably new interpretation proposed by Edward Conze rather than the traditional interpretations. By traditional interpretation, I mean two general views, according to which the *Heart Sūtra* is regarded to have meant, on the one hand, an exoteric teaching, while, on the other hand, an esoteric teaching.[24] According to the former, as evident in the initial half of the text, it inculcates the Mahāyāna insight of *śūnyatā* (emptiness) and the practice of *Prajñāpāramitā* introspection in terms of an exoteric formulation. According to the latter, as the text ends in the latter

---

Apalokita," *Harvard Journal of Asiatic Studies*, vol 1 (1936), 350-362..] Cf. p. 351.

[22] Maitreya (Mi-lê, 弥勒): According to the *Hsien-yu-ching* [「賢愚経」 13 fasc, Taishlō. 4, (No. 202)] or Avadāna Collection called *Damamūka-nidāna-sūtra,* No. 57, Fasc. Po-p'o-li-p'in (「波婆離品」) comprises a story of Maitreya who was a disciple of Śākyamuni. Born as a son of a minister of the king of Vārāṇasī, he became a student of a Brāhmaṇa scholar, but one day having attended Śākyamuni's lecture at the Gṛdhrakūṭa in Rājagṛha, he became a disciple. Cf. *Ta-chi-tu-lun* (the 29th fasc.).

[23] Shan-ts'ai-t'ung-tzù (善財童子).

[24] Komine, Yahiko: "Re-examination of the *Prajñā-Hṛdaya-Sūtra*" (「般若心経再考」), *Mikkyō-gaku Kenkyū* (*Study on Tantric Buddhism*),

half with a prayer verse (*mantra*), it is regarded to promote an esoteric prayer formula as part of Buddhist Tantrism. Like Conze, however, I am inclined to interpret the original intent of the *Heart Sūtra* as re-statement of the Buddhist Truth in terms of dialectical negation of reality in reference to the five *Skandhas*, twelve *Āyatanas*, eighteen *Dhātus*, twelve-link of causation, and finally, four holy Truths. I fully agree with Prof. Conze's view that the *Heart Sūtra* meant to be the second turning of the Wheel of the *Buddha-dharma* in terms of Mahāyāna spiritual salvation in parallel with Śākyamuni's initial turning of the *Dharma*-wheel.

In his article of 1948 entitled "Text, Sources, and Bibliography of the *Prajñāpāramitā-hṛdaya*," Conze analyzed the structure of the *Heart Sūtra* into seven sections and probed their counterparts in the *25,000 Śloka Prajñāpāramitā-sūtra*, so-called *Ta-p'in-pan-jo* (「大品般若経」).[25] He asserted that all the words, phrases, and lines of the short text were extracted from the larger text. Accordingly, this *Heart Sūtra* is meant to be, as Conze says, "a restatement of the four holy Truths for beginners on the method of bearing this teaching in mind as well as on the spiritual advantage of following it."[26] I think that the traditional textual studies and interpretation of the *Heart Sūtra* has not hitherto sufficiently explored the line of Conze's interpretation. As a result, the historical perspective of the textual origin has mostly escaped from their traditional preoccupation.

In general, any authentic scripture ought to begin with an introductory statement in which it is required to make a brief reference to the five-fold background of a given *Sūtra*, namely, (1) the basis of reporting, (2) the time of the reported preaching, (3) the preacher or speaker, (4) the place of the preaching, (5) the assembled audience.[27] Both the translations by Kumārajīva as well as by Hsüan-tzang structurally do not include this introductory portion that comprises five references, but simply replace it by two *ślokas*.[28] The larger versions of the *Hṛdaya Sūtra*, upon which other

---

[25] *Ta-p'in-pan-jo-ching* (「大品般若経」 or 「摩訶般若波羅蜜経」), *Pañcaviṃśati-sāhasrikā-prajñāpāramitā-sūtra* (「二万五千頌」) translated by Kumārajīva, 402-412. Taishō. 8, (No, 223).

[26] Edward Conze: "Text, Sources, and Bibliography of the *Prajñāpāramitā-hṛdaya*," *Journal of Royal Asiatic Society*. 1948, p. 47.

[27] Cf. Komine, *op. cit.*, p. 123. (信成就, 時成就, 教主成就, 住所成就, 衆成就).

[28] Hsüan-tsang's Translation: 観自在菩薩行深般若波羅蜜 ; Kumārajīva's Translation: 観世音菩薩行深般若波羅蜜多時 ; Conze's Sanskrit Equivalents: *Āryāvalokiteśvaro bodhisattvo, gambhīrāṃ prajñā-pāramitā-caryām caramāṇi vyavalokayati sma'*

translations relied, generally comply with the full introductory norms, explaining what the contextual background of the *Sūtra* was.[29] Kumārajīva and Hsüan-tzang both omitted this introductory portion or their Sanskrit original itself omitted it.[30]

---

[29] Those post-Hsüan-tzang translations as referred to above all begin with "Thus have I heard" (如是我聞) and go on to state the circumstance. For instance, this is the introductory portion of Prajñācakra's translation [The *Hṛdaya Sū'tra* in Taishō 8, (No. 254), p. 850a]:

> Thus have I heard. At one time, the World-honored One stayed on the summit of Vulture's Peak together with a great assembly of Bhikṣus and multiple Bodhisattvas who are superior beings. Abiding in the state of *Samādhi*, then, the World-honored One extended his introspection widely and deeply, finding among the assembly a Bodhisattva, "Kuan-*shih-yin-tzŭ-tsai*" by name. [Note that this translator combined with Kuan (觀) both Svara (i.e., 世音) and Īśvara (自在) as 觀世音自在]. While the Bodhisattva is engaged in the practice of profound Prajñāpāramitā introspection (行甚深般若波羅蜜多行時), he illumined and intuited that the nature of Five Skandhas in themselves was entirely devoid of reality, i.e., empty nature (照見五蘊自性皆空). No sooner the Elder Śāriputra received the World-honored One's suggestion, than he joined his both hands respectfully together and spoke to the great being, Bodhisattva Kuan-shih-yin-tzŭ-tsai: "Oh,Your holiness, when one wishes to practice profound Prajñāpāramitā introspection, how should one go about it, sir? Thus requested, the Bodhisattva began to propound, . . ."
>
> *Evam mayāśrutam. ekasmin samaye Bhagavān Rājagṛhe viharati sma Gṛdhrakūṭa-parvate, mahatā bhikṣu-saṅghena sārdhaṃ mahatā ca bodhisattva-saṃghena. tena khalu punaḥ samayena Bhagavān gambhīrāvabhāsaṃ nāma dharmaparyāyaṃ bhāṣitvā samādhim samāpannaḥ. tena ca samayena Āryāvalokiteśvaro bodhisattvo mahāsattvo gambhīrāyāṃ prajñāpāramitāyāṃ caryāṃ caramāna evaṃ vyavalokayati sma: pañca skandhās tāṃśca svabhāva-śūnyān vyavalokayati. atha āyuṣmañcChāriputra buddha-anubhācena Āryāvalokiteśvaro bodhisattvo mahāsattvo āyuṣmantaṃ Śāriputram etad avocat: Yaḥ kaścit kulaputro vā kuladuhitā vā asyām gambhīrāyāṃ prajñāpāramitāyāṃ caryāṃ cartukāmas tena kathaṃ śikṣitavyaṃ? evam ukta-Āryāvalokiteśvaro bodhisattvo mahāsattvo āyuṣmantaṃ Śāriputram etad avocat. yaḥ kaścid ārya putra kulaputro vā kuladuhitā vā asyāṃ gambhīrāyāṃ prajñāpāramitāyāṃ caryāṃ cartukāmas tenaivaṃ vyavalokitavyam.*

In Kumārajīva's as well as Hsüan-tsang's *Heart Sūtra*, this introductory statement was simply dropped.

[30] Here, parallels are shown in diagram between Hsüan-tsang's translation and that of Kumārajīva along with the Sanskrit textual equivalents.

Hsüan-tzan's Tr.	Kumārajīva's Tr.	Conze's Sanskrit Equivalent
INTRODUCTION		
觀自在菩薩行	觀世音菩薩行	*Āryāvalokiteśvarobodhisattvo,*
深般若波羅蜜多	深般若波羅蜜時	*gambhīrāṃ prajñāpāramitā sma/ caryāṃ-caramāṇivyavalokayati*
照見五蘊皆空	照見五陰空	pañcaskandhās tāṃś ca svabhāva paśyati sma/

As indicated in the diagram of the sub-note, the Chinese passage '度一切苦厄' which is equally found in both of Kumārajīva's and Hsüan-tzang's translations, significantly has no Sanskrit counterpart. Except for the translation ascribed to Prajñācakra, the five other translations that appeared after Hsüan-tzang's translation surprisingly do not comprise the Chinese passage '度一切苦厄.' Prajñācakra translated a longer version of the *Heart Sūtra* and initially gives the aforementioned five references as an introduction. Then he introduces the magnanimous figure Bodhisattva Kuan-shih-yin-tzŭ-tsai (観世音自在菩薩摩訶) as engaged in the profound *Prajñāpāramitā* introspection, intuiting that the five Skandhas are nothing but all devoid of reality.[3132] It was at that moment that Śāriputra was suggested by the Buddha to enquire the Bodhisattva Kuan-shih-tsai-tzŭ-tsai regarding how to go about the practice of the introspection.[32] The Bodhisattva replied to Śāriputra, saying:

> When you are engaged in the profound *Prajñāpāramitā* introspection, you shall come to realize an illumination and see how and why the entirety of the five Skandhas is nothing but devoid of their own nature, and then you will be freed from all suffering and distress.[33]

Although the Sanskrit text does not comprise the statement '度一切苦厄' ("to be liberated from all suffering and distress"),[34] it is intriguing to know how and why Prajñācakra's larger text followed those of Hsüan-tzang and Kumārajīva. It is either that there were two different manuscripts, one of which comprises an equivalent passage for '度一切苦厄,' whereas another, not. According to Conze, the absence of the Sanskrit counterpart seems to have been the case as he conjectured that the both texts of Kumāarajīva and Hsüan-tzang may have had it. In his sub-note, Conze says: "There is no trace of this addition in any Sanskrit document, and it may have been made in Central Asia, from where Kumārajīva's text is said to be derived."[35] The remaining five translations all consistently

---

[度一切苦厄] [度一切苦厄] [No Sanskrit equivalent for 度一切苦厄]

31 「時衆中有一菩薩」

32 「即時具寿舎利子、承仏威神、合掌恭敬、白観世音菩薩摩訶薩言、聖者、若有欲学甚深般若波羅蜜多行、云何修行。」Taishō 8 (No. 254), p. 850 a.

33 「行深般若波羅蜜行時、応照見五蘊自性皆空、離諸苦厄。」*Ibid.*

34 「告具寿舎利子言. . .行甚深般若波羅蜜多行時、応照見五自性皆空、離諸苦厄、」*Ibid.*

35 Conze: *op. cit.*, p. 42, note 6.

lack the passage in question, and directly proceed to the dialectical negation of each of the five Skandhas.[36]

§5. VIDYĀ AND MANTRA IN HSÜAN-TZANG'S AND KUMĀRAJĪVA'S *HEART SŪTRA*

The latter half of the text begins with the merit of the foregoing dialectical negation.[37] Accomplishing negation of the reality of the

---

[36] There are a number of excellent research works to establish a synopsis between the *Hṛdaya Sūtra* and *Ta-p'in-pan-jo-ching* (the *25,000 Śloka Sūtra*) as well as between the *Hṛdaya Sūtra* and the *100,000 Śloka Prajñāpāramitā Sūtra*. The following is the synopsis chart referring to these three textual sources. (Cf. Watanabe: *op. cit.*, p. 45 ff):

Hsüan-tz'an Tr.	Kumārajīva's Tr.	Conze's Sanskrit Equivalents
	ŚŪNYATĀ OF FIVE SKANDHAS	
	舎利弗、色空故無悩壊相	
	受空故無受想、想空故無知相	
	行空故無作相、識空故無覚相、	
(*Śūnyatā* of all)	何以故 (*Śūnyatā* of all)	*iha Śāriputra rūpaṃ śūnyat rūpaṃ*
舎利子、色不異空、	舎利弗、非色異空、	*rūpān na śūnyatāiva pthag rūpaṃ yad*
空不異色、色即是空、	非空異色、色即是空、	*rūpaṃ sā śūnyatā yā śūnyatāyā saṃ-*
空即是色、	空即是色	*skāra-vijñānam/evam eva vedan-saṃ-*
受想行識亦復如是	受想行識亦如是。	*jñā-saṃskāra-vijñānam/vijñānam/*
舎利子、是諸法空相	舎利弗、是諸法空相	*iha śāriputra, saarva-dharmāḥ śūnyatā-*
不生不滅、不垢不浄	不生不滅、不垢不浄	*lakṣaṇā aniruddhā amalā* ***anut-***
不増不減、	不増不減、	*pannā aniruddhā amalā* ***avimalā***
		anūnā apari-pūrāḥ/
	是空法、非過去非未来非現在。	
(12 ĀYATANA)		
是故空中、無色	是故空中、無色	*tasmāc chāriputra śūnyatāyāṃ narūpa*
無受想行識,	無受想行識、	*na vedanā na saṃjñā na saṃskārāḥ na*
無眼耳鼻舌身意	無眼耳鼻舌身意	*vijñānam, na cakṣuḥ-śrotra-ghrāṇa-*
無色声香味触法	無色声香味触法	*ihvā-kā\ya-manāṃsi na rūpa-śabda-*
		gandha-rasa-spraṣṭavya-dharmāḥ
(18 DHĀTU)		
無眼界、乃至無意識界	無眼界、乃至無意識界	*na cakśur-dhātur yāvan na mano-*
		vijñāna-dhātuḥ
(12 CAUSAL CHAINS)		
無無明、亦無無明尽、	無無明、亦無無明尽、	*na-avidyā na-avidyā-kṣayo yāvan*
乃至無老死、亦無老死尽、	乃至無老死、亦無老死尽、	*na jarāmarṇaṃ na jarāmaraṇakṣayo*
(4 HOLY TRUTHS)		
無苦集滅道,	無苦集滅道,	*na duḥkha-samudaya-morodha-mārgā*
無智亦無得,	無智亦無得	*na jñānaṃ na prāptir na[aprāptiḥ/*

[37] Hsüan-tz'an Tr. Kumārajīva's Tr. Conze's Sanskrit Equivalents

four holy Truths[38] and that of acquisition as well as non-acquisition,[39] the text asserts that "On account of this unreality of an acquisition,[40] the Bodhisattva relies on the practice of *Prajñāpāramitā* introspection, whereby he has his mind liberated from obstacles,"[41] and "having no obstacle, he has no fear and is free from all up-side-down delusion, suffering and distress. Ultimately he realizes *Nirvāṇa*."[42] The restating of the Mahāyāna truth of *Śūnyatā* as supreme insight is indisputably expressed by the immediately following passage that ends with a prayer (*mantra*) verse:

> On account of the foregoing merits, the Buddhas of three different periods have invariably relied or will rely on the *Prajñāpāramitā* introspection[43] and thereby accomplished or will accomplish the supreme enlightenment (*anuttara-samyak-saṃbodhi*).[44] Therefore, one should know that the *Prajñā Hṛdaya Sūtra* is the great prayer verse,[45] the great wisdom prayer verse,[46] the highest

---

THE MERIT OF PRAJÑĀPĀRAMITĀ TEXT

以無所得故、菩提薩埵、	以無所得故、菩薩、	*tasmāc chāriputra aprāptitvād bodhi*
心無罣礙、	心無罣礙、	*viharaty acittāvarvaraṇaḥ,*
無罣礙故、無有恐怖、	無罣礙故、無有恐怖、	*cittāvarṇa-nāstitvād*
遠離一切転倒夢想、	離一切転倒苦悩、	atrasto viparyāsa-atikrānto,
究竟涅槃、	究竟涅槃、	*niṣṭhā-nirvāṇaḥ; tryadhva-*
三世諸仏、	三世諸仏、	*vyavasthitāḥ sarva-budddhā*
依依般若波羅蜜多故、	依依般若波羅蜜故、	*prajñāpāramitām āśritya*
得阿耨多羅三藐	得阿耨多羅三藐	*anuttarāṃ samyaksambodhim*
三菩提、	三菩提、	*abhisambuddhāḥ*
故知依般若波羅蜜多、	故知依般若波羅蜜、	*tasmāj jñātavyaṃ prajñāpāramitā*
是大神呪、是大明呪、	是大明呪、	*mahāmantro mahāvcidyāmantro*
是無上呪、是無等等呪、	是無上呪、是無等等明呪	*'nuttara-mantro 'samasa-ma-mantraḥ*
能除一切苦、	能除一切苦、	*sarva-duḥkha-praśamanaḥ*
真実不虚故、	真実不虚故、	*satyam amithyatvāt.*
説般若波羅蜜多呪、	説般若波羅蜜呪、	*prajñāpāramitāyām*
即説呪曰、	即説呪曰、	*ukto mantraḥ.*
揭帝揭帝　般羅揭帝	竭帝竭帝　波羅竭帝	*tadyathā oṃ gate gate pāragate*
般羅僧揭帝、菩提僧莎呵。	波羅僧竭帝、菩提僧莎呵。	*pārasaṃgate bodhi svāhā.*

38「無苦集滅道」

39「無智亦無得」

40「以無所得故」

41「依般若波羅蜜多故心無 礙.」

42「無有恐怖、離一切転倒苦悩、究竟涅槃.」

43「三世諸仏依般若波羅蜜多故.」

44「得阿耨多羅三藐三菩提」

45 *mahāmantra*（大神呪）

46 *mahā-vidyā-mantra*（是大明呪）,

prayer verse,[47] the prayer verse that has no equal,[48] and also that this *Hṛdaya Sūtra* is the ultimate truth, with no default whatsoever, removing all suffering."[49] Thus is the word of prayer verse *(mantra)* in praise of the *Hṛdaya Sūtra*:

Whoever has reached, whoever has reached, whoever has reached the yonder shore, whoever has thoroughly reached the yonder shore, he will meet auspicious Enlightenment (*gate gate parāgate parāsaṃgate, bodhisvāhā*).[50]

According to Watanabe's research analysis,[51] the early translations of the *Prajñāpāramitā* texts, such as, *Tao-hsing-pan-jo*[52] translated by Chih-lu-chia-chen[53] as well as *Hsiao-p'in-pan-jo*[54] which was the same *Sūtra* translated by Kumārajīva, agree in rendering "three wisdom verses" as *mahā-vidyā*, *anuttara-vidyā*, and *asamasama-vidyā* respectively as *ta-ming-s-chou* (大明呪), *wu-shang-ming-chou* (無上明呪), and *wu-teng-teng-ming-chou* (無等等明呪). Hence, these renderings are regarded to have meant to be in reference to *Vidyā (明)* and not to *Mantra (呪)*. The same can be said regarding the three wisdom verses that appear in the *Ta-p'in-pan-jo-ching*[55] translated by Kumārajīva on the *25,000 Śloka Prajñāpāramitā-sūtra*.. On the other hand, we find the use of term *mantra* in the *Great Prajñāpāramitā Sūtra* of 600 fascicles translated by Hsüan-tzang, especially in the portion that refers to the Second Lecture Assembly (第二会), which exactly corresponds to the contents of the *very text just mentioned (the 25000 Śloka Prajñāpāramitā).* Hsüan-tzang translated the phrases of *mahā-mantra,* and *anuttara-mantra* and

---

[47] *anuttara-mantra* (是無上呪)

[48] *asamasama-mantra* (是無等等呪)

[49] *sarva-duḥkha-praśamanaḥ satyam amithyātvāt* (能除一切苦真実不虚)

[50] That this prayer verse (*mantra*) is not confined to the *Hṛdaya Sūtra* has been voiced by a number of scholars. The verse is regarded to have been unique to any text of the Prajñāpāramitā as its praise or to the practice of Prajñāpāramitā introspection as means of concentration. Komine: *loc. cit.*, pp. 175-176.*loc. cit.*, p. 77; Watanabe: *loc. cit.*, pp. 73-74

[51] Watanabe: *op cit.*, pp. 69-71. See especially the chart of the synopses.

[52] *The 8000 Śloka Prajñāpāramitā-sūtra* (「道行般若経」)

[53] 支婁迦讖

[54] 「小品般若」

[55] 「大品般若」

asamasama-mantra respectively *as ta-shen-chou* (大神呪), *wu-shang-chou* (無上呪), *and wu-teng-teng-chou* (無等等呪). And these renderings are exactly the same as he translated the *Hṛdaya Sūtra*. The difference between Kumārajīva and Hsüan-tzang once again distinguishes their respective time difference between the olden and new eras of scriptural translations.

Originally, the use of *mantra* belonged to the Vedic rituals, and hence, in the early *Prajñāpāramitā Sūtras*, the anonymous scriptural authors hesitated to use the term that reflects Brahmanical tradition. Watanabe says that the *8,000 Śloka Prajñāpāramitā-sūtra* held no interest in this term and used only either as asserting that the state of concentration acquired through *Prajñāpāramitā* introspection would not be disturbed by any devilish will or a power of any of such spells, nor would a Bodhisattva who has reached the state of non-regression (*avaivartika-bodhisattva*) ever be attracted to any of dubious medicines or incantations. The authors of the earlier *Prajñā Sūtras* regarded *mantra* as merely an item of secular learnings along with poetry (*kāvya*), knowledge (*vidyā*), science (*śāstra*), etc. and often appositively compounding it with *vidyā* as *vidyā-mantra*.[56] On the other hand, when Hsüan-tzang visited India, he met a different circumstance, such that the anonymous authors of the later *Prajñāpāramitā Sūtras* were necessitated to emphasize the power of *Prajñāpāramitā* introspection over against the Hindu usage of magical charms (*mantra*) by compounding the Buddhist term *vidyā* with the Tantric term *mantra*, so that the primary Buddhist wisdom *Vidyā* as power of breaking the primeval force of ignorance (*avidyā*) was well emphasized. Hsüan-tzang's translation of the *Hṛdaya Sūtra* precisely reflects this historical background and a different era from that of Kumārajīva.

Now, I am obliged to bring in Prof. Conze's assertion that the *Heart Sūtra* is not Tantric. In order to defend his point of view, Conze refers to the early Buddhist usage in Pāli Suttas. He points to the fact that we find a similar usage in the *Niddessa*[57] and Pāli commentaries, wherein *paññā* (*prajñā* or 'insight' in Sanskrit) is called *mantra*. Further, he points to one of the earliest *Saṃyutta Nikāya* in Pāli, that "In the First Turning of the Wheel of the Law"

---

[56] *Ibid.*, p. 72.

[57] Of the two extant commentaries of the *Sutta-Nipāta*, the *Niddesa* is the earlier one, ascribed to Sāriputta, a direct disciple of Śākyamuni, and the *Paramatthajotikā* is the later one ascribed to Buddhaghoṣa of the 5th century. Unlike the latter, the *Nidessa* is confined to some parts of the *Sutta Nipāta*.

(*Dhamma-cakka-ppavattana-vaggo*), the knowledge of four holy Truths is equated to *vijjā* (*vidyā* or knowledge or wisdom in Sanskrit).[58] In both of these texts, the term *mantā* (*mantra* in Sanskrit) or *vijjā* (*vidyā* in Sanskrit) is not intended to mean "a secret, mysterious lore of magical potency which can be compressed into a magical formula, a spell." Rather, the term is intended to mean "the knowledge of the four holy Truths which is the fundamental insight (*vijjā*) of the Buddha." In parallel to this first turning of the *Dharma* wheel (*dharma-cakra-pravartana-sūtra*), the main subject of which is the four holy Truths,[59] Conze points out that the Mahāyāna theorists regarded the *Heart Sūtra* as "the second turning of the wheel of the law."[60] This Mahāyāna Buddhist thought enormously appealed to the minds of Chinese and East Asian Buddhists.

§6. LINKAGE OF PRAJÑĀPĀRAMITĀ AND KUAN-YIN BODHISATTVA ATTESTED IN THE FEMININE REPRESENTATION

In China, the cultic worship of Kuan-yin Bodhisattva is believed to have begun shortly after Dharmarakṣa's translation of the *Lotus Sūtra* in 286, but most certainly after the more lucid translation of the same text by Kumārajīva in 406 and quickly spread over the divided continent in the north as well as in the south from the fifth century onward.[61] There is no doubt with the history of the Sui Dynastic unification of the north and south that Buddhist thoughts and their active participation in society contributed toward its realization. I believe that the dominant cultural force of that early Medieval China was motivated by two major sources of spirituality, one being the *Prajñāpāramitā* insight and another being Kuan-yin's activist love and compassion. It was the strike of ingenuity that these two factors were symbolically brought into fusion by Kumārajīva's

---

58 Conze: *Ibid.*, p. 46. *Dhamma-cakka-ppavattana-vaggo*: *The Initial Turning of the Wheel of Dharma* (「初転法輪経」).

59 *Ibid.*, p. 48.

60 *Ibid.*, 47-48.

61 The bibliographical records suggest that there were six translations of the same text, but only three translations ascribed to Dharmarakṣa (「正法華経」286), Kumārajīva (「妙法蓮華経」406), and Jñānagupta and Dharmagupta (「添品法蓮華経」601) are now extant. Nāgārjuna quotes this Sūtra, more often than any other scriptures, in his commentary *Upadeśaśāstra* (「大智度論」) of *Mahāprajñāpāramitāsūtra* [「大品般若経」(translated by Kumārajīva, A.D. 402-412)].

Hṛdaya Sūtra. Kuan-yin as Avalokitasvara in India was a male figure and remained to be so throughout the millennia wherever the image was transmitted. In China, however, despite some of the Indian forms of Avalokiteśvara availed to Chinese Buddhist worship,[62] they developed their own image as an effeminated figure during the T'ang dynasty in accordance with their own cultural and aesthetic taste. This feminine image, or sexually neutral figure, precisely ascertains the fact that the essential nature of the Chinese Kuan-yin was and has been the spirit of *Prajñāpāramitā* personified with the epithet of activist love and compassion.[63]

Lokesh Chandra brilliantly theorized that the Indian Avalokitasvara was a metamorphosis of Brahmā, Lord of the Earth, who was known also as the Hindu deity Lokeśvara or Lokanātha (the lord or the savior of the world).[64] I am obliged to call the reader's attention to an important distinction between the Indian and Chinese Buddhist cults, which were culturally and spiritually different. Lokesh Chandra provides a very persuasive analysis of the origin of the cult of Avalokiteśvara and its iconographic history. But he seems to have missed in recognizing the fact that the Indian Buddhist cult of Avalokiteśvara and the East Asian cult of Kuan-yin are not monolithic in spirituality. He is brilliant in proving Avalokitesvara as a metamorphosis of Brahmā, and on account of Brahmā's potency, he theorized the phenomenon of Avalokiteśvara's multifarious manifestation in Indian iconography. He invoked in part the potency pertaining to the substratum of the metamorphosis, namely, Brahmā, and in part the philosophy of Buddhist assimilation such that the

---

[62] The Hindu deity Śiva was assimilated to Buddhism and gave rise to the name Avalokiteśvara (*avalokita-īśvara*, the lord Avalokita), thereby allowing the emergence of the thousand-armed Bodhisattvas. Lokesh Chandra asserts that "this Avalokiteśvara sometimes appears as a Buddha and at other times as the Hindu deity Īśvara or Maheśvara (Śiva), without clear reason." So came to being several types of Kuan-yin images that were linked to Hindu iconography, like those endowed with one thousand arms, thousand eyes, four faces, eleven faces, a horsehead, a fearless lion head, a blue neck, and so on.

[63] As Kuan-yin moved east, further new variations arose, including the white-robed Kuan-yin, Kuan-yin holding a willow leaf, Kuan-yin with a fishing basket, and the Kuan-yin of easy child-bearing. This last figure, holding a baby in her arm, was sometimes called "Maria Kannon" in Medieval Japan.

[64] Lokesh Chandra: Cf. Chap. 2 in *the Thousand Armed Avalokiteśvara*. Delhi: Indira Gandhi National Center for Arts, 1988. Esp. p. 20. According to this author, when these two names were being used in confusion, 'Avalokita' alone began to be used in later medieval India like the case of the *Bodhicaryāvatāra* by Śāntideva (c. 650-750).

transcendent noumenon descends into the temporary domain as phenomenal manifestation.[65] Here, however, I must pose the following question: Is Brahmā's potency, which was the essential core of Avalokiteśvara, identical in spiritual basis to that which Buddhist thinkers ascribed to Kuan-yin in China?

In reference to the sections of *mantra*, *dhāraṇī*, or hymns, in both the *Lotus Sūtra* and the *Pureland Sūtra*, Lokesh Chandra regards Avalokitasvara as the "master of logos" (*mantra-draṣṭā*) (in parallel to Brahmā in the Brahmanical system), the Seer (*avalokitṛ*) of the Sound (*svara*), who assimilated Hindu deities (*lokeśvara*) by pronouncement of each sacred hymn (*hṛdaya* or *mantra*) unique to each deity[66] As I understand Chap. 25 of the *Lotus Sūtra*, Avalokitasvara's sole concern is to rescue all humans who are in trouble and suffering. Avalokitasvara's virtue of love and compassion is not a self-serving manifestation or self-serving emanation of some transcendent agent or principle. As a Bodhisattva, his virtue must be balanced with the insight of *Śūnyatā*, without which he loses his status and *raison-détre* as a Buddhist personification of love and compassion. The Kuan-yin cult in China was rooted in the insight of *Śūnyatā* and the belief in the original enlightenment proclaimed in the *Lotus Sūtra*, the dual source of the vow of the Bodhisattva career.

There are a few interpretations of how and why the transformation from the male to the female Kuan-yin occurred in China. According to one, it was a result of the cultural melting pot in northwest China during the centuries of the T'ang dynasty (618-907), where a host of different religions rubbed shoulders. The landscape included Buddhism and Taoism, alongside shamanism and Bon, the indigenous religion of Tibet, and Christianity and Manichaeism, alongside Islam and Zoroastrianism.[67] Palmer and Ramsay call particular attention to the figure of Madonna, the one who holds a child in her arm. They think that this representation was itself originally taken from Egyptian statues of the goddess Isis and her divine child Horus. They argue that it is possible to interpret the

---

[65] 「本地垂跡」 Here, Lokesh Chandra borrows Alicia Matsunaga's theory from her *Buddhist Philosophy of Assimilation of the Honji-Suijaku Theory (The Historical Development)*: Tokyo: Sphia University, C.E. Tuttle, 1969. Chandra: *op. cit.*, p. 42. Cf.

[66] Chandra: *Ibid.*, p.16.

[67] Martin Palmer and Jay Ramsay with Man-ho Kwok: *Kuan Yin: Myths of the Chinese Goddess of Compassion*. London: Thorsons, and Imprint of Harper-Collins Publishers, 1995; p. 19.

transformation of Kuan-yin from male to female in a manner consistent with the way in which Virgin Mary became the focus of cultic worship in Christianity. Since Taoist concepts of female deities existed in China before the time of Kuan-yin, the case in question may show that the divine and feminine, once established in a culture, necessarily re-emerge and take on new forms in response to elements of cultural suppression.[68] Blofeld, however, seems to disagree by asserting that the main source of influence came from the female Bodhisattva Tālā of Tibet. Blofeld may have considered the religious and cultural affinity too remote in the hypothesis of an Isis-to-Madonna-to-female-Kuan-yin evolution.69 There is yet a third view on this matter, as proposed by Elena Schmidt in her article in *the Art of Asia,* that the main source of influence may have been the combined forms of the Iranian water goddess Anahita and the Greek fertility goddess Artemis.[70]

However the course of evolution might be, my point of view is that the sudden appearance of a female Kuan-yin during the T'ang dynasty in China came from within the *Prajñāpāramitā* tradition in which the spirit of the *Prajñā Sūtras* was personified as the mother of Buddhas (仏母) and worshipped by late Mahāyāna Buddhists in India as well as in Tibet.[71]

§7. THE PRINCIPLE OF RECONCILIATION EMBODIED IN THE *HṚDAYA SŪTRA*

In my recent visit to China and travelling over the continent, I

[68] Palmer and Ramsay: *op cit.*, p. 21. The authors suggest that among other reasons, popular Buddhism needed a female image to compete with the Taoists and their successful goddesses, such as Queen Mother of the West.

[69] *Ibid.*, p. 40.

[70] Elena Schmidt: "The Little Known Binglingsi, Buddhist Caves," *The Art of Asia,* Vol 27, No. 4, July-August 1997; pp. 132-137.

[71] In China, calling the *Prajñāpāramitā Sūtras* as "Mother of Buddhas" (仏母) began to be seen during the later half of the first millennium in association with Tantric texts. E.g., 「仏母大金曜孔雀明王経」 3 fasc. tr. by Amoghavajra (705-774), the text concerned with Dhāraṇīs; 「仏母出生三法蔵般若波羅蜜多経」 equivalent to the 4th lecture assembly of Hsüan-tzang's 「大般若経」 of 600 fascicles, and parallel with the extant *8000 Śloka Prajñā Sūtra* [「道行般若経」 10 fasc. tr. by Chih-lü-chia-chen, Late Han; 「大明度経」 6 fasc. by Chih-chien in Wu; 「摩訶般若鈔経」 5 fasc.; 「小品般若波羅密経」 25 fasc, by Kumārajīva; 「仏母小字般若経」 1 fasc. 1000; 「仏母般若波羅密多円集要義釈論」 (*Ārya-prajñāpāramitā-saṃgraha-kārikā-vivaraṇa*, 4 fasc.) tr. by Dānapāla, 980, and so forth.

came to witness an age-old tradtion of Chinese art of painting and calligraphy by encountering on several occasions the similar motif of Kuan-yin Bodhisattva and calligraphy of the *Hṛdaya Sūtra* combined together. Some of them are obviously intended to be purchased by potential customers from abroad, but more often times, those displayed works of art are for the interest of local customers. In March 1999, on the way back from attending the 2nd International Conference for Hsüan-tzang Studies held in the city of Tong-chuan, I visited a local museum of a Medieval Agricultural Village set up in the city of Wang-hsian (万県市) in the province of Ssŭ-chuan (四川省). What I came to encounter was a minor landlord family house and the scroll of the Kuan-yin's painting with a calligraphy of the *Hṛdaya Sūtra* hung on the wall of the drawing room side by side with another scroll that depicted a figure of Confucius. I came to realize that a profound cultural force that has survived for ages, once again reclaiming itself even under the Western Communist ideology and system of society adopted by the present regime.

As is known among historians, during the period of the 6th century BC, the central power of the Chou dynasty was steadily declining and the feudal state was rapidly disintegrating. In order to deal with the ills of the time, Confucius championed the Chou aristocracy and culture to regulate their own conduct based on a body of positive rules of propriety, whereas, in its polar opposite camp, Mo-tzu and his followers neither shared the culture of Chou as understood by the Confucians, nor desired to complicate their lives with elaborate etiquette and a code of honor. The guiding principle of the Mohists was always practical utility combined with pragmatic concern. The Mohists felt a deep objection not only to the class division between the aristocrats and the masses, but also to the aristocratic moral code. In contrast to the gradation of love, decreasing according to the remoteness of the relationship, the Mohists introduced the idea of a universal concern or love, loving others just as one's self.

I have been troubled with the general feature of Chinese history, because from the time of Ch'in and Han dynasty, the Confucian ideology has been adopted, by dynasty after dynasty, as singular ideology of the ruling government. Suppose, the Communist revolution that took place half a century ago accomplished a government ruled by the masses for the first time in Chinese history. However, this ideology is not of the Chinese origin. In opposition to the Rationalist theory of innate ideas, the philosophy of modern materialism was brought forth by Lamettrice (109-1751) and Condillac (1715-1780) in France, initially from the problem of mind-body relationship. They theorized that the content of mental activities should come solely from sense-perceptions. From repeated sensations, grow successively attention, recollection, distinction, comparison, judgement, inference, imagination, and expectation of the future, and finally with the help of linguistic symbols, abstraction and the grasping of general principles.[72]

The movement carried out by these, so-called Ideologists, culminated in the *System de la Nature,* a purely dogmatic metaphysics and a heavy armed attack upon all belief in the immaterial world, attributed to Mirabeau's (Pseudonym, 1770).[73] A century later, in opposition to the Hegelian Idealism, Fuerbach inverted the Hegelian system and brought forth a Nominalistic Materialism and theorized that the actual reality is the individual known to the senses, while everything universal, everything mental or spiritual, is but an illusion of the individual. He held that Mind or spirit is "Nature in its otherness," making a purely anthropological explanation of religion, namely that Man regards his own generic nature – what he wishes to be himself – as God.[74] Marx and Engels applied the inverted product of the Hegelian dialectic to their theorization of the socialism's materialistic philosophy of history in terms of economic force as primary cause.

Having said this, I am obliged to quickly add, saying that the Western ideology that applied in Russia has failed to accomplish whatever was originally intended. On the other hand, the transplanted Communist ideology adopted by the contemporary Chinese seems to have been merely a metamorphsis of the Chinese mind and culture. When Hsüan-tzang travelled to India, esoteric Buddhism was at its zenith, but signs of the impending decline of Buddhism were already quite visible. During the few centuries before and after Hsüan-tzang's visit, Hindu iconography and cult movements gradually reclaimed their deities and institutions. If Lokesh Chandra is right in saying that Avalokiteśvara in India was merely a metamorphosis of Brahmā, reverting from Buddhist to Hindu cultic institutions would be a matter of simple switching. In China, on the other hand, esoteric Buddhism was just being introduced during the

72 Cf. Windelband, op.cit., p. 456ff.

73 *Ibid.*, p. 481ff.

74 *Ibid.*, 641, 655.

350.[81] Surely, it was Hsüan-tzang's translation that most effiectively popularized the *Heart Sūtra* based on the great T'ang dynastic patronage, but he was not the initiator of the linkage of Kuan-yin and *Heart Sūtra*, because the linkage was *de facto fait accompli* prior to his translation. It is well known that Chih-i of the T'ien-t'ai school (538-597) wrote the *Profound Meaning of Lotsu Sūtra*[82] in 593 and subsequently *the Profound Meaning of Kuan-yin* and its commentary,[83] as well as the *Short Commentary on the Chapter of Samanta-mukha*[84] These are believed to have contributed to the popularization of Kuan-yin cult movement in the later half of the first millennium.[85] It was the combined cultural force that, I believe, Hsüan-tzansg's *Hṛdaya Sūtra* further successfully released by popularization of the *Heart Sūtra* through early period of the T'ang dynasty and contributed to the greatness of that dynastic rule of the entire continent.

The Buddhist principle of reconciliation is most concisely expressed in the following passage excerpted from the second chapter of the *Ta-p'in-pan-jo-ching* (「大品般若経」):

> Śāriputra spoke to the Buddha: "How should a Bodhisattva, great being, be engaged in the practice of *Prajñāpāramitā*, sir?" The Buddha instructed Śāriputra as follows: "When a Bodhisattva, great being, concentrates in the practice of *Prajñāpāramitā*, he sees no Bodhisattva nor the word of "bodhisattva," nor *Prajñāpāramitā*, nor does he see that he is engaged in the practice of *Prajñāpāramitā*, nor that he is not engaged in the practice of *Prajñāpāramitā*. Why? It is because neither a Bodhisattva nor the word of "bodhisattva has an essential nature of its own. In this insight of *Śūnyatā*, there is neither the *Rūpa-skandha*, nor is there any other *Skandha* like *vedanā*,

---

[81] Cf. E. Cnze: The *Prajñāpāramitā Literature*, The Reiyukai, 1978, p. 13. Watanabe seems to have sided with Conze's hypothesis of the textual origin, although he is critical toward Conze's flaw of substantiation. Watanabe: *loc. cit.*, p. 80, and Note 44 in p. 86.

[82] *Kuan-shih-yin-hsüan-i* (「観音玄義」 2 fasc), Taisho. 34 (No. 1726)

[83] *Kuan-yin-i-shu* (「観音義疏」 2 fasc.), Taishō. 34 (No. 1728).

[84] *P'u-mên-p'in-su*, 「普門品疏」 Taishō. 34, No. 1728).

[85] Chih-i (538-597) systematized the T'ien-t'ai Classification of Buddhist Dcotrines known as "Fivefold Periods and Eight Teachings" (「天台五時八教教判」) on the basis of the *Lotus Sūtra* and *Nirvāṇa Sūtra* (*Ni-p'an-ching*, 「涅槃経」).

seventh century. Its influence was constrained in part by the exoteric Buddhism that had preceded it and established the powerful traditions of the T'ien-t'ai (天台), Hua-yen (華嚴), San-lun (三論), and Wei-shih (唯識、*vijñāna-mātra*) systems of thought. Esoteric Buddhism was further constrained by the Chinese cultural environment which was radically different and alien from that of India. What was crucial to the Kuan-yin cult in China was the insight of *śūnyatā* embodied in the *Prajñāpāramitā-sūtra*, not a Hindu spiritual basis of Brahmā, that has always linked to the Kuan-yin personification of love and compassion.

If the adopted ideology and system of government is a metamorphosis of the Chinese mind and culture, in order to realize people's democratic self rule in the true sense of the term, should it resort to the education of the Western materialist doctrines that are already obsolete? Or should it go back to the age-old Confucian authoritarian principle? There is a greater chance today for Chinese people to seriously investigate into the Moist ideas and principles as an additional study to the contemporary system of education on modern science and technology. In Chinese history, the justice of the people who are governed seems to have often been neglected by making the priority of the prerogative of the governing. Today, no nation can remain independent from international communities, nor can it claim its independent action in violation of human justice, especially, the justice of the governed. The principle of reconciliation is hard to come by. It is my belief that the insight of the *Prajñāpāramitā Sūtras* combined with the activist love and compassion personified in Kuan-yin is one that offers a principle of reconciliation.

§8. CONCLUSION

From the time when Kumārajīva was captured upon the destruction of his patron ruler of Kuchah by a Chinese general Lü-kung (呂光) in 383, he was forced to spend more than a decade of his life non-productively as an exile along with his captor. Of course, he was able to master Chinese linguistics during that time. When he was invited to Chang-an by Yao-hsing (姚興) of Ch'in (秦) in 401, he was ready to carry out his work of translation under Yao-hsing's patronage. He started with the *Twenty-five Thousand Śloka Prajñāpāramitā-sūtra* based on a Uighur text (胡本) not only by editorially examining a previous Chinese translation of the same text, but also newly consulting Nāgārjuna's voluminous commentary

Mahāprajñā-pāramitôpadeśa-śāstra. Thus, when he completed the *Ta-p'in-pan-jo-ching*, he also simultaneously brought forth the *Ta-chih-tu-lun* (「大智度論」) as his translation by the year 404.[75] Importantly, his next step was to translate the *Saddharmapuṇḍarīka-sūtra*, known as *Lotus Sūtra*, and completed it in the year of 406. This year, the eighth of Hung-shih Era (弘始八年), was also marked by the completion of the *Vimalakīrti-nirdeśa-śāstra.*[76] Kumārajīva's productivity seems to have been in full throttle in the year 408 (弘始十年) as he completed the *Eight Thousand Śloka Prajñāpāramitā-sūtra* known as *Hsiao-p'in-pan-jo-ching*,[77] and in the following year, both of the *Madhyamaka-kārikā-śāstra*, and *Dvādaśa-mukha-śāstra*[78] ascribed to Nāgārjuna. Whoever was motivated to link the ideal of Kuan-yin Bodhisattva as depicted in the *Lotus Sūtra* with the *Prajñā Heart Sūtra* in terms of "the second turning of the Wheel of the Law" ought to be someone who thoroughly understood human sufferings and the contents of the *Ta-chih-tu-lun*, because in this commentary Nāgārjuna quotes the *Lotus Sūtra* by far more frequently than any other *Sūtras* and elucidates in detail the Buddhist ideal of love and compassion as the primary epithet of Kuan-yin Bodhisattva.

As to the origin of the *Hṛdaya Sūtra*, two alternative hypotheses ought to be formulated. One of the two alternatives is that a Sanskrit original was composed in India, somewhere from AD 150 through 250 after Nāgārjuna composed the *Ta-chih-tu-lun*, if *Mahāprajñāpāramitā Dhāraṇī(?)* ascribed to Chih-chen's translation[79] in 288 was based on that original. The other alternative is that if the original text of which the Sanskrit manuscript discovered in Nepal was a copy, it may have been a Sanskritization of a Chinese text retransmitted to that subcontinent.[80] In this case, Conze's theory may hold in that the text may have been composed around

---

[75] The 6th year of Kuang-chi Era (弘始六年) was also marked by the completion of the *Śata-śāstra* (「百論」) by Daiva.

[76] 「維摩詰経」

[77] 「小品般若経」 or 「八千頌般若経」

[78] *Chung-lun* (「中論」) and *dvādaśāmukkhaśāstra* 「十二門論」

[79] 「摩訶般若波羅蜜神呪」 ascribed to Chih-ch'ien (支謙) and recorded as lost in one of the early catalogues.

[80] McRae holds that Kumārajīva's 「大明呪経」 may have been finalized after Hsüan-tzang's 「般若心経」 came.. But from the point of view of the linkage of Kuan-yin and Prajñāpāramitā, I cannot follow his view. Cf. J.R. McRae: Ch'an Commentaries on the Heart Sūtra: Preliminary Inferences on the Permutation of Chinese Buddhism, *Journal of International Association of Buddhist Studies*, vol. 11, no. 2, 1988, pp. 87-115.
Kuan-shih-yin-hsüan-i (「観音玄義」 2 fasc), Taisho. 34 (No. 1726).

saṃjñā, saṃskāras, vijñāna, nor is there *Śūnyatā* apart from the *Rūpa-skandha*, nor is there *Śūnyatā* apart from each of the other Skandhas like *vedanā, saṃjñā, saṃskāras, and vijñāna. Śūnyatā* in itself is *the Rūpa-skandha.* The *Rūpa-skandha* in itself is *Śūnyatā. Śūnyatā* in itself is (respectively) the *Skandhas* of *vedanā, saṃjñā, saṃskāras*, and *vijñāna*. Each *Skandha* of *vedanā, saṃjñā, saṃskāras,* and *vijñāna* in itself is *Śūnyatā.* Why? Oh, Śāriputra, just because there is a name-and-word (名字), we call it *Bodhi*, just because there is a name-and-word, we call it Bodhisattva, just because there is a name-and-word, we call it *Śūnyatā*. Why? The ultimate nature of all things (諸法之実性) has neither production nor perishing, neither defilement nor purity. On account of that, when a Bodhisattva, great being, is thus engaged in the practice of *Prajñāpāramitā*, he sees neither the production nor perishing, neither defilement nor purity. Why? Name-and-word is a product out of the concatenation of causes and conditions (因縁和合作法). Only based on the practicality of discrimination and imagination, we designate things as if they are there. This is the reason that when a Bodhisattva, great being, is engaged in the practice of *Prajñāpāramitā* introspection, he sees none of all names and words, and because he does not see them, he is free from attachment.[86]

---

[86]「舎利弗白仏言。菩薩摩訶薩云何応行般若波羅蜜時、不見菩薩不見菩薩字、不見般若波羅蜜、亦不見我行般若波羅蜜、亦、不見我不行般若波羅蜜。何以故。菩薩菩薩字性空、空中無色無受想行識、離色亦無空、離受想行識亦無空。色即是空空即是色、受想行識即是空、空即是識。何以故。舎利弗、但有名字、故謂為菩提、但有名字故謂為空。所以者何。諸法実性、無生無滅無垢無浄故、菩薩摩訶薩如是行、亦不見生亦不見滅、亦亦不見垢亦不見浄。何以故。名字是因縁和合作法、但分別憶想仮名説。是故菩薩摩訶薩行般若波羅蜜時、不見一切名字、不見故不著。」「般若波羅密経」 27 fasc. tr. by Kumārajīva: Taishō. vol. 8, (No. 223) p.221 bc.

ARTICLE ELEVEN

Critical Classification of Buddhist Doctrines and Its Future[1]

§1. Re-evaluation of Chinese Medieval System of Buddhist Philosophy

There has never been a period like today when we need some assured way of transcending cultural and religious differences. Fifty years ago, immediately after the world war II, the so-called "Philosophy East and West movement" was launched at the University of Hawaii by Prof. Moore, etc., and since then, the *Journal of Philosophy East and West* has still been continued today as its legacy. The movement was designed to promote philosophical and cultural communication between the traditions of the East and West toward a global integration of human thought and action. Through the past half-a-century, we have witnessed a remarkable progress toward the said goal of globalization, irrespective of whether or not this result has directly been prompted by an academic movement like that. Soon, scholars of religious studies followed to organize a similar movement in terms of religious dialogue between Buddhism and Christianity, and it would be the next step to include Islamic tradition for such dialogue.

Today, however, we feel to have lost much of the initial wind of East-West movement and have a sense of sorrow over the ineffectuality of academicians' struggle. As we all know, our international society for Chinese philosophy branched off from the Philosophy East and West, because the latter could not provide sufficient incentive within its framework to the demanding interest of Chinese philosophy. Nor was it able to provide similar incentive to the interest of Indian philosophy. As results of it came the off-shoot of an independent *Journal of Chinese Philosophy*, as well as that of the *Journal of Indian philosophy.* After participating in the International Society for Chinese Philosophy more than a decade, I have been reflecting upon what my Buddhist study can do with the ill-deflated movement

---

[1] Presented at the 11th International Conference on Chinese Philosophy, National Chengchi University, Taipei, Taiwan ROC; Aug. 25 - 30, 1999.

of East-West philosophy and the stifled inter-religious dialogue. My conclusion is twofold: (1) that as Buddhists, we ought to pay much more attention to the essential core of Chinese Buddhist philosophy documented well in the so-called *Chiao-p'an* Buddhism (教判仏教) of Medieval China, while resisting the pressure to accommodate inter-philosophical or inter-religious dialogue; (2) that we ought to be more outspokenly critical toward those non-Buddhist thoughts and religions in reference to the essential core of human inability to deal with prejudice and irrational action against other humans of different cultures and religions. In this paper, I intend to present a brief survey on the nature and function of the Buddhist *Chiao-p'an* classification and demonstrate how and why, despite their medieval works in China, these Buddhist intellectual and spiritual endeavors in philosophical terms can provide a new incentive to the scholars and students of Buddhist Studies in the coming 21st century. With that goal in mind, I am obliged to introduce Bruno Petzold's life work: *The Classification of Buddhism Bukkyō Kyōhan* published in 1995 from Otto Harrassowitz, Germany.[2]

Methodologically, the doctrinal classification (*chiao-p'an*) of Medieval China differed from the contemporary discipline of Buddhist Studies in two major ways. *Chiao-p'an* or *chiao-hsiang p'an-shih* (教相判釈) in full means "a systematic classification of Buddhist doctrines based on critical interpretation." It was a form of intelligible systems of Buddhist doctrines constructed as a unified knowledge of Buddhist religion out of a conglomerate of all the doctrines historically developed in India and piece-meal transmitted to China without any chronological order or systematic framework. The principle that underlined the *Chiao-p'an* construction was the Chinese Buddhist acceptance of all scriptures as Śākyamuni's own word and their belief in Śākyamuni's ultimate intention of human salvation. From the contemporary Buddhist Studies' point of view, on the other hand, we not only outright repudiate the belief that all scriptures were records of Buddha's word, but also we feel uncomfortable with the dogmatic integration of different strands of doctrines implied in innumerable scriptures as a meaningful whole of Buddhist salvation.

Contemporary Buddhist Studies was incorporated as part of the department of language or that of history before the 50's, and

---

[2] Bruno Petsold: *The Classification of Buddhism Bukkyō Kyōhan, comprising the Classification of Buddhist Doctrines in India, China, and Japan*, in collaboration with Shinshō Hanayama edited by Shohei Ichimura, published from Otto Harrassowitz Verlag, Wiesbaden, Germany, 1995.

today, it has become a more expansive cross-departmental discipline, irrespective of different fields of enquiry, insofar as resulting knowledge can be comprehended as part of a whole knowledge on Buddhism regarding its spiritual, cultural, and social aspects. In short, Buddhist Studies today is regarded as a scientific discipline primarily based on linguistically and historically valid knowledge on Buddhist teaching, practice and community. Nevertheless, the knowledge based on historical exactness and linguistic and textual critique alone cannot provide a need of those Buddhist practitioners whose practice has globally spread through Theravādin Vipaśyanā, Lamaist Samādhi or East Asian Zen, because they have begun to feel a necessity of some reliable reference for critical examining of their quest of spirituality *qua* their course of practice. The subject of *Chiao-p'an*, which was once abandoned by scholars on the basis that it is not a viable subject of scientific enquiry, nor suited to serious, critical studies in university curriculum, has begun to be re-evaluated today as an indispensable reference for practical as well as intellectual understanding of Buddhist spirituality.

I ought to present three possible factors for explaining this changing trend. First, despite the prevailing Buddhist Studies in the academic world, traditional Buddhist schools, whose *raison d'être* was inseparably linked with their respective doctrinal classifications, have continued to provide their sectarian theoretical as well as practical training on the bases of the respective classifications. The quiet global movement of Buddhist practitioners, though small they may be as a group, but multiple in number, have been gradually changing human perception toward Buddhism, influencing general public throughout the world. These practitioners have entered in the new territory of the higher spirituality where the discipline of contemporary Buddhist Studies alone can no longer provide instructive references.

Second, no sooner the Cold War era came to an end a decade ago, than a series of tragic events has begun to take place through hatred, violence, atrocity, tragic genocide, utterly inhumane in scope and magnitude. We have been witnessing these events in Middle East, African continent, and especially South East Europe, where religious and cultural differences are shaped by different monotheistic religions. Despite the fact that these religions have their common source in thought and literature, they have not been able to prevent such events. On account of these events, in 1997, UNESCO organized in Granada, Spain, the third Seminar on the theme "Contribution by Religions to the Culture of Peace." Participating in this conference, I came to notice the fact that the hardest problem of inter-religious encounter would likely be presented by these monotheistic religions and might prevent any lasting agreement among themselves. It has become my firm conviction that Buddhist scholars should be more outspoken, as critical as possible, on the cause of their inability wrongly resulting from their core religious beliefs.

The third point is the thesis of this paper in itself, because I hold that it is an imperative for Buddhist Study as well as Chinese philosophical study to re-evaluate the meaning of the medieval Chinese *Chiao-p'an* systems and re-instate these subjects as part of academic curriculum, especially as part of Chinese philosophical study. It has long been a main stream to co-ordinate Chinese and Indian philosophies with Western philosophical tradition. Perhaps, this was a necessary step in the beginning to acquire the respectability of Asian thoughts as equal to the status of Western thoughts. From the global point of view, Indian and Chinese philosophies are still behind Buddhist spirituality and philosophical insight that have already become a part of global human life. For these reasons, I believe that Chinese Buddhist accomplishment in the *Chiao-p'an* classification must be re-evaluated as a major part of Chinese philosophical studies.

§2. THE MEANING OF *CHIAO-P'AN* AS BUDDHIST DOCTRINAL CLASSIFICATIONS

In his introductory part (chapter 2), Bruno Petzold compares different attitude of Christian and Buddhist traditions toward the matter of classifying the two different sets of their canons, i.e., respectively, Old Testament and New Testament in the former and Hīnayāna and Mahāyāna scriptures in the latter. He points out that "the attitude of the orthodox Christian Church has always been to discourage on principle any honest attempt to classify the holy scriptures and the divine teachings. And yet it could not openly and decisively oppose such attempts, because by doing so it would have contradicted its own *raison d'être*. For this reason, the attitude of the Church remained ambiguous.[3] Compared with this

[3] *Ibid.*, p.46. On the one hand, the church could not afford to acknowledge the absolute equality of rank between the two Canons of the New Testament and the Old Testament, since by such acknowledgment the New Covenant and the New Testament would have become superfluous. On the other hand, it refrained from appraising the Old Testament as a

attitude, Petzold says that Mahāyāna Buddhism was surely more consistent for classifying the two sets of scriptures, namely, the Hīnayāna Canon as merely propaedeutic, representing a minor truth to prepare the way for learning the Mahāyāna Canon for the sake of higher and highest Mahāyāna truth.[4]

The earliest theory of *Chiao-p'an* is known to have been set forth by Kumārajīva (AD 344-413), great translator, representing the earlier olden translation[5] as a theory of "One Voice Teaching" (一音教). According to his thought, Śākyamuni's one voice affirms all Buddhist teachings, say both Hīnayāna and Mahāyāna teachings, to be true on account of the different understandings on the part of the audience.[6] A century later, Bodhiruci (菩提流支、508-35) who also contributed in the task of translation in Northern Wei, proposed a similar theory as One Voice Teaching. He theorized that the Buddha's one voice in itself implied Hīnayāna and Mahāyāna teachings side by side (如来一音大小並陳). Despite a subtle difference between these two interpretations, both obviously support that the historical evolution of Buddhist teachings was originally imbedded in the Buddha's teaching as truth, and that different stages of historical development were predestined in his teaching as truth apart from the audience.

Simplifying my argument to demonstrate the nature of *Chiao-p'an* to be trans-historical and trans-conventional, I shall try to reduce the complicated T'ien-t'ai and Hua-yen systems to their essential aspect along with some other classifications and reveal what their systems commonly intended to explain. The T'ien-t'ai system is

---

mere elementary and subordinate truth, compared with that of the Evangels.

4 *Ibid.*, p. 47.

5 Analyzing the history of Chinese translations, there were five different periods: (1) ancient translations (古訳、AD 178-375), assembled in Tao-an's catalogue (道安、died in 385), (2) earlier olden translation (旧訳前期、376-501), marked by Kumārajīva and recorded in Sêng-yu's catalogue (僧祐), (3) later olden translations (旧訳後期、502-617), recorded in the Catalogue of Various Scriptures (「衆経目録」) sponsored by dynastic edicts; (4) earlier new translations, (新訳前期、618-959), the period being initiated by Hsüan-tzang (玄奘) and (5) later new translations (新訳後期, 960-1906). Cf. Ono Genmyō: "History of transmission and translation of Buddhist Sūtras," *Bussho Kaisetsu Daijiten* (「仏書解説大辞典」), Additional Vol., pp. 7-8.

6 Strictly speaking, there is some difference between the theories of Kumārajīva and Bodhiruci. The former held that the Buddha's one voice teaching was subdivided into Hīnayāna and Mahāyāna according to the different capacities of the listeners, whereas the latter upheld that the Buddha's one voice teaching implied in itself the two sets of truth (如来一音大小並陳).

known of the criteria for classification as "five different periods" and "eight kinds of teaching" (五時八教). The uniqueness of *T'ien-t'ai Chiao-p'an* (天台教判) was its pseudo-historical principle in classifying the entire scriptures in reference to Śākyuamuni's life career[7]: (1) The *Hua-yen Sūtras* (「華厳」) were classified to be the contents of his teaching at the initial moment of his enlightenment under the Bodhi tree; (2) The group of Hīnayāna scriptures consisted of the three baskets (三蔵) [i.e., Tripiṭaka: Āgama (教), Vinaya (律), and Abhidharma (論)], was classified as the contents of his immediately subsequent teaching given to the initial members of the Saṅgha at the Dear Park (鹿苑); (3) The group of early Mahāyāna scriptures was classified as the contents of his extended teachings (*Vaipulya*, 「方等」) given prior to the Mahāyāna essential teaching; (4) The group of the quintessential Mahāyāna scriptures was classified as the contents of the *Prajñā* or Wisdom teaching (「般若」) lectured at four localities like the Vulture's hill top of Rājagṛha, etc., and (5) finally, the group of later Mahāyāna scriptures was classified as the contents of both the *Lotus* (「法華」) and *Nirvāṇa Sūtra* (「涅槃」) preached toward the end of Śākyamuni's evangelical career.

Despite the fact that these classified teachings appear to be in reference to different times of Śākyamuni's career, the system was not really conceived in terms of historical criterion but entirely based on the principle of Buddhist spirituality exemplified in Śākyamuni's life career. The edifice points to the fact that the entire scriptures that were produced through the first millennium after his Parinirvāṇa were meaningfully organized to structure theoretical and practical teachings as Buddhist spirituality and salvation. It is obvious, therefore, that the system was trans-historical and trans-conventional. I think that the same conclusion can be reached with regard to the *Hua-yen Chiao-p'an* system, which I try to demonstrate how and why the Buddhist doctrinal classification was necessarily trans-historical and trans-convention.

Prabhākaramitra (波羅頗迦羅密多羅、627-633), who arrived in Chang-an in the same year when Hsüan-tzang set out his journey to India, advocated his classification in terms of five teachings[8]: (1) the teaching

---

[7] Five Periods (五時): (1) Hua-yen (華厳); (2) Hīnayāna (鹿苑); (3) Early Mahāyāna (方等); (4) Advamced Mahāyāna (般若); (5) Comprehensive Mahāyāna (法華涅槃).

[8] Prabhākaramitra (波頗 or 波羅頗迦羅蜜多, a South Indian monk, who arrived at Chang-an through Central Asia in the year when Hsüan-tsang left for India, and was engaged in the task of translation, 627-33). His

of the four holy truths (四諦教) comprised in the *Four Āgamas* (「四阿含」), (2) the teaching of the formlessness [or no attributes] of all things (無相教) comprised in the group of *Prajñā Sūtras* (「諸般若」), (3) the teaching of the realization of introspection (観行教) comprised in the *Hua-yen Sūtra* (「華厳」), (4) the teaching of Peace and Happiness (安楽教) comprised in the *Nirvāṇa Sūtras* (「涅槃」), and (5) the teaching of continual adherence to Buddhist spirituality (守護教) comprised in the group of scriptures called *Great Collection of Extended Teachings* (*Mahāvaipulya-mahāsaṃnipāta-sūtra* (「大方等大集経」).[9]

Fa-ts'ang (法蔵、643-721), great systematizer of the *Hua-yen Chiao-p'an* (華厳教判), theorized the classification of "Five Teachings and Ten Schools" (五教十宗)[10] in the order of (1) Hīnayāna (小乗教), (2) early Mahāyāna (大乗初教),[11] (3) later Mahāyāna (大乗終教),[12]

---

theory of Five Teachings (五教説) are as follows:: (1) Teachings on the Four Holy Truths (四諦教) comprised in the Four Āgamas (四阿含), (2) Teachings on the Formless (無相教) contained in various Prajñā scriptures (諸般若), (3) Teachings on the Practice of Dhyāna and Samādhi (観行教) conprised in the Hua-yen Sūtra (華厳), (4) Teachings on Freedom from Suffering (安楽教) comprised in the Nirvāṇa Sūtras (涅槃); and (5) Teachings on the Guarding of Tradition (守護教) comprised in the Assembly of Scriptures (大集経).

[9] 「大方等大集経」[60 fasc. or 30 fasc. Taishō. 13 (397)] translated by Dharmakṣema from Central India (曇無讖 414-26), who also translated the *Mahāyāna Nirvāṇa Sūtra*. The reason that the collected Sūtras in question were regarded as fit for the teaching of continual adherence is that most of these scriptures were due to their contents, namely, numerical collections of various doctrines (法数、法相) centering that of *Śūnyatā* with some addition of esoteric doctrines.

[10] Fa-ts'amg's classification of the ten schools (十宗教判): (1) The school which teaches the existence of both the self and *dharmas* (我法具有宗); (2) The school which teaches the existence of *dharmas* and the nonexistence of self (法有我無宗); (3) The school which teaches the non-existence of *dharmas* in the past and future (法無去来); (4) The school which teaches that there are both the temporal and the real even in the present existence (現通仮実宗); (5) The school which teaches that the phenomena are false and the noumenon is reral (俗妄真実宗); (6) The school which teaches that all *dharmas* are merely Names (諸法但名宗); (7) The school which teaches that everything is Emptiness (一切皆空宗); (8) The school which teaches that the True Virtue is not empty (真徳不空宗); (9) The school which cuts out both Form and Thought (相想空絶宗); (10) The school which teaches that everything has the *a-priori* Nature perfectly and brilliantly (円妙具徳宗). Cp. Petzold: *op cit.*, 421-425.

[11] This group of scriptures asserts that the Hīnayāna practitioners, who are engaged in the Śrāvaka and Pratyekabuddha vehicles, cannot realize Buddhahood (定性二乗不成仏).

[12] This group of scriptures asserts that Mahāyāna practitioners all can

(4) sudden teaching (頓教),[13] and (5) perfect teaching (円教).[14] Of these five, the initial three teachings are based on the principle of gradual teaching (漸教), whereas the fourth and fifth are respectively classified in terms of "sudden teaching" (頓教) and "ultimate perfection" (円教). The last two classifications were initially introduced by the scholar monk Hui-kung (慧光) of late northern Wei (後魏、534-554) along with his teacher Buddhaśānta (仏陀扇多) as part of the three categories: (1) gradual teaching (漸教), (2) sudden teaching (頓教), and (3) perfect teaching (円教). The differentiation of gradual and sudden is said to have been also advocated by Paramārtha (真諦、548-569) in southern China where he arrived. Nevertheless, these three criteria of classification[15] were upheld mainly by those scholars who advocated the *Bodhisattva's Ten-Stage Treatise* (「十地経論」)[16] and subsequently by those scholars of the Hua-yen school (華厳宗), because the *Hua-yen Sūtra* (*Buddhāvataṃsaka-sūtra*) was regarded as the authentic specimen that teaches the criterion of sudden realization (頓悟). The T'ien-t'ai master Chih-i

---

realize Buddhahood (一切皆成仏). This is the theme of the *Mahāyāna Nirvāṇa Sūtra*.

[13] Fa-ts'ang explains "sudden teaching" in his *Essay on the Five Teachings* (「華厳五教章」第一): "Wherever no thought arises, that is the state of Buddhahood" (一念不生成仏); "Sudden" means that "When one suddenly ceases word and conception, the truth suddenly manifest itself, and suddenly realizes the practice of introspection, and sees no single thought to arise. This is the realization of Buddhahood." (「頓者言説頓絶、理性頓顕、解行頓成、一念不生、是仏也」) The teaching refers to such a sudden realization of ultimate illumination without relying on serial stages of practice.

[14] Fa-ts'ang explains perfect teaching (円教) in two criteria: (1) the principle of "ten times ten not exhausted" (十重無尽) and (2) the principle of "each other identical, each other melting" (相即相入). Cf. Sect 5 in this paper. The teaching in question is also explained as the theory of "One in all, all in one" (「一即一切、一切即一」). The third causal context of his ten-fold profound dependent origination (「十玄縁起」第三) explains it as that one and many reciprocally accommodate each other, identifying themselves while remaining as neither one nor many (「一多相容不同門」).

[15] Strictly speaking, another criterion, say, "indeterminateness" (不定教) ought to be added in the order of "gradual," "sudden," "indeterminate," and "perfect."

[16] The leading figures were Hui-kung and his disciple Hui-yüan of Ch'ing-ying-ssù (浄影寺慧遠). The school was based on the *Daśabhūmika-śāstra* (「十地経論」12 fasc.) translated by Bodhiruci, Ratnamati (勒那摩提) and Buddhaśānta during the Northern Wei dynasty.

(天台智者大師、 531-597) is known to have adopted these criteria of classification as part of his four methodical teachings (化儀四教) and four theoretical teachings (化法四教),[17] and so did the Hua-yen master Hsien-shou (賢首大師) Chi-ts'ang (吉蔵、643-712) of T'ang dynasty in his Classification of Five Teachings (五教教判).

I am obliged also to note the teaching of indeterminateness (不定教) to be added to Hui-kung's criteria of gradual, sudden, and perfect, because "indeterminateness" (不定教) was used to differentiate the kind of teaching that neither addresses to gradual realization nor to sudden realization, but to the transcendent Buddha-nature abiding in eternity (仏性常住), for instance, in the *Sūtra on the Lion's Roar of the Queen Śrīmālā* (「勝鬘経」*Śrīmālādevīsiṃhanāda-sūtra*), the *Sūtra on the Golden Light Splendor* (「金光明経」、*Suvarṇaprabhāsottama-sūtra*), and so forth. This notion of indeterminateness, however, was an early interpretation, and it was rectified by the T'ien-t'ai master Chih-i upon its adoption in terms of apparent indeterminateness (顕露不定) and hidden indeterminateness (秘密不定),[18] but these are not essential to my consideration here.

There is no qualm about the principle of gradual realization of enlightenment (漸悟), since it is common that such a result ought to be at hand through one's gradual cultivation of human spirituality. Sudden realization (頓悟), say, of transcendent illumination, or so-called altered consciousness in today's jargon, may be an instantaneous occurrence during the practice of introspection.[19] Fa-ts'ang says that it takes place at the moment when word and thought cease to be (言説頓

---

[17] "Gradual teaching" and "sudden teaching" are included in his Four Methodical Teachings (「化儀四教: 漸、頓、秘密、and 不提」), while "perfect teaching" in his Four Theoretical Teachings (「化法四教: 蔵、通、別、and 円」).

[18] According to Chih-i, "indeterminate teaching" explains the case that the Buddha's one voice necessarily results in varied understandings among the listeners (不定者一音異解). Varied understandings imply two different conditions" (1) In one case, the Buddha's one voice can be grasped immediately by some in terms of sudden realization (頓悟), while by others in terms of gradual realization (漸悟). This is manifest or explicit indeterminateness (顕露不定). (2) In another case, the Buddha's one voice can be understood as sudden realization at one place, but it may also be taken as gradual realization in some other place. Here it is the criterion of hidden or implicit indeterminateness (秘密不定).

[19] Fa-ts'ang exemplifies that some Mahāyāna practitioners directly realize the said state of illumination (直往頓機) without recourse to the practice of Hīnayāna Vehicle (廻小向大) or without going through the serial ten stages of Bodhisattva path (菩薩十地).

絶), where transcendent nature at once manifests itself (理性頓顕) and this is instantaneously experienced (解行頓成). It is apparent that the criterion of sudden teaching was intended to explain how and why transcendence takes place from ordinary consciousness of history and convention. Perhaps the most important criterion in the system of *Chiao-p'an* classification is "perfect teaching" (円教). This criterion appeared both in T'ien-t'ai and Hua-yen systems to reflect their respective philosophical insights on ultimate Buddhist Truth. Both together, I think, the criterion clarifies what the exclusive area of Buddhist concern is. I shall briefly explain why this area of Buddhist enquiry has not been shared by any other system of thought, neither in European nor in traditional Chinese philosophy.

§3. *CHIAO-P'AN* AS THEORETICAL STRUCTURING OF THE LINKAGE BETWEEN *VYAVAHĀRA* AND *PARAMĀRTHA*

As to the criterion of gradual teaching, some systematizers like Tsung-mi (宗密、780-841) included "secular teaching" (人天教) in the lowest stratum of the five teachings,[20] and then listed up Buddhist teachings in hierarchy, starting with the teaching of things that have forms or attributes (有相教), the teaching of the formless (無相教), the teaching of permanence like Nirvāṇa (常住教), the teaching of sudden realization (頓教), and finally the teaching of ultimate perfection (円教). Some other systems, like that of Prabhākaramitra (波羅頗迦羅蜜多、627-33), as mentioned before, lined up five teachings in the order of (1) the four holy truths given in the four Āgamas (四諦教、「四阿含」), which can be renamed as things with form (有相教), (2) the things with no form as expounded in various *Prajñāpāramitā Sūtras* (無相教、「諸般若」), (3) the introspective practice expounded in the *Hua-yen Sūtra* (観行教、華厳), (4) the peace and happiness propounded in the *Nirvāṇa Sūtra* (安楽教、涅槃), and (5) the continual adherence to Buddhist spirituality as enumerated in the *Great Collection of Sūtras* (守護教、大集経). Or like the classification of ten teachings (十種教) by Lay Hua-yen scholar

[20] Five Teachings (五教): (1) Secular teaching on humans and gods (人天教), (2) Hīnayāna (小乗教), (3) Mahāyāna Vijñāna theory that advocates ideation and thought alone real (大乗法相教), (4) Prajñā and middle way (Mādhyamika) repudiation of forms (破相教), (5) One Vehicle teaching that reveals the ultimate truth (一乗顕性教).

Li T'ung-hsüan (李通玄、635-730),[21] whose system goes in the following order:

(1) Initially the Hīnayāna teaching on what is genuinely existent (有);[22]
(2) The Prajñā teaching on repudiation of what is existent and which demonstrates how and why it is of the nature of emptiness (空);[23]
(3) The teaching of *Sandhinirmocana-sūtra* on how to reconcile the theory of reality and that of emptiness and demonstrate how and why it is neither emptiness nor existent (非有非空);[24]
(4) The teaching of *Laṅkāvatāra-sūtra* on the demonstration of how and why the practicality of convention (*prajñapti*(仮) or *vyavahāra-satya,* 俗諦) agrees with primary truth (*paramārthasatya,* 真諦);[25]
(5) The teaching of *Vimalakīrtinirdeśa-sūtra* on the demonstration of how and why whatever goes along with convention (*vyavahāra* or *saṃvṛti,* 俗) is always primary truth;[26]
(6) The teaching of *Lotus Sūtra* (*Saddharmapuṇḍarīka-sūtra*) on the way how whatever is temporary returns to its original reality;[27]
(7) The teaching of *Mahāyāna Nirvāṇa Sūtra* on the way enabling all three Vehicles to return to their common original reality;[28]
(8) The teaching of *Hua-yen Sūtra* (*Buddhāvataṃsaka-sūtra*) on sudden realization of ultimate truth.[29]
(9) and (10) can be grouped together in terms of "indeterminate teaching."[30]

The teachings Nos.2 through 5 (*Prajñā*, *Mādhyamika*, *Laṅkāvatāra*, *Vimalakīrti*, *Sandhinirmocana*) can be collected together on account of their central teaching as emptiness (*Śūnyatā,* 空性) and its

---

21 *An assembled Treatise on the Buddhāvataṃsaka-sūtra*「華厳経合論」120 fasc., A complete commentary on the 80 fascicles *Hua-yen-ching*.

22 第一、小乗:「純有」

23 第二、 般若:「破有、明空」

24 第三、 「解深密経」:「和会空有、明不空不有」

25 第四、 「楞伽経」:「明仮即契真」

26 第五、 「維摩経」:「明俗即常真」

27 第六、 「法華経」:「引権帰実」

28 第七、 「涅槃経」:「令三乗捨権帰実」

29 The Hua-yen explains instantaneous transcendence to surpass ten lives instantaneously, perfectly inter-fusing beginning and ending as non-existent, and yet revealing prior and posterior in total permeation. 第八、「華厳経」、「刹那際通摂十世、円融無始終、明前後通該」

30 第九: 「共不共教、三乗等人同聞、而得益不同」、第十、 「不共共教、来会機会格別、而得益同」

relationship with existence (有). The teachings Nos. 6 and 7 (*Lotus* and *Nehan Sūtras*) can be grouped together as done in the T'ien-t'ai system. Finally the teaching of *Hua-yen Sūtra* is regarded as Sudden Realization and the culmination of all Buddhist teachings. Since Li T'ung-hsüan was a Hua-yen scholar, this is consistent. What lacks in his system is perfect teaching (円教). However, this can be read in his placing of the *Hua-yen Sūtra* as culmination of all *Sūtras*. It is possible therefore to simplify Li T'ung-hsüan's system down to the following four teachings: (1) the Hīnayāna, (2) the early Mahāyāna centered upon Prajñā, etc., (3) the later Mahāyāna teaching of *Lotus Sūtra* and *Nehan Sūtra*, and (4) the culminating Hua-yen teaching which is two-fold: Sudden and Perfect. In parallel with this system of five teachings, the San-lun master Chi-ts'ang (三論宗吉蔵) offered his system as (1) the teaching of Śrāvaka (Hīnayāna) Vehicle (声聞乗), and the teaching of Bodhisattva (Mahāyāna) Vehicle (菩薩乗); the latter was subdivided into (2) the fundamental Dharma wheel (根本法輪) taught in the *Hua-yen Sūtra*,31 (3) the peripheral branch Dharma wheel (枝末法輪) taught in the *Lotus Sūtra*, (4) the teaching on the Singular Vehicle in which the three vehicles are unified (摂末帰本法輪) as taught in the *Nehan Sūtra*.

The Vinaya master Tao-hsüan (律宗道宣、595-667) introduced his three teachings on introspection (三観教) as (1) the teaching on the emptiness of the essential nature of *dharmas* (性空教),[32] (2) the teaching on the emptiness of their attributes (相空教),[33] and (3) the teaching on the theory that the form of things is the subjective Representation-only (*vijñapti-mātratā*) (唯識教).[34] The erudite scholar monk, renowned translator, Hsüan-tzang (玄奘、602-64) who initiated the era of new translation (新訳前期), theorized his classification in terms of three teachings: (1) the turning of the *Dharma* wheel taught in the *Āgama Sūtras* (転法輪、「阿含」), (2) the critical reflection

---

31 「華厳の一因一果法門」

32 The teaching elucidates the emptiness of the nature of psycho-physical elements (*dharmas*) and the absence of self. 「諸法性空無我之教」

33 For the sake of inferior Bodhisattvas, it ought to be taught that whatever is the characteristic of all psycho-physical elements (*dharmas*) is originally empty. 「教説為小菩薩諸法本相是空」

34 For the sake of superior Bodhisattvas, it ought to be taught that all *dharmas* and external defilements are originally devoid of real substance. 「教説為大菩薩諸法外塵本来無実」

of the *Dharma* wheel taught in the *Prajñā Sūtras* (照法輪「般若」), and (3) the continual adherence to the *Dharma* wheel (持法輪) taught in the *Sandhinirmocana-sūtra* (「解深密経」), and so forth. His foremost disciple K'uei-chi (窺基、632-82)[35] also had his own version of three teachings: (1) the teaching on Existence (有教) as Hīnayāna doctrines of the *Āgamas* (.諸「阿含」小乘義), (2) the teaching on Emptiness (空教) as Mahāyāna doctrines of the *Prajñā Sūtras*, *Triple Mādhyamika* treatises, etc. (「般若」and「三論」等), and (3) the teaching on the Middle (中道教) as Ultimate doctrine of the *Hua-yen*, *Sandhinirmocana*, and *Lotus Sūtras* (「華厳」、「解深密」、「法華」等).

Started with Kumārajīva's One-Voice Classification, I briefly surveyed the complex T'ien-t'ai and Hua-yen classifications of theoretical teachings along with several other classifications and have come down to K'uei-chi's three teachings. We are able to see more clearly now what the *raison d'être* of the *Chiao-p'an* or theoretical classification meant in Medieval China. Each classification was neither concerned with the criterion of history, nor with that of convention *per se*, but exclusively concerned with Buddhist spirituality that refers to the relationship between the level of ordinary world[36] and that of transcendence.[37] K'uei-chi's theory of the three teachings as concerned with Existence, Emptiness, and Middle, was fundamentally not different from his master Hsüan-tzang's, because the latter's three *Dharma* wheels (三法輪) refer to the same textual contents of *Āgama*, *Prajñā*, and *Sandhinirmocana-sūtras* as those of K'uei-chi. Li T'ung-hsüan's classification is essentially nearest to Fa-ts'ang's, because my simplified four teachings as his, namely, (1) Hīnayāna Āgama teaching, (2) early Mahāyāna Prajñā teaching, (3) later Mahāyāna Lotus and Nehan teaching, and (4) the culminating Hua-yen sudden and perfect teaching, are parallel with Fa-ts'ang's five teachings: (1) Hīnayāna, (2) early Mahāyāna, (3) later Mahāyāna, (4) sudden and (5) perfect, because, as I mentioned before, Fa-ts'ang's fifth "perfect teaching" can be read into Li T'ung-hsüan's fourth

---

[35] Entitled as Tz'ù-en Ta-shih (慈恩大師), he was the successor of Hsüan-tsang and the systematizer and proper founder of the Fa-hsiang school (法相宗) based on the Representation Only theory (*Vijñapti-mātratā*) (唯識論). The *Sandhinirmocana-sūtra* was translated by Étienne Lamotte as *L'explication des mysthéres*; from the Chinese version translated by Hsüsn-tsang (5 fasc., Taisho. No. 676), Louvain 1935.

[36] *vyavahāra*, *saṃvṛti* (俗諦、世諦 : history and convention)

[37] *paramārtha* (真諦、第一義諦)

"sudden teaching." It is apparent that T'ien-t'ai as well as Hua-yen classifications can be coordinated well in parallel with K'uei-chi's classification of three teachings, especially because K'uei-chi classified the teaching of the Middle in reference to the *Hua-yen*, *Sandhinirmocana*, and *Lotus Sūtras*. And these are the major scriptural sources of "perfect teaching" respectively for the Hua-yen, Fa-hsiang Wei-shih (法相唯識), and T'ien-tai classifications.

§4. THE MIDDLE POSITION DEPICTED AS ULTIMATE AND PERFECT TEACHING

The primary theory of the *Sandhinirmocana-sūtra* (*Sūtra that Elucidates the Profound Meaning*) is known to have been the Vijñānavāda system to explain the traditional concept of Middle Way in terms of representation-only theory (*vijñaptimātratā*) and that of Dependent Origination of twelve causal links in terms of the seed consciousness (*Ālayavijñāna*). According to the Vijñānavada theory of the middle way, all things are mere subjective representation consisting of names and can neither be said "decidedly existent" nor "decidedly non-existent." The realization of this middle way is an active accomplishment of introspection. Briefly explaining, the *Sūtra* presents the transcendent (*tathatā*, 真如、or *paramārtha-satya*, 真諦) as bereft of word and thought beyond all mental dualization and discrimination. Next the *Sūtra* presents the nature of phenomena[38] in terms of eight differentiated faculties of subjective consciousness, and explains all psycho-physical elements (*dharmas*) as ultimately arising from the seed consciousness (*Ālayavijñāna*, 阿羅耶識). The text goes on to introduce the Three-fold Nature of things (*trisvabhāva*, 三性) as imaginary existent (*parikalpita*, 遍計所執性), dependent arising (*paratantra*, 依他起性), and perfect realization (*parinispanna*, 円成実性). This theory alone, however, may be misunderstood as structuring phenomena in terms of real existent (有). The text, therefore, quickly adds another theory as three-fold nature of Emptiness (*triniḥsvabhāva*, 三無性) to demonstrate how and why each of the three natures ought to be viewed as devoid of real existence (空性). In this manner, the text reconciles the antithesis of "existent" and "non-existent" in terms of "neither real existent nor total nothing." In short the Vijñānavādins advocated the middle way in terms of

---

38 *vyavahāra-satya* (俗諦) or *sāṃvṛti-satya* (世諦)

dual negation: "neither decidedly existent nor decidedly non-existent" on the ground of Triple Natures and Triple Empty Natures.

Coming back to the subject of "perfect teaching" (円教) of the T'ien-t'ai and Hua-yen Classifications, I am prepared to introduce Bruno Petzold's explanation of "perfect teaching" by means of paraphrasing his words and few excerpts from his *Classification of Buddhist Doctrines.* He quotes Chih-i to explain *'yüan-chiao'* (円教) by similar usages like *'yüan-miao'* (円妙、perfect, wondrous), *'yüan-man'* (円満、perfect, full), *'yüan-tsu'* (円足、perfect, complete), and *'yüan-tun'* (円頓、perfect, sudden). Accordingly, "perfect teaching" means the highest theory in Mahāyāna Buddhism that teaches the true form of the *dharma*-world (法界、*dharmadhātu*) and leaves nothing hidden or untaught. The "perfect teaching" explains all phenomena in terms of true middle, i.e., not a mere middle or common-sense middle (不但中), by directly (1) identifying whatever phenomenon that arises as emptiness (即空), (2) as temporality (即仮), and (3) as middle (即中). Chih-i called this state of affairs as "perfect harmonization or perfect inter-fusion of three-fold truth (*yüan-jung-san-ti*, 円融三諦). Chih-i adopted these triple principles from Nāgārjuna's renowned work *Madhyamaka-śāstra* (「中論」), especially the 18th verse of the 24th chapter. The verse in question reads as follows:

> Whatever has dependent origination, we call it emptiness (空); it is simply a name that relies on causes (仮);[39] it is indeed the middle way (中).[40]

Petzold asserts that the paramount implication of Chih-i's causal insight is the concrete, spontaneous ontology correlative to that of perfect inter-fusion of the three principles (*yüan-jung-san-ti*, 円融三諦). Whatever arises upon causal dependence (随縁) is endowed (具) with its essential nature (性). This nature is the harmonious realization of the three truths, so that actual (*shih*, 事) and transcendent (*li*, 理), defilement (*kleśa*) and wisdom (*bodhi*), or Saṃsāra and Nirvāṇa, are also harmonized and identified with each other (in terms of *śūnyatā*).[41] Chih-i's theoretical

---

[39] The translation is due to this writer. The term *prajñapti* is translated as name, designation, or representation in the sense of practical convention. 'Upādāya" is interpreted to explain the origin of *prajñapti,* as relying or depending or grasping (執) a given *Skandha* (五蘊) consisting of multiple *dharmas* as a whole.

[40] *yaḥ pratītyasamutpādaḥ śūnyatām tām pracakṣmahe*
sā prajñaptir upādāya pratipat saiva madhyamā//

[41] See *op. cit.*, p. 272.

classification of four teachings (化法四教) represents a system of gradual perfection on the causal insight of Dependent Origination, namely, proceeding to the initial insight of emptiness, then to that of temporality, and finally to that of middle way. These steps were designed to enable practitioners to eventually attain an entirely different significance with regard to phenomenal occurrence. Myriads of phenomena are then reviewed to be no longer separated from the transcendent noumenal principle of ontology, called *tathatā* (真如).[42] In ordinary state of existence, myriads of phenomena arise and perish due to the state of human defilement and delusion. According to the perfect teaching, however, myriads of phenomena or human differentiations become in themselves noumenal manifestation and hence, without relativity or temporality, they are absolute, unthinkable, inexpressible states of ultimate truth.

In contrast to the T'ien-t'ai theory of "perfect teaching" which is depicted as harmonious interaction between phenomena (事) and noumenon (理), the Hua-yen theory of perfect teaching was directed toward the insight of harmonious interaction and inter-fusion between phenomena themselves (事事無礙法界円融). Fa-ts'ang explains the perfect teaching to be two-fold: (1) As one criterion, one may advocate ultimate identity between One Vehicle teaching (同教一乗) with that of three Hīnayāna Vehicles (三乗教：声門、円覚、菩薩). This is the main theme which the *Lotus Sūtra* adheres in terms of gradual realization, i.e., for the sake of guiding three vehicles into the singular vehicle. (2) Likewise, as another criterion, one may advocate difference between One Vehicle and three Vehicles (別教一乗). This is the main theme to which the *Hua-yen Sūtra* adheres, because the highest teaching is destined to be reached by the highest class of beings alone, who are capable of sudden enlightenment. According to the latter interpretation, this ultimate teaching of One Vehicle transcends three Vehicles in terms of two Hua-yen principles. Borrowing Petzold's favored translation, I put the two principles as (1) "ten times ten not exhausted" (十重無尽) and (2) "each other identical, each other melting" (相即相入).

---

[42] The term *tathatā* (真如) is synonymous with *bhūtatathatā* (*ju-ju*, 如如), Buddha-nature, original pristine mind (自性清浄心), often translated as "true likeness," "undifferentiated whole," immutable, beyond changing phenomena, or whatever is true as contrasted to what is false imagination (虚妄); absolute, ultimate source and characteristic of all phenomena. It has never meant to be an active or efficient causal agent, nor a static entity. It is comparable to the term '*yathābhūtam*' which early Buddhists used in literature and Abhidharmas to designate true reality, absolute truth, or anything as it really is. One ought to be cautious about Petzold's use of "ontological source."

The first doctrine "ten times ten not exhausted" may be clarified by the simile of mirrors. For instance, if there are two mirrors directly opposite to each other, then they reflect each other. But when in one and the same room there are hundreds of different mirrors placed at different angles, then each of the will show innumerable reflected mirrors. The relation of the things in the world, to which the aforementioned refers, can be compared to the relation of the mirrors in this simile.[43] The second doctrine "each other identical, each other melting" means the reciprocal identity of things in space and time. The term "*hsiang-chi*" (相即) means the identity of things in space, and '*hsiang-ju*' (相入) means the identity of things in time. Accordingly, there is no contradiction whatsoever between things, all things in the universe being in complete harmony.[44]

Besides these interpretations, it is also inferable from the boundless Hua-yen doctrine of the ten-fold profound dependent origination (華厳十玄縁起無礙法門),[45] which is a good contrast to the T'ien-t'ai's quest of

---

[43] See *op. cit.*, p. 411.

[44] *Ibid.*

[45] It is also called "the ten-fold profound doctrine of the Hua-yen's One Vehicle" (「華厳一乗十玄門」), or "One Vehicle's ten-fold profound doctrine" (一乗十玄門). The following are the theorization of ten different ways of dependent origination ascribed to Chih-yen (智儼、602-668, the second Hua-yen patriarch). Multiple phenomena are thus intuited to arise out of the unhindered mutual interactions and inter-fusion among psycho-physical elements (諸法):

(1) A causal context in which all *dharmas* simultaneously interact and inter-fuse in mutual correlation (「同時具足相応門」);

(2) A causal context compared to multiple gems of Indra's palace curtain mutually reflecting themselves (「因陀羅網境界門」);

(3) A causal context in which all *dharmas*, revealed or hidden, simultaneously establish each other (「秘密蔭顕倶成門」);

(4) A causal context in which all *dharmas*, minor or major, mutually accommodate each other (「微細相容安立門」);

(5) A causal context in which present, past, and future, each having their three times, make up nine, but within a moment of thought (一念) as tenth, these ten different times let temporal succession go on in space and time (「十世隔法異成門」);

(6) A causal context in which similar and dissimilar *dharmas* accommodate admixture as unhindered (「諸蔵純雑具徳門」);

(7) A causal context in which one and many reciprocally accommodate each other as neither one nor many (「一多相容不同門」);

(8) A causal context in which all *dharmas* freely operate without obstruction as interaction and inter-fusion (「諸法相即自在門」);

(9)A causal context in which all *dhamas* are transformed sa morally good within Absolute Mind of purity (「唯心廻転善成門」);

(10) A causal context in which given phenomena and manifest noumenon are grasped as non-different 「託事顕法生解門」).

dependent origination. The T'ien-t'ai's insight explains that phenomena arise from causal interactions of multiple psycho-physical elements, hence they are devoid of substantial reality (i.e., *śūnyatā*), except the fact that they are mere conventional names (*prajñapti*), and thus critically reviewed, they are envisioned as transcendent in the middle domain (*madhyamā*). In contrast, the Hua-yen insight explains how psycho-physical elements make up various causal contexts through inexhaustible accommodation and reciprocal interaction, out of which each phenomenon manifests itself to appear This Hua-yen theory refers to that universe in which dharmas infinitely interact among themselves" in horizontal terms (法界縁起, while the T'ien-t'ai examines phenomena and noumenon and their vertical relationship in reference to dependent origination. The Hua-yen examines the causal contexts in which all *dharmas* (*dharmadhātu*) causally concatenate to produce each phenomenon. Because of this difference, the T'ien-t'ai theory is said from olden times to have clarified the vertical relationship between the world of facts (事) and that of the transcendent (理) in terms of harmonious correlation (理事無礙), whereas the Hua-yen theory analyzed the horizontal relations of all *dharmas* or phenomenal facts themselves (事事無礙).

§5. CONCLUSION: *CHIAO-P'AN* STUDY AND BRUNO PETZOLD'S LIFE WORK

Despite a brief survey of the Buddhist classifications of Medieval China, it is abundantly clear that each and every classification attempted to set forth its own passage from the world of history and convention toward the transcendent goal of the middle way. The T'ien-t'ai and Hua-yen schools surely constructed mutually complementary systems to depict the ultimate insight of Dependent Origination by classifying sets of scriptures in terms of "perfect teaching." The question is: Do these classifications have a meaning in our contemporary secular studies, especially philosophical studies? How and why is it possible to link our secular enquiry with the Buddhist Studies of Classical and Medieval China?

Fa-ts'ang (643-712, the fifth Hua-yen patriarch) reorganized the ten-fold causal doctrine with minor change of terms as follows: (1) 同時具足相応門, (2) 広狭自在無礙門, (3) 一多相容不同門, (4) 諸法相即自在門, (5) 秘密顕了俱成門, (6) 微細相容安立門, (7) 因陀羅網境界門, (8) 託事顕法生解門, (9) 十世隔法異成門, (10) 主伴円明具徳門。Refer to 十玄縁起、「望月仏教大辞典」、pp. 2239c - 2240a.

Buddhist philosophy demarcated itself from all secular philosophy by repudiation of the reality of self and the reality of metaphysical or conceptual reference. This differentiation originally started with Śākyamuni's teaching, which was later classified as Hīnayāna teaching. Although it was in ancient India, yet the philosophical position that repudiated the belief in "permanent self" and "reality of things," has its continual impact on us even today. The Abhidharmist critical enquiry which focused on the reality of *dharmas,* thus called "philosophy of Existence (法有)," however, was soon challenged by Mahāyāna Buddhist thinkers who advocated the insight of *Śūnyatā* (空性) and repudiated the reality of *dharmas* on the same causal ground of Dependent Origination. No wonder, since ancient times, Buddhist thinkers emphasized the importance of this causal insight as the way for their spirituality and religious salvation.

From the point of view of terminology, Śākyamuni's banner of Middle Way as the ultimate way of human salvation has an interesting parallel with Chinese as well as Grecian concept of the "middle" as human virtue. Confucius taught the principle of moderation as middle way (中庸), defining it as an attitude without inclining to either side and admitting of no change. Aristotle defined the principle of "mean" as some median between the vice of excess and that of deficiency. In recent decades, we have often heard the use of word "culture," and ourselves frequently apply this term to characteristic difference of a country, a society, a community, an individual or even characteristic difference of a business company, an educational institution, etc. by referring to some unique way of thought and action different from our own. Human reaction tends to be either extreme or deficient in confronting difference and injustice.

Chinese Buddhists ceased to produce any notable classifications after Yüan and Ming dynasty. One of the driving force of Chinese Buddhist thought was its confrontation with Confucian and Taoist opposition. During the period of six dynasties as well as the following Sui and T'ang dynasties, the contest of the three traditions was intense and stimulative to the creativity of Buddhist thinkers and *vice versa.* A major cause of the decline of Buddhist thought may have been the new trend of syncretic movement (三教融会) that gradually evolved through the times of Yüan (元) and Ming (明), and by entering into the era of Ching (清), all three traditions lost their driving force on account of the prevailing syncretism and ritualized doctrinal contests at the imperial court. I am inclined to think that it is good to have more viable contests among three philosophical and religious traditions of Chinese thought.

It is really not an easy task to read the Buddhist texts of *Chaio-p'an* classifications of Classical and Medieval China and especially to comprehend the doctrinal meanings and transcendent insights as conveyed by the great masters whose works I have quoted in this paper. For one thing, there was no comprehensive introductory book written on the subject matter. As I referred to Prof. Bruno Petzold and introduced his life work on Chinese *Chiao-p'ans*, I believe that his work will be a good substantial text for any one to begin with for his or her study of Chinese Buddhist thoughts, because it was written by a contemporary Western man by our time. Each Buddhist *Chiao-p'an* is a testament of the profound awareness of interaction between the domain of transcendence (*paramārtha*) and that of ordinary consciousness (*sāṃvṛti*). Although every historical religion in the world seems to share such an awareness, as a non-theistic religion, Buddhism is one which offers a much different and unique approach to this matter. Prof. Petzold offers in his book to bring out this Buddhist spirituality geared to that ultimate awareness in comparative terms.

The book testifies that it is possible to bridge the span between traditional *Chiao-p'an* systems of Classical and Medieval China and our contemporary theoretical search for Buddhist truth and the practical pursuit of Buddhist realization. I shall quote my own word from the book as my editor's introduction to ascribe the key of his successful treatise to the dual nature of his comparative insight: The key is "(1) a Westerner's analytical insight into the nature of language and logical thinking, and the identification of the intrinsic classificatory process of the mind which he finds in all Kyōhans [*Chiao-p'an*, 教判], and (2) a Buddhist insight into the paradoxical and dialectical nature of language and logical thinking, intrinsic to the mind at its deepest level, i.e., simultaneous assertion and negation of two opposites."[46] As a scholar of T'ien-tai Buddhism by himself, Prof. Petzold details Chih-i's three-fold truth adopted from the work of Nāgārjuna as *Śūnyatā* (空), *Prajñapti* (仮), and *Madhyamā* (中).

---

[46] Petzold: *op. cit.*, p. xx.

Section Four

BUDDHIST CRITICAL SPIRITUALITY AND CONTEMPORARY WORLD

ARTICLE TWELVE

Buddhist Critical Spirituality in India and the World Today[1]

§1 Introduction

One of the hardest *clichés* to remove from the minds of contemporary Indian thinkers is an erroneous view that Buddhism is a part of Hinduism. Many of modern Westerners of previous days too seem to have strengthened the meaning of this *cliché* by often revealing their misconception of Buddhist spirituality. From earlier days of the academic discipline of Indian Studies, scholars sought the origin of Buddhist spirituality in the background of the Upaniṣadic philosophy, such that the ultimate truth ought to be grasped either as *Tat tvam asi* or *Neti neti.* These esoteric maxims are known as referring to the affirmative presence of ultimate reality as either *Brahman* or *Ātman* permeating the universe. Many Westerners of former days believed that Buddhism was a reformed Hinduism on account of its uncompromising attitude toward the caste system. Buddhism certainly did not compromise with the Hindu ideology of caste system. In any case, the above *cliché* is not only wrong but also harmful to Indian civilization as a whole, because, I think, there is no other time as today when India needs an intellectual power of critique upon its own culture, society, and religion. On the part of Buddhists too, it is the necessary time to participate in the affairs of the country as it did in some ancient and medieval times. With this thought in mind, I try to distinguish Buddhist spirituality from that of Hinduism. The purpose of this paper is to clarify what Buddhist spirituality is, and how and why it is foremost imperative that this Buddhist spirituality ought to be differentiated from that of Hinduism for the sake of Buddhism's speedy revival in contemporary India.

§2. Buddhist Spirituality versus Hindu Spirituality

A little over a decade ago, Lokesh Chandra published a remarkable

[1] Included in Sandhong Rimpoche's Felicitation Volume, *In Search of Truth: A Collection of Articles in Honoour of the Fifth Samdhong Rimpoche, Losang Tenzin on his Sixtieth Birthday*, Alumni of Central Institute of Higher Tibetan Studies, Sarnath, Varanasi, 1999.

work entitled as *The Thousand-Armed Avalokiteśvara.*[2] In this book, he advocated a theory that the Buddhist hypostasis of Avalokitasvara was a metamophosis of Brahmā known as lord of the earth (Sahaṃpati) of the Hindu cult. He was brilliant in proving that the phenomenon of Avalokitasvara's multifarious manifestation in Indian iconography is due to the process of assimilation and interiorization[3] exercised by Brahmā's potency over popular deities. In reference to the sections of *mantra, dhāraṇī*, or hymns, in both the *Lotus Sūtra* and the *Pureland Sūtra*,[4] he sees a linkage between Avalokitasvara of Buddhist personification and Brahmā of Hindu's as "the master of logos (*mantra-draṣṭā*), the seer (*avalokitṛ*) of the sound (*svara*), who assimilated Hindu deities (*lokeśvara*) by pronouncement of each sacred hymn (*hṛdaya* or *mantra*) unique to each deity.[5] In this connection, Lokesh Chandra borrowed Alicia Matsunaga's theory that the Buddhist assimilation that worked in Japan to absorb native gods and various other rites into Buddhism began in India, and that the Buddhist theory of assimilation had its origin in the framework of that early philosophy.[6] He invoked in part the potency pertaining to the substratum of the metamorphosis, namely, Brahmā, and in part the Buddhist philosophy of assimilation, such that the transcendent *noumenon* descends into the temporal domain as phenomenal manifestations.[7]

---

[2] The book was published from Indira Gandhi National Center for Arts in Delhi, 1988.

[3] The author explains the term 'interiorization' as follows: "Mythopoiesis is a fundamental process in culture. It is a continuing relationship between 'inside' and 'outside,' There is no 'inside' without an 'outside.' The inside is interiorised and it becomes 'the inside of the inside.' Avalokiteśvara is an exemplification of these vital courses of cultural renewal." *Ibid.*, p. 16.

[4] The *Saddaharmapuṇḍarīka-sūtra* has a section of *Dhāraṇī* as the 26th chapter immediately after the chapter of Samanta-mukha (Avalokitasvara's facing all directions, or multifarious manifestation) as the 25th chapter in the version of Kumārajīva's Chinese translation; whereas. the extant Sanskrit text has this chapter as the 24th and that of *Dhāraṇī* as the 25th. The *Dhāraṇī* section in the Pureland text also indicates a similar meaning that Avalokiteśvara was responsible for introducing popular deities (*loka-īśvara*) into the Buddhist pantheon by pronouncing each of their *dhāraṇīs* which are supposed to avert evils from the person who obtained his wishes as soon as it is recited. Cf. Lokesh Chandra, *ibid.*, p. 31.

[5] *Ibid.*, p. 16.

[6] *Ibid.*, p. 42. Cf. Alicia Matsunaga: *Buddhist Philosophy of Assimilation of the Honji-Suijaku Theory (The Historical Development)*: Tokyo: Sophia University, C.E. Tuttle, 1969.

[7] *Hon-ji Sui-jaku* (*pên-ti ch'ui-chi*) means the theory that the fundamental locus (*pên-ti, noumenon*) descends into the temporal locus as its traces (*ch'ui-chi, phenomena*).

His theory that Avalokitasvara had the potency of Brahmā as assimilator of Hindu deities, however, had another application in explaining an abrupt and speedy replacement of Buddhist cults by those of Hindu's. From Buddhist legend as well as iconographic representation, we know that Śākyamuni was flanked by Indra and Brahmā before he decided to proclaim his Dharma to the world. Thus, interprets Lokesh Chandra that "with the transcendence of Śākyamuni to Amitābha, Indra and Brahmā were transformed into Mahāsthāmaprāpta and Avalokitasvara."[8] Since Brahmā was the Hindu deity, Lord of the Earth, Lokeśvara or Lokanātha (the lord or savior of the world), Avalokitasvara is said, on the one hand, to have assimilated innumerable Hindu deities as a metamophosis of this deity through his multifarious manifestations, while on the other hand, it is also said to have made it easier and swift for these manifestations to change from Buddhist affiliates to become those of Hindu's. He suggests that at some later period, the Hindu deity Śiva was assimilated into Buddhism and gave rise to the name Avalokiteśvara (*avalokita-īśvara*, the lord Avalokita), thereby allowing the emergence of the thousand-armed Bodhisattvas. And so did likewise several other types of images as linked to Hindu iconography, namely, those of one thousand eyes, four faces, eleven faces, a horsehead, a fearless lion head, a blue neck, and so on.[9] By the mid-seventh century when Hsüan-tzang was travelling in India, the Buddhist cult of Avalokiteśvara was already irretrievably entangled with the cults of various Hindu deities. Lokesh Chandra informs that this Avalokiteśvara sometimes appears as a Buddha and at other times as the Hindu deity Īśvara or Maheśvara (Śīva), without clear reason,[10] and that it was a simple switch on the part of the devotees to change from a Buddhist cultic practice to that of

---

[8] Chandra, *op. cit.*, p. 11. In the Pureland iconography, Avalokitasvara (Kuan-shih-yin) and Mahāsthāmaprāpta (Ta-shih-chih) are the members of the triad as Amitābha's acolytes. The two figures are depicted as sublime as Amitābha and are in possession of a similar set of superior marks only ascribed to the Buddhas. Avalokiteśvara is always on the right of Amitābha while Mahāsthāmaprāpta, a little smaller figure, on Amitābha's left side.

[9] For variations of Avalokiteśvara in India, see Gusto Liebert: *Iconographic Dictionary of the Indian Religions, Hinduism-Buddhism-Jainism.* Asian Arts & Archaeology Series No. 5. Delhi: Indian Books Centre, 1976; pp. 29-30.

[10] Chandra. *ibid.*, pp. 15-16; Hsüan-tsang's travel record reveals that he encountered this kind of indiscriminate enshrinement of Kuan-yin in various sites. Cf. *op. cit.*, p. 114, Note.

Hinduism.

I am obliged to question at this juncture as to whether or not there is a difference between Indian Buddhist and Hindu cultic spirituality, because his theory seems to imply that the spiritual basis of the Buddhist cult of Avalokiteśvara should be identified with that of Hindu cult in terms of the potency ascribed to Brahmā and hence to its metamorphosis. In short, his interpretation bears the aforementioned *cliché* and shares the similar thought background. What is the Buddhist spirituality, then, as distinct from the Hindu's? Is it possible to prove whether or not Buddhist cult embodies an independent spiritual basis from that of Hinduism? Although it is not easy to refute his theory within the Indian context of iconography, I think it is possible and easier to do so in view of the East Asian context, because he seems to have missed recognizing the fact that the Indian Buddhist cult of Avalokiteśvara and the East Asian cult of Kuan-yin are not monolithic in spirituality.

§3. *ŚŪNYATĀ* AS FOUNDATION OF CHINESE BUDDHIST SPIRITUALITY

In China, the cultic worship of Kuan-yin Bodhisattva is believed to have begun shortly after Dharmarakṣa's translation of the *Lotus Sūtra* in 286, but most certainly after the more lucid translation of the same text by Kumārajīva in 406 and quickly spread over the divided continent in the north as well as in the south from the fifth century onward.[11] I believe that the dominant cultural force of that early Medieval China was formulated by two major sources of spirituality, one being the insight of *śūnyatā* inculcated in the group of *Prajñāpāramitā Sūtras* and another being Kuan-yin's activist virtue of love and compassion depicted in the *Lotus Sūtra*. It was the strike of ingenuity that these two principles of spirituality were symbolically brought into fusion in Kumārajīva's particular translation, namely: the *Great Prajñā Prayer Sūtra* (*Mahāvidyā-mantra-sūtra, Ta-miao-chou-ching*) and a couple of centuries later, in Hsüan-tzang's translation in 649: the *Wisdom Heart Sūtra* (*Mahā-prajñāpāramitā-*

---

[11] The bibliographical records suggest that there were six translations of the same text, but only three translations ascribed to Dharmarakṣa (*Chengfa-hua-ching,* 286), to Kumārajīva (*Miao-fa-lien-hua-ching*, 406), and Jñānagputa and Dharmagupta (*T'ien-p'in-fa-lien-hua-ching*, 601) are extant. Nāgārjuna quotes this *Sūtra*, more often than any other scriptures in his commentary *Mahāprajñā-pāramitopadeśa-śāstra* (*Ta-chih-tu-lun*) on the *Pañcaviṃśati-sāhasrikā-prajñāpāramitāsūtra* (*Twenty-five-thousand-verse-pan-jo-ching* translatéd by Kumārajīva, 402-412).

hṛdaya-sūtra, Ta-ho-pan-jo-po-lo-mi-to-hsin-ching), both of which are based on an identical text.[12] In the Indian context Kuan-yin Bodhisattva had two different names. The earlier name was Avalokitasvara rendered as Kuan-shih-yin in Chinese (i.e., one who surveys the voices of the world), and this term was, more or less, finalized during the third through sixth century, reflecting the earlier translation period. The later name was Avalokiteśvara, likely posterior to the time when the Hindu deity Śīva was assimilated to the Buddhist holding, and it was rendered by Hsüan-tzang during the seventh century as Kuan-tzŭ-tzai (i.e., one who excels in introspection or lord of illumination), marking the new translation era.[13] In popularity, this Kuan-yin Bodhisattva was perhaps second only to Śākyamuni Buddha and has remained to be the center of cultic devotion among Mahāyāna Buddhist people throughout ages.

Accepting the history of the partial change from Avalokitasvara to Avalokiteśvara, we ought to notice that the *Prajñā-hṛdaya-sūtra* (*Pan-jo-hsin-ching*)[14] made the most significant moment for the history of

---

[12] The two versions ascribed to Hsüan-tsang and Kumārajīva are not only very *close* in their use of terms and expressions, but also precisely identical in their meaning as "quintessential of the *Prajñāpāramitā* insight." It cannot be refuted that the *Great Wisdom Prayer Sūtra* (*Ta-ming-chou-ching*) was Kumārajīva's translation, because of its *verbatim* identity between this version of the *Heart Sūtra* and a portion of the second chapter of the *Larger Prajñāpāramitā Sūtra* of his translation, known as *Ta-p'in-pan-jo-ching* or the *25,000 śloka Prajñāpāramitā-sūtra* in Sanskrit. On the other hand, trained in Sanskrit and Buddhist Studies in India and experienced in the task of many translations, Hsüan-tsang had no reason to adopt Kumārajīva's use of words and expressions for his version. It is extremely interesting and enticing, therefore, to know how and why similar usage of words and expressions should take place in their respective versions of the *Heart Sūtra*, despite their different centuries and their different cultural orientations. As to the origin of the *Hṛdaya Sūtra*, two alternative hypotheses ought to be formulated. One alternative is that a Sanskrit original was composed in India, somewhere from AD 150 through 250 after Nāgārjuna composed the *Ta-chih-tu-lun*, provided that Chih-chen's translation *Mahāprajñāpāramitā Dhāraṇī(?)* in 288 was based on that original. The other alternative is that if the original text of which the Sanskrit manuscript discovered in Nepal was a copy, it may have been a Sanskritization of a Chinese text retransmitted to that subcontinent. In this case, Conze's theory may hold in that the text may have been composed around 350.

[13] Precisely speaking, the history of Chinese translations ought to be analyzed into five periods, but here I refer to the period of Older Tradition represented by Kumārajīva in the fifth century and the period of New Translation initiated by Hsüan-tsang during the 7th century. 'Kuang-shih-yin' is found in the *Chêng-fa-hua-ching* (10 fasc.) translated by Dharmarakṣa in AD 286; Taishō. 9 (No. 263).

[14] This shortest scripture of all Buddhist texts consists of only 262 Chinese characters. Since Hsüan-tsang did not incorporate it in his super-

Buddhist culture in China, because in this Sūtra Bodhisattva Kuan-shih-yin or Kuan-tzŭ-tsai is made to be the chief expounder of the *Prajñā* insight. In all the texts of *Parjñāpāramitā* literature, there is none other than this single text in which Kuan-shih-yin appears to be the chief exponent of the teaching. And this same Bodhisattva is depicted in the 25th Chapter of the *Lotus Sūtra*, namely, "Kuan-shih-yin's Multifarious Manifestation" (*samanta-mukha*, literally, "facing all directions") as champion guardian and Buddhist savior.[15] In this *Lotus Sūtra*, he inherited the so-called activist virtue[16] to exercise his two-fold expediency, *Prajñā* (wisdom) and *Karuṇā* (compassion), to help humans escape from sufferings for the sake of salvation in lieu of Śākyamuni after his Parinirvāṇa. In the *Prajñā Heart Sūtra*, this activist Kuan-yin Bodhisattva was re-cast, for the first time, as an important part of the scriptural scenario of the *Prajñā* doctrine, namely, as the chief exponent of the transcendent insight of *śūnyatā* and the practice of *prajñā* introspection. What was crucial to the Kuan-yin cult in China was the fact that the insight of *śūnyatā* embodied in the *Prajñāpāramitā-sūtras* has always been linked with the Kuan-yin personification of love and compassion in terms of "skill in means" (*upāya-kauśalya*), and not with a Hindu spiritual basis of Brahmā. I am obliged to challenge Lokesh

---

voluminous, all-inclusive *Great Prajñāpāramitā Sūtra* of 600 fascicles (*Ta-pan-jo-po-lo-mi-to-ching*), he must have regarded it as an independent text. There are eight extant versions of the *Prajñā Heart Sūtra* which are comprised in the 8th volume of the Taishō Tripiṭaka New Edition, and if some non-extant texts are added, the number of its versions is said to go up to as many as thirteen or fourteen, reflecting the enormous popularity of this *Heart Sūtra* in Chinese Buddhist tradition.

[15] The 25th Chapter of the *Lotus Sūtra* begins with the Buddha's reply to Akṣayamati Bodhisattva regarding the meaning of the name Avalokitasvara. The reply points primarily to love and compassion as Kuan-yin's epithet, since he is ever alert to the imploring voices of all sufferers and, should they wholeheartedly chant his name, beseeching him for deliverance, he will come to help them to be free from their suffering. In this chapter, Avalokitasvara is depicted as an activist Bodhisattva engaged in actual and practical tasks of savior with the transcendent faculty of immediately perceiving all voices and in no time, coming to rescue all callers.

[16] Nāgārjuna explains Mahāyāna Buddhist activism in his voluminous commentary *Mahā-prajñāpāramitopadeśa-śāstra* or simply *Upadeśaśāstra* (*Ta-chih-tu-lun*, 100 fasc.) on the *25,000 Śloka-prajñāpāramitā-sūtra*.. He differentiates the love and compassion of Buddhas and Bodhisattvas from those of humans in terms of ultimate effectuation. What is required for the superior virtue of love and compassion (*ta-tz'ŭ and ta-pei*) is that each practitioner not only wishes well for others but also should help them realize it, exercising his skill in means (*upāyakauśalya*). This is the Mahāyāna Buddhist activism distinguished from the orthodox passive virtue of mere wishing or prayer.

Chandra's theory by asserting that in East Asian cultural context, the essential core of Kuan-yin cult was not Brahmā's potency but the insight of *Śūnyatā* embodied in the *Prajñāpāramitā* scriptures.

I am obliged to introduce two factors that can apply to assist my challenge. First, by the seventh century, Chinese Buddhist thought had already set in motion the subsequent development of the East Asian Kuan-yin cult by developing the vow of "Bodhisattva Ideal," so-called vow of self-abnegation for love and compassion toward all other beings, "the vow not to cross to Nirvāṇa for himself, holding mid-stream till all other beings have been successfully rescued and have crossed to the yonder shore." Simultaneously, Chinese Buddhists developed their own image as an effeminated figure during the T'ang dynasty, perhaps, around the 8th to 9th century, according to their own cultural and aesthetic taste, despite the fact that some Indian male forms of Avalokiteśvara were available to Chinese Buddhist worship.[17] Ever since, this feminine form of the Kuan-yin image, often called "goddess of mercy," has remained to be the dominant figure of Kuan-yin Bodhisattva in China and, from the ninth century onwards, spread to the entire continent as well as eastward to Korea and Japan. As the form of this Kuan-yin moved eastward, further new variations came to appear as the white-robed Kuan-yin, Kuan-yin holding a willow leaf, Kuan-yin with a fishing basket, and the Kuan-yin of easy child-bearing, among others. This last figure, holding a baby in her arm, was sometimes called "Maria Kannon" in Medieval Japan. However that may be, my point of view is that the sudden appearance of a female Kuan-yin during the T'ang dynasty in China came from within the *Prajñāpāramitā* tradition in which the spirit of the *Prajñā Sūtras* was personified as the mother of Buddhas (*fo-mu*) and worshipped by the followers of late Mahāyāna Buddhim in India as well as in Tibet.[18]

---

[17] The Hindu deity Śiva was assimilated into Buddhism and gave rise to the name Avalokiteśvara (*avalokita-īśvara*, the lord Avalokita), thereby allowing the emergence of the thousand-armed Bodhisattvas. Lokesh Chandra asserts that "this Avalokiteśvara sometimes appears as a Buddha and at other times as the Hindu deity Iśvara or Maheśvara (Śiva), without clear reason." So came to being several types of Kuan-yin images that were linked to Hindu iconography, like those endowed with one thousand arms, thousand eyes, four faces, eleven faces, a horse-head, a fearless lion head, a blue neck, and so on.

[18] In China, calling the *Prajñāpāramitāsūtras* as "Mother of Buddhas" (仏母) began to be seen during the later half of the first millennium, for instance, Dānapāla's translation: *Fo-mu-ch'u-shêng-san-fa-ts'ang-pan-jo-po-lo-mi-to-ching* (around 980) [Taishō. 8 (No. 228) 25 fasc.] equivalent to the 4th lecture assembly of Hsüan-tsang's *Great Pan-jo-ching* of 600 fascicles, and mostly parallel with the extant *8000 Śloka Prajñā Sūtra* translated as *Tao-hsing-pan-jo-ching* (10 fasc.) by Chih-lü-chia-chen, Late Han; *Ta-ming-tu-ching* (6 fasc.) by Chih-ch'ien of Wu as *Moho-pan-jo-ch'ao-ching* (5 fasc);

§4. MAHĀYĀNA CRITICAL SPIRITUALITY EPITOMIZED IN *PRAJÑĀ HEART SŪTRA*

Traditionally there have been two different ways of looking at the *Heart Sūtra*, but as my primary focus of interest, I advocate a remarkably new interpretation proposed by Edward Conze rather than traditional interpretation. By traditional interpretation, I mean two general views: According to one, the *Heart Sūtra* is regarded as an exoteric open teaching, while according to another, it is an esoteric secret teaching.[19] The former interpretation asserts that the *Heart Sūtra* inculcates the Mahāyāna insight of *śūnyatā* (voidness or emptiness) and the practice of *Prajñāpāramitā* introspection through an exoteric method, and as evident in the initial half of the text, the dialectical treatise culminates in the repudiation of reality from the four holy Truths. The latter interpretation asserts that the text promotes the esoteric teaching as part of Tantric Buddhism, because the ending passage includes an esoteric prayer formula (*mantra*).

Like Conze, however, I am inclined to interpret the original intent of the *Heart Sūtra* as re-stating the Buddhist Truth in terms of *dialectical negation*, irrespective of the five *Skandhas*, the twelve *Āyatanas*, the eighteen *Dhātus*, the twelve-link of causation, or the four holy Truths. I agree with Prof. Conze's view that the *Heart Sūtra* meant to be the second turning of the Wheel of the *Buddha-dharma* in terms of Mahāyāna spiritual salvation in parallel with Śākyamuni's initial turning of the *Dharma*-wheel.

In his article of 1948 entitled as "Text, Sources, and Bibliography of the *Prajñāpāramitā-hṛdaya*," Conze analyzed the structure of the *Heart Sūtra* into seven sections and probed their counterparts in the *Pañcaviṃśatisāhasrikā-prajñāpāramitā-sūtra,* so-called *Ta-p'in-pan-jo-ching* in Chinese.[20] He asserted that all the words, phrases, and lines of the short text were extracted from the larger text. Accordingly, this *Heart Sūtra* is meant to be, as Conze says, "a restatement of the four holy Truths for beginners on the method of

---

Shao-p'in-pan-jopo-lo-mi-ching (25 fasc,) by Kumārajīva]; *Fo-mu-hsiao-tzu-pan-jo-ching* (1 fasc. 1000); *Ārya-prajñāpāramitā-saṃgraha-kārikā-vivaraṇa* (4 fasc.) translated by Dānapāla, 980, and so forth.

[19] Komine, Yahiko: "Re-examination of the *Prajñā-Hṛdaya-Sūtra*" (*Hannya Shingyō Sai-kō*), *Mikkyō-gaku Kenkyū* (*Study on Tantric Buddhism*).

[20] *Ta-p'in-pan-jo-ching* (*The 25000 Śloka Prajñāpāramitā-sūtra*) translated by Kumārajīva, 402-412. Taishō. 8, (No, 223).

bearing this teaching in mind as well as on the spiritual advantage of following it."[21] I think that the traditional textual studies and interpretation of the *Heart Sūtra* has not hitherto sufficiently explored the line of Conze's interpretation. As a result, because of their traditional preoccupation, the historical perspective of the textual origin has mostly escaped from their attention.

Now, I am obliged to bring in Prof. Conze's assertion that the *Heart Sūtra* is not Tantric. In order to defend his point of view, he refers to the early Buddhist usage in Pāli Suttas. He points to the fact that we find a similar usage in the *Niddessa*[22] and Pāli commentaries, wherein *paññā* (*prajñā* or 'insight' in Sanskrit) is called *mantra*. Further, he points to one of the earliest Saṃyutta Nikāya in Pāli, that "In the First Turning of the Wheel of the Law" (*Dhamma-cakka-ppavattana-vaggo*), the knowledge of the four holy Truths is equated to *vijjā* (*vidyā* or knowledge or wisdom in Sanskrit).[23] In both of these texts, the term *mantā* (*mantra* in Sanskrit) or *vijjā* (*vidyā* in Sanskrit) is not intended to mean "a secret, mysterious lore of magical potency which can be compressed into a magical formula, a spell." Rather, the term is intended to mean "the knowledge of the four holy Truths which is the fundamental insight (*vijjā*) of the Buddha." In parallel to this first turning of the *Dharma* wheel, the main subject of which is the four holy Truths,[24] Conze points out that the Mahāyāna theorists regarded the *Heart Sūtra* as "the second turning of the wheel of the law."[25]

My purpose to discuss the *Heart Sūtra* here is two-fold. First, I hold that the Kuan-yin Bodhisattva who became the center of the cult in China was not a metamorphosis of Brahmanical magical potency. While Lokesh Chandra argued that only Avalokiteśvara as a metamorphosis of Brahmā could have successfully accomplished assimilation of Hindu deities, I disagree with his extension of this metamorphosis to the East Asian cultural context. Second, from the foregoing analysis of the *Heart Sūtra*, I hold that Avalokiteśvara or

---

[21] Edward Conze: "Text, Sources, and Bibliography of the *Prajñāpāramitā-hṛdaya*," *Journal of Royal Asiatic Society*. 1948, p. 47.

[22] Of the two extant commentaries of the *Sutta-Nipāta*, the *Niddesa* is the earlier one, ascribed to Sāriputta, a direct disciple of Śākyamuni, and the *Paramatthajotikā* is the later one ascribed to Buddhaghoṣa of the 5th century. Unlike the latter, the *Nidessa* is confined to some parts of the *Sutta Nipāta*.

[23] Conze: *op.cit.*, p. 46. *Dhamma-cakka-ppavattana-vaggo*: *The Initial Turning of the Wheel of Dharma.*

[24] *Ibid.*, p. 48.

[25] *Ibid.*, 47-48.

Kuan-yin Bodhisattva was meant to embody the insight or knowledge of the four holy Truths in terms of No-self as *Vidyā*, and the second insight or knowledge of the four holy Truths in terms of *Śūnyatā* as *Mantra*. Because of different historical and social conditions, the Kuan-yin Bodhisattva in China and East Asia should be understood in terms of the dual (not double) negations and not in terms of the Brahmanical Hindu esoteric assertion or potency.

How then should we view the two faces of Kuan-yin Bodhisattva, one as dispenser of love and compassion, as depicted in the 25th Chapter of the *Lotus Sūtra*, and the other as expounder of the insight of *Śūnyatā*, as depicted in the *Heart Sūtra*? I think that the *Heart Sūtra* provides a point of reconciliation in terms of two human requirements. *First*: Life in general carries varieties of suffering, for which humans have continually sought solutions within the material environment of external nature and within the immaterial inner sphere of human nature. In this human context, Kuan-yin Bodhisattva's vow and skill-in-means are directed toward the fulfillment of the mundane needs of individuals and human-kind in the eradication of suffering and the realization of well-being. *Second*: Kuan-yin Bodhisattva's insight of the four holy Truths is two-fold: (1) the eradication of false conviction in one's self and about things believed to belong to that self (*first negation*), and (2) the eradication of false conviction about the reality of elements of the five aggregates (second negation: *śūnyatā* of the aggregates).

In his article on the *Heart Sūtra*, Conze calls attention to the section which immediately follows the four holy Truths, and he traces in the *larger Prajñā Sūtra*, among others, two important points of discussion on the Bodhisattva's insight of *Śūnyatā*. First, (1) that there is "no attainment" in actual fact, because "attainment" conceptually implies duality in itself, like the duality between "things to be attained" and "an agent of attaining." And second, (2) that there is "no desire for any attainment" on the part of the Bodhisattva, because of his insight of non-duality and hence non-attainment.[26] Here, I must call attention to the fact that a dual negation of "neither nor" underlies the above two points; there is neither "an object of attainment," nor is there "a desire of attainment" in reference to the subjective and objective spheres. This dual negation is extended to encompass loving and loved, knowing and known, acting and acted upon, and so on. From extensive comments made

---

[26] *Ibid.*, p. 45. Literally, it means "there is neither wisdom to acquire nor is there a desire for acquiring it" in Hsüan-tsang's translation.

by Nāgārjuna in his *Ta-chih-tu-lun* (*Mahāprajñāpāramitopadeśa-śāstra*) on this insight, I understand that this dual negation is the heart of the Bodhisattva's vow of self-abnegation to enact his love and compassion for the sake of others.

§5. JAPANESE BUDDHIST CRITIQUE OF HINDU RELIGIOUS THOUGHT

Nearly a decade ago, a revolutionary movement of Buddhist thought has begun to evolve in some Japanese academia under the name of "critical Buddhism" (*'hihan-bukkyō'*). It is an intellectual movement to scrutinize non-Buddhist thought elements from the accepted system of traditional Buddhist doctrines. Although it is still too early to determine the validity of this movement, some of the criteria set forth for this movement seem to be worthy of paying attention, especially because the movement has been a part of finding the way to rectify the cause of social injustice that has continued in practice in Japanese society for some centuries. In 1979, the chief delegate of Japanese Buddhists made an irresponsible statement at the third World Religious Conference for Peace, asserting that Japanese society had no social problem of injustice like that of inequality or discrimination. This was not true in the light of historical facts, because social segregation of some communities of Japan from the general population has been continually practiced, and in the matters of profession, marriage, and social association, their individual members have been suffering from unequal treatment and discrimination by prejudice. Since such hidden practices of injustice are clearly against the spirit of the Japanese constitution, some Buddhist schools have been compelled to examine their past teachings and practices as to whether their sectarian tenets transgressed the spirit of humanity of the constitution.[27]

The primary purpose of this movement was to scrutinize pseudo-Buddhist elements out of what has been hitherto believed as authentic Buddhist teachings. In opposition to the general consensus that the doctrine of "original enlightenment" and the doctrine of "Buddha-nature" (*tathāgatagarbha*) are the foundation of Japanese Buddhism, the leading scholars of this movement suspected that the Japanese uncritical acceptance of these doctrines may have been the primary cause of their failure not to recognize the existence

---

[27] Cf. William Bodiford: "Zen and the Art of Religious Prejudice," *Japanese Journal of Religious Studies*, 23/1-2, 1996.

of social injustice and of their inability of properly facing the matter of its rectification. Thus, two agendas seem to stand out as central to their task of the movement:[28] (1) critical examination of the doctrine of "original enlightenment" inculcated in the *Mahāyānaśraddhotpāda-śāstra* as well as (2) the doctrine of "universal Buddha nature" introduced in the *Śrīmālādevīsiṃhanāda-sūtra* and *Mahāyānaparinirvāṇa-sūtra,* and later on, theorized in the *Mahāyānottaratantra-śāstra, Mahāyāna-sūtrālaṅkāra*, etc.

According to the scholars of the movement, "Original Enlightenment" is defined as "fundamental enlightenment that transcends the phenomenal domain"; it is "universally inherent in all humans from the beginning and hence permanent;" but unless one is awakened of it, it "merely undergoes the cycles of arising and perishing as phenomena." From a superficial looking at this definition, since "original enlightenment" is universally inherent in every individual, the doctrine appears to ascertain the principle of equality, but this is an illusion, they say. The teaching is the sole villain that preserved an element of discrimination.[29] For the reason of this condemnation, they argue that the doctrine ascertains the equality of all individuals in reference to the static transcendent reality (*tathatā* or noumenon) which is universally inherent, and yet the dynamic active *ālayavijñāna* (phenomenal mind or consciousness) of each individual manifests itself as myriad variations due to its external impediments and inner Karmic effectuations. The *Mahāyāna-śraddhotpāda-śāstra (ta-ch'êng-ch'i-hsin-lun)* is generally believed today to have been written in China, but theoretically, it is closely related to some of the Indian Yogācāra textual sources on the subject of *tathāgatagarbha*.[30] Not only Chinese but also Japanese Buddhist thought was enormously influenced by this textual theory. Thus, the leaders of the critical movement argue that the doctrine of original enlightenment was uncritically emphasized as basis of universal salvation, while the discriminatory passages were ignored

---

[28] For best references, see Kenshō Hakamaya's *Hongaku-shisō Hihan: A Critique of the thought of Original Enlightenment*), Tokyo: Daizō Shuppan Ltd., 1989, and Shiro Matsumoto's *Engi-to-Kū (Dependent Origination and Śūnyatā*), Tokyo: Daizō Shuppan Ltd., 1989.

[29] Hakamaya: *Ibid.*, p. 142

[30] The Chinese Tripiṭaka recorded its author as Aśvaghoṣa and translated by Paramārtha (499-569) and the earliest record of this translation is in the *Records of the Three Treasures according to the Imperial Successions* (15 fasc.), mainly comprising the records of the translations from Late Han through Sui dynasty (220-597). Obviously, this Aśvaghoṣa is a different person from the Buddhist poet, author of the *Buddhacaritam.*

or overlooked as an exception or an exclusion with respect to the cases of Icchantikas who are regarded either to have no nature of enlightenment or to meet no future opportunity of enlightenment even despite of it.[31]

The heart of the problem, they say, is an uncritical acceptance of the doctrine of original enlightenment as an ideological premise within their particular indigenous social and cultural environment. For instance, in ancient India, the Upaniṣadic principle of *brahman* or *ātman* was philosophically evolved as ultimate reality within the indigenous social and cultural environment, and though the idea of *ātman* was theorized to be the *a-priori* principle of all humans,, the four Varṇas were also theorized to be the *a-priori* order of society. Originally, Buddhism was one that challenged this established ideology by posing a new insight of dependent origination (*pratītya-samutpāda*). Buddhism challenged the Brāhmaṇism that legitimized the principle of *brahman* or *ātman* as ultimate truth, on the one hand, and yet on the other hand, also legitimized the original order of the caste system in terms of inequal social and cultural status under the Vedic and Upaniṣadic premise. Śākyamuni challenged these two thoughts by posing the principle of no-self (*anātman*) and a caste-free religious community of Bhikṣus. In analogy to this Indian example, the scholars argue in defense of their critical scrutiny as to whether Japanese Buddhists accepted "original enlightenment" as their ideological premise to support their indigenous social and cultural tradition and thereby unawaringly imposed

[31] Here '*buddha-dhātu*' is rendered as "Buddha-nature," but literally it means the locus of Buddhahood. Generally, two interpretations are given: (1) The *Nirvāṇa-sūtra* teaches that "All sentient beings have Buddha nature as inherent in each individual's body," advocating the universalist theory that when humans exhaust all defilements, they become Buddha. The Sūtra, however, contradicts itself by immediately saying that the Icchantika is excluded. [The *Mahāparinirvāṇa-sūtra* translated by Dharmakṣema (385-433); Taisho. 12, 404c] (2) The Icchantikas also possess Buddha-nature, but it is enveloped within a thick shell like a flee which created its hard compartment and hence could not come out unless the shell is broken open. The Buddha nature too cannot break free from the body of Icchantika because of his wrong Karma. It follows that until his cycle of rebirth comes to an end, he is unable to obtain the cause of realizing enlightenment. [*Ibid*., p. 419b] 'Icchantika' means "one who is in possession of desires," etymologically referring to the Lokāyatas. In Buddhist literature, however, the term refers to those who lack a possibility of enlightenment, though one is in possession of Buddha-nature, but no opportunity to realize it. The Wei-shih school admitted such an exception, whereas T'ien-t'ai, Hua-yen and other Mahāyāna schools did not admit it. Thus, the matter of Icchantika became a subject of intense debates between the two camps during the medieval China and Japan.

social injustice upon some groups of Japanese.

The second point of their critique is the doctrine of Buddha-nature or *tathāgatagarbha*. In this regard, I ought to make a brief comment on their claim that Buddhist spirituality in India was invariably affected by Hindu influence in the course of historical passage, and that it eventually succumbed to Hindu influence in developing Buddhist thought in the fashion of '*dhātu-vāda*.' According to one of the leading scholars of the movement, '*dhātu-vāda*' means a doctrine of a singular reality that produces multifarious phenomena as their foundation *(dhātu)*, or simply a theory of existential monism or that of fundamental reality.[32] Thus, *dhātu-vāda* is a theory that advocates "the singular reality as foundation of all things," and it was this type of the Upaniṣadic doctrine, namely, Brahman and Ātman, that Śākyamuni himself criticized as his main target of repudiation. They argue that there is, in fact, a good deal of similarity between the thought of *tathāgatagarbha* and the Upaniṣadic philosophy. It follows that the theory of *tathāgatagarbha* itself ought to be critically examined, and that whatever non-Buddhist thought elements ought to be brought forth as target of critical Buddhist spirituality.

§6. DIALECTICAL NEGATION AS BUDDHIST CRITICAL SPIRITUALITY

Returning to Lokesh Chandra's thesis in which he refers to Alicia Matsunaga's theory that the principle of '*Honji Sujaku*' (*Pên-ti Ch'ui-chi*) which worked in assimilation of Japanese indigenous deities to Buddhist holding had already worked in ancient India in similar way. As regards to the theoretical basis of her theory, Matsunaga calls attention to the *Lotus Sūtra* in which she shows the dual structure separated as the level of transcendent and absolute (*paramārtha-satya*) and the level of phenomenal and relative (*saṃvṛti-satya*) in parallel with the original trans-historical Buddha (*pên-fo*) and the manifested historical Buddha Śākyamuni (*chi-fo*).[33] This structural division was further theorized in the later esoteric doctrines respectively as Vairocana Buddha with the transcendent

---

[32] Cf. Matsumoto: "Possibility for the Critique of Sectarian Zen Study" ('Hihan-shūgaku-no-Kanōsei') – Critical Buddhism and a Critique upon the Tathāgatagarbha Thought, *Shūgaku-to-Genzai* (*A Record of the Open Lecture Series sponsored by Sōtō School Institute*), No. 2; October 1998, pp. 1-118; Matsumoto: *Engi-to-Kū*, *op. cit.*, p. 67 ff.

[33] *Ibid.*, p. 110 f, p. 107 f, p. 211 ff.

body (*dharma-kāya*, *pên-ti-shên*) and the manifested body reflected in the mind of humans as the shadow of Vairocana (*chia-ch'ih/ch'ui-chi-shên*).[34] According to Sêng-chao (374-414), a Chinese scholar monk of the Madhyamaka philosophy and disciple of Kumārajīva, it is said that though the origin and the manifested are different, they are in unthinkable oneness, because without the origin (*pên*) there is no manifestation (*chi*), nor is there any origin without the manifestation.[35] Matsunaga thus probed her thesis that the theoretical basis of Buddhist assimilation of local deities was the dual structure of transcendent and phenomenal and the philosophical negation which underlies it as essential to the Buddhist insight expressed as *prajñā (wisdom)* or *śūnyatā (voidness)*, or dependent co-arising (*pratītyasamutpāda*), or that which is as it is (*tathatā*).

When Buddhism entered new lands whose culture is not advanced, it has always accompanied the transmission of culture into the areas. When it entered a land already culturally advanced, it has transmitted actual Indian gods and also the method of transforming them into Buddhist teaching, whether in Tibet, China, or Japan. Matsunaga exemplifies this process in reference to the innumerable Kuan-yin manifestations by reiterating that the method of assimilation relied on the basic philosophical negation of Early Buddhism and Abhidharma.[36] In the history of Buddhist teachings, the negation of reality has been done twice. The first case was negation of the reality of empirical self on the basis of the Skandhas of sensory and mental elements. Here, the pscyho-physical elements are regarded as real (*dharma-svabhāva*), but a human person is considered unreal (*anātman*). A human is as unreal as a cart which, when broken down into its component parts (wheels, axle, frame, etc.), is after all only a name. This was the position of the orthodox insight of *dharma-svabhāva*.[37] As the second step of negation, the Mahāyāna insight of *Śūnyatā* repudiated the reality of these psycho-physical elements or *dharmas* (*dharma-niḥsvabhāva=śūnyatā*).[38]

I found an interesting parallel between the view of Japanese scholars who have launched the movement of critical scrutiny and Matsunaga's insight. While the Abhidharmists pursued the nature and function of *dharmas*, they were unawaringly falling into the

---

[34] *Ibid.*, p. 213.

[35] *Ibid.*, p. 106.

[36] *Ibid.*, p. 59.

[37] Absence of reality for the existence of an individual person and existence of the reality of *dharmas* (*jên-kung fa-yu*).

[38] *Absence of reality of dharma* (*fa-kung*).

so-called *dhātu-vāda* pattern, because they were compelled to hypothesize the dual domains as (1) phenomenal locus where multiple *dharmas* arise and perish due to causality and (2) trans-phenomenal locus consisting of a collective totality of *dharmas* as foundation, which is called *dhātu.*[39] This Abhidharma system, once again, bears a similar pattern as that of the Upaniṣadic system of reality. And this was one of the major reasons that Mahāyāna Buddhists launched a movement through the group of *Prajñāpāramitā* scriptures, repudiating the reality of *dharmas*. Matsunaga remarks, "Some Mādhyamika scholars began to cling to a false view of *śūnyatā* endowing it with a reality or making it into another type of *ātman*, so this philosophy too fell into the same type of extreme that it had been originally formulated to combat.[40] She points out that "the type of developing denial of previous system is similar to the Indian *neti neti*, and it was the method by which Buddhism was able to maintain its dynamism combating the *natural human tendency* to create static dogma.[41] [The *italic* is this writer's.] Although Matsunaga misinterpreted 'Upaniṣadic *neti neti*' as similar to Buddhist negation,[42] she, at least, managed to convey her insight. In similar tone, the scholars of critical Buddhism in Japan emphasize Śākyamuni's teaching of "dependent origination" to have diametrically opposed to and repudiated the Brahmanical view of *ātman* as universal foundation and sole reality. Now, since the doctrine of *tathāgatagarbha* is understood to have been a *dhātu-vāda*, it was what precisely Śākyamuni intended to critically repudiate. In this respect, Lokesh Chandra's theory may be partially true that Chinese as well as Japanese Buddhist interpretations fell into the pattern of the Upaniṣadic philosophy of *dhātu-vāda* and thus promoted the cultic assimilation of their indigenous gods and spirits. But as Matsunaga stresses, the moment of Buddhist assimilation derived

[39] Matsumoto: *op.cit.*, pp. 5-6.

[40] *Ibid.*, p. 71.

[41] *Ibid.*, p. 73

[42] Matsunaga, author of the book, mixed up the Buddhist negation and the Upaniṣaadic negation of '*neti neti*' here, although her interpretation is not too far because '*tathatā*' is almost parallel with '*ātman*' of the Upaaniṣadic philosophy. This is the ground that the Japanese academics denounce the doctrine of the *Mahāyāna-śraddhotpāda-śāstra* as non-Buddhistic. In the Upaniṣadic as well as Śaṇkara's negation, the existence of Ātman is dogmatically presupposed as the universal reality of all phenomena, and the negation is directed only to the conceptual expressions of language on the basis that language does not cope with that reality. In contrast, the Buddhist and Mādhyamika negation is intended to repudiate the existence of that *ātman* itself.

from the philosophical negation underlying the insight of *śūnyatā* or *tathatā*. I repeat, it is rather the Buddhist critical spirituality of *Prajñā* that repudiates any form of *dhātu-vāda* as major force of assimilation, and not the Brahmanical magical potency ascribed to Hindu deity Brahmā.

§7. Conclusion

The history of Buddhist revival in India has only been a century since Anagarika Dhammapāla organized Mahā Bodhi Society in 1891. Buddhist population in India today is estimated still below one percent. From the point of view of contemporary speed of global economic, social, and political changes, Buddhist revival in India is a staggeringly slow phenomenon. As far as I see it, what is most essential to a real and speedy revival of Buddhism in India is decisive extrication, on the part of Buddhists, from the prejudice that Buddhism is a part of Hindu religion and culture. Attending academic conferences and exchanging arguments with Indian scholars, I have received a distinct impression time and again that the *cliché* in question has never been critically examined by them. In this respect, therefore, I have introduced some recent movement of Japanese Buddhist academics who are steering the course of self-criticism. A parallel between Buddhism and Hinduism is evident as far as the pattern of *dhātu-vāda* is concerned, because it is not only a pattern of Indian intellectual phenomena but also that of everywhere in the world as natural human tendency to create static dogmas, i.e., *dhātu-vāda*. I am convinced that the method, by which Buddhism was once able to maintain its dynamism combating this natural human tendency, ought to be reinstated in Indian academic practice just as it has been attempted or experimented in some other countries. Witnessing on-going religious, cultural and ethnic conflicts resulting in tragic genocide and atrocity in various regions of the world, we are aware how fragile and dangerous it is to advocate any form of human idealism or religious ultimate without critical spirituality.

ARTICLE THIRTEEN

KUAN-YIN BODHISATTVA CULT AND AMITĀBHA BUDDHA[1]

§1. INTRODUCTION

In the Mahāyāna branch of Buddhism, Kuan-yin (觀音) or Kuan-shih-yin (觀世音) is known to be the celestial Bodhisattva personified as the supreme virtue of Buddhist love and compassion. In reference, the name is also identical with that of Kuan-tzŭ-tzai (観自在). These two names were translated respectively from two Sanskrit compounds, namely, Avalokitasvara and Avalokiteśvara (*avalokita-īśvara*). The use of kuan-yin or *kuan-shih-yin* was, more or less, finalized during the third through sixth century, reflecting the earlier period of translation (旧訳). During the seventh century, Hsüan-tzang (玄奘), the renowned scholar monk of the early T'ang dynasty, introduced the latter translation *Kuan-tzŭ-tzai* (観自在), ushering the new translation era (新訳).[2] In popularity, this Bodhisattva was, perhaps, second only to Śākyamuni Buddha and has remained to be the center of cultic devotion among Mahāyāna Buddhist people throughout ages. In Pureland tradition, he is one of the two acolytes of Amitābha Buddha together with Mahāsthāmaprāpta (大勢至) and has remained to be part of the Pureland Trio enshrinement (浄土三尊) throughout history. In the esoteric Buddhist tradition (真言), his image was already transformed before its transmission to China as manifold due to Hindu cultic influence. Many of these forms were forgotten today, and so were the meaning of such remote legacies, while some were absorbed by and incorporated in the popular Kuan-yin cults of later periods.[3] In this paper, I consider those

---

[1] Presented at the 9th International Conference of Shin Buddhist Studies, Honolulu, Aug. 23-25, 1999.

[2] Precisely speaking, the history of Chinese translations ought to be analyzed into five periods, but here I refer to the period of Older Tradition represented by Kumārajīva (旧訳) in the fifth century and the period of New Translation initiated by Hsüan-tsang (新訳) during the 7th century. '光世音' is found in the *Chêng-fa-hua-ching* (「正法華経」 in 10 fasc.) translated by Dharmarakṣa in AD 286; Taishō. 9 (No. 263).

[3] In Esoteric Shingon tradition, Kuan-yin Bodhisattva was depicted in

surviving popular forms of the Kuan-yin cult collectively as an independent religious phenomenon apart from the Pureland and esoteric Shingon traditions.

Since the 1960's and onward, we have continued to witness "inter-religious dialogue" as has been in vogue. And because of the recent tragic events of human atrocity and barbarism derived from religious, cultural, or racial difference, inter-religious and cultural dialogue ought to be an ever more demanded enterprise in the future for discovering human spirituality. In fact, human spirituality is my haunting question. We humans have different religious traditions, theistic as well as non-theistic, and all forms of cultic religions. But what is the ultimate criterion, on the basis of which we can safely determine a given phenomenon to be evidence of "proper human spirituality"?

The cult of Kuan-yin Bodhisattva is a major religious phenomenon within the Mahāyāna Buddhist world that has endured for two millennia. In ancient India, it was one of those Buddhist cults which arose by centering Amitābha, Maitreya, and so on. Its origination was likely contemporaneous with the general trend of the Hindu Bhakti movement. The beginning of the Kuan-yin cult in China was somewhat obscure as to when and how. The popularity must have spontaneously grown along with the developmental course of scriptural translations. My specific question is: What was the Buddhist spirituality of a Kuan-yin cult as differentiated from the spirituality of the Hindu Bhakti movement? What qualified this cult to be called properly as Buddhist spirituality in China? Or in this matter, how can the spirituality of a Buddhist cult like that of Kuan-yin Bodhisattva be determined in comparison with that of other religious traditions and contemporary cultic phenomena? Encountering the multi-religious and multi-cultural world today, we ought to prepare for answering these questions. In this paper, I address to these matters as an insider of Buddhism, but an outsider of the Shin-shū tradition. Hence, my argument may be

---

six forms of manifestation in accordance with the six cycles of life course and states of existence (六道輪廻), at each of which the Bodhisattva is deemed to teach the Dharma and administer salvation for respective residents of hell, hungry ghost, animal, Asura, human, and gods (六道：地獄、餓鬼、畜生、阿須羅、人間、天人). There are a set of six Kuan-yins, that of 15 Kuan-yins, that of 25 Kuan-yins, and so on. For instance, one school advocated the set of Original Kuan-yin (正観音), Thousand-armed Kuan-yin (千手観音), Fearless lion Kuan-yin (獅子無畏観音), Horse-headed Kuan-yin (馬頭観音), Eleven-faced Kuan-yin (十一面観音), Kuan-yin with Cakravartain's Wheel (如意輪観音), and so on.

raised from the general Buddhist point of view unbound to the Shin-shū tradition.

In the Pureland tradition, Kuan-yin Bodhisattva remained to be consistent with the Pureland scriptures by being a sublime male figure as Amitābha-Buddha's deputy dispenser of love and compassion, and carried on the stature of dignity and the aura of spirituality as close as that of Amitābha. The image of the popular Kuan-yin Bodhisattva, however, radically changed its male figure to an effeminated figure in China during the later half of the first millennium as endowed with a maiden like smile and refined celestial womanhood.[4] In East Asia, therefore, the Kuan-yin of the popular cults and the Kuan-yin of the Pureland cult did not seem to have historically influenced each other and remained as parallel entities. Nevertheless, it is attempted in this paper to theorize the spiritual basis of the popular Kuan-yin cult in reference to Chinese Buddhist thought and culture and examine whether it can explain Buddhist spirituality and salvation underlying the Pureland tradition.

§2.. KUAN-YIN BODHISATTVA AND THE BUDDHA: THEIR VIRTUE OF LOVE AND COMPASSION

In the fortieth fascicle of his great commentary *Ta-chih-tu-lun* (「大智度論」), Nāgārjuna refers to Avalokitasvara (Kuan-shih-yin) more than once along with other celestial Bodhisattvas like Samantabhadra (遍吉) and Mañjuśrī (文殊師利),[5] and elsewhere in the text, he refers to Amitābha Buddha and his spiritual realm of peace and happiness.[6] Although thus he knew this Bodhisattva in

---

[4] Although it is not easy to determine precisely when this change took place, this transformation likely occurred during the T'ang dynasty. Cf. Tay, C.N. Kuan-yin: the cult of half Asia. *History of Religions,* No. 162 (now 1976) 147-177; Blofelt, John: *Compassion Yoga; the mystical cult of Kuan Yin.* London (1977) Alternative title, *Bodhisattva of compassion; the mystical tradition of Kuan. Yin.* Boulder, Colo (1978) 158 p; Esp. p. 19.

[5] 「大智度論」Taishō. 25, (No. 1509), p. 350 (a, 14-15) 「如普遍吉菩薩観世音菩薩文殊師利菩薩等」 and (c, 1-3) 「如遍吉文殊師利観世音等」. In this fascicle, Nāgārjuna comments on the nature and function of Buddhist love and compassion while he is commenting on the *25,000 Śloka text* 「大品[二万五千頌]般若経」).

[6] Yamagami Sōgen quotes three passages at the end of his introductory statement on his Japanese translation of the *Ta-chih-tu-lun* in references to the 10th, 29th, and 30th fascicles. 「大智度論」(Taish. 25), *ibid.*, pp. 20-21.

the context of Pureland tradition, he seems to have devoted much of his energy to theorize the paradigmatic Mahāyāna Bodhisattva after the fashion of the 25th chapter Samantamukha (普門品) of the *Lotus Sūtra*. He emphasizes "activist virtue of love and compassion" as characteristic of Mahāyāna Bodhisattva and demonstrates what this activism means by comparing it with the passive nature of love and compassion pertaining to Hīnayāna practitioners (i.e., Śrāvaka and Pratyekabuddha Vehicles). In early Buddhism, the principles of *maitrī* (慈、loving friendliness) and *karuṇā* (悲、compassion) were taught as the basic norms of human ethics, but were soon combined with sympathetic joy (喜、*muditā*) and equanimity (捨、*upekṣā*) as part of the four-fold discipline of spiritual training (四無量心) by the orthodoxy.[7] Nāgārjuna determines that the Hīnayāna virtue of love and compassion as well as that of ordinary humans is inferior (小慈、*hsiao-tz'ŭ* and 小悲、*hsiao-pei*) and that the Mahāyāna superior virtue of love and compassion (大慈、*ta-tzŭ* and 大悲、*ta-pei*) belongs only to Buddhas and Bodhisattvas. The following is his argument to distinguish the fundamental difference between the two:

> The great virtue of love and compassion ascribed to the enlightened is alone true and greatest. The lesser virtue of love (*hsiao-tz'ŭ*) means a mere wishing in thought to make people happier, without the actual ability to do so. The lesser virtue of compassion (*hsiao-pei*) means to empathize with the various physical and mental sufferings which people undergo and feel sympathy for them, without the actual ability to help them rid of these problems. In the case of the superior virtue of love, the Buddha wishes people to be awarded with security and happiness and, in actuality, helps them realize these objectives.

[7] "Four Immeasurable mental Disciplines" (*catvāri apramāṇāni*, 四無量心) (1) In contemplation of *maitrī* (慈) or loving friendliness, one wishes happiness for others beginning with his close relations and then expanding his wishing outward, eventually to encompass all humans. (2) In contemplation of *karuṇā* (悲) or compassion, he empathizes with the suffering of some particular individuals and then expands his empathy outward to eventually encompass all humans. (3) In contemplation of *muditā* (喜) or sympathetic joy, he holds joy for some particular person and for his successful deliverance from suffering, then expands this outward to eventually encompass all humans. Finally, (4) in contemplation of *upekṣā* (捨) or equanimity, he transcends or dissociates himself from the foregoing states of mental involvement, modeling his practice after that of some person who has managed to transcend both suffering and rejoicing. The last of these four practices was clearly established to help maintain a lifestyle of mental balance and spiritual enhancement.

Likewise, with the great virtue of compassion, the Buddha empathizes with people's misfortune and, in actuality, assists them to be rid of their suffering.[8]

Here, the criterion to differentiate the love and compassion of Buddhas and Bodhisattvas from those of humans is clearly expressed in terms of ultimate effectuation, and what is required for the superior virtue is that each practitioner not only wishes well for others but also should help them realize it, exercising his skill in means (方便、*upāyakauśalya*). This is the nature of activism as Nāgārjuna defines it, distinguishing "superior love and compassion" (大慈大悲).

As to the theoretical aspect of Buddhist love and compassion, Nāgārjuna summarily gives three-fold motivational context as criteria in the 20th fascicle of his commentary: (1) the virtue of love and compassion must be motivated by the similarity of one's self with other selves, i.e., common humanity (*sattva-ālambana,* 衆生縁); (2) the virtue of love and compassion must be motivated by the sameness of the psycho-physical elements which form the basis of human existence, i.e., five Skandhas (*dharma-ālambana,* 法縁); and (3) finally the virtue of love and compassion must be totally freed from either one of the two motivational contexts, i.e., independent of motivational context (*anālambana,* 無縁). To explain the foregoing, first, ordinary humans rely on the context of similarity among fellow humans (*sattva-ālambana,* 衆生縁). This is the basis of so-called neighborly love. The Śrāvaka and Pratyekabuddha as well as Bodhisattva[9] initially rely on this first motivational context, but, later on, they necessarily rely on the second motivational context or on the bottom line of human similarity, consisting of human sensory and mental elements, which make up the broader, universal basis of humanity (*dharma-ālambana,* 法縁). In Buddhist terminology, these elements refer to the physiological and psychological facts of

---

[8] *Ibid.*, p. 256b-c: 仏大慈大悲真実最大、復次小慈但心念与衆生楽実無事楽、小慈名観衆生種々身苦心苦、憐愍而已不能令脱。大慈者念令衆生得楽亦与楽事。大悲憐愍衆生苦亦能令脱苦。

[9] In scholastic Buddhism (Hīnayāna), Bodhisattvas were stereotyped together with Śrāvakas and Pratyekabuddhas as "three vehicle followers" (*tri-yāna* or *yāna-traya,* 三乗). It was in Mahāyāna Buddhism that the Bodhisattva ideal was reconceptualized as a threshold Buddha, one who is on the verge of Buddhahood, and was thereby clearly differentiated from the orthodox ideal of discipleship (Śrāvaka) or of the solitary practitioner (Pratyekabuddha). Nāgāarjuna differentiates Avalokitasvara, Samantabhadra, Mañjuśrī from these lower ranking Bodhisattvas.

perception and conception as building blocks of human existence (*dharmas*, 法). This means that the previously independent human individual is lost here as an illusory non-existent being in the wider and more universal landscape of physical, biological, and mental data, which are technically called *dharmas* (or elements).

Then, what does it mean that the Buddha's virtue of love and compassion does not depend on either of the previous two criteria? First, the human virtue of love and compassion must depend on the criterion that all humans are similar. Yet insofar as practitioners have not accomplished the state of Arhat, they are still bound and entrapped by the influence of morally and spiritually defiled propensities (*āsrava*, 煩悩).[10] These practitioners may not transcend the various influencing factors derived from the social and cultural contexts in which the lives of those persons with whom they are concerned are intertwined. When they have realized the state of Arhat, eradicated the idea of self or I-ness, and hence transcended the aspects of identity or difference in the things they experience, they should be freed from the causes of moral and spiritual defilement (*anāsrava*) and comprehend that all humans are merely aggregations of continual flows of sensory and mental elements and ultimately of the empty nature without any substance of identity. At this stage, those saints who are totally liberated become independent from entrapments, social, cultural, and so forth, because they are confronted exclusively by the bottom line, i.e., the five aggregates of sensory and mental operations, neither defiled nor undefiled. One might say that this is the ultimate principle of universality common to all humans, beyond all differences of religion, culture, society, and so forth. This retrospective insight is the second motivational context, within which practitioners are supposed to reassess the world and meet fellow humans with love and compassion.

For Buddhist thinkers, however, this was not enough. Thus came the third non-motivational context only attributed to Buddha's love and compassion. Nāgārjuna again explains this matter as follows:

---

[10] *Yu-lou* (有漏): sāsrava in Sanskrit, āsava in Pāli, means the state of being affected or influenced by passion, defilements, in which the process of life is in full swing; verbal and mental defilement which cause obstruction to enlightenment. Here it is given as "morally and spiritually defiled propensities." 漏尽 (*lou-chin*) or 無漏 (*wu-lou*), opposite of *yu-lou.*, the state of being unaffected or uninfluenced by passion, defilement, in total transcendence from the process of life. Asrava means 'flowing,' 'running,' 'discharge' and is applied in analogy to the discharge or outflow of passions and their faith, impure flux from sense faculties and the mind. It is synonymous with Kleśa or defilement. Āsrava denotes the state of Sāsrava.

The mind of the Buddha ought not to abide either within the domain of ordinary consciousness (*saṃskṛta*)[11] or within the domain of the transcendent (*asaṃskṛta*). His mind relies not on the past, present or future world, because he knows that motivational contexts [of the human world] are unreal, up-side-down, and illusory. Hence, the mind of the Buddha does not depend upon any of these unreal motivational contexts. Since ordinary people do not know how transcendentally real these sensory and mental elements are, they stray into all walks of life (literally, the five cyclical courses of life), attach themselves to sensory and mental elements, discriminating one from another for selection, [thus unable to see *things as they really are* (*yathābhūtam*)].[12] Hence, it is the Buddha's virtue of love and compassion to help humans acquire the same insight [concerning the reality of elements totally freed from defilement]. This is called the independence from motivational context."[13]

In the history of Buddhist teachings, the negation of reality has been done twice. In the first case, as negation of the reality of empirical self on the basis of multiplicity of sensory and mental elements. Here, the pscyho-physical elements are regarded as real (*dharma-svabhāva,* 法有), but a human person is considered unreal (*anātman,* 無我). A human is as unreal as a cart which, when broken down into its component parts (wheels, axle, frame, etc.), is after all only a name. This was the position of the orthodox insight of *dharma-svabhāva.*[14] The aforementioned second motivational context represents this first negation. As the next step, the Mahāyāna insight of *Śūnyatā* repudiates the reality of these psycho-physical elements or *dharmas* (*dharma-niḥsvabhāva*).[15] This second negation

---

[11] *Saṃskṛta* (有為): phenomenal, affected, composite existence is an interplay of multiple subtle, ultimate, not further analysable elements of *nāma-rūpa* (mind and matter) and forces derived from the given causal concatenation of multiple elements. Whatever is phenomenal is therefore subject to the causality of dependent originztion. A*saṃskṛta* (無為): Unaffected, non-composite, absolute, unconditioned, and unlimited, and hence transcendent. Only three *dharmas* were accepted by the Abhidharmists, such as Sarvāstvāda.

[12] 諸法実相.

[13] *Ibid.*, fasc. 20. p. 209c. 無縁者、是慈但諸仏有。何以故、諸仏心不住有為無為性中。不依止過去世未来現在世、知諸縁不実顛倒虚誑故、心無所縁。仏以衆生不知是諸法実相。往来五道、心著諸法分別取捨、以是諸法実相智恵。令衆生得之。是名無縁。

[14] 人空法有.

[15] 法空

then represents the non-motivational context of the Buddha's virtue of love and compassion. In short, Nāgārjuna determines the insight of *Śūnyatā* as basis of the Buddha's love and compassion. But what is the difference between the Buddha and Bodhisattva regarding their virtue of love and compassion, because both are able to see the truth of *Śūnyatā*?

§3. KUAN-YIN CULT AND ITS THEORETICAL BASIS IN THE PRAJÑĀ SCRIPTURES

Around A.D. 286, Dharmarakṣa rendered in his translation of the *Lotus Sūtra* (「正法華経」) 'kuang-shih-yin' (光世音) as translation of *avalokitasvara*, meaning "one who illumines the voices of the world." The use of '光' (*kuang*) essentially connotes an identical meaning as that of Kumārajīva's use of '観' (*kuan*), namely, "spiritual illumination or introspection" '照' (*chao*). Thus, Kumārajīva too rendered 'kuan-shih-yin' (観世音) into the Bodhisattva 'Avalokitasvara,' meaning "the Bodhisattva who surveys the [suffering] voices of the world." Kumārajīva applies this same rendering not only in his translation of the *Lotus Sūtra* (「妙法蓮華経」 *Saddharmapuṇḍariīka-sūtra,* A.D. 406), especially in the 25th Chapter (「観世音普門品」): "Kuan-shih-yin's Multifarious Manifestation," but also in his translation of Nāgārjuna's *Ta-chih-tu-lun* (「大智度論」 or *Mahāprajñā-pāramitôpadeśa-śāstra*) during the years of 402 through 405. It was Hsüan-tzang who made a new rendering in 649 as Kuan-tzŭ-tsai" (観自在菩薩), meaning "the Bodhisattva who excels in [*prajñā*] illumination,"[16] and after his translation, the subsequent translators, such as Fa-yueh (法月), Prajñā (智恵) and Li-yen (利言), Prajñācakra (智慧輪), Dharmasiddhi (法成), Amoghavajra (不空), Dānapāla (施護), all followed his rendering as 'Kuan-tzŭ-tsai Pu-sa' (観自在菩薩), except for Prajñācakra who compounded the two alternatives together

---

[16] Hsüan-ts'ang defends his translation of Kuan-tzŭ-tsai into Avalokiteśvara by saying: "Avalokiteśvara ought to be called in T'ang language as 'Kuan-tzŭ-tsai. Avalokita is kuan (観), īśvara is tzŭ-tsai (自在). His disciple Ch'iung-chi (窺基、632-682) defended his master's rendering in his commentary on the *Mahāprajñāpāramitā-hṛdaya-sūtra* [「般若心経幽賛」巻上、Taishō. 33 (No. 1710)]: In the olden translation, it was Kuang-shih-yin (光世音) or Kuan-shih-yin (観世音) or Kuan-shih-tzŭ-tsai (観世自在), which are all wrong. 'Kuan' means illumining (照), namely, an insight that clarifies non-existence and existence (了空有) and 'tzŭ-tsai' means the proficiency of doing things at one's will (従任)."

as 'Kuan-shih-yin-tzŭ-tsai Pu-sa' (観世音自在菩薩).

Accepting the history of the partial change from Avalokitasvara to Avalokiteśvara, we ought to notice that the *Prajñā Hṛdaya Sūtra* provided the most significant moment for the history of Buddhist culture in China, because the *Sūtra* made the Bodhisattva Kuan-shih-yin or Kuan-tzŭ-tsai to be the chief expounder of the Prajñā insight. In all the texts of *Parjñāpāramitā* literature, there is none other than this single text in which Kuan-shih-yin appears to be the chief exponent of the teaching. And this same Bodhisattva is depicted in the *Lotus Śūtra*'s 25th Chapter "Kuan-shih-yin's Multifarious Manifestation" as champion guardian and Buddhist savior. In this *Lotus Sūtra*, he inherited the so-called activist virtue to exercise his two-fold expediency, *Prajñā* (wisdom) and *Karuṇā* (compassion), to help humans escape from sufferings for the sake of their salvation in lieu of Śākyamuni after his Parinirvāṇa. In the *Prajñā Heart Sūtra*, this activist Kuan-yin Bodhisattva was re-cast, for the first time, as an important part of the scriptural scenario of the *Prajñā* doctrine, to become the chief exponent of the transcendent insight and practice of introspection.

In China, the cultic worship of Kuan-yin Bodhisattva is believed to have begun shortly after Dharmarakṣa's translation of the *Lotus Sūtra*, but most certainly after the more lucid translation of the same text by Kumārajīva and quickly spread over the divided continent in the north and the south from the fifth century onward.[17] From the time when the *Lotus Sūtra* became the basis of the T'ien-t'ai Buddhism, and after Chih-i wrote his powerful exposition on this text and the vows of Kuan-yin Bodhisattva near the end of the sixth century, the Kuan-yin Cult became a major source of Buddhist spirituality throughout Medieval China.[18] There is no doubt

[17] The bibliographical records suggest that there were six translations of the same text, but only three translations ascribed to Dharmarakṣa (「正法華経」286), Kumārajīva (「妙法蓮華経」406), and Jñānagupta and Dharmagupta (「添品法蓮華経」601) are extant. Nāgārjuna quotes this *Sūtra*, more often than any other scriptures, in his commentary *Upadeśaśāstra* (「大智度論」) of *Mahāprajñāpāramitāsūtra* [「大品般若経」(translated by Kumārajīva, A.D. 402-412)].

[18] Chih-i (538-597) systematized the T'ien-t'ai Classification of Buddhist Dcotrines known as "Five Periods and Eight Teachings" (「天台五時八教教判」) on the basis of the *Lotus Sūtra* and *Nirvāṇa Sūtra* (*Ni-p'an-ching*, 「涅槃経」). His authorship covers many writings, but the *Profound Meaning of Lotsu Sūtra* (*Miao-fa-lien-hua-ching-hsüan-i* 「妙法蓮華経玄義」) in 593 [Taishō. 33 (No. 1716)] and *The Profound Meaning of Kuan-yin* [*Kuan-shih-yin-hsüan-i*

with the history of the Sui Dynastic unification of the north and the south that Buddhist thoughts and their active participation in society contributed toward its realization. I believe, therefore, that the dominant cultural force of that early Medieval China was formulated by two major sources of spirituality, one being the *Prajñāpāramitā* insight and another being the *Lotus Sūtra*'s activism personified in Kuan-yin's love and compassion. It was the strike of ingenuity that these two factors were symbolically brought together into fusion by Kumārajīva's *Mahāvidyāmantra-sūtra* (「大明寿経」), and then by Hsüan-tzang's *Hṛdaya Sūtra* in 649. According to Edward Conze's analysis of the *Hṛdaya Sūtra*,[19] there is close parallelism between the contents of the *Hṛdaya Sūtra* and that of the second chapter of the *Twenty-five Thousand Śloka Prajñāpāramitā-sūtra*, so-called *Ta-p'in-pan-jo-ching* (「大品般若経」). He asserted that all the words, phrases, and lines of the short text were extracted from the larger text. Accordingly, this *Heart Sūtra* is meant to be, as Conze says, "a restatement of the four holy Truths for beginners on the method of bearing this teaching in mind as well as on the spiritual advantage of following it."[20] Conze thus concludes that the Mahāyāna theorists regarded the *Heart Sūtra* as "the second turning of the wheel of the law."[21] This Mahāyāna Buddhist thought enormously appealed to the minds of Chinese and East Asian Buddhists. In short, the Buddhist spirituality of Medieval China fundamentally anchored in this *Prajñā* insight and simultaneously galvanized by the activist spirit of Kuan-yin Bodhisattva of the 25th Chapter Samantamukha (「普門品」) of the *Lotus Sūtra*.

A decade ago, Lokesh Chandra, reputed Indian scholar of Buddhist iconography and author of the *Thousand-Armed Avalokiteśvara*,[22] proposed a theory that Avalokitasvara was a metamorphosis of Brahmā.. This deity is known to be the lord of the earth in Hindu tradition, also as Lokeśvara or Lokanātha, the lord or savior of the world. Hindu deity Śakra or Indra was the incarnation of stamina

---

「観音玄義」), its commentary (*Kuan-yin-i--shu*, 「観音義疏」), and the *Short Commentary on the Chap. of Samanta-mukha* (P'u-mên-p'in-su, 普門品疏、Taishō. 34, No. 1728) are regarded to have contributed to the Kuan-yin cult movement.

[19] Edward conze: "Text, Sources, and Bibliography of the *Prajñāpāramitā-hṛdaya*," *Journal of Royal Asiatic Society*. 1948; pp. 33-51.

[20] *Ibid*., p. 47.

[21] *Ibid*., 47-48.

[22] Lokesh Chandra: *The Thousand-Armed Avalokiteśvara*. Delhi: Indira Gandhi National Center for Arts, 1988.

(*sthāman*) and represented the will-to-power and the central active figure of the ethereal world. From Buddhist legends as well as from iconographic representations, we know that Śākyamuni was flanked by Indra and Brahmā before he decided to proclaim his Dharma to the world. Thus, asserts Lokesh Chandra, "with the transcendence of Śākyamuni to Amitābha, Indra and Brahmā were transformed into Mahāsthāmaprāpta and Avalokitasvara."[23] In reference to the sections of *mantra*, *dhāraṇī*, or hymns, in both the *Lotus Sūtra* and the *Pureland Sūtra*, Lokesh Chandra regards Avalokitasvara as the "master of logos" (*mantra-draṣṭā*) in parallel to Brahmā in the Brahmanical system, the Seer (*avalokitṛ*) of the Sound (*svara*), who assimilated Hindu deities (*lokeśvara*) to Buddhist cults by pronouncement of each sacred hymn (*hṛdaya* or *mantra*) unique to each deity.[24]

My immediate reaction in thought was that although it is a very persuasive view of the origin of the Kuan-yin cult, Lokesh Chandra seems to have missed the crucial fact that the Indian Buddhist cult of Avalokiteśvara and the East Asian cult of Kuan-yin Bodhisattva are not monolithic in spirituality. He is brilliant in probing Avalokitasvara as a metamorphosis of Brahmā, in part by focusing on the potency pertaining to the substratum of the metamorphosis, namely, Brahmā, and in part by adopting Alicia Matsunaga's thesis, that the principle of Buddhist assimilation[25] that worked in Japan to absorb native gods and various other rites into Buddhism began in India.[26] I have felt some reservation to decide whether Indian Buddhhist spirituality is traceable in the cult of Avalokitasvara in China, because, according to Lokesh Chandra's theory, the popularity of Avalokitasvara in India was due to the potency of its substratum, namely, Hindu Brahmā. It seems to imply that popularity of Buddhist spirituality in India appears to have been enhanced by the replacement of the Hindu deity Brahmā. In actual history, however, the Avalokiteśvara cult as Buddhist spirituality did not

---

[23] Chandra, *op. cit.*, p. 11. In the Pureland iconography, Avalokitasvara (観世音) and Mahāsthāmaprāpta (勢至) are the members of the triad as Amitābha's acolytes. The two figures are depicted as sublime as Amitābha and are in possession of a similar set of superior marks only ascribed to the Buddhas. Avalokiteśvara is always on the right of Amitābha while Mahāsthāmaprāpta, a little smaller figure, on Amitābha's left side.

[24] Chandra: *Ibid.*, p.16.

[25] 「本地垂跡」

[26] Chandra: *op. cit.*, p. 42. Cf. Alicia Matsunaga: *Buddhist Philosophy of Assimilation of the Honji-Suijaku Theory (The Historical Development)*: Tokyo: Sphia University, C.E. Tuttle, 1969.

last and was quickly reclaimed back by the cults of Hindu gods after several centuries. When Hsüan-tzang traveled to India, esoteric Buddhism was at its zenith, but signs of the impending decline of Buddhism were already quite visible. During the few centuries before and after Hsüan-tzang's visit, Hindu iconography and cult movements gradually reclaimed their deities and institutions. If Lokesh Chandra is right in saying that Avalokiteśvara in India was merely a metamorphosis of Brahmā, then, reverting from Buddhist to Hindu cultic institutions would be a matter of simple switching!

In China, I believe that the history of Kuan-yin cult took a different course of development. During the seventh century, esoteric Buddhism just began to be introduced, and its influence was constrained in part by the exoteric Buddhism that had preceded it and established the powerful traditions of the T'ien-t'ai (天台), Hua-yen (華厳), San-lun (三論), and Wei-shih (唯識、*vijñāna-mātra*) systems of thought. Esoteric Buddhism was further constrained by the Chinese cultural environment which was radically different from and alien to that of India. What was crucial to the Kuan-yin cult in China was the insight of *śūnyatā* embodied in the *Prajñā Heart Sūtra*, which has always linked with the Kuan-yin personification of love and compassion, and not with a Hindu spiritual basis of Brahmā. I am obliged to question, therefore, whether Brahmā's potency, which Lokesh Chandra asserted to be the essential core of Avalokiteśvara, is identical with the spiritual basis which Chinese Buddhist thinkers ascribed to Kuan-yin Bodhisattva?

Kuan-yin as Avalokitasvara in India was a male figure and remained to be so throughout the millennia wherever the image was transmitted, except in East Asia. By the seventh century, Chinese Buddhist thought had already set in motion the subsequent development of the East Asian Kuan-yin cult by developing the vow of "Bodhisattva Ideal." Moreover, despite the fact that some Indian forms of Avalokiteśvara were available to Chinese Buddhist worship,[27] they developed their own image as an effeminated figure during the

[27] The Hindu deity Śiva was assimilated into Buddhism and gave rise to the name Avalokiteśvara (*avalokita-īśvara*, the lord Avalokita), thereby allowing the emergence of the thousand-armed Bodhisattvas. Lokesh Chandra asserts that "this Avalokiteśvara sometimes appears as a Buddha and at other times as the Hindu deity Iśvara or Maheśvara (Śiva), without clear reason." So came to being several types of Kuan-yin images that were linked to Hindu iconography, like those endowed with one thousand arms, thousand eyes, four faces, eleven faces, a horse-head, a fearless lion head, a blue neck, and so on.

T'ang dynasty, probably around the 8th to 9th century, in accordance with their own cultural and aesthetic taste. Ever since, this feminine form of image, often called "goddess of mercy," has remained to be the dominant figure of Kuan-yin Bodhisattva in China and, from the ninth century onwards, spread to the entire continent as well as eastward to Korea and Japan. As the form of this Kuan-yin moved eastward, further new variations came to appear as the white-robed Kuan-yin, Kuan-yin holding a willow leaf, Kuan-yin with a fishing basket, and the Kuan-yin of easy child-bearing, among others. This last figure, holding a baby in her arm, was sometimes called "Maria Kannon" in Medieval Japan. However the course of such evolution might be, my point of view is that the sudden appearance of a female Kuan-yin during the T'ang dynasty in China came from within the Prajñāpāramitā tradition in which the spirit of the *Prajñā Sūtras* was personified as the mother of Buddhas (仏母) and worshipped by late Mahāyāna Buddhists in India as well as in Tibet.[28]

In my recent visit to China and travelling over the continent, I came to witness an age-old tradition of Chinese art of painting and calligraphy by encountering on several occasions the similar motif and construction of Kuan-yin Bodhisattva and calligraphy of the *Hṛdaya Sūtra* combined together. Some of them are obviously intended to be purchased by potential customers from abroad, but more often, those displayed works of art are for the interest of local customers. In March 1999, on the way back from attending the second International Conference for Hsüan-tzang Studies held in the city of Tong-chuan, I visited a local museum of a Medieval Agricultural Village set up in the city of Wang-hsian (万県市) in the province of Ssŭ-chuan (四川省). What I came to encounter was a minor landlord family house and the scroll of the Kuan-yin's painting with a calligraphy of the *Hṛdaya Sūtra* hung on the wall of the drawing room side by side

[28] In China, calling the *Prajñāpāramitā Sūtras* as "Mother of Buddhas" (仏母) began to be seen during the later half of the first millennium in association with Tantric texts. E.g.,「仏母大金曜孔雀明王経」3 fasc. tr. by Amoghavajra (705-774), the text concerned with Dhāraṇīs;「仏母出生三法蔵般若波羅蜜多経」equivalent to the 4th lecture assembly of Hsüan-ts'ang's「大般若経」of 600 fascicles, and parallel with the extant *8000 Śloka Prajñā Sūtra* [「道行般若経」10 fasc. tr. by Chih-lü-chia-chen, Late Han;「大明度経」6 fasc. by Chih-ch'ien of Wu;「摩訶般若鈔経」5 fasc.;「小品般若波羅密経」25 fasc, by Kumārajīva];「仏母小字般若経」1 fasc. 1000;「仏母般若波羅密多円集要義釈論」(*Ārya-prajñāpāramitā-saṃgraha-kārikā-vivaraṇa*, 4 fasc.) tr. by Dānapāla, 980, and so forth.

with another scroll that depicted a figure of Confucius. I came to realize that a profound cultural force that has survived for ages, once again reclaiming itself even under the Western Communist ideology and system of society adopted by the present regime. This feminine image, or sexually neutral figure, embellished with an entire scriptural calligraphy of the *Heart Sūtra* precisely ascertains the fact that the essential nature of the Chinese Kuan-yin Cult was and has been the insight of *Prajñāpāramitā* personified with the epithet of activist Buddhist love and compassion.

§4. KUAN-YIN'S ACTIVISM IN THE CULT AND ITS PRACTICAL BASIS IN THE *LOTUS SŪTRA*

In the history of Mahāyāna Buddhism, no other scripture has ever been so much studied as the *Lotus Sūtra*. The popularity of the text lay in its twofold theoretical framework. First, it illuminated the appointed time at which the original and timeless Dharma revealed by ancient Buddha in the immemorial past would converge with the historical or contemporary Dharma currently realized by Śākyamuni through his enlightenment[29] (Chap. 11: "Beholding the Jewel-inlaid Stūpa"). This moment was symbolized by the dramtic event in which the two Buddhas, trans-historical and historical, would be seated together within the gigantic jewel-inlaid Stūpa that would spring forth from the earth to fill the sky. Second, the *Lotus Sūtra* foretold that at that moment, the immeasurable numbers of Bodhisattvas who had never been seen before would suddenly arise everywhere through the cracked earth from below, to middle of the sky, surrounding the Stūpa (Chap. 15: "Bodhisattvas from Underground"). The scenario points (1) to the beginning of change from the cult of relic worship toward the cult of the anthropomorphic image, (2) to the beginning of revelation of the trans-historical Dharma of original enlightenment by way of the currently revealed Dharma of the enlightened Śākyamuni, and finally (3) to the beginning of the active propagation of the Dharma of the new age by the host of Bodhisattvas charged with the vow of activism for love and compassion. It would be in this dramatic and imaginary arena that Śākyamuni would introduce Kuan-yin Bodhisattva before the multitude of participants (Chap. 25: "Avalokitasvara Bodhisattva").

---

[29] 本門 and 跡門,

The 25th Chap. of the *Lotus Sūtra* begins with the Buddha's reply to Akṣayamati Bodhisattva regarding the meaning of the name Avalokitasvara. The reply points primarily to the virtue of love and compassion as Kuan-yin's epithet, since he is ever alert to the imploring of all sufferers and, should they wholeheartedly chant his name, beseeching him for deliverance, he will come at once to help them be free from their suffering. He is endowed with the transcendent faculty to immediately perceive all voices and, in no time, come to the rescue of all callers. Quite different from what the callers seek for Amitābha Buddha's help, which is confined to the rebirth in his Pureland, Kuan-yin's supplicators pose very different kinds of deliverance, which involve realistic human jeopardies and require immediate care and assistance within this very mundane world. For instance, cases involve some one surrounded by a great fire, swept away by flood water, ship-wrecked and stranded on cannibals' island, threatened by a robber bearing a sword, tormented by ill-minded demons, imprisoned by fetters and chains, imminently attacked by highwaymen, or someone falling into fiery pit, floating on the waves by a shipwreck, pushed away over a precipice, falling from a hilltop, surrounded by the swords of enemies, imminently executed for unjustified reason, suffering from being poisoned, attacked by a horde of wild animals, stepped into a pile of venomous insects, snakes, or scorpions, totally exhausted by pain and fatigue, facing legal suit at a military court, and so on.

Kumārajīva's text mentions altogether thirty-three cases of dangers and predicaments. Indeed, some of these are neither foreign to us even today, nor should people's cry for help and rescue in these cases be put off a moment from the point of view of human rights today. As a matter of fact, the Kuan-yin cult was enormously popular in South Asia during the fourth century. Guṇabhadra (394-468) crossed Southern Ocean by boarding a ship from Siṃhala (present Śrī Lankā) and arrived in Kuan-chou. During the voyage, he is said to have chanted the name of Kuan-yin Bodhisattva.[30] The popularity of the cult goes back further to the 4th or even the 3rd century in India, because Kānheri and Aurangābād cave temples, which began as early as the second century Śaka-Pahlava period in Western India, preserved various *bas-releafs* describing the scenes

---

[30] Cf. A brief biography attached to the *Kuo-ch'ü-hsieny-tsai-yin-kuo-ching* (「過去現在因果経」) translated between 444-453, Taishō. 3, (No. 189), p. 620. Kuan-yin Bodhisattva is called the grantor of fearlessness and safety (*abhayadada*) to any and all sentient beings.

of the Kuan-yin chapter of the *Lotus Sūtra.*[31] Moreover, Nāgārjuna's *Suhṛllekha* or *Friendly Epistle*, translated by Guṇavarman (367-431) before 431, provides evidence of Kuan-yin's popularity already during the second century.[32] In this letter, Nāgārjuna advises his patron Śātavāhana king of South India to honor Buddhist monks for the sake of his learning, help people to be rescued from sufferings like Avalokitasvara is expected to do, and resolve for himself to realize supreme enlightenment.[33]

At this juncture, I am obliged to reflect upon the linkage between this popular Kuan-yin Bodhisattva to be implored by all people as savior, on the one hand, and the saintly Kuan-yin Bodhisattva who was summoned by the Buddha to propound the essentials of the *Prajñāpārmitā* to Śāliputra and others, on the other hand. There seems to be an insurmountable chasm in communication between human wishes of this mundane world and Kuan-yin's response as deputy dispenser of love and compassion in lieu of the Buddha. For, whosoever among people cry for help and rescue are totally adrift amidst the five cycles of life, whereas the Bodhisattva seems to be

---

[31] During the Śaka-Palhava period, ca. from the 2nd CE through 3rd, the bearers of history were those new immigrated peoples of Scythians (Śaka) and Parthians (Palhava) who were engaged in sea-faring in Indian Ocean and caravan land traders. The *Kānheri* complex, located on the *Salsette* Island 16 miles north of Bombay and 6.25 miles northwest of Thānā consists of structures which belonged to the local *Saṅgha* and the universal *Saṅgha* of the four quarters (*caturdiśasaṅgha*), belonging to the Orthodox schools, supported by the local people of Nāsika, Kalyāṇa, and the people of Karṇāṭa and Dhānyakaṭaka of South-eastern India, and included a good number of epigraphic records of that period (165-194). The cult of Avalokitasvara in the religion seems to have been supported mainly by sea-faring communities.

[32] This writer places the life of Nāgārjuna between A.D. 50 and 150 during the Śaka-Pahlava Period. Cf. Ichimura: "Re-Examining the Period of Nāgārjuna: Western India, A.D. 50-150" (「龍樹の年代論再考」), *Journal of Indian and Buddhist Studies*, vol. 40, No. 2, March 1992 (pp. 8-14); "The Period of Nāgārjuna and the Fang-pien-hsin-lun" (「龍樹の年代と方便心論」), Ibid., Vol. 43, No. 2, March 1995 (pp. 20-25). Yasuo Karashina recently pointed out that the term '観音' appears in Guṇabhadra's translation of the *Suhṛllekha*「竜樹菩薩為禅陀迦王説法要偈」、namely:「王当仰学諸賢聖、如観音等度衆生」(Taisho.32, 747c 22). Cf.「法華経の文献学的研究」(2)「観音 Avalokitasvara の語義解釈」: *Annual Report of the International Research Institute for Advanced Buddhology at Soka University*, 1998, pp. 39-66, especially p. 44..

[33] 「龍樹菩薩為禅陀迦王説要偈」Taishō. 32, p. 747, c22; 「王当仰学諸賢聖、如観音等度衆生、未来必当正覚」、Cf. Karashina, S. 「法華経の文献学的研究」 (2) : 「観音 66Avalokitasvara の語義解釈」、*Annual Report of the International Research Institute for Advanced Buddhology at Soka University for the Academic Year 1998*, No. 2; p. 44.

free of these cycles. Irrespective of whether people's desire is spiritual or secular, their calling for help may likely be under the influence of some defiled mental propensities (*kleśas,* 煩悩) caused by the three forces of craving, anger and delusion (貪痴慎). Would Kuan-yin Bodhisattva allow himself to step down to the level of humans since the latter cannot reach his level? If his virtue of love and compassion could actively respond to the needs of people despite their minds being under the influence of moral and spiritual defilement, should not his virtue and motivation be activated in a state of mind similar to that of his recipient human beings? Insofar as communication is required, would his actions not have taken place under the influence of defilement? As a matter of fact, Nāgārjuna poses a similar question for the sake of his readers: "Though I do not intend to be disrespectful to the Buddha," says he, "since he was motivated by love and compassion for his fellow humans and realized enlightenment to discover the way to overcome their suffering, his love and compassion must be in full communication with their minds which are under the influence of defilement."[34]

Nāgārjuna, further, notes some sceptical views. Although the great love and compassion are the foundation of the Buddha-Dharma, some think that these must be of the defiled nature, like a blooming lotus flower rooted in impure mud. Surely the flower is pristine but the mud itself cannot be said to be pure. Hence, the Buddha's love and compassion, as far as its origin is concerned, must be of the defiled nature.[35] Again, since the Buddha comes to being because of his love and compassion for fellow humans, his love and compassion must be of the defiled nature.[36] The underlying thought here is that communication, in general, ought only to be possible between minds which share the same convention.

Kuan-yin's virtue of love and compassion as described in the *Lotus Sūtra* is sublime in light of his transcendent power to survey the world and detect cries of distress. I have long wondered about his vow and its parallel with that of Amitābha who was formerly Dharmākara Bodhisattva. According to the *Pureland Sūtras*, Avalokiteśvara is a deputy dispenser of love and compassion in lieu of Amitābha Buddha, and bears a miniature image of Amitābha in

---

[34] Nāfgārjuna: *Ta-chih-tu-lun* (Taishō. 25), *Ibid*., p. 257, Fasc. 27, 「我不敢不敬。仏以慈悲心為衆生故生、応有漏」

[35] *Ta-chih-tu-lun*, fasc. 27, p.257b: 「大慈大悲雖是仏法之根本、故是有漏、如於泥中生蓮華、不得言泥亦応妙、大慈大悲亦如是。」

[36] *Ta-chih-tu-lun*, fasc. 27, p. 257b: 「仏以慈悲心為衆生故生応是有漏。」

his crown. Amitābha is singularly concerned with and absolutely promises ultimate salvation to all sentient beings, accepting them to his transcendent domain. The locus of Kuan-yin's promise as detailed in the *Lotus Sūtra*, however, is in the human world. Should Amitābha Buddha and Kuan-yin Bodhisattva administer the matter of the Pureland together, these two different domains of salvation ought to be somehow reconciled, although Kuan-yin's love and compassion seems to be consistent with Amitābha Buddha's transcendent love and compassion. But how and why can Amitābha's promise of ultimate salvation and Kuan-yin's promise of this world salvation be reconciled?

In order to have this question answered, I am prepared to introduce the so called "Bodhisattva Vow" especially attributed to a future Kuan-yin Bodhisattva to be. The *Sūtra on the White Lotus of Mercy* (「悲華経」)[37] is not a member of the Pureland texts, but it may rather be regarded to be along with the *Lotus Sūtra* tradition. In contrast to the Pureland group scriptures, this text tells rather a somber human world, except one important message, namely, to convey how and why Śākyamuni's virtue of love and compassion is greater beyond those renowned Buddhas who had been centered in the glorious cults of devotion. Out of many exalted Buddha lands, Śākyamuni chose this mundane, corrupted world for the place of his birth. Undaunted, he was motivated for the sake of multiple sufferers in life on earth to undertake his resolution and realize the supreme enlightenment. After arduous, countless years of training and practice, he finally achieved his goal, and upon his realization, he carried out his initial vow in helping others with the way he accomplished it.

The central legendary episode that is given in the above scripture is not important, but I ought to call attention to the nature of "Bodhisattva Vow" made by a prince upon his resolution to pursue the Bodhisattva career. According to the story, once upon a time, some universal king (Cakravartin, 転輪聖王) Araṇemya or "Discord-free Mind" by name (無諍念王) who ruled the continent, joined the Buddhist path and eventually became Amitābha Buddha. The eldest son, heir apparent, Prince Pu-hün (不) also inclined to take his vow to become a Bodhisattva. The Buddha who initiated the prince's ordination named him Avalokitasvara (*kuan-shih-yin*). The

---

[37] The *Sūtra on the White Lotus of Love and Compassion*, *Karuṇā-puṇḍarīka-nāma-mahāyāna-sūtra* (「大乗悲分陀利経」or「悲蓮華経」10 fasc.), Taishō. 3, 167 (No. 157), translated by Dharmakṣema (曇無讖、414-426).

scripture describes how and why this prince decided his mind to take up the Bodhisattva career and lays out his vow. Indeed, however, the prince's vow was expressed in very identical way as that of Dharmākara who once had resolved his mind at another legendary aeons ago before becoming Amitābha himself. The future Kuan-yin laid his resolution:

> May I resolve my mind for the Bodhisattva career. Should anyone be subjected to suffering, fear and so forth, thereby being forced to abandon the right Dharma, thus to fall into darkness and lose all reliance and protection, yet should he uphold my name in his mind and chant my name, and then shall it be heard by my transcendent faculty of audition and vision, and should he yet remain unliberated from suffering, fear and so forth, shall I not take the supreme enlightenment unto myself.[38]

§5. RECONCILIATION OF PRAJÑĀ INSIGHT AND ACTIVIST VIRTUE OF LOVE AND COMPASSION IN KUAN-YIN CULT

My purpose of discussion on the *Heart Sūtra* in the 3rd section was two-fold. First, I hold that the Kuan-yin Bodhisattva who became the center of the cult in China was not a metamorphosis of Brahmanical magical potency. While Lokesh Chandra argued that Avalokiteśvara could have enabled successful assimilation of Hindu deities only as a metamporhosis of Brahmā, I disagree with his extension of the idea of Hindu metamorphosis to the East Asian cultural context. Second, from the analysis of the *Heart Sūtra*, I showed that Avalokiteṣvara or Kuan-yin Bodhisattva embodies the insight of the four holy Truths in terms of Non-self insight [as *Vidyā*] as well as the higher insight of the four holy Truths in terms of *Śūnyatā* [*as mantra*]. Because of different historical and social conditions, the Kuan-yin Bodhisattva in China and East Asia should be understood in terms of the dual (not double) negation and not in terms of the Brahmanical or Hindu esoteric assertion or potency. In short, the *Prajñāpāramitā* comprises not only the early Buddhist insight of *anātman* (無我) declared by Śākyamuni at the Deer Park but also the later Mahāyāna Buddhist insight of *dharma-Śūnyatā* (法空). Thus saying, however, I do not mean that

---

[38] *Ibid*. (fasc. 3): Taishō. 3, p. 185c: 「願我行菩薩道時、若有衆生受諸苦悩恐怖等事。退失正法堕大暗処、憂愁孤窮無有救護無依無舎、若其為我天耳所聞天眼所見、是衆生等若不得免斯苦悩者、我不成阿　多羅三藐三菩提。」

Avalokitasvara was the metamorphosis of Hindu Brahmā in India either. But to clarify my point of view, it needs another paper.

I demonstrated two faces of Kuan-yin Bodhisattva in our Buddhist terms: (1) one of them being the dispenser of love and compassion depicted in the 25th Chap. of the *Lotus Sūtra*, and (2) another being the expounder of *Śūnyatā* in the *Prajnā Hṛdaya Sūtra*. I think that these two faces ought to be reconciled into one. The *Heart Sūtra* provides a point of reconciliation and a balance of the two as extensively demonstrated in the *Ta-chi-tu-lun*. The point of difference that requires reconciliation lies in two human requirements. (1) Life in general carries varieties of suffering, for which humans have continually sought solutions within the material environment of external nature and within the immaterial inner sphere of human nature. In this human context, Kuan-yin Bodhisattva's vow ought to be directed toward the fulfillment of the mundane needs of individual human-kind in the eradication of suffering and the measurement of their well-being. *(2)* Kuan-yin Bodhisattva's two-fold insight of non-self (無我) and Śūnyatā (空性) elevate his virtue of love and compassion toward the level of unconditional independence from the mundane world upon two grounds (a) the eradication of false conviction in one's self and about things believed to belong to that self (*first negation*), and (b) the eradication of false conviction about the reality of elements of the five aggregates. Now, I contend: What reconciles these points of difference is the Bodhisattva's vow of self-abnegation.

In order to explain my point of view, I should return to the *Heart Sūtra* once again. Kumārajīva's translation (「大妙呪経」*Great Wisdom Prayer Sūtra*) and that of Hsüan-tzang (「般若心経」、*Prajñā Heart Sūtra*) agree one hundred percent with the theme of this short scripture: (1) the practice of deep *Prajñā* introspection leads to the termination of all sufferings,[39] (2) the dialectical negation of each of the five Skandhas leads to the negation of the four holy Truths,[40] (3) the resulting negation of the four holy Truths means neither existence of wisdom nor acquisition of it; there is nothing to be acquired,[41] and hence (4) the Bodhisattva relies on the practice of *Prajñā* introspection realization of Nirvāṇa as well as supreme

---

39 「行深般若、度一切苦厄」

40 「色不異空、空不異色、等、等、無苦集滅道」

41 、「無智亦無得、以無所得」

enlightenment.[42] I introduced Conze's article earlier. In that article he calls attention to the passage which immediately follows the four holy Truths, i.e., the passage that tells "neither existence of wisdom nor acquisition of it, hence there is nothing to be acquired." He traces it in the *larger Prajñā Sūtra* (「大品般若」), among others, and speaks about two important points on the Bodhisattva insight of *Śūnyatā*.

First, there is "no attainment" in actuality, because "attainment" conceptually implies duality in itself, like the duality between "things to be attained" and "an agent of attaining." Second, (2) there is "neither desire for any attainment" on the part of the Bodhisattva, because his insight of non-duality *ipso-facto* views it as non-attainment (無智亦無得、以無所得). Here, attention ought to be called to the fact that a dual negation of "neither nor" underlies the above two points, i.e., "neither attainment" and "nor any desire of attainment," in reference to the subjective sphere and the objective sphere. This dual negation is extended to encompass loving and loved, knowing and known, acting and acted upon, and so on. I understand from extensive comments made by Nāgārjuna in his *Ta-chih-tu-lun* that it is on these grounds that we speak of the Bodhisattva's abnegation of his own enlightenment and Nirvāṇa for the sake of others.

In section two of this paper, I left a question as to what difference ought to be recognized between the Buddha and the Bodhisattva with respect to the three motivational contexts. We understand that a Bodhisattva comes into being when he has been awakened to the fact of human suffering in life and death, and motivates himself to feel love and compassion for all living beings. Upon learning the Buddha's insight, he acquires equivalent insight of sameness (*sama-citta*) toward sentient beings in terms of Non-Self, understanding that every individual self is merely a designation with no everlasting reality. In understanding the dependently arising elements of the five aggregates, he further acquires the insight of *Śūnyatā*, that all elements of the Skandhas have no reality of their own (*niḥsvabhāva* or *śūnyatā*). Thus, the two-fold level of his insight comprise not only an awareness of the sameness of all humans but also an awareness of the sameness of all elements.[43] Now, he

---

42 「依般若波羅蜜多、究竟涅槃、得阿　多羅三藐三菩提」

43 Cf. *Ta-chih-tu-lun.*, fasc. 40, p. 393a: 「所謂大慈悲故、初発度一切衆生心故。学諸仏等心観衆生故、一切法自性空故、如是等因縁故、於一切衆生中生等心、得是等心已、得一切衆諸法等。一切諸法者、如先説衆生等法等義。」

approaches the state of non-duality by transcending the duality of the ordinary world and human convention. By transcending various discriminations like long and short, white and black, male and female, and so on, he envisions the non-dual aspect or rather no-aspect (*wu-hsiang*) of all things. It is within this non-dual context that reconciliation or communication is perfected. Ultimately, this insight is what he wishes all fellow humans to attain.[44]

In the fortieth fascicle, Nāgārjuna speaks of the five kinds of insight eyes (五眼), namely, human eye (肉眼), supernormal eye (天眼), wisdom eye (慧眼), transcendent eye (法眼), Buddha-eye (仏眼). The following is his summary as to how a Bodhisattva's career advances through a series of ever higher insights:

> Observing with his human eyes how those who are near him undergo varieties of suffering in this world, he is motivated with love and compassion for them. The Bodhisattva, great being, initially resolves to pursue the path of enlightenment and undertakes the practice of meditation and concentration to acquire the supernormal eye (*divya-cakṣu,* 天眼). Thus, surveying widely how all other humans undergo varieties of physical and mental suffering by straying into the six spheres of life cycles, the Bodhisattva is all the more motivated with love and compassion for their suffering, and further pursues the way to acquire the wisdom eye (*prajñā-cakṣu,* 慧眼), thereby he wishes to rescue those sufferers. Having acquired the wisdom eye (*prajñā-cakṣu*), the Bodhisattva realizes how varied and diverse the characteristics of human minds are, and thus further pursues the way to acquire the transcendent eye (*dharma-cakṣu,* 法眼), thereby he wishes to help those sufferers realize deliverance by acquiring the same insight for themselves.[45]

The transcendent eye (法眼) means the insight of *Śūnyatā* by which the Bodhisattva enters into the first stage of the final ten sublime states of the Bodhisattva career. Here he is expected to be able to see the characteristic of ultimate reality (*tattva-lakṣaṇam*)

---

[44] Cf. *Ta-chih-tu-lun*, fasc.40, p. 393b: 「復次、衆生中行忍辱慈悲等福功徳無量、功徳無量故心柔軟、心柔軟ゆえ疾得禅定、修禅定故心如意調柔、心如意調柔故、破世間長短男女白黒等。入一相法所謂無相、得是法等已、令一切衆生得是法等。」

[45] *Ta-chih-tu-lun*, fasc. 40, p. 349a-b: 「菩薩初発心時、以肉眼見世界衆生受諸苦患、心慈愍、学諸禅定、修得五通、以天眼遍見六道中衆生、受種々身心苦、益加憐愍故、求慧眼以救済之。得是慧眼已、見衆生心相種々不同、云何令衆生得是実法。故求法眼引導衆生令入法界中、故名法眼。」

as it really is (*yathābhūtam*).[46] At this initial stage, the Bodhisattva should be endowed with the two-fold expedient means (*upāyakauśalya*).[47] Now, the two-fold expediency of the Bodhisattva means (1) the transcendent knowledge or *prajñā* insight as the *Śūnyatā* of all *things (dharma-cakṣu, fa-yen)*, the culmination of the foregoing practice of the six *Pāramitās*, and (2) the great compassion (*mahā-karuṇā, ta-pei*), the very source of the Bodhisattva's original resolution. On account of this two-fold expediency, the Bodhisattva shall not fall into attachment to things of a temporary nature, and neither shall he abandon people as a result of that capacity. While not abandoning his compassionate concern for people, he is, however, fully aware of the unreal nature of all things and of the nature of emptiness (*śūnyatā*). The Bodhisattva maintains these expedient means in proper balance in order to sustain himself in this initial stage, the state of non-regressing or no-back-slide (*avaivartika* or avaivartya) of Bodhisattvahood.[48]

The foregoing features of the activist career of the Bodhisattva ought to have two-fold balanced competence. To repeat, the Bodhisattva sees emptiness in all things that he experiences, and hence he is free from attachment, and yet, he is still said to retain his interest in and compassion for the happiness and well-being of fellow humans. In *Nichomachean Ethics*, Aristotle speaks of the outcome of the perfection of the two virtues. By perfecting practical virtue, we humans are capable of enjoying ideal friendly association with other humans, while by perfecting theoretical virtue, we attain an ideal contemplative life immersed in matters of heavenly and natural law. Representing the Buddhist point of view, Nāgārjuna says that the Buddha revealed three levels of human happiness and well-being, namely, (1) happiness of a human level, (2) happiness of a heavenly level, and (3) happiness of an emancipated level.[49]

---

46 「諸法実相」 (*chu-fa-shih-hsiang*): Both compounds *tattva-lakṣaṇam* and *yathābhūtam* are often come up with verbal terms to see, view, understand, etc. meaning: to intuit the characteristic of ultimate reality as it really is without superimposing one's prejudice or preconception, etc. which necessarily distorts truth to create error.

47 「方便」 (*upāyakauśalya*): skill-in-means, appropriate and excellent expediency, based on the true insight and leading to the goal of religious truth; expedient method to help fellow beings toward the goal of enlightenment.

48 「阿　跋致」 (avaivartika or avaivartya): Cf. *Ta-chih-tu-lun*, fasc. 27. p. 246: 「具足般若波羅蜜多故、知諸法空。大悲心故憐愍衆生。於是二法以方便力不生染著。雖知諸法空、方便力故亦不捨衆生。雖不捨衆生亦知諸法実空。若於是二事等即得入菩薩位。」

49 *Ta-chih-tu-lun*, fasc. 40, p. 355b-c; 人楽、天楽、涅槃楽。

The Bodhisattva should be able to help other humans in their conversion to humanly and heavenly attainment as well as to emancipation. Nāgārjuna then sums up the general difference between the Buddha and the Bodhisattva in relation to common humans, in the following words:

> By acquiring supernormal powers, the Bodhisattva is supposed to know various expedient ways in which to assist fellow humans. But he has not realized Buddhahood, and hence does not have the Buddha eye. He views the world and people with the wisdom eye and the transcendent eye, but is unable to use the Buddha eye. He has reached the ultimate insight that nothing arises or perishes (*anutpattika-dharma-kṣānti*)[50] and thereby clearly sees the causal context in which people [each respectively] realize the ultimate enlightenment. Thus he applies this knowledge to rescue them in various ways, but by not realizing Buddhahood, does not use the Buddha eye.[51] The Bodhisattva has not attained the state of Buddhahood, nor has he attained the Buddha eye. Hence, he is himself afforded three kinds of happiness and well-being, wherefrom he shall help other humans in their conversion, whereas the Buddha helps all humans attain the same conversion while remaining in the state of emancipation.[52]

§6. CONCLUSION

While the East Asian Pureland tradition began to evolve in China, Chinese patriarchs accomplished textual organization under the category of Pureland scriptures and left a number of commentaries. These patriarchs, namely, T'an-luan (曇鸞、476-542),[53] Shan-tao (善導、613-681)[54] and Tao-ch'o (道綽、?-645),[55] led the formative period of the

---

[50] *Anutpattika-dharma-kṣānti* (無生法忍)

[51] *Ta-chih-tu-lun*, fasc. 40. p. 351a: 「得菩薩神通知種々度衆生道。未得成仏故無仏眼慧眼法眼見仏眼不身。菩薩得無生法忍得無生法忍已。能観一切衆生得道因縁、以種々道而度脱之、未成仏故無仏眼。」

[52] *Ibid*., fasc. 40. p. 355c: 「是菩薩未成就仏道、未得仏眼故、以三種楽故。教化可度衆生諸仏但以解脱楽教化衆生。」

[53] The first patriarch of the Pureland tradition in China and author of the *Commentary on Wang-shêng-lun--chu* or *Ching-t'u-lun-chu* (「往生論註」 or「浄土論註」) in two volumes, and the *Verses Praising Amida Buddha* (「賛阿弥陀仏偈」).

[54] The author of the *Commentary of the Four volumes on Kuan-wu-lian-*

Pureland tradition. The earliest advocate of the Pureland cult, Hui-yüan (慧遠、?-416), who organized the Order of White Lotus Flower (白蓮社) as an association of Buddhist monks and laymen for the joint practice of *Nien-fo* (念仏、adoration for Amitābha accompanied by calling his name), was contemporary of Kumārajīva and had his close association with him. These early masters of Pureland teaching had all been acquainted with the critical spirituality of *Prajñā* and activism of Buddhist virtue through Kumārajīva's translation of the scriptures of *Prajñā* and *Lotus Flower*.[56] As to the actual and practical aspect of the Pureland Cult that developed in India, we can only know about it through the contents of the *Sūtra on the Practice of Concentration on the Face-to-face Appearance of the Buddha* (「般舟三昧経」).[57] According to this text, the devotional yearning for

---

shou-ching (「観無量寿経」 *Amitāyurdhyāna-sūtra*). He highlighted the teaching of the *Dhyāna-sūtra* (「観経」) and *Amitāyur-sūtra* (「阿弥陀経」) in terms of the Bodhisattva storehouse that is of the sudden nature (頓経菩提蔵). If one should call the name of the Buddha before his death, irrespective of whether it be for the duration of one day or seven days, by the mere calling of the name, he is predesitned to be born in the Pure Land promptly after his death. This sudden nature of benefit-acquisition is the hallmark of Shan-tao.

55 One of the Pureland patriarchs, author of the Two-fold Classification of Saintly Difficult Path (「難行聖道門」) and Pureland Easy Path (「易行浄土門」): 「二門教判」 in opposition to T'ien-t'ai Ta-shih's commentary on *Amitāyur-dhyāna-sūtra,* 「観無量寿経」). The master was called 'Hsi-ho Ch'an-shih' (西河禅師).

56 Incidentally, the short *Prajñā-Wisdom-Prayer-Sūtra* (「大明呪経」 *Mahāvidyā-mantra-sūtra*), which, though not under the same title as Hsüan-tsang's *Heart Sūtra*, (「般若心経」), may have been Sanskritized and transmitted back to the Indian subcontienent. The title of this small text was not recorded under his name of Kumārajīva in the major catalogue of the six dynasties, such as, the *Collection of the Tripiṭaka Textual Records* (i.e., 「出三蔵記集」) compiled by Sêng-yu (僧祐、420-589), nor did Hsüan-tsang himself seems to have known the existence of such a prior translation. That the *Great Wisdom Prayer Sūtra* (「大明呪経」) was Kumārajīva's translation or composition cannot be refuted because of the *verbatim* identity between this version of the *Heart Sūtra* (「大明呪経」) and a portion of the second chapter of the *Larger Prajñāpāramitā Sūtra* of his translation, known as *Ta-p"in-pan-jo-ching* (「大品般若経」) or the *25,000 śloka Prajñāpāramitā-sūtra* in Sanskrit (「梵文二万五千頌般若」).

57 *The Pratyutpannabuddha-sammukhāvasthitasamādhi-sūtra* translated into Chinese by Chih-ch'en (支讖) in 179. The original scripture probably appeared as contemporaneous to or a little earlier than the appearance of the original *8000 śloka-prajñāpāramitāsūtra* (*Tao-hsing-pan-jo-ching* (「道行

the sublime feature of the Buddha is compared with a caravan leader's passionate yearning for his sweetheart while travelling through ragged terrain and harsh environment under impending fear and anxiety of highwaymen. The practitioners of the cult seem to have been instructed to engage themselves jointly in the intense and concentrated practice of Nien-fo for a certain duration of hours or days for an expectation to see the Buddha's appearance in their altered consciousness. Perhaps, this kind of self-hypnotized state was considered as a means of fortifying human belief in a successful realization of the Pureland or activating human criticial insight by pointing to the truth that "the Buddha neither comes from anywhere nor goes away anywhere." By facing a challenging theory proposed by Lokesh Chandra that the Avalokitasvara cult was essentially based on Hindu spirituality embodied in Brahmā; I feel that we are disadvantaged in order to make a viable response, because his proposal can be extended easily to the early Amitābha cult itself. So I concentrated my counter-argument on the basis of the Chinese Buddhist thought and spirituality.

One thing is very clear to me that the devotional cult movement has its weakness in general when it mingles with other forms of cultures and religions. Unless it has a tight organizational scope and well theorized system on its spirituality, it is difficult to prevent the so-called erosion. Today, we are meeting with multi-cultural and multi-religious society not only in the States but in global terms. A cultic minority, especially a gentle and authentic one like Pureland Buddhism, has been facing real difficulty in the flood of information and countless encounters with different ideas and manifestations. From the point of view of the inner circle of the Shinshū Buddhists, my proposed way of understanding Pureland spirituality may appear to be heretical. I argue, however, to defend my point of view on the ground that the beginning point of Buddhist spirituality was the insight of Non-self and non-reality of things as declared by Śākyamuni. This critical insight is in itself Buddhist spirituality, and I believe, this spirituality can make an enormous impact to all other religions at any time anywhere. Surely, Nāgārjuna himself refers to the cult of Amitābha Buddha and his land of spiritual peace and happiness in the *Ta-chih-tu-lun,* and especially in his *Daśabhūmika-vibhāṣāśāstrạ*, he classified the easy Pureland way (易行浄土門)[58] as an effective means of realizing

般若経」) which was also translated by the same.

[58] The particular chapter "The Easy Practice" (「易行品」) in question

the path as equally as the difficult saintly way (難行聖道門) does.

Let us suppose that the general basis of critical spirituality of Buddhism was once accomplished through the Mauryan Empire in ancient India. In the subsequent period, however, all out movement of Hindu revivalism took place through the devotional and mythological forms of diverse and expansive cult movements, creating a Dark Age to the experience of Buddhist tradition. Lokesh Chandra's theory obviously has this background in mind, because Buddhist cults were an innovation on the Buddhist part in order to respond to the changing socio-cultural trend of those days. When Hsüan-tzang visited India, the Buddhist cult of Avalokiteśvara was declining along with other Buddhist cults, and it eventually succumbed to the Hindu cultic reclaiming just through simple switching. It is very clear to me that the Buddhist critical spirituality or ideology was no longer present as a prevailing thought and norm in Indian society around the time of his visit. It is somewhat ironic, I think, that the Buddhist cult of Avalokiteśvara which originated in India eventually lost its Buddhist spirit under Hindu cultural influence and was quickly reclaimed as a Hindu deity by their cult. In contrast, despite the radical change in its iconographic representation and its increasingly diverse cultural environment, the cult of Kuan-yin Bodhisattva has survived well in East Asia retaining its Buddhist spirituality in the core. Setting a question aside as to whether or not the original Pureland cult in India might be of the nature of Indian Hindu spirituality rather than of Buddhist spirituality, I can assert confidently that the nature of the Pureland faith and cult evolved in China was of the nature of Buddhist spirituality.

It seems very crucial to the prosperity of the Pureland tradition to keep alive this critical Buddhist spirituality and the awareness of human suffering as the crucial source of driving force for differentiating their own spirituality amidst so many other dynamic on-going religious movements, such as Christianity, Islam, Judaism, and so on, all in concentration of this similar awareness in global terms.

---

comes in the ninth of the *Discourse on the Ten Stages* (「十住毘婆沙論」). Cf. Inagaki, Hisao: *Nāgārjuna's Discourse on the Ten Stages* (*Dśābhūmika-vibhāṣā*); (A Study and Translation from Chinese of Verses and Chapter 9..of Verses and Chapter 9); Ryukoku Literature Series V, 1998. Also, Bruno Petsold: *The Classification of Buddhism Bukkyō Kyōhan, comprising the Classification of Buddhist Doctrines in India, China, and Japan* (in collaboration with Shinshō Hanayama and edited by Shohei Ichimura, published from Otto Harrassowitz Verlag, Wiesbaden, Germany, 1995), especially, Pt. XII, Chap. 30, Sect. 3; pp. 694 ff.

ARTICLE FOURTEEN

Natural Law as Basis of Communication between Theistic Religions and Non-Theistic Buddhism[1]

§1. Introduction

Despite the apparent reduction of tension and conflict during the past decade between the major political and social systems of the world, there seems to have been on the horizon an ominous trend growing as religious and communal tensions and conflicts in various parts of the world, resulting in human disasters and sufferings. There is a wise-saying that whatever is divided by one political reason can be reunified by another political reason, but whatever is divided by religious faiths can never return to its former unity. We have witnessed tragic examples in the regions of Palestine, Balkan, or Indian sub-continent attributed to the names of religious difference. The most obvious reason for existing conflicts between different factions, religious or otherwise, is so-called "communication-breakdown." More than anything else what we need today is some form of a "trans-cultural" theoretical foundation upon which each party of the groups involved in conflict can find a middle ground physically as well as psychologically, so as to accomplish mutual understanding and bring forth mutually acceptable concerted action. If the general opinion in the past is right in characterizing Buddhism as one that has held the honor of a name that has created least bloodshed in the name of its religion, I am obliged, as a Buddhist, once again to reflect upon the Buddhist theoretical foundation and see how and why it is contributive to the religious education and cultural dialogue for pluralism and tolerance.

The purpose of this paper is to clarify why Buddhists can advocate the practical and theoretical norms of Human Rights adopted by the architect of the United Nations in reference to the Classical thought of Greek philosophers, to compare the ways through which theistic religions and non-theistic Buddhism

---

[1] The 3rd UNESCO Seminar on the Contribution by Religions to the Culture of Peace, Granada, Spain; April, 1997.

respectively adopt the Classical concept of natural law, and propose how and why the Buddhist way may contribute to the contemporary religious education in the context of pluralism and tolerance.

§2. NATURAL LAW AND THE WORLD OF NATURE

Of all existing systems of ethics, which are more or less bound to their respective religious and cultural traditions, the Aristotelian system of ethics represents the most open and least dogmatic system on earth, because it was conceived on the basis of the rational faculty of humans, the broadest universal denomination of mankind. In his *Nichomachean Ethics*, for instance, Aristotle formulated the concept of "ultimate good as happiness" (*eudaemonia*),[2] meaning the realization of the ideal human nature that ought to be actualized by each and every human being. "Highest happiness" means complete self-realization of this "humanity" given potentially to every individual and knowable by his rational faculty through continual exercise of practical and theoretical virtues. Since the end of World War II, the human rights have been the dominant theme in providing mankind with those indispensable practical norms which are rationally abstracted as universals of natural law. The United Nation's charter specified the contents of this natural law in the Declaration of Human Rights[3] as the right to free exercise of reason and choice, the right to education, the right to political and economic participation, and so forth. All these universally acceptable norms are indispensable practical conditions for realizing the goal of human happiness, the fulfillment of the potential nature of humanity, physical, verbal, and mental.

With abundant faith in humanity, Aristotle conceived human nature as capable of acquiring the "practical virtue" through repeated exercise of reason in terms of the "golden mean," making the best, most precise choice of action under any and each given circumstance.[4]

---

[2] See Aristotle, *Nichomachean Ethics*, Book X, where "highest happiness" is summarily defined. Martin Oswald, trans., introd., notes (New York: Macmillan Pub. Co., 1962) pp. 285-91.

[3] See the "Preamble to the Declaration of Human Rights," *Human Rights: A Compilation of International Instruments* (New York: United Nations, 1988), pp. 1-7.

[4] See *Nichomachean Ethics*, Book II, in which Aristotle investigates the nature of "practical virtue" with regard to emotions and actions. He defines two extremes as well as the median point, stating that, "in

Besides this practical exercise of reason, Aristotle abstracted "theoretical exercise of reason" as a higher faculty for the uniquely human nature that makes an individual a human being, namely, exercise of reason for knowing and contemplating the law and order of society and the universe. While one acquires happiness in life through friendly association with fellow humans through practical virtues, one realizes ultimate happiness (*summum bonum*) in contemplative life through theoretical (or intellectual) virtue in the pursuit of truth. Aristotle thus determined as the highest good a contemplative life in which the faculty of theoretical reason contemplates on the nature of truth as contents of natural law.[5]

§3. ESPOUSAL AND SCHISM OF NATURAL AND DIVINE LAWS IN MODERN TIMES

During the Medieval period, this Classical concept of natural law was challenged by the divine law of Christian Church. Philosophically, not only Aristotle but also his predecessors, Plato and Socrates, sought for ultimate causes to determine what the potential nature of humanity is and how and why it should be fulfilled. Classical philosophy, thus, determined two ultimate causal principles in terms of Forms (*eidos*), essential and teleological goals, and in terms of Matter (*hyle*), corporeal substratum in which the essential nature is given as potential. In a nut-shell, the Grecian system of nature was thoroughly rational, constructed upon the exercise of reason. Medieval theology challenged this characteristic of the Classical thought of nature by opposing it with the mono-theistic being by faith as the primary cause of creation. This ultimate principle, masculine in gender, was of the Judaic origin, volitional in nature, but was conceived by theologians as the source of absolute certainty that precedes the knowledge which appropriates and comprehends it intellectually. Thus, challenge was made gradually but thoroughly by superimposing the divine law based on faith upon the rational

---

emotions and actions, excess and deficiency miss the mark, whereas the median is praised and constitutes success," concluding that "virtue or excellence is a characteristic involving choice, and,. . it consists in observing the mean relative to us, a mean which is defined by a rational principle, such as a man of practical wisdom would use to determine it." (p. 43).

[5] See *Nichomachean Ethics*, Book X, especially pp. 288ff, "7. Happiness, intelligence, and the contemplative life."

concept of natural law in two different ways. Augustine placed the divine law within the same world as that of reason, so-to-speak, thus creating tension and antithesis between the two.6 The scenario was an eventual victory of the kingdom of God over the kingdom of Earth. Thomas Aquinus placed divine law hierarchically as the higher, sacred order of faith over above the lower, profane order of reason.7 With his theology, an espousal was completed between the Classical philosophy of nature and the Christian faith of God within the European continent.

Modern Europe inherited this medieval scheme of the sacred and profane orders, but the faculty of reason soon re-asserted its authority and liberated itself from the status of subservience. The subsequent history of European philosophy seems to have taken the course of gradual dissolution of the medieval espousal. In this respect, the United Nations' declaration of Human Rights which ascertains the freedom of choice in thought and religion among other things seems to have evidenced the completion of this process.[8]

---

[6] The opposite polarity of Augustine's terminology is evident in his doctrine of predestination, so dramatically outlined in *The City of God* (*De Civitate Dei*). Augustine conceived of the divine will as a progressively expanding realm of heaven (the abode of angels and of humans predestined for redemption) within history over against the realm of Nature, the abode of demons and of humans not predestined for redemption whom God has abandoned to sin and guilt. Throughout the course of history, these two groups are related to one another as two different races which mingle only in outer action , while, internally, a strict separations is maintained. See W. Windelband, *A History of Philosophy*, translated by James H. Tufts, 12th ed. (New York: Macmillan Co., 1956), pp. 284-85.

[7] Unlike Augustine, Thomas Aquinas did not regard the political state as a consequence of the Fall, but as a necessary dimension of the world. Aquinas assumes that natural law also flows from the divine nature and must be so conceived, because it is the basis of all human institutions, morality, and social life. The political community is, in fact, the preparatory stage for the higher community of heaven. This assumption justified a system of class hierarchies, whereby the State was subordinated to the Church as a mere means to the end of complete fulfillment of natural teleology. Cf. Windelband, *Ibid.*, pp. 326-27.

[8] The subject of Human Right once became the central issue among philosophers of the Renaissance and Reformation period due to the stimulus of humanism on the one hand and the needs of modern life on the other. Thomas More, for instance, wrote a utopian community based on the principle of religious toleration, and Jean Bodin offered a project to make educated typical representatives of Christianity, Judaism, Muhammadanism, and Heathendom to find a form of worshipping God, which is equally satisfactory to all. Finally, Hugo Grotius proposed a complete separation of

Despite this optimism of the mid-20th century, the ideological war soon began and globally spread, proving the fact that the religious culture of Europe has still been dominating the history of the later 20th century. On account of Medieval espousal with Classical philosophy, the theological culture of Europe preferred the formal cause of ideas to that of corporeal matter. Previously, theologians subsumed the Classical concept of ideas as contents of the creator's omniscience, while rejecting the principle of corporeal matter which directly counters the creation of *ex-nihilo-nihil*. With this background, modern philosophers in Europe developed, on the one hand, the system of idealism by compromising reason with faith, while, on the other hand, also developed the system of materialism by clear separation from religious faith.[9] This kind of analysis alone clarifies

---

divine and human right in the sharp distinctness by placing divine right upon revelation and human right upon reason., and demanded an equally sharp and thoroughgoing separation of the spheres of life to which they apply. (Windelband, p. 427).

[9] Early modern philosophers in Europe, like Descartes, Spinoza, Leibnitz, Kant, Hegel, etc., affirming the existence of God, developed the rationalism based on the reality of universals, whereas in England, succeeding to the Nominalist tradition, Locke, Hume, etc., developed modern Empiricism. The former falls in the line of the Classical causal principle of Form, whereas the latter, in that of Matter. Kant, however, attempted to unify both traditions (i.e., the senses furnish the materials, and the intellect fashion them as knowledge according to the ideas) and examined the faculty of reason that gives forms to the immediate sense data in accordance with the *a-priori* forms of ideas. His major work *Critique of Pure Reason* was designed to examine the *a-priori* forms of reasoning to establish the validity of knowledge. British Empiricism influenced the French Positivist August Comte as well as John Stewart Mill of England, and further crossed the Atlantic to America, where it became Pragmatism of William James, John Dewey, etc. In opposition to the Rationalist theory of innate ideas, the philosophy of modern materialism was brought forth by Lamettrice (109-1751) and Condillac (1715-1780) in France, initially from the problem of mind-body relationship. They theorized that the content of mental activities should come solely from sense-perceptions. From repeated sensations, grow succeessively attention, recollection, distinction, comparison, judgement, inference, imagination, and expectation of the future, and finally with the help of linguistic symbols, abstraction and the grasping of general principles. (Cf. Windelband, op.cit., p. 456ff). The movement carried out by these, so-called Ideologists, culminated in the *Système de la Nature,* a purely dogmatic metaphyscs and a heavy armed attack upon all belief in the immaterial world (*Ibid.*, p. 481ff), attributed to Mirabeau's (Pseudonym, 1770). A century later, in opposition to the Hegelian Idealism, Fuerbach inverted the Hegelian system and brought forth a Nominalistic Materialism and theorized that the actual reality is the individual known to the senses, while everything universal, everything mental or spiritual, is but an

how and why the antithesis has taken hold of the two ideological camps with such volitional and emotional intensity, spilling their conflicts globally beyond the pail of the European continent.

§4. CAUSE OF COMMUNICATION BREAKDOWN AND BUDDHIST SOLUTION

The successful aversion to nuclear confrontation that took place nearly a decade ago, at least, has demonstrated the re-assertion of the human faculty of reason, but a new trend seems to be developing in emboldening the new religious right. Within past few years in America, the two groups of the pro-choice and the pro-life advocates have sharply confronted each other upon their difference. Despite the tradition of well-established separation between religious faith and political reason, the ultra-rightists bombed some abortion clinics, spreading fear and disgust among the pro-choice supporters. The guiding principle of the pro-life advocates seems to be religious conviction, whereas that of the pro-choice is rational decision. Though this is an extreme case, the trend seems to represent a typical form of confrontation between faith and reason within a society of theistic culture. One of the major reasons for which the post-war wisdom of international agencies have not been successfully coping with global conflicts that spread through accelerated speed of human interaction is the out-dated architectural vision, because the problem expected then was, more or less, limited to that of European history and was not the global complexity of religious and cultural confrontations. Without doubt, the hardest problem of the contemporary world is and will be religious difference between theistic forms of faith themselves. The problem of Middle East surmounts the pinnacle of complexity and danger that involves three mono-theistic religions which share not only an identical, as it were, supreme being but also partially the same sacred scripture. The question is: Why can't they communicate among themselves by letting reason work?

From the logical point of view, what is essential to valid

---

illusion of the individual. He held that Mind or spirit is "Nature in its otherness," making a purely anthropological explanation of religion, namely that Man regards his own generic nature – what he wishes to be himself – as God. (*Ibid.*, 641, 655). Marx and Engels applied the inverted product of the Hegelian dialectic to their theorization of the socialism's materialistic philosophy of history in terms of economic force as primary cause.

communication between two interlocutors is the condition that whatever is under discussion must be identical in the minds of speaker and listener. But often times, this simple criterion is hard to come by. Even when the subject matter is expressed by one and the same term, the respective predications create different meanings, resulting in a discrepancy between their references. Here is an example of logical dispute that took place in Medieval India between two Hindu schools. It was concerned with the definition of a "vocal word" or "utterance" (*śabda*). One party asserted that "A word is *impermanent*, because it is a product, just as a pot is." Another party countered it, saying: "A word is *permanent*, because it is audible (communicable), just as any other word is." To the former conventionalist, an utterance is impermanent because it disappears no sooner than uttered, whereas to the latter transcendentalist, it is permanent because it creates a certain ideation in the mind of any listener anywhere when uttered. Although the both parties believed that they were referring to one and the same object of reference because of the same subject term, they, in actuality, were talking about two different things. Consider the underlying universals, namely, "Whatever is a human product is impermanent" which is the cultural basis of the former, whereas "Whatever is audible is permanent" is the cultural basis of the latter. This difference constitutes the cause of communication breakdown.[10]

Evaluating the above logical deadlock, I think that it is impossible for the two parties to resolve their difference logically, nor is there any good reason for either party to choose the claim of the other. Consider the case of dispute between two theistic religions totally

---

[10] In Ancient and Medieval India, inter-sectarian arguments were always carried out on the formal logic of their kind. It was a syllogistic argument consisting of five-member statements, but by the beginning of Medieval India, Buddhist logicians simplified it to become a three-membered formula as their standard, i.e., Thesis, Reason, and Example. Unlike European syllogism, Indian logic in general required a statement of exemplification, indicating its origin inductively. The Discrepancy quoted in the arguments is more apparent in the following chart:

A pot exemplifies a Universal (*vyāpti*): "Whatever is a product is impermanent."

(1) Thesis:	*Śābdo 'nityaḥ*:	A vocal word is impermanent
(2) Reason:	*kṛtakatvāt*:	Because it is a product,
(3) Example:	*ghaṭavat*:	Like a pot is.

A vocal word exemplifies a Universal: "Whatever is audible is permanent."

(1) Thesis:	*śabdo nityaḥ*:	A vocal word is permanent,
(2) Reaspm:	*śravaṇatvāt*:	Because it is audible,
(3) Example:	*śabdatvavat:*	Like any other word.

committed to their respective faiths. Should any conversion occur among their members, each doctrine must be chosen for reasons that are ultimately personal and subjective, or as some sort of mystical apperception, instead of rational choice, precisely because there is no way to prove one faith and disprove another by rational faculty insofar as it is concerned with the efficacy of spiritual salvation. The problem is indeed how to deal with similar difference on an occasion of inter-group dialogue. In this context, the way Buddhist logicians attempted to resolve it in Medieval India seems to be relevant. They approached the above logical dispute with three cautious considerations which seem to be especially relevant to the context of inter-religious dialogue. (1) They lay emphasis on the respective reasons, namely, "being a product" and "being audible," but not on the syllogism as a whole, because each syllogism is valid in the light of syllogistic rules. (2) They also accepted their simultaneous validity within each system of philosophical presuppositions referring to their underlying thoughts, i.e., "Whatever is a product is impermanent," and "Whatever is audible is permanent." (3) They shifted both the mental process and the logical meaning on to a different plane from that of logical laws. Evaluating the Buddhist approach to the above deadlock, Dr. Arnold Kunst, specialist on Indian Buddhist logic, gave the following remark nearly half a century ago: "It is permissible '*in universo*' to juxtapose against "reality" two arguments which appear contradictory to prove one thesis and it is permissible to pose one argument to prove two theses which appear mutually exclusive. It is not permissible to do so at the same time in one system, which, as it were, assumes under these circumstances the weight of reality in the form of an adopted set of dogmas, doctrines or conclusions (*siddhānta*), whichever may be applicable."[11] I am obliged to add to his evaluation by saying: In other words, Buddhist logicians intended to resolve the confrontation, not in the logical and linguistic domain, but in the subliminal domain prior to the logical and linguistic process in the minds of confrontation.

§5. LOGIC OF *CATUṢKOṬI* AND BUDDHIST INSIGHT

From ancient times, Buddhists held the formula of four-fold

---

[11]Arnold Kunst: "The Concept of the Principle of Excluded Middle in Buddhism," *Rocznik Orientalistyczzni*, Tom. XX1, 1957. p. 147.

assertion (*catuṣkoṭi*) as part of their logical theory, that an object of reference can be asserted by four alternative *affirmations*: "x is A," or "x is -A" or "x is both A and -A" or "x is neither A nor -A." From Śākyamuni Buddha onward, this formula was frequently applied to analyze a given logical context. In general, in order to make an efficient communication, two interlocutors need, at least, two elemental propositions for identifying a given object of reference, just as a crossing point can be specified by two lines. Only when a subject term and a predicate term are meaningfully linked, both parties come to know what they are talking about, provided that the linkage can be ascertained as valid by their common culture or religious faith or relevant logic. Language is a system of symbols, thus semantically agreed for referring to certain objects and syntactically agreed for the linkage of symbols. Functionally, naming an object by a symbol is referential, and linking another symbol to it is tendentious or purposive. Śākyamuni and Buddhist thinkers knew that the process of identifying a thing by a name as "A" is necessarily accompanied by the process of differentiating it from another, say, "-A."[12] Accordingly, the linkage of two terms was necessarily examined within the context of the four formulas. The advantage of this four-fold formula is that it actually discloses two different levels of consciousness: (1) On the conscious level engaged in logical and linguistic convention, a propositional linkage is verified either as valid or as invalid by applying a given universal (e.g., "Whatever is a product is impermanent,") to its reference (a vocal word). (2) On the subliminal level where one's consciousness is disengaged from logical and linguistic convention, no singular propositional linkage is ascertained, precisely because what is out there in convention as "A" is accompanied by its opposite "-A,"

---

[12] This subject matter was theorized by Buddhist logician, Dignāga of the fifth century, as *Apoha* (Exclusion Theory); such that the referential use of a word "A" is based on an exclusion of its opposite word "–A." On account of this referential structure, no use of word is regarded to refer to a positive reality as is believed in Naive Realist convention. Suppose, we are listening to an on-going speech, in which phonemes, words, and sentences are incessantly coming and going. Catching a series of rapid sounds, our mind instantaneously configurates them into a word, a series of words into a sentence, and a series of sentences into a unified understanding. Even, underlying this dynamic flow of speech or thoughts, the dual operations of identification and differentiation ascertain or repudiate successive linkages at every moment of consciousness. What regulates a linkage is the four-fold formula, which avid logical reflection alone can *posteriori* abstract.

resulting in the loss of referential existence. Hence, no conventional criterion is at hand for any verification in this subliminal plane of consciousness.

What justifies the two levels of validity determination in terms of convention (*Vyavahāra)* and insight (*Paramārtha*)[13] respectively is the doctrine of the five aggregates of elementary sense data (*pañca-skandha*), the primary basis of Buddhist theory of "Non-Self" (*anātman*), i.e., repudiation of the real existence of an individual self. It appears to be strange from the point of view of convention to repudiate the core of an individual person, believed to be the seat of all vested interest, to be unreal and non-existent by disintegrating his being into the five aggregates of psycho-physical elements. Upon a contact of a sense organ with incoming stimuli, the initial category of data is physical (*rūpa* or form or color) which is fivefold (visual, sound, smell, taste, and tangible) and the following four categories are psychicological in nature in the order of sensation, ideation, configuration, and consciousness (*vedanā, saṃjñā, saṃskāra,* and *vijñāna*). Traditionally, these elementary and momentary psycho-physical elements are regarded more real than an individual person, because these elements are of the nature of ultimate particular, whereas an individual person is a universal that is brought about from the configuration of multiple sense data in terms of direct and indirect causal networks (*hetu-pratyaya-tā*).

Even when a cognition arises as perception of an external object, what underlies this perception is neither an objective entity really out there, nor is there a subjective agent whose core self cognizes it. Given a point of sensation, the symbolic process of the mind is activated to operate referentially and configurate an object as if it were out there, while simultaneously to operate tendentiously to search for a predication through memories of past experiences. What ultimately validates a proposition is not what is believed to be externally existent, but whether a given subject-predicate linkage

---

[13] The meanings of these two terms may be best understood from Nāgārjna's elucidation in his *Mādhyamika-śāstra*, chap. 24, verses 8, 9, and 10:

> In teaching the doctrine (*Dharma*), the Enlightened Ones rely on the two truths, empirical (*vyavahāra-* or *sāṃvṛti-satya*) and transcendental (*paramārtha-satya*). Those who do not differentiate these two truths do not understand the profound reality (tattva) in the doctrine of the Buddha. Without relying on the empirical truth, the transcendental truth cannot be shown; without relying on the transcendental truth, the *Nirvāṇa* cannot be realized.

is correct in the context circumscribed by four formulas prior to the perception of an object. The reason that Buddhist logicians attempted to resolve the sectarian logical deadlock in this subliminal plane of consciousness is that perceptual and conceptual error likely occurs in the subliminal plane due to a variety of biases, as is known from the fact that even a spontaneous perception is an interpretative and unconscious version of what we do after we have perceived. More importantly, they are aware that the subliminal plane provides a middle ground to both parties logically as well as psychologically. Accordingly, for all practical values, what is essential to education, training, experience, and so forth is the efficacy of rectification given to the subliminal domain of human consciousness.

Although the insight of dual truth (*dvaya-satya*), which I referred before as the two levels of validity determination, was not theorized in the early period of Buddhism, it was already implied in Śākyamuni's primary causal insight of "dependent origination" (*pratītyasamutpāda*) and was underlying his initial teaching of the "four noble truths" (*catvāti-āryasatyāni*). On the one hand, the life of engagement in the system of logic and language (*anuloma*) leads to the course of activity, such as, birth, death, and suffering (*duḥkha*), whereas the life of disengagement from it (*pratiloma*) leads to the course of cessation (*nirodha*) and eventually to *Nirvāṇa*. Language constitutes the medium par excellence for culture formation because it depicts, prescribes, and sustains all forms of behavioral patterns that make up subjective and objective institutions of society. Simultaneously cultural forms reinforce the ways of using language. The use of symbols may at times create great liberation in human mind for universal communication, and yet more often it creates bondage and prejudice in it, interfering with proper communication and mutual understanding. In this sense even rational and logical thinking can be said to reflect a particular form of culture and convention. In short, the Buddhist approach to Enlightenment (*Bodhi*) and Emancipation (*Mokṣa*) is to be found in the process of purifying human mind in the subliminal domain of consciousness and, as it were, instilling in it good wills (*karman*) through diligent practices.[14]

---

[14] *Dhamma-padam*: Selection No. 183. W. Rahula: *What the Buddha Taught*, with a Foreword by Paul Demiéville, Bangkok: Hawtrai Foundation Press 2531 (1988).

"Not to do any evil, to cultivate good, to purify one's mind: this is the Teaching of the Buddhas."

§6. BUDDHIST AND CLASSICAL THOUGHTS OF NATURE

I am narrowing my focus to a comparison between the ancient Greek humanist system of thought and that of Buddhist thought. A Buddhist thinker of the 2nd century wrote a voluminous commentary on the text called *Perfection of Prajñā Insight*, in which he classified humanity into four types in accordance with four different goals of life:[15] (1) those who seek happiness in the pursuit of desire, love, and self-preservation as shared by all species; (2) those who seek happiness in the pursuit of practical norms for fulfillment respectively according to individual endowments and circumstances; (3) those who seek happiness in the pursuit of remedy to overcome moral defilements, self-delusion, and ignorant hypocrisy, and (4) those who seek happiness in the pursuit of primary insight (*prajñā*) and ultimate quiescence. The time of this author's active life in Western India was the first half of the second century when Greeks, Persians, Scythians, Parthians, and Kuṣāṇas settled in the subcontinent and participated in Indian civilization through Buddhism. Therefore, his classification carries a remarkable degree of universalism.

Aristotle recognized two different kinds of virtues as practical and theoretical. It is the former which is concerned with the practical conditions, for instance, physical and mental well-being, economic and legal security, familial and community association, moral and political participation, and so forth. These norms are, more or less, found in all human societies, and difference is minor. Insofar as it is the rationally calculable norms of human nature, even including theoretical virtue, communication can be accomplished through the exercise of proper usage of logical and linguistic tools.

---

[15] Nāgārjuna (c. mid-first cent. through mid-second cent.), author of *The Treatise on the Perfection of the Great Prajñā Insight (Mahāprajñāpāramitā-śāstra)*, forefather of Mahāyāna Buddhist philosophy and especially, founder of the Mādhyamika school. Cf. Étienne Lamotte's French translation of its Chinese version *Ta-chih-tu-lun* translated by Kumārajīva of the fifth century; *Le traité de la grand vertu de sagesse de Nāgārjuna*. Louvain Institut Orientliste; Bibliothèque de Muséon, Vol. 18. New reproduction published from the Institut: Tome 1 (vol. 25, published 1981), Tome II (vol 26, 1981), Tome III (vol. 2, 1970), Tome IV (vol. 12, 1976), Tome V (vol. 24, 1980). Lamotte rendered the following French translations: 1. Le point de vue mondain (*laukika siddhānta*), 2. le point de vue individuel (*prātipauruṣika siddhānta*), 3. le point de vue theérapeutique (*prātipākṣika siddhānta*), and 4. le point de vue absolu (*pāramārthika siddhānta*). Cf. Tome I, p. 27ff.

Surely, the initial three Buddhist criteria quoted above go along with the Aristotelian goals of practical virtue. But, does Buddhist theoretical virtue which is directed to the disengagement from the scope of logic and language go along with the Aritotelian theoretical virtue? I think that it does, because disengagement is meant only from the propensity of the referential and tendentious forces of the mind, and it is neither disregarding nor abandoning rational faculty. From childhood, we learn the use of language through listening to others, observing their behaviors, and testing out the efficacy of its usage by ourselves, and along with these experiences, we acquire the mind ingrained with conviction that things exist in the way in which our language depicts. Examining the referential and tendentious forces of the mind, though these are essential to symbolic processes, Buddhist thinkers cast a doubt on the general conviction about the efficacy of logic and language as "faculty of seeing things as they really are."[16]

Buddhist thought does not repudiate the world of nature as depicted by the Classical concept of natural law, and that what it repudiates or applies remedy to is the underlying mental forces of linguistic behavior and culture formation, namely, (1) referential force of the mind directed toward objective existence and (2) tendentious or purposive force of the mind that links one symbol with another depicting existential relations. I believe that the Buddhist insight into the dual truth structure is contributive to successful dialogue between different religious traditions and cultures, because it provides interlocutors with an extra-space for rational faculty and human interaction.

§7. Conclusion: Necessity of Open Comparative Approach

The religious insight of Buddhism can be traced back to Śākyamuni's own experience regarding three basic aspects of human existence, that every phenomenon (*sarva-saṃskāra*) is impermanent (*anitya*), suffering (*duḥkha*), and without its own self (*anātman*). We cannot resist the deepening sense of our experience of impermanence as our age advances. Having seen recurrent conflicts, atrocities, and horrible genocides that have taken place in various parts of the world in

[16] *Yathābhūtam,* adv. "in accordance with fact," "according to what has happened," "according to the truth," [looking at a thing] "as it really is" or "has really happened.". Thus, *yathābhūtam* is used to distinguish an act of seeing as an insight and not an ordinary perception.

recent years, I am compelled to reflect upon Śākyamuni's insight, thinking how important it is to create some way of fundamental communication between the factions, religious or otherwise, to prevent the global trend of tragic human sufferings from further escalation into future generations. It may be true that most of those ethnic conflicts and bloodshed are caused by other factors that have nothing to do with high culture and religions. And also it may be absurd to parallel high culture conflicts among different religious faiths on the one hand and ethnic communal conflicts which strive for basic needs of human survival on the other. I suspect, however, that low culture conflicts may have been perpetuated because of religious or cultural difference, no matter how unsophisticated such difference might be.

Considering the difference between the nature of truth based on human reason and that of truth based on revelation not belonging to human reason, but something that ought to be believed, I agree that it is imperative to build the culture of peace in human mind and that this culture of peace ought to be based on the faculty of reason. The culture of peace ought to be born, nurtured, and developed in an environment in which the faculty of reason can accomplish communication, irrespective of whether it is an inter-religious or inter-cultural dialogue, and also in which reason can exercise its function for rational choice of thought, religion, and culture best fit to every individual. Again, such an environment should persuade any religion, theistic or non-theistic, as well as any thought system to allow rational faculty to conduct comparative approach toward any of the existing thoughts, religions and cultures. Even a revealed truth is a human experience, and when once expressed in language, it becomes a thought to be subjected to equal check and scrutiny as any other literature can be. As to the comparative approach, I subscribe myself to three criteria: (1) how effective a given system of truth is in regulating one's conduct as well as the law and order of society; (2) what kind of ultimate truth is most rationally acceptable to oneself; and (3) how closely this truth is being experienced as part of one's life. I humbly believe that the Buddhist approach in dealing with the mental propensity of referential and tendentious process of language will be contributive to the creation of the culture of peace.

ARTICLE FIFTEEN

Buddha-Dharma and Natural Law towards A Trans-cultural Universal Ethics[1]

§I Introduction

Regardless of the cultural difference between the East and the West, the concept of "natural law" was clearly formulated within their respective histories of ideas to precipitate their systems of human ethics. In the West, the concept of natural law was firmly theorized by Aristotle on the basis of reason and humanity. Later, this was challenged by divine law based on faith, thus creating a perpetual tension and conflict in the Western mind between secular and religious traditions. In the East, especially in ancient India, where Buddhism arose, the concept of natural law was not developed in genuinely rational terms, but on the basis of a semi-religious Brahmanical and Hindu belief. It upheld class distinctions (*varṇa*) as well as communal or caste distinctions (*jāti*). The Buddhist concept of Dharma is essentially religious, assuring spiritual emancipation. It transcends all social convention, upholding the ideal human type of the Arhat and Bodhisattva as a challenge to existing communal norms.

The following has three tasks: (1) a review of the meaning of the Buddhist concept of Dharma within the ancient Indian social context, (2) an examination of why, unlike theistic divine law, it is compatible with the rational concept of "natural law," and (3) a clarification of how it can serve as a trans-cultural basis for universal human ethics.

§2. The Need for the Conscious Choice of A Theoretical Basis of Ethics

In 1950's, as Japan began to rebuild a new nation on democratic principles, Kumatarō Kawada published his concisely written work,

---

[1] Presented at An International Symposium as the first of the Chung Hua Institute of Buddhist Studies, Taiwan Republic of China, January 1990, and its publication included in *Buddhist Ethics and Modern Society, An International Symposium*, edited by Charles Wei-hsun Fu and Sandra A. Wawrytko, Greenwood Press, 1991; pp. 383-405.

Ethics.[2] Because it comprises the result of the author's life-long research on the subject of major ethical doctrines of the world, namely, those of the ancient Greeks, Christian theologians of Medieval Europe, modern philosophers such as Kant and Hegel, ancient Confucian and Taoist thinkers of China, and early (Theravāda) and later (Mahāyāna) Buddhist traditions, it will be entitled *A Comparative Ethics*. Kawada's main objective was to demonstrate how and why we, as human beings are obliged to examine and compare the existing systems of ethical thought in the world, and then to persuasively present his reasons for choosing the Buddhist system of thought as the theoretical foundation of his own ethics. More than ever before, the meaning and method of Kawada's work have become significant today, because we are more clearly aware of the pluralistic nature of the world and consciously choose among systems, irrespective of our previous affiliations. In what follows, Kawada's conscious choice of the Buddhist system of thought as "fundamental ethics" will be defended.[3]

As members of the human race, we share many ethical norms in common, especially practical virtues transcending cultural, religious or ideological differences. Despite this universality, the theoretical foundation of practical virtue exercised in daily conduct may vary, precisely because we have been reared in different societies. For instance, in all major systems of thought and forms of cultural tradition of the world, we find the moral injunction "One ought not to lie." Yet, if each of us is asked: "Why do you uphold this ethical norm?" the answer may vary from one person to another, depending upon one's cultural, religious, or ideological background. Until the later part of this century, scholars of each tradition tended to confine their investigation into the subject of practical virtue or moral conduct to their own system of thought and homogeneous culture, rarely venturing to inquire into other systems. Given present opportunities for travelling and widespread human interaction, the study of ethics increasingly has been compelled to venture into the cultural differences of major theoretical systems of thought and

---

[2] Kumatarō Kawada, *Ethics*, Tokyo: Sekai-shoin Publishing Co., 1956.

[3] "Fundamental ethics" is a rendering of Kawada's phrase '*kompon rinri*' (根本倫理) meaning the "theoretical foundation" or "fundamental thought" that underlies a system of ethics. It also means "intellectual or theoretical virtue" (*chisei-no-toku*, 知性の徳), as distinguished from the "peripheral ethics" (*gi-matsu-rinri*, 技末倫理) or "practical/moral virtue" (*jinrin-no-toku*, 人倫の徳). All English renderings of Kawada's terminology as well as translations of passages from his work are the author's.

tradition. Kawada admirably accomplishes this task in his work prior to presenting his choice of the Buddhist system of thought as his fundamental ethics.

Despite an apparent reduction of tension and conflict among the major political and social systems in the world in recent years, there has been an ominous growth in religious and communal tensions and conflicts, resulting in human disasters and suffering. Whatever is divided by politics can be reunited by another political cause, but whatever is divided by religion can never be reunited.

The most obvious reason for these conflicts, religious or otherwise, is "communication-breakdown."[4] More than anything else what we need is a trans-cultural theoretical foundation wherein each member of the conflicting groups can find a middle ground, physically as well as psychologically, upon which to build mutual understanding and bring forth plans for mutually acceptable concerted action. If the general opinion in the past is correct in characterizing Buddhism as one of the most peaceful religions on Earth, we, as Buddhists, are obliged to reflect upon our theoretical foundation of ethics and respond to this honorable evaluation and challenge.

Although Kawada's work is based on his extensive studies into the theoretical foundations of ethics in historically universal systems,[5] the focus here will be a comparison of the ancient Greek humanist system and that of Indian Buddhism. The reason is that the former system is regarded as most universal in terms of the natural (i.e., rational) aspect of humanity, while I will argue that the Buddhist system of thought harbors no rational, emotional, or volitional conflict with it.

---

[4] This terms is borrowed from Thomas Kuhn's work, *The Structure of Scientific Revolutions*, 2nd ed. (Chicago, Illinois: University of Chicago Press, 1970).

[5] "Universal systems" refers to the major world doctrines of ethics formulated by Aristotelian and Stoic philosophy, Christian theology, Confucian and Taoist thought, and the Buddhist philosophy of "trans-empirical knowledge" (*chi-ken-no-tetsugaku*, 知見の哲学). Unlike peripheral or practical virtue, whose universality depends on the similarity of human nature above and beyond temporal or spatial differences, theoretical virtue is not necessarily universal in terms of human nature, but only within a given group on the basis of historical continuity (Kawada, pp. 82-83). For instance, the idea of philosophy as "the study par excellence of ultimate principle and cause," the core of the humanist tradition, constitutes the theoretical foundation of humanist ethics. Likewise, in Buddhist philosophy "trans-empirical knowledge" (*chi-ken-no-tetsugaku*, *shyŭō-ken* (正見), *sammādiṭṭhi*, or *samyag-dṛṣṭi*) has been upheld within Buddhist society from its inception as the fundamental theoretical virtue and thus is rightly described as "historical universal."

§3. THE WORLD OF NATURE AND MOKṢA IN RELATION TO HUMAN ETHICS

Among all existing systems of ethics, generally bound to their cultural or religious traditions, the Aristotelian system represents the most open and least dogmatic system, being conceived on the basis of the human rationality. In his *Nichomachean Ethics*, Book X,[6] for instance, Aristotle formulated the concept of ultimate good as "happiness" (*eudaemonia*), meaning the realization of ideal human nature that ought to be actualized by everyone. "Highest happiness" means complete self-realization of this potential in everyone and knowable by reason, i.e., a complete and continual exercise of practical and theoretical virtues.

Since the end of the World War II, human rights have been the dominant theme in providing humankind with indispensable practical norms rationally abstracted as practical universals of natural law[7] - rights to material fulfillment, free exercise of reason and choice, education, to political and economic participation, and so forth. These universally acceptable norms, are indispensable practical conditions for realizing the goal of human happiness, fulfilling the potential nature of humanity, physically, verbally, and mentally.

With abundant faith in humanity, Aristotle conceived of human nature as capable of acquiring the "practical virtue" through the repeated exercise of reason, namely, observing the "golden mean" in conduct by making the best, most precise choice of action under each and every circumstance.[8] In addition, Aristotle abstracted the

---

[6] See Aristotle, *Nichomachean Ethics*, Book X, where "highest happiness" is summarily defined; Martin Oswald, trans., intro., notes (New York: Macmillan Pub. Co., 1962, pp. 286-91.

[7] See the "Preamble to the Declaration of Human Rights," *Human Rights: A compilation of International Instruments* (New York: United Nations, 1988), pp. 1-7.

[8] See Nichomachean Ethics, Book II, in which Aristotle investigates the nature of "practical virtue" with regard to emotions and actions. He defines two extremes as well as the median point, stating that, "in emotions and actions, excess and deficiency miss the mark, whereas the median is praised and constitutes success," concluding that "virtue or excellence is a characteristic involving choice, and . . it consists in observing the mean relative to us, a mean which is defined by a rational principle, such as a man of practical wisdom would use to determine it" (p. 43).

"theoretical exercise of reason" as the higher faculty of our unique human nature, namely, the exercise of "theoretical virtue" for knowing and contemplating law and order in society and the universe. While one acquires happiness in life through friendly association with fellow humans in accordance with practical virtues, one realizes ultimate happiness (the *summum bonum*) in the contemplative life, in which the faculty of theoretical reason contemplates the nature of truth.[9]

In ancient India, the goals of life were conceptualized somewhat differently, although parallels exist. For instance, Kauṭilya, known as the state councillor to the founder of Maurya dynasty, Candragupta (c. 324 to 313 B.C.), a contemporary of Alexander the Great, classified the four goals of human life,[10] as (1) *kāma*, gratification of sensual desire in pursuit of love and pleasure, (2) *artha*, acquisition of material wealth in pursuit of economic and political success, (3) *dharma*, observance of religious and moral values in pursuit of fulfilling the duties prescribed to social hierarchies of Hindu society, and (4) *mokṣa*, realization of emancipation in pursuit of spiritual release. While the initial three [Kāma, Artha, and Dharma] known as the group of three (trivarga), constitute the pursuits of worldly happiness, the goal of Mokṣa or "other-worldy pursuit" in Weberian jargon[11] was the ultimate goal of life, the final human good.[12]

In the Buddhist literature, these four aims of life were reconceptualized. Thus, the author of the *Mahāprajñāpāramitopadeśa-śāstra* (i.e., *Ta-chih-tu-lun*, 「大智度論」; *the Treatise on the Great-Wisdom Perfection*),[13] classified humanity into four types in accordance with

---

[9] See Aristotle, Book X, especially pp. 288ff, "7. Happiness, intelligence, and the contemplative life."

[10] Kauṭilya, *Arthaśāstra* (*The Treatise on Polity*, or literally translated, *On the Realization of Wealth*). See R. Shastry, ed., 2nd rev. ed. (Mysore: 1919). A translation was published in Bangalore, 1915, 1923, Bārhaspatya *Arthaśāstra*, ed. and F. W. Thomas, trans. (Labore, India: Punjab Sanskrit Series, 1921), pp. 76-77.

[11] See Max Weber, *The Sociology of Religion*, Ephraim Fischoff, trans., Talcott Persons, intro. (Boston: Beacon Press, 1963). Weber introduced four typologies of religion from the sociological point of view, which he considered to encompass the widest spectrum of types of religions: (1) other-worldly mysticism, (2) other-worldly asceticism, (3) inner-worldly mysticism, and (4) inner-worldly asceticism. See also Weber's *The Religion of India: The Sociology of Hinduism and Buddhism*, Hans H. Gerth and Don Martindale, trans. and eds. (Glencoe, Ill.: Free Press, 1958).

[12] See Heinrich Zimmer, *Philosophies of India* (New York: Meridian, 1956), pp. 34-47.

[13] Although the author is generally accepted as Nāgārjuna, the great dialectician and author of the *Madhyamakakārikā-śāstra*, *Vigrahvyāvartanī*,

the four different goals (*siddhāntas*, *hsi-t'an*, 悉檀)[14]: (1) those who seek happiness in terms of fulfillment of desire, love, and self-preservation as shared by all species (*loka-siddhānta*, shih-chien, 世間悉檀); (2) those who seek happiness in terms of good conduct according to their individual inclinations and circumstances, as adequate to themselves (*pṛthagjana-siddhānta*, *ko-ko-wei-jên*, 各各為人悉檀); (3) those who seek happiness in the pursuit of the eradication of all Karmic defilements which may cause an individual to fail to grasp what is right, resulting in wrong action (*pratipakṣika-siddhānta*, *tui-chih*, 対治悉檀); and (4) those who seek happiness in the pursuit of knowledge of the paramount objective that transcends the pursuit of the world, i.e. beyond convention (*paramārtha*, *ti-i-i*, 第一義悉檀).

There are evident similarities and differences between the ancient Greek and Buddhist conceptions. The initial three Buddhist criteria of human life correspond to the Aristotelian realization of happiness in all the aspects of human nature. However, the fourth, i.e., pursuit of the paramount goal of quiescence as ultimate happiness (*paramārtha-siddhānta*), is radically different from the Aristotelian goal of ultimate happiness for the following reason. Whereas Aristotle spoke of ultimate happiness within the scope of logic and language (*logos*), whereby the rational faculty contemplates the nature of ultimate truth, in the Buddhist conception, ultimate happiness is conceived as transcending the faculty of logic and language, and hence reason.

§4. BUDDHIST DUAL TRUTH: TRANS-EMPIRICAL AND CONVENTIONAL

The classification of spiritual release (*mokṣa*) as the ultimate goal of life expresses a pan-Indian cultural formula. The thinkers of the Brahmanical and *Upaniṣadic* thought referred to such realization as the state in which self (*ātman*) is identified with the principle of the universe, Brahman (i.e., "*tat-tvam-asi*" or the state in which ultimate truth can be expressed in language only negatively "*neti neti*").[15] Since Buddhist thought repudiated the idea of "Brahman"

---

and so forht, the problem of authorship has been bracketed in the present discussion.

[14] See *Taishō Daizō-kyō*, vol. 25, p. 49b; also, Ryūjō Yamada, *Daijō Bukkyō Seiritsu-ron Josetsu* (「大乘仏教成立論序説」 *The prolegomena to the Theory of the Establishment of Mahāyāna Buddhism*) (Kyoto: Heirakuji shoten, 1995), p. 312.

[15] See respectively the *Chāndogya-Upaniṣad* (VI, i. 6. 12-13) in R. E.

as the ultimate principle of the universe, as well as that of "*ātman*" as the ultimate principle of each individual self, the Buddhist goal of emancipation, or Nirvāṇa, was differently viewed in terms of "dual truth" (i.e., *satya-dvaya*, *êrh-ti*, 二諦). Conventional truth (*saṃvṛti-* or *vyavahāra-satya*, *shih-su-ti*, 世俗諦) corresponds to our ordinary world of reason (*anumāna*) and sense perception (*pratyakṣa*), while ultimate truth (*paramārtha-satya*, *ti-i-i* or *chên-ti*, 第一義諦 or 真諦) transcends the faculty of reason and perception by means of the introspective transcendent faculty (*prajñā*, *pan-jo*, 般若).[16] The uniqueness of this dual-truth conception consists in the dialectical relation between the two truths.

In the West, natural law, as abstracted by scientific reasoning, soon was superimposed upon divine law in terms of Christian faith in two different ways. Augustine placed the divine law within the realm of reason, creating tension and antithesis between the two,[17]

Hume, trans., *The Thirteen Principal Upanishads* (Oxford: 1921), pp. 247-48; and the *Bṛhadāraṇyaka-Upaniṣad* (IV. v. 15), Hume, under "*neti neti*," p. 147.

[16] Nāgārjuna first introduced the doctrine of "dual truth" in his *Madhyamakakārikā-śāstra*, 24: 8-10 (i.e., "Examination of the Four Holy Truths"; *āryasatya-parīkṣā-nāma*).

> Based on the two kinds of truths, Buddhas teach the Dharma in two ways, in terms of "contingent practicality" (saṃvṛti-satya) and "unconditioned transcendence" (*paramārtha-satya*) (k.8).
>
> Those who do not understand the difference between these two truths cannot know the profound meaning of the Buddha's teaching (k.9).
>
> Without depending on the truth of contingent practicality, the truth of unconditioned transcendence cannot be shown. Without realizing unconditioned transcendence, Nirvāṇa cannot be experienced (k.10).

For a detailed study of the meaning of '*saṃvṛti*' or *vyavahāra*,' see Gaddjin Nagao's "An Interpretation of the Term '*Saṃvṛti* (convention) in Buddhism," *Silver Jublee Volume of the Zinbun-kagaku Kenkyusyo* (Kyoto: Kyoto University, 1954), pp. 550-61. The term '*paramārtha*' literally means the primary, foremost, or highest meaning or object of pursuit, thus approximating the Latin term *summum bonum*. The concept of *paramārtha* is clarified when contrasted with *saṃvṛti*.

[17] The oppositional polarity of Augustine's terminology is evident in his doctrine of predestination, so dramatically outlined in the *City of God* (*De Civitas Dei*). Augustine conceives of the divine will as a progressively expanding realm of heaven (the abode of angels and humans predestined for redemption) within history over against the realm of Nature, the abode of demons and of humans not predestined for redemption whom God has abandoned to sin and guilt. Throughout the course of history, these two groups are related to one another as two different races which mingle only in outer action, while, internally, a strict separation is maintained. See W. Windelband, *A History of Philosophy*, James H. Tufts, trans., 12th ed. (New York: Macmillan Co., 1956), pp. 284-85.

whereas Thomas Aquinas posited a hierarchical scheme,[18] in which divine law represented a higher, sacred order above the lower, profane order of reason. These Medieval schemes of the sacred and profane orders, however, proved incapable of retaining their influence in the modern era, when the faculty of reason re-asserted its authority and liberated itself from the status of medieval subservience to theological concerns.

In the Buddhist system of thought, however, the two truths were conceived neither in terms of the Augustinian antagonism nor in that of the Thomistic hierarchy. Especially in Mahāyāna, the two orders are dialectically conceived as "totally identical and totally different simultaneously,"[19] to borrow the Mādhyamika expression. In the Yogācāra system of three-fold nature (*tri-svabhāva*), the state of absolute quiescence (*parinispanna*, *yüan-ch'eng-shih*, 円成実) is distinguished from the state of phenomenal delusion (*parikalpita*, *pien-wai-sho-chih*, 偏計所執) and yet, the respective referential spheres of these two coincide in "dependent nature" (*paratantra*, *i-t'a-ch'i*, 依他起).[20] Again, in the *Mahāyāna-śraddhotpāda-śāstra*, the ultimate truth of "thusness" (*tathatā*, *chên-ju*, 真如) is considered to be identical with the totality of (psycho-physical) phenomena, because the obstructed vision of human beings temporarily views their appearance due to the presence of avoidable obstacles or inessential presence of obstacles (i.e., *k'o-ch'en-fan-nao,* 客塵煩悩, or

---

[18] Unlike Augustine, Thomas Aquinas did not regard the political state as a consequence of the Fall, but as a necessary dimension of the world. Aquinas assumes that natural law or right also flows from the divine nature and must be so conceived, because it is the basis of all human institutions, morality, and social life. (See Windelband, p. 326) The political community is, in fact, the preparatory stage for the higher community of heaven. This assumption justified a system of class hieararchism, whereby the State was subordinated to the Church as a mere means to the end of complete fulfillment of natural teleology (Windelband, p. 327).

[19] One of the best passages referring to this insight is found in Nāgārjuna's *Madhyamakakārikā-śāstra*, 25: 19-20 (i.e., "Examination of Nirvāṇa"). Despite the fact that, from the point of view of conventional truth (*vyavahāratas*), the realms of Saṃsāra and Nirvāṇa ought to be clearly distinguished, Nāgārjuna declares that (from the point of view of transcendental truth or *paramārthatas*) no such distinction exists.

[20] This structure derives from the *Mahāyānasaṃgraha* by Asaṅga, in which dependent nature (*paratantra*) is invariably presented first, followed by the two other natures (*parikalpita* and *parinispanna*), which constitute the worlds of delusion and transcendence respectively. Strictly speaking, however, the ultimate referential world is constituted by the trans-empirical insight of Dependent Origination, assumed to encompass the structure of all three.

kleśa, karmic defilements).[21] In Buddhism, therefore, the higher order, the world of transcendence, was not conceived as existing apart from the lower order, the world of delusion, although this type of expression sometimes brought about misinterpretations of the Buddhist system of thought as a form of pantheism.[22] Strictly speaking, the relationship between the higher and lower truths is dialectically expressible only as "simultaneously identical (immanent) and different (transcendent)," or "neither identical nor different" (*fei-i fei-erh*, 非一非二).

From the logical point of view, it is contradictory to apply the terms both "totally identical" and "totally different" to a single object simultaneously, nor does it make sense linguistically to do so without jeopardizing the meaning of that reference. Thus, it is more frequently spoken of a "dual negation" or "bi-negation," that is, what is neither identical nor different. This simultaneous affirmation of logical opposites, "both identical and different," and their simultaneous negation, "neither identical nor different," which constitute the latter two members of the four alternative pairs in logic,[23] traditionally have been accepted by Buddhist thinkers, whether Indian, Chinese, or Japanese. This fact is reflected in the expressions *pratītya-samutpāda* (*yüan-ch'i*, 縁起), *śūnyatā* (*kung-hsing*, 空性), and *tathatā* (*chên-ju*, 真如).

---

[21] Philosophically, the core doctrine of the *Śraddhotpāda-śāstra* is that "the on-going phenomena arising and perishing in the universe" (*traidhātuka/san-chieh*) are ultimately identical with the real presence of "thusness" or *tathatā*, or the way in which "things arise and perish as they really are" (*hsen-hsiang-shêng-mieh-chi-chên-ju-shih-tsai*, 現象生滅即真如実際). Hence, practically, when extraneous dust is wiped away, the pristine, orginal mind becomes manifest (*tzu-hsing-ch'ing-ching-hsin*, 自性清浄心) as things in themselves.

[22] Benedict de Spinoza's pantheistic definition of God is a case in point. Spinoza's doctrine of the nature of substance closely parallels the Hindu concept of Brahma (neuter noun) as the ultimate material cause of the universe in possession of infinite substance-attribute relations. Hence, God is Nature - the universal world-essence, the sum total of the individual things that are modifications of the divine essence. However, such a view does not represent the Buddhist dialectical relationship of 'simultaneous identity and difference." See Windelband, pp. 408-09.

[23] Catuṣkoṭi: "x is A," "x is not A," "x is both A and not –A," and "x is neither A nor not–A;" There are many articles on this subject, at least two of which are recommended: K. N. Jayatrilleke, *Early Buddhist Theory of Knowldge* (George Allen & Unwin, 1963), especially chapter VII, "Logic and Truth," pp. 333-68; and D. Seyfort Ruegg, "The Uses of Four Positions of the Catuṣkoṭi and the Problem of the Description of Reality in Mahāyāna Buddhism," *Journal of Indian Philosophy*, Vol. V (1977), 1-74.

§5 LOGICO-LINGUISTIC CRITERION FOR DEMARCATING DUAL TRUTH

The primary criterion which ancient Buddhist thinkers in India used to distinguish the trans-empirical and the conventional dimension of this world was whether or not linguistic symbolism was intrinsic and indispensable. Nāgārjuna, forerunner of the Mādhyamika School, clearly focused his dialectical critique on this logically and linguistically bound world of convention, thereby formulating the doctrine of *śūnyatā* ("emptiness," "voidness," '*kung-hsing*,' 空性). He concluded that language ought not to be granted absolute status, but must be treated cautiously, as temporary, relative, and culturally formulated. In his dialectical demonstration, Nāgārjuna frequently resorts to grammatical case categories [i.e., syntactical relations; *kāraka-śabda-vyavahāra*),[24] especially in the nominative (*kartṛ*), accusative (*karman*), and instrumental (*karaṇa*) cases. In this way, he denies reality to each of these case categories because they are contrary to belief and practice (*laukika-vyavahāra*). In the second chapter of the *Madhyamakakārikā-śāstra*, for instance, Nāgārjuna analyzes the agent of motion (*gantṛ*), the destination of the movement (*gantavya*), and the act of motion (*gamana*), then dialectically denies the reality of these categories, denouncing them as merely "relative," "temporary" and "conditioned." Hence each category is seen to lack an independent self-identity or reality (*niḥsvabhāva, śūnyatā*).[25] Undeniably, these categories are practical universals found in any and all forms of human language, and make it possible for us to translate one language into another. Yet, the Buddhist insight of Dependent Origination (*pratītyasamutpāda*),

---

[24] The *Siddhāntakaumudī*, Vol. I, S. C. Vasu, ed. and trans. (Delhi: Motilal Banarsidass, 1962) chapter 16, p. 327, gives the Pāṇini's definition of "*kāraka*" as "anything that helps toward the accomplishment of an action." Thus in cooking, the fire, the furnace, the vessel, and the cook all help to accomplish the action. For example, Rāma is the agent, food is the object, the vessel is a locative, fire is an instrument, the furnace is the ablative, and the master is dative, each being *kāraka*. Out of seven cases in which a Sanskrit noun is declined, six represent such relations to an action, excluding the genitive case, which is not directly related to an action.

[25] In *Madhyamakakārikā-śāstra* Chap. 2 ("Examination of Motion"; *gatāgataparīkṣā-nāma*), Nāgārjuna utilizes these case categories: 'gantṛ' as nominative; '*gati*,' '*gata*,' '*agata*,' '*gamyamāna*' or 'gantavya' as accusative, and '*gamana*' as instrumental, and completes his *reductio-ad-absurdum* demonstration in Kārikās 22-25.

emptiness or voidness (*śūnyatā*), or non-essentiality or absence of self-nature (*niḥsvabhāva*), or middle path (*madhymāpratipad*) directly challenges our common belief in the reality of the foregoing logico-linguistic system.

Hindu schools of thought, for instance, invariably asserted that the linguistic universals are real and permanent. Even the Naiyāyika Hindu logicians, though admitting, on the one hand, that linguistic usage is an agreed-upon convention, followed suit in asserting that the perfect usage of language (namely, Sanskrit) would yield realization of heavenly happiness. This meant that if people are capable of correctly formulating words and sentences, they can realize any goal within that language. The renowned commentator of this realist school of logic, Vātsyāyana, author of the *Nyāyabhāṣya*, was obliged to defend their logical system against the Buddhist critique by asserting the reality of the aforementioned syntactical cases (*kāraka-śabda*). The defense was directed to Nāgārjuna's critique of the Naiyāyika system in his *Vigrahavyāvartanī*.

The Nyāya scholars distinguished four kinds of *pramāṇa*: as direct perception (*pratyakṣa*), Inference (*anumāna*), vocal word (*śabda*), and analogy (*upamāna*), and theorized that these means of cognition are necessary components for acquiring knowledge.[26] Now, in the above text, Nāgārjuna repudiates the reality of *pramāṇa* by demonstrating its relative nature and function within an epistemic action context (*kārakas*). Briefly explaining, according to Nāgārjuna's *reductio-ad-absurdum* argument, a *pramāṇa* [i.e., an act of cognizing] is correlative to its *prameya* (i.e., an object of cognition) and cannot function by itself, just as a fact of illumination ought to be explained by an interaction of "light" and "dark." Because if these opposites are granted with an absolute reality or self-identity respectively, there follows an absurdity such that "light" and "dark"

---

[26] Hindu philosophical schools, such as Mīmāṃsaka and Naiyāyika, also asserted the power of the spoken word (*śabda*) in terms of the efficiency of meaningful utterance. The Mīmāṃsakas upheld the efficacy of prescriptive language, because verbal commands can invoke actions on the part of the listener. The Naiyāyikas, on the other hand, were interested in the logical and descriptive use of language and viewed words as capable of producing cognition in the listener. Thus, they accepted verbal communication as a valid means of knowledge (*śabda-pramāṇa*). The Buddhists, however, never accepted verbal instruction or communication as an independent *pramāṇa*, but rather included it in the category of *anumāna* (inference). In other words, Buddhist logicians accepted the efficiency of linguistic symbols only with reference to the mental process of which language is merely a super-structure. This critical examination of the nature of verbal communication is, indeed, one of the objectives which Nāgārjuna accomplished in the *Vigrahavyāvartanī*.

could never meet together on account of their difference. Nor would it be free of absurdity even when "light" and "dark" are granted an identical nature, precisely because it is superfluous to think of a meeting of two luminous things to explain a fact of illumination or that of two darkening things to explain its contrary (i.e. absence of illumination). Thus, in either case, a *pramāṇa* (an act of perceiving) and a *prameya* (an object perceived) cannot be made to encounter each other.

What Nāgārjuna thus reveals is that, while conventionally conceived as opposites, in the transcendent higher order (*paramārtha*) light and dark must be accepted as simultaneously identical and different.[27] In other words, if the Naiyāyika logicians wish their system of *pramāṇa* to work as authoritative convention, Nāgārjuna succinctly points out that they must accept the dependent nature (*pratītya-samutpāda*) of the *pramāṇa*, the nature of non-essentiality or no-self (*niḥsvabhāva* or *anātma*), and hence that of emptiness or voidness (*śūnyatā*), rather than upholding its self-existent self-nature (*svabhāva or ātma*). The Naiyāyika theorists obviously misunderstood the intent of Nāgārjuna's critique as undermining the authority of their system. Vātsyāyana sought to counter the Buddhist critique through the assertion of the reality of *kāraka* categories,[28] precisely because the system of *pramāṇa* has no other basis than that of logico-linguistic convention.

The structural foundation, upon which Aristotle conceptualized an agent of action, an intended goal of action, and a morally right or wrong act expressible by the instrumental case has the same grammatico-linguistic structure used by ancient Indian thinkers, Buddhist as well as Hindu. Hindu thinkers insisted on a static view of language, according to which the world of Nature can be described accurately in realistic terms by logico-linguistic categories, such as *kārakas*. In contrast, Buddhist thinkers held a dynamic view of language based on the trans-empirical insight into the higher order and hence accepted the world of nature only conditionally in conventional terms (i.e., as *saṃvṛti* or *vyavahāra*). A similar

---

[27] See Shohei Ichimura, "An Analysis of Mādhyamika Dialectic in Terms of the Logical Principle of *Anvaya-Vyatireka*," *Amala Prajna Aspects of Buddhist Studies (Professor P. V. Bapat Felicitation Volume)*, N. H. Samtani and H.S. Prasad, eds. (Delhi, Indian Book Center, 1989), especially section IV, p. 334ff.

[28] Vātsyāyana (*Bhāṣya* II, i, 15) insists on pramāṇa and prameya in terms of the Kāraka arrangement, by resorting to the idea of *samākhyā-nimitta-vaśa*; and states (II, i, 16): *'kārakaśabdas caivam pramāṇam prameyam iti.'*

difference holds true between ancient Greek thinkers who wholeheartedly accepted the rationally constructed world of ideas or concepts, on the one hand, and Buddhist thinkers, on the other, who accepted the same world with reservations as relative, temporary, culturally conditioned, and most of all, bound by logico-linguistic conventions.

In Chinese Buddhist translation, the Sanskrit terms '*asaṃskṛta*' and '*saṃskṛta*' were rendered '*wu-wei*' (無為) and '*yu-wei*' (有為) respectively. Although '*wu-wei*' and '*yu-wei*' are originally of Taoist jargon to mean "to do nothing" or "being natural with no human effort" and "to do something" or "being unnatural with human contrivance," these were borrowed by translators to render the above Sanskrit originals, meaning respectively "totally quiescent or transcendent" (*nirvāṇa*, *tathatā*, or *śūnyatā*), and "causally produced" (*hetu-pratyayaiḥ kṛta*) or "totally involved (in the world of) delusion" (*abhibhūta-parikalpita*). What Buddhist thought designated the "ordinary world" or "world of convention" (*laukika* or *vyavahārika*), and Chinese Buddhists translated as '*yu-wei*' to mean "the world of purposive action," is equivalent with the world of nature, that of on-going phenomena, that of humanity, in which ancient Greeks spoke of human nature, goals of happiness, and morally right or wrong actions.

§6. THE TRANS-CULTURAL FOUNDATION WITHIN THE DUAL TRUTH STRUCTURE

Given the Buddhist expression, "the higher truth is immanent and transcendent simultaneously in the lower truth," one may hypothesize that the dual truth structure underlies pre-linguistic and post-linguistic processes of the mind. This is supported by the fact that Buddhist thinkers, Indian as well as Chinese, asserted that these dual dimensions act in perfect harmony, without any obstruction or discord existing between them (*tathābhūta*, *tathatā* or *paramārtha* on the one hand and *loka-saṃvṛti* or *vyavahāra* on the other). The renowned Hua-yen patriarch Fə-ts'ang (法藏、643-713) envisioned a perfect interaction (*wu-ai*, 無礙] between the world of transcendent (*hsing*, 性 or *li*, 理) and that of phenomena (*hsiang*, 相; *shih*, 実). The T'ien-t'ai master Chih-i (智□ 、538-597) expressed the same feature between the two spheres as 'perfect permeation' (*yüan-jung*, 円融), and similarly the San-lun master Chi-ts'ang (吉蔵、

540-623) referred to it as "perfect accordance" (*hsiang-chi*, 相即).[29] What was meant by these terms?.

Buddhist logicians, e.g., Dignāga and Dharmakīrti, admitted only two valid means of knowledge: (1) direct perception (*pratyakṣa*) that transcends logico-linguistic processes of the mind, undifferentiated moment of time like a point-instant (*kṣaṇika*), lacking (*nirvikalpaka*) in all subsequent logico-linguistic processes (*sa-vikalpaka*), and (2) inferential knowledge (*anumāna*) for which logico-linguistic processes serve as superstructure (*sa-vikalpaka-jñāna*). While the former type of knowledge transcends space and time, the latter type constitutes empirical knowledge, although referring to a given point-instant, the latter is interpretative in nature and links symbols in terms of subject-predicate relationships. It was argued that whatever is asserted in terms of logico-linguistic terms and relations has no real object of reference, as is generally assumed, but merely reflects the substructural mental process as a negation of correlative terms and relations. This '*Apoha*' theory is attributed to the fifth century thinker Dignāga.[30]

However, the theory presupposes the three features cited by Nāgārjuna and his Mādhyamika dialecticians: (1) that a given *pratyakṣa*, momentary (*kṣaṇika*) and non-dualistic (*nirvikalpa*),

---

[29] The insight of "simultaneous identity and difference" or "simultaneous immanence and transcendence" was already clearly expressed in the works of the early Chinese Buddhist Mādhyamika thinker, Sêng-chao, a disciple of Kumārajīva, although Sêng-chao's dialectical method consists of paradoxical formulae rather than the Indian *reductio-ad-absurdum* argument, he demonstrates that any opposites treated in his argument ought to have their common, identical reference. Following Sêng-chao, Chi-ts'ang further developed the Mādhyamika doctrine in terms of "dual negation" (i.e., the "neither this nor that" formula) as embodying the primary Buddhist insight. See Shohei Ichimura, "A Determining Factor that Differentiated Indian and Chinese Mādhyamika Methods of Dialectic as *Reductio-ad-Absurdum* and Paradoxical Argument respectively," *Journal of Indian and Buddhist Studies* (*Indogaku Bukkyōgaku Kenkyū*) Vol. 33, no. 2 (1985), 831-41; "On the Dialectical Meaning of Instantiation in terms of *Māyā-Dṛṣṭānta* in the Indian and Chinese Mādhyamikas," *Ibid.*, Vol. 36, no. 2 (1988), 971-77; "The Sino-Indian Trans-cultural Method of Mādhyamika Dialectic: Nāgārjuna to Sêng-chao to Chi-ts'ang," *Buddhism in India and Aborad*, G. Kuppuram, ed. (1990)

[30] See Th. Stcherbatsky, *Buddhist Logic I*, Bibliotheca Buddhica 26 (1-2), (Leningrad: 1930; New York: Dover, 1962), p. 457ff. As to the causal relationship between Nāgārjuna's dialectical method of critique and Dignāga's theory of *Apoha*, although it appears to be paradoxical to say that the ultimate fact that transcends the mental process is also immanent in it by way of negation, this is what Buddhist logicians in effect proposed in their ontology and logic. I believe this is what Nāgārjuna intended to demonstrate through his dialectic.

activates the mind to comprise any two correlative terms (e.g., light and dark); (2) that an immediately following assertion, whether it asserts a fact of illumination or its opposite, i.e., that of dark, is accompanied by the exclusion of its contrary (i.e., when 'light' is asserted, 'dark' is *ipso-facto* negated, and *vice versa*); and (3) that underlying this activated logico-linguistic process of the mind (*nāmakalpanā*) is the causal concatenation of psycho-physical elements (*upādāya-skandha*) or the reciprocal interdependence of any given set of correlative symbols.[31] Accordingly, the Buddhist theory of language was dynamic in nature, whereas that of the Naiyāyika was static.

Thomas Kuhn, a contemporary historians of science, seems to have proposed a structure similar to that of the Buddhist logicians. He distinguished the epistemic process of the human mind into (1) stimulus-to-sensation, containing tacit intuitive knowledge, and (2) logico-linguistic. In the first of these, the pre-linguistic area, Kuhn locates our neural apparatus, and neural programming or reprogramming, which he assumes is constantly interacting with the logico-linguistic processes. Kuhn presents two reasons for this assumption: (1) even a spontaneous perception is an interpretative and unconscious version of what we do after perceiving something, and (2) much of neural processings that take place between receiving a stimulus and awareness of a sensation can be altered by education, through language, culture, and so forth.[32]

Kuhn's suggestion for resolving communication-breakdown seems to support my hypothesis that the dual truth of the Buddhist doctrine can be made intelligible by taking account of Kuhn's dual dimension of the human mind. Even in the field of science, Kuhn asserts, communication-breakdown can occur. For instance, scientists who support the heliocentric theory of the universe and those who support the Ptolemaic geocentric theory of the universe may agree to a similar set of conceptual terms and relations, allowing them to produce exactly the same calendars with accurate dates, times, and constellations, and so forth. Neither party can prove one theory as true, while disproving the other as false. Kuhn suggests that through translation any two contesting parties can remold each other's stimulus-to-sensation process, apparently meaning "neural reprogramming." Kuhn cites the key factors in translation: (1) recognizing each other as members of different language communities,

---

[31] See Ichimura, "An Analysis of Mādhyamika . . ," especially section IV, pp. 337-39.

[32] Kuhn, pp. 193-95.

(2) trying to discover the differences of terms and locutions for extra- and inter-group discussions, (3) elucidating the problems in those isolated areas of difficulty by using shared, every day vocabularies, (4) discovering what the other sees and says when presented with a stimulus to which one's own verbal response would be different, (5) translating the other's theory and its consequence into one's own language, and (6) simultaneously describing in one's own language the world to which that theory applies.[33] This working-out of logico-linguistic route of the mind and a gradual tuning of the pre-linguistic perceptual processes creates a suitable climate toward mutual communication and consensus regarding a theory-choice, i.e., determining which of the contesting theories ought to be supported.

Kuhn's approach was intended to resolve conflicts among scientists. Implementing it in matters of religious, cultural, or ideological differences would be a formidable task, due to the multiple factors, emotional as well as volitional, to be considered in addition to rationality. Historically, religious or ideological differences frequently have led to violent confrontation and bloodshed. In today's nuclear age humankind has realized that this is no longer a feasible approach. We are compelled to choose either some new system of thought or one from among existing systems of thought able to provide a viable channel for resolving the problems of communication-breakdown as a means of engendering cooperation rather than conflict. The question is: What kind of criteria should we rely on to choose successfully?

Kawada suggests three criteria for making such a choice: (1) the effectiveness of a given system of truth for regulating one's conduct, as well as establishing social law and order; (2) the rational acceptability of the ultimate truth offered; and (3) the degree to which this truth can be experienced in one's life.[34] Since the initial criterion is an obvious one, only the remaining two require classification, by reference to some of Kawada's remarkable insights.

As to the nature of truth, Kawada distinguishes truth based on human reason, and truth based on divine revelation, i.e., not belonging to human reason, but something that ought to be believed (without recourse to reasoning). Insofar as ethics is the subject of philosophical investigation, based on human reason, the revealed truth itself may avoid direct scrutiny. But since even the nature of

[33] Kuhn, p. 202.
[34] Kawada, pp. 226-27.

revealed truth is a human experience, once it is expressed in logical and linguistic symbols, it becomes subjected to rational analysis and investigation. Thus Kawada justifies his assertion that the nature of truth, which is an ethical system's theoretical foundation, ought to withstand rational investigation and must be acceptable to human reason. Moreover, each individual must be allowed to examine the nature of a given system of truth to decide whether it represents the best choice of a theoretical foundation of ethics for that person.[35]

Next, Kawada defines truth as a mean between two extremes, such as the extremes of excess and deficiency. As such, truth reveals the opposition between the extremes, while simultaneously serving as a middle ground. Here, however, Kawada brings forth a dialectic: "The nature of this truth is such that by being a middle, it is neither an opposite extreme nor a middle (*anantamadhya*)."[36] He explains this middle by critically evaluating major philosophies, including those of the ancient Greeks, Christians, Kant and Hegel, Confucianism and Taoism. Then, he turns to the Buddhist concept of middle, i.e., the middle path evolved from the insight that whatever arises from the causality of Dependent Origination (*pratītya-samutpanna*) is empty (*śūnya*) because it has no substantial identity (*anātmatā*), nor any independent nature (*niḥsvabhāvatva*). Since this middle path constitutes the truth that whatever arises from causes and conditions (*hetu-pratyaya-sāmagrī*) is empty in nature, this middle is neither an extreme nor a middle (*anantamadhya*). That is, it is not a middle that is believed to exist as real or substantial. Insofar as one sees any truth in this manner in the middle, one is obliged to accept the Buddhist philosophical insight of "Dependent Origination" and "Middle Path" as his foundation of ethics.[37]

In support of the third criterion - that a system of truth ought to be anchored in personal experience - Kawada observes that all historically existing systems of truth, insofar as they have become a theoretical foundation of anyone's ethics, were not merely products of thought, but also were actually lived. Since such experience can neither be seen nor heard by another, anyone can make a false claim to others about the experience as well as deceive themselves.[38] He explains his choice of the Buddhist system over the sysstems of the ancient Greeks, Christian theologicans, modern philosophers, or

---

[35] Kawada, pp. 229-30.
[36] Kawada, p. 231.
[37] Kawada, pp. 233-34.
[38] Kawada, p. 235.

Confucians and Taoists as follows:

The fundamental ethics (*konpon rinri*, 根本倫理) of the Buddhist philosophy of trans-empirical insight (*chi-ken*, 知見) consists of humanity's basic experience of the nature of impermanence (*anityatā*, 無常). Therefore, whoever sees through trans-empirical insight (*prajñā*) that every phenomenon (*sarva-saṃskāra*) is impermanent (*anitya*), that every phenomenon is suffering (*duḥkha*, 苦), and that every phenomenon is without its own self (*anātman*, 無我), abhors the nature of suffering (intrinsic to all things). It is said that this is the path of purity (*Dhamapadam*, *maggavaggo*, vv.5-7). Seeing the nature of impermanence in this manner is the fundamental experience which enables an individual to activate his fundamental ethics (i.e., theoretical ethical foundation) derived from the truth of "dependent origination" (*yüan-chi*, 縁起). We cannot resist the deepening sense of our experience of impermanence as our age advances. Because of this experience of impermanence, one knows that it is clearly different from a sense of nihilism though it appears to resemble it. Borrowing the Hegelian word, this is "the truth acquired by us through experience."[39]

§7. FUNDAMENTAL ETHICAL MOTIVE OF THE BUDDHA

After studying the history and thought of Buddhism for many years, one comes to a point at which one is obliged to ask a fundamental question about why Śākyamuni Buddha started a new religious movement by organizing a new order (Saṅgha) of professional monks and lay followers.[40] Scholars rightly assert that Śākyamuni's religious movement and path of emancipation harmoniously resolved the pre-existent socio-cultural antitheses, thereby serving as a guide for the realization of a universal welfare state, such as the Mauryan Buddhist empire. Nevertheless, such abstract, pan-Indian theorization cannot really explain why Śākyamuni as an individual daringly stood up, kindled his spiritual and mental flame, and having thrown away his prestigious hereditary position in society and

---

[39] Kawada, pp. 237-38

[40] See Ichimura, "A Re-evaluation of Inceptive Buddhism Through De-mythologization of Śākyamuni Buddha," in *Professor Upendra Thakur Felicitation Volume*, 1988. This same article will appear in *The Recent Researches in Indian History, Culture, Society and Religion Essays*, Harchanran Singh Sobti, ed. (Delhi, India: Sundeep Prakashan, 1990).

worldly glories and prosperity, exerted his life force single-mindedly toward religious emancipation. Indeed, mere presentation of a universal theory cannot reveal the acute and urgent problem that may have been behind Śākyamuni's motive of renunciation and pursuit of religious austerity.

However, the *Pāli Jātaka* implies that Śākyamuni confronted a crisis. The *Bhaddasāla-jātaka* clearly records the deadly dilemma Śākyan clansmen faced concerning their survival due to the Kosala king's marital proposition:[41] If they accepted the proposition, they were convinced that their clan-state would disintegrate because the purity of their blood would no longer be maintained. If they rejected it an equally deadly result would ensue, because the overlord state could endanger the continued existence of their state.

At the time of Gautama, an absolute monarchical state of ancient India was based on the Brahmanical world view. By definition they were obliged to protect and promote the authority of Brāhmaṇa caste as the apex of the social system of four castes (*varṇas*).[42] The Śākyan society, on the other hand, was a republican polity with a clan-oriented religion, in which there was neither a Brāhmaṇa nor a Śūdra caste (the lowest of the Varṇa).[43] Legitimate clan members had economic and political privileges associated with clan membership and were guaranteed of equal rights. Naturally, for them, the security and maintenance of the clan-oriented society must have been their highest priority. Yet the Brahmanical world-view, bearing a higher degree of universalism, gradually eroded the aforementioned clan-oriented ideology in both religious and social spheres.

From the available bits of information, it is apparent that the crisis the Śākyan faced involved an increasing antithesis between the general social system consisting of four Varṇas controlled by the Brāhmaṇa and the clan-oriented system controlled by the landed clansmen. It is possible that within the life time of Śākyamuni, armed conflict broke out between the Kosala absolute monarchism and the Śākyan tribal republic, while the rapid process of Brahmanization (i.e., Hinduization) was taking place in Śākyan

---

[41] No. 465 (*The Jātaka* IV, 145).

[42] The four *Varṇas* and their social duties (*dharmas*) are clearly prescribed in the *Mānavadharmaśāstra*. Though the *Dharmaśāstra* attributed to Manu was a product of the post-Mauryan period, it probably reflects the Brahmanical world-view and legal concepts. See VII, *Rājadharma*, sections i and ii, and also X. *Jātidharma*, sections i and ii.

[43] The Śākyan social structure can be inferred from the Weberian analysis of the agrarian development in ancient times. See Weber, *The Religion of India*, p. 47ff.

society.[44]

Perhaps, the most negative aspect of Indian culture seems to have been the fact that the caste system has been sustained and reinforced throughout the history of India till modern times, and that one of the primary factors for this continuity has been the mind of general populace prone to superstitious belief in magical power. The gravity of the dilemmatic problem which the Śāyan clansmen faced can not be properly evaluated without referring to the force of such superstitious belief.

As analyzed by Weber, the nature of the caste system in India, the continuity and reinforcement of the Indian caste system depends on, among other things, the principle of endogamy (i.e., the requirement that marriage take place within one's caste).[45] It must be especially noted that the normative force or motivation for the caste system is not found in an individual's rational judgment or ethical virtue, but in the superstitious belief in the magical power of blood. Only once throughout the Pāli and Āgama texts does Śākyamuni directly address the issue of racial prejudice in the *Ambaṭṭha-sutta* of Dīgha Nikāya, No. 3, and its Chinese counterpart, *A-mo-chou-ching (*「阿摩書経」*)* of the *Ch'ang-a-han-ching* (「長阿含経」、*Dhīrgha-Āgama*, No. 20).[46] Unlike the ancient Greek city states, the idea of equality

---

[44] Weber refers to the Śākyan-Kosala conflict in *The Religion of India*, pp. 43-44. There seems to have been some historical basis for the legendary tragic destruction of the republic by the new Kosala king Virūdhaka (Vidūdabha in Pāli), son of King Prasenajit, who was the son of a Śākyan woman (Vāsabhakhatiyā, a daughter of Mahānāman, the Buddha's paternal uncle, according to Buddhaghoṣa) and Nāgamuṇḍa. Indian civilization can be studied in reference to innumerable cases of alien racial migrations and hence, in reference to the processes of acculturation and social integration known as "Hinduization" or "Indianization."

[45] A detailed analysis of the caste system in India can be found in chapters II and III of Weber's *Religion of India*, pp. 55-133.

[46] Briefly, the story is as follows: The Buddha's evangelical movement in Kosala alarmed the Brahmans. Thus, the renowned Brahman Pokkharasadi sent his student, a proud young Brāhmaṇa named Ambaṭṭha, to meet with the Buddha. The young fellow, however, challenged the Buddha three times, denouncing the rudeness of the Śākyan clansmen. As a Brāhmaba, he was personally insulted by not having been welcomed by the clansmen in his previous visit to Kapilavastu, capital of the Śākyan republic. In response to the charge that the Śākyans were vulgar and failed to honor the Brāhmaṇa whose familial lineage was nobler and superior, Śākyamuni attacked Ambaṭṭha's belief in his familial lineage and hereditary right by reference to the Śākyan tradition. The Śākyans believed themselves to be descended from a ruling family, whereas Ambaṭṭha, like all Brahmans, was considered a descendant of slaves. The story is the general basis for the Buddhist tradition that Śākyamuni's claim that he was of the Kṣatriya family did not refer to the Kṣatriya of the Brahmanical society, but the

among citizens and rational individuals was not fully developed in ancient India. Hence, the Indian concept of natural law, with its practical norms, distinguished as the four major goals of life was not as universal as that of the ancient Greeks. There is good reason to assume that it was this deficiency that, at least in part, motivated Śākyamuni to make progress with his new religious movement.

The Pāli literature amply demonstrates, Śākyamuni was already subjected to apotheosis while still active in life. He was believed to have been endowed with superhuman qualities and merits accumulated through his innumerable life cycles. Only due to such qualities could the people of his days comprehend his accomplishments in renunciation, enlightenment, and the formation of the Saṅgha. Yet, we must demythologize the Buddha as a human being and make detailed analyses of his historical context before we can clarify the historical significance of the rise of Buddhism by reference to the personal conduct of the founder. Only by so doing alone, will we be able to fathom the Buddha's true intentions in forming the Buddhist Saṅgha. Such findings can then serve as criteria for examining the subsequent history of Buddhism's institutional development.

Like any other institution, the Buddhist Saṅgha inherited theoretical and practical goals and tasks as inherited from its founder. The prevailing thought at the time of Śākyamuni classified people in terms of four *Varṇas,* along with all the implications of such a system. Theoretically, therefore, it would have been Śākyamuni's major task to analytically penetrate into the nature and function of human mentality underlying this socio-cultural propensity and to uncover ways of dealing with such problems. Classifying people in terms of the four *Varṇas* involves the use of language, without which no communication and no understanding is possible. Yet, the use of language also creates sets of traditions and prejudices, channelling human actions in specific ways. For good or ill, language involves thinking and constitutes a form of cultural convention. From this point of view, it is not difficult to see why Śākyamuni set as the theoretical task of the Saṅgha the perpetuation of the path of transcendence from worldly convention,

---

Kṣatriya of Indo-Arian lineage. The textual teaching, of course, addressed the nature of the Saṅgha as transcending social stratification. In this rare passage the Buddha strongly admonishes the young man for his haughty pride by stating that as long as anyone is fixated on marriage ties, birth, family, or self-conceit, they are totally incapable of understanding the truth represented by the Buddha and his Saṅgha.

including the conventions of the Indian socio-cultural context of his time. Such a path of transcendence was then and continues now to be applicable to any socio-cultural conventions, as evidenced in non-Indian cultural regions of East Asia.

Remarkably, from the practical point of view, the Buddhist Saṅgha from its inception established concrete measures in its practical norms for countering caste conventions. The principle of endogamy binds a man to one caste, as it does preceding generations, and likewise binds one to a single profession associated with that caste. The caste system also is regulated by the principle of commensalism which prohibits eating together with members of other castes, a direct corollary to the superstitious belief in pollution through inter-caste physical contact. In contrast, the Buddhist Saṅgha prohibited its members from engaging in any productive profession, requiring them to accept food from all households, regardless of caste associations. These were bold and innovative practical measures at the time.

From the foregoing analyses, it is evident that Śākyamuni may well have foreseen the dismal future of a small clan-oriented society in conflict with Brahmanical society. He was aware of the inherent limitations of Śākyan society, its bondage to a tribal mentality, but also knew the irrational nature of the Brahmanical social system (specifically, the *Varṇas*). His response, therefore, was to transcend both the Śākyan and the Brahmanical socio-cultural systems, since both were equally bound by irrational superstitious beliefs concerning the magical power of blood. His alternative was a celibate community of professional monks adapted to the Indian socio-cultural environment. In abandoning a society bound by the aforementioned force of superstitious beliefs, they sought Nirvāṇa, in the process transcending their own socio-cultural context as well as all other socio-cultural forms of human mentality.

§8. CONCLUSION

Although the conception of dual truth was not formulated in the early period of Buddhism, the insight into the causality of Dependent Origination implied the later development of the doctrine. The structure of the dual truth is anchored in this insight distinguishing the world in which symbolic system of language operates and the world that transcends it. When an object of reference is perceived as having an independent nature (*svabhāva*) through symbolic system, it is known as empirically existent. When it is intuited as having a merely dependent nature (*pratītyabhāva*) because of causes and conditions (*hetu-pratyaya*), it is known as transcendentally non-existent (*Śūnyatā*), thereby discounting the reality of symbolic system. It is clear that Buddhist thought does not repudiate the empirical world of ethics found in ancient Western philosophers. However, it does repudiate underlying mental forces of linguistic behavior and culture formation, namely, (1) the referential force of the mind toward its objective reference, and (2) the tendentious or purposive force of the mind that links one symbol with another.

Language constitutes the medium par excellence for culture formation because it depicts, prescribes, and sustains all forms of behavioral patterns that make up subjective and objective social institutions. Simultaneously cultural forms reinforce the ways language is used. Though symbols may serve to liberate the human mind for universal communication, more often they create bondage and prejudice, interfering with proper communication and mutual understanding. In this sense even rational and logical thinking can be said to reflect a particular form of culture and convention. The important point is how one should deal with the force of the mind tied to a particular form of culture and not to another, and how that mind can be opened to what lies beyond a given culture.

Śākyamuni set forth the saintly path *Śrāvaka-yāna* of Arhat-hood, striving upon the ever upward path that is the path of mental purification. In this context, Nāgārjuna's dialectical method analyzes the logico-linguistic route of the mind saturated with a particular cultural perspective and allows for purification of the pre-linguistic route of neural programming. The intent is not to prepare the way for another particular cultural form, but to liberate us from all forms of cultures. This transformation can be understood more clearly when seen within the Indian social and cultural context. Later, Buddhism introduced the path of the Bodhisattva for the downward passage from transcendence into the world of convention. This ideal human type, having once achieved mental purity through the upward path and thus firmly established in freedom, is ready to adapt to any culture and convey to fellow humans that dual passage (i.e., upward and downward) dialectically linking the dual truth .

Kawada expresses his sense of the dialectical method of the middle path as follows:

> As the last stage of our methodology for philosophical investigation of various systems of thought, (I am obliged to explain that)

this dialectical method of (the) middle path means that after having chosen one's system of thought, one must examine one's self as well as others very seriously in order to become a better person than one's previous self and others. Hence, what guides one's step to exercise the dialectical method of the middle path is the middle path itself that transcends both opposites or two extremes. Therefore, this middle path is the fundamental truth which is neither an extreme nor a (fixed) middle.[47]

[47] Kawada, p. 243.

BIBLIOGRAPHY AND INDEX

Bibliography

Abhidharma-mahāvibhāṣāśātra or a detailed commentary on the *Abhidharma Jñānaprasthāna-śāstra* that belonged to the Sarvāstivāda school (「阿毘達摩大毘婆沙論」 or A-p'i-ta-mo-*t'a-p'i-po-sha-lun,* 200 fasc.) translated by Hsüan-tzang (玄奘). Taisho. 27, (No. 1545).

Agarwala, V.S., *Harṣacarita Eka Sāṃskṛtika Adhyayana*, Patna, 1953, pp.197-198.

Ambaṭṭhasutta (Dīgha Nikāya III in Pāli Tripiṭaka), and from the Sanskrit Dīrgha Āgama Chih-ch'ien translated it as「仏説解梵志阿摩昼経」, which is included in *Chang-a-han-chin (* 「長阿含経」 第二十); Taoshō 1, (No. 20).

Aristotle: *Nichomachean Ethics* translated by Martin Oswald, with introduction and notes; New York: Macmillan Pub. Co., 1962.

Arthaśāstra by Kauṭilya, edited and translation by R. Shastry, 2nd rev. ed. (Mysore: 1919). A translation published by Bārhaspatya, Bangalore, 1915, 1923.

Basham, A. L.: A New Study of Śaka-Kuṣāṇa Period, *Bulletin of School of Oriental and African Studies (BSOAS),* XV (1953), 80-97.

________: The Succession of the Line of Kaniṣka, *Bulletin of the School of Orieental and African Studies* (BSOAS), XX (1959), 77-88.

________: *The Wonder that was India (A survey of the culture of the Indian sub-continent before the coming of the Muslims)*, London: Sidgwick and Jackson, 1954,

Beal, Samuel (tr.): *Buddhist Records of the Western World.* translated from Hsüan-tzang's *Ta-t'amg-hsi-yu-chi* (「大唐西域記」), 1884

Bhaddasālajātaka No. 465, IV, 144-153

Bhattacharya, K. (edited and translation): *The Dialectical Method of Nāgārjuna: Vigrahavyāvartanī* (2nd edition.), Delhi: Motilal Banarsidass, 1978.

Bhavya: *Ta-ch'êng-changchen-lun* (「大乘掌珍論」 2 fasc.) *or The Mahāyāna Treasure within the Hand,,* translated by Hsüan-tzang (玄奘); Taishō 30 (No. 1578), 268 ff; Sanskritization from Chinese text by N. Aiyasvami Sastri, *Visva-Bharati Annals* II, (1949).

Biography of Bodhisattva Āryadeva, the (*Ti-p'o-p'u-sa-chuan,* 「提婆菩薩伝」 1 fasc.) tramslated by Kumārajīva, Taishō. (No.2048), pp. 186f.

Biography of Bodhisattva Aśvaghoṣa, the (Ma-ming-p'u-sa-ch'uan, 「馬鳴菩薩伝」 1 fasc.) tramslated by Kumārajīva, *Taishō* (No. 2046), pp183.

Biography of Bodhisattva Nāgārjuna, the (*Lung-shu-p'u-sa-chuang,* 「龍樹菩薩伝」 1 fasc.) translated by Kumārajīva, Taisho 50 (No. 2047), p. 184a-185b; A second version, (1 fasc.), also translated by Kumārajīava, *ibid.* pp.185b-i86c.;

Biography of Bodhisattva Nāgārjuna, the, (*Lung-shu-p'u-sa-chuang,* 「龍樹菩薩伝」 1 fasc.), *Taisho* 50 (No. 2047), p. 184a-185b; a second version, (1 fasc.) also translated by Kumārajīava, *ibid.* pp.185b-i86c.;

Blofelt, John: *Compassion Yoga; the mystical cult of Kuan Yin*. London (1977) Alternative title, Bodhisattva of compassion; the mystical tradition of Kan. Yin. Boulder, Colo (1978)

Bloom, A. H.: The Linguistic Shaping of Thought. New Jersey: Lawrence Erlbasum Associates, 1981.

Bochenski, I. M.:*A History of Formal Logic*, tr. and ed. by T. Thomas. New York: 1956.

Bodiford, William: "Zen and the Art of Religious Prejudice," *Japanese Journal of Religious Studies*, 23/1-2, 1996.

Brgess: *The Buddhist Stupas of Amaravati and Jaggayyapeta, Archaeological* (Survey of Southern India), London: 1887),

Buddhaghoṣa's *Sumaṅgalavilāsinī* (A Commentary on Dīgha-Nikāya (*Dīghanikāya-aṭṭhakathā*) edited by Rhys Davids and Carpenter, PTS. Pt. I, 258 ff).

________: *Paramaṭṭha-jotika* (Commentary on *Khuddakapāṭha*) translated by Bhikkhu Ñāṇamoli; P.T.S. translation Series No, 32, London , Luzac and co., 1960.

Buddhāvataṃsaka-mahāvaipulya-sūtra (*Ta-fang-kuang-fo-hua-yen-ching*, 「大方広仏華厳経」 translated by Buddhabhadra (359-429). Taishō. 9 (No. 278), amd also the 80 fasc. version 「大方広仏華厳経」 translated by Śikṣānanda (652-710). Taishō. 10 (No. 279).

Bukkyō Kaisetsu Daijiten (*Dictionary of Buddhist Books with Expositions*) vol. 9, Tokyo: Daito Shuppan, 1933-36.

Burgess: *Notes on the Amarāvatī Stūpa* (Madras 1882).

Bus-ston: *History of Buddhism*, Eng. trans. by E. Obermiller, Heidelberg, 1932, Pt II, pp.120-130;

Carakasaṃhitā, Vimāna Section of Agniveśa's *Carakasaṃhitā*; Text with English Translation and Critical Exposition based on Cakrapani Datta's *Ayurveda*; Varanasi: Chowkhamba Sanskrit Series, 1976.

Cardona, G.: "Anvaya and Vyatireka in Indian Grammar," *The Adyar Library Bulletin*, 31-32, (1967-68), pp. 313-352.

Catalogue of Buddhist Scriptures Newly Determined in the Era of Chen-hüan (「貞元新定釈経目録」, ca. the 9th century).

Ch'u-san-ts'ang-chi-chi (「出三蔵記集」 15 fasc.) compiled during 510-518 by Sêng-yu (僧祐、445-518) of Liang. Taishō 55, (No. 2145)]. The catalogue integrated an anterior *Catalogue* compiled by Tao-an (道安、314-385, which was known as *the Catalogue of the Various Scriptures through General Survey* (「綜理衆経目録」) on those Buddhist texts brought to China as well as translations, covering the period from the late Han dynasty down to the Eastern Chin (東晋、317-419).

Chaturbhuj, Sri: "The last Abbot of Nalanda," *Maha Bodhi*, 82, 6, (1964).

Chi-ts'ang's (吉蔵) referemce to the Mohist logic in his major work: *The Profound Meaning of Three (Mādhyamika) Treatises* (「三論玄義」), Taishō. 45, (No. 1852).

Chih-i (538-597), the systematizer of the T'ien-t'ai Classification of Buddhist Dcotrines known as "Fivefold Periods and Eight Teachings" (「天台五時八

教教判」), T'ien-t'ai Ssŭ-chiao-i (「天台四教義」12 fasc.)' Taisho 46 (No. 1929).

_______: *The Profound Meaning of Lotus Sūtra* (*Miao-fa-lien-hua-ching-hsüan-i* 「妙法蓮華経玄義」) in 593; Taishō. 33 (No. 1716).

_______: *The Profound Meaning of Kuan-yin* [*Kuan-shih-yin-hsüan-i* 「観音玄義」), its commentary (*Kuan-yin-i-shu*, 「観音義疏」), and the Short Commentary on the Chap. of Samanta-mukha (P'u-mên-p'in-su, 「普門品疏」、Taishō. 34, No. 1728).

_______: *The Great Discipline of Śamatha and Vipaśyanā* (*Mo-ho-chih-kuan*, 「摩訶止観」), Fasc. 10, No. 2 of two vols.

Conze, Edward: "Text, Sources, and Bibliography of the *Prajñāpāramitā-hṛdaya*," *Journal of Royal Asiatic Society*. 1948.

Coomaraswamy, Ananda K.: *Yakṣa,* Smithsonian Miscellaneous Collections, vol. 80, no. 6.

Das, S. C. (ed): Sumpā-mKhan-po: dPg-bSam-īJon-bZan. Calcutta: 1908;

Dayal, Har: *The Bodhisattva Doctrine in Buddhist Sanskrit Literature,* (originally published in 1932 by Routledge & Kegan Paul, London). Reprint by Delhi: Motilal Banarsidass, 1970.

Dhamma-cakka-ppavattana-vaggo (Saṃyutta Nikāya.: Book XII, Chap. 2: Tathāgatena vutta Nos. 11 and 12): *The Initial Turning of the Wheel of Dharma* (Saṃyutta-Nikāya). The equivalent Chinese translation appears as the Sūtra of the Initial Preaching of Dharma (「初転法輪経」) in the Saṃyukta-Āgama, No. 15 (「雑阿含経」No. 15, Sect. 17).

Dialogues of the Buddha II, III tr. by T. W. S. and C. A. F. Rhys Davids; The Sacred Books of the Buddhists III, IV), London 1910 & 1921.

Dutt, B. N. and U. N. Ghoshal (Eng. trans.): *Tāranātha: Mystic Tales* (the relevant portion). IHQ XXVIII, 1952, p.41 ff.

Dīgha Nikāya No. 17: *Mahā-sudassana-sutta* ("The great Sun" = Sudassana = Cakravartin), and No. 26: *Cakkavatti-sīhanāda-sutta* ("The Lion's Roar of the Universal Ruler").

Dīpavaṃsa (*The Chronicle of Ceylon*) edited and translated by B. Law, *Ceylon Historical Journal* , Vol. 7, 1948.

Fo-mu-hsiao-tzu-pan-jo-ching (1 fasc.); *Ārya-prajñāpāramitā-saṃgraha-kārikā-vivaraṇa* (4 fasc.) translated by Dānapāla, 980.

Fu, Charles Wei-hsun and Sandra A. Wawrytko (ed.): *Buddhist Ethics and Modern Society, An International Symposium*, edited by Charles Wei-hsun Fu and Sandra A. Wawrytko, Greenwood Press, 1991.

Fu-fa-ts'ang-yin-yüan-chuan (*Record of the Histories of Dharma-Transmission,* 「付法蔵因縁伝」6 fasc.) translated by Kiṅkaya and T'an-yao in A.D. 472). Taishō. 50, (Nol 2058).

Fukui, Bunyū: A Historical Study on the Prajñā Heart Sūtra (「般若心経の歴史的研究」). Tokyo: Shunjūsha, 1987.

Go-lo-tsa-ba gZon-nu-dpal: *The Blue Annals*, Eng. trans. by G. N. Roerich, 2 parts, Calcutta, 1949, 1953.

Graham, Charles A.: *Later Mohist Logic, Ethics and Science*, The Chinese University Press, Hong-kong, 1978.

Great Prajñā Prayer Sūtra (*Mahāprajñāpāramitā-vidyā-mantra-sūtra, Mo-ho-pan-jo-po-lo-mi Ta-ming-chou-ching,* 「摩訶般若波羅蜜大明呪経」 1 fasc.), translated by Kumārajīva, Taishō. 8, (No. 250).

Guṇavarman (求那跋摩、367-431): translated the *Āryanāgārjuna-bodhisattva-suhṛllekha* in A.D. 431 under the title: *Bodhisattva Nāgārjuna's Essential Teaching in Verse for King Ch'an-t'o-chia-wang* (「龍樹菩薩為禅陀迦王説法要偈」 1 fasc.). Taisho. 32, (No. 1672), pp. 745b-748a.

Hahn, Michael: A new edition of Nāgārjuna's *Ratnāvalī,* Vol 1, The Basic Texts (Sanskrit, Tibetan, Chinese); Bonn: 1982, which also contains the text of the canonical Tibetan version and a photocopy of the Chinese translation by Paramārtha..

Hakamaya, Kenshō: *Hongaku-shisō Hihan (A Critique of the Thought of Original Enlightenment)*, Tokyo: Daizō Shuppan, 1989.

Harṣacarita or *The Life of King Harṣa* (Chaukhamba ed., Varanasi, 1958), Ucchvāsa (8th bk.).

Hattori, M.: *Dignāga, On Perception*, Harvard Oriental Series 47 (1968).

History of Buddhism (*Chos-ḥbyun*, or literally *Record of the Doctrine*) by Bu-ston.

Hsüan-tzang: *Ta-t'amg-hsi-yu-chi (*「大唐西域記」 1 2 fasc.*)* by and his disciples [Taisho (No. 2067)]. *The Buddhist Records of the Western World during the Great T'ang- Dynasty.* translated by Samuel Beal, originally published 1884 London; Two volumes bound in one, Motilal Banarssidass, Delhi: 1981.

Hu-shih (胡適): *The Development of the Logical Method in Ancient China*, Shang-hai: The Oriental Book Co., 1928.

Hume, R. E. (trans.): *The Thirteen Principal Upanishads* (Oxford: 1921).

Hye Ch'o Diary, The : Memoir of the Pilgrimage to the Five Regions of India, translated text and editing by Yang, Han-sung, Jan, Yün-hua and Iida, Shotaro and Laurence W. Preston. Seoul. Korea: Asian Huamanities Press, Po Chin Chai Ltd.

Hṛdaya or Prajñā Heart Sūtra Grooup: See *Prajñā Heart Sūtra* Group.

I-ching (義浄、635-713): translated in A.D. 637 the *Āryanāgārjuna-bodhisattva-suhṛllekha* under the title: *Bodhisattva Nāgārjuna's Exhortation in Verse for the King (*「龍樹菩薩勧誡王頌」 *Lung-shu-p'u-sa-ch'üan-chieh-wang-sung*, 1 fasc.), *Taisho* 32, (No. 1673), pp.751a-754b.

_______: *Nan-hai-chi-kuei-nei-fa-ch'uan* [「南海寄帰内法伝」 Taishō. 54 (No. 2125)] translated by J. Takakusu under the title: *A Record of the Buddhist Religion as practised in India and the Malay Archipelago.* Oxford: The Clarendon Press, 1896.

Ichimura, S.: "An Analysis of Mādhyamika Dialectic in terms of the Logical Principle of Anvaya and Vyatireka," *Amalā Prajñā Aspects of Buddhist Studies (Professor P.V. Bapat Felicitation Volume)* edited by N. H. Samtani and H. S. Prasad [Bibliotheca Indo-Buddhica No. 63; Delhi: Indian Book Centre, 1989.

_______: "On the Paradoxical Method of the Chinese Mādhyamikas: Sêng-chao and the Chao-lun Treatise," *Journal of Chinese Philosophy* 19 (1992) 51-71.

_______: "A Determining Factor that Differentiated Indian and Chinese Mādhyamika Methods of Dialectic as *Reductio-ad-Absurdum* and Paradoxical Argument Respectively," *Journal of Indian and Buddhist Studies (Indogaku Bukkyōgaku Kenkyū)* (*JIBS*) Vol. 33, no. 2 (1985), 831-4.

_______: "A Study of the Mādhyamika Method of Refutation, Especially of its Affinity to that of *Kathāvatthu*," *Journal of International Association of Buddhist Studies* (*JIABS*) III, 2(1980), 7-15.

_______: "Ābhidharmika Logical Deadlock in *Kathāvatthu* and Nāgārjuna's Madhyamaka Dialectic," *JIBS*, Vol. 39, No. 2, March 1991, 20-24.

_______: "An Approach to Dōgen's dialectical thinking and method of instantiation (a comparative study of *Shōbō Genzō*)," *Journal of the International Association of Buddhist Studies* (*JIABS*), IX, 2(1986) 79-80.

_______: "Buddha's Love and Human Love," included" in *Chung-Hua Buddhist Journal*, No. 13, pp. 195-254; Taipei: The Chung-Hwa Institute of Buddhist Studies, March, 2000.

_______: "Buddhist dialectical methods and their structural identity," presented at the 31st International Congress of Human Science in Asia and North Africa, and its résumé included in the Proceeding, Tokyo: The Toḥo Gakkai, 1984, pp.149-150; The full text included in *The Dr. S. V., Sohoni Felicitation Volume, Journal of Bihar Research Society* (*JBRS*), 1987.

_______: "Contemporary Significance of Chiese Buddhist Philosophy," *Journal of Chinese Philosophy* (*JCP*), 24 (1997) 75-106.

_______: "Is Sêng-chao's method of demonstration an authentic Mādhyamika?" presented at the 194th annual meeting of the American Oriental Society, 1983, and included in *The Professor L. M. Joshi Memoarial Volume*, Central Institute of Higher Tibetan Studies, Sarnath, Varanasi, India, 1987.

_______: "*Śūnyatā* and Paradigm-Shift: Dialogue between Buddhism and Science" included in *Śramaṇa Vidyā Studies in Buddhism, Prof. Jagannath Upadhyaya Commemoration Volume I*, Sarnath, Varanasi, India: Central Institute of Higher Tibetan Studies, 1987, pp. 81-100.;

_______: "Nāgārjuna as author of *Suhṛllekha* and *Ratnāvalī* and his Eventual Center of Activity as Southern Kosala," Hyderabad, Dec. 26-28, 1997.

_______: "Nāgārjuna as author of *Suhṛllekha* and *Ratnāvalī* International Seminar on Contribution of Andhra Desa to Buddhism under the title:and his Eventual Center of Activity as Southern Kosala," Hyderabad, Dec. 26-28, 1997.

_______: "Nāgārjuna's Dialectic and Indian Logic (2)," *Journal of Indian and Buddhist Studies* with the following titles:Vol. 46, No. 2, 1998, pp. 1024-1020.

_______: "On the Dialectical Meaning of Instantiation in terms of *Māyā-Dṛṣṭānta* in the Indian and Chinese Madhyamikas," *JIBS.*, Vol. 36, no. 2 (1988), 971-77.

_______: "On the Relationship between Nāgārjuna's Dialectic and Buddhist Logic (1)," *JJIBS*, Vol.45, No. 2, 1997, pp. 1029-1025.

_______: "Re-Examining the Period of Nāgārjuna: Western India, A.D. 50-150" (「龍樹の年代論再考」), *JIBS*, vol. 40, No. 2, March 1992 (pp. 8-14).

_______: "The *Madhyamaka* and the Future," *Buddhism into the Year 2000 (Studies in Buddhology)*, Bangkok: Dhammakāya Foundation, 1994, pp.

67-85.

_______: "The Period of Nāgārjuna and the *Fang-pien-hsin-lun*", *JIBS.*, Vol. 43, No. 2, March 1995 (pp. 20-25).

_______: "The Period of Nāgārjuna and the Fang-pien-hsin-lunor *Upāyahṛdayaśāstra* (「龍樹の年代と「方便心論」」), *JIBS,* Vol. 43, No. 2, 1995, pp. 2033-2028.

_______: "The Sino-Indian Trans-cultural Method of Mādhyamika Dialectic: Nāgārjuna to Sêng-chao to Chi-ts'ang," *Buddhism in India and Aborad*, G. Kuppuram, ed. (1990).

_______: Buddhagaya Temple in Indian Buddhism (1-10), *World Buddhism* (Sri Lanka) XVIV, 4-12, 1975 and XXV, 1 (1976).

_______: Nāgārjuna's Dialectic and Buddhist Logic (3)," *Journal of Indian and Buddhist Studies*, Vol. 47, No. 2, 1999, pp. 1021-1016.

Inada, K. K.: *Nāgārjuna: A Translation of His Mūlamādhyamikakārikā*. Tokyo: Hokuseido Press, 1970.

International Encylopedia of Psychiatry, London: Roughsh Co. , 1972.

Jacobi, H.: "On the Dates of the Philosophical Sūtras," *Journal of the American Oriental Society* (*JAOS*), 3.

Janusz Chmielewski's series of articles: "Notes on Early Chinese Logic (I-VI)," *Rocznik Orientalistyczny* (RO): Vol. 26, No. I, (1962), 7-22 and No. 2, (1963), 91--105; Vol. 27, No. 1, (1963), 103-121; Vol. 28, No. 2, (1965), 87-111. Vol. 29, No. 2, (1965), 117-138; Vol. 30, No. 1 (1966) 31-52..

Johnston, E. H. and A. Kunst: (eds): The *Vigrahavyāvartanī* of Nāgārjuna with the author's Commentary, [*Mélanges Chinois et Buouddhique*, Vol. 9, 1951, (Appendix, pp. 99-152)].

Johnston, E. H.: *The Buddhacarita or Acts of the Buddha*, Pt I (Sanskrit edition) and II (English translation): Canto i to xiv translated from original Sanskrit supplemented by the Tibetan Version; published by the Univ. of Punjab, Lahore: Calcutta: Baptist Mission Press 1936.

Joshi, L. M.: "Life and Times of the Madhyamaka Philosopher Nāgārjuna," *Maha Bodhi* 73, 1(1965) and 2(1966), 42-49. Joshi's survey covers the following: Bu-ston: *History of Buddhism*, Eng. trans. by E. Obermiller, Heidelberg, 1932, Pt II, pp.120-130; Go-lo-tsa-ba gZon-nu-dpal: *The Blue Annals*, Eng. trans. by G. N. Roerich, 2 parts, Calcutta, 1949, 1953; Tāranātha: *Mystic Tales*, Eng. trans. by B. N. Dutt. Calcutta 1944, pp. 8-11; *Geschichte des Buddhismus in Indien*, German transl. by Von A. Schiefner, St Petersbury, 1869; Eng. trans. by N. Dutta and U. N. Ghoshal in *IHQ* of the relevant portion in *Indian Historical Quarterly* XXVIII, 1952, p.41 ff;

K'uei-chi (窺基、632-682): *Suttle Complement on the Mahāprajñāpāramitā-hṛdaya-sūtra* (「般若心経幽賛」巻上) Taishō. 33 (No. 1710).

Kajio, Kōun: *A Study on the Developmental History of Mahāyāna Buddhism* (「大乗仏教の成立史的研究」), Tokyo: Sankibō, 1981.

Kajiwa, Kōun: *A Study on the Formation of Mahāyāna Buddhism* (「大乗仏教の成立史的研究」). Tokyō, Sankibō, 1981).

Kajiyama, Y.: "Epistemology and Logic" included in *the Lectures on Mahāyāna Buddhism* IX (「講座大乗仏教」第九巻), Tokyo: Shunjūsha, 1984.

Karashina, Yasuo: 「Avalokitasvaraの語義解釈」、*Annual Report of the International Research Institute for Advanced Buddhology at Soka University*, 1998, pp. 39-66. The term '観音' appears in Guṇabhadra's translation of the *Suhṛllekha*「竜樹菩薩為禅陀迦王説法要偈」:「王当仰学諸賢聖、如観音等度衆生」(Taisho.32, 747c 22) included in「法華経の文献学的研究」. Pt. 2 of "the Study of the *Lotus Sūtra* based on Textual Critique," *Annual Report of the International Research Institute for Advanced Buddhology at Soka University for the Academic Year 1998*, No. 2; p. 44.

Karuṇā-puṇḍarīka-nāma-mahāyāna-sūtra, translated by Dharmakṣema (曇無讖, 414-426) as「大乗悲分陀利経」or「悲蓮華経」(10 fasc.) [*The Sūtra on the White Lotus of Love and Compassion*]. Taishō. 3, 167 (No. 157),

Kathāvatthu edited by A. C. Taylor for PTS, 1894-97; reprint by Routledge & Kegan Paul, 1979.

Kathāvatthuppakaraṅa-Aṭṭhakathā included in the *Pañcappakaraṅa-aṭṭhakathā* named *Paramaṭṭhadīpanī* and critically edited by N. A. Jayawickrama (Text Series No. 169); London: PTS, Routledge & Kegan Paul, 1979,

Kau-sêng-fa-hsien-ch'uan (「高僧法顕伝」1 fasc.) or *the Biography of the Eminent Monk Fa-hsüiang* (or *the Record of his Journey to India*). Taishō. 51, (No. 2085).

Kitagawa, Hidenori: *A Study of Indian Classical Logic* - Dignāga's System, Kyoto: Suzuki Foundation, 1965.

Komine, Yahiko: "Re-examination of the *Prajñā-Hṛdaya-Sūtra*" (「般若心経再考」), *Mikkyō-gaku Kenkyū* (*Study on Tantric Buddhism*).

Kuan-yin-ching (「観音経」), i.e., Chapter 25 'Sammanta-muckha' (「観世音菩薩普門品第二十五」) of the *Lotus Sūtra* (「法華経」), the 25th in Kumārajīva's text with its title in English as "Kuan-yin's Manifestation in All Gates"; Dharmarakṣa's translation has it as the 23rd chapter with its title as Kuang-shih-yin's manifestation in all gates (「光世音普門品」), and the last translation of 601 has it as the 24th with the same title as Kumārajīva's. The extant Sanskrit text has all chapters closely parallel with the last Chinese version, but the chapter in question is the 24th.

Kuhn, Thomas: *The Structure of Scientific Revolutions*, (2nd ed.). Chicago, Illinois: University of Chicago Press, 1970.

Kumārajīva (鳩摩羅什) and his major Translations within the decade of 401-410:

Miao-fa-lien-hua-ching (「妙法蓮華経」7 fasc.) Taishō from *Saddharma-pṇḍarīka-sūtra*, in 408; Taishō and in the year of 409,

Mo-ho-pan-jo-po-lo-mi-to-ching (「摩訶般若波羅蜜経」27 fasc.) [Taishō. 8, (No, 223] on *Pañcaviṃśatisāhasrikāprajñāpāramitā-sūtra* (「二万五千頌般若経」) or *Twenty-five thousand Verse Wisdom Sūtra*, 404, which is generally known as the Larger Prajñāpāramitā Sūtra (*Ta-p'in-pan-jo-ching*,「大品般若経」);

Mūlamadhyamakakārikāśāstra of Nāgārjuna (「中論」4 fasc.) Taishō 30, (No. 1564) in the year 409 as well as *Dvādaśamukhaśāstra* (「十二門論」1 fasc.) Taishō 30, (No. 1568) in that same year.

Smaller Prajñāpāramitā Sūtra (*Hsiao-p'in-pan-jo-ching* 「小品般若経」) in the year of 406 from the *Aṣṭasāhasrikā-prajñāpāramitā-sūtra* or *Eight Thousand Verse Prajñā Sūtra* (「八千頌般若経」 10 fasc.);

Ta-chih-tu-lun (「大智度論」) *from Nāgārjuna's* voluminous commentary *Upadeśaśāstra* or *in full, Mahāprajñāpāramitopadeśaśātra, the year Of 404;*

Wei-mo-chieh-so-shuo-ching (「維摩詰所説経」 3 fasc.) Taishō 13 (No. 475)

Kunst, Arnold: "The Concept of the Principle of Excluded Middle in Buddhism," *Rocznik Orientalistyczny* XXI, (1957),

________: "The Two Membered Syllogism," *Rocznik Orientalistyczny*, XV (1939-40), p. 76;

La Vallée Poussin, Louis de: *Mūlamadhyamakakārikās* (*Mādhyamikasūtras*) de Nāgārjuna avec la *Prasannapadā* Commentaire de Candrakīrti. [Bibliotheca Buddhica, IV, St-Pétersbourg, 1903-1913],

Lamotte, E.: *Histoire du Buouddhisme Indien, des Origines á l'ére Śaka*, originally published in 1958 as part of publication of the Oriental Institute of Louvain. An English translation by Sara Webb-Boin came out in 1988 as 36th volume of the institute.

________: *Le traité de la grand vertu de sagesse de Nāgārjuna. Ta-chih-tu-lun* (「大智度論」 100 fasc.); Taishō. 25, (No. 1509]: Bibliothèque de Muséon, Vol. 18. New reproduction published from Louvain Institut Orientliste: Tome 1 (vol. 25, published 1981), Tome II (vol 26, 1981), Tome III (vol. 2, 1970), Tome IV (vol. 12, 1976), Tome V (vol. 24, 1980).

Liebenthal, W: *Chao-lun: The Treatise of Sêng-chao*, comprising a full textual translation in English, from Peking in 1948 (a revised edition published by the Hong Kong University Press in 1968);

Liebert, Gusto: *Iconographic Dictionary of the Indian Religions, Hinduism-Buddhism-Jainism.* Asian Arts & Archaeology Series No. 5. Delhi: Indian Books Centre, 1976

Lintner, Chr.: *Nagarjuniana, Studies in the Writings and Philosophy of Nāgārjuna.* (Buddhist Traditions Vol. II), Motilal Banarsidass, 1982

Ta-ch'êng-changc-hen-lun (「大乘掌珍論」 2 fasc.) *or A Treatise on the Mahāyāna Treasure within One's own Hand* by Bhavya and translated by Hsüan-tzang (玄奘); Taishō 30 (No. 1578), 268 ff; Sanskritization from Chinese text by N. Aiyasvami Sastri, *Visva-Bharati Annals* II, (1949).

Lokesh Chandra: *The Thousand Armed Avalokiteśvara.* Delhi: Indira Gandhi National Center for Arts, 1988.

Lotus Sūtra, Saddharmapuṇḍarika Sūtra, Group:

Chêng-fa-hua-ching (「正法華経」 in 10 fascicles), translated by Dharmarakṣa in AD 286; [Taishō. 9 (No. 263)].

Miao-fa-lien-hua-ching (「妙法蓮華経」 7 or 8 fas.) translated by Kumārajīva in 406; , Taishō. 9 (No. 262);

Pei-hua-ching (「悲華経」 or 「大乗悲分陀利経」 or 「悲蓮華経」) 10 fasc., translated by Dharmarakṣa 414-426. Taishō. 3, (No. 157),

Saddharmapuṇḍarīka-sūtra in Sanskrit: edited by Kern and Nanjō, 1912, Bibliotheca Buddhica 10. Three translations of the *Lotus*

Sūtra (「法華経」) are as follows:

T'ien-p'in-miao-fa-lien-hua-ching (「添品妙法蓮華経」 in 7 or 8 fascicles), Taishō. 9 (No. 264), translated by Jñānagupta and Dharmagupta in 601.

Lüders, Heinrich: *List of Brahmī Inscriptions from the Earliest Times about A.D. 400 with the Exception of Those of Aśoka*, Indological Book House, Varanasi, 1973;

Lung-shu-p'u-sa-chuang (「龍樹菩薩伝」 or *the Biography of Bodhisattva Nāgārjuna* (1 *fasc.*) translated by Kumārajīva, *Taisho* 50 (No. 2047), p. 184a-185b; Also a second version (1 fasc.), *ibid.* pp.185b-186c.;

Mahāyāna-ṣraddhotpāda-śāstra (*The Treatise on the Awakening of Faith in Mahāyāna* 「大乘起信論」) ascrobed to Aśvaghoṣa and recorded as translated by Paramārtha, but some argue that the textual compilation might have been in China; Taishō 32 (No. 1666).

Mahāparinirvāṇa-sūtra translated by Dharmakṣema (385-433) as *Mahā Parinirvāṇa Sūtra* 「大般涅槃経」、40 fasc.); Taisho. 12, (No, 374).

Mahāyānaparinirvāṇa-sūtra (「大乗涅槃経」 40 fasc.) translated by Dharmakṣema (385-433); Taishō. 12 (No. 848).

Malefjit, Taylor A. de Waal: *Image of Man (A history of Anthropo[ogical Thought)*, NY: Alfred A. Knopf, 1976

Maspero, H.: "Sur la date et l'authenticité du Fou-ta-tsung-yin-yuan," *Mélanges d'Indianisme*, Paris.]

Matsumoto, Shiro: *Engi-to-Kū* (*Dependent Origination and Śūnyatā*), Tokyo: Daizō Shuppan, 1989.

________: "Possibility for the Critique of Sectarian Zen Study" (Hihan-shūgaku-no-Kanōsei) – Critical Buddhism and a Critique upon the Tathāgatagarbha Thought, *Shūgaku-to-Genzai* (*A Record of the Open Lecture Series sponsored by Sōtō School Institute*), No. 2; October 1998, pp. 1-118; Matsumoto: *Engi-to-Kū, op. cit.*, p. 67 ff.

Matsunaga, Alicia: *Buddhist Philosophy of Assimilation of the Honji-Suijaku Theory (The Historical Development)*: Tokyo: Sophia University, C.E. Tuttle, 1969.

Meditation of Marcus Aurelius Antoninus, The, translated by A.S.L. Farquharson and edited by R. B. Rutherford. Oxford world's Classics, Oxford Univ. Press 1989.

Mochizuki Bukkyō Daijiten, vol. 2, p. 1755b. "Ssŭ-hung-shih-yüan" or "Shigu-seigan" (「四句誓願」).

Mystic Tales of Tāranātha, Engl. trans. by B. N. Dutt, Calcutta 1944, pp. 8-11; *Geschichte des Buddhismus in Indien*, German transl. by Von A. Schiefner, St Petersbury, 1869; Engl. Trans.

Mūrti, T. R. V.: *The Central Philosophy of Buddhism (A Study of the Mādhyamika System)*. London: George Allen and Unwin Ltd., Ruskin House*Museum Street, 1955

Nagao, Gaddjin: "An Interpretation of the Term 'Saṃvṛti (convention) in Buddhism," *Silver Jublee Volume of the Zinbun-kagaku Kenkyusyo* (Kyoto: Kyoto University, 1954), pp. 550-61.

Nāgārjuna: *The Biographical Record of Bodhisattva Nāgārjuna* (*Lung-shu-p'u-sa-chuang,* 「龍樹菩薩伝」) translated into Chinese by Kumārajīva in 405

A.D.

Nāgārjuna: *Mūla-madhyamaka-kārikā-śāstra* (「中論」), *the Fundamental Middle Through Versified Composition*:

Mūlamadhyamakakārikās (*Mādhyamikasūtras*) de Nāgārjuna avec la *Prasannapadā* Commentaire de Candrakīrti; edited by Louis de La Vallée Poussin. [Bibliotheca Buddhica, IV, St-Pétersbourg, 1903-1913],

Āryanāgārjuna-bodhisattva-suhṛllekha:

(1)translated by Guṇavarman (367-431), A.D. 431 (「龍樹菩薩為禅陀迦王説法要偈」 *Bodhisattva Nāgārjuna's Essential Teaching in Verse for King Ch'an-t'o-chia-wang,* fasc.), Taisho. 32, (No. 1672), pp. 745b-748a;

(2) by Saṅghavarman, (A.D. 434), (「勧発諸王要偈」 *Lung-shu-p'u-sa-h'üan-fa-chu-wang-yao-chieh* (1 fasc.), Taisho. 32, (No. 1673), pp. 748a-751a,

(3) by I-ching (635-713), A.D. 637, (「龍樹菩薩勧誡王頌」 *Lung-shu-p'u-sa-ch'üan-chieh-wang-sung,* 1 fasc.), Taisho 32, (No. 1673), pp.751a-754b.

Prajñāpāramitopadeśaśāstra (「大智度論」 *Ta-chih-tu-lun*) translated by Kumārajīva in the year of 404, Taishō. 25 (No. 1509), 100 fascs.

Rājaparikathā-ratnamālā in Tibetan version or *Pao-hsing-wang-chêng-lun* (「宝行王正論」 1 fasc.) translated during 558-569 by Paramārtha (A.D. 499-569); Taisho 32, No. 1656. Some Sanskrit fragments of the *Ratnāvalī* have been discovered by G. Tucci, and he subsequently published its edited text and English translation in *Journal of Royal Asiatic Society* 1934, pp. 307-325; 1936, pp. 237-252, also 423-435.

Vaidalyaprakaraṇasūtra (「広破経」): Y. Kajiyama (ed): "The Vaidalyaprakaraṇa of Nāgārjuna, " Tibetan passage in the appendix; Miscellanea Indologica Kiotiensia, Nos. 6-7 (1965).

Vimalakīrti-nirdeśa-śāstra (「唯摩詰所説経三巻」 translated by Kumārajīva in the year of 406. Taishō. 13, (No. 475

Vigrahavyāvartanī 「回諍論」 the *Treatise on Turning Around (Doctrinal) Disputes*: Kunst and Johnston: A Sanskrit edition of the *Vigrahavyāvartanī, Mélanges Chinois et Bouddhiques* (1948-1951).

Nagasawa, Kazutoshi (Japanese trans.): *The biography of Fa-hsien and Travelogue of Sung-yun* (「法顕伝、宋雲行紀」), Tokyo: Heibonsha 1971

Nakamura, Hajime: *Jihi* (「慈悲」 *Buddhist Love and Compassion*). Kyoto: Heirakuji Shoten (11th ed), 1994.

Nakamura: "The Influence of the Concept of *Śūnyatā* on Buddhist Logic," *Bukkyo no Kompon Shinri* (*The Fundamental Truth of Buddhism*), Tokyo: 1956, p. 32, and also included in the *Indian Buddhism: A Survey with Bibliographical Notes,* (Osaka: 1980).

Niddesa, the earliest commentary on *Sutta Nipāta* ascribed to Sāriputta, a direct disciple of Śākyamuni,

Nikāya III, 16. The banished four princes of King Okkāka, third successor of the Īkṣvāku,

Nyāyapraveśakasūtra by Śaṃkarasvāmin: Sanskrit edition included in Gaekwad Oriental Series, 38 (1930).

Obermiller, E. (E. trans.): *Bu-ston's History of Buddhism*. Heidelberg: 1932, Pt II, pp.120-130;

Ono, Genmyō: "History of transmission and translation of Buddhist Sūtras," *Bussho Kaisetsu Daijiten* (「仏書解説大辞典」), Additional Vol., pp. 7-8.

Palmer, Martin and Jay Ramsay with Man-ho Kwok: *Kuan Yin: Myths of the Chinese Goddess of Compassion*. London: Thorsons, an Imprint of Harper-Collins Publishers, 1995

Paramatthajotikā: the later commentary on Sutta Nipāta ascribed to Buddhaghoṣa of the 5th century.

Paramaṭṭha-jotika (Commentary on Suttanipāta) I, 232-6. Also Dīgha Nikāya III, 16.

Pathaka, S. K., "Life of Nagarjuna" from Pag Sam Jon Zang, *IHQ* XXX, p. 93f.

Petsold, Bruno: *The Classification of Buddhism Bukkyō Kyōhan* (「仏教教判論」), *Comprising the Classification of Buddhist Doctrines in India, China, and Japan* (in collaboration with Shinshō Hanayama and edited by Shohei Ichimura, published from Otto Harrassowitz Verlag, Wiesbaden, Germany, 1995.

Prajñā Heart Sūtra (Hṛdaya)「般若心経」Group:

Fen-pên-pan-jo-po-lo-mi-to-hsin-ching (「梵本般若波羅蜜多心経」) translated by Prajñā-cakra (智慧輪) in 861; *Ibid.*, (No. 254).

Mahāprajñāpāramitā-hṛdayasūtra Pan-jo-po-lo-mi-to-hsing-ching (「般若波羅蜜多心経」) tramslated by Hsüan-tzang (玄奘); Taisho. 8, 1 fasc. (No.. 251).; (3) *Pu-pien-chih-ts'ang-pan-jo-po-lo-mi-t-hsin-ching* (「普遍智蔵般若波羅蜜多心経」) re-translation by Fa-yueh (法月), T'ang dynasty; Taishō 8, (No. 252).;

Pan-jo-po-lo-mi-t-hsin-ching (「般若波羅蜜多心経」) by Dharmasiddhi ? (Fa-chêng, 法成) in 855; *Ibid.*, (No. 255).

Pan-jo-po-lo-mi-to-hsin-ching「般若波羅蜜多心経」translated by Prajñā (般若) and Li-yen in 790; *Ibid.*, (No. 253).

prajñā 1Mahāprajñāpāramitā Mahā-vidyā-manta Sūtr (Mo-ho-pan-jopoi-lo-mi-ta-ming-shoù-ching or「摩訶般若波羅蜜大明呪経」*translated* by Kumārajīva (羅什); Taishō 8, 1 fasc, (No. 250).

Sacred Mother of Buddhas Prajñā Heart Sūtra expounded by the buddha「仏説聖仏母般若波羅蜜多心経」by Dhānapāla (施護) in 980-? of Sung dynasty [*Ibid.*, (No. 257)] and by the same translator, 「仏説帝釈般若波羅蜜多心経」; *Ibid.*, (No. 249).

Sanskrit version *Prajñāpāramitāhṛdayasūtra* 「梵本般若波羅蜜多心経」 by Amoghavajra (不空金剛) in 771-775 [*Ibid.*, (No. 256)]. In textual introduction, this *Hṛdaya Sūtra* is said to have been transliterated from a Chinese original by Amoghavajra (不空), thus entitled as "*A Sanskrit Prajñā Heart Sūtra transliterated from T'ang Chinese version*" 「唐梵翻対字音般若波羅蜜多心経」[Taishō 8, (No. 256)]. The text was discovered from the Tung-huang excavation and is said to have been the version upon which Hsüan-tzang translated.

Prajñāpāramitā Wisdom Sūtra Group:

Aṣṭasāhasrikā-prajñāpāramitā-sūtra or *Eight Thousand Verse Prajñā Sūtra* (「八千頌般若経」) extant in the following three translations:

Hsiao-p'in-pan-jo-po-lo-mi-ching 「小品般若波羅蜜経」 (The Smaller Prajñā Text), 10 fasc.) translated by Kumārajīva from the *Aṣṭāsāhaseikā-prajñā-pā ramitā-sūtra (8000 Verse Prajñā Sūtra)* in 408; Taishō. 8. (No. 227).; Taishō. 8, (No. 227).

Mo-ho-pan-jo-po-lo-mi-ching 「大品般若経」 (The Larger Prajñā Text) or 「摩訶般若波羅蜜経」 translated by Kumārajīva from (27 fascs.) translated by Kumārajīva from the *Pañcaviṃśatisāhasrikā-prajñāpāramitā-sūtra.* Taishō. 8, (No. 223) in the year of 409 simultaneously with 「大智度論」

Pañcaviṃśatisāhasrikā-prajñāpāramitā-sūtra (The twenty-five thousand Verse Prajñā text 「二万五千頌般若波羅蜜経」).

Ta-chih-tu-lun (「大智度論」 100 fasc.s), translated by Kumārajīva from the *Mahāprajñāpāramitopadeśa-śāstra* ascribed to Nāgārjuna. Taishō. 25, (No. 1509). The treatise was Nāgārjuna's commentary on the *Pañcaviṃśatisāhasrikā-prajñāpāramitā-sūtra (the 25,000 Śloka Text),* and Kumārajīva produced both the text and this treatise in 409.

Ta-ming-tu-ching (「大明度経」 6 fasc.) translated by Chih-ch'ien (支謙) of Wu (呉), Taishō 8, (No. 225);

Ta-pan-jo-po-lo-mi-to-ching (「大般若波羅蜜多経」 600 fascs.) translated by Hsüan-tzang from the *Mahāprajñāpāramitāsūtra consisting of 100,000 Ślokas*; comprising the 「八千頌般若」 as well as 「二万五千頌般若」 together with other Prajñā Sūtras. Taisho. (No. 220), Vol. 5 (1 to 200th fasc.), Vol. 6 (to 400th fasc.), and Vol. 7, (to 600th fasc.).

Tao-hsing-pan-jo-ching, (「道行般若経」 10 fasc.), translated by Chih-lou-chia-ch'en (支婁迦讖) in A.D. 179; Taishō. 8, (No. 224); and by as

Preamble to the Declaration of Human Rights, *Human Rights: A Compilation of International Instruments* (New York: United Nations, 1988), pp. 1-7.

Rahula, W.: *What the Buddha Taught*, with a Foreword by Paul Demiéville, Bangkok: Hawtrai Foundation Press 2531 (1988).

Raja, K. Kunjuni: *Indian Theories of Meaning*, Adyar Library and Research Center, 1963.

Rājataraṅgiṇī or *The Records of Kaśmīra Kings* compiled by Kalhaṇa, historian or chroncler, during the eleventh century.

Randle. H. N.: *Indian Logic in the Early Schools (A Study of the Nyāya Darśana in its Relation to the Early Logic of Other Schools)*, Oxford Univ. Press, 1930, Reprint by Oriental Book Reprint Corporation 1976.

Ratnākara: *Antarvyāptisamarthana*, edited by Haraprasad, Bibliotheca Indica new series, No. 1226; (Calcutta: 1910), p. 103 (15-16).

Rhys Davids and Carpenter (ed.): Buddhaghoṣa: *Sumaṅgalavilāsinī* (ed. by PTS. Pt. I, 258 ff);

Rhys Davids, Mrs.: The Points of Controversy or Subjects of Discourses.

PTS, 1915]: A Translation of the *Kathāvatthu*, London: PTS, Luzac & Co., 1960.]

Robinson, R. H.: *Early Mādhyamika in India and China*. University of Wisconsin Press, 1967. (an inclusion of partial translation of the *Chao-lun* (「肇論」).

Roerich, G. N. (Eng. trans: *Go-lo-tsa-ba gZon-nu-dpal: The Blue Annals* 2 parts.). Calcutta, 1949, 1953;

Roerich, George and A. S. Altekar: *The Biography of Dharmasvāmin* (Chag-lo-tsa-ba Chos-rje-dpal) English translation; Patna: 1959.

Ruegg, D. S.:"Towards a Chronology of the *Madhyamaka* School," *Indological and Buddhist Studies* (Volume in Honor of Professor J.W. de Jong on his Sixtieth Birthday), Bibliotheca Indo-Buddhica No.27, Delhi: Indian Books Centre, 1982,

Śaṅkarasvāmin: *Nyāyapraveśaka-sūtram*, the edited Sanskrit text included in the *Gaekaward Oriental Series*, 33 (1930), p. 1 ff.

Śrīmālādevīsiṃhanāda-sūtra (「勝鬘獅子吼一乗大方便方広経」1 fasc.) Taishō 12, (No. 353) translated by Guṇabhadra.

Sandhong Rimpoche: *Felicitation Volume, In Search of Truth: A Collection of Articles in Honoour of the Fifth Samdhong Rimpoche, Losang Tenzin on his Sixtieth Birthday*, Alumni of Central Institute of Higher Tibetan Studies, Sarnath, Varanasi, 1999.

Saṃdhinirmocana-sūtra (Chieh-shên-mi-ching, 「解深密経」5 fasc.) or *Sūtra that Elucidates the Profound Meaning*), translated by Hsüan-tzang in 647; Taishō. 16 (No. 676).

Saṅghavarman (僧伽跋摩), A.D. 434, trasnslated the *Suhṛllehha* as *The Essential Teaching in Verse Recommended to all Kings* (「勧発諸王要偈」 *Lung-shu-p'u-sa-h'üan-fa-chu-wang-yao-chieh* (1 fasc.); Taisho. 32, (No. 1673), pp.748a-751a, in which the name "Ming-sheng" (明勝、Udayana?) appears in the first verse.

Schayer, S.: "Über die Methode der Nyāya-Forschung," *Zeitschrift Winternitz*, (Leipzig: 1932),

Schmidt, Elena: "The Little Known Binglingsi, Buddhist Caves," *The Art of Asia*, Vol 27, No. 4, July-August 1997;

Searle, J. R.: *Speech Acts: An Essay in teh Philosophy of Language*, Cambridge: Cambridge University Press, 1969.

Sêng-chao (僧肇): *Chao-lun* or *The Treatise of Sêng-Chao* consists of four short essays and two epistles written on Buddhist doctrines, regarded as the earliest extant Chinese Mādhyamika text composed by the native Chinese mind. 1 fasc., Taishō Daizōkyō 45, (No. 1858),

Sêng-yu (僧祐、420-589): *Collection of the Tripiṭaka Textual Records* (「出三蔵記集」)

Shastri, R.: *Kauṭilya's Arthaśāstra* (*The Treatise on Polity*, or literally translated, *On the Realization of Wealth*). 2nd rev. ed. (Mysore: 1919). Translation from Bārhaspatya, Bangalore, 1915, 1923,

Shwe Zan Aung and Caroline Augusta Foley Rhys-Davids, *The Points of Controversy* originally published 1915.

Sinha, Narendra Krshna and Anil Chandra Banerjee: *History of India*, Calcutta: A. Mukherjee & Co., 1952

Spengler, Oswald: *The Decline of the West*, abridged English edition prepared by Arthur Helps, from the translation of Charles Francis Atkins; N.Y.: Alfred A. Knoph, 1962

Staël-Holstein, A. von. "The etymological origin to two Pāli verbal roots apalok and olok," *Harvad Journal of Asiatic Studies* 1(1936) 350-362..

Stcheerbatsky: Th.: *The Conception of Buddhist Nirvāṇa*was, Leningrad: the Academy of Sciences of the USSR, 1927 (Indo-Iranian Reprints, 1965).

Stcherbatsky, Th.: *Buddhist Logic* (I and II), originally published by the Academy of Sciences of the USSR, Leningrad as Bibliotheca Buddhica XXVI (Pts I and II) and by Constable and Company ltd. in England, 1930, and its reprint by Dover Publications, Inc., 1962.

Sūtra on the Original Action of the Garland of the Bodhisattva, The [*P'u-sa-ying-lo-pênyeh-ching*(「菩薩瓔珞本業経」、2 fasc.)] translated by Chu-fo-nien (竺法念、Buddhasmṛti) in 376-378. Taishō. 24 (No. 1485).

Ta-ch'êng-changc-hen-lun (「大乗掌珍論」2 fasc.) *or A Treatise on the Mahāyāna Treasure within One's own Hand* by Bhavya andtranslated by Hsüan-tzang (玄奘); Taishō 30 (No. 1578), 268 ff; Sanskritization from Chinese text by N. Aiyasvami Sastri, *Visva-Bharati Annals* II, (1949).

Ta-chuang-yen-ching-lun (「大荘厳論経」) translated by Kumārajīva; Taishō 4 (No. 201).

Takakusu, Junjiro: *The Essentials of Buddhist Philosophy*, University of Hawaii Press, 1947

Tāranātha wrote that Nāgārjuna lived his last 200 years at Śrīparvata practising Tantras with Yoginīs till he was beheaded by prince Suśakti, the grandson of king Udayana. Cf.

Tāranātha: *History of Buddhism*, chap. xv, *IHQ*. XXVIII, 1952, trans. by N. Dutt and U. N. Ghoshal, pp. 41-50;

Tattvasaṅgraha-pañjikā (GOS, 30-1, 1926)],

Tay, C.N. Kuan-yin: the cult of half Asia. *History of Religions*, No. 162 (now 1976) 147-177.

Taylor, Edward Burnett (1832-1917): has soften been called the father of this disicpline. Cf.

Tibetan scholar monk Chag-lo-tsa-ba Chos-rje-dpalv's Auto-Biography: *The Biography of Dharmasvāmin*

Tibetan sources for Buddhist History: *Blue Annals* by Gos-lo-tsa-ba gZon-nu-dpal (AD 1392-1481); *History of Buddhism* by Bu-ston; the *Mystic Tales* by Tāranātha (circa. AD 1574), and the *History of Buddhism in India* by Sumpā-mKham-po (AD 17th or 18th century), and so forth

Toynbee, Arnold: *A Study of History*, abridged one-volume edition by the author and Jane Caplan, Oxford University Press, 1972

Tsukamoto, Z.: The Jōron no Kenkyū (*The Study of Chao-lun*), a full textual translation in Japanese. Kyoto: Heirakuji, 1955

Tucci, G.: An edition of the Sanskrit frgments and English translation, "The *Ratnāvalī* of Nāgārjuna: Part I," *Journal of the Royal Asiatic Society*, 1934, pp. 307-325; "Part II," *ibid*., 1936, pp. 239-252];

_______: Minor Buddhist Texts, II (Rome 1958),

_______: *Pre-Diṅnāga Buddhist Texts on Logic from Chinese Sources*,

Translated with an Introduction, Notes and Indices; Baroda: Gaekwad Oriental Institute, 1929;

_______: Sanskrit fragments corroborated by the Tibetan version, verses 1 through 34: "A Numerical Problem in Nāgārjuna's *Ratnāvalī*," *Indological and Buddhist Studies* (*Volume in Honour of Professor J. W. de Jong on his Sixtieth Birthday*), Delhi-India: Sri Satguru Publications, 1982, pp. 161-185.

Ui, Hakuju: "A Study on the *Hōben-shin-ron* with Annotations" (「方便心論の註釈的研究」); Publilshed as part of his monograph, *Indian Philosophical Studies* II (「印度哲学研究」), pp. 472-585.

_______: *Vaiśeṣika Philosophy according to the Daśapadārthaśāstra*. Royal Asiatic Society, London, 1918

Upadeśaśāstra or Mahāprajñāpāramitopadeśa-śāstra: See the Prajñāpāramitā Sūtra Group.

Vācaspati Miśra in his *Nyāyavārtikatātparyaṭīkā*. Cf. Vidyabhusana, *op. cit.*, pp. 281-282.

Vasu, I, S. C., ed. and trans.: *The Siddhāntakaumudī*, (Delhi: Motilal Banarsidass, 1962.

Vidyabhusana, Satis Chandra: *A History of Indian Logic*, Motilal Banarsidass reprint, 1971 [Originally published from the University of Calcutta in 1931].

Vinaya in Four Divisions (*Ssŭu-fên-lü* (「四分律」 *Dharmaguptaka-vinaya*), in Chinese translation (Taisho. vol. 22, p. 101b)

Von A. Schiefner (German trans.): *Geschichte des Buddhismus in Indien,*. St Petersbury, 1869.

Waal Malefjit, A. de: *Image of Man (A history of Anthrolopogical thought)*, by, NY: Alfred A. Knopf, 1976,

Watanabe, S.: 「「般若心経成立序説」－「摩訶般若波羅蜜大明呪経」と「大品般若経」の関係を中心として」, *Journal of Buddhist Studies* (「仏教学」) No. 31, pp. 41-86.

Watanabe, Shōgo: An introduction to the theory on the formation of the *Prajñā-hṛdaya-sūtra* (「般若心経成立論序説」), Buddhist Studies (「仏教学」 No. 31, July 1991), p. 42.

Watanabe, Shōgo: An introduction to the theory on the formation of the *Prajñā-hṛdaya-sūtra* (「般若心経成立論序説」), Buddhist Studies (「仏教学」 No. 31, July 1991), p. 42. Also Cf. Kajiwa, Kōun: *A Study on the Formation of Mahāyāna Buddhism* (「大乗仏教の成立史的研究」 Tokyō, Sankibō, 1981), p. 171;

Webb-Boin, Sara (tr.): *History of Indian Buddhism from the Origins to the ŚakaEra*, translated into English by Sara Webb-boin, Universitér Catholique de Louvain, Institut Orientaliste, Louvain-La-Neuve, 1988 as 36th volume of the institute.

Weber, M. *The Religion of India: The Sociology of Hinduism and Buddhism*, Hans H. Gerth and Don Martindale, trans. and eds. (Glencoe, Ill.: Free Press, 1958).

Weber, M.: *General Economic History* (Glencoe, Ill.: Free Press, 1950

Weber, Max: *The Sociology of Religion*, Ephraim Fischoff, trans., Talcott Persons. Boston: Beacon Press, 1963.

Windelband, W.: *A History of Philosophy* translated into English by James H. Tufts, New York: Macmillan Co., 1956; p. 171. [orignally written in German and publlished by Macmillan, 1893].

Winternitz, M.: *History of Indian Literature* II, Univ. of Calcutta Press, 1933, pp. 343-344).

Yamada, Ryūjō, *Daijō Bukkyō Seiritsu-ron Josetsu* (「大乗仏教成立論序説」 *The Prolegomena to the Theory of the Establishment of Mahāyāna Buddhism*) (Kyoto: Heirakuji shoten, 1995).

Yamagami, Sōgen: Japanese translation of Ta-chih-tu-lūn,

Yamaguchi, S.: "Nāgārjuan's Śāstra on the Nyāya School - *Vaidalyaprakaraṇa*, (Shōrigakuha ni taisuru Ryūju no Ronshō I)." *Buiddhist Studies* (*Bukkyō Kenkyū*), IV, 2(1927),

Yamaguchi, S.: "Nāgārjuna's Treatise Challenging the Naiyāyika School - on the *Vaidalyasūtra* (*Shōrigakuha-ni-taisuru-Ryūju-no Ronsho - Vaidalya ni-tsuit*) *Shūkyō Kenkyū* (*Journal of Religious Studies*) 4, No. 1 (Tokyo: 1927),, and

Yamaguchi, S.: Susumu: French translation of the Tibetan translation of *Vigrahavyāvartanī*, *Journal Asiatqiue*, 215, p. 1-86.

Yamaguchi, Susumu: "Shōrigakuha ni taisuru Ryūju no Ronshō: Vaidalia," Pts 1 and 2, (Nāgārjuna's Treatise against the Naiyāyika School), *Shūkyō Kenkyū*, IV, 2 & 3 (1927), 80-100, No. 2 (1927), 87-110.

Yogācārabhūmiśāstra ascribed to Maitreyanatha, tramslated by Hsüan-tzang **as** *Yü-chia-shih-ti-lun*(「瑜伽師地論」 100 fasc.). Taishō 30, (No. 1579).

Zimmer, Heinrich: *Philosophies of India*, edited by Joseph Campbell, New York: MeBibilog.Ā@Final and usedridian Books, 1957

INDEX

D

G

H

I

L

M

O

Ś

S

T

U